LEARNING

An Introduction
to the Principles
of Adaptive Behavior

Under the General Editorship of
JEROME KAGAN
Harvard University

—LEARNING—

An Introduction
to the Principles
of Adaptive Behavior

J. E. R. STADDON
Duke University

R. H. ETTINGER
Eastern Oregon State College

Harcourt Brace Jovanovich, Publishers

San Diego   New York   Chicago   Austin   Washington, D.C.
London   Sydney   Tokyo   Toronto

Requests for permission to make copies of any part of the
work should be mailed to: Permissions, Harcourt Brace Jovanovich,
Publishers, Orlando, Florida 32887.

Copyrights and Acknowledgments appear on pages 427–429,
which constitutes a continuation of the copyright page.

ISBN 0-15-550351-0

Library of Congress Catalog Card Number: 88-82142

Printed in the United States of America

Preface

The study of learning has always occupied a privileged position in biopsychology because learning is such a distinctive feature of human behavior. One of the main justifications for any scientific research has always been its potential application. Hence, the study of learning in animals has always been a popular endeavor that could be justified not only by its intrinsic interest, but also by the promise of human betterment.

After its heyday in the 1950s and 1960s, other ways of approaching the study of human intelligence, particularly cognitive psychology in its several forms, displaced animal learning from the limelight. Nevertheless, since its inception nearly 90 years ago, the modern study of animal learning has racked up an impressive track record. The number of research papers reporting experiments on various aspects of learning in animals now runs to many thousands. To this mountain of data has been added over the years a growing number of theoretical foothills. Moreover, interest in how animals learn, and in what this learning can tell us about the nature and neural mechanisms of intelligence, has revived with the growth of neuroscience and the theory of neural networks. How should an introductory textbook cope with this mass of information? Comprehensive coverage is impossible. A glance at some venerable graduate texts, such as the massive book by Osgood (1953), the two versions of Hilgard and Marquis' text (1940; Kimble, 1961), and Mackintosh's survey (1974) which, even 14 years ago, renounced any claim to completeness, shows the futility of any attempt to provide adequate coverage of the experimental literature.

In the face of this flood of data and theory, most learning texts follow a familiar course. Certain experiments have become well known, sometimes because of their uniqueness (Skinner's 1948 "superstition" experiment and Garcia's taste-aversion studies are good examples), but sometimes through a more or less accidental follow-my-leader process. The plethora of theoretical approaches is handled by presenting each in sketchy form and called "balanced coverage." Because space limitations prevent any approach from being discussed in depth, little attempt can be made to resolve conflicting views or to show in detail how any given view can handle a range of data. The student is often left with the impression that knowing this field is a matter of learning a number of names, conclusions, and definitions by heart—rather than an adventure in which familiar ideas are seen in a new light and novel concepts impress by their power to explain complex behavior.

We believe there is a better way. The study of learning in animals is a relatively mature field, and the basic phenomena and experimental techniques are known. Good textbooks in other mature fields such as physics and biology do not require students to learn only long strings of names and definitions. They describe the objects of study—heat, light and sound, communities, organisms, cells—and the principles that underlie these objects—quantum mechanics and Newton's laws or genetics, cell metabolism, and evolution through variation and natural selection. We have tried to do the same for the field of animal learning. We have described a variety of basic phenomena—from the orienting behavior of bacteria through simple reflexes and reflex-like behavior in mammals and birds and on to Pavlovian and operant conditioning in their many varieties—as well as simple and complex discrimination. After we have described a phenomenon, we have tried to show how it depends on underlying theoretical processes and how it functions as an adaptation.

We have not adhered to one familiar dichotomy found in other textbooks on learning—the one between functional and mechanistic accounts of behavior. Most behavior *is* adaptive, so the study of adaptive function is an indispensable part of any text on behavior. But it is equally certain that every behavior is the product of some process; so the study of process is also essential. We present these two aspects, process and adaptation, as complementary, not conflicting, aspects of behavior.

We have also tried to describe in some detail—because in the study of behavior, procedural details are usually critical—the experimental procedures through which each learning phenomenon is demonstrated.

The emphasis of the book is on learning in animals, but we have not hesitated to bring in examples from research on humans where these would be helpful. We have taken a cautious position on the application of basic behavioral research with animals to human problems, however, because so many applications have been based on little more than superficial similarities. We discuss the problem of applying basic research results to practical problems in several contexts. We conclude that principles and processes can often be applied widely, but that using animal experiments directly as models for human mental malfunction can be misleading.

The first part of Chapter 1 provides a brief historical context, and deals with many of the philosophical puzzles that have influenced theoretical approaches to learning: the false dichotomy between learning and instinct, the mind–body problem, types of explanation for behavior, the relation of teleology to mechanism. We state our position on the relationship between the psychology of sub-human animals, human psychology, and what might be called the psychology of intelligent machines. The last part of the chapter deals with the biology of development and its relation to the study of learning—a topic neglected in many texts, even though developmental changes and changes due to learning are interwoven throughout life.

Chapter 2 describes some very simple mechanisms for behavior guided by its consequences—operant behavior. We use as examples the orienting behavior of plants and single-celled animals. Some of these processes, hill-climbing and adaptation, for example, turn up later as components of complex behavior. Our main intention here is to show how quite complex outcomes, such as tracking down a nutrient source, may be achieved by astonishingly simple means. The notion of learning as a process of search is introduced in this chapter.

Chapters 3 and 4 introduce the basic phenomena of Pavlovian and operant conditioning. Pavlovian conditioning—learning about the motivational significance of stimuli—is treated as a component of operant conditioning—guidance of behavior by its consequences, rather than as independent processes. The theoretical concept of an integrator is introduced in Chapter 3 and used to explain some simple reflex properties such as temporal summation and sensitization. Chapter 4 also discusses organisms as dynamic systems and describes elementary dynamical systems concepts such as stability and deterministic chaos. Boxes in these two chapters give brief historical accounts of some of the important figures and movements in the study of learning.

Chapter 5 describes learning in a variety of species. It shows how all learning can be looked at, from a functional point of view, as a process of inference. The differences between phenomena such as imprinting, bird song learning, and Pavlovian conditioning are in what is to be inferred and in the prior information provided to the animal by its genetic endowment.

Chapter 6, on stimulus control and cognition, introduces more complex ideas. It discusses the measurement of excitatory and inhibitory stimulus control, and control by time. The chapter goes on to discuss the role of memory in discrimination and its relation to temporal control. A variety of experimental techniques, such as generalization testing, delayed matching to sample, the radial and water maze, and a number of time-based schedules of reinforcement are discussed in this chapter. It ends with a discussion of parallel distributed processing and the idea of a distributed memory representation.

Chapter 7 discusses in greater depth several discrimination phenomena related to behavioral contrast. And the notion of behavioral competition as an ingredient in inhibitory effects is introduced.

Chapter 8 discusses the relationship between Pavlovian and operant conditioning. The first part of the chapter discusses the functional properties of a variety of Pavlovian and operant phenomena such as blocking and US preexposure. The middle part of the chapter discusses the phenomenon of operant "shaping" and the nature of behavioral variation. The last part of the chapter deals with the necessary and sufficient conditions for operant conditioning—the role of temporal contiguity and contingency. The chapter concludes with a discussion of a simple dynamic model for reinforcement, built out of ingredients that should be familiar from earlier chapters, adaptation (the integrator), competition, arousal, and variability. The model shows both standard operant conditioning phenomena and the "misbehavior" effects discussed in the first part of the chapter.

Chapter 9 takes up in more detail the phenomenon of conditioned reinforcement, in simple and choice situations, and extinction. It shows in quantitative detail how the complex patterns of results from concurrent chain experiments conform (or fail to conform) to the optimal policy, and it shows how they can be derived from a simple timing process related to reward delay (proportional or scalar timing).

Chapter 10 discusses aversive stimuli. We describe the basic phenomena and procedures that use aversive stimuli and discuss the relationships between avoidance schedules and many of the arrangements under which people must live. The chapter also takes up the controversial topic of learned helplessness, both as a phenomenon and as a theory for clinical depression. The chapter ends with a description of how the reinforcement model introduced in Chapter 8 can account for the basic phenomena of aversive control.

Chapter 11 is an extended account of choice and behavioral allocation. It is the most quantitative chapter in the book, because the theory in this area is quantitative: optimality and economic models and dynamic models for choice. We believe that we have been able to explicate these ideas without skimping on anything essential and in a way that is accessible to students with nothing more than high school algebra and the ability to understand simple graphs. We show in the last part of this chapter how the scalar timing process discussed in Chapter 9 seems to underlie many well-established quantitative properties of simple reinforcement schedules and of the choice between schedules.

ACKNOWLEDGMENTS

We are very happy to acknowledge the contributions of a number of people who were kind enough to read early drafts of several chapters—Nancy Innis, Kimberly Kirby, Art Kohn, John Pearce, and Alliston Reid—and a number of people who provided reviews—E. A. Wasserman, University of Iowa; Tom Minor, University of California, Los Angeles; James Matthews, New York University; and Warren Meck, Columbia University. Their comments and criticisms greatly improved the book. We are also grateful to Cambridge University Press, who permitted us to use some material from Staddon's earlier book *Adaptive behavior and learning* (1983).

Contents

CHAPTER

6

Stimulus Control and Cognition   153

CHAPTER

7

Stimulus Control and Performance   215

CHAPTER

8

Learning and Behavior   240

CHAPTER

9

Conditioned Reinforcement, Chain Schedules, and Extinction   278

CHAPTER

10

Aversive Stimuli   321

CHAPTER

11

Behavioral Allocation and Choice   356

1

The Analysis of Adaptive Behavior

Like many common words, *learning* means something rather different when used in a technical context than when used in common speech. People "learn" algebra, learn a language, learn to ski, skate, or play the violin, learn where the candy machine is, learn to recognize people and social situations, and learn to see well-camouflaged birds or critical features in X-ray pictures. Can all these kinds of learning be identical? Is this book about all of them?

Different types of learning often have different properties and may be different in some respects from one animal species to another. For example, language learning is not possible for most animals. In this book, we spend a great deal of time discussing some types of learning and little on others. We describe how animals learn to find food, how they learn to recognize cryptic prey, and how they learn to react to signals for pleasant or painful events. But because our emphasis in this text is on animals, we say rather little about language learning or the subtleties of social interaction. We discuss a number of aspects of animal behavior that are closer to economics or decision making: how animals choose between attractive alternatives that differ in amount

B   O   X

1.1

Animal Psychology in the United States

Animal psychology in the U.S. has suffered from being oversold. A few years ago "rat psychology" *was* psychology. Legions of eager "rat runners" trained in the traditions of Clark Hull or B. F. Skinner performed experiments designed to test theories that were assumed to be universal. No one who studied for an advanced degree in psychology (even in areas apparently remote from the animal lab such as personality or clinical psychology) was permitted to graduate without first becoming steeped in the study of animal learning. In many cases, this practice was borne out by the facts. For example, the effects on learning of practice (spaced versus massed) and reward (delayed versus immediate, large versus small) and many of the properties of memory are quite similar in rats and people. But even if early theories were called into question, as they often were, it still seemed legitimate to interpret animal experiments as "models" for human problems. For example, Martin Seligman (1967) and his associates found that dogs that were given severe, unavoidable electric shocks on one day failed the next day to learn to jump over a low barrier to "safety"—something that unshocked dogs learn quickly. This phenomenon, known by the catchy label of *learned helplessness* is still widely taken as a model for human depression, despite wide differences in the causation and properties of the two phenomena. As another example, compulsive gambling was labeled a simple effect of ratio schedules of reinforcement, even though this theory completely fails to explain why some people become compulsive gamblers and others do not. The ratio property of most gambling situations (the more you do it, the more you get—or fail to get—in strict proportion) may have something to do with typical gambling patterns, but it is obviously only part of the story.

Several years ago, Harry Harlow and his students performed a number of ingenious experiments in which baby macaque monkeys were reared apart from their natural mothers. Some of the infant monkeys were provided with artificial "mothers" made of terry cloth; others were given artificial mothers

or delay, and above all, how their behavior is changed by *valued* events, by reward and punishment.

Why animals? The appropriate motto for psychology might seem to be "The proper study of mankind is man" but we disagree. The history of science argues for viewing humans as part of a larger universe and not something qualitatively different and separate from the rest of nature. The Copernican and Einsteinian revolutions removed humans from the center of the universe, and the Darwinian revolution returned them to the world of animals and plants from which many religions had displaced them. The problem of understanding human behavior is that were somewhat less "cuddly." Some of the artificial mothers dispensed milk; others did not. Harlow compared the behavior of the infants when they grew up and found that only the ones that had had the terry-cloth mothers behaved normally in social relationships. His work was taken to show the importance of physical contact to normal human upbringing. You can probably trace the bumper sticker "Have you hugged your kid today" to Harlow's work. Such an extension from animals to humans was inherently plausible (who can doubt the value of a hug?), but as several ethologists pointed out, the validity of the extension depends more on its inherent plausibility than on the method used. For example, if Harlow had used any one of a number of other monkey species, he would have found different results.

Criticisms of the supposed link between animals and humans combined with an increasing interest in aspects of human behavior that are only weakly if at all echoed in the behavior of animals, such as language and symbolic skills, have led to a reaction against animal psychology. For example, some of the more extreme advocates of cognitive psychology assert that *only* human beings are capable of cognition. Whether this statement is true or not (and much recent work suggests that it is not), the implication that animal learning and behavior have nothing to teach us about human learning and behavior by no means follows. The failure of many previous efforts to insist on humankind's apartness from the rest of nature suggests that this attempt also will fail.

Humans are not rats, sweet peas, *Drosophila, E. coli,* or any of the other species that have been used as aids in the study of human biology. Nevertheless, by understanding the way that these organisms work—their genetics, molecular biology, and behavior—rather than using them as explicit models of human beings, we may learn about aspects of humanity that cannot be learned in any other way.

part of a larger problem, the understanding of intelligence, which can be advanced in many ways. One way is by studying human beings but also (and perhaps better) by studying simpler creatures that show some aspects of intelligent behavior—(infrahuman) animals, and machines. We see the psychological study of adaptive behavior in animals as the biological counterpart to artificial intelligence, which is the study of the adaptive behavior of artificial devices. Artificial intelligence may be seen in hardware (e.g., special-purpose electronic computers) or software (programs, mathematical structures). We find the study of the intelligence of animals an exciting and worthwhile activity in its own right. We have faith that such study may lead to a deeper understanding of human nature. Just as Michael Faraday, the "father of electricity," had faith that his experiments with wires and magnets would one day contribute to human betterment, we believe that animals are interesting in their own right and that we should not be too eager to leap from experiments with animals to conclusions about humans (Box 1.1).

For the past ten years, the study of learning in animals and humans has increasingly drawn on biology and ecology. We no longer view an organism's behavior as solely determined by simple stimulus–response mechanisms, for example. It no longer seems sufficient to study how animals learn without also studying why they learn and what is the function of their learning in their natural environment.

BIOLOGY AND BEHAVIOR

Organisms are machines that are designed by evolution to play a certain role. This role, together with the environment within which it is played, is termed the organism's ecological *niche* (Box 1.2). For example, most cats (tigers, leopards, mountain lions) play the role of solitary hunters, wolves and wild dogs are social hunters, antelope are social grazers, and so on. The animal's niche defines the patterns of adaptive behavior essential for survival and reproduction, what Charles Darwin termed *fitness* (Box 1.3). Ecological considerations such as these are involved in our understanding of learned as well as instinctive behavior.

For simple niches, such as those filled by most nonsocial invertebrates, direct responses to specific kinds of stimuli are all that is required. The animal needs to keep no record of its past history to succeed; for animals, it is sufficient to avoid "bad" things and approach "good" ones. A modest memory for the immediate past allows a creature to respond to changes in stimulation. Direct stimulus–response mechanisms, plus some sensitivity to rates of environmental change, are sufficient for a wide range of surprisingly intelligent behavior. For example, consider the *kineses* (indirect orientation movements) of many bacteria along a chemical gradient or the *taxes* (direct orientation movements) of photosensitive insects: Bacteria can move toward concentrations of food, and insects can move toward or away from light without remembering anything about the distant past. Their physiological "computers" (neural and biochemical) need only record the concentration now and the concentration a little while ago to be able to assess whether their situation is getting better or worse. A simple hill-climbing rule such as "if things are getting better, continue as before, otherwise change direction" generally works well to keep an animal in a favorable environment.

As the niche grows more complex, however, adaptive behavior requires greater dependence on the animal's past, which carries two kinds of cost. First, the animal must *have* a past (memory) if its future behavior is to be guided by it. Such memory implies an increase in brain structures and a lengthening of in-

B   O   X

1.2

The Concept of Niche

Niche is one of those almost undefinable terms that are nevertheless essential to sciences that deal with "organized complexity" (e.g., ecology, economics, psychology and behavioral biology). Like most such terms (other examples are "market," "social class," "response," and "stimulus"), the term niche is best defined by example: It is fairly obvious that the talents required of a leopard are quite different from those needed by an antelope. Among the former are powerful means of attack, a digestive system that works on meat, and a visual system adapted to attend to one thing at a time. Among the latter are a good means of evading attack, multiple stomachs, a lengthy gut able to cope with the poor diet provided by grazing, and a visual system able to detect threat from any quarter. Thus, the claws and teeth of the leopard and its forward-facing eyes and short digestive tract find functional explanation, as well as do the speed and maneuverability of the antelope and its lengthy digestive tract and sideways-facing eyes.

The behavioral adaptations required by different niches are usually less apparent than morphological differences, especially if they involve differences in the way that past experience affects present potential. However, the match between adaptation and niche is no less close because it is hard to see.

The basis for the modern idea of niche is Charles Darwin's discussion of an organism's "place in the economy of nature." References to his later work, including mathematical definitions of the concept, can be found in any ecology text.

fancy and adolescence, which necessarily delays reproductive maturity and places the individual at a reproductive–fitness disadvantage when compared to others that mature more quickly. It is sometimes better to be dumb and fast than intelligent and slow. Second, there is a growing bookkeeping cost: The behaviors acquired through past experience and some representation of the environments in which they are appropriate must be "stored," with minimal duplication, in such a way that the animal has ready access to the most appropriate response. It is no good to remember what to do if you do not also remember when to do it— and both are useless if it takes too long to reach a decision.

Representing data in the most flexible, economical, and easy-to-retrieve manner is a problem that confronts all data storage systems, natural as well as artificial. Much work in computer science and artificial intelligence (AI) is concerned with such database management. Efforts to automate vision and speech recognition have shown how complex this task really is. For example, early speech

B   O   X

1.3

Darwinian Fitness

The term *fitness* has a special meaning in biology: It refers not to the physical vigor of an organism (the colloquial meaning) but to its relative success in reproducing itself. Since only genes (with rare exceptions) actually reproduce, fitness is a property of the genetic material—of the *genotype*, not the *phenotype*. For example, consider a simple creature with only two possible gene loci, that is, its genotype is a word with only two letters (let's call them locus 1 and locus 2). Suppose that each of these loci can be occupied by only two different alleles (here an alphabet with just two letters), giving us four possible genotypes (Figure B1.1). The fitnesses of these four genotypes are then determined by how many of them appear in the next generation, relative to the number in the present generation.

For example, suppose the genotypes all began with 1000 individuals in the first generation and resemble Table B1.1 in successive generations. Clearly genotype D is reproducing itself faster than the other three, going from 1000 to 1418 individuals in 10 generations, whereas type A only goes from 1000 to 1090. In fact, all four types are growing geometrically (like compound interest) at rates of 1, 2, 3 and 4 percent per generation. The fitness of type D, therefore, is twice that of type B, even though both types increase from generation to generation.

In nature, of course, there are always factors that limit this growth, so that the total population size (which here increases from 4000 to 4997 individuals) is more or less constant from generation to generation. Consequently,

TABLE B1.1   Numbers of Individuals with Genotype

Generation	A	B	C	D	Total
1	1000	1000	1000	1000	4000
2	1010	1020	1030	1040	4100
3	1020	1040	1060	1081	4201
4	1030	1060	1091	1124	4305
5	1040	1081	1123	1168	4412
6	1050	1102	1156	1214	4522
7	1060	1124	1190	1262	4636
8	1070	1146	1225	1312	4753
9	1080	1168	1261	1364	4873
10	1090	1191	1298	1418	4997

continued

BOX 1.3 (*continued*)

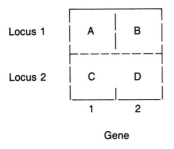

FIGURE B1.1   Four possible genotypes.

if the relative rates of growth are constant from generation to generation, the proportion of the fittest type will increase until it eventually drives out all others. However, natural populations are almost never homogeneous for two reasons: The fitness of a given genotype is almost always frequency dependent, that is, it decreases as the population numbers increase; and in real organisms, the number of loci and possible genes to fill them are both so large that genotypes are never repeated. For example, an organism with 100,000 loci each of which can be filled by 10 alleles implies $10^{100,000}$ possible genotypes, an unimaginably large number. Since sexual reproduction causes genes to be rearranged in an unpredictable way from one generation to the next, it is obvious that a given genotype is unlikely to recur, save by explicit cloning. Thus in reality, we cannot analyze an organism's fitness in this simple way. We must make assumptions (which may be questionable) about how different genes combine to affect fitness. Instead of measuring directly the fitness of genotype A (i.e., 1,1), B (1,2), and so on, we are reduced to studying the frequency of the genes at each locus in successive generations and using this information to estimate the fitness of specific genes, even though no gene acts in isolation.

Fitness is the ultimate measure of *natural selection,* which is the major agent for systematic evolution. Any adaptation, behavioral or morphological, must always be analyzed in terms of its probable effects on the fitness of the organisms that possess it, even though the difficulties involved in measuring fitness and in identifying the heritable aspects of the adaptation often render the results of such an inquiry inconclusive. We cannot always be sure how or whether a given feature contributes to fitness.

recognition systems took so long to search through all the possible interpretations of a sentence that they were of no practical use. In vision and hearing, and the correct and appropriate performance of learned acts, living organisms can somehow search through the alternatives quickly, which demonstrates the complexity of the task the brain performs almost without effort. The difficulty of performing electronically with computers what animals do easily with nervous systems shows how early stimulus–response learning theories underestimated the information-processing task implied by the behavior of mammals and birds.

Because identical situations rarely recur from day to day, the animal's representation of past environments must also allow it to behave appropriately in environments *similar* to those it has already encountered. For example, a chipmunk that has just received a painful bite from a spider will learn to avoid not just that spider but other spiders—and perhaps a few insects, as well. The chipmunk's concept of "spiderness," or *similarity* in the language of psychology, is determined both by the animal's evolutionary history and its own experience in ways that are slowly being unraveled.

LEARNING AND INNATE BEHAVIOR

As niches grow more complex, the need for simple mechanisms does not diminish. All animals, even humans, need reflexes, but in addition, more complex learning processes are also required. An animal's past experience can affect its future in a variety of ways. It used to be conventional to divide experience into learned behavior and innate behavior: *Innate behavior* was assumed to be completely independent of experience, whereas *learned behavior* was thought to be entirely dependent on experience. Critics soon pointed out that nothing is truly innate, in the sense of independent of *any* experience. For example, certain kinds of malnutrition can produce blindness, so that behavior, learned or otherwise, that depends on vision cannot develop. Nevertheless, many behaviors are almost independent of any specific kind of experience. As an example, many small invertebrates avoid light; they need no special training or nasty shock in a lighted place to show this pattern. Most mammalian reflexes are similar; for example, as soon as an infant can move at all, it will automatically withdraw its hand from a flame. The knee jerk in response to a tap, pupillary contraction in response to a bright light, and many other reflexes all develop normally in a variety of environments and are common to normal members of the human species.

But many other effects of experience don't fit into the innate/learned dichotomy. For example, age slows responses and hardens joints, fatigue reduces muscular strength, hunger (food deprivation) and thirst change preferences in systematic ways, and so on. The effects of fatigue and food deprivation are reversible, but (despite the propaganda of health-fad magazines) the effects of aging generally are not. Yet, none of these effects corresponds to the usual meaning of the term *learning*, which refers to a more specific and only partly reversible change, often related to a positive or negative outcome: The animal learns where food is to be found or to avoid places where it is vulnerable to predators. The change is *specific* because it refers to particular stimuli (environment) and responses (actions). It is only partially reversible because having once learned that food is to be found in a specific place, say, the animal will always treat that place differently from a place where food has never been found. In this text, we are primarily concerned with such types of behavioral changes, which are usually termed *associative learning,* but the definition is not exact, and there is probably no single physiological process that underlies associative learning, even in a given species. Experience can change behavior in many ways that do not involve learning, as well as in ways of which we are not sure. In other words, no hard-and-fast line separates learning from other kinds of behavioral change. No neat dichotomy exists between "learned" and "innate" behavior; rather, there is a spectrum of ways in which past experience affects future behavior, and learning is perhaps the most interesting, and certainly the least understood, of these.

The concept of *innate* is nevertheless useful. The mechanism that permits learning is innate, even if what is learned is not. For example, the sonatas that Mozart wrote when he was six years old depended on his prior learning of the 12-tone keyboard, musical notation, the sonata form, and so on. But, his brain structure permitted him to put together his experiences in a way impossible for most six-year-olds. How much was innate? How much depended on experience? These questions are impossible to answer. We might ask how much additional musical training would be required for an average six-year-old to perform like Mozart. The answer must surely be between 10 years and infinity. How many years of additional training are equal to how much innate endowment? Despite our natural tendency to try and compare the apples of natural endowment to the oranges of experience, the question is almost meaningless. However, it is certain that *any* learning depends on natural endowment, so that all learning is in a sense innate.

The concept of "innate" in the innate/learned dichotomy also relates to a useful distinction better expressed by the term *canalization,* which refers to the sensitivity of a phenotypic character. Canalization might be behavioral or morphological (i.e., to do with the physical characteristics of the organism) to the environment in which the organism matures. For example, some behaviors develop in almost any environment. Physical characteristics such as the four-chambered heart of mammals, bilateral symmetry, as well as most reflexes are strongly canalized; they develop in almost any environment that allows the organism to survive to maturity. On the other hand, a trait such as competence in the English language or the ability to do algebra is not at all canalized, since these traits are critically dependent on a specific environment. Competence in *some* language is an intermediate case: Evidently just about any linguistic environment is sufficient to produce language learning in a normal infant, even in the absence of explicit instruction. In a similar way, male chaffinches and white-crowned sparrows develop some adult song if they are allowed to hear it at the critical time in their first year of life, but the kind of song they develop depends on what they are permitted to hear (the model), as well as the species. That is, language and song development are canalized; the specific song or language to be learned is not.

What an animal learns and the way that it learns it is much affected by its niche. Since niches differ in many respects, so do learning mechanisms. Niches, however, do not differ in every respect, and there are also similarities among learning mechanisms. For example, space and time are common to all niches. The properties of causality, whether an important event is dependent on or independent of a prior event or the animal's own behavior, also vary little from one niche to another. Consequently, a wide range of animal species adapt to the temporal, spatial, and causal properties of the environment in similar fashions. There are also some general rules that apply across niches: For example, old information is generally less useful than new information; consequently animals forget, and they forget less about things they learned recently. Conversely, an animal's environment around the time of birth usually has a special significance, thus behaviors learned at that time may be especially resistant to change. Food, water, sex, and habitat are vitally important to all species. Hence these things are better remembered than "neutral" events, and they have special properties as guides of behavior.

This book is mainly concerned with the way that animals adapt to these special properties that are common to all niches. Our major emphasis is on adaptations that depend on learning about rewards and punishments.

PHILOSOPHICAL BACKGROUND

Animals and people seem to have purposes, beliefs, attitudes, and desires; they seem to know some things and not others, to want some things and disdain others, and so on. These beliefs are what philosophers call *intentional systems*. They may seem to set psychology apart from the physical and biological sciences: After all, the chemist doesn't worry about the beliefs of his or her compounds nor is the physicist concerned about the purposes of protons or the quirks of quarks. Does this mean that psychology is not scientific? Is psychological study different in kind from study in the physical sciences? No, not at all; the difference is quantitative and lies in the variety, responsivity, and historicity of what psychologists study. Even simple animals can perform a great variety of activities. Moreover, what they do almost invariably depends in subtle ways on their environment: Even the lowly ant may forage in the cool evening but seek shade in the midday sun and rush to its nest when it smells a hostile neighbor. Behavior is exquisitely responsive, and in "higher" animals, it depends greatly on individual history. For example, a key element in a Dorothy L. Sayers detective story is the inexplicable shying of a horse when at a seaside rock—to which (it turns out) he had days earlier carried a man who committed a murder. In mammals and birds, especially, present behavior can be affected in complex ways by events in the remote past.

The language of intentionality is simply the everyday way that we deal with complex historical systems. The original version of this book was written with the aid of a microcomputer that used an operating system called MS-DOS. Examine how the instruction manual refers to MS-DOS and its associated programs: "MS-DOS *could not find* a disk . . . ," "COPY *assumes* that a . . . character . . . ," "MS-DOS *does not know* that . . . ," "Seven commands are *recognized* by MS-DOS . . . ." No one assumes that a little man inhabits the microchips and has "real" knowledge, beliefs, desires, and understanding. The most striking examples are provided by chess-playing programs. A good one elicits precisely the

B   O   X

1.4

René Descartes (1596–1650)

The French philosopher René Descartes is famous for discussions on what he termed "method of doubt" (Cartesian method of doubt), in which he found that he could doubt everything except his own thoughts, hence his aphorism *cogito ergo sum* ("I think, therefore I am"). He is also famous for his stunning discovery of the relationship between algebra and geometry (Cartesian coordinates). His contribution to psychology reportedly grew out of his acquaintance with the bronze nymphs and satyrs then common in public parks. These ingenious mechanical devices were activated by a footfall, at which point they leapt out in front of startled strollers. Crude as these models may seem to a generation reared on Disney animatronics, they appeared strikingly lifelike and apparently gave rise to Descartes's conclusion that animals were merely more elaborate mechanical devices of this nature. Reflexes apart, humans were conveniently excluded, apparently for religious reasons.

Descartes was a man of modest private means that for the most part allowed him to follow his own pace and think his own thoughts. A late riser, he used the mornings for reflection. Anxious to avoid interruptions, even in an age much less intrusive than the present, he moved frequently and kept his address secret from all but a select few. He died relatively young in Sweden, where, out of mistaken respect for royalty, he had taken a job as tutor to the cold-loving, energetic, early-rising, and inconsiderate Queen Christina only a few months before. His great work, *Discourse on method,* contains his account of analytic geometry. His *Treatise on man* contains his contributions to psychology and physiology.

same kinds of comments we would expect from a human player: "It is attacking the queen," "It wants to gain control of the center of the board," and so on. Yet no one doubts that the underlying program provides a precise and mechanical account of the machine's behavior. Anything that responds to varied stimuli in varied ways, especially if its behavior depends on past history (as with computer operating systems), is understood at a common-sense level in intentional terms.

Nevertheless, as artificial intelligence advances, we may become even more intrigued by questions such as do machines *really* have beliefs, attitudes, and desires? The great Renaissance philosopher René Descartes argued persuasively (and without the benefit of AI) that animals, at least, are nothing but machines. His discussion has great relevance for our study of learning in animals. Since the most committed AI advocates are also convinced that humans, too, are machines (Box 1.4).

METHODOLOGICAL BEHAVIORISM

Two questions are important here: First, are there such things as beliefs, desires, and so on? And second, if so, do machines possess them? Two schools of thought exist on these questions: One says that beliefs and so forth are real but that machines probably don't have them (and who cares about machines anyway?); the other (the school we follow in this text) finds questions of this type not scientifically useful.

According to the first school, human beings have "real" desires, attitudes, and so on, and it is the business of "real" psychologists to study them. Sometimes attitudes and beliefs are deemed to be worthy of study in their own right. Although more commonly, they are studied as causes of action—people do what they do because they believe what they believe. This school's approach leaves little room for work with nonhuman animals, tends to keep the study of behavior at a verbal level, and attends *first* to the "meaning" of people's actions, verbal and otherwise, rather than focusing on the details of the actions themselves. This school espouses the psychology of the paper-and-pencil test, interview, and verbal report.

Its point of view has some practical benefits. The power of advertising rests in some measure on the correct assessment of people's attitudes toward, for example, bodily appearance and sexual attraction. Products are promoted to enhance whatever is generally favored (slenderness, a tan skin, white teeth, the appropriate odor, etc.), and for this to work, advertisers must have reliable ways of measuring people's attitudes (toward weight, skin color, teeth, armpits, etc.). Nevertheless, this approach has both experimental and theoretical limitations. Experimentally, its problem derives from the difficulty of separating *correlation* from *causation.* It presents the old question: Do we run because we are afraid, or are we afraid because we run? "Fear," like "attitudes," is a property of the subject's internal state, not something external that the experimenter can manipulate directly. Consequently, you can never be certain that the running and the fear are not both simultaneously caused by the same external conditions. The problem is not insuperable: There are ways that intentional terms like "fear," "hope," and so on can be made methodologically respectable and tied to observables. The theoretical limitation of this approach is whether the labor involved is worth it. The entire enterprise rests on the presupposition that intentional terms like "fear," "belief," "attitude," and the like form the best basis for theoretical psychology.

Our discussion of clever computer programs showed that such terms represent only one level of explanation. They enable someone ignorant of the details of the computer program to make some sort of sense of what the machine is doing. Despite their usefulness, study of the actual program rarely reveals anything that corresponds directly to intentional terms. It is rash, therefore, to base a program of psychological research on the assumption that intentional terms represent the ultimate form of explanation. Throughout this text, we attempt other levels of understanding—understanding in terms of the mechanisms and the functions of behavior. In the computer program described, such comprehension would correspond to an understanding of the details of the program itself as well as to what the program does and why it does it.

According to the second school, the answer to the question "Are there *really* such things as beliefs, desires, and so on?" is "Maybe . . . but how important is this question to a scientific picture?" These terms are useful ways of coping with some complex systems, but the question is metaphysical, and we have no reason to suppose that these terms will prove especially useful in unraveling the mechanisms of behavior. In this text, we are concerned with *methodological behaviorism,* the behaviors of people and animals measured in physical terms (i.e., with a minimum of interpretation). This school of study is the dominant stance among psychologists and biologists interested in learning and animal behavior. Methodological behaviorism is not untheoretical; it simply takes no advance position on the nature of appropriate theory. In particular, it does not presume that psychological theory should be based on the intentional language of everyday speech.

THE MIND–BODY PROBLEM

The mind–body problem is the set of philosophical problems raised by the common-sense notion that mental phenomena such as volitions, thoughts, attitudes, and the like cause behavior. Like many philosophical riddles, the mind–body problem has acquired an air of permanence and insolubility that tends to produce a defeatist attitude (e.g., If so many great thinkers of the past have failed to solve this problem, then what chance have we?) It consists of two main aspects. The first is practical: measuring "mental" phenomena and demonstrating their causal efficacy. Again, the difficulty here is that correlation does not imply causation: Even if a given mental event is invariably associated with some action, we cannot thereby prove the one causes the other, because we cannot directly manipulate the mental event. However, we should still study mental events, because invariable association under a variety of circumstances may be interesting enough no matter what the logical deficiencies. The second aspect of the mind–body problem is more serious and concerns the role of mental events as extraphysical causes of behavior. The idea is that mental events have "a life of their own," they occur independently of any physical cause, and they themselves cause action. This idea can only be disproved by exclusion: Only when we can explain every conceivable behavior of animal or human in purely physical terms, then there will be nothing left for nonphysical causes to account for. Clearly, nonphysical causes are safe for a while.

Many researchers follow a sort of Cartesian dualism that allows them to perform their scientific investigations. (Descartes proposed that although human behavior is largely automatic, some important aspects, being determined by the soul, are not.) The dualistic view may be epitomized as follows: "Well, clearly there *are* mental effects not completely traceable to physical causes, but the

B   O   X

1.5

Free Will, Truth, and Determinism

If behavior is determined, is real knowledge then impossible? If everything we do is determined by "purely mechanical" processes, then how can we attach any truth-value to our conclusions? The capacity to discover the truth seems to presuppose the capacity for error (i.e., for "spontaneity," "free will," "choice," etc.) The Marxist conclusion that all beliefs are simply a reflection of social and economic conditions seems inherently paradoxical, since if true, the statement itself is also a reflection of the conditions to which Marx himself was subject. If true, then it is determined, hence not true (or at least not necessarily true). In a similar way, for many people it makes no sense to ask if a conclusion is true if it can also be shown to follow from a completely deterministic process.

Yet, there is nothing essentially implausible about this concept of belief. Natural selection provides a way out for the behavioral determinist (if not for Karl Marx). For example, quite early in the history of artificial intelligence, computers were programmed to discover and prove simple theorems in mathematical logic. For this purpose, it was only necessary that the machine be programmed to generate logic statements (i.e., that it have some mechanism of behavioral variation) and then apply to them a set of logical tests (i.e., rules of selection), rejecting statements that failed (false propositions) and retaining those that passed (true propositions). To be sure, there is often a random element in the generation process, as there is in the behavior of organisms; yet the process as a whole is perfectly comprehensible from a deterministic point of view. Consequently, there is nothing paradoxical in the notion that animal (and human) behavior (including consciousness and "mental life") is determined by the physical activity of the nervous system and that it follows comprehensible, deterministic laws. Animal and human modes of thought and be-

part of the nervous system (type of behavior, species of animal, etc.) that I happen to work on is in fact perfectly deterministic and can be understood by the usual scientific methods."

Some take this Cartesian position for religious reasons, others because the application of determinism to human behavior seems to pose problems. The dualistic stance is open to criticism in part because science must assume determinism. That is, science must assume that there are lawful regularities and that it is the business of science to discover them. If determinism applies to the lower animals, considered worthy subjects for psychology, then evolutionary continuity requires that it also apply to humans (Box 1.5).

liefs have evolved under the rigorous rules of natural selection. In this view, we have faith in logic and reason, which are the bases for the rejection (not the origin) of scientific hypotheses because these modes of thought have survived the test of natural selection. The human scientist may differ from an "intelligent" computer only quantitatively—in the range of different hypotheses he or she can entertain and in the subtlety of the tests for truth that he or she can apply.

This view of belief systems precludes the possibility of "absolute truth," because truth is always relative to the set of alternatives that have been considered and the criteria used for selecting from them. Truth does not assert that *nothing* is true (as some have argued), just that we can never be sure we have the truth. Nor does truth imply that everything is equally uncertain. Some things are clearly much more likely to be true than others. Paraphrasing Dr. Johnson in response to Bishop Berkeley's *idealism* (the notion that everything exists only in our minds): "I refute it thus!" as he kicked a rock. The reality of the external world may be uncertain, but it is clearly less uncertain than the philosophizing of Bishop Berkeley.

As the human species evolves and our cultural heritage develops, better criteria and more powerful hypotheses may appear, so that deeper truths may become possible. This kind of relativism is widely accepted by scientific workers of all philosophical persuasions.

For views of the mind–body problem different from the one sketched here see Sperry (1969). For discussions of evolutionary epistemology, see Campbell (1975), Popper (1968), and Toulmin (1967).

THE NATURE OF EXPLANATION

The emphasis of this book is on explanations for behavior in purely environmental terms, that is, on methodological behaviorism. How does the animal's past history interact with rules built in to the animal by its evolutionary history and individual development to produce future behavior? We spend little time discussing the animal's internal structure (because this book is not about neurophysiology, fascinating though that field has become in recent years). We also do not delve into intentional states that we can relate to our own introspections (because the history of the field gives us little hope that this direction is a promising one, especially for the behavior of animals). Because there is often confusion about the meaning of explanations at the level we emphasize, we briefly discuss "black-box" explanations. As an example, we show how the simple notion of *negative feedback* provides a purely mechanical account of purposive behavior and, by extension, of motivation in general.

Levels of Explanation

Scientific explanations can be at many levels. For example, the behavior of a moth circling a flame might be explained as

1. An "instinct"
2. A form of taxic reaction (e.g., orientation toward light)
3. A specific kind of control system
4. The response of a specific neural network connected to a set of receptors and effectors
5. In terms of intentions (e.g., the moth wanted to get near the light)

LEVEL 1: CLASSIFICATION   The instinct account (level 1) says nothing about the process involved; it is simply a kind of classification. It places the moth's behavior in a group that contains all the behaviors that depend little on experience. Although this explanation is relatively primitive, it is not empty; it may in fact be essential to go through such a "natural history" stage at the beginning of any science.

LEVEL 2: TAXES   Explaining the behavior as a *taxis* (level 2) (a form of phototropism, for example) is also classificatory but now in terms of the results of experiments. For example, blinding in one eye causes continuous turning movements in some phototropic animals. Phototropisms that behave this way are classified in one way; others are classified differently. This approach moves closer to the underlying process of the behavior in question.

LEVEL 3: CONTROL SYSTEMS   The control-system account (level 3) explains the moth's behavior in terms of a negative-feedback mechanism sensitive to a given illuminance difference between the two eyes (Figure 1.1). This account rests on experimentation and quantitative results and constitutes an explanation in terms of a process. The basic idea is simple: For any given discrepancy between the moth's actual heading and the setpoint heading (i.e., the heading that maintains an angle (α) between the moth's heading and the direction of the light), there is a tendency to turn in a direction that reduces the discrepancy (negative feedback). A feedback model gives the "rules of the game," those aspects of the behavior that are invariant, that is, independent of specific inputs and outputs. This control-system account is analogous to the wiring diagram for sensors, a thermostat, or a furnace. However, it is still a *black-box* account: The equations of

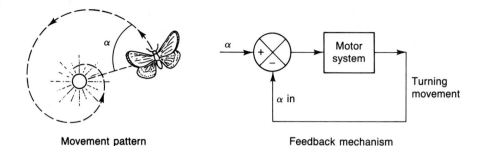

Movement pattern   Feedback mechanism

FIGURE 1.1   A control-system model for moth phototropism. The idea is that the insect flies in such a way that there is a constant difference between the amounts of light that fall on the two eyes, which means that the moth will always fly at a certain angle (α) to the light. If α is less than 90°, this behavior causes the moth to spiral in toward the light. Note that this mechanism works to keep the animal in a fixed direction with respect to the sun (see Chapter 2, "Direct Orientation (Taxes)"); it fails when used with artificial lights. If we specify how quickly the animal adjusts to forced deviations from its preferred angle, we have a dynamic control-system model for the behavior.

the model and the boxes and connecting arrows that make the model easier to understand may have little to do with an account in terms of neural and other structures (level 4). Nevertheless, the control-system account says what the neural structures must *do,* and it hints as to how they might do it (as do the symbols in an electrical diagram). Note: Block diagrams cannot be interpreted literally as connections among neural circuits.

LEVEL 4: BLACK BOXES   In terms of neural structures, black-box accounts provide a natural preliminary to accounts at level 4. Many would argue that a complete explanation of behavior must include descriptions of neural structure and function. However, we are a long way from explaining even the simple behavior of simple organisms in these terms.

LEVEL 5: INTENTIONAL SYSTEMS   Finally, the intentional account (level 5) leaves such term as "wanting" yet to be explained. It also adds nothing to the simple observation that the moth follows the flame. Intentional explanations, like the instinct account, are useful as an initial step, especially if there are many ways in which a given objective can be attained. Although, our moth example is simple enough that a complete control-theory account can be given, and reference to intention is unnecessary.

In summary, each level of explanation has its uses. Explaining the moth's circling in terms of instinct is a useful starting point for the student of behavioral development, and it may have implications for the evolution of behavior. The taxis account relates the behavior to other orientation reactions, and it may be useful for understanding species differences. The control-system account is useful for making quantitative predictions and as an element in accounts of the integration of behavior. That is, the control-system account is useful in theories that bring together a number of mechanisms so as to account for something approaching the organism's total behavioral repertoire. Studying behavior at the neural level has led to understandings of physiological systems and a great appreciation of the neural complexity of simple behavior. The use of intentional terms may also be a useful starting point when behavior is especially complex and we are a long way from identifying underlying causes.

PURPOSE, TELEOLOGY, AND MECHANISM

The concept of *purpose* has occupied a prominent place in the history of psychology. Although criticized by the behaviorists, it is covertly retained even by them in the form of so-called "control of behavior by its consequences." Some readers may have noticed that the setpoint of a feedback mechanism (the set temperature of a heating system, the α angle in the moth example) corresponds closely to the intuitive idea of a "goal" or "motive." This connection was pointed out some years ago in a classic philosophical paper by Roseblueth, Wiener, and Bigelow (1943). These researchers showed that the idea of feedback provides the conceptual link between *mechanistic accounts* of behavior, that is, explanations in terms of antecedent events (proximal causes), and *teleological* (or *functional*) *accounts,* that is, explanations in terms of goals or motives (final causes). The superiority of a feedback account rests in its self-contained ability to answer both for those cases where the goal is attained and those where it is not.

Functional Versus Mechanistic Explanations

Common-sense explanation in terms of purpose does not easily account for failures to achieve a goal. For example, a student may do well on an organic chemistry examination, which might be attributed to his or her goal of getting into medical school. But, suppose the student had failed the exam, despite a strong motivation to succeed. Explanation in terms of goals or motives must then postulate some competing motivation (the student may have spent too much time with friends?) or else say something about the student's capabilities and methods of study, that is, resort to a mechanistic account. In short, conventional motivational accounts offer only two explanations for failures to achieve an objective—competing motives (time with friends) or unsuspected structural limitation (poor memory for lists of chemical reactions). Both these escape routes have an ad hoc look to them, yet they roughly correspond to respectable explanatory alternatives: an optimality (or functional) account provides the laws by which motives compete, and a mechanistic account dispenses with motives entirely and explains behavior through antecedent conditions and structural properties of the subject.

Different fields emphasize different types of explanation. Classical economics, for example, explains people's allocation of time and money between different commodities, or between work and leisure, in terms of a balance of motives (a functional account). The individual is assumed to optimize his or her total utility by allocating resources so that the marginal gain from switching from one commodity to any other is constant. That is, he or she spends so that every last nickel will buy the same benefit, no matter where it is spent. In this way, total benefit is usually maximized. *Optimality analyses* (about which much more will be said in later chapters) are the ultimate form of functional account, because they specify precisely the "rules" by which goals are obtained. On the other hand, the field of ecology (which has much in common with economics as the similar name implies) has generally favored mechanistic accounts: The distribution of species within and between habitats is usually explained in terms of the species' feeding strategies and reproductive rates, for example.

Psychology and behavioral biology have at different times favored both approaches. Reinforcement theory is basically functional, in the sense that behavior is assumed to be guided by access to a key event, the reinforcer, which *in effect* functions as a goal (although we will look at the process mechanistically): The animal works for food or to avoid electric shock. Purposive terminology is studiously avoided (the phrase "works for" is frowned on in the young, and it is only employed in the privacy of the laboratory), but the lack of any general agreement on the details of the reinforcement mechanism means that the term *reinforcement* is in effect much closer to *goal* than many who use it would like. For example, when several experiments showed that hungry rats would sometimes press a lever for food even if free food were available (so-called *contrafreeloading*), a popular explanation was that the lever-pressing behavior was "self-reinforcing." This term is not really any different from saying that the animal "likes" to press the lever, although it sounds more scientifically respectable. As we shall see in later chapters, reinforcement, both as an effective procedure and an explanation of behavior, is usually defined in terms of restriction of access to a specific activity (eating, for example). Thus, the notion of self-reinforcement (as a sufficient explanation for behavior) is paradoxical: If lever-pressing is (self)-reinforcing, why doesn't the animal press all the time—as it would for an unrestricted food reinforcer?

Other areas of learning psychology have emphasized mechanistic accounts. For example, the Hullian theories of learning were a praiseworthy, if largely unsuccessful, attempt to specify the causal links between the stimulus as cause and the response as ultimate effect. More recent mathematical theories of conditioning and the effects of food and other stimuli on general activity (arousal) are strictly mechanistic, looking to antecedent, rather than consequential, events for explanation of the behavior. Theories that explain choice and the distribution of behavior in terms of competition between the tendencies to engage in different activities are also, like their ecological counterparts, mechanistic in spirit.

Both mechanistic and functional accounts have their uses, although mechanistic theories are obviously desirable when possible. Although, when the means by which an organism, or an economy, can attain some end state are many and poorly understood, but the goal is relatively clear, then a functional theory may be the best that is available. For example, for Winnie-the-Pooh, honey is clearly a goal or reinforcer. Much of his behavior can be explained as an attempt to get at the honey, even though our knowledge of Pooh psychology is limited, so that we do not know how he comes up with specific plans. An adequate teleological explanation (like the empirical principle of reinforcement in which x is a reinforcer if behavior that leads to x becomes more likely) is certainly better than a premature mechanistic theory, as the early followers of Hull found to their cost.

The explanation of the chess-playing program described earlier is mechanistic in terms of the program itself and the individual instructions that determine each move as a function of prior moves by both players. But when designing such a program as well as when trying to understand it, it is usually convenient to divide it into two portions—a part that generates potential moves, that is, variation, and a part that evaluates each move in terms of a set of criteria, that is, selection. The dichotomy between variation and selection was independently discovered by Charles Darwin and Alfred Russel Wallace as their theory of evolution by natural selection, but the distinction is more general: All adaptive, purposive behavior can be analysed in this way. The dichotomy leads to the two explanations for adaptive behavior, that is, mechanistic (causal) explanations, which define both the rules by which behaviors are generated (variation rules) and the rules by which adaptive variants are selected (selection rules) and functional explanations, which specify (perhaps in simplified form) the selection rules. Mechanistic accounts deal just in antecedent causes; functional accounts work in terms of final outcomes. Thus, the form of the shark is explained functionally by its hydrodynamic efficiency, the taking of a computer opponent's queen in a chess program in terms of the improved position that results, and performance on simple reinforcement schedules in terms regulating food intake.

Functional explanations are often way stations to mechanistic explanations. In studies of learning, they help identify important variables and draw attention to the constraints that limit an animal's ability to attain functional goals. For example, mammals and birds can easily learn to use stimuli as guides to the availability of food; a hungry pigeon has no difficulty learning that a peck on a red disk yields food, whereas a peck on a blue disk does not. But mammals and birds are much less capable of using *past* stimuli as guides. In the delayed-match-to-sample task, one of two stimuli is briefly presented, then after some delay both are presented, and a response to the one that matches the first is rewarded. Delays of more than a few seconds between sample and choice presentations gravely impair most animals' abilities to choose correctly. The constraint is a memory constraint. Other psychological constraints have to do with animals' abilities to process information and with their perceptual abilities. Identification of limitations of this sort is the first step toward understanding behavioral mechanisms.

In addition to internal (psychological) constraints, constraints are also imposed by the environment. For example, animals cannot perform more than one activity at a time, so that the total amount of their activity is limited; spatial arrangements limit the order in which food sites can be visited and the time between visits. Reinforcement schedules, either natural (as in picking up grain, one peck per grain, or in natural replenishment processes) or artificial (ratio and interval schedules, for example) further constrain the distribution of activities. Precisely expressed in the form of optimality theory, functional explanations allow, indeed force, you to take account of these external constraints.

In the field of psychology, it is traditional to belittle functional accounts (although they often come in the form of vaguely expressed reinforcement theories). Indeed, one of our most influential figures boasts in his memoirs that in planning his major work he deliberately avoided any discussion of adaptiveness. Few maintain that position today. Studying behavior both in terms of its adaptive (evolutionary) function and in relation to current goals (reinforcers) is useful in identifying important variables and in distinguishing environmental from psychological constraints. We hold functional and mechanistic explanations with equal regard in this book.

The idea that organisms attain goals, either through natural selection for the best form of wing or individual reinforcement of the most effective foraging strategy, derives naturally from the concept of selection/variation: A behavioral variant occurs, the best (in terms of flight efficiency or eating frequency) is preferentially selected, the next round of variants contains a few that are even better, and so on. The validity of this argument depends on two notions:

1. That we have the selection rule correct (that better fliers really have more offspring)

2. That the *correct* variants occur

In other words, an animal may fail to behave in what seems to us to be the optimal fashion if we have misread what it is "trying" to achieve (the selection rule) or because it never generates the necessary behavioral variant. That is, the most efficient foraging strategy cannot be selected (reinforced) if it never occurs. The memory constraints illustrated by the delayed-match-to-sample task limit behavioral variation in this manner. Thus, failures to optimize are if anything even more informative than successes, as they offer clues to the underlying behavioral mechanisms.

THE EVOLUTION AND DEVELOPMENT OF BEHAVIOR

The processes that guide an individual's development (ontogeny) are the product of the species' past evolution. Developmental processes affect future evolutionary possibilities for the species, and they often incorporate the effects of past experience on the behavior of individuals in ways that contrast with, and thus help define, learning.

Organisms change throughout their lifetimes, and the processes by which they change are the outcome of past evolution. As Darwin noted, organisms bear their evolutionary history both in their structure and in the manner of their historical development. Rudimentary organs provide some of the most striking examples—the human appendix, the rudimentary breasts of male mammals, the vestigial lung of snakes (that have only one functional lung), the teeth of fetal whales that vanish in the adult. None of these organs have any function in the adult, yet they remain. There are behavioral parallels in the inappropriate "grass flattening" of domestic dogs and in the exaggerated fears of human children (e.g., of the dark, of insects, of strangers). In many cases, these vestigial behaviors disappear with age, as in some of Darwin's examples.

Such examples illustrate the half-truth that "ontogeny recapitulates phylogeny," that is, the idea that the stages through which an organism passes, from embryo to adult, represent a history of the race in an abbreviated form. Gill slits in the human fetus were once taken to mean that the fetus at that stage resembles the ancient fish from which mammals are descended. The actual relations between ontogeny and phylogeny are more complicated and derive from the fact that evolution acts via the mechanisms of development.

At conception the organism is essentially undifferentiated and "pluripotent," that is, many avenues for development are possible. With progressive cell divisions, differentiation increases, and the options for further development are reduced. This process of progressively finer differentiation and the concomitant reduction in future options takes place throughout life. The process eventually ends in death, which is not a wearing out but the largely predetermined end of a course charted by prior evolution. A typical lifespan, like other characteristics, is determined by its costs and benefits, weighed in the delicate balance of natural selection.

The Gene–Environment Interaction

Genes determine the direction of the developmental process that occurs throughout the life cycle of an individual, although we don't yet know exactly how this process works. A recent theoretical account begins: "Despite our relatively detailed understanding of molecular biology, the processes which control the development of a multicellular organism from a single cell, the fertilized egg, are almost completely unknown" (Caplan & Ordahl, 1978, p. 120). Nevertheless, the genetic changes that provide the raw material for evolution act not directly on morphology or behavior but on the course of development. That is, a stage may be added or missed entirely, and stages may be accelerated or retarded. These changes in the development path are the raw material for formation of new species. For example, if the genital system matures relatively faster than the rest of the body, the result may be a sexually mature "larval" animal, as in the case of the Mexican Axolotl (*Ambystoma tigrinum*), a salamander that can become sexually mature while still a tadpole. Continued selection might adjust this situation, so that the terrestrial stage is completely abolished and a new species of entirely aquatic amphibian results.

The action of a gene depends on its environment, which includes the rest of the genotype, the cell of which it is a part, the constitution of neighboring cells, circulating metabolites such as hormones, and the neurotransmitters released by nerve impulses. For example, during the development of the fruit fly *Drosophila,* the polar cytoplasm influences the nuclei that migrate through it to differentiate into the reproductive cells. If this section of cytoplasm is removed from the egg so that migrating nuclei do not encounter it, the reproductive cells do not develop, and a sterile animal results. The polar cytoplasm affects the expression during development of genes responsible for the reproductive system.

Because the organism's internal environment is intimately affected by its external environment, the course of development is a joint product of genotype and the environment in which the organism matures. In effect, therefore, the action of genes and the environment are symmetrical—each depends on the other. The main difference between environmental and genetic effects is that because the genotype is fixed but the environment can vary, environmental effects on behavior may be reversible. Since the sensorimotor systems that bring the animal into contact with its environment develop with age, the effects of environment on development are likely to become richer and more subtle as the organism grows older. The environmental effects on an embryo or a newborn may be great, but they are unlikely to involve the transmission of as much information as interactions later in life. On the other hand, environmental effects are likely to be self-limiting, owing to the accumulation of irreversible changes, so that mid-life might often be the time of maximal sensitivity to external influences.

Gross morphological changes are not readily reversible, which is why traces of an organism's evolution are retained in its development. But behavior, and presumably the changes in brain state that correspond to behavior, is almost by definition easily altered. Consequently, it is not at all clear what we should expect of the relation between behavioral and morphological development. Is it reasonable to assume, for example, that behaviors that appear early in ontogeny only to disappear later are of the same sort as human fetal gill slits? Were these the behaviors of our immature ape ancestors? In the case of some primitive reflexes, such a guess may be reasonable. For fear of strangers or of the dark, we cannot be sure. This question will not be settled until we understand how brain structure and physiology relate to behavior. How is past experience represented neurophysiologically? How does the current environment interact with this representation and the animal's motivational state to produce action? Unfortunately, we are a long way from answering these questions.

Genetic Assimilation

The subtleties of gene–environment interaction are nicely illustrated by some ingenious experiments by the geneticist Charles Waddington. Using fruit flies, Waddington (1960) showed that environmental changes can act as a sort of probe to uncover latent characteristics of the genotype. In one experiment fruit fly pupae were subjected to heat shock at an age when this treatment was known to produce adults with various kinds of altered wing-vein patterns (venation phenocopies) (Figure 1.2). Individual fruit flies that showed a specific kind of phenocopy were then selectively bred together. Soon, fruit flies were produced that responded to this kind of stress with high frequencies. Continued intense artificial selection made it possible to produce strains of flies in which the selected-for abnormality appeared even in the absence of heat stress. Waddington termed this phenomenon *genetic assimilation,* which is the process by

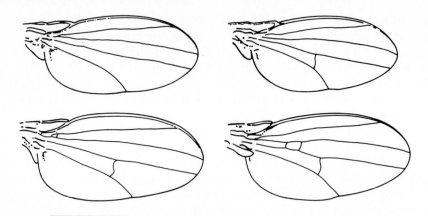

FIGURE 1.2   Four typical *Drosophila* wing types (venation phenocopies) induced by subjecting the pupa to heat stress (from Waddington, 1960, p. 394).

which the environment can uncover genetic characteristics that are no longer expressed by most members of a species.

Many other examples of genetic assimilation also exist. Consider the familiar phenomenon of the formation of skin calluses in response to (and as a protection against) abrasion: Calluses form much more readily on some parts of the body (such as the hands and feet) than on others, which reflects differential selection pressure. Indeed, calluses can even form on the feet of a bedridden person, that is, in the absence of the usual environmental stimulus. The phenomenon also shows an evolutionary vestige in the form of knuckle calluses, which form spontaneously in many individuals. Knuckle calluses are of no use now, but presumably they served an adaptive function in our knuckle-walking ancestors. Evidently, past selection for callus development in response to abrasion leads to the spontaneous development of calluses in some people.

In higher animals, training procedures may be regarded as genetic probes whose effects can be interpreted in the same way as Waddington's heat shock. For example, the ease with which an individual learns some skills such as music or mathematics may be an indication of how close his or her genotype is to one that would produce this behavior with minimal or no training. You might speculate that a program of selective breeding for precocious musical ability would eventually lead to Mozarts capable of writing symphonies at age six and finally, perhaps, to infants capable of spontaneous, high-order musical expression in the absence of *any* explicit training—human songbirds.

Imprinting

Such a scenario may seem improbable, either because it seems unreasonable that something as complex as musical proficiency should be entirely innate, or because we are accustomed to think of *learned* and *innate* as opposites. There is no basis for either objection. For example, sheepdogs are selected for their ability to learn to herd sheep, although training a professional sheepdog takes years. Nevertheless, components of herding, such as circling and attempting to "group" people or animals, appear spontaneously in pets that have never been specifically trained. Speech is learned, yet adult intonation patterns and a large number of phonemes (speech-sound units) occur spontaneously in infants. Precocial birds learn to identify their own species early in life, via the process termed *imprinting;* nevertheless, the type of object accepted for imprinting, especially later sexual imprinting, cannot deviate too much from the natural stimulus if it is to be effective. For example, young male swamp sparrows learn their song from adult males, but they are quite specific in what they will accept as a model. In all cases, the learned ability is put together with ingredients provided innately.

Complex behavior may be innately programmed, and thus complexity by itself is an unreliable guide to whether a behavior is learned or innate. Almost all the intricate behavior of insects develops independently of experience, for example. Some songbirds such as the song sparrow develop their elaborate song without any specific experience, whereas others such as the chaffinch require early exposure to their much simpler species' song if they are later to sing normally. Most dramatic, perhaps, is the inheritance of navigational ability by migratory birds. The golden plover breeds in northern Alaska and migrates during the fall to Argentina by way of Labrador; it returns in the spring over Central America, heading north and west along the Mississippi river. The bobolink travels from Maine to Brazil, Wilson's petrel from the Falkland Islands to Newfoundland. Marine animals such as whales and salmon perform comparable migratory feats. Migratory birds use navigational aids such as sun direction, assessed both directly and through sky polarization on partly cloudy days; time, via an internal clock keyed to the light-dark cycle; the direction of the earth's magnetic field; low frequency sounds (infrasound) such as the sound of surf on a distant beach, which may be audible hundreds of miles away; visual terrain cues; and perhaps other features not yet identified. These cues are combined to guide flight in ways that are far from being understood, even in the short flights of homing pigeons. The capacity to carry out these long migrations is little dependent on experience. Thus, the complexity of a behavior pattern is an unreliable cue to its developmental origins.

Environmental effects on development can occur at any time, from conception to senescence. For example, experiments by the pioneering developmental psychobiologist Zing-Yang Kuo (1932) showed that the passive movement of the head and beak in embryonic chicks caused by their heartbeat plays a role in their later development of pecking. Gilbert Gottlieb (1966) has shown that ducklings' abilities to follow the repetitive call of their mother depends for its selectivity on prehatching experience with sound frequencies above 1500 Hz. Normal ducklings are able to hear their mother while in the egg. When given a choice between a recording of the normal call and a call with higher frequencies filtered out, Gottlieb found that normal ducklings reliably chose the normal call. However, birds deprived of hearing the mother while in the egg choose both alternatives equally. Under normal circumstances, all ducklings receive the required experience, both by hearing their own calls while in the egg and by hearing the calls of their siblings in adjacent eggs.

These dependencies of later behavior on apparently unrelated earlier experience may seem odd and even capricious, but they fit in well with an epigenetic view of development that stresses the interaction between genes and the environment. Gene action is strictly conditional and dependent on the gene environment and thus, in many cases, on the environment of the organism. Natural selction favors any genetic change that reliably has a beneficial effect on the phenotype. If the expression of that genetic change depends on the presence of a specific environmental feature, then as long as that feature is a reliable accompaniment of normal development, the gene is favored, and an environmental dependence becomes established.

Imprinting is the best-known example of this kind of dependency. Precocial birds such as chicks and ducklings generally form a permanent attachment to individuals that they see and can follow during the first day or two of life. This behavior is part of the process by which these species learn to identify their own kind. In these animals, species identification might have developed in several ways: For example, ducklings might be provided at hatching with an essentially built-in "template" that enables them to recognize members of their own species immediately. Many species are provided with such a template, for instance, almost all insects, brood parasites such as the cuckoo and the North American cowbird, which never see their own parents and could not function without the innate ability to recognize their own species. But even with such a template, the ducklings would also require a propensity to follow (following the mother when she calls is essential if the duckling is not to end up inside a predator). Such following implies some learning, so that the animal doesn't follow *any* female duck but only the mother. Under normal circumstances, of course, the first individual that the chick or duckling sees is a member of its own species. If not, its future is likely to be dim—an orphan is not likely to contribute to future generations. Therefore, given the existence of some learning mechanism, an efficient solution to the species–identification problem is the existence of a critical period during the first few days of life when the individual learns about the characteristics of its own species through those of the individual it follows. Most genes act only during specific stages of development, so that only small changes in genotype over many generations may have been necessary to change from the built-in template kind of behavior to imprinting. As imprinting evolved, less of the template was necessary, and mutations that tended to degrade the template may have been selected.

Vestiges of the template mechanisms from which imprinting may have evolved can still be detected. Ducklings imprint most rapidly to stimuli that resemble members of their own species. Their imprinting is weak to a severely abnormal stimulus such as a moving box, although this problem can be overcome later by exposure to the natural stimulus.

SUMMARY

The introductory chapter of any book must always anticipate the presuppositions of its readers. We assume that many readers know more about psychology than biology but that they may still hold common-sense mentalist views about the causes of human and animal behavior. To this end, we discussed animals as machines and intentional terms and their limited usefulness as explanations of behavior.

We introduced several philosophical problems that have plagued the study of behavior from earliest times. The mind–body problem is the set of philosophical puzzles that is raised by the notion that human behavior is caused by such mental phenomena as beliefs, attitudes, volitions, and the like. In describing the problem of the appropriate form of scientific explanation, we found that teleological (functional) explanations are useful explanations of behavioral phenomena, especially where mechanistic explanations are not yet possible. Optimality theory allows functional explanations to be formululated precisely, and it forces us to specify what is important to an animal and what are the constraints, both internal and external, within which behavior must operate. These constraints, in turn, provide clues to the underlying mechanisms that allow the animal to behave in a goal-directed manner.

The common distinction between learned and innate behavior requires modification. Some years ago, a perceptive psychologist (Verplanck, 1955) wrote a paper entitled "Since Learned Behavior Is Innate, and Vice Versa, What Now?" The paper correctly identified the problem: Learning depends on inherited mechanisms and is constrained by them. Additionally, we discussed how past experience affects later behavior in many ways, only a few of which we call "learning." The best way to get a feeling for the range of possibilities is to study ontogeny: how it reflects past evolution and how it incorporates environmental effects, sometimes in an apparently capricious and idiosyncratic way. Our discussion led to an epigenetic view of development, which holds that changes in morphology and behavior during ontogeny reflect a process of differentiation in which some options are chosen and others given up. In addition, development is guided at every instant by the joint effects of genotype and environment.

2

Simple Mechanisms for Adaptive Behavior

Orb-web spiders have devised a most efficient net for catching flying insects, yet we can trace no history of trial and error in the life of an individual spider that could explain the excellence of the web's design. Spiders don't *learn* how to weave good webs; no spider tries different designs and discards all but the most efficient. It is their instant perfection that sustains mystical beliefs in the power of instinct. Yet surely there was trial and error by ancestral spiders who built webs with varying efficiencies. Those who built best were better nourished and had more offspring. Since variations (i.e., individual differences) in web-building ability are to some degree inherited, the ability to build better webs evolved not by selection of good webs by individual spiders (i.e., by learning) but by selection of spiders who made better webs. Web building depends on history—but it depends more on the history of the species than on the history of the individual spider.

In "higher" animals, however, behavior is more often selected in the life of the individual, not by differential reproduction of individuals with innate talents. For example, the adaptive behavior of a rat depends not only on mechanisms that have developed with little input from the environment (as in the web building of spiders) but also on a complex individual history.[1] For the rat, built-in mechanisms interacted with the environment, laid down memories, which caused behavior to be different, and so on in a complicated circular process whose workings soon become quite difficult to disentangle (we nevertheless make the attempt in later chapters!). But in simple animals, like the protozoa and invertebrates discussed in this chapter, behavior depends little on past history and not at all on the animal's distant past (no "Rosebuds" for the invertebrates![2]). Such simple animals are easier to discuss, thus we begin with them. The rudimentary mechanisms that underlie the behavior of simple animals nevertheless allow for remarkably subtle adaptations to diverse environmental conditions. Such behaviors are essential to the survival of simple animals and are essential ingredients of adaptive behavior in higher animals.

SIMPLE ORIENTATION MECHANISMS

Finding the proper habitat, a place not too hot or cold, too dry or wet, safe from predators and with a supply of food, is a major behavioral problem for all animals. For simple animals such as protozoa and primitive invertebrates, it is their main problem. These organisms possess either no or only the most rudimentary nervous system. Many have only primitive vision and hearing, that is, they have no *distance receptors* (sensory systems able to register the direction and distance of a remote object such as a predator or source of food). Hence, they must solve the problem of orientation—avoiding bad places and seeking out good ones—in an exceedingly economical fashion. Their orientation mechanisms illustrate the properties of adaptive behavior in their starkest form.

The movement of climbing plants is a good example of an orientation problem and of a simple solution to it. Green plants feed on sunlight, and all organisms need food: Thus, it is important for any green plant to gain access to sunlight. Other plants with similar requirements present obstacles to growth. Where the need for light is not outweighed by other considerations, such as avoidance of predation, extremes of temperature, or the effects of wind, plants grow vertically and seek the highest, best-lighted point.

---

[1] Note the distinction between *mechanism* and *behavior*. The mechanism (*program* is another term) the spider uses to build a web develops with little specific input from the environment. But, the spider's behavior that is guided by that mechanism often depends critically on environmental inputs, as the spider adjusts construction to conform to the local environment and to repair damage.

[2] Movie buffs may recall the classic Orson Welles film *Citizen Kane,* in which the hero keeps recalling the name "Rosebud," whose meaning is resolved at the end of the film in a flashback to his youth. The delayed effects of such old memories are a mainstay of fiction. If protozoa could write, they would be restricted to memories of only few seconds or minutes.

B   O   X

2.1

Charles Darwin (1809–1882)

It seems almost superfluous to devote a special section to someone as well-known and universally influential as Charles Darwin. Yet, perhaps it is possible to describe a few new aspects of this important person. Darwin was born in 1809 to an affluent English physician and his wife, on the same day as Abraham Lincoln. He grew up conventionally. He greatly enjoyed the outdoor life, to the point that in his late teens his father thought him "an idle sporting man" unlikely to achieve much of note. He attended medical school in Edinburgh (where he "put forth no very strenuous effort" to learn medicine) and college at Cambridge (he was then destined for the clergy), where he spent much time hunting and riding—and prophetically, collecting beetles and other natural objects—as well as talking with the botanist J. S. Henslow. He pursued his collecting, and his report of at least one new species was published in a pictorial collection. He always declared that he learned little from his college work; but he obviously learned much from Henslow and Adam Sedgwick, the geologist with whom he went on field trips. In conformity with the rest of his family, Darwin was devout as a youth, but to his wife's sorrow, he lost any belief in conventional religion in later life.

The formative experience of Darwin's life was his five-year trip as an unpaid naturalist on the Royal Navy survey vessel HMS *Beagle,* captained by the young eccentric aristocrat James FitzRoy. Like many great scientists, Darwin's true education was directly from nature. During landfalls (Tenerife, South America, the islands of the Pacific), he collected rocks, plants, animals, and birds in prodigious abundance. In the long sea-spells in between, he classified, wrote, and thought deeply about the significance of his growing collection. The voyage developed in him the "habit of energetic industry and of concentrated attention." Like Sir Isaac Newton, when asked how he made his great discovery, Darwin could also have answered "by always thinking unto it." He tested his first elegant theory, conjectured in England before the trip, on the formation of coral reefs. He pondered the reasons for the diversity and relatedness of organisms, and wrote notes on this topic during the several years after the voyage.

Darwin was hesitant to publish on evolution for fear of religious censure, but he became almost obsessive about gathering evidence to buttress what now seems to us an already overwhelming case first for evolution and second (and most important) for natural selection as its chief agent. A few years after his return from sea, Darwin retired to Down House (now a museum) in Kent, England, well-supported by his father's money. There, Darwin became a semi-invalid, with an illness still not identified. He used his illness well, though, to avoid professional obligations and to organize his family as assistants in his great work. He wrote, corresponded, and performed experiments on climbing

continued

BOX 2.1 (*continued*)

plants, pigeon breeding, the survival properties of seeds in sea water, and many others. He worked for eight years on the classification of barnacles (his is still the standard work), to the point that his young son, visiting a friend's house for the first time, asked "And where does *your* father do his barnacles?" In 1858, he received from the young biologist Alfred Russel Wallace, who was recovering from fever in what is now Indonesia, a manuscript that contained an independent discovery of natural selection (Wallace even used the same name!) and its role in evolution. The story of how Wallace and Darwin amicably reported their work together in a paper to the Linaean Society (whose unremembered president at the end of that year commented that "little of note" had occurred) has become a famous example of honor between Victorian men of science. In the year after their joint paper, Darwin hurriedly put together a 500-page "abstract" of the much larger book he had planned to write—*Origin of Species*. His text has changed the world and influenced scientists and scholars in fields as diverse as geology, biology, psychology, and political science. (Karl Marx dedicated *Das Kapital* to Darwin and sent him a copy. It is still at Down House. The pages are uncut.)

Darwin died in 1882 and is buried beside Newton in Westminster Abbey.

Besides the *Origin of Species,* and his lively account of the *Beagle* voyage, Darwin's short autobiography, written for his children, is a wonderfully simple account of the life and thoughts of the greatest biologist.

Charles Darwin (Box 2.1) studied growing plants of several varieties and noticed that the growing tip always *moves* as it grows. He identified this rotation (which he called *circumnutation,* meaning "circular nodding") as a key element in plant orientation. He describes circumnutation as follows:

> When the shoot of a hop (*Humulus lupulus*) rises from the ground, the two or three first-formed, whilst very young, may be seen to bend to one side and to travel slowly round towards all points of the compass. . . . From seven observations made during August . . . the average rate during hot weather and during the day is 2 hrs 8 m for each revolution. . . . The revolving movement continues as long as the plant continues to grow; but each separate internode, as it becomes old, ceases to move (1875, pp. 2–3).

Two forces can be seen at work here: one directed and one undirected. The upward growth of the plant is a directed movement, the direction is opposite to the force of gravity (*negative geotropism*). But, the turning movement is undirected until the tip encounters a vertical obstacle such as a stick or the stem of another plant. Once such an obstacle is encountered, the turning movement, together with upward growth, ensures that the plant will twine about the obstruction and be lifted to a higher (and generally more satisfactory) location.

Green plants also possess a second orientation mechanism: *phototropism,* which combines with upward growth to direct the tip of the plant (on the average) toward the lightest portion of the sky. The efficient light-seeking of the plant can therefore be explained by the combined effects of three separate adaptive mechanisms: negative geotropism, circumnutation, and positive phototropism.

This example is quite simple. Nevertheless it illustrates how all adaptive behavior grows out of the interplay between variation and selection. Circumnutation plays the role of variation: The plant tip sweeps out an arc "searching" for a bright spot of sky or (in climbing plants) for some vertical support. The environment, in the form of vertical obstacles, plays the role of selection, blocking the moving tip and constraining it to a specific location. So long as these three underlying processes work in harmony, the plant steadily improves its situation.

Following this pattern, the study of plant movement by Darwin and others led eventually to the discovery of *auxins,* which are powerful regulators of the differential growth that underlies movement in plants. The movement of bacteria, can also be traced to biochemical processes. As we study more complicated behavior, the mechanisms that underlie variation and selection are less easy to see, although careful study will always find them underlying any adaptive behavior.

Analysis of Behavior

A plant's light-seeking illustrates two aspects of the study of adaptive behavior: analysis of behavior as the route to understanding and the link between physiology and behavior. The analysis of behavior can be studied as component processes, such as the three previously described, and is the main theme of this book. The aim of behavioral analysis is the explanation of all behavior of an organism in terms of a limited number of fundamental processes and their rules of interaction. We come closest to achieving this aim when analyzing simple orientation mechanisms.

The Link Between Physiology and Behavior

The second aspect of the study of adaptive behavior is its relation to physiology: Once an adaptive mechanism has been identified at the purely behavioral level, it becomes profitable to look for its physiological basis, that is, for the structures and chemical processes that underlie it. In the behavior of higher animals, the best-understood processes tend to be those that involve the peripheral parts of the nervous system—sensory processes, simple perception, and some aspects of the organization of motor behavior such as reflexes.

INDIRECT ORIENTATION (KINESES)

All living creatures behave; not even a virus is completely inert. Quite primitive animals often show extraordinarily clever behavior. For example, in the 1880s biologists discovered bacterial chemotaxis: the ability of bacteria such as *Salmonella* to move up or down a chemical gradient. By inserting a capillary tube containing a suspension of an attractive substance into a medium containing bacteria, Engelman and Pfeffer showed that more bacteria entered the capillary than would be expected if they simply moved randomly. Such behavior is quite extraordinary for an organism that is only two millionths of a meter long, has only the most primitive sensory and motor apparatus, and has no nervous system at all.

Hill-Climbing

Bacterial chemotaxis is actually a kinesis, because its movements are not directly guided by the chemical source. Bacteria have no distance or directional receptors; they cannot detect the source of a chemical in the way that we can look, from a distance, and detect an illumination source. Of course, we have no distance receptors for chemical gradients either. Given these constraints, the simplest way to find the source of a diffusing chemical is by means of a process called *hill-climbing*, in which the hill to be climbed is the chemical gradient. Hill-climbing can be explained by the simile of a blind person trying to find his or her way to the top of a hill. The simplest course: Sample a direction; if it is downhill or level, sample again; if it is uphill, follow it for one step; then sample again; and so on. A more efficient type of hill-climbing is to use repeatedly, until it fails, the information provided by a successful sampling. The rule here: Sample until you find an "up" direction; then keep going until it becomes a "down" direction (we call such sampling "tumble and swim," for reasons that will become apparent in a moment). The logic of these two hill-climbing strategies is illustrated by flowcharts in Figure 2.1. Both require a small memory that is sufficient to store a single slope value. Nevertheless, more complex and efficient variants of hill-climbing are possible. Indeed, all adaptive behavior can be thought of as a form of hill-climbing (Box 2.2).

Hill-climbing is essentially a process of comparing two heights: The difference between them defines the gradient. There are only two ways bacteria can detect a chemical gradient. One is by comparing chemical concentrations across the minuscule length of the body (simultaneous comparison). Such a procedure would involve detection of concentration differences of as little as one part in 10,000—a formidable task. If the bacteria could do so, they would be able to move up the gradient more or less directly, a *taxis* in the classification of Fraenkel and Gunn (1940). But, the actual movements we see seem almost random with respect to the gradient (Figure 2.2a shows a computer simulation of a *random walk*, the kind of pattern shown when there is no gradient).

The only other way to detect movement across a chemical gradient is to make comparisons across time (*successive comparison*). Such comparison might allow some kind of modulation of a largely undirected pattern of movement by increases and decreases in concentration. This kind of orientation mechanism is termed a *kinesis*.

Successive Comparisons

In some ingenious experiments, researchers McNab and Koshland (1972) showed that successive comparison is the key. First, they found that the movement pattern of the bacteria was the same at different absolute concentrations of an at-

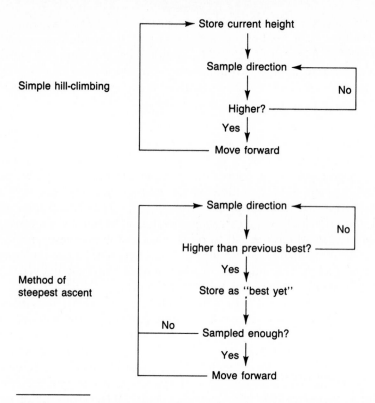

FIGURE 2.1   Flowcharts define the logic of two kinds of hill climbing.

tractant—providing the organisms were given some time to settle down. They then subjected the bacteria to a sudden "step" change in concentration (with no gradient) and studied them immediately after mixing was complete. If the organism's behavior were guided by comparison between the concentrations at its "head" and "tail," there should be no effect of the sudden change (because there is no gradient). But if their movement was determined by a difference across time, then a sudden drop in concentration should produce the same effect as swimming down a gradient—and so it proved.

These simple organisms showed essentially only two modes of movement: straight-line swimming, and "tumbling." Bacterial tumbling increased dramatically if attractant concentration decreased, as it would when swimming down a gradient. Tumbling decreased when attractant concentration increased, as when swimming up a gradient. These bacteria have reduced a complex problem in three-dimensional orientation to simple on-off control of a random pattern: Tumble when conditions worsen; swim straight when they improve. They find their way up the attractant gradient by means of the simple hill-climbing strategy illustrated in Figure 2.1: Straight swimming corresponds to "move forward"; tumbling corresponds to "sample direction." The tumbling performs the role of a

B   O   X

2.2

Optimizing Mechanisms and Searching in Problem Space

All adaptive behavior can be thought of as a search for the best (or a better) alternative. A simple way to analyze this concept is in terms of a spatial metaphor: Imagine all possibilities as making up a space of one, two, or more dimensions. In the case of the protists that are the topic of this chapter, there is no need for metaphor, since their problem truly is spatial—finding the best place to be. (One reason that we spend a great deal of time studying the protists is that their literal problem is a metaphor for the more general one.)

But, learning even such a simple task as balancing a pole can be thought of as an optimizing problem. Andy Barto and his associates (Barto, Sutton, & Anderson, 1983) at the University of Massachusetts have pursued this analogy in the form of a computer simulation. Their subject of study has been a deceptively simple problem first tackled by the Edinburgh AI researchers Michie and Chambers (1968): Imagine a trolley that can move back and forth along a limited stretch of track (Figure B2.1). A pole is attached to a hinge in the middle of the trolley, so that the pole can only move back and forth. The trolley contains a motor, which can drive the wheels forward and backward at a constant speed. A computer controls the motor. *Problem:* What should the computer tell the motor to do to maintain the pole in an upright position? The problem is one of physics, and it can be solved precisely. But, the AI researchers' aim was different: They wanted to devise a set of rules that would enable the computer to *learn* how to balance the pole. To do so, they defined a four-dimensional abstract *state space*, whose dimensions were the angle of the pole to the vertical and whose rate of change was the position of the trolley and its velocity. You can't draw such a space of course, and it would be cumbersome to build a real trolley. But, there is no mathematical difficulty in working with the con-

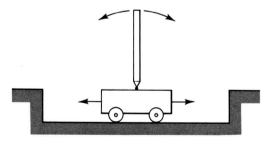

FIGURE B2.1   The trolley and the state space problem.

continued

BOX 2.2 (*continued*)

cept, so they put trolley, controller, and the relevant equations of motion into a computer program. They then computed the result of any action by the trolley. Since the entire experiment was contained in a computer program, "trials" were short, thus "learning" could proceed rapidly.

In the simulations, the state of the combined pole-trolley system is defined by a single point in the four-dimensional state space. Since the system is simulated on digital computer, the states must be finite in number: Researchers allowed for three regions of position, six of pole angle, three of trolley velocity, and three of pole angular velocity—for a total of 162 (3 × 3 × 6 × 3) states. In each of these states, the computer can tell the motor to move left or right. In the simulation, as trials are repeated a history is built up that allows the computer to assess which states are "good" and which "bad": "Good" states are those that are followed by long periods before the pole falls or the trolley runs out of track; "bad" states are typically followed by only short periods of success. The computer then "hill-climbs," picking for each state whichever response (left or right) leads to the next "best" state. In this manner, the computer learns to balance the pole within an extraordinarily small number of trials—less than 100 trials.

The point: A simple hill-climbing rule can be used to solve what is an apparently different problem from that of orienting in a chemical gradient. The pole-balancing maneuver shows how any problem can, usually with profit, be thought of as a problem of *spatial search.*

Simple motor learning, such as to catch a ball or throw a frisbee, must be acquired via processes that surely resemble the trolley simulation more than they resemble a standard control mechanism that already has the equations of motion built into it. Certainly, the laws of physics are not built into us in any kind of literal way. Yet we, and our ancestors, had had ample opportunity to learn by trial and error and to "remember" parameter values and response biases that make adapting to new situations—even completely novel ones such as weightlessness—possible and even easy.

random, slow search of the environment; when the search reveals a slight improvement, the organism follows that direction: "By taking giant steps in the right direction and small steps in the wrong direction, [*Salmonella*] biases its walk very effectively in the direction which aids its survival" (Koshland, 1977, p. 1057). Figure 2.2b illustrates a computer simulation of the "tumble-and-swim" strategy.

These experiments show that bacteria are able to detect a gradient by making successive, rather than simultaneous, comparisons. Over how much distance can they compare? This distance is determined by a process of *sensory adaptation* that is in effect a simple memory (recall that some memory is essen-

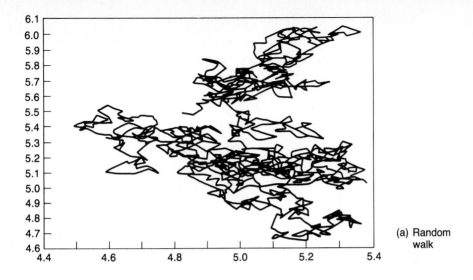

(a) Random walk

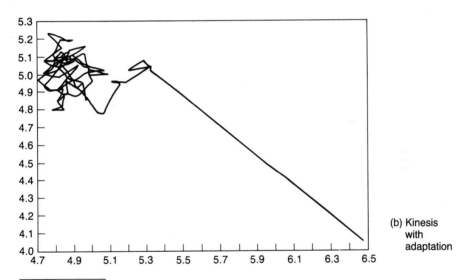

(b) Kinesis with adaptation

FIGURE 2.2 **(a)** A typical random walk. Starting at position (5,5) at each instant, the computer moves a dot across a small fixed amount in a random direction, tracing out a jagged, directionless path. **(b)** Tumble-and-swim pattern in a linear gradient. Attractant concentration increases from left to right. The computer keeps a running average of the concentration values it experiences. The difference between the current attractant concentration and the running-average concentration corresponds closely to sensory adaptation, since this difference is zero in a stable environment (current = average), positive when changes are for the better (current > average), and negative when changes are for the worse (current < average). The dot initially follows a random walk ("tumble"), but if this random movement takes it up the gradient (so that the current attractant concentration is significantly greater than the running average), it stops moving randomly and persists in its current direction. As you can see, this rule is relatively efficient in taking an animal up a gradient.

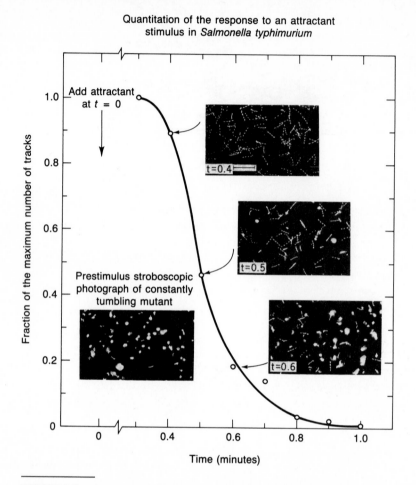

Quantitation of the response to an attractant
stimulus in *Salmonella typhimurium*

FIGURE 2.3   The photographs, taken through a dark-field microscope, show that an increasing proportion of bacteria cease tumbling and begin swimming in a straight line: The field is illuminated stroboscopically, so that when the camera shutter is left open for a brief period a smooth-swimming bacterium appears as a series of white dots. The graph shows the proportion of organisms tumbling as a function of time, since the attractant (serine) was added at time zero (from Koshland, 1977).

tial to hill-climbing).[3] It can be measured as follows: In the increased attractant experiment, the initial effect is an increase in smooth swimming and a decrease in tumbling. As time elapses, however, fewer bacteria swim smoothly, and even-

---

[3]Unfortunately the term *adaptation* is frequently used in biology to mean two quite different concepts: adaptation to an environment (a fin is better adapted to swimming than a paw) and sensory adaptation (our vision adapts to the darkness after coming in from the sunlight). The sensory adaptation meaning is intended here in connection with bacterial orientation.

tually all resume tumbling. This reversion to tumbling under constant conditions meshes with McNab and Koshland's initial observations that pattern of movement was the same at different attractant concentrations. Figure 2.3 shows a graph of the adaptation process. The graph illustrates the proportion of bacteria that swim smoothly at different times after mixing; the numbers were obtained from photographs like those in the figure. The graph shows the curve to be declining, which means that fewer bacteria are swimming smoothly as time passes.

The adaptation mechanism allows these organisms to make comparisons across a distance of between 20 and 100 body lengths, which reduces the analytical problem from 10,000 to 1 to between 100 and 1,000 to 1: Thus, a comparison across time remains difficult but is easier than when using simultaneous comparison.

Bacteria tumbling responds symmetrically to attractants and repellants: An increase in attractant concentration as well as a decrease in repellant concentration tends to suppress tumbling. This relatively simple process thus provides the animal with a complete motivational system that is able to deal adaptively with both positive and negative events.

As we move from bacteria to more complex, single-celled animals, kinesic orientation also becomes correspondingly more complex. For example, in a classic account Herbert S. Jennings (1906) described how ciliates such as *Paramecium* and *Oxytricha* avoid a region that is unfavorable because of conditions such as its temperature or pH. Figure 2.4 is taken from Jennings's book, and it shows the reaction of a single animal to a heated zone at the top of the figure. When it first enters the unfavorable region, the animal stops, backs, turns to the right, and starts to move in a new direction; if the unfavorable area is encountered again, the animal repeats the process until it finds a successful direction. The direction of each turn is unrelated to the actual direction of the boundary. This trial-and-error mechanism is obviously similar in many ways to the initiation of tumbling by bacteria when circumstances worsen; but this animal's activity is more efficient, because its reaction is actually to reverse its direction of movement. It would be even more efficient if the turn were reliably away from the boundary, but such a process requires localization of the point of maximal stimulation on the animal's body (which may be beyond the sensory capacities of *Oxytricha*).

Paramecium and many other ciliates show essentially the same movement patterns as *Oxytricha*, reacting to negative gradients by retreating and turning. As with the bacteria, this process serves both to avoid bad regions and locate good ones. If a bad region surrounds a good one, the process keeps the animal within the good region.

DIRECT ORIENTATION (TAXES)

Kinesic (indirect) orientation works by means of successive comparisons. Animals orient in this manner either when the gradient to be detected is too shallow to permit simultaneous comparison (when the source of stimulation cannot be

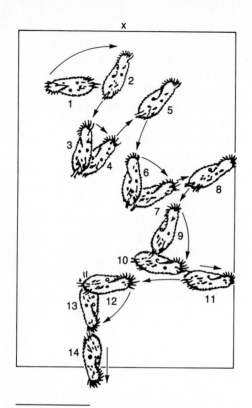

FIGURE 2.4　Reaction of *Oxytricha fallax* to heat applied at the top of the figure (at "x"). The animal moves backward from position 2 to position 3, then swivels its posterior end to position 4, and then moves forward to position 5. The set of movements 2–5 constitutes one turn. This turn did not take the animal out of the warmed area, and thus turning was repeated in 5–8, 8–11, and 11–14. Evidently it was cooler at position 14, from which point the animal then began movement in a straight line (from Jennings, 1906, Figure 84).

sensed at a distance because the direction of local gradients is not perfectly related to the direction of the source) or if the organism does not possess a sensory system capable of simultaneous comparisons. The possession of visual and auditory receptors allows for a more efficient strategy: The steepest local gradient usually points to the source, and gradients are often quite steep. Thus, simultaneous comparison in animals with more advanced receptors can allow for direct (*taxic*) orientation toward a source with no wasted motion. Any movement provides immediate feedback about the organism's progress. (We have more to say about feedback in Chapter 4.)

Although there are several different types of taxic reactions, they don't appear to correspond to completely different orientation mechanisms. We discuss four of these types as we describe the experiments used to identify them. All show the essential role of feedback in taxic orientation, a solid appreciation

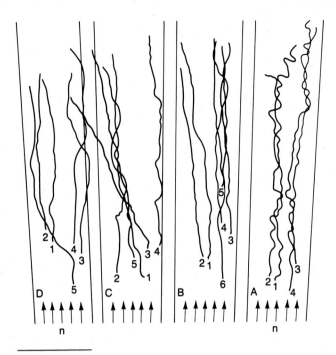

FIGURE 2.5   Tracks of four photophobic maggots (A to D) in a beam of horizontal light (arrows). Each maggot was tested four to six times (from Mast, 1911).

of which will be helpful in our discussions of learning and motivation in later chapters.

Klinotaxis

The first taxic reaction, *klinotaxis*, is really an intermediate case, since it involves both undirected orientation by successive comparisons and directed orientation by simultaneous comparisons. Figure 2.5 shows the results of an experiment conducted by Mast (1911) using maggots. Mast tested each of four maggots (*Lucilia sericata*) four to six times for its orientation to a beam of horizontal light. Movement was always directly away from the light (negative phototropism), although the tracks were not perfectly smooth. Substantial head movements (wiggles in the record) are especially apparent in the track of maggot A. These head movements provide a clue to the underlying process. Fraenkel and Gunn write:

> During steady forward crawling the head is sometimes put down symmetrically in line with the axis of the body, but from time to time it comes down alternately to the right and to the left. When the maggot first begins to crawl, these lateral deviations of the head are usually considerable, and may even result in the body assuming a U-shape (1961, p. 60).

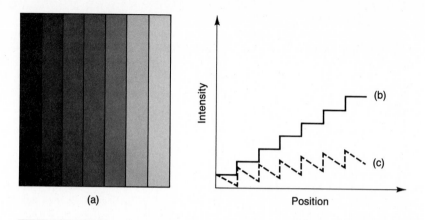

FIGURE 2.6   **(a)** Gradient of luminance across a striped array. **(b)** Perceptual effect of this luminance distribution: a staircase pattern of progressively increasing brightness (solid line). **(c)** Actual gradient (dashed line).

The animals look as if they are searching for the direction of the light. Once they find it, they move in the opposite direction. They find their direction by successive comparison, which can be shown by tricking the animal—turning on an overhead light when the animal is turning in one direction and turning it off when it faces the other direction. Under these conditions, a negatively phototactic animal moves in the direction associated with the low light level.

This process is similar to so-called trial-and-error learning, but it is still much simpler than the learning of higher organisms. No long-term memory is involved; the animal does not remember where the light was. The maggot has fewer modes of reaction than an animal such as a rat, and it can therefore be led into maladaptive behavior by relatively simple means. For example, the maggots may move away from a directional source, even if it means moving into a region of higher but nondirectional (e.g., overhead) illumination. They can also be induced to move up (rather than down) a gradient of illumination by turning on a second light only when the animal is facing down the gradient. In the absence of long-term memory, the maggot has no way of discovering that its situation, although improving on a moment-by-moment basis, is worsening overall—which is the weakness of all simple hill-climbers.

Lest you begin to feel superior to such lowly creatures, we point out that similar tricks can be played on the human visual system. Figure 2.6a shows a gradient of illumination: From left to right, the illumination grows repeatedly dimmer and then rapidly brighter. Figure 2.6b shows how this pattern looks to the human eye. Because of inhibitory, rate-sensitive mechanisms, the rapid increases in illumination have a greater perceptual effect than the slow decreases. Consequently instead of a series of "notches," we see a staircase pattern of progressively *increasing* brightness. The stripes in Figure 2.6c show the actual appearance of such a gradient.

The most dramatic perceptual illustration of rate sensitivity in humans is the effect of so-called stabilized retinal images. By using an electromechanical

B   O   X

2.3

Sensory Adaptation and the Videophone

All sensory systems show adaptation—which is no accident. As human communication technology has advanced, it has become clear that the visual images, especially, contain enormous amounts of information. Because of this fact, use of the videophone has not become commonplace: To use it with conventional video technology would require a coaxial communication channel much more expensive than the cheap copper or aluminum wire that now carries local telephone conversations from pole to home. Audio signals contain much less information, so they can travel comfortably on wires.

The solution now being proposed is not to send information on every pixel (the colored spots on the television screen, of which there are approximately 250,000 in a standard TV picture) every .03 seconds, as is now done, but just to send information on the pixels that have *changed*. This method represents nothing more than an electronic version of sensory adaptation. The problem for the nervous system is not so much transmission (the optic nerve has millions of fibers) as the extraction of relevant information. Adaptation is the first step in extracting information from the retinal image.

control system (or by actually mounting a tiny projector on the surface of the eye), it is possible to arrange that the image on the human retina always stays in the same place, even if the eye moves (and the eye is always moving, although the excursions are quite small if the person is looking at a fixed location). Under stabilized conditions, perception is soon eliminated; parts of the image begin to fade, and soon all that can be seen is a uniform gray (Pritchard, 1961).

These effects arise because sensory systems and the orientation mechanisms that depend on them are usually more sensitive to the *rate of change* of the relevant stimulus than to its absolute value: The important variables are changes over space and (especially) time rather than the stimulus value itself. Sensory adaptation is one of many labels for this sensitivity to rate of change, since it refers to the waning effect of a constant stimulus. This mechanism is enormously useful to animals, and in most cases it represents a great improvement over dependence on absolute stimulus values (Box 2.3). As we have seen, however, in the absence of other, longer-term memory processes, this mechanism can sometimes lead to maladaptive behavior.

The mechanistic details of klino-taxis in *Lucilia* or any other species that show the pattern (e.g., the protozoan *Euglena*, earthworms, the ascidian *Amaroucium*) have not been fully worked out by researchers. It is likely that the behavior of head-swinging (which also guides the animal) occurs only when the rate of change of illumination of the receptor(s) exceeds some threshold value.

In a stable, uniform light field, the animal moves little and swings its head from side to side in a relatively narrow arc; but if the light falling on the receptors increases greatly, a large head excursion occurs, followed by a smaller return swing. If any of these subsequent swings again produces an increase in receptor illumination, further swings are produced. As time passes, the effect of increases in receptor illumination diminishes because of adaptation, so that successive head swings are likely to be of smaller amplitude. If the source of illumination is fixed, the animal will, in the meantime, become oriented away from it, so that tracks similar to those in Figure 2.5 result. If the source of illumination is moving, then the animal's ability to orient away from it depends critically on quantitative details involving its rate of movement, head-swinging, and sensory adaptation.

The remaining taxic orientation reactions—tropotaxis, telotaxis, and the light-compass reaction—all involve simultaneous comparison of the stimulation of two or more bilaterally symmetrical receptors (two eyes or two ears). One clue to the type of reaction an organism displays is provided by its track while orienting in a uniform gradient: The track is convoluted if the mechanism is a kinesis, wavy for klinotaxis, and straight for the taxes that rely on simultaneous comparisons.

Tropotaxis

The two-light experiment is critical to the identification of tropotaxis (Figure 2.7). The figure shows the tracks of several pill-bugs (*Armadillium* sp.: terrestrial crustaceans that live under rocks and decaying wood) placed some distance from a pair of equally bright lights. *Armadillium* behaves in a positively phototactic fashion in this experiment; it approaches the lights. But when placed equidistant between the two lights, the animal often follows a path between them, rather than moving straight toward one or the other. At a certain point, it heads for one of the lights.

Tropotaxis is the outcome of a balancing process: The animal moves about until its two eyes are stimulated equally, at which time it proceeds forward. As the animal approaches a certain point between the two lights, it moves toward one or the other, as the tracks in the figure show. What triggers the shift is not certain, after all, if balance is the only component of the behavior, the animal could go on for ever along the median line. Its change in direction is probably caused by a kinesic component that causes the animal to begin turning when light intensity begins to decrease. As in essentially every case we discuss, several mechanisms work together to produce adaptive behavior.

Another way to identify tropotaxis is to eliminate the stimulation on one side of the animal, either by blinding it in one eye or painting over the eye if possible. The result is then *circus movement:* In a uniform light field (e.g., an overhead light), elimination of the use of one eye means that stimulation appears to come from only the other eye. If the animal is positively phototactic, it turns continuously toward the illuminated side; if it is negatively phototactic, it turns continuously toward the blinded side. In a normal animal with an eye-level light

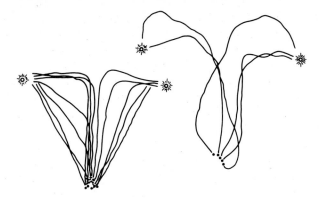

FIGURE 2.7   Tracks of photopositive *Armadillium* toward two equal lights (after Müller, 1925).

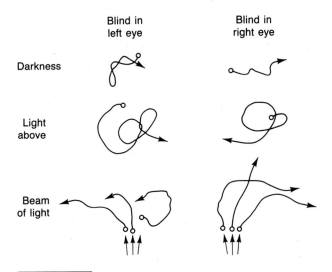

FIGURE 2.8   Tracks of photonegative *Ephestia* larvae, blinded on one side, under three illumination conditions (after Brandt, 1934).

source, these reactions eventually lead to equal stimulation of both eyes and leave the animal facing either toward or away from the light source. Figure 2.8 shows circus movements produced in unilaterally blinded *Ephestia* larvae.

Telotaxis

Tropotactic animals usually orient between two equal, symmetrically disposed lights and only directly approach one of them when the angle subtended by the lights is large. In *telotaxis*, the animals generally head straight for one of the two lights (although they may switch from one to the other as they approach them) even if the lights are quite far away. Fraenkel and Gunn provide a graphic natural-history description of telotaxis as follows:

> Large numbers of [the little mysid crustacean, *Hemimysis lamornei*] are to be found in the aquarium tanks of the Marine Biological Stations at Plymouth and Naples. When a single light is placed at the side of a glass tank containing *Hemimysis*, the animals swim to and fro continually, always keeping in line with the beam of the light. They swim about 10 cm towards the lamp, then turn sharply through 180° and cover about 10 cm again before turning back towards the lamp, and so on. If an additional light is arranged so that the two beams cross at right angles, some of the mysids are quite unaffected in their behaviour while others switch over to this second light and behave as if the first one were non-existent. The result is that the mysids form two streams which, so to speak, flow through one another, crossing at right angles and not interfering with one another (1961, p. 90).

The mechanisms involved in telotaxis depend on the type of receptor the animal possesses. If its eye is capable of forming a rudimentary image, that is, of immediately identifying the bearing of a source of stimulation (rather than just a gradient direction), then the animal has the necessary information available on the receptor surface. It therefore can orient correctly by placing its walking apparatus under the control of one image exclusively. This problem is not a trivial one, since the image-identification system must discriminate one source from another and compensate for changes in retinal position caused by the animal's own movement. Both the lensed eyes of vertebrates and the compound eyes of insects and other arthropods provide such directional information.

Many animals with image-forming eyes prefer to orient toward a light using the tropo-tactic balance mechanism (shown both by orientation between two lights and by circus movements when unilaterally blinded), even though the same animal may respond telotactically under other conditions. For example, at first a unilaterally blinded bee will show circus movement, but after a time, it heads straight toward a light source. The preference for tropotactic orientation may be a reflection of the complex computations required for telotaxis.

Light-Compass Reaction

The fourth type of taxic reaction common in animal orientation is the *light-compass reaction.* For example, bees use the light-compass reaction when returning to the hive. In addition, although often able to rely on odor trails, ants can also orient with respect to the sun, finding their way back to the ant hill by keeping a fixed angle between their path and the direction of the sun. Moreover, many species are able to compensate for the movement of the sun by a change in the light-compass angle, thus maintaining a fixed direction. This behavior is sometimes termed *sun-compass orientation,* and it appears to be one of the main components of navigation performed by migrating birds. The compensation depends on an "internal clock" that is tied to the 24-hour cycle (a *circadian rhythm*). The sun-compass reaction seems more complex than the straightforward equal balance of tropotaxis, but of course an *un*equal balance achieves the same result (if the degree of imbalance varies with time-of-day).

Animals also show many other simple orientation reactions. For example:

skototaxis (approach to dark areas or objects)

a variety of reactions to temperature gradients (usually favoring a specific temperature zone either because it is appropriate for the organism's metabolism or because it is a signal of the animal's prey [as when ticks prefer the skin temperature of their host])

postural reactions to light and gravity (geotaxis and the dorsal light reaction)

reactions to physical contact (many small and vulnerable animals seek out and conform to crevices and corners)

reactions to fluid flow (rheotaxis, e.g., fish generally face upstream, flying insects orient into the wind, some tidal crustaceans orient using cues from wave currents)

reactions to chemical and humidity gradients

orientation in sound fields (sound localization).

Similar principles, those of simultaneous or successive comparison, feedback, and time-dependent effects, are involved in all these reactions. Despite the relative simplicity of each reaction analyzed in isolation, in combination they can lead to complicated, "intelligent" behavior.

REFLEX ACTION

The beauty of simple orienting mechanisms is that at once we can see the animal's entire behavioral repertoire. The familiar, ancient (and probably misleading) psychological categories of motivation, cognition, sensation, and perception are all fused into a simple set of processes that respond to stimulation, initiate action, and guide the animal to aid its survival and reproduction. With more complex animals such as birds or mammals, it is more difficult to see how these processes fit together. Their behavior is so varied and dependent on individual history, and their niches are so complex, that we cannot grasp as a whole the functional relations among the various elements in their repertoire. Thus, there is a natural tendency to look for some specific behavioral mechanism as the key to understanding behavior in general, when the real key is no specific mechanism but rather how the different mechanisms fit together to yield adaptation to a niche.

Earlier we described the simple avoidance reaction of the ciliates *Paramecium* and *Oxytricha* when confronted with a sudden change for the worse. *Paramecium* can vary only its rate and direction of movement. Its rather rich sensitivity to a variety of chemical, photic, and thermal stimuli must therefore be funneled into these limited modes of reflex action. It is perhaps easy to see such a simple creature as jerked hither and yon by simple stimulus–response reactions. But "higher" animals are not so limited: Not only can they sense even more aspects of their physical environment, they can perform many additional behaviors. The avoidance reaction of *Paramecium* is just one extreme of a continuum of reactions that serves the function of bringing the animal into a congenial environment. The reflexes of higher animals serve a similar function. Most reflexes serve to avoid, escape from, or minimize the effect of, noxious stimuli.

Thus, reflexes are a part (actually a rather small part) of the adaptive repertoire of organisms. Yet they have historically had a special role because of the apparent simplicity of the relation between stimulus and response. Reflex stimulus and response look like *cause and effect*, the discovery of which is often supposed to be the chief object of experimental science. The immediacy of reflexes and their relative independence of the animal's past history make them easy to study. Moreover, the obvious adaptiveness of reflex properties and the similarity between reflex properties and some aspects of the properties of "higher" behaviors suggested to many early physiologists and psychologists that a complete psychology might be built out of reflexes. This view is almost certainly mistaken, at least in its original form. Nevertheless, for historical reasons and because it makes sense to begin with relatively simple processes, a discussion of reflexes is a natural preliminary to discussion of more complex kinds of behavior.

The idea of *reflex behavior* has a long history, beginning in the modern era with the French philosopher René Descartes (Box 1.4), who was perhaps the first to propose that all animal, and much human, behavior can be explained mechanistically—rather than by reference to a "soul" that directs the animal from within. This idea was elaborated on by the Russian physiologist I. M. Sechenov (1829–1905) who also carried out experimental work on spinal reflexes, that is, the built-in protective and integrative responses that can be demonstrated in animals in which the higher brain centers have been severed from the spinal cord (so-called "spinal preparations"). His work was continued by the British physiologist C. S. Sherrington, whose work followed a familiar pattern. Rather than attempt to study sensory and motor integration as a whole, a confusing and impossible task, Sherrington attempted to reduce such behavior to its simplest elements. Instead of working with an intact dog or cat, Sherrington operated on the animal so as to disable the higher brain centers. These "spinal" animals cannot learn and behave in an automatic way that can be easily studied. In his stately fashion, Sherrington describes the properties of his experimental preparation as follows:

> Experiment today put[s] within reach of the observer a puppet-animal which conforms largely with Descartes' assumptions. In the more organized animals of the vertebrate type the shape of the central nerve-organ [i.e., the brain] allows a simple operation to reduce the animals to the Descartes condition. An overlying outgrowth of the central nerve-organ in the head can be removed under anaesthesia, and on the narcosis passing off the animal is found to be a Cartesian puppet: it can execute certain acts but is devoid of mind. . . . Thoughts, feeling, memory, percepts, conations, etc.; of these no evidence is forthcoming or to be elicited. Yet the animal remains a motor mechanism which can be touched into action in certain ways so as to exhibit pieces of its behaviour (1947, p. xi).

With such a reduced, decerebrate animal, it is possible to study in full quantitative detail the simplest level of reflex—sensorimotor integration—free of the complications introduced by spontaneity and "volition."

Reflexes are automatic, but they are not crude or undifferentiated, nor are they without a clear function in the normal life of the animal. Sherrington continues with a number of examples:

> The movements are not meaningless; they carry each of them an obvious meaning. The scope commonly agrees with some act which the normal animal under like circumstances would do. Thus the cat set upright . . . on a "floor" moving backward under its feet walks, runs or gallops according to the speed given the floorway. Again in the dog a feeble electric current ("electric flea") applied by a minute entomological pin set lightly in the hair-bulb layer of the skin of the shoulder brings the hind paw of that side to the place, and with unsheathed claws the foot performs a rhythmic grooming of the hairy coat there. If the point lie forward at the ear, the foot is directed thither, if far back in the loin the foot goes thither, and similarly at any intermediate spot. The list of such purposive moments is impressive. If a foot tread on a thorn that foot is held up from the ground while the other legs limp away. Milk placed in the mouth is swallowed; acid solution is rejected. Let fall, inverted, the reflex cat alights on its feet. The dog shakes its coat dry after immersion in water. A fly settling on the ear is instantly flung off by the ear. Water entering the ear is thrown out by violent shaking of the head. An exhaustive list would be much larger than that given here. . . . But when all is said, if we compare such a list with the range of situations to which the normal dog or cat reacts appropriately, the list is extremely poverty stricken. . . . It contains no social reactions. It evidences hunger by restlessness and brisker knee-jerks; but it fails to recognize food as food: it shows no memory, it cannot be trained or learn: it cannot be taught its name (1947, pp. xi–xiii).

The deficiencies of the reflex animal are in the simplicity of the stimuli to which it can respond and in the absence of any but the briefest memory. It can neither learn new behaviors nor recall past experiences: Like Louis XIV, it learns nothing and forgets nothing. It is just this absence of history that makes reflex study of such analytical interest: The assurance that what is observed *now* can be traced to causes in the environment that are either present or no more than a minute or two in the past much simplifies the scientist's task. The absence of spontaneous movement completes the picture. How different and more difficult to study is the normal animal, whose behavior may reflect experiences months or years ago and whose ability to adapt to situations may allow for a variety of novel, spontaneous behaviors.

Sherrington was a physiologist, and his concern was with the function of the nervous system. He defined a reflex as a sensorimotor (stimulus–response) relation that involved at least two neurons between receptor and effector, that is, at least one *synapse,* the then-hypothetical, now much-studied point of contact between communicating nerve cells. However, most of Sherrington's experiments on reflex function were purely behavioral, and the reflex properties that emerged from them turn up even in organisms that lack a nervous system.

LAWS OF REFLEX ACTION

Sherrington's concept of the reflex is far from the simple, inflexible, push-button caricature sometimes encountered in introductory textbooks. To be sure, reflexes always have a stimulus and a response. But the ability of the stimulus to produce the response depends on the reflex threshold, which depends not only on the state of many other reflexes but also (in the intact animal) on higher brain centers that retain, in memory, the effects of an extensive past history. We examine some of the well-defined rules of reflex expression and interaction that make this possible.

Threshold

The stimulus for any reflex must be above a certain minimum level if it is to elicit a response. This minimum level of intensity is called the *absolute threshold* for the response. For example, a minimum level of tone is necessary to elicit the ear movement of a dog. A level below this threshold does not elicit a response. This threshold is not fixed, however; it depends on several factors that include the stimulus situation, the animal's state of attention, and its immediate as well as past history. In Sherrington's animals, the threshold was mainly affected by immediately preceding events.

The concept of a *threshold* is basically statistical in nature. It varies even when conditions are absolutely fixed. For practical purposes, the absolute threshold is usually taken to be the intensity of stimulus sufficient to elicit the response 50 percent of the time.

Latency

The time between the onset of a stimulus and the occurrence of the response is termed *reflex latency,* and it is perhaps the most useful measure of the strength of a reflex. The shorter the latency, the stronger the reflex. Latency depends on the same factors as threshold, and the two often go together; for example, factors that lower threshold usually shorten latency. Latency also depends on stimulus intensity, as a more intense stimulus typically elicits a vigorous response with a short latency. Thus, the strength and speed of most reflexes are directly related to the intensity of the eliciting stimulus.

Temporal and Spatial Summation

Two or more stimuli that are below their absolute thresholds may elicit a reflex if they are presented at or near the same time (*temporal summation*) or at or near the same location (*spatial summation*). For example, a cat will turn toward an unexpected sound with its ears pricked forward, pupils dilated, and every muscle tensed and ready to receive additional information or to act immediately if necessary. This *orientation reflex* may be elicited by two subthreshold sounds provided they are presented in close succession.

Competition

Different reflexes cannot occur simultaneously if they each involve similar neural and muscle groups. Therefore, they must compete for the same final motor pathway for expression. Any stimulus that acts to elicit reflex A must also act to

(a)

(b)

FIGURE 2.9   **(a)** Posture of a dog greeting its master (submissive). **(b)** Posture of a dog with hostile intentions (aggressive) (from Darwin, 1872).

inhibit reflex B. Thus incompatible reflexes often show up as behavioral as well as muscular opposites.

Darwin pointed out that each emotional "state of mind" tends to be associated with a stereotyped set of reactions and that opposite "mental states" are often associated with physically opposed actions (the *principle of antithesis*). For example, people who are perplexed may scratch their heads or roll their eyes. People who disagree with a proposition are likely to shift about or close their eyes; whereas if they agree, they look straight with open eyes. In greeting its master, a dog typically displays a submissive posture such as that shown in Figure 2.9a: The forelegs are bent, the coat smooth, and the tail is wagging. This position is incompatible with the dog's posture when facing a potential enemy (Figure 2.9b). The principle of antithesis is an example of the reflex principle of competition between opposing reflexes.

Cooperation

Reflexes need not always compete for expression, however. In some cases, reflexes that share response components facilitate each other by summation. This *cooperation* can be demonstrated by presenting a subthreshold stimulus for a leg contraction while at the same time presenting a stimulus for the scratch reflex. Postural reflexes (the mechanisms that maintain balance) must coexist and combine adaptively with others. Thus, the result of the summation of stimulation may be a leg withdrawal, as both require movement of the same muscles.

Reflex laws describe one aspect of behavior of all vertebrates. However, little behavior of higher animals, especially humans, is purely reflexive: Remote past history has multiple effects on present responsiveness, the same stimulus need not elicit the same response, and stimuli are often so complex that they are difficult to define in purely physical terms. Nevertheless, the mode of analysis we have adopted throughout this chapter has been to break down complex behavior into simple, interacting mechanisms. Such methodology has become the standard method of attack on even the most complex problems. Although the highest flights of the human intellect may ultimately resist this analytic approach, as yet behavioral science knows no other as effective.

SUMMARY

Kineses, taxes, and reflexes are all limited in a critical way: They depend only on events in the present or the immediate past. These mechanisms represent the best that animals can do when limited to what might be termed *local memory,* that is, a brief memory of the immediate past. Reflexes are limited in an additional way: They are *ballistic,* that is, they occur in response to an eliciting stimulus and are not readily modified by their consequences. As such, they are almost independent of feedback. On the other hand, kineses and taxes are behavioral mechanisms that are guided in a simple way by the environment; that is, they are dependent on some form of feedback. Although simple and relatively easy to analyze, kineses, taxes, and reflexes can nevertheless produce remarkably flexible behavior that allows for adaptation to a changing environment.

The differences between reflexes and orienting mechanisms simply reflect their different functions. Kinesic and taxic orientation mechanisms have a large random component, because simple organisms are not in a position to predict important features of their environment. Consequently, a large pool of behavioral variation is necessary if the right variant (movement to the best location) is to be found. Conversely, reflexes have evolved to deal with highly predictable contingencies (e.g., limb withdrawal is almost always the best response to painful stimulation of an extremity).

3

Operant
Behavior and
Mechanisms
for Learning

The situations with which any animal must cope can be ranged along a continuum in terms of their *certainty*, of how sure the animal can be of the proper response.[1] At one end of the continuum are simple hazards such as stepping on a thorn or touching a hot stove. In such cases, the proper reaction is highly predictable—lift the paw or withdraw the hand. Reflexes have evolved to deal with such simple, predictable situations. At the other end of the continuum are problems such as finding food or a mate, for which the appropriate action is usually uncertain. In such cases, the best that evolution can manage is to bias the animal in favor of certain classes of activity and provide it with a means of learning from experience. Evolution says: "If this is a food situation, try these activities first, and then let the outcome decide which method of finding food is most effective." As we will see, the phenomenon known as *classical*, or *Pavlovian, condition-*

---

[1] We mean to imply no conscious deliberation here, of course. Animals cannot decide whether or not to behave reflexively. Our statement is simply a shorthand for saying that during the life of a species some situations recur that can be handled in a predictable fashion from generation to generation, whereas in others the correct response cannot be known in advance.

ing subserves the first two functions: It tells the animal what kind of situation it is in (food-related, hazardous, etc.) and provides it with a set of candidate activities to try. *Instrumental,* or *operant, conditioning* subserves the second function: It allows the animal to learn from experience which activity is the most effective. In practice, these two aspects of learning from experience, defining the set of candidate activities and selecting the most effective, work together, and the term *operant conditioning* is applied to the entire process. In this chapter we discuss the evolutionary basis for operant conditioning in this broader sense.

PREDICTABLE VERSUS UNPREDICTABLE SITUATIONS

Predictable situations imply that behaviors that evolved to deal with them will have predictable antecedent stimuli. Unpredictable situations, if they are analyzable at all, must be described in terms of the outcomes of behavior. Thus, reflexes are best described in terms of well-defined eliciting stimuli and the responses they elicit; whereas operant behavior is best described in terms of its apparent goal.

Responses Based on Stimuli

The type and vigor of a reflex response is often closely related to the type and intensity of the eliciting stimulus. Reflexive behavior is also ballistic; once it is elicited by a stimulus, it is not readily modified by what happens as a consequence. Even humans find it difficult to suppress automatic reactions to painful or surprising stimuli, and the situation is no different when the results are bad. For example, many auto accidents have been caused by the distracting effects of a bee in the car. The essential feature of reflexive action is that it is almost independent of feedback.

Responses Based on Outcome

Kineses, or orienting responses, evolve to deal with an unpredictable situation such as the location of a safe or nutritious place. The movement of the orienting bacteria from moment to moment is unrelated to any single stimulus, yet its behavior as a whole can be understood in relation to the prevailing chemical gradient. The organisms aggregate in high concentrations of an attractant, and they disperse from high concentrations of a noxious substance. Behavior of this type is guided by its consequences: Under normal conditions, the location of the bacteria is determined by the chemical gradients in its environment. Because the antecedent causes of its behavior are many, but the "final cause" is one, we can best describe the behavior by its outcome—the bacteria find the food.

The psychologist Burrhus F. Skinner termed behavior that was guided (or "controlled," see Box 3.1) by its consequences *operant behavior,* and the term

B   O   X

3.1

"Control" by Consequences

B. F. Skinner was the founder of the radical school of behaviorism, for which he developed a series of operant-conditioning techniques. He, as well as those who have worked with his techniques, was fond of the word *control,* frequently applying it to the action of reinforcers: Skinner developed the concept of operant behavior as behavior "controlled by its consequences." Since we argue that reinforcers are better thought of as *selective* agents, Skinner's usage may be puzzling to some students. In fact, there is no contradiction: When selection is severe, the relation between environment and the selected feature is very much like control. For example, the various species of finches that Darwin studied in the Galapagos have adapted to deal with different kinds of food: The birds that feed on grain have small, slender beaks, whereas those that feed on nuts have large, "nutcracker" beaks. Nevertheless, within each species considerable variation exists in beak size and diet. Boag and Grant (1981) kept records over the years of the typical beak sizes of various species. They found that even two years of severe drought, which reduced the availability of grain and nuts, caused the average beak size of one species to increase by some 60 percent. It is no exaggeration to say that beak size here was controlled by the requirements of the available food, even though nothing more than (severe) natural selection was at work.

In similar fashion, when the selective effect of reinforcement is strong, the animal's behavior seems almost to track the reinforcer. For example, the rate at which hungry pigeons peck colored lights for food reward (reinforcement) can be sharply modulated by the rate at which pecks produce food. Thus, if food is delivered at a high rate when a green light is pecked and is never delivered when a red light is pecked, pecking soon occurs at a high rate when the green light is on and ceases as soon as the light turns red. Under these conditions, behavior is said to be controlled by reinforcement.

When selection is strong, the selective factors exert control very much like the setpoint of a feedback system: The control is feedback control. For example, in a conventional feedback-tracking system, as the target moves, so too does the gun. If tracking is good, the illusion is that the weapon is physically attached to the target. Similarly, the control of a car's road wheels by the steering wheel when the car is equipped with power steering is also feedback control. "Control" by reinforcement—by the consequences of behavior—is of this sort. In both cases, the behavior moves so as to reduce the discrepancy between the present state of affairs (e.g., "no food") and some better state ("food")—which is an example of *negative feedback.*

has become generally accepted. The word *operant* refers to an essential property of goal-directed behavior: that it have some effect, in other words, that it operate on the environment. If a bacterium cannot move, or if movement has no effect on the organism's chemical environment, then its behavior will not appear to be guided by a goal.

Skinner was interested in the concept of learning (and like most psychologists, whether they study animals or not, really had his eye on humans), and he restricted his definition to operant behavior that reflects learning. It is useful however to have a term for the larger concept of learning, so we use operant behavior to refer to any behavior that is guided by its consequences, whether or not learning is involved. We reserve the term *operant conditioning* for operant behavior that is learned.

The consequence that guides conditioned operant behavior has historically been termed a *reinforcer,* because reinforced behavior often increases in frequency. That is, the frequency or rate of an activity (a directly measurable property) is often taken as a measure of its strength (an inferred property); thus, responses are said to be reinforced or strengthened by their consequences. As we will see, there are several arguments against this simple, traditional view of reinforcement (Box 3.2). Reinforcers are best considered as agents of selection that eliminate ineffective behavioral variants. Through arousal and Pavlovian conditioning, they also generate behavioral variants in ways that we discuss in Chapter 5.

MECHANISMS OF OPERANT BEHAVIOR

We can learn something about the mechanisms that must underlie operant conditioning by asking how the operant behavior of mammals differs from the orienting behavior of protozoans. There are of course trivial differences: Protozoans are small, and mammals are big; protozoans can move about but can't do much else, whereas mammals can climb, run, talk, and press levers, for example. These same sorts of differences also exist among different mammal species; they have nothing to do with the essential, goal-directedness feature of operant behavior. Yet, there are differences. For instance, let's consider how the operant behavior of a simple animal differs from that of a mammal or a bird. Such a comparison can also tell us something about the evolution of learning and the mechanisms that must be involved.

Operant Behavior in Simple Organisms

One of the most beautiful examples of intelligent behavior by protozoans is provided by Herbert S. Jennings's account of how a *Stentor,* a single-celled pond animal, copes with a mildly irritating substance introduced into the water in its vicinity (Figure 3.1 and Box 3.3):

B   O   X

3.2

The Concept of "Strength"

As we saw in Chapter 2, the threshold and latency of simple reflexes provide measures of the "strength" of the reflex: The lower the threshold and the shorter the response latency, the stronger the reflex. In his early theoretical work (e.g., 1938), B. F. Skinner devised a unit of study, which he termed the *operant*, for conditioned operant behavior such as pressing a lever or pecking a key for food reward. The operant was derived from Ivan Pavlov's conditioned reflex, but it dealt with ongoing, freely emitted behavior. Consequently, the concepts of threshold and latency were not applicable. Hence, Skinner proposed the rate of behavior (e.g., lever presses per minute) as an appropriate measure for the strength of an operant.

In our lexicon, an operant is no more than a habit, and as we have seen, there is really no basis for attempting to apply reflex ideas to what is now termed operant behavior. Although Skinner expressly disavowed any allegiance to Pavlov, he was in fact perpetuating Pavlov's error of thinking that the effects of conditioning can be explained in terms of reflexlike units. Reflexes, which have evolved to deal with highly predictable situations, really have nothing to do with operant behavior, which has evolved to deal with more or less unpredictable situations.

Such experiments in the area of learning theory present examples of psychology's continuing propensity to attempt to become a "hard" science by embracing concepts from supposedly "harder" fields. For Gustav Fechner (the "father of psychophysics") and learning theorist Clark Hull, physics was the maiden to be embraced; for Pavlov and Skinner, it was physiology (of course Pavlov had an excuse, since he *was* a physiologist).

Let us now examine the behavior under conditions which are harmless when acting for a short time, but which, when continued, do interfere with the normal functions. Such conditions may be produced by bringing a large quantity of fine particles, such as India ink or carmine, by means of a capillary pipette, into the water currents which are carried to the disk of *Stentor.* . . .

Under these conditions the normal movements are at first not changed. The particles of carmine are taken into the pouch and into the mouth, whence they pass into the internal protoplasm. If the cloud of particles is very dense, or if it is accompanied by a slight chemical stimulus, as is usually the case with carmine grains, this behavior lasts but a short time; then a definite reaction supervenes. The animal bends to one side. . . . It thus as a rule avoids the cloud of particles, unless the latter is very large. This simple method of reaction turns out to be more effective in getting

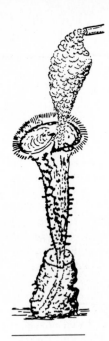

FIGURE 3.1   *Stentor roeselii* attached to its tube and drawing a cloud of carmine particles into the ciliary disk as part of its normal feeding pattern (from Jennings, 1906, Figure 111).

rid of stimuli of all sorts than might be expected. If the first reaction is not successful, it is usually repeated one or more times. . . .

    If the repeated turning to one side does not relieve the animal, so that the particles of carmine continue to come in a dense cloud, another reaction is tried. The ciliary movement is suddenly reversed in direction, so that the particles against the disk and in the pouch are thrown off. The water current is driven away from the disk instead of toward it. This lasts but an instant, then the current is continued in the usual way. If the particles continue to come, the reversal is repeated two or three times in rapid succession. If this fails to relieve the organism, the next reaction—contraction—usually supervenes.

    Sometimes the reversal of the current takes place before the turning away described first; but usually the two reactions are tried in the order we have given.

    If the *Stentor* does not get rid of the stimulation in either of the ways just described, it contracts into its tube. In this way it, of course, escapes the stimulation completely, but at the expense of suspending its activity and losing all opportunity to obtain food. The animal usually remains in the tube about half a minute, then extends. When its body has reached about two-thirds its original length, the ciliary disk begins to unfold and the cilia to act, causing currents of water to reach the disk, as before.

    We have now reached a specially interesting point in the experiment. Suppose that the water currents again bring the carmine grains. The stimulus and all the external conditions are the same as they were at the beginning. Will the *Stentor* be-

3.3

Micropsychology:
Jacques Loeb (1859–1924) and
Herbert Spencer Jennings (1868–1947)

Around the turn of the century, there was great interest in the behavior of microorganisms, because it was felt that they could act as a guide to principles that might be applied to the higher animals and humans. The two principal proponents were Jacques Loeb, a Jewish-intellectual emigré from Germany, and Herbert S. Jennings, a man born of modest circumstances in rural Illinois.

Loeb's parents died while he was young, but they left him with resources sufficient to attend a university (then a privilege of the few) and begin an academic career. He studied medicine and did research on brain function in dogs in Germany. In 1885 Loeb received an assistantship in Berlin, but he gave it up after a year, mainly because of his growing reluctance to inflict brain lesions on his dogs. He moved to Würzburg and there became interested in the reactions of simple animals and plants to light. Out of this rather limited experimental experience, Loeb developed his theory of *tropisms*. His concepts were considerably elaborated in later years, but the basic notion was simple: Movements such as phototropism are automatic reactions to stimulation (like the tropotaxis described in Chapter 2 that worked by equalization of stimulation to two symmetrical photoreceptors). In 1891 Loeb came to the United States when job scarcity (and anti-Semitism) in Germany made the U.S. an attractive option. He soon found a job at the then-new University of Chicago, where he remained for several years. He later worked at the University of California, Berkeley, and finally went to the Rockefeller Institute (now called Rockefeller University).

Herbert S. Jennings, son of an evolutionary-minded physician father (his other son was first-named "Darwin"), went to the University of Michigan where he got a degree in biology. He entered Harvard in 1894 and received a Ph.D. after two years for work on the early development of a rotifer (a microscopic animal). He did research at Jena, in what is now East Germany, and Naples, where he did much of the work on protozoic behavior later written in his classic work *The behavior of the lower organisms* (1906). Jennings returned from Europe to become professor of botany at Montana State A&M, then instructor in zoology at Dartmouth, and then instructor and assistant professor at the University of Michigan. In 1903 he went to the University of Pennsylvania as assistant professor in zoology. In 1906 he went to Johns Hopkins as an associate and then full professor of experimental zoology. He remained at Hopkins until his retirement in 1938. After finishing his book on behavior, Jennings become more interested in genetics and published numerous papers and books on the topic.

continued

BOX 3.3 (*continued*)

Loeb had a greater influence on the early development of psychology than Jennings did, probably because his ideas were simpler, and he readily provided prescriptions for action. Loeb's tropism theory was based on two simplifying assumptions that Jennings, quite correctly, resisted: that an organism is passive, remaining quiet unless forced into action by an external stimulus, and that the reaction to a stimulus does not depend on the state of the organism. Loeb's conviction that behavior of microorganisms is exceedingly simple and automatic led naturally to preoccupation with the control of behavior. He was not sympathetic to placing animal psychology within an evolutionary context. John B. Watson, polemical promoter of behaviorism (see Box 3.4), later found Loeb's ideas an easy model for his own highly simplified and rigidly deterministic view of behavior.

In contrast to Loeb, Jennings's ideas were based on extensive and careful observations and experiments on protozoa. He noticed that spontaneous activity was far from being a rarity, it is the rule. In actuality, it is reflexlike behavior that is the exception. Thus, Loeb's idea of "forced action" could not be generally correct. We now know that variability in behavior is essential to adaptation to unpredictable conditions, whereas a "Loebian" animal could learn nothing new. Like Loeb, Jennings saw many similarities between the behavior of protozoa and higher animals, but unlike Loeb he drew the conclusion that both were complex, not that both were simple:

> ". . . if Amoeba were a large animal, so as to come within the everyday experience of human beings, its behavior would at once call forth the attribution to it of states of pleasure and pain, of hunger, desire and the like, on precisely the same basis as we attribute these things to the dog. . . ."

Nevertheless, contrary to the assertions of some later historians, Jennings was not arguing that protozoans were "conscious," he meant that simple stimulus–response rules (although this terminology is from a later period) are not adequate to describe protozoic behavior. His idea that much behavior is spontaneous, in the sense that it cannot be traced to currently present stimulation, is an unacknowledged anticipation of the notion of operant behavior. But, Jennings was an experimenter rather than a theorist; he could see what was wrong with Loeb's tropisms, but he lacked the theoretical tools necessary to provide a testable alternative. Today we possess the tools: The digital computer makes it relatively easy to discover the often complex effects of simple processes; and modern molecular biology offers techniques for dissecting the physical basis for the behavioral process. It remains to be seen whether Jennings's experimental analysis of protozoic behavior can now be brought to fruition through deeper theoretical analysis.

For a brief discussion of the relation between simple mechanisms and complex behavior see V. Braitenberg's *Vehicles* (1984) and a review by J. E. R. Staddon (1987). For a fascinating discussion of the historical context for the Loeb–Jennings debate, see Robert Boakes's history of animal psychology, *From Darwin to behaviourism* (1984).

B   O   X

3.4

John Broadus Watson (1878–1958)

John B. Watson is one of the most turbulent figures in the history of psychology. Born in the South (unusual for an academic at that time), his religious upbringing failed to take, and after a wild adolescence he went to the local college, Furman University. He had a stint of high-school teaching and then went on to doctoral work at the University of Chicago, finishing up with a dissertation entitled "Animal education: The psychical development of the white rat." Watson was attracted to Chicago because of the writings of the philosophy professor John Dewey, an influential and not altogether beneficial figure in the history of American education. But Watson, showing an admirable disdain for obscurity and a fine eye for the Emperor's new clothes, found Dewey's writings opaque (what a pity that more social scientists don't share his impatience with pretentious nonsense!). He was more attracted by the hard-headed mechanism of Jacques Loeb (see Box 3.3) and a younger psychologist named James Angell. Under Angell, Watson did his thesis work on rat learning, beginning a trend that was to dominate United States psychology for several decades.

Watson carried on his psychobiological work at Chicago for several years as well as followed up an interest in what would now be termed *ethology*. In 1907 he began a series of ethologically oriented visits to the Dry Tortugas, off the coast of southern Florida, to study the natural behavior of terns. The papers he wrote at that time, although they achieved little fame, are nevertheless scientifically among Watson's best.

After eight years at Chicago, Watson left for a prestigious professorship at Johns Hopkins University, where he flourished for several years as one of the most popular (and by all accounts best-looking) young teachers. Early in his time at Hopkins, Watson became interested in the exciting behavioral physiology being done in Russia, in particular the work of V. M. Bekhterev and Ivan Pavlov. His interest in this work and his own work with infants led him to a new philosophical position, first expressd in a journal article and later in a highly influential polemical book called *Psychology from the standpoint of a behaviorist* (1919). This work was brilliant, albeit one-sided. Watson argued powerfully that not only was objectively measured behavior the only legitimate datum for psychology (something now generally accepted as *methodological behaviorism*) but also, and wrongly, that all behavior was to be explained in stimulus–response terms. For Watson, thought became covert speech, measurable by imperceptible movements of the vocal chords, emotion and purpose were all reduced to muscular movements or to the perception of sensations produced by muscular movement. In contrast to the wordy verbage that characterized much psychology before behaviorism (and, it must be admitted, not a little afterwards!), Watson's new approach was a refreshing dose of clarity. His views on behaviorism dominated experimental psychology for many years

continued

BOX 3.4 (*continued*)

and had several neobehavioristic descendants: Hullian and neo-Hullian theory, Edward Tolman's purposive behaviorism, and B. F. Skinner's radical behaviorism. But, its simplicity, and reactions to that simplicity, continue to propel this area of psychology from one extreme to another in a series of oscillations that persist to this day.

Two of Watson's students, Karl Lashley and Curt Richter, went on to become highly influential psychobiologists. Watson's career at Hopkins ended after World War I, because, caught in a bad marriage, he became attached to a bright and attractive graduate student, Rosalie Rayner, with whom he had done collaborative research. His wife, at first complaisant, later obtained evidence of the affair and, urged on by relatives, set her lawyers to work. Fearing for his job, Watson left academia at age 42 and pursued a highly successful career in advertising. He and Rosalie eventually married, and he evidently found lifelong satisfaction in both his new career and his new marriage. Advertising's gain was probably psychology's loss: For all his oversimplification, Watson's energy and clarity might well have matured into a highly creative psychobiology. Instead, he is remembered more for a youthful polemic than for his many careful experimental and observational studies.

have as it did at the beginning? Will it at first not react, then bend to one side, then reverse the current, then contract, passing anew through the whole series of reactions? Or shall we find that it has become changed by the experiences it has passed through, so that it will now contract again into its tube as soon as stimulated?

We find the latter to be the case. As soon as the carmine again reaches its disk, it at once contracts again. This may be repeated many times, as often as the particles come to the disk, for 10 or 15 minutes. Now the animal after each contraction stays a little longer in the tube than it did at first. Finally it ceases to extend, but contracts repeatedly and violently while still enclosed in its tube. In this way the attachment of its foot to the object on which it is situated is broken, and the animal is free. Now it leaves its tube and swims away. In leaving the tube it may swim forward out of the anterior end of the tube; but if this brings it into the region of the cloud of carmine, it often forces its way backward through the substance of the tube, and thus gains the outside. Here it swims away, to form a new tube elsewhere (Jennings, 1906, pp. 174–175).

The behavior of *Stentor* as Jennings describes it is marvelously adaptive. How might we explain it? We present both a mechanistic and a functional account of *Stentor's* behavior. Although mechanistic accounts are usually preferable to functional ones (because they pave the way for understanding physical mechanisms, for example) we find that behavioral systems frequently become too complex for completely mechanistic explanations. Sometimes there is no practical way to decide among several possible mechanisms, even though the goal of the behavior is clear. Thus, we often settle for the convenience of a functional account.

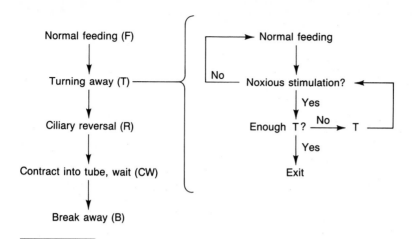

FIGURE 3.2   Chain-reflex model for *Stentor* avoidance behavior. Left: Feeding and the four types of avoidance reaction, in the order they normally occur. Right: A program for each link in the chain.

A MECHANISTIC ACCOUNT OF *STENTOR* BEHAVIOR   *Stentor* has four levels of response to escape from the carmine, each more costly (but also more likely to be effective) than the preceding one:

1. Turning away (T) uses little energy and doesn't interfere with feeding (F)
2. Ciliary reversal (R) uses little energy but is an interruption of feeding
3. Contracting into the tube and waiting for a while (CW) is energetic and seriously interferes with feeding
4. Breaking away (B) is most energetic of all and means abandoning a known feeding site

We don't know what causes the animal to shift from one mode of behavior to another. Jennings is typically cautious: ". . . shall we find that it has become changed by the experiences it has passed through. . . ?" He avoids saying what aspect of the animal's past experience might be responsible for the change from CW to B, the most drastic change in the sequence.

Several simple mechanisms explain the succession of avoidance reactions, one of which is illustrated in Figure 3.2. The figure shows on the left the sequence of five activities and on the right the sequence of decisions that allows each activity either to be repeated or to be followed by the next. The basic idea is that each activity is repeated for a while ("enough?"), and then if the noxious stimulation persists, the next avoidance response is tried. "Enough" might correspond to number of repetitions, time spent in the activity, or some combination of time and number.

The model in Figure 3.2 is an example of a reflex chain, in which each ac-

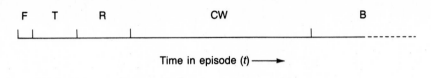

FIGURE 3.3   A temporal decision rule for *Stentor* avoidance.

tivity is the cause of the next one in the sequence.[2] Chains come to mind first when one ponders how a simple animal might put together a sequence of acts, and they were popular with early stimulus–response psychologists. But, chains represent a rather rigid form of behavioral organization; for example, if one activity fails to occur or is blocked in some way, the next activity cannot occur. Perhaps for this reason, chain reflexes are rarely found—even in something like walking in arthropods, in which it might seem reasonable that the movement of one limb should precipitate the movement of the next (it turns out that the centipede has better ways to orchestrate its parade of legs!).

An alternative way to organize avoidance behavior is by means of a *temporal program*. The risk to *Stentor* is directly related to the time the carmine is present. The four avoidance reactions listed previously are progressively more costly. The animal needs a rule that will match the cost of the avoidance response to the risk. Therefore, one way to determine which behavior should occur is simply to identify three cutoff times (t_T, t_R, and t_{CW},) such that $t_T < t_R < t_{CW}$. Then activity R (say) will occur when $t_T < t < t_R$, $t > t_T$, where t is the time since the beginning of the episode. The temporal rule that describes the animal's behavior is shown graphically in Figure 3.3. Thus, an internal clock that starts running with the onset of the carmine, with settings corresponding to changes in behavior such as $T \rightarrow R$, $R \rightarrow CW$, and so on, is an alternative method of generating the observed sequence of avoidance reactions.

This temporal decision rule is also a mechanism for the *Stentor* behavior clock; each avoidance reaction has an associated cutoff time that initiates successive reactions. This one-dimensional mechanism has limitations, however, in that it says nothing about the possibility of different concentrations of carmine or any other noxious substance and any differences in amounts of time the concentrations are present. As risk is directly related to both concentration and time, let's examine a slightly more complex model that takes us from the domain of simple mechanism (clock or reflex chain) to the domain of a functional, in this case economic, analysis. We give up some details about the process so as to arrive at a comprehensive explanation. How the model works will be clear from the example.

[2]The chain diagrammed in Figure 3.2 is actually more complicated than a traditional chain, which is of the form $A \rightarrow B \rightarrow C$, in which each activity occurs for the same brief period. Such a process generates sequences of the form ABC. . . . The process in Figure 3.2 contains small loops that permit each activity to occur for variable amounts of time; such a process generates sequences of the form AAABBCCCCCDD. . . .

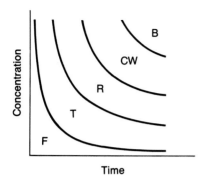

FIGURE 3.4   A time–concentration decision rule for *Stentor* avoidance.

A FUNCTIONAL ACCOUNT OF *STENTOR* BEHAVIOR   The economic (functional) analysis for our model is illustrated in Figure 3.4. It describes the results of a simple hypothetical experiment in which the concentration of a noxious substance is increased from zero to some fixed value at time zero. The experiment is repeated for a number of different concentrations, and the times at which transitions from one activity to another take place are recorded. If both time and concentration affect the times of behavioral transition, these data should be describable by a set of decision curves (convex to the origin) that define the combinations of time and concentration when the animal should change from one activity to the next.

The rationale for these curves is that the four escape activities are progressively more costly to the animal (ciliary reversal, which is an interruption of feeding, is more costly than turning; contract-and-wait is more costly than ciliary reversal; etc.). Thus, the animal should switch from one to the next only when the damage potential of the aversive stimulus is higher than some predetermined level. Presumably danger is directly related to both the duration and intensity of the stimulus (e.g., danger = duration × intensity), hence the approximately hyperbolic curves.[3] Thus, as the product of duration multiplied by intensity increases, the animal shifts to more costly avoidance tactics: Reaction T will occur first, blocking the others; if T is ineffective, thus allowing stimulus duration to continue to increase, or if the concentration increases, the animal will switch to reaction R; and so on.

Although this explanation has added only one risk factor (concentration) to the temporal rule described previously, this two-dimensional case makes it clear that an explanation by decision rules is functional—not mechanistic. That is, the explanation is based on the final outcome (avoidance) rather than on a specific mechanism (the curves in Figure 3.4 are equivalent to what economists call *indifference curves,* in which all points along a given curve are equivalent in terms of the decision to change from one level of activity to the next). It is not

---

[3] A rectangular hyperbola is an equation of the form xy = constant.

at all obvious what mechanism the animal uses to compute the relative importance of time and concentration in deciding on an avoidance reaction, nor does this analysis say anything about *dynamics,* how quickly the animal adapts to changes in concentration. It is possible to invent potential processes, but discriminating among them would require careful behavioral and perhaps physiological experiments. In Box 3.5 we show how a dynamic model for this behavior might be developed.

STENTOR CONCLUSIONS   The functional account is more general than the specific mechanism that underlies it, because it applies not just to *Stentor* but to any small animal similarly situated (even though different species, and perhaps different individual *Stentors* might perform the activity in different ways, i.e., using different physiological processes). If we can think of more than one way to solve a behavioral problem, there is sure to be a comparable diversity in nature's solutions.

An animal's ability to behave according to the prescriptions of a functional account depends on specific mechanisms. Our example here is of the reflex type, that is, requiring nothing more than local memory; but in other cases, mechanisms can be more complicated. For some purposes, the functional account is more useful; for others, we might like to know more of the details of how the animal performs the activity. For example, if we are interested in how an animal's behavior relates to its niche, the functional account is better; but if we want to explore the physiological basis for the behavior, the mechanistic account is more useful.

Clearly the more intelligent the animal, the more possible mechanisms may underlie a given example of adaptive behavior. Consequently, when we are dealing with mammals and birds, functional theories often fare better than mechanistic ones.

OPERANT BEHAVIOR AND LEARNING

How does the avoidance behavior of *Stentor* stack up against the operant behavior of higher animals, for example, Edward L. Thorndike's original learning situation in which a cat is to escape from a puzzle box? At one level, the similarity is great. In both cases, a change for the worse in the animal's environment causes a change in its behavior. Further changes continue to occur in a systematic way until the irritating condition is relieved (variation and selection). The increasing rapidity of contraction (CW) in response to successive applications of carmine resembles the increasing efficiency with which the cat escapes on successive trials. The cat's improvement would probably be called "learning"; does *Stentor*'s behavior also qualify?

The same external situation—carmine plus normal feeding behavior by the animal—initially leads just to turning away but later to breaking away. Such be-

B   O   X

3.5

The Dynamics
of Adaptation and Summation

It is hard to discuss in the abstract the difference between functional (e.g., economic) and mechanistic models for behavior. It may be helpful, therefore, to describe an actual mechanistic model for *Stentor* avoidance that shows the relations between adaptation and the reflexlike properties of temporal summation and sensitization.

Every model is built of elements. Here, we use only two: an integrator and a threshold. The concept of *threshold* should be familiar from Chapter 2, in which an absolute threshold is the level of a variable above which some activity will occur. The *integrator* sounds more complicated, but it behaves simply and familiarly. Figure B3.1 shows a bucket with a hole in the bottom sitting in a stream. We call the depth of water in the bucket *V. V* is the *dependent variable,* since it depends on the depth of the stream (X), which is therefore the *independent variable.* When the bucket is first placed in the stream, $V = 0$; but as water leaks in, eventually $V = X$. The bigger the hole, the faster the bucket fills with water. Conversely, if the stream level falls, V is at first greater than X, but then the two become equal. In such a situation, V lags X and also represents a sort of average of X over the recent past. The difference between V and X behaves like anything subject to *adaptation:* large following any change in X, but decreasing so long as X remains unchanged. Adaptation is quick if the hole is large, slow if the hole is small.

To generate predictions, we must find a mathematical form for the integrator. The simplest way is via *discrete* (rather than *continuous*) mathematics (Ralston, 1986). Instead of assuming time to be continuous, we let it be

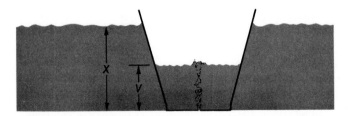

FIGURE B3.1   A physical system that behaves as an integrator. X is the level of a stream in which stands a leaky bucket. Just after the stream level rises, the water level in the bucket (X) is below the stream level; after a while, the two will be equal.

continued

BOX 3.5 (*continued*)

discrete, divided into brief "clock ticks" (like the time in a digital computer). We then can specify how V (our dependent variable) in clock-tick N depends on the current X (the independent variable) and V in the preceding instant $(N - 1)$. Our integrator corresponds to the following *difference equation:*

$$V_N = (1 - \alpha) V_{N-1} + \alpha X_N \qquad \text{(B3.1)}$$

where α is a constant between 0 and 1. The α corresponds to the size of the hole in the bucket; thus, the larger α is, the more quickly V tracks X (when $\alpha = 1$, V tracks X perfectly [i.e., V always equals X]). Equation B3.1 may look complex, but it simply says that the water level in the bucket (V_N) at any instant (N) is a (weighted) average of the level an instant ago (V_{N-1}) and the current level outside (X_N). It is easy to see that the equation has the same properties as the leaky bucket. For example, when $V_N = V_{N-1}$ (i.e., when V ceases to change), then $V = X$ (to check this conclusion, try setting $V_N = V_{N-1}$ in the equation). That is, $V = X$ is the *steady-state* solution to this difference equation—which means that after a long time, the water level in the bucket will equal the water level in the stream.

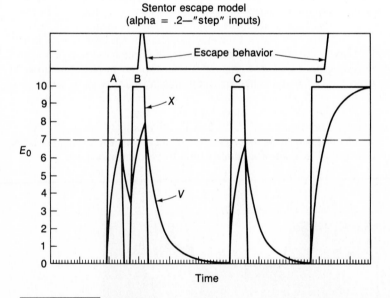

Stentor escape model
(alpha = .2—"step" inputs)

FIGURE B3.2   Temporal summation as the effect on an integrator. The figure describes a hypothetical experiment in which "pulses" of noxious substance (A–D) occur at different time intervals. The curved lines show the integrator output. The event record at the top of the figure shows when the integrator output exceeds a threshold value ($E_0 = 7$). The response to pulse B, but not to pulse C, shows the effect of temporal summation.

continued

BOX 3.5 (*continued*)

How can this process explain the escape behavior of *Stentor?* Quite easily, if we let V represent the animal's tendency to make an escape reaction and then define an escape threshold (E_0) above which escape displaces feeding. (For simplicity, we consider only one escape reaction, but the approach can easily be extended to any number of reactions). The independent variable (X) corresponds to the concentration of noxious substance. Figure B3.2 presents data from a hypothetical experiment, which shows how the process works. The vertical bars A–D show episodes for which the concentration of noxious substance suddenly increased from zero to a high value ($X = 0 \rightarrow X = 10$). The figure shows that the first episode (A) was not sufficient to elicit the escape reaction, because the integrator value (V) did not rise above the escape threshold (E_0), which we set at 7. But, the second episode (B) follows soon enough after the first episode that V has not yet declined to zero, so that V rises above 7, and there is a brief escape episode (shown at the top of the figure). (The second example is one of *temporal summation*). The third "spike" of noxious substance (C) is too brief to elicit the avoidance reaction, but the final episode (D) occurs for a long time and produces a prolonged escape reaction.

We can now see the entire sequence of *Stentor* reactions, none of which is mysterious. But, notice that this simple process already shows the reflex phenomenon of temporal summation (episodes A and B compared with episode C), which also fits the definition of *sensitization* we discuss later in the

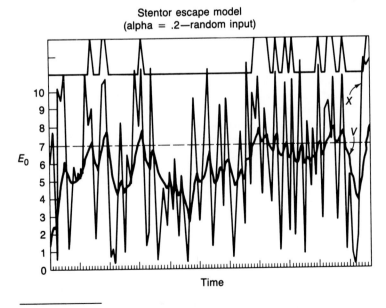

FIGURE B3.3   Response of the integrator system in Figure B3.2 to a randomly varying input.

continued

BOX 3.5 (*continued*)

chapter. Hence these two phenomena, discovered and defined separately, are probably due to the same process—namely the presence of an *integrator*, which is a primitive form of short-term memory.

Notice also that our model can predict the animal's reaction not just to these simple "step" stimuli but to any time–concentration pattern. For example, Figure B3.3 shows the *Stentor* response to random variation in concentration. Although the economic model discussed in the text can well explain the steady-state behavior of this model, it cannot explain dynamic properties such as temporal summation or the system's response to a variable input like the one shown in Figure B3.3.

The rate constant (α) provides an easy way to extend this model to any number of escape activities. In the new model, the more costly activities have lower α values (so they would take longer to gain "strength"); but higher asymptotes (the maximum values attained when V ceases to change) require a second parameter (β) that is greater than 1 for each additional activity. We also assume that only one activity can occur at a time and that the activity with the highest V displaces all others. Equation B3.1 becomes the following:

$$V_N = (1 - \alpha) V_{N-1} + \beta \alpha X_N \qquad\qquad \textbf{(B3.2)}$$

which implies an asymptote (when $V_{N+1} = V_N$) at $V = \beta X$. The slower-growing "strengths" take longer to attain their maximum values, but since their maxima are assumed to be larger, these activities will eventually occur unless the noxious stimulus is removed. In general, the lower the value of α and the higher the value of β, the later an activity will occur in the escape sequence. Thus, if a noxious substance persists, the slower-growing, but potentially stronger, higher-level escape activities will supersede the faster-growing, but weaker, lower-level escape activities.

Not enough is known about *Stentor* escape behavior for us to say whether this model is entirely true, but it explains most of what *is* known and provides a basis for further experimentation. That mechanisms like the integrator are involved in these phenomena is certain; we are only uncertain about what else may be necessary for a full explanation. Ultimately, we would like to know what biochemical mechanisms are responsible for the behavioral processes we have identified.

havior means that there has been a change in *Stentor*'s internal state. These changes must have been occurring all along, otherwise the initial avoidance reaction, turning away, would have persisted indefinitely. Thus, the animal shows one essential feature of learning—a change in behavior potential as a result of experience. Thus far our *Stentor* is doing about as well as Thorndike's cat. What is the crucial difference?

Memory and Discrimination

The big difference is in the effect on the animal's behavior of either lapse of time or change in situation. The same *Stentor* exposed to carmine after 24 hours will almost certainly behave as it did when first exposed, not as it did at the end of the first exposure. A small lapse of time will have lesser effects, but some new experience during that time (e.g., a new chemical stimulus) is likely to abolish the effect of the earlier experience. But the cat that escapes efficiently from the box after a few successive trials will not be the same cat one week later that it was when first put in the box. It may not escape quite as rapidly as it did on its last trial, but it will certainly do better than it did on its first trial. The cat's ability to respond correctly after a lapse of time is not immune to the effects of intervening experience, but it is likely to be much less affected than the behavior of *Stentor*. What does this difference between cat and protozoan mean?

The obvious answer is that the protozoan cannot remember as long as the cat. Leaving aside for a moment the problem of exactly what we mean by "remember," a problem is: Why *doesn't Stentor* remember as long as the cat? The difficulty is unlikely to be some general limitation on the persistence of behavioral changes in small animals. In theory and in fact, it is a simple matter to set a molecular "switch" that affects behavior after long delays. Even precisely timed delays are not rare in nature. Many simple animals show periodicities that extend over long periods, for example, circumannual rhythms, the periodicity of the 17-year locust, and so on. Nature has no problem in building clocks or retaining changes over long periods.

We can get an idea of the real difference between a cat and our *Stentor* by looking at what each creature *ought* to do in its respective situation—given what we can guess of their different discriminative abilities. The cat faces a much more clear-cut problem. It can discriminate puzzle boxes from the many other things it is familiar with. When it sees the box again, it is unlikely to confuse it with anything else and has no reason to suppose that its previous solution is not appropriate. The *Stentor*, however, is unlikely to be able to discriminate carmine from many other chemical mixtures. Consequently, when it encounters the carmine on a later occasion, it may simply be unable to identify it as the same event. Even if the carmine has exactly the same sensory effect on both occasions, that effect may be sufficiently similar to that of other chemicals experienced before and later that the *Stentor* may still be unable to identify its second carmine experience as a repeat of its first. Even a highly intelligent *Stentor* might be well advised to treat a second exposure (especially if much delayed after the first) as a completely new situation.

Stentor reacting to carmine may be like a person with poor vision meeting again someone he or she has met before: If he or she must rely entirely on vision, he or she will necessarily be unsure whether or not he or she has really met the person before, a situation quite different from any intelligence and ability to remember a face. The poorly sighted person (like the hearing-impaired person) may appear dumb not because he or she cannot remember and understand but because he or she cannot discriminate. In other words, *Stentor* probably doesn't

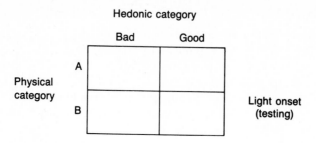

FIGURE 3.5   Contingency table for a simple animal that divides all stimuli into two categories (A and B).

have sufficient information to justify repetition on the second carmine exposure of the behavior it had developed in response to the first exposure. Therefore, *Stentor* may fail to learn not because it cannot remember but because it cannot be sufficiently sure when the same situation has recurred.

The abilities of animals are usually in harmony with one another; an animal will not evolve one ability to a high level if lack of another makes the first useless. For example, an animal that can only move slowly may not have highly developed distance vision, a short-lived animal such as a butterfly may have little ability to repair injuries, and a fish that lives in caves is often blind. In similar fashion, the persistence of memory is functionally related to the number of things that can be identified. This relation can be illustrated as follows: Imagine a simple animal that can classify stimuli in only four ways: good; bad; and two other, "neutral" categories unrelated to good or bad (e.g., two categories of physical size or intensity). Every situation that the animal encounters must then fit into one of the four cells defined by a 2 × 2 table (Figure 3.5). For it to be worthwhile for an animal to form an association between a given state of the world and its hedonic (good or bad) consequences, there must obviously be a *real* association. For example, if our animal can only partition neutral events into the two categories of "intense" and "weak," then there must really be some general correlation between the intensity of a physical event and its hedonic consequences; that is, loud noises must generally be associated with "bad" and soft noises with "good" or "neutral."

It is obvious that the more possible categories the animal has available, the greater the correlation between events in a given category and their hedonic consequences. For example, many loud noises are quite harmless, but loud, staccato noises coming from long objects may potentially be dangerous. The more qualifiers (additional categories) the animal has available, the more accurately it can identify the concomitants of good and bad, and the more accurately the animal can identify signals for good and bad, the more worthwhile it becomes to remember them.

We conclude that *Stentor*'s poor, long-term memory is much more likely to reflect a limitation on its ability to classify physical events into a number of categories than some limitation on storage or the persistence of physical change. The problem is one of information processing. To react to carmine later as it did on the first occasion, that is *learn*, *Stentor* must be able to identify the relevant features of its environment accurately enough to minimize the chance of two possible errors: reacting to the wrong stimulus and failing to react to the correct one. If its categories are so few that carmine does not uniquely occupy one of them, then it lacks the ability to tell whether a given chemical stimulus is carmine or something else—thus *Stentor* cannot detect the special properties of carmine presentations. The major difference between animals that can and cannot learn—between protozoans and pigeons, for example—is in their ability to differentiate among states of nature. The difference is in what they can discriminate rather than in how well they can remember.

LEARNING MECHANISMS

We pointed out in Chapter 1 that there are many ways that past experience can affect the future behavior of organisms and that only a few of these reflect learning. In each case of learning, the basic operation is the same: That is, learning involves using something as a signal for something else. For example, in the case of Pavlovian (classical) conditioning, the ticking of a metronome becomes a signal for food. In the case of operant (instrumental) conditioning, the small chamber with a response lever sets the occasion for, or becomes a signal for, the pressing of a lever. The signal for learning can also be used in other ways—corresponding to habituation, sensitization, and pseudoconditioning. Sometimes only operant and Pavlovian conditioning are classified as learning, but for lack of a general term, we refer to all five types—habituation, sensitization, pseudoconditioning, operant conditioning, and Pavlovian conditioning—as *learning*. We reserve the term *associative learning* for what typically occurs only in classical and operant conditioning. We now define the five types of learning in a general way. Chapter 4 discusses the specific operant and Pavlovian conditioning procedures in more detail. The mechanisms of Pavlovian and operant conditioning are discussed at length in later chapters.

Every stimulus has two aspects: good–bad (hedonic quality) and other, nonhedonic properties. For example, an electric shock is "bad," but it also has a certain "tickling" quality, a duration, a limited spatial extent, and so on, all of which have no specific good–bad aspect to them. Similarly, food is "good," but it also has a certain taste, texture, temperature, and color. Sometimes the hedonic and nonhedonic aspects are distinct; sometimes they are not. For example, spatial location rarely has any hedonic quality, but the taste of a food and its value may be inseparable. Whether separable or not, every stimulus has its hedonic and nonhedonic aspects. In the simplest kinds of learning, the animal uses the nonhedonic characteristics of a stimulus as a cue for its hedonic qualities.

Habituation

Habituation is the selective waning in strength of a response to repeated stimulation. For example, anything novel is potentially dangerous. Hence any sudden novel sound tends to be treated as potentially harmful: *Stentor* retreats into its tube; a rabbit pricks up its ears, turns toward the sound, and gets ready to bolt for its burrow. But as the sound is repeated and is not accompanied by any bad consequences, its nonhedonic properties, which at first were taken as potentially alarming, are eventually treated as a "safety" signal, and the sound alarms no more. Habituation is therefore a kind of learning in which the nonhedonic aspects of a stimulus are treated as a signal for safety or neutrality. The stimulus is thus reclassified as "harmless."[4]

In higher animals, the effects of habituation may be long-lasting or not, depending on the stimulus. For example, wild birds may take alarm at a new feeding station, but their alarm will habituate and will not reappear even after a few days away. On the other hand, the effects of habituation to a series of pistol shots will not persist unless the experience is repeated many times. The more intense the stimulus, the more transient the habituation to it. In lower animals, the effects of habituation rarely persist.

Habituation can often be abolished by some new experience (*dishabituation*). For example, if an animal has become habituated to a series of loud noises and is now placed in a new situation or presented with a bright light, another animal, or some other striking stimulus, another loud noise will often cause alarm.

Sensitization

Sensitization and the other three types of learning (pseudoconditioning, Pavlovian conditioning, and operant conditioning) all involve two kinds of stimuli: a stimulus with hedonic value and a stimulus with less or no hedonic value. These types of stimuli can also be termed a *reinforcer,* also known as an *unconditioned stimulus (US)* (terms derive from the use of hedonic stimuli such as food and electric shock in operant and Pavlovian conditioning situations, respectively), and a nonhedonic *conditioned stimulus (CS)*. A noxious hedonic stimulus such as an electric shock or a loud sound will usually elicit a startle reaction from a human or an animal. A loud sound will startle, a weak sound will not; but a weak, nonhedonic sound (CS) presented after one or two shocks (US) may cause startling again. These facts hold true not because the animal has learned

---

[4]Adaptation, habituation, and fatigue are often-confused processes that all refer to the waning in strength of behavior under repeated stimulation. They have similar properties but differ in their physiological implications: *fatigue* is presumed to be a property of the motor system (i.e., muscles and the neural systems that serve them); *adaptation* refers to the sensory system (visual adaptation, adaptation to touch, etc.); and *habituation* is presumed to be a property of the central nervous system. Thus, animals can habituate to complex properties of their environment (e.g., to the sight of specific individuals), whereas sensory adaptation and fatigue are the effects of relatively simple physical properties such as illumination level and energy expended.

anything about the relation between the shock and the sound, but because the sound is not a signal for the shock. Sensitization has a sort of confusion effect: The animal is anticipating the shock; sudden shock and sudden sound share non-hedonic qualities; so sound after shock is reacted to like shock.

The term *anticipation* here is more than necessary, because sensitization in our example is quite similar to the reflex property of *temporal summation* (see Box 3.5). All that is involved is that the shock changes the animal's state in such a way that another shock or a stimulus like shock will be reacted to more strongly than if the first shock had not occurred. In the same way, after a second or two exposure to carmine, *Stentor* reacted differently to further carmine: The initial few seconds sensitized the animal, so that further exposure elicited more extreme reactions. Only local memory is involved here; a weak sound long delayed after shock will elicit no reaction, just as a second dose of carmine delayed after the first produces the same effect as the first rather than a stronger effect.

Note that sensitization reflects a real property of the world: that things usually change relatively slowly (the world now is not too different from the world a few seconds ago). Thus, even if *Stentor* cannot uniquely identify carmine, it can be fairly sure that a "sensation" (i.e., sensory effect) that repeats itself after a few seconds is likely to reflect the same objective event, whereas a repeat after a longer interval is less likely to be the same event. It makes sense for the effects of two carmine exposures in close succession to summate.

All learning is a sort of inference. In this case, the question is: Did A cause B? (Did the sensation associated with carmine "cause" the subsequent noxious effects?) The people who study artificial intelligence call this problem the *assignment of credit problem:* Who is responsible for the bad (or good) thing that just happened? The ecological basis for sensitization is that a given sensation that is repeated after a short interval, with no intervening event, is much more likely to represent the same objective state of the world than if the two occurrences are separated by a long interval, or if other events intervene. Dishabituation reflects the ecological fact that the same sensation, repeated without an intervening different sensation, is more likely to reflect the same objective event than if a different sensation intervened.

Any frightening situation sensitizes the animal (again reflecting the basically inferential nature of the process); it is not always necessary to present a noxious stimulus. For example, the following situation provides a good classroom demonstration of a sensitized human startle response: A student is invited to participate in front of the class in an experiment to measure skin resistance. He or she is asked to place two fingers on two metallic contacts protruding from an unfamiliar piece of obviously electrical apparatus. At the instant that the finger touches the (completely harmless) contacts, the demonstrator sounds a loud siren. The siren produces no, or at most a weak, startle when presented without the potentially harmful electrical apparatus. However, when it coincides with what the student fears may be a painful, or at least a novel, experience, the reaction is vigorous. This response is owing to the effects of sensitization. Although, much more is involved here than the simple integrator that is sufficient to account for similar effects in primitive animals.

Shock onset
(training)

	Sudden	Gradual
Sudden	2/7	7/9
Gradual	8/10	1/8

FIGURE 3.6   Summary results from a pseudoconditioning experiment by Wickens and Wickens (1942). Cells show numbers of animals per group for the four possible results.

Pseudoconditioning

Pseudoconditioning is similar to sensitization. In both cases, prior presentation of a US (hedonic stimulus) causes a CS (nonhedonic stimulus) to elicit the same reaction. The effect is called sensitization if the CS at a stronger intensity can elicit the reaction (shock → startle, loud sound → startle, weak sound → startle unless preceded by shock or loud sound). The effect is called *pseudoconditioning* if the CS never elicits the reaction on its own.

An experiment by Wickens and Wickens (1942) is a neat demonstration of the role of confusion or generalization in these effects. The researchers trained two groups of rats in a box with two chambers to run to the second chamber when shocked in the first. For one group, the shock came on suddenly; for the other, its onset was gradual. One-half the animals in each group were then tested with a light that came on suddenly; the other half with a light that came on slowly. As you can see from Figure 3.6, the light nearly always elicited running when its speed of onset matched the training condition; it rarely did so when the speed did not match the training condition.

Sometimes animals habituate to a stimulus, sometimes they are sensitized by it, so that their reaction increases with successive stimulus presentations. We seem to have things both ways here, since a reaction can only decrease or increase. Fortunately, the effect to be expected from a given stimulus does seem to depend on measurable stimulus properties, most notably stimulus intensity. Animals seem to habituate to stimuli of low or moderate intensity; but they become sensitized by intense stimuli. For example, a sudden, loud tone elicits a startle response from rats, but after repeated presentations, the response habituates. However, if the same loud tone is presented against a background of loud white noise, the reaction not only fails to habituate, it increases across tone presentations. The critical factor seems to be the damage potential of the situation.

Pavlovian Conditioning

If a hedonic stimulus (US) is reliably preceded (signaled) by a neutral, non-hedonic stimulus (CS), many animals can learn to use the CS as a signal for the US. The process differs from sensitization and pseudoconditioning in at least two ways:

1. It is persistent. Sensitization and pseudoconditioning both depend on the CS being presented a relatively short time after the US, whereas after training a CS will be effective a day or more after the previous US presentation.
2. The CS must really be a good predictor of the US. It is not sufficient that they occur more or less close together in time (i.e., be contiguous).

We describe how *contiguity* (temporal succession) is separated from *contingency* (*regularity* of succession) in Chapter 4.

In the standard procedure studied so extensively with dogs by Ivan Pavlov, a US such as food is repeatedly preceded by a neutral CS such as a tone. After a few such pairings, the salivation originally produced only by food is now produced by the tone as well. The reaction to the US is called the *unconditioned response (UR)*; the reaction to the CS is called the *conditioned response (CR)*. A comparable experiment with *Stentor* would involve pairing brief carmine presentations (US) with some other stimulus, such as a change in illumination or temperature (a potential CS). The carmine elicits turning away; the light-change initially elicits nothing. If after a few pairings the light produces turning, then we *may* have Pavlovian conditioning. Additional control experiments in which the order of CS and US is varied (to rule out sensitization and pseudoconditioning) are then necessary to ensure that it is the predictive relation between the CS and the US that produces a change in behavior. Further additional tests with the CS alone are necessary to see if the change is a relatively permanent one, as it usually is in higher animals. In practice, of course, protozoa rarely pass all these tests; most of their learning is habituation, sensitization, or pseudoconditioning.

Pavlovian conditioning is the prototype for all signal learning. The CS is a signal for the US, and the animal reacts to the CS as if it were the US—although careful scrutiny usually shows that the reaction to the CS is anticipatory rather than a copy of the reaction to the US.

Operant Conditioning

Suppose we pair a tone with food a few times in Pavlovian fashion, but then we present the tone alone: What will the animal do? Pavlov knew that his dogs would not sit quiet under such conditions (which is one reason he restrained them in a harness). Given the opportunity, the dog tries to produce food: If the experimenter is in the room, the dog begs. If he or she is not in the room, the dog paws at the food bowl and tries to leave the room to explore. Suppose one of these explorations is in fact effective, as it might be if the experimenter has merely hidden the full food bowl, for example. The dog then eats and is removed from the room. If the experiment is repeated on the following day, the tone, the room, and the various other stimuli will not now produce the random searching we saw the day before. Instead, the dog is likely to go directly to the place where he previously found the food.

This is a two-phase process:

1. The first phase (variation) is more or less unsystematic behavior that eventually leads to something good (or avoids something bad).

2. The second phase (selection) is the recurrence of efficient behavior when the animal is later returned to the same situation.

The two phases together are called *operant conditioning* (an essentially equivalent term is *instrumental learning*). The first phase fits the control-by-consequences definition of operant behavior. The second phase is referred to as the control of operant behavior by a discriminative stimulus, which is described in detail shortly.

The Relation Between Operant and Pavlovian Conditioning

The processes involved in operant and Pavlovian conditioning are intimately related. The parallel between the two is easy to see in avoidance or escape conditioning. A situation that signals shock or some other aversive stimulus elicits a range of avoidance and escape reactions of three types: fight (attack any plausible target, such as a conspecific), flight (escape from the situation), or "freeze" (immobility). These reactions tend to occur in a systematic sequence (as in the *Stentor* example), depending on the severity and duration of the threat and the opportunities offered by the environment. If no reaction is successful in escaping from the threat, then the animal settles on the final reaction in the series, which in the case of shock, is generally immobility. Such learning is usually described as Pavlovian conditioning, in which an aversive CS produces conditioned immobility or helplessness.

But if one of the reactions *is* effective in eliminating the threat, then repeated recurrence of the situation is likely to lead to reliable repetition of this effective avoidance response. Such learning is operant conditioning. The response is an operant response.

The relation between Pavlovian and operant conditioning is clear:

1. Pavlovian conditioning is the name we give to the process that permits an animal to detect that the CS predicts the US. In this way, the animal is able to identify the hedonic qualities of the situation: Is it "good" or "bad?" What kind of "good" or "bad" is it?

2. Given this information, the animal (be it rat or *Stentor*) has available a repertoire of potentially useful reactions that nature (in the case of *Stentor*) or nature and past experience (in the case of the rat) has given it to try. Pavlovian conditioning allows the animal to pick the be-

havioral repertoire most likely (as determined by its evolutionary and individual history) to be useful in the context of a given US.

3. If some reaction is effective, it is selected (in ways that are discussed in Chapter 4) and recurs when the situation recurs. This control of operant behavior by the situation in which it has developed is termed *discriminative control.* The environmental features that are effective in controlling behavior are collectively termed the *discriminative stimulus* for the response. Pavlovian conditioning obviously sets the stage for response selection and discriminative control.

GENERALIZATION AND DISCRIMINATION[5]

Adaptive behavior demands as a minimum that animals respond differently in different situations. The different kinds of learning just discussed define "situation" in different ways. In habituation, the period immediately following a stimulus is treated by the animal as a different situation from other times. Sensitization and pseudoconditioning work in the same manner, as the period immediately following a US is different from other time periods. In operant and Pavlovian conditioning, the animal further differentiates the world according to stimuli in addition to the US. The CS and its associated context (discriminative stimulus) define not only a specific hedonic quality but also, in the operant case, a behavioral pattern that is perhaps unique.

Just what the term "situation" signifies in the operant and Pavlovian conditioning of birds and mammals is the topic of later chapters. For now, let's consider the idealized view illustrated in Figure 3.7. The figure shows along the vertical axis the various states of the world ("stimuli") that can be discriminated by an animal; the various modes of behavior of which the beast is capable are similarly arranged along the horizontal axis. Suppose that in the situation defined as A behavior B_A develops as a consequence of operant conditioning. Physical situations never recur identically, for instance, one day is sunny, the next is overcast or rainy, and so on. Consequently, animals are able to accept minor variations in stimulus situation. They never repeat a response identically either—nor should they, since some variants are more effective than others, and variability itself is sometimes advantageous in avoiding traps (as noted in Chapter 2). These two sources of variation—physical situation and response—mean that the pattern of behavior that develops in situation A is better represented as a region, or *probability distribution,* in the stimulus–response area of Figure 3.7. It is not represented as a point at which a unique stimulus produces a perfectly stereotyped response. You can think of this relation between situation and action,

---

[5] The core ideas in this section have recently been elaborated in a series of important papers by Roger Shepard (e.g., 1987).

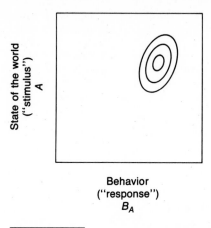

State of the world ("stimulus") A

Behavior ("response") B_A

FIGURE 3.7   Definition of an operant as a region in a stimulus–response space. Closed contours are lines of equal probability.

termed an *operant* (*habit* is the older term), as a hillock in the space centered on the point (A, B_A), where the third dimension, off the page, corresponds to response strength.

Generalization

This picture presents an enormous simplification, but it enables us to define generalization and discrimination in an easy manner. *Generalization* refers to the effect of systematic variation in the physical stimulus situation on the operant response controlled by that situation. Usually the effect is to reduce the probability of the measured response, as suggested by the hillock picture in Figure 3.7. Thus a pigeon trained to peck a green disc for food reward will peck less frequently on a yellow or red disc. Generalization leads to two kinds of "confusion": A given operant response can occur in situations other than (but similar to) the training situation; and responses other than the given operant can show up in the training situation.

The extent of generalization obviously depends on the animal's individual and racial experience of variability and the reliability of correlations between physical properties of the world and appropriate behavior. Aspects of the environment that never vary can be ignored: For example, most lizards can move up or down a temperature gradient to find the temperature that suits them best, but some tropical rain-forest species have lost this ability. Because of the unvarying temperature of their environment, such animals have apparently lost the capacity to respond to temperature variation; many deep-sea fish are similarly deficient. This lost capacity is an extreme deficit in discrimination and reflects the animals' racial history. An animal reared in an experimental environment in which large changes have little significance is likely to generalize more broadly than an animal reared in an environment in which large significance is routinely attached to small changes. Such a situation illustrates true generalization, an effect of individual history. Measured generalization reflects both individual and racial history. The essential feature of generalization is that it represents the animal's estimate (based on some combination of racial and individual experience) that two different physical stimulus complexes require the same response and thus can be treated in the same manner.

Discrimination

Discrimination refers to the limits on an animal's ability to treat similar situations differently. Generalization and discrimination are loosely, and asymmetrically, related. Generalization refers to the stimulus variations the animal is willing to accept and still defines the situation as essentially unchanged in terms of appropriate action. Discrimination refers to the minimal variations in situation (stimulus) that the animal is *capable* of treating as different. A pigeon may be able to detect the difference between wavelengths of 500 and 600 nm (they look green and yellow to humans), yet it remains willing to treat them alike, because in the past they have been associated with the same consequences. On the other hand, wavelengths of 500 and 501 nm can be associated with consequences as different as we like, yet the pigeon does not treat them differently, because it cannot tell them apart.

An animal may be able to detect small differences in situation but be inclined to accept large ones as of no significance. Hence, broad generalization need not imply poor discrimination. But, an animal cannot treat similar situations as different if it cannot tell them apart. Hence, poor discrimination implies broad generalization.

SUMMARY

This chapter dealt with four related topics:

1. the difference between the operant behavior of simple animals and higher animals
2. the relation between mechanistic and functional explanations of behavior
3. the similarities among learning mechanisms
4. generalization and discrimination

From the topics we arrived at several conclusions.

The most important difference between the operant behavior of the tiny protozoan *Stentor*, for example, and the operant behavior of higher animals is the richness with which the animal's environment is represented internally. The behavior of *Stentor* depends only on its current environment and the environment of the immediate past (local memory). The *Stentor* has no memory of the distant past, thus its current behavior cannot be guided by it. Higher animals such as mammals and birds can behave in a variety of ways, however, and these behaviors depend on both their current environment and their past history (associative learning). It is likely that *Stentor* has failed to evolve the capacity to learn not because memory mechanisms in themselves are complex but because to be useful they must work with complex discriminative and information-retrieval apparatus—which are beyond the capacity of an organism that lacks a nervous system.

Mechanistic and functional explanations of behavior answer different questions. Mechanistic accounts are specific and lead naturally to physiological questions: that is, how the mechanism is represented physiologically and how it operates. If we are curious about *how* an organism works, we should pursue a mechanistic explanation. A functional account is much more general, and it tells us something about the animal in relation to its niche—not necessarily as an individual, but as a member of a species. Although mechanistic explanations are often scientifically preferable, functional accounts are often a necessary first step in situations where specific mechanisms cannot be identified or where different mechanisms all produce similar effects.

Learning involves using something (e.g., a stimulus or a context) as a signal for something else (another stimulus or a specific pattern of behavior).

We defined several learning mechanisms. Habituation is the selective waning of a response to repeated stimulation. It may be either long-lasting or short term, usually depending on the intensity of the stimulus. Sensitization is the selective increase in a response to repeated stimulation. It is a sort of confusion effect. When an organism is "anticipating" a nasty stimulus and a neutral stimulus is presented, the organism often treats the neutral one as if it were the nasty one, because the two share properties. Pseudoconditioning (which is similar to sensitization) may occur when prior presentation of a US causes a CS to elicit the same response as the US. The difference between pseudoconditioning and sensitization is that for pseudoconditioning the CS never elicits the reaction on its own. For example, if a nasty shock is presented prior to a novel tone, the tone may elicit a fear reaction. If the tone would not have elicited fear on its own, the effect is pseudoconditioning; if the tone (perhaps at a louder level) elicits fear, the effect is considered sensitization. Pavlovian conditioning is the prototype for all signal learning. If a hedonic stimulus (US) is reliably preceded by a neutral, nonhedonic stimulus (CS), many animals can use the CS as a signal for the US. The response that occurs to the CS *if and only if* it predicts the US is termed a conditioned response (CR). Pavlovian conditioning differs from habituation, sensitization, and pseudoconditioning in that its effects are persistent, and the CS must reliably predict the US for learning to occur.

Generalization refers to an organism's willingness to treat two physically and discriminably different situations as equivalent. Discrimination refers to the limits on an organism's ability to treat different situations as different. An animal may be willing to behave in the same fashion, even when it can tell that two stimuli are not the same (generalization). On the other hand, if it cannot tell one stimulus from another, it must generalize because it cannot discriminate.

Both generalization and discrimination have something to do with the consequences of action in different situations. The limits to discrimination presumably reflect evolutionary forces that have favored the development of sensory capacities up to, but not beyond, a certain point: If pigeons cannot tell the difference between light wavelengths of 500 and 501 nm it is presumably because in nature such small differences rarely signify anything of importance. Pigeons can tell the difference between 500 and 550 nm, but they may nevertheless treat them the same, because in the history of the individual animal, the same behavior was effective in securing reward in the presence of both stimuli (generalization).

4

Reinforcement and Behavior

All functional explanations of behavior depend on some notion of what is "good and bad"—its hedonic value (as described in Chapter 3). If we are speaking of evolutionary adaptation, hedonic value boils down to Darwinian fitness, which is a well-defined notion in principle but is usually hard to measure in practice. If we are speaking of the operant behavior of individual animals, good and bad correspond to reinforcement and punishment, that is, to situations better or worse than the current situation. This chapter discusses the concept of *reinforcement*, how it is defined, and the procedures used to study its effects. When studying reinforcement, we must ask two kinds of questions:

1. What makes situations good or bad? Can we define hedonic value independently of the behavior of the animal (i.e., do all good situations share common features)? Or, must we always see the effect of a situation on an animal before we can be sure of its hedonic value?

2. Granted that we know the hedonic properties of a situation, how does it affect behavior? That is, what are the mechanisms (the

rules) that determine the effects of positive and negative hedonic events (reward and punishment) on behavior?

The problem of defining "the good" has always been a preoccupation of philosophers. G. E. Moore, an early twentieth century Cambridge morals philosopher, summed up the modern consensus in dry but exact fashion: "I have maintained that very many things are good and evil in themselves, and that neither class of things possesses any other property which is both common to all its members and peculiar to them" (1903, p. x). In other words, all that good things have in common is that they are good, and all that bad things have in common is that they are bad.

Early behaviorists were undeterred by the philosophers' failure to find an independent yardstick for value. Deceived by the apparent simplicity of the white rat, they tried to reduce motivated behavior to a small set of "primary drives": hunger, thirst, and sex. For the rat, at least, the definition of "good" was that it led to the reduction of one or more of these three drives. But, opinions differed about what should be done when rats sometimes acted in ways that could not be explained by one of the three. For example, rats in a new environment will eventually explore it; given a weak electric shock for pressing a lever, they are likely to press again rather than avoid the lever after their first press; and so on. One school added new drives to the list: curiosity, habitat preference, freedom, sleep, and aggression. Another school, more parsimonious, held to the original trinity and proposed to solve the problem of additional motives by linking them to the basic three. For example, exploratory behavior might be explained not by a "curiosity drive" but by a past "reinforcement history" in which exploration had led to food, water, or sexual activity.

Neither course was wholly satisfactory. Among those willing to entertain additional drives, there was no general agreement beyond the basic three. Indeed, someone acquainted with desert animals might question thirst as a primary drive, since such animals rarely drink in nature, obtaining the water they need from their food. The modern version of the multiple-drive view is the economic concept of a *preference structure*. This idea is more ambitious than earlier drive theories in that it proposes to accommodate not only more than one drive (or desirable consequence) but also shows how competing drives are to be reconciled. For example, drive theory could not easily explain how an animal that is both hungry and thirsty could choose between food and water. The view that there are primary and secondary motives and that all behavior can be derived from a small primary set has no real contemporary descendant. However, recent attempts within economic psychology to derive a universal preference structure from a limited set of motivational characteristics are clearly in the same tradition.

The question of what makes a situation good or bad from an animal's point of view, interesting as it is, has not led to conclusive answers. Psychologists have been driven back to Moore's conclusion that there is nothing beyond the animal's reaction that marks a situation as good or bad. This fact has led to an animal-defined concept of reinforcement: A situation is good if the animal does something to approach it and bad if the animal does something to avoid it.

The question of how situations with known hedonic properties affect behavior has attracted much more attention for two reasons. First, it suggests many more experiments. If we have something an animal wants, such as food, and we know what the animal can do in a gross sense, then we can require all sorts of activities of it as a condition for giving it the food. The way in which the animal copes with the problems we set tells us something about the machinery (both thought and action) that it has for improving its situation. Second, and most important, the more we know about that machinery, the closer we are to answering the first question about what defines value for the animal. It is well to begin with simple, extreme cases. For example, if we understand how animals avoid and escape electric shock or how hungry animals cope with finding food, then we will be in a better position to understand their behavior in situations in which the rewards and punishments are less potent and their behavior more subtle.

This chapter discusses the main experimental arrangements—both Pavlovian and operant conditioning—that have been used to study the effects of hedonic events on the behavior of animals. We describe in general terms the effects that these procedures have on animals, leaving more in-depth accounts to later chapters.

PAVLOVIAN CONDITIONING

The study of conditioning begins with the Russian Ivan P. Pavlov, whose work made its major impact in the West with the (1927) publication of an English translation of his lectures on conditioned reflexes. The lectures had been given in 1924 to the Petrograd Military Medical Academy, and they summarized several decades of active work by a large research group. The subtitle of his book *Conditioned reflexes* is "An investigation of the physiological activity of the cerebral cortex"—which gives us a clue to Pavlov's objectives. As a physiologist, Pavlov was interested in behavior as a tool for understanding the functioning of the brain. However, like C. S. Sherrington, his experiments involved little surgical intervention; most were purely behavioral. Pavlov also often interpreted his results physiologically (e.g., inferring that waves of excitation and inhibition spread across the cortex). Unlike Sherrington's speculations about reflexes, however, later physiological work has not supported Pavlov's conjectures. Nevertheless, Pavlov's observations and his theoretical terms continue to be influential (Box 4.1).

Experimental Methods

Pavlov's basic procedure was one of *delayed conditioning*, in which a brief stimulus of a few seconds' duration, such as a tone, a bell, or a flashing light, is periodically presented to a dog that is restrained in a harness (Figures 4.1 and

B   O   X

4.1

Ivan Petrovich Pavlov (1849–1936)

The findings of Ivan P. Pavlov and his approach to behavior are still subjects of lively debate in the West and continue to dominate Soviet experimental psychology—even though much of his work is nearly a century old. Pavlov was born in a small town in Tsarist Russia and was educated for the priesthood. Nevertheless, he eventually graduated from college in natural science and received his doctorate at the Imperial Medico-Surgical Academy in St. Petersburg (now Leningrad). He subsequently studied physiology with C. F. Ludwig in Leipzig (now in East Germany) and with R. Heidenhain in Breslau (now Wroclaw in Poland). His research interest was digestive physiology. He discovered the secretory nerves of the pancreas in 1888 and perfected operations that made visible the functions of the digestive system. He eventually received the Nobel Prize for this work in 1904. Pavlov ascended to a position of dominance in Russian academia, and for the last several years of his life, he headed a large research institute at the St. Petersburg Military Medical Academy—an establishment quite different from the modest operations of most other biologists of his time. Much of Pavlov's later research was therefore carried out by others, albeit under his active supervision. Even after the Communist Revolution in 1917, Pavlov retained his reputation, and his resources were only augmented; Lenin evidently felt that Pavlov's work could provide a sound materialistic basis for the new "Soviet Man."

Pavlov's work made its impact in the West with the (1927) publication of an English translation of his lectures on conditioned reflexes. His ideas were taken up in the United States by the energetic and polemical John B. Watson (see Box 3.4).

4.2). The dog has recovered from a minor operation in which the duct of its salivary gland has been brought to the outside of the cheek, so that the saliva can be collected and measured. At the end of this brief stimulus (CS) some food powder (the US) is placed in the animal's mouth. The food powder induces salivation, which produces the unconditioned response (UR). This sequence of operations and effects—tone → food → salivation—is repeated several times, and soon a new effect can be seen. Salivation now begins to occur when the tone comes on, before food has actually been placed in the animal's mouth. This response is termed the conditioned response, or conditional response (CR); it is conditional because it depends on the relationship between CS and US during prior training. (The term *conditioned response* has become standard for what Pavlov observed, although *conditional* is closer to the Russian meaning. The term *condi-*

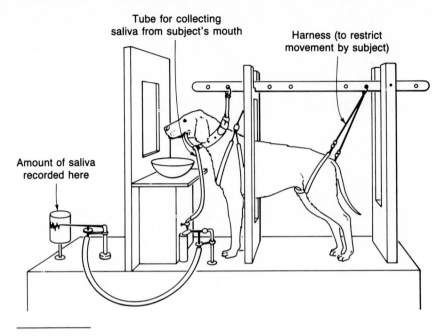

FIGURE 4.1   Pavlov's conditioning apparatus.

tional is now normally used to refer to a type of discrimination in which one of two simultaneously presented stimuli is signaled as positive by the presence or absence of a third stimulus: e.g., given two stimuli A and B, A is rewarded when a third stimulus, C, is present; otherwise B is rewarded.)

Pavlov's basic observation can hardly be called startling, and it must have been observed by anyone who kept animals and fed them on some kind of schedule. Irish playwright George Bernard Shaw, a vegetarian and leading literary figure when Pavlov's fame was at its height, in his satire "The adventures of the black girl in her search for God," parodies Pavlov as follows:

> "This remarkable discovery cost me twenty-five years of devoted research, during which I cut out the brains of innumerable dogs, and observed their spittle by making holes in their cheeks for them to salivate through. . . . The whole scientific world is prostrate at my feet in admiration of this colossal achievement and gratitude for the light it has shed on the great problem of human conduct."
>
> "Why didn't you ask me?" said the black girl.
>
> "I could have told you in twenty-five seconds without hurting those poor dogs."
>
> "Your ignorance and presumption are unspeakable" said the old myop.
>
> "The fact was known of course to every child; but it had never been proved experimentally in the laboratory; and therefore it was not scientifically known at all. It reached me as an unskilled conjecture: I handed it on as science . . ." (1946, p. 36).

Shaw's parable reminds us that selling as behavioral "science" what is really commonplace knowledge embedded in jargon is nothing new. The spirit of Shaw's caricature may delight the more rabid animal-rights activists today, but in this

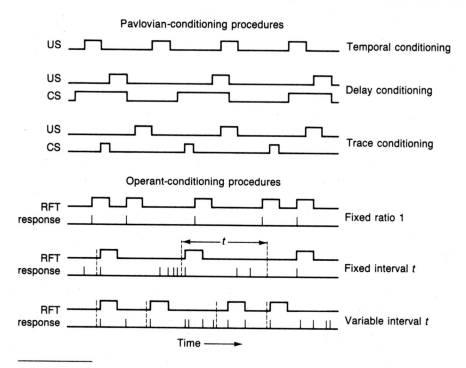

FIGURE 4.2   Event diagrams of common Pavlovian- and operant-conditioning procedures. Time is on the horizontal axis, and the occurrence of the labeled event (CS, US, response, RFT [reinforcement]) is indicated by upward deflection of the line. In the Pavlovian procedures, the occurrence of the US (unconditioned stimulus) is independent of responding, but it is systematically related to a CS (conditioned stimulus), post-US time, or post-CS time. In the operant procedures, the reinforcer depends on a response and (on all schedules other than fixed-ratio 1) on some other time, response, or stimulus condition. Thus in a fixed interval, a certain time (t) must elapse before a response is reinforced; on fixed-ratio N, $N - 1$ responses must occur before the Nth response is effective.

case, his criticism is not just: Pavlov's contribution was not the discovery of anticipatory salivation but its measurement and use as a tool to study behavioral processes (the "physiology of the cerebral cortex" in his terminology). For example, Pavlov found that if the duration of the CS is longer than a few seconds, the saliva does not begin to flow at once and is delayed until just before the delivery of food. (Pavlov called this fact *inhibition of delay.*) However, this period of delay is fragile, in the sense that any unexpected change in the situation immediately causes a copious flow of saliva. This phenomenon, a sort of dishabituation (see Chapter 3), is found in operant as well as Pavlovian conditioning, and its study has revealed important information about memory and the organization of action. Pavlov was able to develop for learned behavior a set of principles comparable to those earlier derived by Sherrington in his studies of spinal reflexes. He did so by

Studying the effects of varying the type of CS and the time between CS and US

Pairing one stimulus with the US and another with its absence

Researching what happened when the CS was presented without the US

Numerous other similar manipulations

Pavlov came to the conclusion that the essential ingredient for conditioning was the close temporal relation (*temporal contiguity*) between the CS and the US. He had good reasons for his belief, although he overstated the case. (In actuality, the first experiments that showed temporal contiguity and point to a sort of alternative were conditioning experiments that looked at variables not studied by Pavlov and his associates.)

Pavlov could point to many data that suggest the importance of temporal contiguity. For example, compare delay conditioning with *trace conditioning* (Figure 4.2). Both procedures involve a delay between CS onset and the occurrence of the US, but in trace conditioning, the CS ends some time before the US begins. Trace conditioning is much more difficult to achieve than delayed conditioning, which suggests that any delay between CS and US is detrimental to conditioning. Many other early experiments demonstrated the bad effects on conditioning of CS–US delays. The only discordant note was provided by *temporal conditioning* (Figure 4.2), which is simply periodic presentation of the US such as a fixed-interval schedule without the response requirement. (Temporal conditioning is also known as a *fixed-time schedule*.) In temporal conditioning, the US serves as a (temporal) CS, like the neutral CS in trace conditioning. Despite the delay between CS and US, temporal conditioning is quite effective, even with long delays. This difference between temporal and trace conditioning seems to depend on the properties of memory, which also accounts for other examples of long-delay conditioning discovered subsequently. Temporal conditioning attracted little attention until relatively recently, and the main attack on contiguity came from another quarter.

Stimulus Contingency or Temporal Contiguity?

An important paper by Yale psychologist Robert Rescorla (1967) made a major advance—he showed that contiguity (pairing) is not all that matters. According to Rescorla, it is also important for conditioning that the potential CS *predict* the US in a special sense we explain shortly.

Rescorla used a procedure, invented by William K. Estes and Burrhus F. Skinner in 1943, that does not involve salivation at all. The Estes–Skinner procedure, known as *conditioned suppression* or the *conditioned emotional response (CER)* is used to study Pavlovian conditioning, but it is a mixture of both operant- and Pavlovian-conditioning procedures. The key ingredient is a variable-interval (VI) schedule of food reinforcement. On a VI schedule, the animal receives a small bit of food (or other reinforcer) for the first lever-press after a period of time that varies from one food delivery to the next. Because the time of food delivery is unpredictable, most animals learn to respond at a more-or-less steady rate on VI schedules. Hence, responding on VI schedules is an admirable

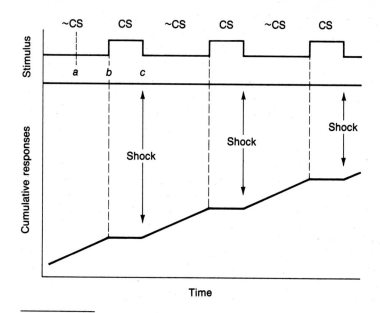

FIGURE 4.3   The suppression of a response maintained by a variable-interval (VI) schedule of reinforcement during a stimulus (CS) ending with a brief electric shock. The degree of suppression is measured by comparing response rate during the stimulus (period *bc*) with responding during the same period before stimulus onset (period *ab*).

baseline with which to study the effects of other independent variables; since the animal responds at a steady rate, any change in rate associated with the presentation of a stimulus can safely be attributed to the stimulus, rather than to accidental variation.

Estes and Skinner made use of a VI baseline to study the effect of occasionally presenting a relatively brief, neutral stimulus of the type used by Pavlov. After an initial "novelty" effect, the animal (usually a rat) continues to respond at about the same rate when the stimulus is present as when it is absent. This condition is the control condition, which establishes that the stimulus by itself has no effect. In the next phase, the rat is briefly shocked (through the metal-grid floor) at some time during the stimulus presentation. After a few such stimulus–shock pairings, the stimulus produces a clearly recognizable suppression of lever-pressing (Figure 4.3).

Conditioned suppression behaves in essentially the same way as the salivation of Pavlov's dogs, but it has several practical advantages: Rats are cheaper than dogs; no operation is required; and there are fewer physiological limitations on lever-pressing than on salivation. Although other Pavlovian conditioning methods are sometimes used in Western laboratories (e.g., measurement of skin resistance, blinking, or the nictitating-membrane response in rabbits), the conditioned-suppression method is widely favored.

A simplified version of Rescorla's procedure is shown in Figure 4.4. In the

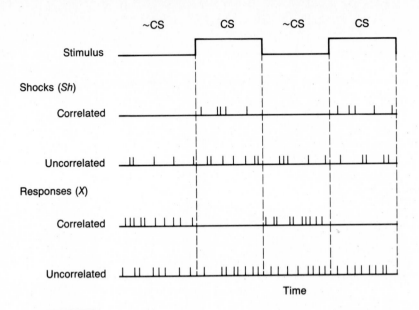

FIGURE 4.4   Stimulus contingencies in classical conditioning. The top panel shows the alternation of two stimuli. The next two panels show correlated and uncorrelated stimulus contingencies. The last two panels show the effects of correlated and uncorrelated stimuli on responding maintained by a VI food schedule.

figure, there are two stimuli (e.g., a tone versus a light or buzzer versus absence of buzzer) labeled CS and ~CS ("not-CS," the absence of CS). These stimuli last 60 sec., and in this simplified version, they occur in strict alternation, with about 50 such cycles making up a daily experimental session (only two cycles are shown in the figure). In the correlated condition (second row in Figure 4.3), brief, randomly spaced shocks occur only during the CS. In the uncorrelated condition, the shocks occur throughout the experimental session, that is, indiscriminately in the presence of both CS and ~CS. This uncorrelated condition is sometimes also called a *truly random control* condition (Rescorla, 1967).

The effect of these two procedures on lever-pressing maintained by the VI schedule is shown in the bottom two rows of the figure. In the correlated condition, animals typically respond for food only in the presence of the ~CS, which is not associated with shock—which is the conditioned suppression just discussed. An interesting result is obtained in the uncorrelated condition (bottom row): In this condition, animals respond indiscriminately in the presence of both stimuli, although at a somewhat lower rate than with the ~CS in the correlated condition.

This result rules out CS–US contiguity as a complete explanation for Pavlovian conditioning. Simple pairing of US (shock) and a CS cannot be sufficient for conditioning, since this pairing occurs in both the correlated and uncorrelated conditions of Rescorla's experiment. Yet, conditioning occurred only in the correlated condition. What, then, are the necessary and sufficient conditions for Pavlovian conditioning?

STIMULUS CONTINGENCY   Intuitively, the answer is clear: The animals show conditioning to a stimulus only when it is a reliable signal for—predicts—the US. The CS and US must therefore be correlated for conditioning to occur. This conclusion, first advanced by Leon Kamin over 20 years ago, is appealing and widely accepted, but it is deceptive: As with a bikini, what it reveals is suggestive, but what it conceals is vital. "Predictability" is something quite different from "contiguity." Contiguity is a perfectly unambiguous time relation between two events. Event A is said to be contiguous with event B if event B always follows A. On the other hand, the predictability of something depends on the *knowledge* of the observer. For example, because of Isaac Newton's work with astronomy, we can predict with accuracy when Halley's comet will return, whereas before none could do so; we know something Newton's predecessors did not, namely the laws of planetary motion. The situations used to study conditioning in rats are so simple, and our understanding of them so intuitive, that it is hard to define just what is involved in detecting the kinds of correlation depicted in Figure 4.3—it is hard even to realize that correlation is not a simple property like weight or duration. Nevertheless, an explanation of conditioning in terms of correlation or predictability is a functional explanation, because it specifies only the result of a procedure, not the process by which the animal achieves that result. The predictability explanation for Rescorla's result is better than Pavlov's contiguity account of conditioning, but its success carries a cost: A gain in comprehensiveness has also meant a loss in precision. (We describe in Chapter 5 the mathematical theory of Rescorla–Wagner, which is a mechanism sufficient to allow animals to detect contingent relations of the sort studied by Rescorla.)

The idea of contingency can be made more precise with the aid of a common device—the *contingency table.* Figures 4.5 and 4.6 are contingency tables computed for the correlated and uncorrelated (random) conditions in Figure 4.4. The rows correspond to conditions (CS and ~CS), and the columns correspond to the occurrence or nonoccurrence of shock. (Shock and ~Shock). Thus, the entry in the upper right cell in Figure 4.5 is the number of occurrences of the CS when at least one shock occurred (both presentations of the CS are accompanied by shock in Figure 4.4). The bottom right cell displays the number of times when the ~CS occurred and was accompanied by shock (zero), and so on. The concept of a *stimulus contingency* is obvious from the comparison of Figure 4.5 and 4.6: When the presence or absence of the stimulus is a predictor of shock, entries in the major diagonal of the table are high, and entries elsewhere are low (Figure 4.5). When the presence or absence of the stimulus is uncorrelated with the presence or absence of shock, the rows are the same (Figure 4.6). Figure 4.7 shows an intermediate case in which the CS is partially correlated with shock. Because Figure 4.7 more closely resembles Figure 4.5 than Figure 4.6, conditioning occurs. The entries to the right of the tables are *conditional probabilities,* for example, the probability of shock given a stimulus ($p(Sh|CS)$, in which shock is labeled Sh).

	~Shock	Shock	
CS	0	2	$p(Sh|CS) = 1.0$
~CS	2	0	$p(Sh|{\sim}CS) = 0$

FIGURE 4.5   Correlated condition (Sh = shock).

	~Shock	Shock	
CS	0	2	$p(Sh|CS) = 1.0$
~CS	0	2	$p(Sh|{\sim}CS) = 1.0$

FIGURE 4.6   Random condition (Sh = shock).

	~Shock	Shock	
CS	2	3	$p(Sh|CS) = .6$
~CS	4	1	$p(Sh|{\sim}CS) = .2$

FIGURE 4.7   Partially correlated condition (Sh = shock).

The amount of conditioning to a stimulus in a Pavlovian-conditioning situation is directly related to the degree of contingency between the stimulus and the unconditioned stimulus. Figure 4.8 illustrates an especially clear example of this relation: Data from an experiment by Rescorla show that the suppression ratio is linearly related, with negative slope, to the value of ϕ, the coefficient of contingency between CS and US. Since low suppression ratios mean high sup-

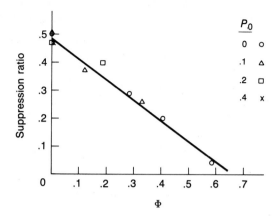

FIGURE 4.8   Suppression ratio as a function of φ for experimental results from Rescorla (1968). Suppression ratio is response rate in the CS divided by rate in the CS plus rate in its absence ("no suppression" = ratio of .5, which is the value for both noncontingent points in which φ = 0). Increasing suppression is indicated by smaller suppression values (from Gibbon, Berryman & Thompson, 1974, Figure 3).

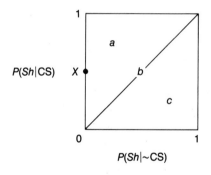

FIGURE 4.9   Stimulus–stimulus (CS–US) contingency space (Sh = shock).

pression and thus good conditioning, these data show a direct relation between the effectiveness of a conditioned stimulus and its correlation with shock.

CONTINGENCY SPACE   Contingency tables form the basis for the general, two-dimensional *contingency space* shown in Figure 4.9. Since the row totals of conditional probabilities in a contingency table always add to 1.0 (i.e., $p(\sim Sh|CS) + p(Sh|CS) = 1.0$), a given contingency space can be represented by just one of the two columns. By convention, the right-hand column is usually chosen, that is, $p(Sh|CS)$ and $p(Sh|\sim CS)$. Thus, each such contingency table defines one point in contingency space. The contingency space is divided into three regions:

1. Above and to the left of the major diagonal is the region of *positive*

contingencies, in which $p(Sh|CS) > p(Sh|\sim CS)$ (shocks are more likely during CS).

2. Below and to the right of the major diagonal is the region of *negative contingencies,* in which $p(Sh|CS) < p(Sh|\sim CS)$ (shocks are less likely during CS).

3. The major diagonal itself defines the absence of contingency between *Sh* and CS, in which $p(Sh|CS) = p(Sh|\sim CS)$ (the uncorrelated, or truly random, condition as defined by Rescorla (1967), in which shocks are equally likely during CS and $\sim$CS).

Positive contingencies generally produce *excitatory conditioning;* that is, the contingent stimulus produces an effect of the same sort as the US (e.g., suppression of food-reinforced responding in the CER experiment). Negative contingencies generally produce *inhibitory conditioning,* that is, effects of a sort opposite to those of the unconditioned stimulus. For example, imagine a CER experiment in which shocks occasionally occur on the baseline (i.e., in the absence of any CS). We can present two kinds of CS: a stimulus in which no shocks occur (a "safety signal," which is an inhibitory CS) and a signal in which the shock rate is higher than the baseline (a "warning signal," which is an excitatory CS). The safety signal will produce an increase in lever-pressing (suppression ratio > 0.5, an inhibitory effect in this context), whereas as the shock-correlated CS will produce suppression relative to the baseline (suppression ratio < 0.5, an excitatory effect in this context).

For both excitatory and inhibitory conditioning, the stimulus, or its absence, predicts something (e.g., shock). If visits to your dentist always elicited warnings (the excitatory CS) of impending pain (the US), the warning would come to elicit fear. Such conditioning is excitatory conditioning, because $p(\text{Pain}|\text{Warning}) > p(\text{Pain}|\sim\text{Warning})$. On the other hand, if you are more likely to suffer on visits where no warning is given than on the occasions in which it is given, then the warning serves as a "safety signal" and comes to inhibit fear. Such conditioning is inhibitory conditioning, because $p(\text{Pain}|\text{Warning}) < p(\text{Pain}|\sim\text{Warning})$. In either case, we can learn about signals for pain. More common perhaps is the dentist whose signal falls on the diagonal line in our contingency space; thus, pain is equally likely whether the dentist signals it or not. It is no wonder that visits to the dentist make us anxious!

Temporal and Trace Stimuli

Up to this point, we have described contingent relations only between stimuli and USs that overlap in time—the delay conditioning procedure. Other arrangements are possible and are shown in Figure 4.2. In temporal conditioning, the US is contingent on time since the previous US. For a contingency to exist, the spacing of US presentations must be fixed. In trace conditioning, the CS occurs several seconds before the US. If the time between the CS and the US becomes quite long, conditioning becomes more difficult to demonstrate. These temporal procedures raise two questions:

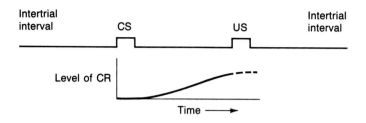

FIGURE 4.10   Typical time relations between conditioned response (CR) and trace-conditioned stimulus (CS) in salivary conditioning.

1. What is the effect of the trace CS on the conditioned response (CR)? Is the CR more or less likely to occur when the CS occurs compared to when the CS is not presented?

2. When does the CR occur? Is it during the CS, immediately after, or after a delay?

The answer to the how-likely-is-the-CR question: "It depends." It depends on the temporal relations among the CS, the US, and the other stimuli in the situation. If the time between the CS and the US is quite short, conditioning may be good, and therefore the CR is quite likely. As the temporal relation is extended, the likelihood of the CR decreases. The timing of the CR also depends on these factors to some extent. The CR almost never occurs during a trace CS; it typically occurs afterward. It is also delayed more or less in proportion to the CS–US interval: The longer the interval, the longer the trace CR is delayed after the CS offset. Figure 4.10 shows the typical time course of a trace-conditioned response.

Let's think through why trace conditioning is so hard to achieve. We begin by looking at the four conditioning sequences diagrammed in Figure 4.11. The sequences are typical Pavlovian-conditioning procedures, consisting of an *intertrial interval,* the period between the end of the US and the onset of the CS (period US–CS), and the *trial period* between the CS and the ensuing US (period CS–US). In the diagram these two periods add to a constant, which is the US–US interval. The intertrial interval and the trial period are formally analogous to the ~CS and CS periods in the CER procedure previously described. Of course, they may not be analogous from the animal's point of view, because they depend on its ability to remember the event that initiates the period. Remember that the CER procedure imposes no such memory requirement, because the stimuli overlap in time. The behavior to be expected from these four procedures depends entirely on how the animal uses the temporal information available to it.

What is the effect of the CS on the probability of a CR in these procedures? When does trace conditioning occur? When does it fail? We consider two possibilities: The animal has perfect memory (i.e., can use either the CS, the US, or both as time markers); the animal's memory is imperfect.

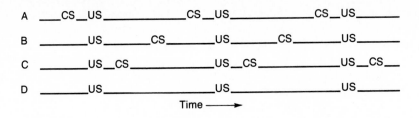

FIGURE 4.11   Three CS placements in trace conditioning (A, B, and C), compared with temporal conditioning (D).

CONDITIONING WITH PERFECT MEMORY   If we don't have to worry about memory constraints, then the effect of the trace CS should simply reflect the time relations in the situation. In every case in Figure 4.11 the CS is always the closest in time to the next US. The CS might be said to predict the US, and trace conditioning should occur. However, since the times between US and US and between CS and US are both fixed, the animal might use either or both as time markers. We know that temporal conditioning yields excellent conditioning (sequence D in Figure 4.11), thus we know that animals can use the information provided by a fixed US–US interval. If it uses the US, then the CS has no special effect, and trace conditioning does not occur. But since the accuracy with which an animal can tell time is roughly proportional to the time interval involved (i.e., it is better at estimating short times than long ones), the animal obviously does better to use the CS, which is the stimulus closest to the next US. Moreover, this advantage is greater the closer in time the CS is to the US: Sequence A should therefore produce the most reliable trace conditioning, B next, and C the worst. If the animal can use either CS or US as a trace stimulus, it should always use the CS.

CONDITIONING WITH IMPERFECT MEMORY   However, if the animal's memory is imperfect, then some events may make better time markers than others. In particular, a highly salient stimulus such as a US may be a much better time marker than a "neutral" CS. In this case, we have two factors that act in opposite directions: The CS is always closer than anything else to the US. Hence, trace conditioning to the CS is favored over trace (temporal) conditioning to the US. But if the US is better remembered (makes a better time marker) than the CS, then other facts being equal, temporal conditioning should be favored over trace conditioning. Trace conditioning should therefore occur only under three conditions:

1.   When the CS–US interval is much shorter than the US–US interval

2.   When the US–US interval is variable, so that post-US time cannot be used to predict US occurrence

3.   When the US is not favored over the CS as a time marker.

Predictions 1 and 2 have generally been supported; the conditions necessary for prediction 3 are rarely encountered. Therefore, USs make better time markers than almost any neutral stimuli.

Obviously, animals behave adaptively in Pavlovian-conditioning experiments, much more so than the earlier notion of automatic conditioning-by-contiguity suggests. For the most part, animals become conditioned to the stimulus that best predicts the US, and apparent failures to do so in trace conditioning seem to reflect special attention to the US, which is undoubtedly adaptive in other contexts. The subtlety of this behavior poses considerable problems for theory. So long as simple pairing seemed to be the critical operation for Pavlovian conditioning, attention could be focused on procedural details (e.g., the relation between conditioned and unconditioned responses, the effects of CS–US delays, and the effects of CS salience) with the assurance that the basic mechanism was known. However, it was not, and we still know little about the computational process that allows animals to identify and react just to those aspects of their environment that predict hedonic events.

OPERANT CONDITIONING

The modern, experimental study of reinforcement is usually dated from the work of Edward L. Thorndike (Box 4.2). During the last years of the nineteenth century, while a graduate student first at Harvard University and then at Columbia, Thorndike studied the behavior of cats and other animals escaping from puzzle boxes (Figure 4.12). The cats could escape from the box by clawing on a wire loop or a bobbin or by making some other response of this sort to unlatch the door. After each successful escape (trial), Thorndike gave the animal a brief rest, then put it in the box once again. This process was repeated until the animal mastered the task. Thorndike measured the time the animal took to escape on successive trials, producing for each a *learning curve* like the ones shown in Figure 4.13.

As the figure illustrates, Thorndike's learning curves can be quite variable, which is due to the fact that they only measure times—not activities. What seems to be happening is that on early trials the cat tries various methods for escaping from the box, such as pawing at the door, scratching the walls of the box, mewing, rubbing against parts of the apparatus, and so on. Most of these methods are ineffective in operating the latch. Because these activities occur in an unpredictable sequence from trial to trial, the effective response occurs at variable times after the beginning of a trial. Trial times improve because the ineffective acts gradually drop out.

The Law of Effect

Thorndike concentrated on trying to find the selection rule that determines how the effective act is favored over ineffective ones. He decided that temporal contiguity between an activity and the hedonic value of the outcome was the critical factor. He stated his conclusion as the law of effect:

B   O   X

4.2

Edward Lee Thorndike (1874–1949)

Edward L. Thorndike was an undergraduate at Wesleyan University, and he there became interested in the work of the great psychologist William James, chiefly through James's classic textbook *Principles of psychology,* a vivid and entertaining account of psychology that remains enjoyable to this day. Because of James, Thorndike went on to graduate work at Harvard University, where he found few facilities for work with animals. James was hospitable, allowing Thorndike to experiment with cats, chickens, and other small creatures in his basement. The *law of effect* emerged from Thorndike's Ph.D. dissertation on cats learning to escape from a puzzle box. It was a breakthrough in two ways: Thorndike suggested a simple mechanism for rewarded learning, and he wrote lengthy works on animal learning *without* mentioning Charles Darwin and evolution (cf. Galef, 1988). The first step was clearly an advance: George J. Romanes and other disciples of Darwin were full of speculations about the functional significance of learning and animal intelligence, but they had little interest in the mechanisms that might underlie either. (Darwin, however, as always was interested in both the functional and proximal causes of behavior). But, Thorndike's step away from evolutionary biology was a mistake that has only recently been redressed by collaborations among psychologists, ethologists, and behavioral ecologists.

Thorndike drifted away from basic research into applied work soon after he left graduate school. He ended a career marked by voluminous publication, mostly about mental testing and learning in human subjects, as a prestigious professor of educational psychology at Columbia Teachers College.

Of several responses made to the same situation, those which are *accompanied or closely followed by satisfaction* to the animal . . . will, other things being equal, be more firmly connected with the situation . . . ; those which are accompanied or closely followed by discomfort . . . will have their connections with the situation weakened. . . . The greater the satisfaction or discomfort, the greater the *strengthening or weakening of the bond* (our italics, Thorndike, 1911, p. 244).

This principle provided a framework for American studies of learning for the next 60 years. The first phrase in italics identified as critical the close temporal relation between reinforcement (or punishment) and subsequent behavior. The term *satisfaction* identified reinforcement and punishment as necessary for learning, and it raised the issue of the definition of what was subsequently to be termed *reinforcement.* The term *bond* led to the view that learning involves the formation of links or associations between specific responses and specific stimuli

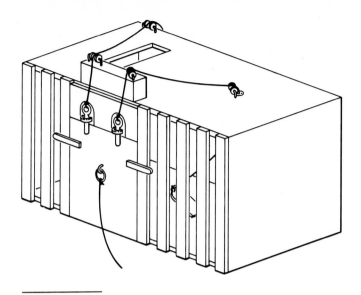

FIGURE 4.12   A typical puzzle box used by Edward Thorndike.

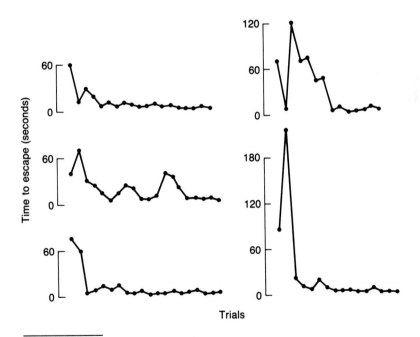

FIGURE 4.13   Time taken to escape from a puzzle box on successive trials by five different cats (from Thorndike, 1898).

(situations). These three ideas have been more or less severely modified by later work. Let's look at each of them.

The law of effect would be of little use without some independent measure of what is meant by "satisfaction." If we want to train an animal according to Thorndike's law, we must know what constitutes satisfaction for it; otherwise the principle is of no help. Thorndike solved the problem by making use of the fact that animals are able to perform more than one activity to obtain something they want—A satisfying state of affairs is anything the animal "does nothing to avoid, often doing such things as to attain and preserve it." This idea is now known as the *transsituationality* of the law of effect: If something such as food serves as a reinforcer for one response, it should also serve for others. Another way to deal with the same problem is to study approach and withdrawal as reference responses. A "satisfier" (positive reinforcer in modern terminology) is something the animal will approach; a "discomforter" (punisher, aversive stimulus, or negative reinforcer) is something it will withdraw from. Reinforcers are thus unconditioned (hedonic) stimuli (USs).

Thorndike's definition of a reinforcer is the aspect of his law that has been least altered by later work. It has been extended somewhat by the notion of a preference structure, but its essential feature—that hedonic quality is revealed by the animal's own behavior—has been retained.

Comparison of Thorndike's law with the discussion of learning in the previous chapter shows that Thorndike made no distinction between local and long-term memory. Learning to escape from a puzzle box is one matter; recalling the effective response after a delay or after being removed from the situation is quite another. For example, a cat may learn today to escape from a puzzle box, just as *Stentor* (Chapter 3) may "learn" to escape from carmine; but, neither may be able to repeat the feat tomorrow. The availability of a rewarding consequence is certainly necessary for such adaptive behavior, but its role in enabling the animal to remember what it learned is not obvious. We certainly cannot assume, as Thorndike did, that reinforcement is necessary for memory (i.e., the formation of Thorndike's "bonds"). (In later chapters, we will see that valued events seem to be better remembered than neutral ones, but that is another matter.)

The third element in Thorndike's law is his assumption that the effective response is directly "strengthened" by its temporal contiguity with reinforcement. It turns out that contiguity is terribly important; but it is not the only aspect that is important. Thorndike's emphasis on the strengthening of single, effective response at the expense of the many ineffective responses has been misleading in some ways. For example, when Michelangelo was asked how he was able to sculpt so beautifully, he is reported to have said: "No, it is really quite easy: I just take away all the marble that is *not* the statue, and leave the rest." Thorndike's law does not emphasize that reinforcers act by a process of selectively eliminating unsuccessful behaviors, although he was certainly aware of that aspect.

Later experiments have shown that response–reinforcer contiguity is not sufficient for a reinforcer to be effective, and it may not always be necessary.

Problems are soon revealed with strengthening-by-contiguity as the *sole* explana-tion for instrumental learning. For example: where does the to-be-strengthened behavior come from? What about learning with long delays between response and reinforcer (we discuss some striking examples later on)? How quickly do reinforcers have their effects? How quickly does behavior weaken when re-inforcement is lacking? There are two ways to deal with the incompleteness of contiguity as an explanation. One is to consider what additional processes may be necessary. The second is to look in more detail at the functional properties of operant behavior: To what procedural properties is it sensitive? In what sense do animals maximize the amount of reinforcement? Functional questions are much easier to explore than ones about additional mechanisms. Moreover, the more we know about the functional properties of operant behavior, the more educated our guesses can be about the underlying processes (mechanisms).

Experimental Methods

All science begins with taxonomy. If we want to understand the properties of reinforcement and punishment, the first step is to gather some examples of how they act and then begin classifying. How are examples to be gathered? You could collect anecdotes: "Little Freddie used to pick his nose, but when I thrashed him soundly for doing it, he soon stopped." Such a method is obviously un-satisfactory: We don't know how soundly Freddie was thrashed, how soon the thrashing followed the offense, or how quickly Freddie desisted. We have no precise measure of the response, the punishment, or the frequency with which one followed the other. We don't know Freddie's past history. Useful data on the effects of reinforcement and punishment cannot be gathered like bugs at a picnic. They require planning, design, and experimentation—but what kinds of experiments?

Experiments on reinforcement are of two general types: experiments in which the animal can improve its situation by moving about and experiments in which movement is irrelevant, but the animal can improve its situation by making a spatially localized response. The first category includes studies in which the animal must find food in a maze or runway or avoid electric shock in a shuttle box (Figure 4.14). Mazes are of two main sorts: the Hampton Court variety, in which there is one goal box and many blind alleys, and the animal's task is to learn the one path to the goal;[1] and the newer, radial maze, in which every goal box contains food, and the animal's task is to visit each goal box without repeti-tion. Early studies of learning all used situations of the kind that requires loco-motion as essential for reinforcement. The second category comprises mainly so-

---

[1]Hampton Court is a magnificent sixteenth-century palace outside London that was built by King Henry VIII's Lord High Chancellor, Cardinal Wolsey, a "man for all seasons" but not averse to the ac-quisition of great wealth. The splendor of Hampton Court, whose gardens contain one of the earliest recreational mazes, is reputed to have contributed to Henry's envy—and Wolsey's fall (after which the palace passed into Henry's possession).

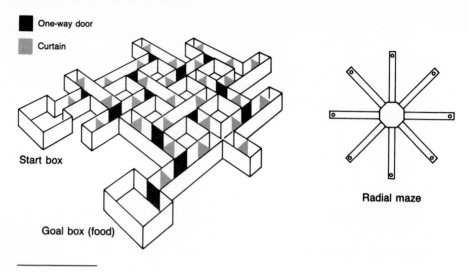

One-way door

Curtain

Start box

Goal box (food)

Radial maze

FIGURE 4.14   Typical mazes used to study spatial learning.

called free-operant or Skinner-box experiments, in which the animal must press a lever or peck a lighted key for reinforcement, which is delivered in a fixed place by an automatic mechanism.

Maze-type experiments are useful if spatial behavior is of special interest, or if you want to make use of animals' natural tendency to approach some objects and withdraw from others. For example, no special training is required for an animal to move from the part of a shuttle box where it has just been shocked to a part where it has never been shocked. Rats can explore the goal boxes of an eight-arm radial maze without having to be led down each arm. Spatial tasks are less useful if you are interested in time relationships, such as between reinforcement and response, between successive responses, or between stimuli and responses.

Skinner-box experiments usually require that the animal first be trained to make the instrumental response (e.g., a lever-press), but they are ideal for the study of time, because the experimenter can measure exactly when a specific response occurs and arrange for reinforcement or punishment to occur in a precise temporal relation to it. The Skinner box also lends itself easily to automation: Given a food-pellet dispenser, a transducer for measuring specified aspects of the animal's behavior, and a computer to record response information, present stimuli, and operate the feeder according to a rule specified by the experimenter, human intervention is required only to place the animal in the apparatus and type in "GO" at the terminal.

Thorndike looked at changes in behavior across learning trials; in contemporary terms, he studied the *acquisition* of behavior. If he had persisted in running his cats even after they had mastered the task, he would have been studying *steady-state* behavior, which are the properties of a developed habit. Steady-state behavior is more interesting if reinforcement does not follow every response (*intermittent reinforcement*). It is easier to study if the animal need not be reintroduced into the apparatus after each occurrence of the reinforcer. Both these requirements favor Skinner's method over Thorndike's, and the Skinner box has become the preferred apparatus for studying steady-state operant behavior (Box 4.3). Let's look at some common arrangements.

Skinner boxes come in many varieties (Figure 4.15). For a rat, the standard version is a small, metal-and-plexiglass box about 20 cm. on a side. On one wall is a lever, often retractable, so it can be presented or withdrawn under remote control. A feeder, for either pellets or liquids, dispenses food at an aperture in the middle of the wall. Stimuli sources, in the form of a loudspeaker or buzzer, and lights above the levers are also on the wall. The version for a pigeon is a little larger, food comes from a grain hopper, and the stimuli and response transducer are combined in the form of a translucent pecking key, on which colored lights or other visual stimuli can be projected. Pecks on the key or presses on the lever go to a controlling apparatus (originally a tangled mess of wires, timers, and electromagnetic relays, today it is usually a computer) that operates the feeder and turns the stimuli on or off according to the experimenter's program.

This basic plan can be modified in several ways. Additional transducers (for the same or different responses) can be added, or the transducers might be modified for different species. For example, Oxford ethologists have studied Great Tits (small European perching birds) in a Skinner box with a pair of perches to record hops and a conveyer belt to present mealworms as reinforcers.

SIMPLE FEEDBACK SYSTEMS   The essential features of all Skinner-box arrangements are represented in Figure 4.16, which has two parts: the programming computer (R), which provides reinforcers (at a rate we usually denote $R(x)$, to indicate that it depends on x) for the animal, and the animal (O), which provides responses (at a rate x) for the computer. The animal and apparatus constitute a *feedback system.* Anything we measure about steady-state operant behavior, such as the animal's rate of lever-pressing or the rate at which it is rewarded with food, generally reflects properties of both halves of the system: the animal *and* the programming computer. This system is analogous to the simple feedback system used to control room temperature; in such a case, R refers to room temperature that feeds back to thermostat O. Figure 4.16 is a model for all interaction between an animal and its environment (compare it with Figure 1.1); the Skinner box simply represents a highly controllable environment.

R and O are *functions:* R defines how the response the animal makes (x) will be translated into the reinforcers it receives ($R[x]$). R is of course known, since the experimenter determines the program for delivering reinforcers. Program R is termed a *feedback function* (or *schedule function*). Other names for R are *contingencies of reinforcement* or *reinforcement schedule.* The *control function* (O) defines how the reinforcers the animal receives will be translated into responses. Another name for O is the *laws,* or *mechanisms,* of behavior. O is generally not known; the aim of the experiment is to help refine our understanding of it.

Figure 4.16 can be converted from an illustration to a formal model once we

B   O   X

4.3

Burrhus Frederick Skinner (1904–)
and Radical Behaviorism

Burrhus F. Skinner is the best known psychologist of modern times, and he may be the most influential since Sigmund Freud. Skinner grew up in a modest rural household in Susquehanna, Pennsylvania. Like Freud, he always had a strong interest in literary matters—at one time he contemplated becoming a professional writer—but he also enjoyed the American gadgeteering tradition whose most famous exemplar is Thomas Edison. As a graduate student at Harvard, Skinner combined these two talents most effectively in his work on the instrumental learning of rats. Skinner's thesis work led to a theoretical system, cleverly adapted from the reflexology he had encountered as a graduate student, which was published as *The behavior of organisms* (1938), his major conceptual work.

His writing style is most engagingly exemplified in a famous article from the late 1950s, commissioned for a philosophically pretentious compendium ponderously entitled *Psychology: A study of a science* (it is almost true to say that any subject that calls itself a science is unlikely yet to be one—"mortuary science" is a good example). The article was called "A case history in scientific method," and it was supposed to display the "axioms and postulates" of Skinner's theoretical system. Skinner, along with several other holdouts, declined to follow these stultifying instructions and instead described in clear and entertaining prose the series of steps he went through in discovering what was later to become known as the "Skinner box" (Skinner has never favored the term, preferring the more modest "experimental chamber").

The Skinner box, and the reinforcement schedules that it made possible, was discovered through a combination of accident and laziness. Skinner was a graduate student experimenting on the motivational properties of eating. His initial experimental arrangement was a runway along which the animals ran to reach food at the other end. Running speed was taken as an indicator of hunger. This apparatus required Skinner to lift the rat after each "run" and replace it in the starting position. Seeking to ease his task, Skinner's first modification was to put in one-way doors and a return path, turning the runway into a basically circular affair, so that the rat could return itself to the start position. He then saw that instead of bringing the rat to the food, it would be even easier to bring the food to the rat—in return for a simple arbitrary response, like pressing a small lever. Response rate, lever-presses per minute, could then be used as a measure of motivation. Thus was the Skinner box born. Accident then entered in when Skinner, working on a weekend in days before the 24-hour grocery store, saw that he was running out of food pellets. So he tried rewarding the animal only intermittently, for every second or third lever-press. To his surprise, the animals not only continued to respond but did so with even greater vigor than before. Skinner soon tried out many other rules for determining when food should be delivered. Because of his later experiences on a research project during World War II, he subsequently switched from rats to pigeons. His results were eventually published in a somewhat disorganized volume, coauthored with Charles Ferster, *Schedules of reinforcement* (1957).

Skinner is notable for his lifelong, single-minded advocacy of *radical behaviorism,* the position that psychology should confine its attentions strictly to physically measurable behavior. He has consistently argued against the elaborate theories that were dominant when he was a young man, but he has never come to terms with contemporary theories (such as mathematical and computer models) that are not vulnerable to criticisms aptly leveled at older views. His view of theory is similar to comedian Mort Sahl's view of the liberal Republican: "There are liberal and conservative Republicans. A conservative Republican believes that nothing should ever be done for the first time. A liberal Republican believes that things should sometimes be done for the first time—but not now!" Skinner has always said that certain kinds of theory (such as those in the physical sciences) are acceptable in principle—but somehow, for Skinner, the time has never seemed right to take any of them seriously.

In place of theory, Skinner, and even more the Skinnerians, has substituted a persuasively argued advocacy of the principle of reinforcement: the notion that all, or almost all, behavior is to be explained as the outcome of the organism's "history of reinforcement." This point of view echoes the first behaviorist John B. Watson's assertion of the power of early training. It has been especially successful in the United States (it has been less well received in Europe) because it appeals to the "can do!" spirit: If everything is the outcome of reinforcement contingencies, anything might be changed in the same way by finding the right schedule of reinforcement. Accordingly, much effort, some of it quite successful, has been devoted to clinical and educational applications of reinforcement. Nevertheless, the practical success of these programs probably owes as much to the evangelical spirit of their practitioners as to the scientific soundness of the principles on which they are (often loosely) based.

It is hard to predict what history will make of Skinner's work. Certainly the experimental methods he pioneered and the varied empirical findings to which they led represent an enduring contribution. But, his scientifically shaky, although rhetorically persuasive, advocacy of the reinforcement principle may well turn out to have had a retarding effect on our understanding of the processes that underlie behavior.

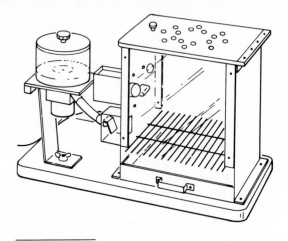

FIGURE 4.15   One example of a Skinner box.

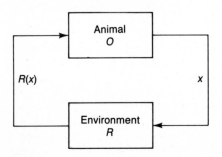

FIGURE 4.16   Feedback relations in an operant-conditioning experiment: $x =$ response measure, $R(x) =$ reinforcement produced by x, $R =$ feedback function (reinforcement schedule), and $O =$ control function (behavior laws).

decide on the proper way to measure x (responding) and $R(x)$ (reinforcer presentation: *reinforcement*, for short). We now look at some commonly used programs (reinforcement schedules) and how the animal adapts to them.

SCHEDULES OF REINFORCEMENT

Response-Based Schedules of Reinforcement

The simplest feedback function (reinforcement schedule) is when every lever-press yields a food pellet. This function is also the simplest *ratio schedule:* *fixed-ratio 1* (FR 1), also known as *continuous reinforcement.* Figure 4.17 shows how one hungry (i.e., food-deprived) rat first learned to respond for food

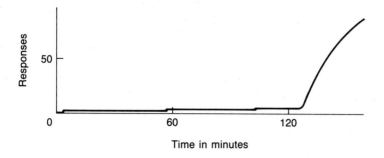

FIGURE 4.17   Cumulative record of the acquisition of lever-pressing by a rat reinforced with food on a fixed-ratio 1 schedule. The first three feedings had little effect; the fourth is followed by a rapid increase in lever-press rate (from Skinner, 1938, Figure 3. Reprinted by permission of Prentice-Hall, Englewood Cliffs, N.J.).

pellets delivered on a fixed-ratio 1. The rat had previously been exposed to the Skinner box and given occasional opportunities to eat from the automatic feeder, but responses to the lever had no effect. Such exposure is known as *magazine training,* and it simply allows the animal to become used to eating from the feeder. On the day shown in the figure, the lever was connected to the feeder for the first time. The rat's lever-presses are shown as a *cumulative record:* Time is on the horizontal axis, and each lever-press increments the record on the vertical axis (each response produces only a small vertical increment, so that cumulative records appear quite smooth so long as response rate changes gradually). The first three lever-presses (at time zero, close to 60 min., and about 95 min.) produce food but not additional lever-pressing. On the fourth response, the animal evidently "catches on," and it presses rapidly thereafter; the rapidity of the presses show in the steepness of the record. The record begins to tip at the extreme right of the figure, as the animal's rate of pressing slows—presumably because it becomes less and less hungry.

FIXED-RATIO SCHEDULES   Skinner discovered that a hungry rat will continue to press a lever even if food doesn't follow every lever press. When the number of presses required for each food delivery is constant, the resulting arrangement is termed a *fixed-ratio schedule.* For example, on a fixed-ratio 4, four lever-presses are required for each food delivery. When the number of responses varies from food delivery to food delivery, it is termed a *variable-ratio schedule.* A variable-ratio 10 would require an average of 10 responses to produce food. The ratio value is the ratio of responses made to food deliveries received over some period of time. When the time interval involved is a single experimental session (typically 30 min. to 3 hours), the relation between responses made and reinforcers received (i.e., between response and reinforcement rates) is known as the *molar feedback function.* For ratio schedules, this function takes a uniquely simple form:

$$R(x) = x/M \qquad\qquad\qquad\qquad\qquad \textbf{(4.1)}$$

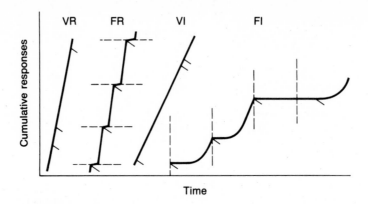

FIGURE 4.18   Stylized cumulative records of steady-state performance on fixed-ratio, variable-ratio, and interval schedules. Rate of responding (response time) is represented by the slope of these curves. Dashed lines show when a reinforcer is available for the next response.

where M is the ratio value, $R(x)$ is the frequency of feeder presentations per unit time (food rate), and x is the rate of lever-pressing. Thus, if an animal responds at 20 responses per minute ($x = 20$) on an FR 4 schedule ($M = 4$), the rate of reinforcement ($R[x]$) would equal 20/4, or 5 per minute. The feedback functions for a ratio and an interval schedule are presented in Figure 4.18. An understanding of feedback functions is useful both in analyzing the behavioral adjustments to different reinforcement schedules and in studying the regulatory properties of motivational systems. These topics are studied in Chapter 11.

VARIABLE-RATIO SCHEDULES   Fixed- and variable-ratio schedules have the same *molar* feedback function, but they differ in their local, *molecular* properties. This difference shows up in cumulative records of steady-state (that is, well-learned) behavior, which are shown in stylized form in Figure 4.19. The diagonal "blips" on the record indicate food (reinforcer) deliveries. The dashed horizontal lines through the fixed-ratio record are separated by a constant vertical distance, indicating that each reinforcer occurs after a fixed number of responses. Records such as this one have been produced by pigeons, rats, people, monkeys, and numerous other animals—performance on simple reinforcement schedules usually differs little across a range of mammal and bird species. Both fixed-ratio and variable-ratio schedules generate high rates of responding, as shown by the steep cumulative records in the figure. But, the local structure of behavior is different: Animals typically pause briefly after each food delivery on fixed-ratio schedules, and they respond steadily on variable-ratio schedules. This brief pause is termed the *preratio pause,* and its duration has been shown to depend on the value of the following fixed ratio: the higher the ratio, the longer the pause. The difference between behavior on fixed-ratio and variable-ratio schedules is a reaction to the fact that food never immediately follows food on fixed-

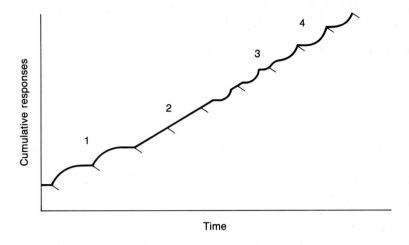

FIGURE 4.19   Schematic cumulative record of the changing patterns of responding as a pigeon adapts to a fixed-interval schedule (adapted from Ferster & Skinner, 1957, p. 117).

ratio schedules, but sometimes does so on variable-ratio schedules. Food predicts a period of no food on fixed-ratio schedules, but on variable-ratio schedules the number of responses required varies randomly from one food presentation to the next. Thus food predicts nothing, and there is no reason for the animal to deviate from a more or less steady rate of responding.

Time-Based Schedules of Reinforcement

The feedback rule for ratio schedules is that reinforcer occurrence depends on a fixed or variable number of responses. In addition, there are two other simple possibilities: dependence on time or joint dependence on time and the number of responses. Pure dependence on time is an open-loop procedure (temporal conditioning), in the sense that reinforcer occurrence is then independent of the animal's behavior, so that the response input (labeled x in Figure 4.16) doesn't exist. Pavlovian-conditioning procedures are all open-loop procedures. Therefore, the only remaining operant possibility is joint control by time and responses. The most frequently used procedures of this type are *fixed-* and *variable-interval schedules.* Both require the passage of a certain amount of time followed by a single response for the delivery of the reinforcer. The sequence is important: A response that occurs too early is ineffective; to be effective, it must occur after the time interval has elapsed.

FIXED-INTERVAL SCHEDULES   Figure 4.17 showed how a rat learns to respond on an FR 1 schedule. How might an animal learn to respond on a fixed-interval (FI) schedule? The process takes much longer than on the simple FR 1, because the animal must learn both the response contingency (the fact that a response is necessary for each crack at the food) and the minimum interval between food deliveries (i.e., the FI value). For a FR 1, it must learn only the response contingency.

Let's begin with a magazine-trained pigeon maintained at about 80 percent of its normal body weight (i.e., very hungry!), with the controlling computer set to limit food deliveries to no more than 60 within a single daily session (so as to prevent the animal from gaining weight from day to day). The pigeon has been trained to peck, and so far it has received food for every effective key-peck. Let's now introduce it to the fixed-interval procedure, with the interval set to 60 sec.

Figure 4.19 shows in stylized form the stages that the pigeon's key-pecking goes through as it converges on the final steady-state performance. These stages are by no means clear cut, nor are the transitions between them perfectly sharp, but we nearly always see the four patterns shown in the figure succeed each other in this order. Each stage takes up many interfood intervals, perhaps 50 or more (i.e., up to several daily experimental sessions). At first (Stage 1), each peck-produced food delivery (indicated by the blips in the cumulative record) produces a burst of further pecks, which slowly dies away; the animal pecks slower and slower when these pecks do not result in food. After 60 sec. have elapsed, and the response rate is now low, an isolated response immediately produces food, which at once elicits a further pecking burst.

In Stage 2, the temporal pattern of pecks between food deliveries changes from negatively accelerated to approximately constant. The pigeon now responds at an approximately steady rate for many intervals. This pattern is succeeded by (Stage 3) breaks in the steady responding that take the form of brief periods of acceleration followed by returns to a lower rate of response. This pattern shifts gradually to the final form, which involves a pause in responding after each food delivery, followed by accelerating responding (Stage 4). Figure 4.19 illustrates the so-called fixed-interval "scallop," a highly reliable pattern that is shown by many mammals and birds.

As the figure shows, the steady-state, fixed-interval pattern is quite similar to the fixed-ratio pattern. The differences are the higher "running" rate (rate after the preratio pause is over) in the fixed-ratio schedule, the slightly shorter pause (in relation to the typical interfood interval), and the "scalloped" pattern of the fixed-interval record. These differences indicate a gradual acceleration in responding, rather than the "break-and-run" pattern characteristic of fixed-ratio patterns.

Each stage of *fixed-interval acquisition* (as this process is termed) makes good adaptive sense. The first stage—a burst of rapid responding after each food delivery—seems to be an innate adaptation to the fact that food often occurs in patches. Finding some food after a lull strongly suggests that there is more where that came from, so that foraging efforts should be stepped up. The spatial equivalent is *area-restricted search:* for example, when a pigeon foraging in nature finds some grain after a period of unsuccessful search, its rate of turning increases (i.e., it continues to look in the same vicinity), and its rate of movement may increase as well. The process is a kinesis, adapted to keep the animal in the "hot" area. An animal on a fixed-interval schedule is restricted to the same "food patch," but it can follow the temporal part of this rule by looking especially hard for more food immediately after it receives some.

The final stage is also adaptive: The animal pauses after receiving food, because it has learned that no more food is likely for a while, and it is free to occupy that time in some other manner. The two intervening stages represent the transition period when the animal is gradually giving up its initial, "default" rule (area-restricted search) in favor of a new rule (the FI scallop) adapted to changed circumstances. Since the animal cannot be certain from day to day that the new pattern of food delivery will persist, it makes sense that it should change only gradually from one pattern of behavior to another.

The pause after food on a fixed-interval schedule is obviously adaptive, but it is nevertheless usually too short: The efficiency of steady-state, fixed-interval performance is surprisingly low. Strictly speaking, only a single response need be made for each food delivery—namely, the first response after 60 sec. Yet, a pigeon might make 30–40 key-pecks in an average interval, only one of which is essential. Part of the explanation for this inefficiency lies in limitations on the animal's ability to estimate the passage of time (the rest of the explanation is described in detail in Chapter 6).

VARIABLE-INTERVAL SCHEDULES The difference between fixed-interval and variable-interval schedules parallels that between fixed-ratio and variable-ratio schedules: On variable-interval schedules, the probability that a response will produce food is constant from moment to moment. The probability of receiving food on fixed-interval schedules increases with time. Furthermore, food delivery in variable-interval schedules has no special predictive significance, as it does with fixed-interval schedules because interfood times are not constant. The animal on a variable-interval schedule learns little about the spacing of food, so it does not engage in other behavior immediately after receiving food. Thus, animals on a VI schedule tend to respond at a more or less steady rate that is a bit slower than the rate at which an animal responds on comparable fixed-interval schedule.

Fixed-interval schedules must be treated differently from variable-interval schedules, because the animal can predict when food will be available on FI schedules almost perfectly; whereas VI schedules are explicitly designed to prevent such predictability by establishing random interreinforcement intervals. For example, for a VI 60 sec schedule, the average time between reinforcements is made up of two time periods: the prescribed minimum interreinforcement interval (the VI value, 60 in this case), which can be written as $1/a$, where a is the maximum possible reinforcement *rate* (1 per minute), and d, which is the delay between the time when reinforcement is available for a response and the time when the next response actually occurs. Thus,

$$D(x) = \frac{1}{R(x)} = \frac{1}{a} + d \qquad\qquad (4.2)$$

where $D(x)$ is the actual mean time between reinforcements and $R(x)$ is the obtained rate of reinforcement. If we specify the temporal pattern of responding, then d can be expressed as a function of x, which is thus the average rate of responding. In the simplest case, if responding is random in time, then

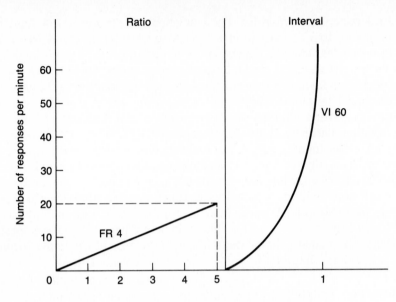

FIGURE 4.20   Ratio- and interval-schedule feedback functions. The solid lines represent the average food and response rates determined by the schedule.

$$d = \frac{1}{x} \tag{4.3}$$

The expected time from reinforcement setup to a response is simply the reciprocal of the average response rate. Combining Equations 4.2 and 4.3 yields the actual feedback function:

$$R(x) = \frac{ax}{a + x} \tag{4.4}$$

which is a negatively accelerated function that moves toward a as $x \to \infty$ and to x as $x \to 0$; that is, it has asymptotes at $R(x) = a$ and $R(x) = x$ (Figure 4.20).

Let's continue with our example and compute one point on the feedback function. Given a VI 60 sec schedule ($a = 1$) and an average response rate of 30 per minute ($x = 30$), we can compute $R(x)$ as follows

$$R(x) = \frac{1(30)}{1 + 30}$$

$$= .97$$

As the response rate increases, $R(x)$ approaches the maximum scheduled reinforcement rate (a), which in our example is 1.

If responding is not random, or if it depends on postreinforcement time (as in fixed-interval schedules), the delay (d) may depend on properties of responding in addition to the average rate. In this case, the properties of the schedule cannot be captured by a simple response rate versus reinforcement rate feedback function; something more complicated is required. This difficulty emphasizes that although the concept of a feedback function is perfectly general, to form one simple enough to be useful may mean drastically simplifying assumptions about behavior. Perhaps surprisingly, the FI feedback function is more difficult to derive than the VI function, because we know that animals can tell time and thus do not respond randomly (which they do, to an approximation, on VI schedules).

The procedures for fixed-ratio, fixed-interval, and variable-interval schedules are summarized in the form of event diagrams in Figure 4.18. These operant procedures can be compared with the open-loop (Pavlovian-conditioning) procedures discussed earlier in the chapter.

Behavioral Equilibrium on Reinforcement Schedules

The four patterns shown in Figure 4.19 are the outcome of a converging process. In the acquisition phase, the animal at first shows more or less an innate pattern of reactions to occasional, unpredictable (from its point of view) food deliveries. As food continues to be produced by this interaction, food deliveries begin to take on a predictable pattern; this pattern, in turn, guides future behavior until the process converges to produce the steady-state pattern of behavior shown in the figure. For example, on fixed-interval schedules, the major regularity, the fixed time between successive food deliveries, depends on the animal's behavior as well as on the schedule. If the pigeon pecked slowly or erratically, so that many food deliveries were obtained well after the time at which the apparatus had "set up" (i.e., well after the dashed vertical lines in Figure 4.19), then the time between food deliveries would not be fixed, although the *minimum* interfood interval might still approximate the fixed-interval value. By varying its behavior early in training, the animal is able to detect invariant properties of its hedonic environment: On fixed-interval schedules, the FI value is detected, and it controls behavior; on fixed-ratio schedules, it is the ratio value; on variable-interval schedules, it is the mean, minimum interfood interval.

These examples illustrate a general characteristic of operant behavior: The stimuli that come to control behavior are often themselves dependent on behavior. This kind of interaction is not restricted to the somewhat artificial conditions of the Skinner box. For example, a young squirrel learns about the tastiness of various nuts by first opening them in an exploratory way and then sampling the contents. This procedure allows the squirrel to learn that some nuts are better than others, so that it will seek out and respond to especially tasty types that it ignored previously. With additional experience, the animal may come to learn that hazelnuts (say) are to be found in the vicinity of hazel trees or under hazel leaves. Thus at each step, the animal's initial explorations reveal correlations—between the appearance of a nut and its taste and between a habitat and the occurrence of desirable nuts—that guide future behavior. The fixed-interval case is simpler only because the situation is artificially constrained. The only relevant explorations on fixed-interval schedules are along the single dimension of time. The animal varies its distribution of responses in time, and the correlation that emerges is the fixed minimum time between food deliveries. The correlation then guides the future distribution of responses, which conforms more and more closely to the periodicity of the schedule, and in turn, sharpens the periodicity of food deliveries. The process finally converges on a stable pattern of behavior, and it defines a state of equilibrium between the animal and the environment.

With only slight exaggeration, we can say that animals' "learning systems" treat reinforcement schedules in the same way that their perceptual systems treat visual inputs. In both cases, through behavioral variation (in response pattern or direction of gaze) the animal is able to detect the invariant properties of the "stimulus" and respond appropriately. The major differences are speed, as the perceptual system acts quickly, and verisimilitude. Given the long evolutionary history of adaptation to the perceptual world and the relative rarity in nature of procedures that resemble standard reinforcement schedules, perception is usually more accurate and adaptive than behavioral adjustment to reinforcement schedules.

The fixed-interval scallop and other properties of such stable performances are aspects of the equilibrium state reached by the feedback system illustrated in Figure 4.16. This equilibrium is dependent both on the fixed-interval feedback function (schedule) and on the mechanisms that underlie the organism's operant behavior. However, the examples given should make it clear that a specific equilibrium need not be unique. The final equilibrium depends on two behavioral aspects: the range of sampling, which is the variability in the animal's initial response to the situation and the number of different responses it tries, and the speed of convergence, which is the rapidity with which the animal detects emergent regularities and is guided by them. Too little sampling or too rapid convergence may mean an equilibrium far from the best one possible. In Chapter 10 we discuss phenomena such as "learned helplessness" and electric-shock-maintained behavior that represent maladaptive equilibria.

Equilibria can be stable, unstable, neutral, or metastable in response to environmental changes. Stability is not an absolute property of a state but a label for the observed effect of a perturbation. A state may be recoverable following a small perturbation but not after a large one. For example, the physics of soap bubbles shows that their form is the one with the lowest free energy for the number of surfaces: Thus, a spherical bubble returns to its original, efficient shape after a slight deformation. The spherical shape is a stable equilibrium under moderate perturbations. A more drastic deformation will puncture the surface, at which time the bubble collapses to a drop, and the original state cannot be recovered. The bubble's spherical shape is stable under slight deformation, but it is metastable in response to a severe deformation.

The four types of equilibria can be illustrated by a visual metaphor: Imagine that the state of our hypothetical system is represented by the position of a ball in a terrain of hills, valleys, and plains. On the plain, the ball stays where it is placed (neutral equilibrium). In a valley, if the ball isn't moved too far, it returns to the valley floor (stable equilibrium). On a hill, even a small displacement lets the ball run down to the valley (unstable equilibrium). If the ball starts in a valley, it returns to the valley only if it isn't moved too far up the hill; too large a displacement, and it rolls into the next valley (metastable equilibrium).

The valley metaphor is also realistic in one other way—it implies oscillatory behavior as the ball rolls from one valley wall to another after a perturbation. This kind of oscillation is common in many natural systems. For example, consider the swings in population of both predator and prey or the oscillation in body weight of most animals. In other words, some systems may never settle down to a steady constant pattern. They may show fixed oscillations (like a frictionless pendulum), more complex oscillations, or even chaos—behavior that appears utterly random, even though it may be the outcome of a perfectly deterministic process.

Simple reinforcement schedules generally yield stable equilibria: A given schedule usually yields the same pattern of behavior, and this pattern can be recovered after some intervening procedure. Exceptions are of two kinds. Occasionally a pattern is unstable in the sense that it persists for a brief period (which may be several days or even weeks), but then without any change in the schedule, it alters in an irreversible manner. For example, occasionally an animal will show instead of the typical scallop pattern a more or less steady rate of responding on a fixed-interval schedule. Indeed, all animals pass through such a period. However, once this pattern changes to the scalloped one, the original pattern never reappears. It therefore represents an unstable equilibrium.

A more interesting exception is metastability. In this case, the pattern of behavior under a given schedule remains stable, but it is not recoverable when the schedule is reimposed after an intervening treatment. This effect is quite common. So-called *spaced responding* provides an example. Hungry pigeons can be trained to space their responses in time by delivering food only if a keypeck is separated from the preceding one by at least t seconds, where t is approximately 10–20 sec. They adapt to this procedure with difficulty, because the better they adapt, the more frequently they receive food; the more frequently they receive food, the more inclined they are to peck. Since more frequent pecking reduces the rate of access to food, the stage is set for a slow and oscillatory process of adaptation. Pigeons do eventually settle down, but at first their performance is far from optimal. For example, an animal initially exposed to a 10-sec timing requirement may after several weeks still space most of its pecks less than 5 sec apart, and the mode of the interpeck interval distribution may be at only one or two seconds. However, if the spacing requirement is changed, on returning to the original requirement, the pigeon will perform much better than before: The average spacing between pecks will be greater, and the modal peck will be closer to the timing requirement. As the animal is exposed to different timing requirements, the performance at each requirement becomes better, until the mean and modal interpeck time periods come to approximate the spacing requirement. This pattern represents a stable equilibrium. Mean and modal interpeck time periods that are shorter than the timing requirement are metastable equilibria.

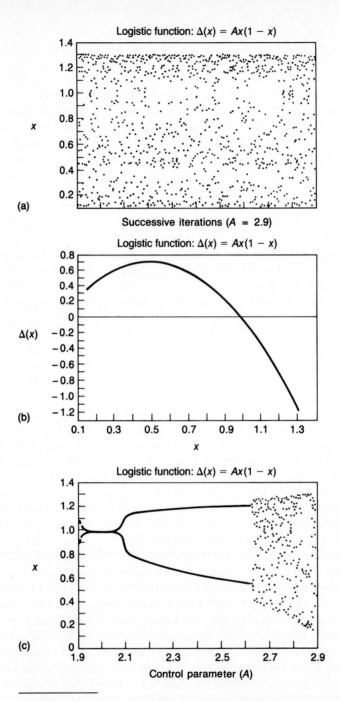

FIGURE 4.21 Behavior of the logistic difference equation: $\Delta(x) = Ax(1 - x)$, where $\Delta(x)$ is the change in x from one iteration to the next. For example, if we begin with $x = .1$ and $A = 1$, then $\Delta(x) = .09$, so that successive x values are 0.1, 0.19, 0.34, 0.57, 0.81, and so on. For many values of A, $\Delta(x) = 0$ when $x = 1$ (a stable equilibrium), but when A is greater than about 2.9, the equation is highly unstable, and successive x values appear almost random.

Perhaps surprisingly, almost all the steady-state, reinforcement-schedule performances that have been studied are stable or metastable. There are no reliable examples of even oscillatory behavior. Nevertheless, the microstructure of operant performances (e.g., the values of successive interresponse times on VI schedules) often appears highly variable and close to random. It is intriguing to speculate that perhaps some of the apparent randomness in measures of operant behavior is not really random at all—that perhaps we are looking at chaotic behavior of a fully deterministic system. Figure 4.21 suggests that this speculation may not be far-fetched: Figure 4.21a shows apparently random data, a set of highly variable points varying as a function of time. Figure 4.21b shows the effect of plotting each data point $(x[N])$ against the difference between that point and the next point in the sequence: That is, $x(N + 1) - x(N)$, which yields a completely regular parabola. Figure 4.21c shows that *chaotic* behavior is only one pattern derivable from the simple, nonlinear, logistic difference equation shown $\Delta(x) = Ax(1 - x)$; for other values of the control parameter (A), the function shows orderly, stable behavior (see Crutchfield, Farmer, Packard, & Shaw, 1986; and Gleick, 1987, for entertaining accounts of recent research on chaos).

Response Contingency or Temporal Contiguity?

Both Pavlov and Thorndike thought that temporal contiguity was the only, or at least the major, factor behind the changes in behavior produced by hedonic events (i.e., learning). Later experiments have shown that temporal contiguity is not sufficient to account for learning. As we discussed earlier in this chapter, animals are able to detect correlations between CS and US in Pavlovian-conditioning situations. As you might expect, the same is true of operant conditioning, although the theoretical analysis is a bit more complicated.

POSITIVE RESPONSE CONTINGENCIES   The problem for an animal in a Pavlovian-conditioning experiment is to detect which stimuli predict the US and how well they predict it. The problem in an operant-conditioning experiment is similar, namely, to discover what aspects of the animal's own behavior (i.e., what responses) predict the US (reinforcer) and how well they predict it. The only difference between the problems of stimulus and response selection is that the animal can control its own behavior in the operant-conditioning case, whereas it cannot control the CS in a Pavlovian-conditioning experiment. Hence, an animal in an operant-conditioning experiment need not take at face value a given correlation between its behavior and reinforcer occurrence: It can increase or decrease its response rate or vary its response in other ways and see if the correlation is maintained. This difference means that in an operant-conditioning experiment the animal can go beyond correlation to arrive at the cause(s) of the reinforcer. Because the animal cannot control the stimulus–stimulus relations in a Pavlovian experiment, it is limited to detecting correlations between the CS and the US; it can never conclude that the CS causes the US.

Let's look at contingency in operant-conditioning experiments in the same way we did earlier for Pavlovian-conditioning (CER) experiments. Figure 4.2 shows two event records for responding on a fixed-interval schedule: The animal's

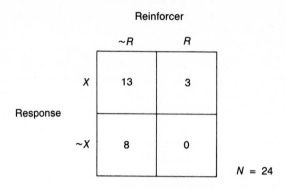

FIGURE 4.22   Response-contingent reinforcement.

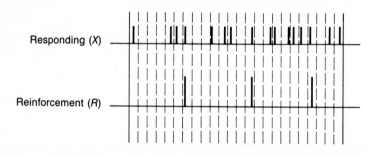

FIGURE 4.23   Analysis of response-reinforcement contingency by time bins.

responses are on the top, and the reinforcers delivered on the fixed-interval schedule are on the bottom. The vertical dashed lines represent time bins for isolating instances where responses and reinforcers occurred simultaneously.

To find out if the response predicts the reinforcer, we can ask: How many times is a reinforcer accompanied by a response (i.e., both in the same instant)? How many times does it occur without a response? How many times does a response occur unaccompanied by a reinforcer? How many times does neither response nor reinforcer occur?

The contingency table in Figure 4.22 shows the answers for the sample of responses and reinforcements shown in Figure 4.23. The table in Figure 4.24 shows the same data in conditional-probability form: The entries are the same entries in Figure 4.22 divided by the row totals (i.e., $13/16 = .81$ for $p[\sim R|x]$). They show the conditional probabilities that R or $\sim R$ will occur, given x or $\sim x$. An obvious difference between the contingency tables for response and stimulus selection (i.e., between operant and Pavlovian conditioning) is that the response table is partially under the animal's control. For example, if the animal responds more slowly on the FI schedule in Figure 4.23, the entries in the upper left cell (unsuccessful responses) will decrease much more rapidly than entries in the

	~R	R
X	.81	.19
~X	1.0	0

FIGURE 4.24   Response-contingent reinforcement in conditional-probability form.

upper right cell (reinforced responses). That is, responding predicts reinforcement much better—the contingency between the two improves—as the response rate decreases, which follows from the properties of a FI schedule (the more slowly the animal responds, the more likely that each response will produce a reinforcer). With further decreases in the response rate, the entries in the upper right cell will also begin to decrease. As the response rate decreases to zero, entries in all but the lower left cell vanish. The lower right cell in Figure 4.22 is always zero for the standard reinforcement schedules: The animal doesn't receive the reinforcer unless it responds at least once. The natural variability in the response rate means that this argument is not just academic: The animal has the relevant information available to it. It shows by its behavior that it is indeed sensitive to these relations: For example, rats press a lever for food delivered on a VI schedule more slowly if occasional "free" food deliveries are given, because the free foods increase the entries in the off-diagonal ($P[F|$no response]) cell.

NEGATIVE RESPONSE CONTINGENCIES   Up to this point, we have restricted our discussion to positive contingencies, that is, situations in which the reinforcement rate increases with increases in the response rate. Negative contingencies are also possible, and they are most common on escape, avoidance, and omission schedules. On these schedules, the reinforcement rate decreases as the response rate increases. For example, animals learn quickly how to avoid electric shock or to escape from noxious stimulation. For both the escape and avoidance procedures, the reinforcer is something to avoid or escape from; thus it is termed a *negative reinforcer*. On omission schedules, animals are reinforced for withholding responses. In general, reinforcement affects behavior in a consistent way. Animals cease to respond if responding produces shock (i.e., an aversive stimulus, which is the procedure of punishment) or if responding prevents food (the omission procedure). However, there are some exceptions: It is possible to have too much of a good thing, and some things are reinforcing only in certain quantities (which is even true of food, although not, perhaps, of money or other human goodies). Even if the reinforcer maintains its value, paradoxical effects can be produced under special conditions. For example, animals can respond in such a way as to produce electric shock, and hungry pigeons can be induced to peck even if pecking prevents food delivery. Such exceptions are of interest for the light they shed on the mechanisms of operant behavior, and they are discussed in more detail in later chapters.

SUMMARY

The effects of reinforcement on behavior are obvious. Unaided by experimental psychologists, humanity managed long ago to discover that children and animals desist from punished behavior and persist in rewarded behavior. Science has added to this foundation in at least three ways:

1. It defines precisely reinforcement and punishment. This work has led to the present concept of a reinforcement contingency. We have shown that animals are sensitive to changes in both stimulus–reinforcer and response–reinforcer contingencies.

2. It emphasizes the importance of time delays between either stimuli or responses and reinforcement.

3. It designs simple situations that allow us to explore the limits of animals' abilities to detect reinforcement contingencies.

In this chapter we presented a brief history of operant and Pavlovian conditioning. In their early stages, temporal contiguity was emphasized as the mechanism of association. Later work has shown this statement to be incorrect, or at least incomplete. Animals are sensitive to the degree to which stimuli (as with Pavlovian conditioning) or responses (as with operant conditioning) predict hedonic events. The main difference between operant and Pavlovian conditioning is that animals can have an effect on the contingency in operant situations, whereas behavior has little relation to contingencies in Pavlovian conditioning. Animals in operant-conditioning experiments are able to go beyond correlation to the detection of causation. We have only begun to understand the intricate mechanisms that allow mammals and birds to detect subtle correlations among external stimuli (including time), their own behavior, and events of value.

This chapter also introduced the concept of feedback functions for some simple reinforcement schedules. An understanding of feedback functions is helpful in analyzing the behavioral adjustments to reinforcement schedules and in studying the mechanisms of motivational systems. These subjects are taken up again in Chapter 11.

5

Learning and Inference

Most animals are small and don't have long life-spans—flies, fleas, bugs, nematodes, and similar modest creatures comprise most of Earth's fauna. A small, short-lived animal has little reason to evolve much learning ability: Because it is small, it can have little of the complex neural apparatus needed; because it is short-lived, it has little time to exploit what it learns. Life is a trade-off between spending time and energy learning and exploiting knowledge already known. The longer an animal's lifespan and the more varied its niche, the more worthwhile it is to spend time learning.

It is no surprise that learning plays a rather small part in the lives of most animals. Therefore, learning is not necessarily the key to the study of animal behavior (as it was once thought to be). Nevertheless, learning is interesting for other reasons: It is involved in most "intelligent" behavior, and it is central to human behavior.

THE ASSESSMENT OF LEARNING

Learning and *memory*—without which there can be no learning—are terms derived from common speech. Because they are familiar, we think we understand them. Yet attributing an observed change in behavior to "learning" must be done with caution, because learning cannot be directly observed: It is an inference from what we know of an organism's behavior and past history. Learning is a change in an animal's *potential.* We say that an animal has learned something when it behaves differently now because of some earlier experience, but no number of failures to find a difference in behavior are sufficient to assert that *no* learning has occurred, and success in finding a difference is no guarantee that learning is the cause. Moreover, the precise definition of exactly *what* is different when we talk about "behaving differently" is far from obvious. We expand on these topics shortly.

Learning and Performance

All (associative) learning is situation specific: The animal behaves differently in some situations but not in others. Hence, a conclusion about whether or not an animal has learned is true only for those situations we have actually studied. That is, we cannot know whether Jack has learned to ride a bicycle unless we give him a bicycle and provide some motivation for him to ride it. Any number of failures to find evidence for learning can be invalidated by a change observed in some new situation not previously tried. For example, a student may fail to answer a question about a specific topic on the final examination, but he or she might have answered correctly had the question been phrased a little differently. In such a situation, the instructor's inference that the student had learned nothing based on his or her answer to the first question would have been premature. Unfortunately, we cannot test this idea by asking the same student both questions, because the first question may so confuse the student that he or she forgets what he or she knew and fails the second question—although he or she might have succeeded had it been given first. In addition, different students learn differently, thus giving the second question to another student tells us nothing about the first student. In short, negative evidence—evidence for no learning— is never conclusive.

Psychologist Tony Dickinson (1980) has coined the term *behavioral silence* to refer to learning that does not appear in most learning tests. (Of course, it must appear under *some* conditions, or else we have no basis for asserting its existence.) In a moment we discuss several examples of behavioral silence, some involving quite primitive creatures. The concept is related to that of *unobservability* (Box 5.1), which shows that there may be effects of experience that are undetectable *even in principle.*

In practice, we can never accomplish every task that is logically required to demonstrate learning, because what must be compared is not two different individuals but the *same* individual (physically the same and with the same history) with and without a specific experience. Even if we could find two identical animals (e.g., clones), there is no way we can be sure that they have exactly the same set of past experiences. Consequently, any difference between the two animals, given that animal A has a specific learning experience and animal B does not, cannot *conclusively* be attributed to the experience. The difference might

5.1

Unobservability

The behavior of a system or an organism is defined by only two aspects: the stimuli to which it is sensitive and the responses it makes. A stimulus can have only two effects: to produce a response (the familiar effect) and to change the future behavior of the system. This second effect of a stimulus on behavior potential is usually referred to as a change of *internal state*. An event that produces neither a response nor a change in future behavior is not a stimulus for that system. Given these definitions, it is relatively easy to show that simple systems exist whose properties we cannot even in principle understand fully. For example, under some conditions, we can never discover the initial state of a system.

This limitation on our understanding of systems and organisms holds because the tests themselves can eliminate the evidence they are intended to elicit. Stated formally, E. F. Moore's *uncertainty-principle theorem* is that "there exists a [finite-state] machine such that any pair of its states are distinguishable, but there is no simple experiment which can determine what state the machine was in at the beginning of the experiment" (1956, p. 138). This definition sounds formidable, but we can give an easy example. Imagine a simple black box (Figure B5.1) that has two inputs (stimuli, which are buttons 1 and 2) and three outputs (responses, which are red, green, and yellow lights). The relationships among these stimuli and responses are determined by three

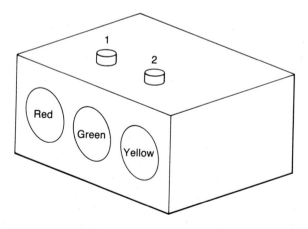

FIGURE B5.1   A black box with two inputs (stimuli) and three outputs (responses).

continued

BOX 5.1 *(continued)*

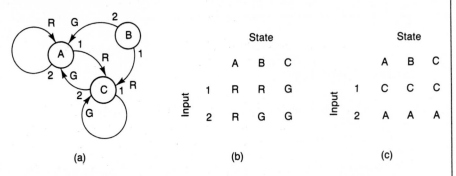

		State		
		A	B	C
Input	1	R	R	G
	2	R	G	G

(b)

		State		
		A	B	C
Input	1	C	C	C
	2	A	A	A

(c)

(a)

FIGURE B5.2   **(a)** State diagram for a simple finite-state system with three states (A, B, C), two inputs (1 and 2), and two outputs (R and G). Arrows show state transitions in response to the stimulus at the beginning of the arrow, with the response shown at arrow end. **(b)** Response table for the process (e.g., in state A, input 1 causes output R). **(c)** State-transition table for the process (e.g., in state A, input 1 causes a transition to state C).

possible states of the box (A, B, and C). The state determines which input produces which output and which change of state.

These relations are summarised by the diagram in Figure B5.2. In Figure B5.2a, the three circles show the A, B, and C states of the box. The arrows coming out of the circles show the effects of the stimuli buttons 1 and 2. At the ends of the arrows are the letters G (green), R (red), or Y (yellow), indicating which light comes on when the corresponding button is pushed. Notice that any pair of states can be distinguished. For example, states A and B are distinguished by the fact that button 2 yields red when the box is in state A and green when it is in state B. Similarly, states B and C and A and C give different responses to stimulus 1.

Looking at Figure B5.2a (and remembering that the observer sees only the lights and buttons not the internal states), we can see that the observer can be certain about the initial state of the box only under certain conditions. For example, from Figure B5.2b you can see that if pushing button 1 produces a green light, then the observer can be sure the box is in state C; if pushing button 2 lights the red light, the observer can be sure the box is in state A. But, both the other possibilities—1 → R or 2 → G—are ambiguous. In the first case (1 → R), the box can be in states A or B; but after the input (Figure 5B.2c), the box is in state C, so that information about the initial state is lost. The same is true for case 2 → G, in which the box can be in states B or C; in either case, it moves into state A after the stimulus (Figure B5.2c), thus initial-state information is lost.

Everyday experience shows that this phenomenon is relevant to psychology. For example, asking someone to recall an event may actually cause him or her to forget it, although some less direct test might have shown that he or she had in some sense remembered it. Many people have had the experi-

continued

BOX 5.1 (*continued*)

ence of being asked to recall verbally a familiar telephone number and being unable to do so; yet they could have dialed the number without difficulty. Sometimes the ability to dial correctly is retained even after failure of verbal recall; but more commonly, failure to recall also abolishes (often only temporarily) the ability to dial correctly.

In addition to this logical difficulty, problems are also posed by unavoidable limits on the total amount of data that can be gathered in any behavioral experiment. Many sequential processes can be identified only by analyzing data samples that are much larger than those typically available. Again, we conclude that there is no experimental method that guarantees an answer to the question: What kind of a system is this one? Guesswork and ingenuity play a much larger role in the understanding of behavioral mechanisms than is generally realized.

conceivably reflect some other variation in their individual histories. Of course, these logical difficulties don't mean that we can never discover anything about learning, although they do mean that there is no method that guarantees an answer. In any case, we must always proceed in the usual scientific manner: by "guess and test," by making inferences about what is probably going on in one situation, and then retesting in a new situation.

A Definition of Learning

In defining a change as due to "learning," some kinds of experience are usually excluded. A change in behavior potential is necessary but not sufficient. For example, a change brought about by physical injury or restraint or by fatigue or illness doesn't count—a man who has lost an arm behaves differently than before, but few of the changes may be due to learning. Short-term changes such as those termed habituation, adaptation, or sensitization (cf. Chapter 3) are also excluded—the change must be relatively permanent. *Forgetting* holds an ambiguous status: The change is usually permanent and does not fall into any of the forbidden categories, yet it is paradoxical to call forgetting an example of learning. Evidently, not every quasi-permanent change qualifies as learning. Learning is a category partly defined by exclusion.

There is probably no point in attempting a definition for learning that covers all the bases. What we need is some understanding of the variety of ways in which an animal's environment can produce long-lasting changes in its behavior. If we can understand how these effects come about, and especially, if we can find the general principles that underlie them, then learning phenomena can be explained. An adequate theory of learning must be just one aspect of an adequate theory of behavior in general.

The first step in understanding how the environment produces persistent changes in behavior is obviously to classify, but to classify *what?* Not types of change, per se—we would not expect the behavior affected (e.g., pecking, lever-pressing, singing) to be especially revealing. Rather, it is the way in which the animal's past experience guides its future behavior that is important. Thus, we first must classify animal histories. If we can also come up with a description of the changes produced (the problem of "what is learned?"), we will have a solid basis from which to make generalizations.

For convenience, we distinguish two main types of learning: *template learning* and *reinforced learning.* The first type tells us much about the kinds of change produced by learning; the second tells us much about how these changes occur. These two aspects of learning are not independent. Imprinting and the song learning of birds are discussed first in the template-learning section. Pavlovian conditioning and related forms of learning are discussed in the reinforced-learning section.

TEMPLATE LEARNING: IMPRINTING

The young of many precocial birds (i.e., able to walk and see immediately after hatching), such as ducks and chickens learn about their parents during their first day or so of life. This type of learning, known as *imprinting,* occurs spontaneously, without any explicit "training" by the parents. It has been a well-known phenomenon for many years, being first studied scientifically by the British naturalist Douglas Spalding in the 1870s. Spalding died prematurely, and the topic was taken up more extensively by the German ethologist Oskar Heinroth and his more famous student, Konrad Lorenz. The function of *filial imprinting,* that is, imprinting on the mother, is to bring the young under the mother's control, so that they will attend to her warnings of danger and follow her when necessary. In some species, filial imprinting also leads to *sexual imprinting,* which enables sexually mature animals to seek out for mating individuals of the correct sex and species.

Imprinting is not restricted either to birds or to visual stimuli. Goats and shrews imprint to olfactory signals; ducklings in the egg form preferences for the frequency of the maternal call; Pacific salmon imprint to the odor of the stream where they were hatched; touch, temperature, and texture are important in the attachment of a young monkey to its mother. But, we know most about the imprinting of precocial birds.

Chicks imprint in two steps. First, the chick tends to follow moving objects. If the only object it sees is a box with flashing lights, it will follow it. After a little experience of this sort (a few minutes can be sufficient), the young bird learns enough about the characteristics of the followed object to pick it out from others and to follow it on future occasions. With further experience, the young animal begins to treat the imprinted object as a member of its own species. In a few species, filial imprinting may persist into later life and lead to abnormal mate choice. In the laboratory, the imprinting of chicks can appear strikingly unintelligent, in the sense that the young bird can become imprinted to a variety of strange objects (e.g., a human experimenter, a hand, a box with flashing lights). Described in this fashion, the imprinting process seems quite mechanical and mindless.

Yet on closer examination, the mechanisms that underlie imprinting are more selective than may at first appear. For example, if provided with a choice of moving objects during the first posthatch day, the young bird is much more likely to imprint on the object that resembles its natural parent. Even after imprinting on some artificial object, the initial imprinting may wear off if the animal is exposed to the natural object later. Such a change is more likely if the original imprinting object is quite unnatural.

Imprinting also involves more than just a stimulus–response connection. For example, in one experiment mallard ducklings were raised by the adults of another species. When the mallards were later released as adults onto a lake that contained dozens of species of geese and ducks, the males attempted to mate almost exclusively with females of the species that raised them. Clearly the birds learned more than just to remain near their foster parents; they learned about mate selection as well.

The Critical Period

There seem to be two essentials for imprinting to occur. First, the bird must be exposed to an object of a certain type. Typically, this object is the bird's parent, but experiments have shown that nearly any moving or flickering object will do. Second, the bird must be exposed to this object during its first one or two posthatch days. This early time period is referred to as a *critical period*. The critical period was once thought to be fixed, but later work has shown it to be flexible. The period can be extended by limiting imprinting experience: That is, an unstimulated bird is open to imprinting experience for longer than one that has already imprinted. In addition, the length of the critical period depends on the quality of the imprinting stimulus: A good stimulus will continue to be effective at later ages than a poor stimulus.

There has been much argument about the importance of this critical period for several reasons. Imprinting when it occurs is hard to reverse, so that the animal's *first* experience with an imprintable object blocks any effect of later objects. And after the early period, young birds become *neophobic* (afraid of new things), which interferes with potential imprinting. The growth of neophobia leaves a brief time "window" when the young bird can imprint to a novel, moving object; afterward, such objects elicit only fear. Of course, neophobia implies prior learning, since the unfamiliar is defined only in contrast to the familiar, and familiarity is learned. Until it has learned about the familiar, the animal cannot even recognize what is unfamiliar, much less be afraid of it. The critical feature of imprinting may therefore be its irreversibility, plus a built-in tendency for young birds to fear the unfamiliar.

Maternal Calling

In nature, the female duck interacts with her chicks in ways that are not possible for an artificial imprinted object. *Maternal calling* is an important part of these interactions. It is likely that this calling serves to confirm imprinting in nature and make it less easily altered than some imprinting in the laboratory.

Classification of Filial and Sexual Behavior

The essential change produced by imprinting seems to be one of classification. Young precocial birds seem to be innately equipped with an empty mental "slot" labeled "parent." The imprinting experience provides them with a set of natural objects to put into that slot. The animals have a ready-made repertoire of filial and, later, sexual behavior. Imprinting simply allows them to direct their behavior toward the appropriate objects.

The Role of Reinforcement in Template Learning

Experiments have also shown that the imprinting object can function as a reinforcer, in the sense that the young animal learns to make some more or less arbitrary response to bring the imprinting object closer. Chicks are clearly "comforted," in some sense, by proximity to the imprinted object: They cease making "distress calls" and begin to make "comfort calls," they move around more, and so on. Yet the concept of reinforcement misses what is most interesting about the chick's learning: the critical period, the relative irreversibility of the process, and its relation to evolutionary and ontogenetic factors. It is not surprising that chicks are "reinforced" by proximity to their mother. What is truly interesting is that precocial (but not altricial, i.e., slow-maturing, born helpless) animals show the imprinting process and that it is somewhat selective and limited to a restricted time period.

The young animals act as if they have a "need" to fill an empty slot labeled "mother." The slot may initially be empty, but it is not shapeless. Clearly some objects fit it better than others, since the young birds imprint much more effectively to some objects than to others. This basis places imprinting under the category of *template learning,* a term that was originally coined to describe song learning in birds.

TEMPLATE LEARNING: SONG LEARNING IN BIRDS

Songbirds differ in the extent to which song development depends on experience. Song sparrows (*Melospiza melodia*), with one of the most intricate and beautiful songs, need relatively little experience. In one experiment, song sparrows were foster-reared by canaries in a soundproof room. The songs of the adults were indistinguishable from the songs of wild-reared birds. That is, song development was not impaired by foster rearing, and the sparrows showed no

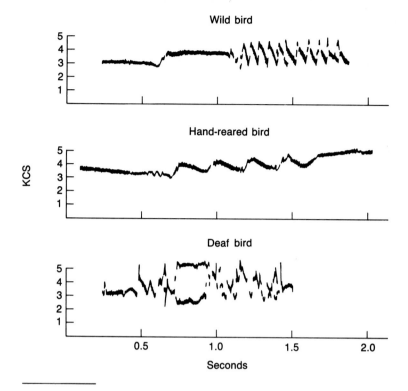

FIGURE 5.1   Sonograms of songs of three white-crowned sparrows raised in different auditory environments: a wild bird, a hand-reared individual, and a bird deafened before the onset of singing. The sonograms show frequency as a function of time. Since most songbird song is close to being a pure tone (so-called whistle song), the sonograms mostly show just a single line of varying frequency (from Konishi & Nottebohm, 1969).

tendency to imitate the canary song. Other experiments have shown a small effect of depriving song sparrows of early experience, but clearly much of the information for the song sparrow song is innate. At the other extreme, white-crowned sparrows (*Zonotrichia leucophrys*) develop severely abnormal songs if deprived of the opportunity to hear their species' song during the first six months of life. The upper sonogram in Figure 5.1 shows two seconds of the song of a wild, white-crowned sparrow; the middle sonogram shows the much simpler song of a deprived bird; the bottom sonogram shows the song of a deaf bird for comparison purposes.

The Oregon junco (*Junco oreganus*) is an intermediate case. After early isolation, adults produce wild-type songs but with a simpler syllabic structure. But juncos raised in isolation in groups, or in general laboratory rooms in which they could hear other species, produce more complex syllables and larger song repertoires—including sound patterns present neither in wild junco populations nor copied from other species. The song pattern of isolated juncos is important because it shows that the inability to develop a normal song in isolation does not preclude the ability to copy and to improvise new sounds.

Song learning in birds is not always easily disrupted, although it is in the case of the white-crowned sparrow. In addition, some song learning may be short-lived. For example, mocking birds, starlings, mynah birds, and many parrot species imitate other sounds soon after hearing them, but such learning is usually reversible. Starlings, for instance, seem to have a new repertoire every season, and most other imitative birds continue to add and delete items from their repertoire throughout life.

The Phases of Song Learning

The song learning of male white-crowned sparrows and many other songbirds proceeds in two phases. For white-crowns, the first phase occurs during a critical period from 10 to 50 days after hatching, when the immature males must have the opportunity to hear adult male song. Birds kept in isolation or deafened during this critical period never sing normally. But, if the animals are prevented from hearing song either before or after this period, the later development of adult song is unimpaired. The second phase begins at about eight months. At this age, the birds become sexually mature and begin to sing. The onset of singing is not immediate; it is preceded by a period of *subsong,* a twittering unorganized pattern quite different from adult song. The adult song emerges gradually from the subsong over a period of several weeks.

FORMATION OF A TEMPLATE   Experiments have shown that the first of these phases is essential for the bird to store a model (template) of the adult song. As in imprinting, the animal is selective in what it stores. For example, white-crowned sparrows exposed during the critical period only to songs of the song sparrow incorporate none of the normal adult song into their model; their song development is just as impaired as if the birds had been reared in complete acoustic isolation. On the other hand, in the wild, the birds' early receptivity permits them to learn the local "dialect" of white-crown song. In fact, the dialect may be the evolutionary function of song learning in this species. Figure 5.2 shows sonograms of white-crowned sparrow dialect variations in the San Francisco Bay area. Although the dialects are different from one another, there is obviously a family resemblance. Evidently the birds' mechanism for template formation restricts the class of possible templates. It is as if the bird were a musician programmed to learn a single piece of baroque music. Such an individual would be immune to the charms of Johannes Brahms or the Beatles, but he or she would instantly learn anything by Johann S. Bach or Antonio Vivaldi.

PRACTICE AND AUDITORY FEEDBACK   Even after the template has formed, song learning is not complete. The period of *practice,* when bird sings subsong and incomplete versions of adult song, is also essential. The final song is evidently built up by a circular process in which the bird sings, hears the results of its own singing, and slowly modifies what it sings until its production matches the stored template.

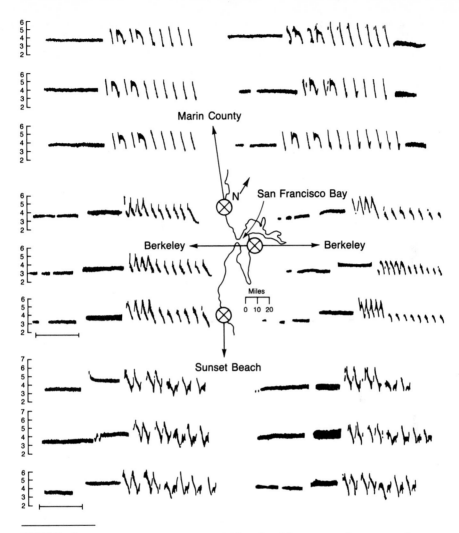

FIGURE 5.2 Sonograms of the songs of 18 male white-crowned sparrows from three different localities within the San Francisco Bay area. Songs from a given area are similar to each other, and they are different from the songs of other areas (after Marler & Tamura, 1964).

This loop can be interrupted in two places: by disrupting the motor apparatus to prevent practice and by deafening the bird to prevent it from hearing its own production. Experimentally deafened birds show normal subsong, but it never evolves into normal adult song. An example of the grossly abnormal song of an early-deafened bird is shown in the bottom panel of Figure 5.1. Moreover, the deafened bird's song is not owing to some disruptive effect of the deafening operation. Birds reared in a noisy environment, so that they cannot clearly hear their own song, also develop abnormal songs. These results prove the importance of auditory feedback. It is obviously difficult to impair motor function in a reversible way so as to prevent practice but permit singing in adulthood. Nevertheless, it might be conceivable that a bird denied the opportunity to practice would sing normally as an adult when motor function was restored—although this possibility seems unlikely. Almost certainly, both halves of the loop—motor and perceptual—are essential for normal song development in white-crowned sparrows, chaffinches, and many other songbirds.

Once song sparrows, white-crowns, and other songbirds have developed their adult song, it is largely immune to further interference. For example, white-crowns deafened as adults continue to sing essentially normal songs for many months.

The Ecological Basis of Song Learning

These diverse processes of song learning presumably have an ecological basis, although this basis is not always obvious. For example, the sensitivity of young white-crowns allows them to learn the dialect of their location. What advantage is conferred on a male that learns a dialect rather than being innately provided with an adequate song? White-crowns occupy a wider range of habitats than some other similar species, which suggests that genetic subpopulations may be especially well adapted to specific habitats. There are probably other possibilities, for example, the imitative abilities of mockingbirds may be related to the evolutionary benefits of a large song repertoire, something which is itself not well understood.

TEMPLATE LEARNING: A SUMMARY

In summary, for all their apparent differences, imprinting and the song learning of songbirds share three central features. First, in both cases, behavior is based on a stored model or template. Second, the perceptual learning that leads to template formation is selective. That is, only objects or songs that satisfy certain general characteristics are accepted as models. And third, there is a critical period when imprinting or song learning can occur. Isolation from objects or songs during this period prevents normal learning.

REINFORCED LEARNING

Reinforced learning has been a major concern of psychologists since Edward L. Thorndike and Ivan P. Pavlov. The field has become increasingly divided into two topics: Pavlovian conditioning and operant conditioning. Pavlovian conditioners tend to be interested in *learning;* whereas operant conditioners are more interested in *performance.* Pavlovian conditioners tend to use what is termed "between-groups" methodology, in which two or more groups of animals are given different, and presumably irreversible, treatments. They infer learning from the differences between the groups. Operant conditioners tend to use "within-subjects" methodology, in which successive treatments are given to the same individual. They study aspects of behavior such as the effect of reward size, rate, probability, or type of choices made between two or more alternatives. Their successive treatments are presumably reversible in their effects.

Neither the Pavlovian conditioners nor the operant conditioners have fully confronted the difficulties we discussed earlier in the chapter of making inferences about learning. Since animals are not replicas of one another, experiments that compare different treatments on different animals (i.e., between-group experiments) can only reveal simple, universal properties of learning. Since few experiences are ever completely erased (and we cannot be sure which are and which are not), within-subject experiments are also always confounded to some degree.

The division between operant and Pavlovian conditioning conforms to no characteristic of the processes involved in learning: The distinction is much more a matter of procedure (e.g., open-loop versus closed-loop, cf. Chapter 4) than of process. Nevertheless, for historical reasons and reasons of convenience, much research in the two "camps" tacitly assumes that there is a single learning "process," and each camp designs experiments that sometimes preclude any other possibility. A safer tactic is to look at a range of learning phenomena in different species and see what useful generalizations emerge. In this section, we look at the learning of bees, taste-aversion learning, and several experiments on Pavlovian conditioning. A fair conclusion is that although there are some general learning principles, there is no single learning process. Moreover, the different processes correspond not at all to the classical and instrumental procedures. Learning is almost certainly not the slow, continuous "strengthening" that was once believed. Rather, it is a discrete process that involves the assembly of many elements, both performed and remembered, that form new programs for action.

Elements of Insect Learning

The learning of insects is most easily analyzed. Careful experiments have often been able to break down apparently complex learning into simple elements. Some examples can cut through many of the confusions engendered by the more complex learning of mammals and birds.

Honey bees (*Apis mellifera*) learn the color, shape, location, odor, and payoff schedule (many flowers secrete nectar only at certain times of day) of their food sources. In their searches for new food sources and their exploitation of old ones, they do not seem to be significantly inferior to many "higher" species. Yet, their learning is built from simple elements. For example, the color of a flower is clearly visible to the bee before landing, while standing on the flower, and while circling the source after takeoff; yet the color of the flower is learned *only* during the final three seconds before the bee lands. A naive bee carried from the hive to a distinctively colored artificial feeder will circle after taking on a load of sugar water, but it will not be able to pick out the correct feeder color on a second trip a few minutes later. But if the bee is interrupted during its first feeding, so that it must take off and land again, it can remember the feeder color perfectly. In the same manner, bees learn landmarks only when taking off—the circling flight that reliably follows takeoff presumably serves to scan the environment for this purpose. Therefore, a bee feeding at a new location and that is removed before finishing has no recollection of the location, even though it had the opportunity to scan landmarks when first arriving (see Gould & Gould, 1981).

These peculiarities are necessary adaptations to the bee's limited mental capacity: Like a small computer, the bee can perform only one activity at a time, and it cannot afford to store useless information. It makes functional sense for the animal to note landmarks only after leaving, because it is at this time that the bee knows whether the place is valuable enough to be worth recording. This idea is supported by the fact that bees don't circle when leaving a potential food site that provided no food. Bees presumably learned color when landing because that activity can be done equally well before or after landing, although learning landmarks belongs better to the takeoff phase. While on the flower, the bee looks for and gathers nectar. Evidently this activity is sufficiently demanding that no processing resources are left over for learning color. Since the bee must obviously look at the flower to land on it, learning color can occur most efficiently at that time.

The learning of a bird or a mammal is not so perfectly sequential as the learning of bees. Nevertheless, when a pigeon homes on its loft or a swallow returns to its nest after a foraging flight, it must process the same kind of information as the bee, even if not in such a rigid order. Moreover, the phenomenon of *attention* (discussed in Chapter 6) represents exactly the same kind of constraint as the compartmentalized learning of the bees. Mammals, birds, and humans have limited processing resources; therefore, if the task at hand is difficult, dealing with it effectively limits the amount of attention that can be paid to other tasks. We may all be able to walk and chew gum at the same time, but few can perform mental arithmetic at the same time as they answer questions or read a book. The larger brains of mammals and birds allow them an advantage over bees: They can shift attention in relatively flexible ways, rather than being preprogrammed to attend to specific tasks at specific times.

Learning as Program Assembly

Analysis into elements reduces the process of learning to the building of a *program*, in which rules and elements are combined to produce a system that can solve a specific problem such as finding a food source. In bees, the process is often relatively simple, since steps are added one at a time, as in a small digital computer. Moreover, bee learning largely seems to involve the defining of variables (e.g., color, location) to be operated on by built-in programs—rather than building the programs themselves. Thus, the worker honey bee is innately provided with a set of routines for reacting to landmarks and colored food sources. Its learning consists largely of applying those routines to specific landmarks and flowers. The bee is like a handheld-calculator that knows innately how to multiply and relies on the environment only for the input of numbers.

In mammals and birds, the process is much harder to unfold, because in addition to defining variables (the process termed *stimulus control*), program elements, or rules, are combined in new ways during learning. Further entangling the task of analysis, many elements seem to happen at once, or at least in rapid succession, often with no obvious behavioral accompaniment. These difficulties force us to deal with learning in birds and mammals at a more abstract level, in terms of poorly defined concepts such as "template," "coordinate system," "internal representation," and "response strength." Our objective remains to reduce this learning to the level of elements, but our task is greatly complicated.

Learning and Reinforcement

The bee-learning example provides some insight into an old issue in learning theory—the role of reinforcement in learning. The question: Does reinforcement affect *learning* or just *performance?* We know that reinforcement affects performance, that is, action, because we can train animals to perform tasks by rewarding them for it. Often they will not perform the activities unless they are rewarded for it. But, is action *all* that is affected by reinforcement?

This question is difficult to answer, because learning is often vaguely defined, and reinforcement seems to be retroactive. If we can't define learning precisely, we can't expect to answer detailed questions about it. The relation between reinforcement and its effects is indirect and delayed: A reward comes *after* the behavior being rewarded, so the immediate effect of reward must be on the animal's internal state rather than directly on the behavior being rewarded. Presumably the animal's state is changed in such a way that the rewarded behavior becomes more likely. Perhaps our question should be rephrased as follows: Are changes in the animal's state (of the sort we might like to term *learning*) produced only by reward or punishment, or can they take place independently of reward and punishment?

Bee learning provides an answer. Bees encode (i.e., show a change in future performance that we interpret as a change in the state of their memory) the color of a flower *before* they have landed on it, hence before they have any opportunity to be rewarded. Clearly color, an essentially neutral stimulus, can cause a change in the bee's state independently of reward. On the other hand, bees encode information about landmarks only after, and if, they have been rewarded (found nectar). In experimentation, it is necessary to reward bees, so that failure to choose correctly can be attributed to something other than lack of reward. Moreover, it is quite likely that information about flower color is erased from the bee's modest memory if the flower fails to yield nectar, although this fact may be hard to demonstrate behaviorally.

The question as originally posed is an example of one of those undecidable propositions about black-box systems discussed earlier in the chapter. Since we must infer learning from performance, and we know that reward is often necessary for performance, we simply cannot give a general answer to the question of whether reward is necessary for learning. As the bee example illustrates, it is easy to come up with a learning process in which reward is essential to the demonstration of learning, yet in-depth analysis shows learning effects that are independent of reward.

Based on experiments with bees, we can say with certainty that reward and punishment are not the only events that can cause a persistent change in an animal's internal state. For example, we can decide experimentally whether a given behavior is learned before or after the animal is rewarded. Bees encode flower color before being rewarded by the flower, but they learn landmarks only after reward. Thus, it seems that learning involves a balance of both encoding that precedes and is independent of reward and encoding that follows and depend on reward.

LEARNING AS A PROCESS OF INFERENCE

The evolutionary function of "reinforced learning" is to detect regularities in the environment that are related to things of value to the animal. For example, the function of bee learning is to identify and locate sources of food. Learning of this sort can be thought of as a process of *inference,* in the sense that certain environmental features such as landmarks and colors are taken as signals for food. In this section we explore how different kinds of inference require different kinds of information, so that many of the differences between "different types of learning" reflect differences in the task—not necessarily in the learning process.

Any inference can be mistaken, for instance, if the environment changes in between observations or if too few observations are made. For example, if the experimenter changes the color of the feeder after the bee's first visit, the animal will be unable to locate the food source. That is, its initial inference that the original color predicts food will be wrong. Or if the feeder is full only some of the time, a single observation will provide unreliable information. Therefore, an initial visit to a full feeder can lead to the incorrect inference that the feeder will be full on subsequent visits.

As we saw in previous chapters, some cues are more predictive than others. Let's imagine an experiment with artificial feeders that have two properties: a color and a pattern. An experimenter can arrange a predictive relation between food and either color, pattern, or both. Suppose there are two patterns (X and Y) and two colors (A and B). Suppose that pattern X predicts food (all X-type feeders contain sugar water), but pattern Y does not (all Y-type feeders are empty). Color is made irrelevant (both A- and B-color feeders contain food one-half the time). These contingencies are illustrated in Figure 5.3, which shows the four possible feeder types (AX, AY, BX, BY) and the probability of finding food at each. If the bee can learn about only one aspect at a time (as seems likely), and if it learns on first exposure, then its choice of whether to attend to color or pattern is critical. If it attends first to color, it will always be wrong. Clearly, in this case the animal must make several observations before it can detect the correlation between visual appearance and food potential.

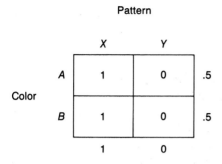

FIGURE 5.3   Probability of food for feeders with different color and pattern combinations.

This need for more observations is almost independent of the animal's computational capacity. Even if the bee can attend to both color and pattern on each trial, it still does not know which one is more important until it has sampled several flowers, that is, until it can fill in from its own experience the probabilities set out in Figure 5.3.

This example shows why (in a functional sense) animals learn some activities rapidly and others more slowly. The speed of learning is determined both by the processing limitations of the creature and by the necessity to sample the environment a sufficient number of times to obtain a reliable estimate of significant correlations—either between signals and food (as in Pavlovian conditioning) or between behavior and food (operant conditioning). Learning is the process of improving these estimates (inferences) about environmental contingencies.

Following any given observation, the animal's action (i.e., what it "infers" about the likelihood of food or other important event) is based both on the experiences it has already had and initial "biases" that are based on built-in factors. For example, we will see in the next section that many animals selectively pick out the taste (rather than color or location) of a novel food as the probable cause of subsequent sickness. This initial bias may be termed a *prior probability,* and it reflects experience of the individual animal and of past generations.

Causal Attribution and Sampling

The animal that learns must deal with two related problems:

1. Causal attribution: What (in my behavior or in the environment) is the cause (or predictor) of the "good" and "bad" that happen to me? It is interesting that this problem, long familiar to psychologists, has also come to the fore in studies of machine learning, for which it is known as the *assignment of credit problem.*

2. Sampling: Given that action must eventually be taken, how much effort should be devoted to gathering additional information? How certain

can I be (based on experience to date) about assigning credit? Is this degree of certainty sufficient for action?

Learning mechanisms have evolved so as to provide adequate answers to these questions.

The problem of how much sampling an animal should do is an exceedingly difficult one even in a simple environment. The answer, as you might expect, depends on several factors:

1. How much does the animal already know?
2. How large is its computational capacity? That is, how many features or stimuli can it assess on each trial?
3. How important are the consequences of being correct or incorrect?

How much the animal already knows is likely to be related to the variability of the environment. Properties that are variable should be learned more slowly than properties that are fixed, because the animal can be less certain of the meaning of a given conjunction. For example, should the child bitten by a German shepherd be afraid of all furry animals, all dogs, just German shepherds, or just *this* German shepherd? Without some knowledge about the hostile propensities of dogs and other animals, either built-in or based on previous experience, to help rule out some of these possibilities, more data are obviously needed. Providing the risk is not too great, the child should sample a few more dogs. But the child's genetic code, which is determined through natural selection by the experience of his or her ancestors, may help limit the possibilities—just to dogs, for example. An initial bias to fear all dogs after being bitten by one might be termed an *innate prior.* Subsequent experience with dogs may further affect the tendency to be afraid or unafraid of specific dogs and change this initial probability. The prior probability and subsequent experience together determine the level of fear induced by canines experienced later in life.

Taste-Aversion Learning as Inference

In simple animals these initial biases or prior probabilities are nearly always innate. Bees do not learn colors more rapidly if raised in an environment in which fixed colors are always reliable predictors of food. Nor can bees learn to be less impulsive about learning odors. Even in mammals and birds, examples of innate priors of this sort are common. For example, a rat made sick by a harmless injection of lithium chloride 30 min after tasting a new food in a new cage will develop a strong aversion to the novel taste but not to the new cage. Such *taste-aversion learning* follows the Pavlovian-conditioning paradigm (an unconditioned stimulus [US], sickness, follows a conditioned stimulus [CS], the taste of food), but it has several unusual properties. Taste-aversion learning is relatively insensitive to long delays, whereas conventional Pavlovian conditioning is almost impossible with a CS–US delay of 30 min or more. In addition, taste-aversion learning is highly selective (a taste CS is much more effective than a place CS), and it occurs on a single trial. The dominance of taste and the occurrence of learning on a single CS–US trial is evidence of a strong prior probability.

However, previous experience does play a key role in taste-aversion learning. If a rat is made sick some time after having tasted both a familiar and a novel food, an aversion develops only to the novel food. Here is a perfect example of an inference: The prior probability that the familiar food is poisonous is low, because it has been eaten safely on previous occasions; on the other hand, the prior probability that the unfamiliar food is poisonous is uncertain. If the animal must make a decision to avoid a food based on a single exposure, then the novel food is obviously the preferred candidate. This sort of learning is familiar to humans as well. If after eating tofu (novel) and fish (familiar) at a Japanese restaurant you become quite ill, you will most likely blame the illness on the tofu rather than on the real culprit—the raw fish. Even more interesting, such inferences are completely automatic and immune to reason: You are likely to form a strong aversion to the taste of the novel food no matter how intellectually compelling is the evidence to incriminate the fish. Taste-aversion learning is a completely automatic inference process: It has nothing to do with the linguistic processes we normally associate with the term. Animal learning inferences are all of this automatic, preverbal sort.

The characteristics of taste-aversion learning are also highly adaptive in context. The aversion to taste rather than to some other feature of the environment follows from the (almost)[1] invariable relationship between food and sickness. Animals may feel sick for reasons other than poison, such as disease, but nonfood stimuli rarely cause sickness. The rapid learning, because of a high innate prior probability, follows from the severe risk associated with eating poisonous substances. The cost of omitting a safe item from the diet generally is small, whereas the cost of eating poison is quite high. This large difference clearly biases selection in favor of conservatism, that is, rapid taste-aversion learning and neophobia (avoidance of novel objects, especially foods). Indeed, rats are quite cautious when confronted with new foods. They eat only a little at first and wait some time, usually without eating any other food (which would confound the "experiment"), before incorporating the new food into their diet.

IS TASTE-AVERSION LEARNING PAVLOVIAN CONDITIONING?   The long delay between the CS (taste) and the US (illness) typical of taste-aversion learning is not characteristic of other kinds of Pavlovian conditioning. Is taste-aversion learning something special, unique, or at any event different from more familiar kinds of Pavlovian conditioning? This difference has been the source of considerable controversy. From a scientific point of view, the controversy boils down to two questions:

1. What are the procedural differences between conventional and taste-aversion conditioning?
2. Are there residual differences between the two types of conditioning that require different processes?

---

[1] We say "almost" because, as a historical curiosity, the taste-aversion learning phenomenon was first brought to the attention of experimental psychologists in a study by Garcia et al. (1961), in which sickness was induced by X-rays (one of the few noningestive methods of producing sickness).

As we shall see, procedural differences account for much of the disparity between taste-aversion and conventional conditioning. Similarity differences between taste and nontaste stimuli may account for the rest.

The main procedural difference is that in taste-aversion learning there are usually no stimuli of the same qualitative sort (i.e., tastes) intervening between the CS and the US; whereas in conventional, Pavlovian conditioning with a long delay, there are usually other sights and sounds that intervene between the CS (a tone or a light) and the US. Such extraneous stimuli offers opportunities for confusion. Perhaps taste is an effective stimulus after long delays because tastes and other stimuli (such as lights and sounds) are not easily confused: A single taste experienced half an hour before sickness can still be remembered clearly despite all the nontaste stimuli experienced in the interim. Conversely, the main reasons that long-delay Pavlovian conditioning with nontaste stimuli fail may be because

1. There is nothing to distinguish the CS from stimuli that occurred before and after the CS, so that the animal has no way of knowing which stimulus to associate with the US (attribution of credit).

2. These other stimuli impair recall for the CS and thus prevent the animal from making any connection between it and the US.

Such effects are proactive and retroactive interference, and they are familiar to all of us who have failed to remember one individual's name after many introductions at a party. *Proactive interference* is the deleterious effect of event *A,* at time t_1, on recall of information about event *B,* at *later* time t_2. *Retroactive interference* has the reverse effect of event *B* on recall of *earlier* event *A.* An event in the middle of a series is subject to *serial-position effect,* which means it is subject to both proactive and retroactive effects; hence it is worse recalled under most conditions, than events at the beginning or end, which are subject to only one of the two effects. If the animal cannot remember a specific stimulus that occurred 30 min ago, it is in a poor position to show a conditioned response to that stimulus as a consequence of a US that just occurred.

Two kinds of experiment are necessary to back up this argument. One shows that when interfering stimuli are eliminated, conventional Pavlovian CSs like lights and tones can become conditioned even with long delays. The second shows that taste-aversion learning can be impaired if interfering tastes are allowed to occur before the initial taste or between it and the US.

Both types of experiment have been performed. For example, experiments with conventional visual stimuli can be successful with long delays if the stimuli are highly salient and if interfering stimuli are minimized. The effects of interference on taste-aversion learning have also been shown in several studies by Sam Revusky (1971). In one study, four groups of rats were allowed to drink 2 ml of saccharin solution. After 15 min, each group was allowed to drink water that contained varying concentrations of vinegar (a novel taste). Later, all the rats were made sick by an injection of lithium chloride. After three days, each group received a series of preference tests in which the animals were offered a choice between saccharin water and dilute coffee. Figure 5.4 summarizes the results:

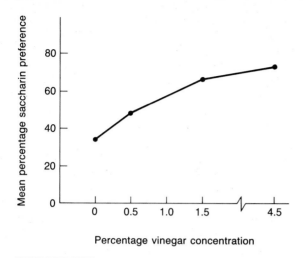

FIGURE 5.4   Preference of rats for drinking saccharin solution versus a novel coffee solution. Preference is a function of the concentration of vinegar drunk in between original experience with saccharin and lithium-chloride-induced sickness. The groups that tasted the stronger vinegar solutions showed greater preferences for (i.e., less aversion to) saccharin (after Revusky, 1971).

The weaker the intervening vinegar solution, the less saccharin water was drunk, that is, the stronger the aversion to saccharin.

There are two possible reasons for the interfering effect of the vinegar taste in Revusky's experiment:

1. The vinegar coming after the saccharin interfered with the animal's re-call of the saccharin; consequently, the animal could not associate the saccharin with the sickness one hour later. The experience here would be retroactive, because it was caused by the following stimulus.

2. The vinegar was closer in time to the sickness than the saccharin, so that the animal associated the vinegar rather than the saccharin with sickness. This experience would be an example of an innate prior, since recent events are much more likely to be the cause of something than more remote events.

The dominance of one potential CS over another is termed *overshadowing*. In either case, we might expect the rats to form an aversion for vinegar, which pre-sumably occurred, although Revusky did not test for it.

Let's now ask: What would have happened had both vinegar and saccharin been familiar? What would happen if the experiment (vinegar → saccharin → sickness) were repeated several times? Common sense and data from other ex-periments can answer these questions: When the two events are equal in every other respect, the rats will avoid the taste closer in time to the sickness. Proper-ties of memory, of which retroactive interference is one, reflect regularities in the causal properties of the environment, in particular, the fact that a recent event (i.e., sacchrin) is more likely than an earlier event (i.e., vinegar) to be the cause of sickness. In other words, as new information is made available, older information becomes less useful.

Inference and Backward Conditioning

Learning that occurs on one trial, such as color learning in bees or taste-aversion learning in rats, must require at least some acquisition of information or change of state before the occurrence of the reinforcer. The rat must record the novel taste if it is to acquire an aversion to it, just as the bee must record the color of the flower. On the other hand, this information need not dominate over subsequent information, and additional processing may continue after a reward has occurred. For example, in an experiment by Lucas and Guttman (1975), rats were given a single electric shock while taking a pellet from a small hole in the center of a striped pattern (novel stimulus) display. After a brief delay, a rubber hedgehog was suddenly introduced into the chamber. The next day the rats were tested for their aversion to the CS (stimulus display) and to the toy hedgehog. The animals tended to avoid the hedgehog most, even though it had been introduced *after* the shock, and it illustrates *backward conditioning*—something which is not supposed to occur, and usually doesn't. Backward conditioning makes little causal sense, because if *B* occurs after *A*, it cannot be the cause of *A*.

Of course, from another viewpoint, the animals were acting perfectly sensibly. It is impossible to be certain of the validity of a causal inference on the basis of a single instance. The prior probability, from the rat's vantage point, that a striped pattern (the CS in this experiment) will be dangerous is small, whereas the prior probability that a lifelike dummy will be dangerous is much greater. Repeated experiences would serve to correct mistaken inferences drawn on the basis of this single experience. But given just one trial, the animal's "guess" that the toy hedgehog—and not the striped pattern—was the source of a single, painful experience seems reasonable.

This result also shows that considerable processing continues after the US has occurred. Here the rats evidently acquired some fear of the hedgehog, which was presented after shock. It is likely that a subsequent trial in which presentation of the hedgehog was soon followed by shock would rapidly confirm this fear and produce long-lasting avoidance. On the other hand, if the hedgehog were continually presented only after shock, the fear would come to be elicited by the striped CS and not the hedgehog. Thus the first conditioning trial not only produces some learning, it also creates a set of CS candidates to which the animal can attend on later trials. These later trials will rule out some of the CS candidates and confirm others.

Blocking: Expectation and Surprise

The effect of any event on an animal usually depends on its current state of knowledge. Thus an answer to the question about what are the necessary and sufficient conditions for learning depends on what the animal already knows and what is to be learned. *In general, animals learn only when something violates their expectations or when they have only weak expectations* (as in a novel situation). All the examples of reinforced learning discussed thus far fit this generalization. For example, when two tastes have an identical temporal relation to poisoning, conditioning develops only to the novel taste. In another example, when a compound stimulus such as a tone-light combination is used in one of the standard Pavlovian-conditioning arrangements (cf. Chapter 4), the amount of conditioning that occurs with each element (tone and light) depends on what the animal already knows about each.

Evidence for this *surprise hypothesis* came first from a series of conditioned-suppression experiments by Leon Kamin (1969). In Kamin's experiments, rats were trained in two steps: First they received several tone-shock pairings, then the combination of tone *and* light was paired with shock for some additional trials. Kamin wanted to find out how much conditioning would accrue to each element. Because the probability of shock in the presence of light is greater than in its absence, $p(Sh|CS) > p(Sh|\sim CS)$, we might expect some conditioning to the light. On the other hand, the light, which was added after several tone-shock pairings, did not provide additional information about shock, so that when shock occurred, an animal's initial expectation about shock was not violated: The shock followed the tone as before. Kamin's hypothesis predicted that the rats should not learn about the light or should learn less than if there had been no prior tone-shock pairings—and his prediction held true. This effect is called *blocking*, in which prior conditioning of one element of a stimulus compound prevents learning about another.

What if the intensity of shock is increased for the trials with both tone and light? If the animal attends only to the tone as before, it will be surprised by the new level of shock! In other words, its expectancy was violated. Under these conditions, we would predict learning about light as well as tone. Indeed, this prediction typically holds true.

In general, the greater the violation of expectation, the greater the learned change in behavior. For example, if two stimuli are presented in alternation, with shocks occurring only in the presence of one of them (CS+), then the other (CS−) becomes a *safety stimulus*. That is, the CS− signals the absence of shock. If this CS− is now presented with a novel stimulus (X) as a compound and is paired with shock, then X acquires a greater increment in its power to suppress lever-pressing than when it is presented alone.

We can conclude that learning is initiated by a violation of expectation (or *surprise*) and that the change in behavior that occurs depends on prior probabilities or initial biases toward certain expectancies. If the prior probabilities are strong, as with taste-aversion learning, learning occurs with the novel CS as opposed to familiar stimuli. However, when prior probabilities are weak or don't exist, as with Kamin's experiments, learning about the novel CS of a stimulus compound will not occur unless there is a violation of expectancy. The following section on mathematical models of conditioning shows how these "expectancy" effects may correspond to simple processes. For example, the rat's version of the term *expectancy* may be much less elaborate and "cognitive" than the word implies.

THE RESCORLA–WAGNER MODEL FOR CONDITIONING

A number of mathematical models have been proposed to account for the joint effects of surprise (violation of expectation) and inference (the change in behavior caused by the violation) on conditioning. The effects are joint in the sense that the animal's expectation must be violated before any change in behavior (and presumably learning also) can occur. We discuss here the *Rescorla–Wagner model*, whch is one of the simplest and certainly the best-known model, to give you an idea of how such models work and show you that simple processes can often display subtle behavior.

One way to represent the joint dependency of learning on surprise and inference is to assume that the *associative strength* (associative value) of a stimulus is proportional to the product of two functions (one representing the surprise aspect and the other representing the inference aspect). The joint function can be represented as follows:

$$\Delta(V) = f(\text{surprise}) \times g(\text{inference})$$

where $\Delta(V)$ is the change in associative strength after one trial, f is something that measures surprise, and g is something that measures inference (i.e., the amount or direction of change in behavior associated with a given amount of surprise). We assume $f(0) = 0$, so that when surprise $= 0$, $\Delta(V) = 0$; thus with no surprise, there is no change in V, which conforms to the assumption discussed earlier that surprise is necessary for learning.

A Mathematical Representation of Surprise

How can we represent surprise? Perhaps the simplest assumption we can make is that surprise corresponds to a discrepancy between all that we can learn about a situation after many consistent pairings of a CS with a US, which is referred to as the maximum associative value (V_{max}), and what we actually know at any given time (V). On the first trial, V must be zero. As conditioning proceeds, V approaches V_{max}, which is the maximum amount of conditioning. Thus, as a first simple guess, we say that $f(\text{surprise}) = V_{max} - V$; that is, the bigger the difference between the current and maximum associative strengths, the greater the surprise.

If the CS is a compound, V may be represented as the sum of the associative values of the elements ($V = V_1 + V_2 + \cdots + V_N$). Therefore, for two elements,

$$f(\text{surprise}) = V_{max} - (V_1 + V_2)$$

A Mathematical Representation of Inference

The simplest inference assumption is that all stimuli are equally likely candidates for conditioning, except that some are more *salient* (more intense, more noticeable) than others. The more salient candidates are conditioned more quickly, condition faster which implies that the inference function is a constant that may take on different values for different stimuli. Inference can thus be represented as follows:

$$g(\text{inference}) = S_i$$

where S_i is a measure of the salience of the ith stimulus. S_i represents a prior stimulus. If S_i is large because of prior conditioning, for example, the animal treats the stimulus as a likely predictor of a US or its absence; if S_i is small, the animal requires convincing that the stimulus has any signal value.

If we now combine the equations that represent surprise and inference, we get

$$\Delta(V_1) = S_1[V_{\max} - (V_1 + V_2)]$$

where $\Delta(V_1)$ is now the increment in associative strength of one of the elements of the compound stimulus after one reinforced trial. This equation is the well-known model proposed by Robert Rescorla and Alan Wagner in 1972. It is a simple extension of an older, one-stimulus, *stochastic learning model* proposed by Bush and Mosteller in 1955.

The effects of extinction (omission of the US) are handled by setting $V_{\max}$ equal to zero, so that $\Delta(V)$ becomes negative. Changes in the intensity of the *US* (e.g., reward magnitude, motivational level) are handled by increasing or decreasing $V_{\max}$. Thus, the final equation of the Rescorla–Wagner model is as follows:

$$\Delta(V_i) = S_i(V_{\max} - \Sigma V_i)$$

where $\Delta(V_i)$ is the increment in strength to stimulus i on a given trial, and ΣV_i is the sum of the associative strengths of all stimulus elements. Notice that this equation is the *integrator* discussed in Chapter 3, and we are dealing with a familiar and commonly encountered process. All that the Rescorla–Wagner model adds to the basic integrator is application to compound events (stimuli), which it handles by means of the assumption that associative strengths are additive.

Applications of the Rescorla–Wagner Model to Overshadowing and Blocking

Simple as it is, Rescorla–Wagner is nevertheless complicated enough to predict overshadowing and blocking. In a compound made up of elements with high and low salience, when learning is complete ($\Delta(V) = 0$), $V_1 + V_2 = V_{\max}$, but most of the associative strength will have gone to the more salient stimulus: Thus, if $S_2 > S_1$, then as conditioning progresses, stimulus 2 will overshadow stimulus 1. The way that V_1 and V_2 change during conditioning, assuming that both begin at zero, is shown in Figure 5.5.

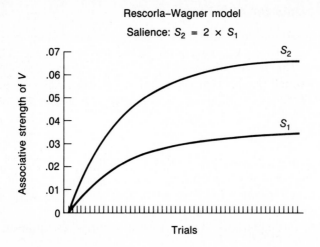

FIGURE 5.5   Rescorla–Wagner Model: The effects of stimulus salience. The growth in associative value for two stimuli of unequal salience, in which stimulus 2 is twice as salient as stimulus 1. If both stimuli begin at zero, stimulus 2 will always have twice the associative value of stimulus 1.

Blocking is accommodated by the fact that after the first phase, in which S_1 alone is paired with the US, V_1 must be close to V_{max}. Thus even though V_2 is initially zero, $V_{max} - (V_1 + V_2)$ is also close to zero when S_1 and S_2 are presented together at the beginning of the second phase. Consequently, little or no further change can occur in either V_1 or V_2 in the second phase; the conditioning of S_2 is blocked by the prior conditioning of S_1. Notice that this argument predicts an actual *loss* in associative strength for V_2 if for some reason it has a high V value when introduced as part of the compound late in training. Experiments have shown just such a paradoxical loss of strength by a stimulus element that continues to be reinforced, which indicates that the Rescorla–Wagner model captures an essential feature of the conditioning process.

Let's now study an example of blocking of conditioning to a light (stimulus L) by previous conditioning to a tone (stimulus T). To begin, we assign a value to V_{max}, which represents the intensity of the US. A value of zero represents extinction or no US. Larger values represent more intense USs. We also assign values to the salience of each stimulus element (S_L and S_T). A value of zero represents an unnoticeable stimulus, and it results in no conditioning. A value of one represents a salient stimulus. If we set $V_{max} = 1$, and both $S_L = 0.25$ and $S_T = 0.25$, so that the tone and the light are equally salient, we get

$$\Delta(V_i) = S_i(V_{max} - \Sigma V)$$

On the first trial, with V_T (tone) equal to zero and no light, we get

Trial 1: $\Delta(V_T) = 0.25(1 - 0) = 0.25.$

Continuing for three more trials, we get the following table:

	V_T	$\Sigma(V_T + V_L)$
Trial 1: $\Delta(V_T) = 0.25(1 - 0)$ = .25		.25
Trial 2: $\Delta(V_T) = 0.25(1 - .25)$ = .188		.438
Trial 3: $\Delta(V_T) = 0.25(1 - .438)$ = .141		.579
Trial 4: $\Delta(V_T) = 0.25(1 - .579)$ = .105		.684

Now let's introduce the light—remembering that if it had been introduced at the beginning, the first $\Delta(V)$ would have been 0.25:

	V_L
Trial 5: $\Delta(V_L) = 0.25(1 - .684)$ = .079	

Clearly, introducing the light late, after there has already been conditioning to the tone, means that it gains much less associative value than it would have if it had been introduced early on, either alone or together with the tone. Figure 5.6 shows three curves: the course of V_T (tone), the course of V_L (light) when the light is introduced after some conditioning to the tone, and the course of what would have happened if the light had been the sole stimulus element from the beginning. The figure shows the gradual rise in conditioning to the tone, then the much slower rise in the strength of conditioning to the light, which is introduced midway. The dashed line shows the conditioning to the light that would have oc-curred if it had been present from the beginning.

This simple model also accounts for the results of Rescorla's "truly random control" procedure (discussed in Chapter 4). Single-stimulus conditioning can be considered as compound conditioning when *contextual cues* (the physical environment of the test apparatus) constitute the other element. In the stan-dard, delay-conditioning arrangement, in which the US is paired only with the CS (stimulus 1), the CS and the contextual cues (stimulus 2) receive the same num-ber of increments in associative value during conditioning. However, the context also receives a substantial number of decrements during ~CS + ~US trials. For example, if the CS is paired with shock half the time, and a brief shock occurs on the average of one per minute, then in one hour there will be 30 increments in both CS strength and background stimuli strength. However, there will also be 30 occasions for which no shock was presented in the absence of the CS but in the presence of the context. This situation will cause reductions in the strength of the context. It is easy to show that this process will result in eventual control by the CS—that is, good conditioning.

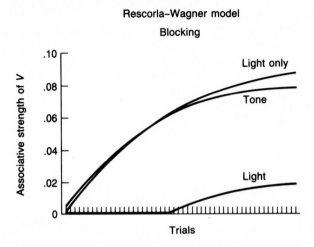

FIGURE 5.6   Rescorla–Wagner Model: Blocking. The curve labeled "tone" shows the associative value for a tone that is present throughout conditioning. The curve labeled "light" shows the associative value of a light presented only after the tone has already acquired some associative value. The curve labeled "light only" shows the associative value the light would have had if it had been presented alone from the beginning.

However, in the truly random control condition, the US is equally likely in the presence or absence of the CS. Therefore, the CS continues to receive 30 increments every hour, but the context now receives twice as many. This situation eventually leads to predominant control by the context and no conditioning (zero associative value) to the CS.

Failures of the Rescorla–Wagner Model

The Rescorla–Wagner model is able to do a great deal with simple assumptions. However, we should not be surprised that it fails to account for absolutely everything; for example, blocking can be reduced by a decrease as well as an increase in the expected level of shock (V_{max}) coincident with the introduction of the new stimulus element. This finding is difficult for the model because for any conditioning to occur to S_L (light) in our example, there must be an increase in V_{max}. If V_{max} decreases, the model predicts a decrease in the associative strength to S_T (tone) and a negative value (inhibitory conditioning) to S_L. Under other conditions, however, inhibitory conditioning does occur.

Perhaps the most difficult result for the Rescorla–Wagner model is *latent inhibition*, which is the delay in conditioning produced by presenting a stimulus without any consequence (US) for several trials, before presenting it on trials followed by a US. According to the model, preexposure to S cannot change the associative value from zero, because without V_{max} there can be no conditioning. Notice however that this effect does follow from the verbal account: During preexposure, the animal can learn that the CS does not predict a US; consequently, when conditioning begins, it must overcome existing learning as well as learn something new. Overcoming existing learning to learn something new certainly takes longer than just new learning alone.

Several researchers have suggested modifications and extensions of the Rescorla–Wagner model to deal with its failures, but their formulations are more complicated, and none has gained universal support. We have described the Rescorla–Wagner model in some detail not because it is completely correct but because it helps to clarify the meaning of terms such as expectancy and surprise, and it clearly captures one aspect of conditioning in an exact fashion.

SUMMARY

This chapter avoids a formal definition of learning in favor of a definition based on exclusion. We can conclude that learning involves a specific and relatively permanent change in an animal's potential produced by the environment. But, there are unavoidable, logical and practical limits to how much we can discover about what individual organisms learn.

We distinguished between two kinds of learning: template learning and reinforced learning. Imprinting and song learning in birds were discussed as examples of template learning. Template learning is a specific kind of change that is dependent on the perception of certain objects (for imprinting) or songs during a limited, critical period in development. Relatively little is known about the function of this kind of learning in higher animals, including humans (the study of language, which some have compared to song learning in songbirds is a partial exception). Perhaps we know so little about template learning because the behavioristic approach to learning grew out of the older, philosophical tradition of *associationism,* with its tabula rasa (clean slate) view of human nature that put all weight on individual experience (i.e., on the effects of reinforcement) and gave none to ancestral experience. In this chapter we attempted to combine what is valuable from the older tradition—its emphasis on the details of temporal contiguity and predictiveness—with the innate biases—priors—given by heredity and representing the experience of an animal's ancestors. All learning involves an intimate mixture of both built-in biases and mechanisms for extracting information about causation from the stream of experienced events. As we pointed out in Chapter 1, it makes no sense to draw a line between learned and innate factors, because learning itself involves innate factors and cannot occur without them.

The role of reinforcement in learning and performance was introduced through an analysis of color and landmark learning in bees. We saw how bees learn about some features of their environment before reinforcement and others only afterwards. We concluded that reward and punishment are not the only events that can cause a change in an animal's internal state, although they are usually necessary for the performance of learned activities.

The function of reinforced learning is to detect regularities in the environment that are related to things of value to the animal. Such learning can be described as a sort of inference, in the sense that certain environmental features are taken as signals for valued events. How rapidly an animal learns about these regularities depends on how much it already knows because of its evolutionary history (innate prior probabilities) and because of its personal history (learned prior probabilities). When the expectation about a valued event is violated on a given trial or observation (surprise), learning occurs, and the prior probability is updated.

The Rescorla–Wagner model of learning provides a simple mechanism or rule that is capable of detecting correlations between signals, behavior, and valued events. Each observation or learning trial can be viewed as making an estimate (inference) about these correlations. Learning occurs only when these expectancies are violated.

6

Stimulus Control and Cognition

The ability to recognize when specific adaptive behaviors are appropriate has been taken for granted in previous chapters. In this chapter, we look at some aspects of recognition and the organization of individual knowledge.

To behave adaptively is to behave differently in one situation than in another. As we move from *Paramecium* to pigeons and people, the number of modes of possible behavior increases enormously, and with it the number of different situations for which a unique behavior is appropriate. How do animals organize this knowledge? How are situations recognized? The two questions are not really separate, since some kinds of organization make recognition quick and accurate, whereas others make it slow and unreliable.

THE DEFINITION OF RECOGNITION

What does it mean to *recognize* something? We can give a simple formal definition in terms of the concepts of internal state, stimulus, and response introduced in Chapter 5: To recognize something is to be in a unique state, so that in the presence of object w, the animal is always in state W, and state W never occurs at any other time. Such a condition is also necessary for the animal to discriminate w from objects that are not w. But, this formal definition conceals a great deal. For example, it isn't much help in constructing machines that can recognize, for which much more specific information is required. To construct a machine that can recognize, we must know how to process specific visual (auditory, touch, etc.) inputs and how to direct the visual apparatus on the basis of past information: Where should the machine look next? How does it distinguish objects from their backgrounds? How does it identify the same object from different points of view? How does it encode this information so that it provides a useful basis for action? All of these problems must be solved if behavior is to be adaptive.

Most of these questions about adaptive behavior center around *perception*, and we can't do this topic justice here. In this text we take for granted the processes that translate a specific physical environment into some internal representation that allows the animal to recognize the environment on subsequent occasions. More cautiously phrased, we take for granted the processes that allow the animal to behave in *essentially* the same manner every time it is in the same environment. Perceptual processes are not trivial; in many respects they are more complicated than the topics dealt with in this text. We pass them by only because our main interests lie elsewhere. This chapter involves the last step in the perception process: the encoding of information in ways useful for action. Concern is not with how the animal "sees" a Skinner box or a colored light, but with how these objects resemble or differ from others in its world and how they serve to guide behavior.

To address the question of what it means to recognize something, we begin with a functional definition, which largely avoids the difficult perceptual problems we have just described. We go on to discuss the traditional concept whereby a stimulus is some specific, physically defined event. We discuss stimuli and stimulus elements, then we describe how control by simple stimuli is measured in transfer tests. The results of transfer tests can often be summarized by rules that describe the effects of stimulus compounds in terms of the effects of their constituent elements. Tests are also useful for assessing the effects of reinforcement on stimulus control. We discuss stimulus representation and how animals use complex stimuli as guides to behavior in natural environments. In addition, the second half of the chapter takes up the problem of memory, the set of processes through which an animal's past affects its present and without which animals could never learn to discriminate one stimulus from another. We conclude by demonstrating how what we have learned about memory can help us understand spatial learning.

THE DEFINITION OF STIMULUS CONTROL

Discriminative and Eliciting Stimuli

The word *stimulus* implies the existence of a response. That is, a stimulus is usually thought of as a stimulus *for* something. As previously discussed, this definition may be too narrow, because a stimulus may change the organism's internal state without immediately eliciting a response. However, some stimuli are clearly more important for the actions they produce, others for their changes of state: Some stimuli are goads to action; others function more as signals. The stimulus for an "ideal" reflex is a goad—the response follows the stimulus invariably and at once. A "pure" eliciting stimulus is one that produces a reaction but has no other effect on the animal. Obviously, few, perhaps no, stimuli fit this description exactly, but stimuli for simple protective reflexes of decerebrate organisms (light for pupillary contraction, air puff for blinking, touch for the scratch reflex) come close. Of course in reality, even eliciting stimuli have effects on the animal that go beyond the response they produce. Normal (not decerebrate) animals can remember past stimuli, which can therefore affect future behavior after long delays. At the other extreme, a stimulus such as "you've won!," although it may well elicit a great deal of activity, is much more important for the change of state that it produces.

The distinctive property of *discriminative,* or *controlling, stimuli* is that they define a certain state of the organism. This state is defined as a set of stimulus–response and stimulus–state–change relations different from those associated with other states. Discriminative stimuli serve as signals defining situations in which a specific course of action is appropriate. For example, young bluejays will attack and eat butterflies. Monarch butterflies are mildly poisonous and make birds sick. After some unfortunate experiences with monarchs, the birds learn to avoid them. The distinctive red and black pattern of the monarch signals (*controls* in the conventional terminology) a pattern of behavior different from that normally elicited by butterflies. Thus, discriminative stimuli often elicit a response; but their special property is that in the presence of a specific discriminative stimulus, the animal behaves according to a set of rules different from those that apply to other discriminative stimuli.

The signal that defines the situation need not be the object to be attacked or avoided (e.g. the butterfly); the signal may be different from the stimulus responded to. For example, on rainy days birds may look for worms brought to the surface by waterlogging of their burrows, whereas on dry days they may look for other prey. In this case, the weather is the signal, although it is the worm that is to be attacked. A hungry zoo animal may rush to its food bowl at the sight of the keeper. The number of caterpillars a female digger wasp brings back to each of her separate larvae is determined during a daily checkout visit. The food store for each larva is the signal that controls subsequent foraging. Even primitive animals show such contextual reactions. This kind of conditional dependence of a behavior pattern on a situation may be termed *systematic variation.* For the digger wasp, the rules are built-in, and they are not altered by experience. But for mammals, birds, and a few other animals, systematic variation is acquired during the lifetime of the individual (i.e., learned). The stimuli involved are termed discriminative stimuli, and the process is known as *associative learning*.

STIMULUS–RESPONSE RELATIONS   This view of stimulus effects is not too different from the common-sense notion that animals percieve the world as a set of situations, each with its own regularities. Note though that this view has not always been the dominant one in experimental psychology. We began our discussion with the concept of *situation* because the history of this field fosters the deceptively simple alternative that operant behavior can be understood solely in terms of stimulus–response relations, in which both stimuli and responses are defined as simple physical events.

B. F. Skinner enlarged the definitions of stimulus and response to embrace classes of physical events linked by a common consequence. For Skinner, a discriminative stimulus is the class of all physical stimuli that signals a reinforcement contingency. Likewise, a response is the class of all acts (behavior) that satisfies the contingency. But, Skinner was silent on the relations among these classes of stimulus and response events and their structural properties. The stimulus–response view, in either its simple or enlarged form, is experimentally convenient, but it provides few clues to understanding how animals work, either conceptually (e.g., in terms of possible working computer models) or physiologically (in terms of neural mechanisms). Because it never goes beyond a single stimulus or stimulus classes to the relations among them, it is little help in understanding how animals get about in natural environments, why some complex stimuli appear similar whereas others seem different, how pigeons differ from people, or why stimuli that are psychologically simple to identify (e.g., faces and other natural objects) are often physically complex.

THE PERCEPTUAL APPROACH TO STIMULUS EFFECTS   There are two main approaches to these questions. One is perceptual and physiological. This approach seeks to identify the transformations imposed on the physical stimulus by the animal's nervous system that allow it to detect complex invariances. An example is the fixed shape of a three-dimensional object perceived from different angles or the constant size of the same object seen at different distances, in different lights, and with varying exressions. Perception is hard to study with animals, and our knowledge of perceptual processes still falls short of answering these questions.

THE FUNCTIONAL APPROACH TO STIMULUS EFFECTS   The second approach is functional. The evolutionary function of knowledge must be as a guide to action. Hence, the animal's task is always to organize the mass of physical stimulation in ways that enable it to deploy its behavioral resources with maximum efficiency. Physical stimuli that signal the same set of regularities (in the life of the individual or its ancestors) should be treated as equivalent and should come to control the same pattern of adaptive behavior. Lions, tigers, and leopards look similar to us not because they are related, but because they behave in similar ways and require similar actions from us. In some ways a leopard is more similar to a zebra than to a lion (leopard and zebra both have black and white markings, neither has a mane, etc.); nevertheless, we (and other mammals) give more weight to characteristics that are distinctively feline and predatory about leopard and lion that the zebra does not share. Presumably we link leopard, lion, and tiger because of biases built into our perceptual and cognitive systems that lend more weight to features such as teeth, claws, and the position of eyes on the head than to color and pelage. We can assume these biases stood our lion-vulnerable ancestors in good stead.

The class of "similar" physical stimuli constitutes a stimulus in the functional sense.[1] The relations of similarity and difference between stimuli so defined constitute the animal's knowledge about its world. The functional approach to stimulus control therefore begins with the study of similarities and differences among stimuli and hopes to end with some way of representing this knowledge and rules for how organisms use it.

Stimulus Generalization

The experimental study of stimulus effects boils down to the question of *stimulus generalization,* also known as *stimulus equivalence.* That is, what stimuli are equivalent, or nearly equivalent, in their effects to a given stimulus? When stimuli have similar effects on an organism, they are said to belong to the same stimulus class.

Species differ greatly in the complexity of their stimulus classes. Small invertebrates are often guided by signals that can be identified with relatively simple physical properties. For example, a tick locates its prey by placing itself at a certain height above the ground. There it waits, until a warm-blooded animal passes close enough to provide the necessary chemical stimulus, whereupon the creature releases its hold and drops on its unwitting host. For a tick, the world seems to be divided into different heights—most bad, a narrow range of good—and the presence or absence of butyric acid. No doubt the animal can also identify acceptable ranges of temperature, illumination, and humidity, although other features, such as the music of Mozart, the beauty of a summer evening, the difference between one grass and another, are ignored. The tick asks rather few questions of the world, and it is content with simple answers. The more intelligent the animal, the less simplistic is its world. Mammals and birds can identify dozens or hundreds of different situations and react to complex properties of their environments. Occasionally birds and mammals can be tricked by simple *sign stimuli* such as the male robin's foolish attacking of a red piece of fluff or the stickleback's attack on primitive models (Box 6.1). These instances attract experimental attention in part because they are easily studied exceptions to the prevailing complexity.

---

[1]Notice that this use of the word *functional* is not quite the same as the biological sense of *adaptive* or *optimal.* It is closer to the common-sense idea of *function:* what is something *for?*

B   O   X

6.1

Sign Stimuli, Releasers, and Motivated Behavior

The influential German ethologist Konrad Lorenz (1950) collected many striking examples of apparently automatic reactions of animals to simple physical stimuli: sticklebacks attacking painted red dummies, gull chicks pecking at spotted pencils, gulls' mindless retrieval of any spherical object, even grotesquely large ones. A well-studied example is the springtime behavior of male English robins, who will attack small balls of red-dyed cotton, which are substitutes for the red-breasted male bird. There is no doubt that the animal's perceptual apparatus can discriminate between a ball of fluff and a male robin, but the *innate-releasing mechanism (IRM)* that Lorenz believed to underlie such reactions was thought to be a much more stupid beast. Even so, it is tempting to take such simple reactions as a model for the organization of all adaptive behavior, seeing apparently complex reactions to complex stimuli as merely bundles of stimulus–response elements.

This view has not turned out profitably: We no longer expect animal behavior to be reducible to stimulus–response elements. Nevertheless, the IRM remains interesting for its motivational if not its perceptual aspects. For example, one of Lorenz's more interesting observations was what he called *vacuum reactions:* Predators like cats and hawks, when deprived for some time of the opportunity to hunt, often show hunting behavior in the absence of any prey. Anyone who has had a pet cat will have seen such behavior. Even without these dramatic examples, it is easy to show that most predators become less fussy about their choice of prey if they are hungry or have not hunted for a while. Lorenz summarized these observations by means of a motivational model that actually has quite wide applicability, at least as a memory aid.

His *hydraulic model* works as follows (Figure B6.1). The water level in a tank represents the tendency to engage in some innate activity, such as prey-catching or aggression. As time passes without opportunity to act, water continues to fill the tank. The water flows in more quickly if the animal is more motivated (e.g., hungry). Eventually, the water in the tank causes the spring-loaded valve to release, and the act occurs even without a stimulus. But if there is a stimulus (weight in the pan connected to the outflow valve), the reaction occurs earlier—the better the stimulus (heavier the weight), the sooner the reaction occurs. After the reaction occurs, it then is some time before the water level rises to the point that it can occur again.

Some readers may recognize that this metaphor is another variant of the integrator, introduced in Chapter 3. In formal terms, the growth of the tendency to respond (water level) is

$$V_{N+1} = V_N + M \tag{B1.1}$$

continued

BOX 6.1 *(continued)*

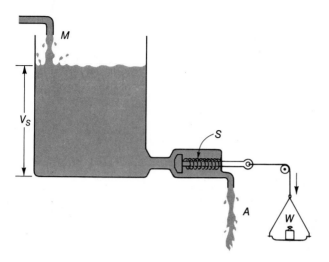

FIGURE B6.1   Lorenz's hydraulic model. With no weight acting against the valve spring (S), a certain water level (V_S) is required before the valve will be pushed out to allow water to flow and an action (A) to occur. However, as weights (W) are added, V_S declines: The weights represent the effect of stimulus appropriateness, indicating that the more appropriate the stimulus, the lower action threshold. Water flows in at a rate (M) that is proportional to the animal's motivational level. Although the "flush-toilet" metaphor can be understood by everyone, a simple difference equation (B1.1) captures the essentials of Lorenz's model without the superfluous metaphor of the tank, the spring, and a fluid, "action-specific energy."

where M is the *motivational level* and V_N is the value of what Lorenz called *action-specific energy.* By picking a starting value for V and a constant value for M, you can see that this equation describes a linear growth in V with time: For example, if $V_0 = 0$ and $M = 1$, successive values of V are 1, 2, 3, and so on. When V_N exceeds some threshold value (V_S, where S denotes that V depends on the quality of the eliciting stimulus), then the activity occurs, and V is reset to zero. If the animal is more motivated (greater value of M), the threshold is reached sooner; in other words, if the stimulus is good, then the threshold is low. The model can be made more accurate by allowing the action not to reset V outright but to cause it to decline at a rate proportional to itself, so that during the performance of the act $V_{N+1} = aV_N$, where a is a positive constant less than 1, with the act shutting off when V reaches a lower threshold (V_E). Other small modifications can generate a rather rich repertoire of behavior from this essentially simple process.

Even in its simplest form, Lorenz's model captures three important properties of many motivated (as opposed to reflexive) actions:

continued

BOX 6.1 *(continued)*

1. Their tendency to become more likely with time

2. The refractory period after they occur (during which they are less
    likely) to occur

3. Their sensitivity to stimuli

For example, eating follows such a pattern: It is increasingly likely to occur as
deprivation time increases (although, to be sure, it does not occur in the complete absence of a stimulus—food); unpalatable foods become more acceptable as hunger increases; and eating is much less likely to occur immediately
after a meal.

The needs of a tick are simple, its responses few, and its information-
processing capacity limited. It functions rather like a heat-seeking, guided missile, using an easily measured cue sufficient to identify its intended host. Butyric
acid is evidently an adequate signal for a meal, just as heat suffices to guide the
Sidewinder missile to a plane or a tank. More complex animals can and do recognize greater numbers of signals, and their niches demand more complex relations between what they can recognize and what they can do. Whether simple or
complex, animals must differentiate among states of nature only to the degree
that the states make a difference, both in terms of consequences of value and in
terms of the animal's ability to respond appropriately.

CONSEQUENCES OF VALUE AND APPROPRIATE RESPONSES   "Consequences of value"
are simply the events termed reinforcers. States of nature that make no difference, now or in the lives of ancestral animals, are usually not differentiated. That
is, they do not produce different states of the animal. The "ability to respond
appropriately" is more difficult to define. Animals are limited in three ways: by
the physical properties to which they are sensitive, by the responses they can
make, and by their ability to integrate stimulus information and use it as a guide
to action.

For example, bees are sensitive to near-ultraviolet light, but humans are
not; hence bees can respond to an aspect of the world that we cannot. Sensitivity
to the appropriate physical property is a necessary but not a sufficient condition
for adaptive response. Similarly, birds can fly, pigs cannot. Some responses are
physically possible for an animal, others are not.

The most interesting behavioral constraints are information-processing
ones. Octopi are reported to have difficulty in discriminating between a figure
and its vertical reflection (e.g., between \ and /). The necessary information is
evidently available at the retinal level (the octopus can discriminate between \
and |), but information-processing limitations prevent the animal from making
appropriate use of the information. The digger wasp is subject to an especially
interesting limitation. A female usually maintains several burrows, each contain-

ing a larva. Hence, she must keep track of the provisioning requirements at several locations—a considerable feat of memory. Yet she updates her information on each burrow only on the first visit each morning. Experiments show that the information is not updated on subsequent provisioning visits, even if circumstances have changed. For example, if between visits some food is removed, the animal does not make up the loss that day. Again, the information is available, but the animal cannot process it appropriately. The functional explanation for this limitation is the absence of such interventions in the life of wasp ancestors. That is, a predator that removes the larva's food is likely also to remove the larva.

The most widespread information-processing limitations derive from the imperfections of memory. Most animals are poor at learning sequences. For example, rats cannot learn to make a perfect sequence of choices that follows a simple rule (e.g., ABAABBAAABBB . . .), to get food. Instead, they make A and B choices in an irregular fashion, so that occasionally the correct sequence occurs and food is delivered. For the rat, the key property that it uses to predict food may be not the sequential arrangement of As and Bs but their relative frequency. The rat is said to generalize across sequences that differ in order but share the same relative frquency. For example, it may behave similarly after experiencing ABAABBAAABBB and BBBAAABBAABA.

To identify patterned sequences accurately, the animal must either learn the rule behind the pattern or have a very good memory. It can either learn that the number of As and Bs keeps doubling, or it must memorize the exact sequence. People need not rely completely on their memory for events, because symbolic representation—language, numbers, and so on—provides a way of encoding rules that nonlinguistic species appear to lack. "Lower" animals appear to encode past events in a relatively unprocessed form, so that accuracy decreases as sequence length increases. Thus, a rat finds it difficult to learn sequences of As and Bs, whereas people can learn them easily if there is an underlying rule. Nevertheless, in situations in which symbolic coding is difficult or impossible, humans' abilities to respond selectively to sequences of events are far from impressive. For example, when similar events occur in temporal alternation, as in changes of "serve" during a tennis match, after several alternations it may be hard to remember which event occurred most recently, that is, "who's serve is it?"

The situations into which animals organize their world are therefore limited by their ability to detect certain kinds of relations and not others. Animals are usually good at detecting the times at which food will occur and at identifying when it occurs with highest frequency. They are typically not good at picking up complex stimulus sequences.

Measurement of Stimulus Control

Stimulus equivalence can be studied with simple stimuli by training an animal with one stimulus and seeing to what extent the response trained to that stimulus will occur when other stimuli are presented. This approach raises two questions: How is control established? How do the physical properties of stimuli affect stimulus equivalence? The answer to the first question was foreshadowed in Chapter 4. A stimulus comes to control behavior when it predicts something about positive or negative reinforcement. For example, suppose we take a hungry pigeon and place it in a Skinner box in which every minute or so a red key light comes on for 8 sec. Now imagine two possible experiments with this basic procedure. In the first, the animal is given brief access to food 60 times per hour, with the occurrence of food and onset of the red light determined by independent, random processes: Both occur 60 times per hour, but they are uncorrelated. In the second experiment, food again occurs 60 times per hour, but it now always occurs at the end of the 8-sec light: Food and light are correlated. In the first experiment, the pigeon will look at the light the first few times it comes on, but soon it will ignore it. The pigeon will spend no more time near the light than near any other feature of the box—although there is no doubt that it will spend more than a chance amount of time near the feeder.

The result of the second experiment is quite different. The bird will attend more and more to the light instead of less and less, and within 30 or 40 food deliveries, the bird is likely to peck at the red key. Once it has developed this behavior, the pecking is maintained indefinitely. (This procedure, which is known as *autoshaping*, was discovered by Paul Brown and Herbert Jenkins in 1968. As we will see, it had a strong influence on theories about the relationship between Pavlovian and instrumental conditioning.) The specific response to be directed at the stimulus will depend on details of the apparatus and the species of animal. For example, rats are notoriously unwilling to peck a key, but they may press or chew an illuminated lever. Most species will learn to approach the signal stimulus when it comes on, and many will also learn something about its fixed duration, approaching the food hopper as the end of the 8 sec approaches. Thus, the rule for the development of stimulus control is that there be a stimulus–reinforcer contingency in the sense described in Chapter 4.

TRANSFER TESTING   The only way to find out which physical properties of a stimulus are important to the behavior it controls is to vary the stimulus and study the effect. This type of testing is termed *transfer testing*, since the idea is to see how much of the original behavior transfers to the control of the stimulus variants during the test. Transfer testing involves two steps. The first is to identify a physical stimulus that controls an identifiable aspect of behavior. Sometimes the control has been established through training, but it may also be a natural relation. The second step is to vary aspects of the stimulus under conditions where any associated change in behavior can be attributed solely to these stimulus variations.

Vocal communication of the American brown-headed cowbird (*Molothrus ater*) provides an example of natural stimulus control. The cowbird is a brood parasite: Like the European cuckoo, it lays its eggs in other bird's nests. This unlovely habit has made it of great interest to biologists from Charles Darwin onward, but for present purposes, the important behavior is the male's vocal repertoire. The male cowbird produces a song that consists of a series of whistlelike sounds that elicits a distinctive "copulatory posture" from a receptive female. This response is rapid and easily recognizable, so it provides an excellent bio-

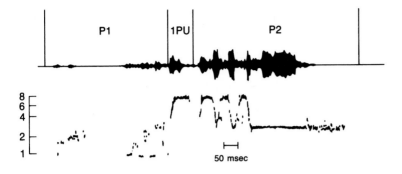

FIGURE 6.1   Typical song of male cowbirds reared in isolation. The upper display shows the changes in amplitude (intensity) through the song. The lower display shows the associated changes in instantaneous frequency (frequency in kilohertz on the vertical axis) (from West, King, Eastzer, & Staddon, 1979, Figure 1).

Song Variant	Percentage Response
S	75
S – IPU	38
P1 + IPU	62
P1	27
P2 + IPU	46
P2	19

FIGURE 6.2   Level of responding to parts of the male cowbird song. S = whole song, IPU = interphrase unit, P1 = phrase 1, P2 = phrase 2. Notice that the effect of the two phrases is almost additive, in the sense that probability (p) (percentage) of response when both are presented is the value expected if each exerts an independent effect: $p(P1 + P2) = 1 - (1 - p1)(1 - p2) = p1 + p2 - p1p2$; S – IPU (= P1 + P2) = $0.38 \cong 0.27 + 0.91 - 0.19 \times 0.27 = 0.41$.

assay to measure the effectiveness of song variants. A picture of a typical song of male cowbirds reared in isolation is shown in Figure 6.1. In one experiment, preliminary tests with tape-recorded songs showed that the song can be divided into three significant units: phrase 1 (P1), phrase 2 (P2), and the interphrase unit (IPU). In subsequent tests, songs in which one or two of the three segments had been deleted were played to females.

Figure 6.2 shows the results, represented as follows: S = complete song; P1, P2 = phrases 1 and 2; IPU = interphrase unit; S – IPU = complete song with IPU deleted (the same as P1 + P2); P1 + IPU = phrase 1 followed by IPU; P2 + IPU = IPU followed by phrase 2. (Data are not shown on the IPU presented in isolation, because it had no effect.) Each of six receptive females heard about 200 songs, equally divided among these variants. The figure shows the percentage of positive responses over the whole group for each song variant. The results can be summarized by two statements:

1. P1 and P2 contribute to song effectiveness in an independent, additive manner. That is, the percentage response to P1 + P2 (S − IPU = P1 + P2) is greater than either P1 or P2 in isolation in approximately the amount implied by independent effects.

2. Addition of the IPU approximately doubles the effectiveness of a song variant (compare P1 + IPU with P1, P2 + IPU with P2). That is, it appears to interact in a multiplicative fashion.

This example illustrates the plan of attack when attempting to measure stimulus control. First, you need some idea of the general features of the physical stimulus that are likely to be important. (In the cowbird case, preliminary work showed that the amplitude of the signal was less important than changes in its frequency over time [frequency modulation]). Then these critical features are varied, either by selective omission (as in the cowbird) or by graded variation, as in generalization testing, which is discussed shortly.

In either case, the spacing and frequency of tests must be chosen with care, so that the response does not change for reasons unrelated to the stimulus. These confounding effects are principally habituation for naturally occurring stimulus–response relations (as in the cowbird example) and reconditioning or extinction for relations established through differential reinforcement. Habituation is the eventual weakening of a response following repeated elicitation (cf. Chapter 3). Female cowbirds habituate during repeated song playbacks unless the playbacks are relatively infrequent, as they were in this experiment. *Reconditioning,* the establishment of control by a test stimulus that would otherwise be ineffective, can occur if reinforcement continues to occur during tests for stimulus control. Conversely, the response may become *extinct (EXT)* if reinforcements are omitted during the test.

If the critical stimulus features have been correctly identified, the results of the tests should lend themselves to a simple description of the sort just offered for the cowbird song. If no simple pattern can be discerned, then it may be either that no simple pattern exists or that we have failed to define the essential stimulus features.

Testing for Stimulus Generalization

Cowbirds need no training either to make or to respond to calls of the type shown in Figure 6.1. Indeed, one result of this experiment was to show that isolated male cowbirds have more effective songs than males that live normally, in the company of their fellows. Every animal species shows examples of stereotyped, innate relations of this sort. For many, these reactions, together with primitive orienting mechanisms of the type described in Chapters 2 and 3, constitute the animal's entire behavioral repertoire. However, in mammals, birds, and a few other species, much behavior consists of reactions acquired to relatively arbitrary stimuli.

A simple procedure for studying learned stimulus control of this type is as follows (Guttman & Kalish, 1956). A hungry pigeon is first trained to peck a key for food reinforcement. The food is delivered on a variable-interval schedule of intermediate value (e.g., VI 60 sec). The response key is illuminated with the stimulus of interest (termed $S+$ or S^D for *discriminative stimulus*). In early studies, $S+$ was usually chosen to be physically simple (i.e., light of a single wavelength, a single vertical line, a tone). More recently, complex stimuli such as pictures of scenes or of animals and people have begun to receive more attention.

After the pigeon has learned to peck $S+$ for food, variants on the test stimulus are presented for relatively brief periods. For example, if five variants are tried, each may be presented for 1 min in an irregular order, for a total of perhaps 60 presentations. Thus, each variant is presented repeatedly, so that any slow changes in the tendency to respond are shared equally by all. No reinforcement occurs during a *generalization test* of this sort, so as to avoid reconditioning. Extinction is prevented, or at least mitigated, by the VI training. On a VI schedule, long periods without food are common; hence, the animals persist in responding even when food is omitted entirely. The *extinction curve* is quite gradual, and over a 60-min period, responding generally shows little decline. Thus, the average rate of response in the presence of each test stimulus is likely to be an accurate measure of its tendency to facilitate or suppress responding relative to S+.

Figure 6.3 shows the unaveraged results of a typical generalization test. The horizontal axis shows the physical values (here intensities of a monochromatic green light) of eight test stimuli. The vertical axis shows the average number of pecks/minute made by an individual pigeon to each of these values during a single 60-min test session. The resulting symmetrical curve is typical: Responding is highest to $S+$, and it decreases more or less smoothly as the physical value of the test stimulus departs from the $S+$ value. Because the value is highest at $S+$ and declines on either side, the gradient in Figure 6.3 is termed an *excitatory, or decremental, generalization gradient.*

A great many physical stimulus properties—wavelength of light, line tilt, roughness, spatial frequency, and others—have been tested in this fashion. The almost universal result—using pigeons, rats, monkeys, octopi, goldfish, people, and many other species—is the kind of gradient shown in Figure 6.3: Responding is maximal at (or near) $S+$, and it falls off systematically with the physical stimulus difference between $S+$ and the test stimulus.

In some respects this result is unsurprising: Why shouldn't behavior bear an orderly relation to the properties of the physical world? Often the physiological basis for the relation seems obvious. For example, tonal frequencies are spatially represented on the basilar membrane of the cochlea; many neural transducers, such as those for pressure and light, fire at a rate directly related to physical stimulus intensity. In other cases, the result is puzzling. For instance, color perception depends on central integration of information from three or four types of photoreceptors, each with a different wavelength-absorption peak. As a continuum, wavelength finds no simple representation in such a system. Yet wavelength generalization gradients are among the most orderly, and show no sudden

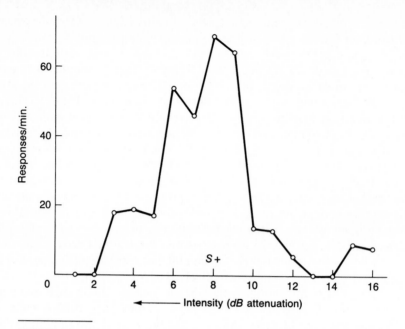

FIGURE 6.3   Key-peck rate of an individual pigeon as a function of the intensity of a green key light during a single, 60-min generalization test (Staddon, unpublished data).

slope changes, even at color boundaries. From these kinds of experiments, it appears that the form of generalization gradient represents a cognitive property— a judgment of stimulus similarity—rather than a purely sensory or physiological property.

Compounding of Stimulus Elements

We have described two kinds of stimulus control: by a stimulus *element* (the cowbird example) and by a stimulus *dimension* (the generalization examples). These two kinds of control are reflected by different test operations. When a stimulus dimension is varied but the stimulus element is always present, then we are measuring dimensional control by a stimulus. When the stimulus element is either present or removed entirely, we are measuring control by the stimulus element.

Elements and dimensions of stimuli can be defined by simple physical properties such as wavelength. For example, rather than splitting up the cowbird song into elements, we could have considered the "proportion of total song" as a stimulus dimension. This dimension presents a perfectly objective property, but it is not very useful, because as we have seen, the elements (P1, P2, IPU) vary greatly in their effectiveness as elicitors of the response, and two of them combine additively, whereas the other seems to act multiplicatively. In other words, in a generalization test, the aspects we choose to vary cannot be arbitrary; we must judge the correctness of our choice by the comprehensibility of the results. The justification for labeling P1, P2, and IPU as elements in the cowbird song is that they do behave in sensible ways when compounded.

Subjective experience suggests two ways that stimulus elements can combine, and these seem to correspond to different algebraic rules (see Garner, 1962; Lockhead, 1970). For example, a visual stimulus element such as a triangle must have some color, as neither form nor color can exist in isolation. People and animals tend to perceive colored objects as wholes; they don't normally attend to form and color separately. Dimensions treated in this manner are described as *integral,* and they roughly follow a multiplicative rule. That is, a value of zero on either dimension, and the stimulus has no effect—in other words, a form without color cannot be seen. On the other hand, it is easy to imagine visual displays whose elements are not so intimately related: For example, a pigeon might attend to the stars or to the stripes in a picture of the American flag. Stimulus elements of this sort are termed *separable,* and they follow an additive rule. In the cowbird experiment, P1 and P2 appear to be perceived by the birds as separable elements, since their effects were independent. But, the IPU seems more like an integral element, since it had little effect on its own but greatly enhanced the effect of other elements with which it was compounded.

Animals must behave with respect to objects or states of the world, not to stimulus dimensions or elements. Therefore, one use for generalization testing is to shed some light on the way that animals classify objects as guides to behavior. Since objects differ not in one dimension but in many, the interactions among dimensions have first claim on our attention. Unfortunately, rather little is known about multidimensional stimulus generalization. One reason is technical: It is no simple matter to create and manipulate at will multidimensional stimuli. There are also practical difficulties. For instance, to map out a single dimension, perhaps 10 stimuli are sufficient; but to map out two dimensions with the same 10 × 10 resolution, 100 stimuli are required. Obtaining an adequate sample of behavior in the presence of each of 100 stimuli, while at the same time ensuring no changes in behavior due to extraneous causes such as extinction, is difficult indeed. When three dimensions are involved, it is impossible.

A third reason is that once invented, techniques take on a life of their own. We know that rewarding an animal for pecking a key illuminated with a monochromatic light will cause it to attend to wavelength. Why not look at the effects of reinforcing two or more wavelengths, of alternating reinforced and unreinforced stimuli of different wavelengths, of successive versus simultaneous comparison, and so on? All these variations have been tried, usually with orderly results not devoid of interest (we discuss such variations further in Chapter 7). But, the relation between these neat manipulations and the animal's knowledge about its world, its *umwelt,* is not always clear. Therefore, generalization testing is often used to study the effects of reinforcement rather than stimulus equivalence.

Stimulus Control and Reinforcement: Attention

Although unidimensional gradients (e.g., Figure 6.3) leave us rather far from understanding cognition, they are useful tools for the study of reinforcement mechanisms. The steepness of the gradient is a measure of the degree to which the animal's natural tendency to vary—to respond indiscriminately—is restrained by the reinforcement schedule. Gradient steepness is also affected by the availability of other sources of control.

For example, Hearst, Koresko, and Poppen (1964) trained pigeons to peck a key on which a vertical line is projected. They then looked at the effect of overall rate of reinforcement on the steepness of the gradient for line tilt. Different groups of birds were trained with different VI schedules. The researchers found that the higher the rate of reinforcement, the steeper the gradient (Figure 6.4). Others have found similar results. Evidently, the better the correlation between a stimulus and food, the tighter the control of a given stimulus dimension over operant behavior, that is the greater the restraint of the animal's natural tendency to vary. The critical factor is the predictive nature of the stimulus. In general, the stimulus or stimulus element that best predicts reinforcement is the one with the sharpest control.

A related effect is that control by a highly predictive stimulus element tends to weaken control by a less predictive element. Thus in another condition of the Hearst experiment, pigeons were trained to peck a vertical line, although this time the schedule required spaced responding. That is, food was delivered only for pecks separated by more than 6 sec. This procedure is termed a differential reinforcement for low rates (DRL) or a *spaced-responding schedule*. On a DRL schedule, postresponse time is the best predictor of food delivery. The stimulus on the response key guides the actual peck, but it has no other significance. On a VI schedule, postresponse time is only weakly predictive of food (food is somewhat more likely following longer postresponse times, but the difference is small when animals respond as fast as pigeons typically do in these experiments). As this difference between VI and DRL may lead you to expect, a generalization test showed that control by the line-tilt dimension was much worse for spaced-responding animals than for VI animals (Figure 6.5).

These results lead naturally to the concept of *attention* and to the generalization that animals attend preferentially to stimuli and stimulus properties that best predict the availability of reinforcement. The steepness of the generalization gradient provides an objective measure of attention in this sense: A steep gradient indicates that the animal is attending to a given dimension; a flat gradient indicates that it is not. However, attention may be more subtle and complex than this simple view suggests.

Matching-to-Sample Tasks and Selective Attention

In the preceding examples we defined attention as control of behavior by a stimulus. When only a fragment of a stimulus array exerts control over behavior (e.g., fragments of the cowbird song), attention is considered to be selective. However, what happens when several elements of a stimulus array equally pre-

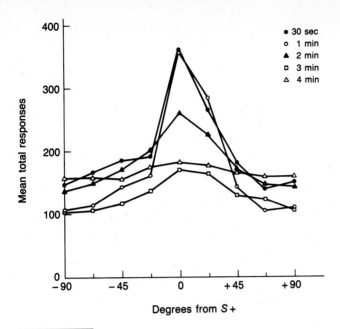

FIGURE 6.4   The total number of key pecks made by five groups of pigeons, each trained with a different VI schedule (ranging from VI 30 sec to VI 4 min) to a line-tilt stimulus during a generalization test. $S+$ was a vertical line (0°) (from Hearst, Koresko, & Poppen, 1964).

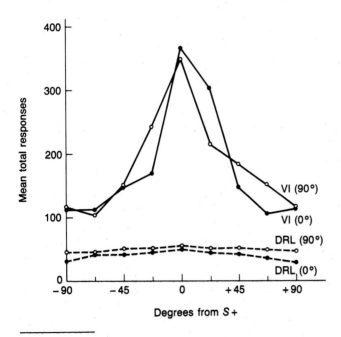

FIGURE 6.5   Generalization gradients of line tilt following VI or spaced-responding training. Two groups are in each condition: one trained with a vertical line as $S+$, one with a horizontal line as $S+$ (from Hearst, Koresko, & Poppen, 1964).

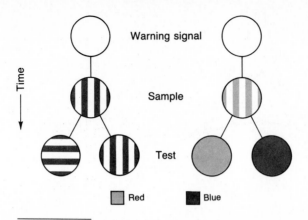

FIGURE 6.6   Two typical matching-to-sample sequences as used by Maki and Leith (1973). An element trial is depicted on the left. A compound trial appears on the right. Warning signals and samples appear on the center key. The two test stimuli appear on the side keys.

dict reinforcement? To address this question, Maki and Leith (1973) used a *matching-to-sample procedure.* They trained pigeons to peck on white warning keys. Immediately after pecking the warning key, it turned off and was followed by a sample key. The stimulus presented on the sample key typically included black-and-white vertical stripes or red-and-white vertical stripes. No responses were required on the sample key, and after a brief delay it was turned off and was followed by the illumination of two test keys. On one test key the stimulus matched the sample key, and a peck on it was considered correct (and produced food reward); the other key did not match, and a peck on it was considered incorrect (Figure 6.6).

   Two types of trials were included in Maki and Leith's matching tests. On one type (element trial), the sample stimulus and the matching stimulus contained identical elements. For example, if the sample stimulus contained black-and-white vertical stripes, one of the matching stimuli was identical and also contained black-and-white vertical stripes. For the other type of trial (compound trial), the matching stimulus contained only one element of the compound sample stimulus illustrated in Figure 6.6. That is, the matching stimulus for the compound trials could contain either a line or a color element.

   How well do animals perform on matching-to-sample tasks? What does their performance tell us about attention? The answer to the first question is illustrated in Figure 6.7, which shows how performance on both types of trials (element and compound) changed as sample duration increased. Clearly animals do better on element trials in which they are only required to process information on a single element. On both types of trials, performance improves as the animals are given more time to process the sample, but compound-trial performance is never quite as good as element performance. Of interest, however, is why they do as well as they do on compound trials. If the animals could attend to

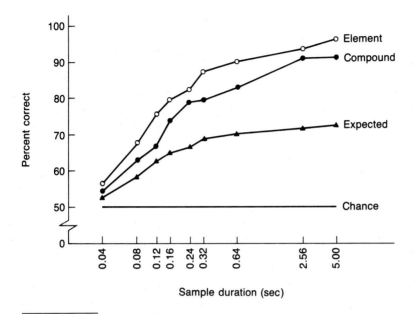

FIGURE 6.7   Matching-to-sample performance for two birds. The open and closed circles represent performance on element and on compound trials, respectively. The diamonds represent performance that would result from a hypothetical bird attending to only one element per compound trial. The resulting curve is a combined average of element performance (perfectly attending to the to-be-tested dimension) and chance (perfectly ignoring the to-be-tested dimension) (data taken from Maki & Leith, 1973).

only one element of the compound sample on each trial, their performance would fall on the line that represented expected performance. That is, it would fall halfway between chance performance (50 percent) and element performance: On one-half of the trials, the animals would be attending to the correct element; on the other half, their performance would be dictated by chance. Given that the animals perform better than expected if they were attending to a single element, they must be attending to both. That is, their attention is shared between the elements of the compound sample. Performance is not as good on the compound trials because the elements seem to compete for processing (or remembering) in a system with limited capacity. The processing capacity seems to be maximally taxed during short presentations of complex compound samples.

The idea that there is a limit to the amount of information that can be processed and that this information competes for processing (or memory) is referred to as the *inverse hypothesis*. According to this hypothesis, the amount of processing a stimulus element receives is inversely related to, or shared among, the number of predictive elements in a compound display. Baldly stated, the inverse hypothesis is a fact of physics—the bandwidth of any information channel (such as a pigeon or a person) is always limited. The real issue is whether or not the tasks being studied are in fact pushing against that limit. Maki and Leith's data show that even simple tasks can challenge pigeons' information processing capacity.

Stimulus Representation and Memory

We are clearly much farther along in understanding the ways in which physical stimulus elements come to control the behavior of animals than in understanding how they put these elements together internally to represent their world. Yet, intuition suggests that underlying the flexibility of behavior in response to shifting contingencies of reinforcement must be some invariant structure that corresponds to the unchanging aspects of the physical world. Time, three-dimensional space, and the properties of solid objects in relation to one another are all independent of the animal. Although by careful manipulation of rewards and punishments we can cause animals to perform different activities with respect to different physical features, the features themselves are not changed. In a properly designed organism, there should be some representation of these invariances that remains constant, even as behavior shifts in response to contingencies of reinforcement. Some promising beginnings have been made toward *stimulus representation*, which measures how people represent objects. Some of these ideas have implications for animal studies.

COGNITIVE MAPS   Perhaps we have learned the most about stimulus representation from studies of how animals orient themselves, find their way about their natural environments. For example, there is ample proof that rats usually find their way about by means of a map that represents the distances and directions of objects in relation to each other. This idea, once heretical in the behavioristic world, was first proposed by the famous psychologist Edward C. Tolman (Box 6.2). A *cognitive map* implies that the function of specific stimuli is not so much to elicit approach or avoidance directly but rather to tell the animal where its map is in relation to the visible world, to anchor the map to landmarks. We saw a primitive example of such mapping in the light-compass reaction discussed in Chapter 2. Many animals, such as bees, use this reaction (modulated by an internal clock) to define north–south by the position of the sun. Thus given a single landmark or a cue for latitude, bees can then locate themselves perfectly.

The idea of a map is not well-developed in psychology, although most people accept that rats, for example, have such things. We first illustrate the idea by describing some experimental results. We then try to infer what properties cognitive maps must have to be consistent with the data.

EXPERIMENTS WITH COGNITIVE MAPS   The eight-arm radial maze illustrated in Figure 6.8 was first studied extensively by David Olton and has turned out to be an ideal arena for demonstrating the properties of spatial memory in rats. The standard experiment involves an open, eight-arm maze with food concealed in a small cup at the end of each arm. Hungry rats are placed in the center of the

B   O   X

6.2

Edward Chace Tolman (1886–1959)

Edward C. Tolman was one of a handful of major learning theorists during the heyday of experimental psychology 50 years ago. (Others were Clark Hull, Edwin Guthrie, and a little later, B. F. Skinner.) Tolman was born into a wealthy, Quaker family in Newton, Massachusetts. He did his undergraduate work at MIT in science and mathematics, and he then transferred to Harvard after acquiring an interest in psychology. He received his doctorate there in 1915. He did no work with animals at Harvard nor at Northwestern, where he taught for three years before going to the University of California, Berkeley. He gave a comparative psychology course at Berkeley and remained there for the rest of his career. Tolman soon became skeptical of the simplistic, Watsonian view that all learning involves nothing but the association of muscular movements to specific physical stimuli. His rats were smarter than that. For example, given a choice of routes to reach a goal (some long, some short, some dangerous), the rats always made the best compromise, eventually picking the shortest, least-painful route. The route they picked was not easily traceable to any property such as recency or frequency of previous choices.

Tolman's mature views are summarized in his book *Purposive behavior in animals and men.* He called his approach *purposive behaviorism,* and he contrasted it with the simplistic views of John B. Watson and Edward L. Thorndike. Tolman made a late attempt to formalize his views in 1959, just before the potentialities of digital computers became widely known. His account is striking in that it outlines what would now be called an *information-processing model:* Tolman was the first cognitive psychologist, in the modern sense.

In the 1930s, 40s, and 50s, Tolman's views played second-fiddle first to those of Clark Hull and then to Skinnerian theories. Although the recent growth of cognitive psychology, of both animals and people, and the revival of interest in spatial learning, promises to bring Tolman to prominence as the source of many modern ideas.

maze and are allowed to choose freely among the arms, until either all eight arms have been visited or a fixed amount of time has elapsed. One trial of this type is typically given each day. After a small number of daily trials, rats soon learn to visit each arm without repetition. That is, they only visit an arm once, and they leave after they have eaten the piece of food in the cup.

Experiments have shown that this efficient performance typically depends on the animal's *memory* for arms that it has previously visited rather than on any kind of strategy (e.g., as "always turn right when leaving an arm" or on an

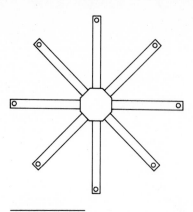

FIGURE 6.8   Eight-arm radial maze.

odor trail). In fact, each rat may develop a completely different pattern of moving from arm to arm. How do rats perform this activity so efficiently?

In the laboratory, experiments have shown that visual cues outside the maze act as landmarks. Because rats learn quickly to pick up each piece of food without revisiting an arm, they must know where each arm is in relation to their current position. They seem to form a map of the maze using *extramaze cues* as landmarks. Thus, if after picking up four pieces of food (i.e., visiting four arms), a rat is covered up in the center of the maze and the arms are rotated, it will revisit some arms. However, these revisited arms will be in the spatial position (in relation to the rest of the room) of arms the animal had *not* visited before the maze was rotated. This result shows that the rats identify the arms by their spatial position, not via odor marks. Well-trained rats do not explore the maze in a rote way; rather, they "know" the spatial location of each arm and can remember the locations they have not visited.

A recent innovation makes these points dramatically. Richard Morris placed rats in a circular pool of milky water. Somewhere in the pool, concealed from view, is a small platform a centimeter or so beneath the surface. Rats swim until they find the platform, which allows them to rest with their heads above water. In a series of ingenious experiments, Morris has tested normal and brain-operated rats to study their ability to find the platform and remember its position. Normal rats learn to find the platform after only a few trials. They obviously rely on cues outside the pool, since they cannot even in principle use response strategies or odor.

A clever radial-maze experiment shows that extramaze cues act to fix the map; they are not push-pull stimuli that directly control approach or avoidance. Suzuki, Augerinos, and Black (1980) used a radial maze that was covered with a black cloth dome onto which stimuli could be fixed. In a series of tests, this stimulus array was altered in various ways to see if individual stimulus elements were guiding the animals. The results showed that the animals were using the whole array to orient their map with respect to the maze. Small changes in the array produced no effect; large changes caused the animals to behave as if in a new maze.

Other evidence for the existence of maps that are independent of cues comes from the spatial learning of rats blinded either before or after learning a radial maze. If the rat is allowed to learn the maze and is then deprived of vision, its relearns the maze almost immediately—to the point that such an animal is almost indistinguishable from a normal rat. But if the rat must learn the maze initially without the aid of vision, learning is slow and imperfect. Evidently, it is a great deal easier to learn to identify a familiar landmark through another modality (such as hearing or smell), which is all that the maze-experienced blind rats need to reorient their preexisting map, than to build up the entire map from scratch without the aid of vision.

This sort of cognitive map is familiar to humans as well. For example, people quickly learn to get about efficiently in new environments and can often plan shortcuts through unseen territory. There are also times when you become aware that your behavior depends on a map. That is, most people have had the experience of being disoriented after emerging from an unfamiliar subway station or department store exit and then feeling the world "rotate into position" as the brain orients its map by means of familiar landmarks.

This phrase is not just metaphorical. If you think about it a bit, you will see that navigating by a (two-dimensional) map requires just two reference points: one is necessarily the observer, the other is simply any landmark. Once the observer knows where he or she is in relation to a landmark, he or she also knows where the map is in relation to the world and knows which direction to take to reach any goal. Therefore, when you enter a familiar environment from a novel position, the necessary "mental operation" is indeed a rotation of the mental map until any landmark in the map is in registry with its real-world counterpart.

These mentalistic ideas would normally elicit scorn from dyed-in-the-wool behaviorists, but they have become more respectable since psychologist Roger Shepard (e.g., Shepard & Metzler, 1971) found a way to measure "mental rotation" in an objective manner. Shepard showed human subjects an asymmetrical target object (a set of cubes arranged to form a "nonsense figure," although a picture of a left hand would have done as well). They were then shown pictures either of the same object rotated by some amount (i.e., the hand turned through some angle) or of its mirror image (a right hand). The subjects were told to respond one way if the object was the same, another way if it was different. Shepard's research found that the time taken to respond correctly to the "same," rotated, object was proportional to the angular difference in orientation between it and the reference object. Evidently, the subjects had to rotate (at a constant speed!) their mental image of the reference object to bring it into registry with the projected figure before they could decide whether or not the two were the same. In this case, the images were of three-dimensional objects projected on a screen, but the alignment of cognitive maps by means of landmarks is probably a similar process.

SPATIAL REPRESENTATION   The idea that behavior can be understood in terms of *spatial representation* applies to more than just the representation of physical space. The world of simple animals, such as that of the tick referred to earlier, lends itself easily to a spatial description. The animal is sensitive to relatively simple physical properties such as temperature, illumination, altitude above ground (although this aspect may be computed indirectly from illumination, temperature gradient, crawling time, etc.), humidity, time of day, and various chemical stimuli. The physical values of each of these aspects together define a multidimensional space. Therefore, any given environment at a given time would represent a point in such a space. The representation itself immediately solves the problem of recognition: Since the space is defined by just those physical dimensions that are important to the animal, the location of the representative point constitutes "recognition" of a situation. The beast comes equipped by its heredity with a set of preferences (preferred positions) in this "world space." By moving around, the animal changes its location not only in the real world but also in its world space. Simple orientation mechanisms of the type discussed in earlier chapters can then be used to hill-climb up the value gradient. In this way, the tick finds the right height, temperature, humidity, and other factors its genes tell it will promote survival.

Spatial representation is not just a theoretical trick. It is an efficient way to represent environmental features that are vital to ticks (or any other animal) in a form that allows the animal to compare any set of dimensional values and make a decision about where to go next. No matter what environment the tick, say, finds itself in, it is never at a loss to evaluate it or decide what to do about it. Spatial representations are efficient, but that doesn't necessarily mean evolution has built organisms to use them. Nevertheless, some form of internal representation is probably our best current guess about how animals, including people, represent their worlds.

TEMPORAL CONTROL AND MEMORY

Learning implies memory; yet the behaviorists studied learning for many years without using the word "memory" at all. They were right to be cautious, because the word, drawn as it is from folk psychology, has no precise meaning. In fact, it has too many meanings. *Memory* is probably the most protean term in psychology, having many technical and nontechnical meanings. Psychology has a long history of "definitive dichotomies," which at the time were the last word in classifying types of memory. Most of you have heard of at least a few of the following: long- and short-term memory, working and reference memory, episodic and semantic memory, primary and secondary memory, procedural and declarative memory (or knowledge), and probably several others we have forgotten. Not all these divisions are useless, but their very number shows that memory is not fully understood.

In the discussion of unobservability in Chapter 5, we defined memory simply as a change of state caused by a stimulus: Memory is involved if how the animal behaves at time t_2 depends on whether event A or event B occurred at previous time t_1. Of course, breaking a leg is a change of state in this sense, so as with learning, we must restrict our definition to effects that are specific and to some extent reversible. The difference in behavior at t_2 should bear some sensible, informational relation to the difference between prior events A and B. In addition, we should be able to change the effect through additional experience. Nevertheless, the advantage of a formal definition of memory is that it commits us to no specific theoretical position, and it draws attention to the memorylike (although not traditionally considered memorial) properties of habituation, dishabituation, spontaneous recovery, and especially temporal control.

Much is known about *temporal control*, which is the ability of many animals to learn about time intervals. The first part of this section reviews the properties of temporal control and derives some general principles about the discrimination of recency. We then show that these principles also apply to more traditional situations used to study memory in animals, such as successive discrimination reversal and delayed matching-to-sample tasks. We conclude by showing how the idea of internal representation can be combined with the principles of memory to explain many of the properties of spatial learning in the radial maze.

Temporal Control

Animals readily detect periodicities: If a pigeon is regularly rewarded with food for the first key peck T sec after eating (i.e., a fixed-interval, T-sec schedule: FI T), it will usually not begin to peck again until perhaps half the time has elapsed. That is, the pigeon's *postreinforcement pause*, or *waiting time*, stabilizes at close to $T/2$ sec (see experiments reviewed in Richelle & Lejeune, 1980). The animal is able to adjust waiting times by using food delivery as a *time marker*. Control of behavior by a past event is termed temporal control, to distinguish it from control of behavior by a currently present stimulus, which might be termed *synchronous control*.

A simple, if not totally accurate, way to describe temporal control by food reward is to say that the food "resets" the animal's "internal clock," and that pecking is initiated when the clock reaches a value that is an approximately constant proportion of T. Theoretical and experimental work in recent years by John Gibbon, Russell Church, and their associates has pursued this internal-clock metaphor quite successfully. They show how it can help us understand not just how animals tell time but also the effects of drugs and reinforcement mechanisms on them.

Many features of temporal control are consistent with the clock idea. For example, as in a real clock, the *error* in timing is proportional to the interval to be timed: A clock that is one minute fast after one hour will be six minutes fast after six hours. If instead of a constant error, the clock is simply variable from day to day, then the variation in its error over an actual time T is proportional to T and is termed the *scalar timing property* (Gibbon, 1977). The *reset property* of the time marker can be demonstrated by omitting it or replacing it with some-

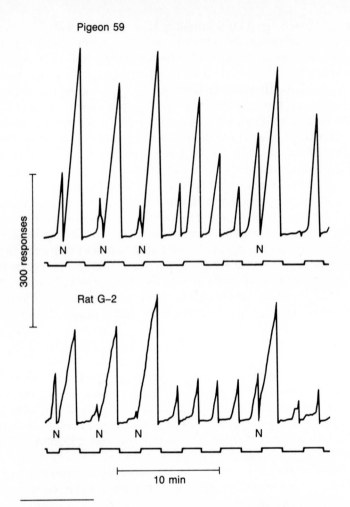

FIGURE 6.9   Sample cumulative records of stable performance in an experiment in which animals were trained on a fixed-interval, 2-min schedule. At the end of intervals marked "N," food delivery was omitted, and a brief, 3-sec stimulus was presented in its stead. The record at the top is from a pigeon; the record at the bottom from a rat. The recorder pen was reset at the end of every interval (from Staddon & Innis, 1969, Figure 3).

thing that is not treated as a time marker. For example, John Staddon and Nancy Innis (1969) trained pigeons and rats on a fixed-interval, 2-min schedule and then shifted to a procedure in which food was delivered at the end of only 50 percent of the intervals. The change this type of scheduling produces is shown in Figure 6.9. Intervals ending with "no food" (a brief blackout of the same duration as food delivery) are indicated by "N" in the figure. The animals show the usual pause after receiving food, but if food is omitted at the end of a fixed interval, then the animals continue to respond until the next food delivery. Thus in the absence of a "reset" (food), responding continues. With continued experience of reinforcement omission, some animals learn to pause a bit after the nonfood stimulus, but for most, the "run-through" effect persists indefinitely. This absence of pausing after a nonfood stimulus is known as the *reinforcement-omission effect*. The effectiveness of food versus nonfood as a time marker has implications for memory that we discuss shortly.

Synchronous discriminative stimuli seem to tell the animal what to expect at a certain time, rather than affecting its estimate of time directly. For example, Russell Church (1978) trained rats on a procedure in which 30-sec and 60-sec fixed intervals were intermixed, each with its own distinctive (synchronous) discriminative stimulus (this schedule is known as a multiple FI FI schedule). The animals soon developed pauses appropriate to the signalled interval. Then in test sessions, the stimulus in the 30-sec interval was changed abruptly to the 60-sec stimulus. The change could occur 6, 12, 16, 24, or 30 sec after food. The rats behaved as if they had a single, postfood clock, and they used the stimulus to scale their rate of responding to the clock setting. Thus an animal's rate of responding t sec after food in the presence of the 60-sec stimulus was the same, whether the stimulus appeared just after the food (i.e., simple FI 60) or at some later time. Rats always seem to know what time it is; the synchronous stimulus simply tell them whether or not to expect food at that time.

The simplest possible clock model has two variables: a clock rate (how fast the clock runs) and a clock setting (the remembered time, position of the "hands," at which the animal should begin to respond). The two-variable model is the essence of the Gibbon–Church timing hypothesis. Experiments (e.g., Roberts, 1981; see also Dews, 1962) have shown that the clock is under (synchronous) stimulus control, since animals can learn to disregard variable-length "timeout" stimuli in between a time marker and food, timing only in the presence of the nontimeout stimulus, which is of fixed duration. For example, the effects of drugs on the two variables can be distinguished by the speed of their effects: A drug that affects clock rate has an immediate effect on waiting time, because the remembered setting is reached sooner or later than before. But, an effect on the (memory for) the setting itself shows up as increased variability in timing or as a delayed effect as the waiting time progressively increases or decreases to a new value.

The clock idea is a convenient simplification, although in a moment we show that the reset property is far from absolute: Under many conditions, events that precede the resetting stimulus can affect behavior. These interference effects and the conditions under which they occur show that temporal control reflects the same process studied in more conventional memory experiments, thus temporal control and memory are different aspects of the same process.

Excitatory and Inhibitory Temporal Control

We know that (synchronous) discriminative stimuli can either enhance or suppress an instrumental response (inhibitory and excitatory control are discussed in detail in Chapter 7). Temporal control can also be excitatory or inhibitory, depending on circumstances. All the examples discussed thus far are inhibitory,

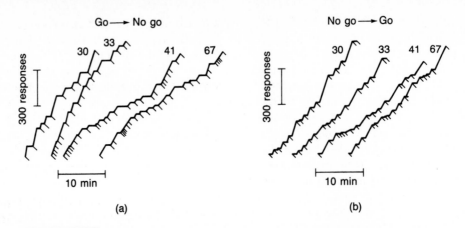

FIGURE 6.10   Cumulative records of four pigeons trained **(a)** either on a
procedure that reinforces a high rate after food (go → no-go schedule) or **(b)** a
low rate after food (no-go → go schedule). Diagonal "blips" indicate food deliveries
(from Staddon, 1972, Figure 2).

since the instrumental response is suppressed immediately after the time marker.
As with inhibitory synchronous control, suppression of the instrumental response is usually associated with facilitation of competing responses. These responses are called *interim activities:* The postfood "pause" is a pause only in
instrumental responding; other activities such as pacing in pigeons and drinking
or wheel-running in rats occur at their highest rates during the pause.

   Animals can learn to respond rapidly after a time marker just as easily as
they can learn to pause. Excitatory temporal control is as easy as inhibitory control. For example, in one experiment (Staddon, 1972) pigeons were trained on a
VI 60-sec schedule in which the response required for food was either pecking or
refraining from pecking for at least 10 sec. The signal telling the animals which
response was required was the postfood time: At postfood times of less than 60
sec, pecking was required to obtain food; at longer postfood times, refraining
from pecking was required. Cumulative records in Figure 6.10a show stable performance on a temporal "go → no-go" schedule of this sort. The animals show a
sustained period of high rate responding for about 60 sec after each food delivery (indicated by the blips on the record) followed by no responding until the
next food delivery. The records in Figure 6.10b show the FI-like behavior
produced by the "no-go → go" schedule, in which no pecking is required at postfood times of less than 60 sec, with pecking required at longer time intervals.

   Like synchronous control, temporal control shows generalization decrement: Variation in an inhibitory temporal stimulus produces increases in subsequent responding; variation in an excitatory stimulus produces decreases. Because the effect of a temporal stimulus is delayed, discrimination is not as fine
as in the synchronous case. Larger changes in the stimulus must be made to
produce comparable percentage changes in the response rate.

It is easy to show the effects of variation in the stimulus complex associated with food delivery on FI pausing. For example, in one study (Kello, 1974) with pigeons, fixed intervals ended unpredictably with one of three events: food paired with 3-sec offsets of the key and house lights and 3-sec illumination of the feeder light (F), all these events without feeder operation (NF), or offset of the lights alone (N). The pigeons paused longest after F, least after N, and an intermediate amount after NF, and response rates over the interval following each kind of event were in the reverse order. Comparable experiments with the excitatory procedure have shown the opposite result: slowest responding after N, highest after F (Figure 6.10a). In both cases, the effect of the test time marker is of the same sort as the training time marker, although weaker. The difference provides a measure of similarity.

These experiments are examples of control by stimulus elements (cf. the previous section "Compounding of Stimulus Elements" and the Chapter 5 sections on "The Rescorla–Wagner Model for Conditioning"). It is trickier to demonstrate temporal control by a stimulus dimension, simply because it is harder to establish temporal control by "neutral" stimuli such as colored lights and line tilts (we'll see why in a moment). Nevertheless, when good stimulus control is established, gradients of the standard sort are obtained. If the time marker is inhibitory, then instances of responding that follow the stimuli increase as the test stimulus varies from $S+$; if the time marker is excitatory, then instances of responding that follow the stimulus decrease as the test stimulus varies from $S+$.

Conditions for Temporal Control

Under what conditions will a stimulus such as food come to serve as a time marker? The general answer is the same for both temporal and synchronous stimuli: when it predicts something about the time to reward. A temporal stimulus acquires control when it reliably signals. Indeed, any detectable, time-related variation in the probability of reward. For instance, it acquires control when it reliably signals a period free of food delivery (e.g., the early part of each interval on a fixed-interval schedule) or a period when the conditions of reinforcement are different from those of earlier or later periods (e.g., the go → no-go schedule).

The signaled period need not immediately follow the time marker. Consider a modified, fixed-interval, 6-min schedule in which food is sometimes available (in perhaps 50 percent of intervals on a random basis) at a postfood time of 1 min, as well as always available after a postfood time 6 min (Figure 6.11). (We call this schedule a modified FI schedule, but it could also be called a variable-interval schedule, since it has two different interfood intervals.) Figure 6.11a shows the probability of food delivery at two postfood times: one vertical line of height 0.5 at postfood time $T/6$, the other of height 1.0 at time T. Figure 6.11b shows the average response rate as a function of postfood time for a pigeon that has adapted to this procedure. It shows a high rate just after food (roughly corresponding to the first probability "spike"), followed by a period of low response rate, ending with a high response rate toward the end of the T-sec interval.

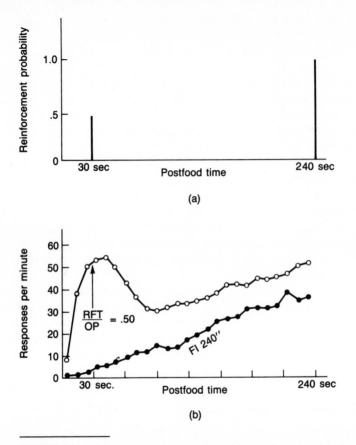

FIGURE 6.11   **(a)** Food reinforcement probabilities as a function of postreinforcement time on a modified fixed-interval schedule. Reinforcement occurs with a .5 probability 30 sec after food and with a 1.0 probability 240 sec after food. **(b)** Average rate of key pecking as a function of time since food for a pigeon trained on this schedule (from Catania & Reynolds, 1968, Figure 19).

Thus, a time marker can initiate a sequence of alternating respond–not respond periods.

If the availability of food is random in time, then at any instant the probability that food will become available for a response is constant—food is no more likely at one postfood time than another. This scenario demonstrates a *random-interval schedule*. With such a schedule, we would not expect, nor do we find, much patterning of responding as a function of postfood time: The average response rate is approximately constant. However, the probability of food does increase as a function of postresponse time on these schedules, since the longer the animal waits, the more likely that food will be delivered. We might expect, therefore, that the probability of response will be low immediately after a response, which is true to some extent, although the effect is somewhat masked by the tendency of pigeons to respond in bursts of or two or three pecks at a time. However, animals on concurrent random-interval schedules (i.e., two response keys with different RI schedules for each) show in their patterns of choice that they are quite sensitive to this property of RI schedules (termed *momentary maximizing* by Hinson & Staddon, 1983; Shimp, 1966, see Chapter 11). Spaced-responding schedules make the temporal requirement explicit, in that they only reinforce responses that are longer than time T. If T is fairly short (less than a minute or so), pigeons and rats adapt by spacing their responses appropriately.

What determines exactly when an animal will begin to respond after a time marker? The functional answer is that it will depend on the accuracy with which the animal can tell time, how sure it can be of the time of food availability, and what other activities are available to it. For example, suppose that in addition to pecking the key for food, the animal has at least one other activity it likes to do. On a fixed-interval schedule, the amount of time available for the other activity is critically determined by the accuracy with which the animal can estimate the interfood interval. If it is quite accurate (most waiting times before pecking are close to the mean), then it can defer key pecking until just before the end of the interval (i.e., to a late setting of his internal clock). Thus the animal will only rarely respond too late, and so it will receive food after a longer wait than necessary. On the other hand, if the animal is inaccurate (waiting times widely scattered about the mean), it cannot safely defer pecking until almost the whole interval has elapsed (i.e., set the mean to a high value). If it were to try to defer pecking, it would often wait too long. Of course, if there is likely to be any variability in the time of food delivery, even animals that can tell time fairly accurately will miss some opportunities for food. The possibility of future variation, plus limitations on the timing mechanism and the low cost of key pecking, all favor rather inaccurate timing, in which the bird typically responds much sooner than is apparently necessary.

In fact, timing behavior on FI schedules is just about what we would expect: Under usual conditions, there is considerable variability in the FI pause, but the average is well under the FI value. But if offered an attractive competing (interim) activity (e.g., a running wheel for a rat), pauses shift to longer values. Conversely, pigeons trained in a small box or restrained in a bodycuff (so there is no opportunity for interim activity) show shorter pauses than animals responding in large enclosures (Frank & Staddon, 1974).

Characteristics of the Time Marker

Food is not the only stimulus that is effective as a time marker, but it is more effective than "neutral" stimuli such as tones, lights, or even the animal's own response (recall that pigeons and rats can only learn to space their responses if the delay times are quite short). For example, consider again the procedure illustrated in Figure 6.9. In that experiment, food was omitted at the end of half the fixed intervals, but even at the end of no-food intervals, the light on the response key went out (for the pigeon) and the "house" lights went out (for both rat and pigeon) for about 3 sec. This "timeout" period was equal to the duration of access to food at the end of food intervals. It tells the animal exactly as much about the time until the next food opportunity as does actually receiving food: In both cases, the next food opportunity is after two minutes. Yet, both the rat and the pigeon paused after receiving food but not after the timeout. Why?

There are two possibilities: Either the original hypothesis—that the pause is determined solely by the predictive properties of the time marker—is wrong, or there is something special about food (and electric shock and other "hedonic" stimuli) that makes it more effective than a neutral stimulus such as a light. We have already discussed too much support for the predictive property of the marker to give up that idea, but there is also much evidence that supports the special nature of hedonic stimuli such as food. Perhaps hedonic stimuli can override predictive stimuli because they are more easily remembered.

INTERFERENCE WITH THE TIME MARKER BY OTHER STIMULI   Let's consider some other experimental results that demonstrate interference of memory. In the first experiment (Staddon, 1970; see also Lowe, Davey & Harzem, 1974), pigeons were trained on a fixed-interval, 1-min schedule in which each interval ended with food reinforcement, with the special proviso that the duration of access to food varied unpredictably from interval to interval. Five different feeder durations ranged from 1.3 sec to 9.0 sec. In this experiment the pigeons had food available as a time marker in every interval; thus there is no obvious reason why they should not have paused in much the same way as on the usual FI schedule in which all food deliveries are of the same duration. But, they did not. The results for three pigeons are shown in Figure 6.12. The upper panel shows the average rate of responding over the entire interfood interval: For all the pigeons, response rate decreased as food duration increased (an inverse relation). The bottom panel shows the average pause after each of the five food durations: For all the pigeons, the longer the food duration, the longer the pause (a positive relation).

There is an uninteresting explanation for this result. Perhaps the pigeons simply take longer to swallow their food after eating for 9 sec as compared to eating for 1 sec or 2 sec? This plausible explanation is wrong for at least two reasons. First, it implies that pigeons should pause after food on any schedule, not just fixed-interval; but as we know, they do not. For example, they show minimal pauses on variable-interval schedules. As we have seen with the go → no-go schedule, it is also relatively easy to train animals to respond especially fast after receiving food rather than pausing. Second, and more directly relevent, other experiments (e.g., Hatten & Shull, 1983) have shown that this differential-pause effect depends on the animals experiencing different food durations within the same experimental session or at least in an intermixed fashion. If instead of daily experiencing of five different food durations, the animals are given several days at one duration, then several more days at another, and so on, then pausing after the short durations increases from one session to the next (or decreases, if the food duration is long). Soon all differences disappear, and the animals pause about the same amount after any food duration. The differential-pause effect

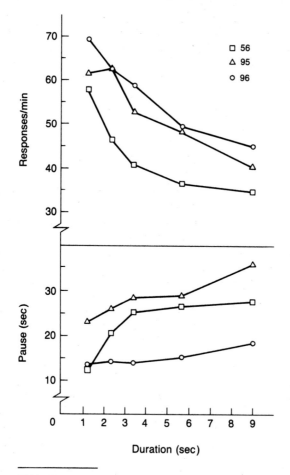

FIGURE 6.12   Top panel: Response rate for intervals following the access-to-food durations shown on the abscissa for three pigeons trained on a fixed-interval, 60-sec schedule in which intervals terminated unpredictably with one of five different food durations. Bottom panel: time-to-first-response (postfood pause) following different food durations (from Staddon, 1972b, Figure 1).

appears to depend on the insertion of different food durations from moment to moment.

The destructive effects of interference between stimuli can be shown directly. In another experiment (Staddon, 1975), pigeons' abilities to use a brief stimulus as a time marker were impaired by presenting it with another stimulus with no predictive significance. The birds were first trained to respond for food on a variable-interval, 1-min schedule. After a little experience, the birds showed characteristic steady responding, with no postfood pausing. In the second phase, every two minutes a brief (3-sec) stimulus (three vertical lines) was projected

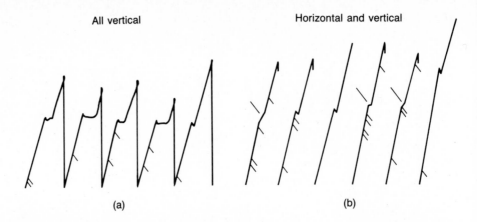

FIGURE 6.13   **(a)** Cumulative records of stable performance on a variable-interval, 1-min schedule in which a brief vertical-line stimulus (indicated by depression of the response record) occurred every 4 min: The stimulus signaled a 2-min fixed-interval schedule. The record reset at the end of each FI 2 reinforcement. **(b)** Performance on this schedule when some 4-min periods were initiated by a brief, horizontal-line stimulus (arrows) signaled "no change" (i.e., the VI 1 schedule continued in effect) (from Staddon, 1975, Figure 3).

on the response key. This stimulus signalled that the next reinforcement would be programmed on a fixed-interval, 2-min schedule. Thus after food or at any other time, the animal could expect food after some unpredictable time averaging one minute; but, after the 3-sec, vertical-line stimulus, the animal knew that food would be available only after exactly 2 min.

The pigeons adapted to this new time marker by developing a poststimulus pause appropriate to the 2-min, fixed-interval duration. This pattern is illustrated for one animal by the cumulative record in Figure 6.13a. The record reset at the end of each 4-min cycle (i.e., after each FI 2-min food delivery), and the recording pen was depressed during the fixed interval. The pause after the brief stimulus is clear in four of the five intervals in the figure, which is a typical proportion. This result shows that when there are no interfering events, pigeons can learn to use even a brief, neutral stimulus as a temporal cue.

Figure 6.13b shows the effect of an apparently trivial modification of this procedure. Instead of scheduling the 2-min, fixed-interval schedule exactly once during each 4-min cycle, it was scheduled on only one-half the cycles. By itself, it is not likely that this change would have had any significant effect, providing that the brief, vertical-line stimulus continued to be a reliable temporal cue. However, during those cycles when no fixed interval was scheduled (i.e., when the VI 1-min schedule remained in effect), a brief horizontal-line stimulus was projected on the response key. The first effect of this change was that the pigeons paused indiscriminately after both horizontal- and vertical-line stimuli, which of course led to their sometimes waiting longer than necessary after the horizontal-line stimulus. Eventually, the animals ceased to pause after either stimulus (Figure 6.13b).

Pigeons have no difficulty in telling vertical from horizontal lines when they are required to do so in standard simultaneous or successive discrimination procedures. Thus, their failure to pause differentially after the two stimuli in this experiment doesn't reflect some kind of perceptual limitation. They can recognize a vertical-line stimulus, and they learn to respond differently in the presence of vertical and horizontal lines. The problem seems to be that in this experiment the animals were not required to respond in the presence of the stimuli. Instead, they had to behave differently *after* the stimuli had come and gone, pausing after the vertical lines, not after the horizontal lines. In the mixed (horizontal and vertical) condition, the vertical lines produced only brief pauses: The effect of the stimulus was restricted to a relatively brief poststimulus period. Why?

A common-sense explanation is that in the mixed condition, the animals could not remember for more than a few seconds which stimulus had just occurred. In other words, the effect of the informative, vertical-line stimulus was abolished by prior presentation of the (uninformative) horizontal-line stimulus, an effect which is termed *proactive interference* (impairment of a stimulus recall by occurrence of a prior stimulus).

There is a complementary, well-known effect in human memory studies that is termed *retroactive interference* (impairment of earlier stimulus control by the interpolation of a later one). Is there a parallel effect in the study of temporal control? The evidence is less clear than for proactive interference, but a common phenomenon may be related: If a novel stimulus is presented during the pause on a fixed-interval schedule, animals will often begin responding at once. This sort of disinhibition was first seen by Pavlov in delayed-conditioning experiments. Its effect may be owing to retroactive memory interference, the later event (the novel stimulus) impairing recall of the earlier one (food, the time marker). The converse effect, insulation from proactive interference by means of differential stimuli during the fixed interval, has also been demonstrated. (Proaction and retroaction are discussed in more detail later in the chapter.)

If the interference demonstrated in these experiments has something to do with memory, we can make some additional predictions. All theories of memory agree that under normal circumstances an event is better remembered after short times than after long. Therefore, if the effects of reinforcement omission reflect failure of memory, they should be reduced when the time intervals involved are short. This case seems to be true: For example, if we repeat the fixed-interval, reinforcement-omission experiment with 15-sec or 30-sec intervals rather than 60-sec or 120-sec intervals, the pigeons pause as long after brief stimuli presented in lieu of food as they do after food.

REDUCING INTERFERENCE WITH NEUTRAL STIMULI   Interference between to-be-remembered events can also be reduced if they are associated with different situations or contexts. For example, if a person is required to learn two lists of similar items (words or nonsense syllables) one after the other in the same room and then is asked to say whether a specific item comes from the first or the second list, the person will often make mistakes, identifying an item from list B as coming from list A, and vice versa. If the same experiment is performed with the two lists either separated in time learned in different rooms, or learned from different experimenters, confusions of this sort are much reduced.

A similar experiment has been performed with temporal control (Staddon, 1974). Two pigeons were trained on a fixed-interval, 2-min schedule in which intervals ended either with food or a brief blackout. The response key was either red or green during each fixed interval. Both stimuli gave the same information about the outcome of an interval: In either case, the probability the interval would end with food was $\frac{1}{3}$. When the stimulus during the interval was green, that interval had *begun* with a blackout—thus the green stimulus was a consistent context for remembering blackouts (green retroacted blackouts). When the stimulus during the interval was red, the context was ambiguous, because red intervals began indiscriminately with blackouts or food.

The critical question was whether the animals were better able to use the neutral time marker that began green intervals than the time marker that began red intervals: Would they pause longer following blackouts in green than following blackouts in red? The answer: Yes. The two pigeons and two others similarly trained with a shorter fixed interval all paused almost as long after blackouts as after food in green, but they paused much less after blackouts in red. Evidently, the distinctive context was able to mitigate the usual interference between blackouts and food in fixed-interval, reinforcement-omission procedures.

Some "neutral" stimuli are more memorable than others. For example, the extraordinary human capacity for remembering faces has often been noted. The reason why people are able to identify hundreds or even thousands of faces but only a few, say, telephone numbers is still the object of active research. A popular hypothesis is that this memory capacity has something to do with the multi-dimensional property of "natural" stimuli such as faces and scenes. There is some evidence that animals' abilities to use a stimulus as a time marker in fixed-interval schedules is similarly affected by stimulus complexity. For example, in our laboratory we have seen that if instead of the usual simple color or blackout stimulus a color slide of a pigeon was presented as the neutral omission stimulus, the birds showed essentially normal, fixed-interval pauses. In this case, the pigeon was better remembered than a neutral stimulus.

Conclusion: The Discrimination of Recency

The reinforcement-omission effect—shorter pausing after a neutral stimulus presented in lieu of food than after food on fixed-interval schedules—seems to reflect a competition for control of the animal's behavior between two past events: food, which is the earlier event, and the later neutral stimulus. The animal must attend to the most recent event and ignore the earlier one. Both events have the same temporal significance, but food is more valued. Evidently, a few seconds after the neutral stimulus, the animal attends to food rather than to the neutral stimulus. Since the last food delivery is relatively remote in time, the animal's responses (long postfood times signal further food) result in a too-short pause after the neutral stimulus (the reinforcement-omission effect). The same process accounts for diminished pausing after short FI feeder durations when long and short are intermixed.

The general conclusion is that temporal stimulus control is vulnerable to the kinds of proactive and retroactive interference studied in memory experiments. Aspects that give a stimulus value, such as reinforcing properties, stimulus complexity, or "meaningfulness," facilitate temporal control. Separation, in time or by context, minimizes interference between events. Conversely, the occurrence of similar interfering events (the horizontal-vertical experiment) or more memorable events with similar significance (the reinforcement-omission effect) impair temporal control. When the interfering event is similar in properties but different in temporal significance to the event of interest, the resulting impairment of temporal control may be termed a *recency confusion effect,* since the animal is evidently uncertain about which stimulus just occurred. When the interfering event is highly salient or valued, the resulting impairment is better termed a *recency overshadowing effect,* since the more salient, older event exerts control at the expense of the more recent, less salient event.

Other Methods for Measuring Temporal Control and Memory

PRODUCTION METHOD VERSUS PEAK PROCEDURE   Fixed-interval schedules might be termed a *production method* for studying temporal discrimination in animals, in the sense that the animal determines how long it waits. A related method is the so-called *peak procedure* (Roberts, 1981), in which food is available for a response after a fixed period T. On one-half of the trials, food is presented after T sec, and on the other trials food is omitted. Trials when food is not available last $2T$. In these double-length trials, when the animal begins to respond, it gives us an estimate of the rat's timing ability—typically the response rate is highest (or peaks) at a time close to T under these conditions.

SIGNAL-DETECTION PROCEDURES   Animals and people can also be asked to estimate time intervals. For example, in one popular, discrete-trial procedure, the animal is provided with two response alternatives (e.g., two pecking keys for a pigeon), one signifying "too long," the other "too short." Each cycle of the procedure has two parts: In the first part, the keys are dark and ineffective; after a variable period of time (t), the key lights come on, and the animal must respond. If t is less than some target time (T), a response on the left key, say, is reinforced with food, and a response on the right key is either unreinforced or mildly punished by a timeout. If $t > T$, a response on the right-hand key is reinforced, and one on the left-hand key is punished. The advantage of this procedure is that the costs and benefits to the animal associated with different kinds of errors and correct responses can be explicitly manipulated; they are not simply accidental consequences of the cost of responding and the benefits of the interim activities that happen to be available (as in the fixed-interval situation). In this manner, we can get some idea of the limitations on the timing process itself, apart from biases to respond or not respond associated with competition from activities other than the measured response.

This time-estimation experiment is best analyzed using a method originally invented for evaluating physical communication systems but that has found wide use in psychology—*signal-detection analysis*. The key idea is that two main factors affect decision making under conditions of uncertainty (e.g., deciding whether an intruding aircraft is a "hostile" or a "friendly"): the intrinsic difficulty of the task and the costs and benefits associated with its two possible responses (yes for hostile and no for friendly). The intrinsic difficulty of the task, that is, the organism's perceptual capabilities, sets a limit to what can be achieved. The costs and benefits associated with the two outcomes determine the relative cost-liness of the two kinds of errors that can be made: false alarms (saying "yes" when the craft is friendly) and misses (saying "no" when it is hostile). For ex-ample, if the cost of a miss is quite high (you are attacked with a nuclear device) compared to the cost of a false alarm, then the rational observer is likely to say "hostile" even when he or she is quite unsure about whether or not the invading aircraft is hostile or friendly. Conversely, if the cost of a false alarm is quite high (you shoot down a friendly pilot), then the observer must be sure of his or her identification before saying "yes." Even if the costs of the two errors are quite comparable, the rational observer is more likely to say "yes" if "hostiles" are more common than "friendlies," and vice versa.

The major contribution of signal-detection analysis, for our purposes, is to show us a way of representing two contributions to choice, *task difficulty* and *bias*, in a single graph that allows us to separate them. The idea is to plot two experimentally determined probabilities—the probability of saying "yes" given that the signal ("hostile") is really there (the probability of a "hit") against the probability of saying "yes" given that there is no signal ("friendly," which is the probability of a false alarm). Such curves can be obtained by varying either or both of the two aspects that affect bias: signal probability (the relative frequency of "hostiles" and "friendlies") and the relative costs of the two kinds of errors. Each value of relative cost (say) gives a single point on the graph; the set of points then defines what is called an ROC curve (which stands for *receiver-operating characteristic*). The shape of the ROC curve defines the intrinsic difficulty of the task (which we show in a moment), and the position of each point on the curve defines the degree of bias.

This analysis can be applied to our time-estimation experiment in the fol-lowing manner. The two choices are "too long" (pecking one key) and "too short" (pecking the other key). Bias was manipulated by varying the costs of errors (timeout periods) and the benefits (rewards) produced by correct and in-correct responses.

We plot p(too long–long), that is, the probability that the bird says "too long" when the stimulus really was too long, against p(too long–short), that is, the probability the bird says "too long" when the stimulus really was too short (Figure 6.14). The results in the figure are from a pigeon experiment by Alan

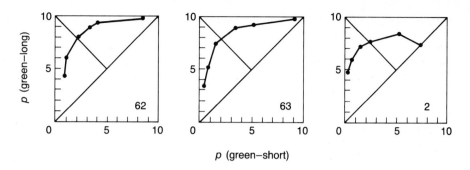

FIGURE 6.14   ROC plots for three pigeons trained on a procedure in which the duration of a time interval was judged. Responses on a green key signaled "too long"; responses on a red key signaled "too short." Abscissas show the probability of a green key response given a sample interval that is shorter than the target duration; ordinates show the probability of a green key response given a sample interval that is longer than the target duration (from Stubbs, 1976, Figure 2).

Stubbs (1976), in which three pigeons were trained to peck a green key as the correct response for a "long" stimulus and to peck a red key as the correct response for a "short" stimulus. All three pigeons showed typical ROC curves, which are pushed far into the northeast corner of the unit probability square, indicating quite good discrimination of time intervals. (Where should the curves lie if there is *no* discrimination at all?)

DELAYED-MATCHING-TO-SAMPLE PROCEDURE   A similar procedure, the *delayed-matching-to-sample procedure* (*DMTS*), can also be used to study memory interference. In this procedure, a pigeon, say, is confronted by three response keys. At the beginning of each cycle, only the center key is illuminated with one of two stimuli (S_1 or S_2). One or a few pecks on this sample key turns it off. After a delay of a few seconds, the two side keys come on, one showing S_1 the other S_2. The animal's task is to peck the key that shows the sample stimulus. A correct response yields food; an incorrect response yields a timeout, which delays the next trial. After either event, the cycle resumes. The location of S_1 and S_2 in the choice phase varies unpredictably from trial to trial, so that the animal must recall the most recently presented sample to make a correct choice.

This procedure offers the same possibilities for confusion as the temporal-control experiments previously described. For example, on each trial, the animal must be able to discriminate between the most recent sample and earlier samples. This criterion suggests that there should be fewer errors if the delay value is short or if the sample stimulus duration is long—both effects are generally found. One also suspects that performance is likely to be better if there is a substantial interval between trials, because each sample is then more widely separated in time from preceding samples, which should reduce their interference. This intertrial effect has not been shown reliably with pigeons and nontemporal sample stimuli, although experiments with rats have shown the effect (Riley & Roitblat, 1978; Lett, 1975).

The DMTS procedure nicely demonstrates that it is the memory for the sample that is important, not the subsequent choice arrangement. In an experiment by Harrison and Nissen (1941) with chimpanzees, the procedure was as follows: The animal was presented with two buckets, one covering food, the other not. The animal saw the trainer baiting one or other bucket. After a delay, out of sight of the buckets, the animal was released and allowed to select one. In between baiting and choice, the buckets were moved closer together or farther apart. Nissen concluded that it was the separation of the buckets at the time of baiting that was important to accurate choice, not their separation at the time of choice. Evidently, it is the manner in which the sample is represented or coded by the animal that determines how well it can be responded to after a delay. If the baited and unbaited buckets are coded with different spatial coordinates, they are not confused, even after substantial delays. But if their spatial coordinates (or other properties) are similar, then with a lapse of time the animal cannot reliably distinguish between the buckets.

As might be expected from the importance of stimulus value to recall, performance in this task depends on the magnitude of the bait. If large and small baits are shown on different trials, accuracy is better on trials with large baits, even if the animal is always rewarded with bait of the same, small size.

All these experiments illustrate what Honig and Thompson (1982) have called *retrospective encoding:* The animal's behavior is determined at the moment of choice by the historical *memory array,* the series of events in the immediate past, of which the sample stimulus is presumably the most salient. However, it is worth noting that many experimental arrangements permit a simpler strategy, one that pigeons and rats are not slow to adopt. Consider the following DMTS arrangement: Four sample stimuli (A, B, C, and D) are similar line orientations. (We assume that the similarity among the line orientations will make them difficult to distinguish, thus biasing the task.) There are only two test stimuli: red and green. The reinforcement contingencies call for a red response if the sample stimulus is A or C or a green response if it is B or D. Clearly, the animal can do better on this task if, instead of trying to remember at the moment of choice which of the four hard-to-discriminate stimuli was most recent, it decides at the time the sample stimulus is presented and *remembers the choice,* not the stimulus on which it was based. Honig and Thompson call this strategy *prospective encoding,* and it implies that the animal actively decides on and then remembers its upcoming choice at the moment it sees the sample stimulus.

A number of experiments have shown that animals behave as this model predicts. For example, Roitblat (1981) performed a DMTS experiment with three sample stimuli (red, orange, and blue) and three choice stimuli (responses) (line orientations at 90°, 12.5°, and 0° to the vertical). A response to the 90° orientation was correct following the red stimulus, the 12.5° orientation was correct following the orange stimulus, and so on. The two similar colors, red and orange, required dissimilar responses (90° and 12.5°), whereas the two dissimilar colors (orange and blue) required similar responses (12.5° and 0°). Roitblat then increased the delay between sample and choice (the *retention interval*) and found that his pigeons tended to confuse not choices 90° and 12.5°, which would imply growing confusion between the memories for the similar samples red and orange, but choices 12.5° and 0°, which implies the animals made a decision at the time the sample stimuli were presented and then remembered their choices. Given that colors are generally easier for pigeons to remember than line orientations, it is not obvious why Roitblat's pigeons settled for prospective encoding in this experiment. But, notice that no matter which method the animal adopts, it still must cope with potential interference from earlier events. For example, on trial *N*, the pigeon may remember that 0° is correct; then on the next trial, perhaps 12.5° is correct. As the retention interval progresses, confusion between the 12.5° orientation and the preceding 0° orientation is still possible: In these repetitive procedures, the animal must always discriminate recencies of choices if not of the stimuli. From this point of view, perhaps the greater forgetability of line orientations is an asset, in that there may be less interference from previous trials if the animal is remembering a line orientation rather than a color. No doubt there are other possibilities. Researchers are still trying to understand these interactions, and the problem of the factors that favor one or other type of encoding is an active area of animal memory research.

Proactive and Retroactive Interference

The laws of memory define the limits on control of present action by past events. These limits are of two kinds: *proaction effects,* in which an earlier event (S_1) interferes with control of behavior by a later event (S_2), and *retroaction effects,* in which a later event interferes with control of behavior by an earlier event. The degree to which one event interferes with control by another depends on two properties: the similarity of the two events (including similar times of occurrence) and the difference between the behavior controlled by each. For example, suppose that S_1 normally elicits R_1 and S_2 normally elicits R_2. In the DMTS situation, S_1 might be a red sample key and S_2 a green sample key. R_1 would then mean pecking the red choice key and R_2 pecking the green choice key. In a DMTS, R_i is always the next response required after S_i, so that only proaction effects are possible. Since the responses required by S_1 and S_2 are different (S_1 and S_2 are not confused when both are present), interference in this situation depends on the similarity of the stimuli: The more similar are S_1 and S_2, the worse the performance. If instead of red and green we used red and pink, say, as sample stimuli, we could expect choice accuracy to decrease. As we just saw, animals make more accurate choices when the two baited buckets are far apart than when they are close together. Response similarity makes much less difference than stimulus similarity, because the responses are usually available all the time and are not subject to interference or decay: The animal always knows what the response alternatives are on each trial; it is less sure about which alternative is correct. Indeed, this asymmetry is a logical necessity, since the animal cannot even learn the task unless it can perfectly discriminate the choices. Knowing the

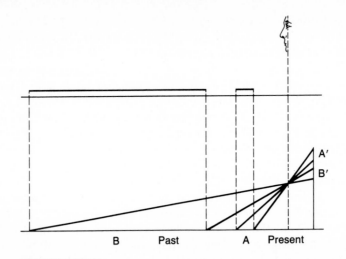

FIGURE 6.15   Perspective metaphor for the temporal resolution of memory. Top: The "mind's eye" viewing past events (B: long duration, remote past; A: short duration, recent past). Bottom: Perspective projections of A, B, A', B' from the viewpoint of the present.

choices requires only that the animal have learned a discrimination; knowing which choice to make additionally requires it be able to remember which of the discriminated events occurred last.

In temporal-control experiments, the responses controlled by the interfering events can be either the same or different: In the FI reinforcement-omission experiments, food and blackout control the same behavior (pausing); in the first condition of the horizontal-vertical experiment (Figure 6.9, left), food and blackout (vertical lines) control different patterns (pausing and responding). Interference is less when the two events controlled different patterns. Therefore, under some conditions interference seems to depend on response as well as on stimulus aspects of the task.

Proaction and retroaction effects in these experiments measure the *temporal resolution* of memory (cf. D'Amato, 1973). That is, they answer the question: How close can two events be in time without affecting an animal's ability to remember which is the more recent? A useful metaphor is shown in Figure 6.15. This model assumes that past events are separately represented by the animal, and it implies that the (temporal) similarity relationships among events change continuously with the passage of time. The upper portion of the figure shows the "mind's eye" looking back over the record of past events, which are arranged in a time line so that the distance of the event from the eye (the present) is proportional to how long ago the event occurred. The bottom portion of the figure shows how recalled events appear in the mind's eye. Let's suppose that this eye (unlike a normal visual system) perceives the size of events solely in terms of their retinal size. Therefore, the salience of the various events is given by their projected size, as shown by the vertical line on the bottom, right-hand side of the figure. Thus a long-lasting but remote event may appear only as large as a shorter but more recent event: B' is the same size as A', even though B is an event of longer duration than A. Moreover, the relative sizes (saliences) of events changes with lapse of time, that is, as the vantage point moves further toward the right.

The various effects we have described are generally consistent with the metaphor in the figure. For example, events of longer duration are obviously easier to "see" than events of short duration, which meshes the results of reinforcement-omission experiments in which longer events produce longer postevent pausing. Events that are widely separated in time are easier to tell apart (i.e., interfere less) than events that are close together in time, which is consistent with the effect of long, intertrial intervals in improving DMTS performance. Moreover, the interference (proximity in the projected "memory image") between adjacent events should increase with time. No matter how brief an event, with short delays it should appear more salient than any earlier event; but as time elapses, longer, long-past events gain relative to shorter, more recent events. Just as a house will blot out a mountain behind it when the viewpoint is close to the house, but the mountain will loom over the house when both are viewed from a distance. As time passes, A' (the representation of event A), will therefore lose in size relative to B' (the representation of earlier, but longer, event B). This principle in the study of memory can be summed up by *Jost's Law:*

> Given two associations of the same strength, but of different ages, the older falls off less rapidly in a given length of time (Hovland, 1951, p. 649, after Jost, 1879).

This principle accounts for the ability of even a not-very-salient event to control behavior over a brief time interval.

Figure 6.15 shows that any limit on the animal's visual acuity means that in a given context, only a limited number of past events can be distinguished. The model therefore implies a limit to the capacity of *short-term memory* or as it is frequently termed, *working memory.* (However, the metaphor suggests that there may be no real basis for many memory dichotomies—that everything may follow from a single process.)

Hedonic value, as an important factor in memorability, can be represented in this analogy by the dimension of height: Just as a distant, high structure looms over a lower, closer one, as the viewpoint recedes, so does a preceding reinforcement seem to overshadow a neutral stimulus in the fixed-interval, reinforcement-omission paradigm. Therefore, both confusion and overshadowing effects fit easily into the analogy.

Memory Limitations

We end this section on methods of studying animal memory with an account of two procedures much used to study species differences in intelligence. These procedures exemplify the memory processes already discussed, and they also illustrate the fallacy of comparing species in terms of their performance on some task rather than in terms of the processes that underlie performance differences.

Memory limitations enter in an interesting way into two tasks originally devised to study "higher mental processes" in animals: *discrimination reversal* and *learning set.* Both tasks were intended to assess animals' flexibilities by requiring them to learn a new task frequently, either a discrimination opposite to the one already learned (discrimination reversal) or a completely new discrimination (learning set). There are several versions of each procedure.

THE DISCRIMINATION-REVERSAL PROCEDURE   One procedure that has been used with pigeons (Staddon & Frank, 1974) is as follows: The animals are trained on a multiple schedule, that is, one in which two different stimuli (called *components*) are presented successively on the same response key. The two 1-min components occur in strict alternation. In one component, key pecks produce food according to a VI 60-sec schedule; in the other, pecks are ineffective (extinction). The extinction stimulus ($S-$) changes to the VI stimulus ($S+$) after 60 sec only if no peck has occurred in the preceding 30 sec; thus by pecking on $S-$, the animal can prolong its duration indefinitely. This "correction" procedure imposes a cost for responding to $S-$ and also provides an additional cue to the identity of $S+$ each day (if a stimulus changes within 30 sec of a peck, it must be $S+$). The stimuli are red and green key lights. After an initial period during which the animals learn a specific discrimination (e.g., green: VI, red: EXT), the significance of the two stimuli is changed daily. Therefore, green signifies VI reinforcement on odd-numbered days and extinction (EXT) on even-numbered days.

The obvious question: Do the pigeons improve in their reversal performance from one discrimination reversal to another? Figure 6.16 shows the percentage of "correct" (i.e., VI stimulus) responses on the first day of each reversal for six pigeons reversed every day, every second day, or every three days. The results for all six pigeons are similar: a steady improvement in performance, settling down to perhaps 90 percent correct responses after several reversals.

What does this result tell us about the flexibility of these animals' learning processes? Two other results from this experiment—the effects of a shift to a new pair of stimuli and of days off (i.e., no experimentation took place)—shed some light on this question. After a good performance had been achieved on the red–green reversal problem, the two stimuli were changed from red and green to blue and yellow. The pigeons were given a total of 11 daily reversals with this new pair of stimuli. Then the animals were simply not run for a period of four days, then run for a single day, then not run for a further eight days. The effect on discrimination performance is shown in Figure 6.17: The animals performed quite well on the first day with the new stimuli, but discrimination was poor the next day, that is on the first reversal after the change, and they took several further reversals to recover their previous level of ability. In a similar fashion, the pigeons performed well after the four days off and after the next eight days off, but on the first reversal after the eight days off, their performance was poor and remained so for several subsequent reversals.

To interpret these results, consider the two aspects that are necessary for good performance on this task, bearing in mind that pigeons seem incapable of what is called *spontaneous reversal* (are not able to learn to avoid the previ-

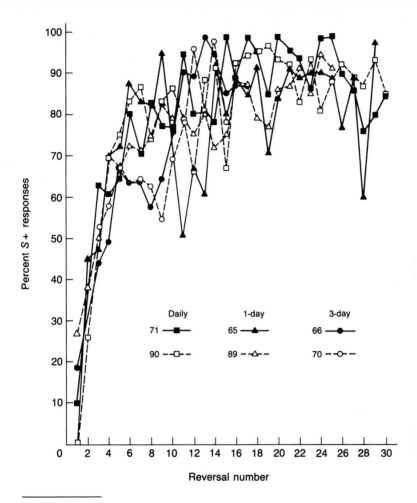

FIGURE 6.16   Performance of six individual pigeons exposed to daily reversal of a red–green successive discrimination, in which $S+$ was reinforced according to a VI 60-sec schedule, no reinforcement occurred in $S-$, and the change from $S-$ to $S+$ occurred only if no $S-$ response preceded the change by less than 30 sec. The animals had learned the simple red–green discrimination perfectly before being exposed to reversal training; this experience, plus the correction procedure, accounts for the close to zero percent $S+$ responses on the first reversal (from Staddon & Frank, 1974, Figure 1).

ously rewarded stimulus). Given that the pigeons must cope with the problem in some simpler manner, they must presumably at least ignore on Day N the significances established for the stimuli on Day $N - 1$. Throughout the experiment, they also must attend each day to the cues to the correct stimulus, that is, the delivery of food reinforcement in the presence of $S+$ and the delay contingency for pecking on $S-$. Good performance depends on their balance of these two fac-

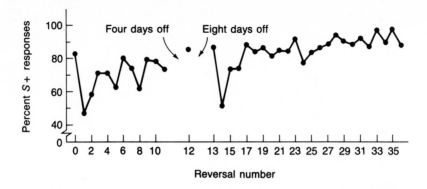

FIGURE 6.17   Average percent of $S+$ responses for six pigeons following a shift to blue–yellow reversal after extended training on red–green reversal (from Staddon & Frank, 1974, Figure 8).

tors. For example, if the animal is good at detecting the cues for $S+$ and $S-$ but poor at disregarding the significance established for red and green on the previous day, then performance each day will not be good: The animal will always begin by responding a lot to $S-$ (yesterday's $S+$) and not much to $S+$, thus ensuring a mediocre discrimination score. Conversely, if the animal treats the stimuli afresh each day but is poor at detecting $S+$ and $S-$, performance will also be inferior. The properties of memory are involved in the first prerequisite—control of behavior on Day N by the significances established on Day $N - 1$.

We can get an idea of the relative importance of memory and speed of learning about reward cues from the way that performance changes within and across experimental sessions and from the results shown in Figure 6.17. For example, consider an animal that has such poor long-term memory that it essentially starts afresh each day, being unable to remember which stimulus was $S+$ on the previous day. If such an animal learns quickly within each day (i.e., has good short-term memory), then the absolute level of performance will be quite good, although there will be no improvement across successive reversals. Neither the days-off manipulation nor the shift to a new problem (i.e., new pair of stimuli) should have any effect. Certainly, there is no reason to expect any special effect on the first reversal.

Procedural Versus Declarative Memory. There is one qualification to this conclusion: In recent years, researchers have become aware of a difference between what is called procedural memory and declarative memory. *Procedural memory* is what is involved in learning to ride a bicycle or some other motor task: It is memory of *how to do* something, not verbal knowledge about it. On the other hand, *declarative memory* is *knowledge about* something. In humans, the distinction is brought out most dramatically by certain kinds of brain damage (e.g., Korsakov's syndrome, which is a frequent effect of alcoholism). Individuals with hippocampal damage of this sort will retain their "how-to" knowledge (e.g., how to solve the Tower of Hanoi puzzle), but they will strenuously deny ever having encountered the task before (e.g., see papers in Weinberger, McGaugh &

Lynch, 1985). When asked why they perform so well, like other brain-damaged people (e.g., split-brain patients) in similar situations, they will make some rationalization that bears no relation to the truth. Pigeons cannot verbalize, but there is nevertheless a resemblance between signal learning—learning which stimulus is $S+$—and declarative knowledge and between learning about procedural cues to $S+$ and procedural knowledge. Therefore, it may be that an animal could have rather poor declarative memory but good procedural memory. Such an animal would not remember anything of stimulus value from day to day, but it might well retain some memory of the reliable procedural cues that signal which stimulus is $S+$ each day. Such an animal would show progressive improvement in the daily reversal task as it learns about the procedural cues, but it would not show any special effect of the days-off or new problem manipulations.

What about the case of an animal that always remembers perfectly the previous day's $S+$, that is, has good declarative as well as procedural memory? It will presumably do *worse* than an animal with poor day-to-day recall, because it always remembers perfectly the wrong response each day and must overcome this bias before it can respond correctly. It may or may not show progressive improvement, depending on which learning process, procedural or declarative, is faster, and it will show no special effects of days off or a new problem.

The most interesting possibility is the intermediate case: the animal with good enough declarative memory to remember yesterday's $S+$, providing there is not too much proactive interference from the day before yesterday and earlier days. Such an animal will show progressive improvement not because it is learning more but because it is *forgetting* more (forgetting more each day about the previous day's $S+$ because of proactive interference from the growing number of earlier days). Early in training, you might expect such an animal to remember quite well. In particular, on the second day with any new pair of stimuli, there will be no sources of interference, and the animal should remember well the significances established on the first day. But since on the second day of a new problem the correct response is now opposite to the well-remembered, first-day response, we might expect to see especially *poor* performance on the second day (the first reversal) of any new problem. These facts are illustrated in Figure 6.17. In short, anything that improves the animal's memory for what happened in the previous experimental session should impair its discrimination-reversal performance.

A new problem is one such factor; days off is another. We might reasonably expect that the longer the time elapsed since discrimination $N - 1$—especially if discriminations $N - 2$, $N - 3$, and so on precede $N - 1$ and provide sources of proactive interference—the smaller the effect the significances established should have at the outset of discrimination N. These facts also proved true in the experiment shown in Figure 6.17. After a days-off period, performance is slightly better than before the days-off period (reversals 12 and 13 in the figure). For example, if the pigeons are run on Saturday but then not run again until the following Thursday, performance on Thursday is good. But, the very factors that minimize interference on Thursday from what was learned on Saturday act to maximize interference on the next day, Friday, from the significances established on Thursday. Thursday is temporally isolated from the discrimination sessions preceding it, so that its effect on Friday is unimpaired by the contrary stimulus significances established on the preceding Saturday. The result is poor performance on Friday.

This same line of argument leads us to expect that performance at the beginning of each experimental session should change systematically with successive reversals. Early on, the animal should respond incorrectly at the beginning of each session, responding most to $S-$ (i.e., the previous day's $S+$). But with continued training, recall of the previous day's $S+$ and $S-$ should be progressively impaired, so that at the beginning of each experimental session the animal should respond more or less equally, at an intermediate level, to both stimuli. These facts are more or less borne out with pigeons. At first, errors are high chiefly because the animal consistently picks the wrong stimulus at the beginning of each session; with continued training, this initial bias disappears, and the animal appears more hesitant, responding at a slower rate but more or less equally to both stimuli. (Presumably, the hesitancy reflects the ambiguous status of both stimuli: The animal cannot, at this state, recall which stimulus was $S+$ yesterday, but it has no difficulty recalling that both stimuli have served as both $S+$ and $S-$.)

The discrimination-reversal task is not ideal as a test of intelligence in animals, because good performance can be achieved in several ways, not all of which correspond to superior ability (the problem may also be with the concept of "intelligence" itself, but that is another story). For example, poor temporal resolution of memory, that is, a relative inability to distinguish yesterday's $S+$ from the $S+$ the day before that, can aid performance on the task. It is possible to imagine three types of performance on the task, depending on the temporal resolution of memory:

1. At the lowest level, temporal resolution is exceedingly poor (which simply amounts to local memory). Hence, each day is treated as a separate experience, and discrimination-reversal performance is little different from simple discrimination performance. There should be no improvement across successive reversals (but note the preceding comments about the procedural/declarative distinction).

2. At an intermediate level, temporal resolution is intermediate. Hence, discrimination-reversal performance is initially poor, but it improves as proactive interference accumulates and weakens the effect of Day $N - 1$ training on Day N performance.

3. At the highest level, temporal resolution is sufficiently good that the animal may show spontaneous reversal, using the $S+$ on Day $N - 1$ as a cue to $S+$ on Day N. Spontaneous reversal is not possible at the two earlier stages, because late in training, the $S+$ for Day $N - 1$ cannot be recalled, thus cannot be used as a cue on day N.

Although, spontaneous reversal may fail to occur even if memory permits because of performance constraints. The animal may in some sense know that today's $S+$ is opposite to yesterday's, but it may be constrained to respond to the most recent $S+$—yesterday's—anyway, as in the autoshaping-omission procedures discussed in Chapter 7. Pigeons are one example of this phenomenon. All three of the listed cases permit good steady-state reversal performance. They differ in the means used to achieve it, but these differences can be revealed only by appropriate tests. For example, available results suggest that goldfish correspond more or less to Case 1, pigeons and rats to Case 2, and some higher primates to Case 3.

THE LEARNING-SET PROCEDURE   The learning-set task, in which a new pair of stimuli must be discriminated each day, seems like a better test of "learning ability," whatever that might be, because the role of temporal resolution is minimized. However, performance in this task depends on something that might be termed *cognitive resolution:* the ability to keep separate (not confuse) a number of different pairs of stimuli, since if new stimuli are confused with old ones, then on some days the animals will pick the wrong stimulus as $S+$, which will retard acquisition of the discrimination. Thus, the learning-set procedure is subject to the same dual process as discrimination reversal: Any improvement across problems (i.e., pairs of stimuli) can reflect improvement in attending to the procedural features (differential reinforcement, correction) that signal $S+$ and $S-$. But improvement may also reflect increasing confusion among past stimuli with concomitant reduction in the ability to affect preferences for new stimuli.

If the pairs of stimuli used each day are quite different (i.e., the animals have good cognitive resolution), then the animals will treat each day as a fresh discrimination. If the animals are pretrained on discrimination reversal, they should transfer perfectly to such a task, having already learned how to identify $S+$ each day, as did the pigeons in the experiment discussed.

Memory and Spatial Learning

The discussion of discrimination reversal and learning set emphasizes a major difficulty in studying learning and memory: We see and can measure *performance,* but the same performance can usually come about in several ways, and even simple tasks can call on more than one ability. Performance can never be taken at face value; we must always ask about the component abilities that make it up. An analysis into components can never be satisfactorily proved by a single, "crucial" experiment. The best we can do is to take our hypothesized basic abilities or processes and show how by putting them together in various combinations we can bring together a wide range of facts. The smaller the number of processes and the larger the number of facts explained, the more profitable our choice.

In this section, we take the principles of memory just discussed and put them together with the notion of spatial representation discussed earlier to provide a general theory that can explain many of the properties of spatial learning in rats and other animals.

Recall that rats learn rapidly and well not to revisit arms in the eight-arm radial maze. Even more dramatic learning of this sort is shown by several species of food-hoarding birds. For example, in collaborative research, Sara Shettleworth (University of Toronto) and John Krebs (Oxford University) have shown that marsh tits, a small European bird, can remember with the greatest accuracy and for a long time where they have stored seeds. In one experiment (Shettleworth, 1983), the birds were allowed to store a small number, say 12, of hemp seeds in a large aviary filled with tree branches into which had been drilled a total of 100 holes, each covered with a little flap, that could be used as storage sites. Each bird was returned to a holding cage after it had stored all its seeds. Some hours later, it was allowed to retrieve the stored seeds. Notice that this experiment is a little more sophisticated than the radial-maze experiment in that it allows for both kinds of errors: failing to visit a full storage site and visiting an empty storage site. The design of the radial maze usually permits only errors of the second variety. Notice also that Krebs and Shettleworth's experiment readily lends itself to analysis using signal-detection terms. Nevertheless, analyzed by any method, these little birds perform impressively. Even after hours of delay, they recover an average of eight of the 12 stored seeds within a short time, and they visit few empty sites. Moreover, their accurate performance is not due to favoring a few sites, that is, if the birds are allowed two separate opportunities to hoard, they avoid on the second opportunity sites already filled the first time.

DIFFERENCES BETWEEN MATCHING AND SPATIAL TASKS   What is going on in these experiments, which seem to show memory abilities much greater than earlier results obtained using the DMTS procedure? For example, DMTS experiments show that performance falls off after delays on the order of seconds, whereas the radial-maze and seed-storage experiments show rats and birds remembering unvisited sites after delays of hours. Is there something unique about spatial memory? Are similar processes involved in DMTS and these spatial situations, so that it is something about the procedures, not the processes, that accounts for the differences in performance?

The answer seems to lie much more in procedural than in process differences. Without a doubt, there are some process differences. Rats, marsh tits, and many other animals have a much better memory for spatial locations than for colored lights or tones—the types of stimuli typically used in DMTS experiments (although recent studies have shown that pigeons, for example, can remember accurately hundreds of colored slides of natural scenes for many months: Vaughan & Greene, 1984). There are also differences in innate response tendency: Rats and many other animals have a spontaneous tendency to avoid places recently visited. This tendency was first termed *spontaneous alternation* in T-mazes, but the same tendency is exhibited as *patroling* in residential mazes (mazes with more than two alternative goal-routes) and in the radial maze. This least-recent tendency makes adaptive sense. The least-recently visited place is the one where circumstances are most likely to have changed. Consequently, if there is value in keeping up to date about the state of the world, the least-recent rule is the one to follow. For an opportunistic forager like the rat, many food sources correspond to a random-interval schedule: They are depleted by each visit and are replenished unpredictably with time. The least-recent strategy is optimal for exploiting such sources. Of course, the hoarding behavior of rats and marsh tits is also built-in and requires no training, thus such tendencies make radial-maze training much more rapid than DMTS tasks.

The major difference between DMTS and these spatial tasks seems to be in the challenge to the *recency discrimination* the different procedures pose. DMTS makes the most severe demands on recency discrimination, since the animals see the same stimuli repeatedly, intercalated at relatively short intervals. Identifying the stimuli themselves is no problem (after all, there usually are only two), but identifying which one occurred last is quite difficult. Radial-maze experiments (and the marsh tit studies) usually involve only one or two trials a day, and the larger number of stimuli (eight arms versus two sample stimuli) is actually an advantage, since the animal rarely experiences the same stimulus twice in close succession. When trials are massed, radial-maze performance deteriorates: If the animal is trained on two different mazes in close succession, performance deteriorates when the two mazes are physically close together, so that their *spatial coordinates* are similar (remember the Harrison and Nissen experiment discussed previously).

Moreover, animals can learn to perform quite well after long delays on two-choice, DMTS-type tasks if the demands on recency discrimination are reduced. Lett (1975) has done a series of delayed-alternation and delayed-reward experiments, in which rats learned either to avoid or return to one arm of a T-maze, even though they were rewarded only after delays of from 1 min up to an hour or more. For example, in one experiment, Lett gave rats one trial per day on a simple T-maze discrimination, removing the animals to their home cages as soon as they entered the correct arm and then rewarding them in the start box after a 60-min delay. Over a period of 10 days or so, the rats learned to perform correctly. Two features of the experiment seem important to its success: removal of the rat from the goal box as soon as it entered and the long intertrial interval in relation to the delay interval. Removal from the goal box seems to be important to minimize context-specific, retroactive interference from activities that may occur in the goal box after it is entered. The long intertrial interval is necessary for the animal to be able to discriminate the most recent goal entry from previous goal entries. The task in this experiment is to discriminate between the memory for the correct goal box, visited 60 min ago (the retention interval) and the memory for the wrong box, visited perhaps as recently as the previous trial (i.e., with a time separation equal to the intertrial interval plus twice the retention interval). Therefore, the animal must discriminate between two traces originating t and $2t + I$ sec ago.

In short, once the procedural differences are taken into account, most of the differences between radial-maze and DMTS performances make perfect sense.

SIMILARITY, GENERALIZATION, AND DISTRIBUTED MEMORY

In this chapter we have discussed stimulus discrimination, stimulus generalization, and memory as separate topics. We have also used the term representation without giving an exact definition or describing possible mechanisms that might allow organisms to build up representations. In this section, we describe an ex-

6.3

Neural Modeling and Behavioral Psychology

Behavior is generated by the nervous system, so that knowledge about the nervous system, its structure, and how it works has always held a special status as a potential source of theories for behavior. The early reflexologists, I. M. Sechenov in the nineteenth century and Ivan Pavlov in the early twentieth century, were perfectly explicit about the direct relation between behavior and the nervous system. Sechenov proposed that all behavior could be explained in terms of reflexes, and Pavlov viewed behavior as a way of understanding the function of the cerebral cortex. When Pavlov measured stimulus generalization of the salivary response, he believed it to be a direct measure of the spread of neural excitation within the brain. But, his conclusions were for the most part premature. The radical behaviorism of B. F. Skinner was a reaction against the too-eager application of an imperfect understanding of the brain to explain an equally imperfect understanding of behavior. Much better, said Skinner, is to achieve a solid understanding of behavior, in its own terms, before attempting to explain it neurally.

While this debate raged between the biological and behavioral psychologists, work in a completely different intellectual tradition was laying the groundwork for contemporary work in neural modeling. At the University of Chicago in the 1930s, mathematician Nicholas Rashevsky, following a line of thought begun by the British biologist D'Arcy Wentworth Thompson, organized a discipline that he termed *mathematical biophysics,* which attempted to explain not only behavior but many other aspects of biology in mathematical terms. Rashevsky was a brilliant mathematician, but he was a poor biologist. Both aspects prevented his work from having much impact on everyday, nonmathematical, biology. Nevertheless, he pioneered the study of neural networks and attempted to explain many conditioning phenomena in neural

citing research direction that suggests how all these topics may be related and gives some hints about the way that experiences are represented in the brain.

Recent research in cognitive science and the theory of neural networks is beginning to provide simple model examples of brainlike processes that can learn and show associative memory (for reviews of this work, see Grossberg, 1987; McClelland & Rumelhart, 1986; see Box 6.3 for a historical summary). One aspect that makes these models intriguing is that they show stimulus generalization automatically: It doesn't have to be built in as a separate property. The models are brainlike in that they are built of many repeated elements, connected terms much more sophisticated than Pavlov's. A little later, a group at the Massachusetts Institute of Technology, excited by the work on machine computation then just beginning, pursued the analogy between neurons and computation. Their work led to a landmark paper by Warren McCulloch and Walter Pitts, "A logical calculus of the ideas immanent in nervous activity" (1943), which showed in exact detail how simplified, symbolic neurons could solve logical problems.

But, the decisive step in bringing the idea of neural modeling to the attention of a wider scientific audience was taken by the Canadian neuropsychologist Donald Hebb in *The organization of behavior*, (1949) in which he suggested both a simple learning rule for neural networks and also patterns of activity that might correspond to psychological entities such as "habits" and "emotions." *Hebb's learning rule*—that the strength of a connection is increased if the two connecting neurons are simultaneously active—has been widely studied in recent years, and although better rules have been found, the Hebb rule is usually good enough to produce adequate learning.

After Hebb, interest in neural networks languished for several years. But in the mid-1970s, several research groups achieved notable successes in two areas: visual perception and associative memory. David Marr and his associates at M.I.T. made striking advances in our understanding of the computational processes involved in vision and how these processes must involve parallel processing by many neural units. Several other groups showed how matrixlike arrangements could reproduce the puzzling features of associative memory that make it so different from memory in digital computers. There is an excellent review of these recent developments in James McClelland and David Rumelhart (1986).

together in all possible combinations. These elements resemble neurons (nerve cells) and the synaptic junctions between them, although they are generally much simpler than the "real thing." Information is represented in such networks in a completely different manner than in a digital computer, the old cognitive psychology metaphor for human information processing. Instead of each item (stimulus) being "stored" in a specific location, like a computer bit being stored at a specific location in memory, information is represented by the strengths of interconnections between elements. This pattern of connection strengths is termed a *distributed representation*. The ability to categorize and respond to stimuli that are similar to the training stimulus, that is, to show stimulus generalization, is an intrinsic property of distributed representations.

One-Layer Networks

Figure 6.18 shows a one-layer network that illustrates a simple distributed representation (such unidirectional, feed-forward networks as this one are called *perceptrons:* Rosenblat, 1959). The figure shows four input units (A, B, C, and D) and four output units (a, b, c, and d). You can think of the inputs as receptor cells and the outputs as neurons, but they are obviously much simpler and more homogeneous than real receptors and real neurons. The figure illustrates the kind of connections that such networks can make, not create a model of a real neural network, which would be so complicated that its essential principles of operation would be obscured. Thus bearing in mind how simplified our model is, let's see how it works. It has three essential properties:

1. Each unit can take on a range of values.
2. The value of an input unit depends solely on the input stimulus. For example, if the input stimulus is 1, −1, 1, −1, then unit A has the value 1, B is −1, C is 1, and D is −1).
3. The value of an output unit depends on the weighted sum of the inputs to it. For example, let's suppose that all the weights are equal to 1, then with the stimulus 1, −1, 1, −1, the inputs to output unit a are 1, −1, 1, −1, which add up to 0; thus the value of unit a is 0. In fact, with equal weights, all four output units are equal to 0, since each output unit receives an input from all four input units.

We'll see in a moment what happens when the weights are not all equal, but first we need a better way to represent the network than the cumbersome picture in Figure 6.18. Each input is connected to every output, and vice versa, so there are 4 × 4 = 16 connections. Each of these connections is associated with a weight, which allows some connections to be more important than others. For example, if the connection between A and a is less important than the connection between A and b, we might assign the weight .25 to the Aa connection and .75 to the Ab connection. The weights (connections) can be excitatory or inhibitory. The two just described are excitatory, because the weights are positive. If the connection between A and c is inhibitory, it has a negative weight, −.25, say. The essential information about this one-layer network can be represented by a 4 × 4 matrix of 16 positive and negative numbers that represent the weights of the 16 different connections (Figure 6.19). The inputs are at the top of the figure, and the outputs are on the left. The cell entries are the weights of the indicated connections.

Figure 6.20 shows an input/output connection matrix with some actual numbers in place. We have also moved the input stimulus to the left and output response to the right for easier reading. Check for yourself that the output numbers are correctly derived from the input numbers (a = A.Aa + B.Ba + C.Ca + D.Da = 0 × .25 + 1 × .25 + 0 × .25 + 1 × .25 = 0.5, and so on).

Input (stimulus)

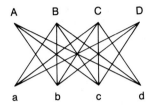

Output (response)

FIGURE 6.18   A one-layer network illustrates a simple distributed representation.

Input

	A	B	C	D
a	Aa	Ba	Ca	Da
b	Ab	Bb	Cb	Db
c	Ac	Bc	Cc	Dc
d	Ad	Bd	Cd	Dd

Output

FIGURE 6.19   A 4 × 4 matrix that represents the weights of 16 different connections. The inputs are at the top; the outputs are on the left.

	Input		Weights			Output	
A	0	0.25	0.25	0.25	0.25	0.5	a
B	1	0	0	0	0	0	b
C	0	0	0	0	0	0	c
D	1	−0.25	−0.25	−0.25	−0.25	−0.5	d

FIGURE 6.20   A 4 × 4, input/output connection matrix with numbers in place.

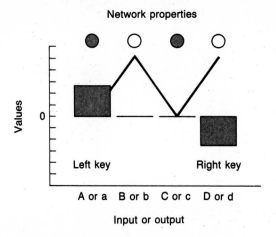

FIGURE 6.21   A graphic depiction of the input/output matrix shown in Figure 6.20. The four circles represent the stimulus, which is either "on," "off," or some intermediate stage. The solid line represents the input; the shaded bars represent the output, which correspond to the responses keys beneath them.

The information in the preceding input-output matrix is shown graphically in Figure 6.21. The four circles at the top represent the stimulus, which you can think of as four lights that can be completely on, completely off, or at some intermediate brightness. "On" corresponds to a value of 1, "off" to −1. The intensity of the lights (i.e., the input) is also represented by the solid line. The shaded bars represent the output, which you can think of as pigeon key pecks on the left-hand or right-hand response keys. Assume that the rate of pecking is proportional to the height of the bar above the zero line but that it is zero if the value is negative (i.e., below the line).

Figure 6.22 shows how this network responds to various configurations of stimuli, ranging from all "on" (1, 1, 1, 1) to all "off" (−1, −1, −1, −1). Each panel shows the input (solid line) and the output (shaded bars). Notice that with the weights shown, the network acts as if it has learned to discriminate between "white" (all inputs "on": 1, 1, 1, 1), in which case it responds strongly on the left (panel 1), and "black" (all inputs "off": −1, −1, −1, −1), in which case it responds strongly on the right (panel 13). The network has several interesting properties:

1. It categorizes its inputs: No matter what the input, the network only responds on one side, either left (unit A > 0) or right (unit D > 0).

2. It shows stimulus equivalence: For example, panels 2 and 3 show different inputs but the same response. Evidently this network attends to the number of units that are "on," but it does not attend to which units are on. Consequently all inputs with the same total "energy" (same number of lights on) are treated identically.

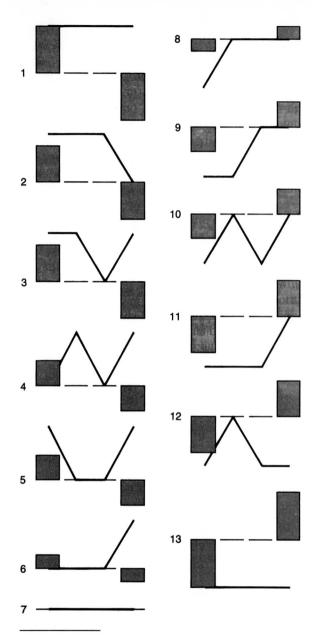

FIGURE 6.22 How the input/output network illustrated in Figure 6.21 responds to various configurations of stimuli, ranging from all "on" (1, 1, 1, 1) to all "off" (−1, −1, −1, −1). Each panel shows the input (solid line) and the output (shaded bars).

3. It shows generalization decrement. The network responds maximally on the left-hand side when all the inputs are all "on" (panel 1) and maximally on the right-hand side when all are "off" (panel 13). But, intermediate configurations produce intermediate results: For example, when all four inputs are at an intermediate level (0), the network makes no response (panel 7). If more lights are on than off, some responses are made to the left; if more lights are off than on, some responses are made to the right.

(Note that in the figure the inputs are all either zero or greater than zero or all zero and less than zero. Check for yourself that mixtures of positive and negative inputs still conform to these rules.)

We have described this network as a model for a stimulus–response relation, but it can also serve as a model for stimulus–stimulus associations, if we think of the input pattern as one property of an object (e.g., its color) and the output pattern as another (e.g., the form of the object). Then since this linear network operates perfectly symmetrically, presentation of the color will evoke the form, and presentation of the form will evoke the color. One-layer networks such as this one can show what psychologists used to call *redintegration,* that is, the ability to recreate an entire stimulus given only parts of the stimulus. There are many familiar examples: Most people can anticipate the melody of a favorite record after hearing just the first few notes; we can identify a friend after catching just a glimpse of him or her; and so on.

However, the one-layer network has limitations that prevent it from performing some relatively simple tasks. For example, it cannot solve what has been called the *exclusive-or (XOR) problem,* that is, it cannot both respond when either of two stimuli occur and *not* respond when both are presented together. For example, suppose we have a one-layer network that produces output 1 to inputs 01 and 10 and produces output 0 to input 00; there is no way that it can fail to respond with a positive value (other than 0) to input 11. Since rats and pigeons (not to mention people!) can easily learn an XOR discrimination, responding to two stimuli presented separately but not to their combination, the one-layer network is obviously an inadequate model for their behavior.

Two-Layer Networks

The XOR limitation can be overcome, however, by adding a threshold nonlinearity and a second layer of so-called "hidden units." Many two-layer networks are adequate for the job; an especially simple one is shown in Figure 6.23. This network has two inputs and a single output. The inputs are connected in all possible ways to the two hidden units with positive weights, thus stimulus 11 produces inputs of +2 to both hidden units. These hidden units have different thresholds (+1 and −1), but since 2 is greater than both thresholds, both inputs are transmitted to the output, but with opposite signs, since one hidden unit transmits with a weight of −1, the other with a weight of +1. Therefore, the summed input to the output unit is 0. Input 00 produces the same result. Input 01 transmits 0 through the top pathway but 1 through the bottom, for an output of 1.

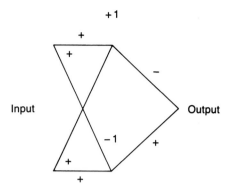

FIGURE 6.23   A two-layer, linear threshold network. The network has two inputs and a single output. The inputs are connected in all possible ways to the two hidden units with positive weights.

Input 10 transmits 1 via the bottom hidden unit and 0 (because it is equal to, not greater than, the threshold) via the top hidden unit, again for an output of 1. Thus, this two-layer, linear threshold network can solve the XOR problem.

Great progress has been made in extending the idea of distributed representations in other ways. For example, the computation performed by each node can be more complicated than merely summing weighted inputs. Indeed, there are great advantages to nonlinear networks that involve thresholds as well as other kinds of nonproportional relationships between the input to a unit and its output. All units need not be identical. The network need not be *symmetrical* (i.e., the connection between A and a does not have to be the same weight as between a and A). Most important, the weights do not need to be set in advance; they can change with time according to various rules that allow the network to learn a representation.

THE DELTA RULE AND BACK PROPAGATION   Several learning rules have been proposed. One of the most widely studied, the *delta rule,* is essentially the same rule we have already seen in our discussion of the Rescorla–Wagner model (Chapter 5). In the present context, it works as follows. Suppose that the weights in the network shown in Figure 6.20 are initially all 0.25. We present the positive stimulus as 1, 1, 1, 1; the desired response is the output configuration 1, 0, 0, 0; and the actual response is 1, 1, 1, 1. To achieve the desired result, we simply decrement the weights of all the connections that give an output greater than the one desired, and we increment the weights of all the connections that give an output less than that desired. Thus, weights Aa, Ba, Ca, and Da (Figure 6.19) are left unchanged (since a = 1, the desired value), and all other weights are decremented. Let's now suppose that the weights decrease from .25 to 0.2. On the next presentation of the stimulus 1, 1, 1, 1, the output is 1, .8, .8, .8—not perfect, but better. After a few repetitions, reducing the incorrect weights each time, the correct output will be produced, at which point the weights cease to change. The new set of weights is thus a learned representation of this discrimination.

Learning in two-layer networks is more complicated than that in one-layer networks—the delta rule does not apply. But other methods, most notably a rule called *back propagation,* have been found that allow multilayer networks to learn effectively.

SUMMARY

This chapter began with the problem of how animals recognize and attend to different situations. We took recognition and attention for granted in earlier chapters, in which we looked at how animals adapt to various procedures without asking how they know when a specific strategy is appropriate. Traditionally, this problem was handled by the concept of stimulus control: Specific physical stimuli or classes of physical stimuli were said to control specific responses or classes of responses. This concept worked well enough, but it cannot explain how animals represent relationships among complex stimuli. To answer these and other questions, some notion of an internal representation is required. A simple and powerful notion is to represent objects in a multidimensional abstract space. The problem of recognition is thus solved in a natural way, because any given environment defines a specific point in such a space. If, either innately or as a consequence of past training, different regions of this space have different values, then this representation provides a guide for action, in the sense that it lets the animal know whether its actions have made things better or worse. For example, by following a hill-climbing rule (or one of the more efficient variants that are now becoming better understood), an animal can act to improve its situation. Thus some kind of spatial representation is our best current guess about how animals encode information about their worlds.

But it is only a guess: Traditional methods of transfer testing with varied elements or physical stimulus dimensions are directed at different questions, and thus far they tell rather little about the problem of representation. They do tell us something about the rules that describe how physical stimulus elements combine and about the effects of reinforcement on stimulus control. Stimulus elements can combine additively, multiplicatively, and according to other quantitative principles, many of which can be represented spatially. Stimulus control, which is measured by the steepness of generalization gradients, is directly related to how well a stimulus feature predicts a valued outcome. But for both technical and historical reasons, we lack much information on control of behavior by multidimensional stimuli.

Stimuli come to control behavior only because the animal remembers something about its past. Memory in the most general sense is implied by any difference in behavior that can be traced to a difference in an organism's past history. Control of behavior by a time marker (temporal control) is one of the simplest examples of a memory effect. We showed that control by a time marker can be impaired by both prior and subsequent events—interactions that correspond to the proactive and retroactive interference much studied in human and animal memory experiments. These interactions limit animals' abilities to discriminate between the absolute and differential recency of events, which is sometimes known as working memory.

Recency discrimination depends on the specific properties of time markers. Hedonic stimuli such as food and electric shock are especially effective as time markers. Hedonic events preempt the animal's attention, so that a remote hedonic event may control behavior even though a more recent, but less salient, event is a better predictor. When interference is minimized, neutral events can serve as time markers, and they then behave in the same way as synchronous stimuli: Excitatory temporal stimuli show decremental generalization gradients; inhibitory stimuli show incremental gradients. This encoding of the properties of specific stimuli is sometimes known as reference memory.

The temporal aspects of memory can be represented by a "perspective" metaphor, in which the perceived recencies of events are represented by projections of their actual recencies in a "mental retina." Such a model implies a context-specific limit on the number of events that can be separately represented in event memory, thus there is a limit to short-term or working memory. The model also implies that as time passes, older events gain in memorability relative to newer ones, which is a long-established fact about memory (Jost's law). Animals that learn tasks such as successive, discrimination reversal and delayed-matching-to-sample seem to behave according to Jost's law: Reversal performance improves with practice, is unaffected by a lapse of several days or by shifting to a new pair of stimuli, but is usually impaired on the first reversal after the shift.

The chapter also analyzed how trace discrimination, together with spatial discrimination, can explain a variety of experimental results about spatial memory (rats in the radial maze and marsh tits in an artificial forest). Our analysis showed that most of the differences between spatial memory tasks, in which performance is relatively insensitive to delay, and tasks such as *delayed-matching-to-sample,* which are highly sensitive to delay, seem to be traceable to the greater demands placed on recency discrimination by DMTS. (This conclusion echoes Chapter 5, in which we found that most of the differences between long-delay, taste-aversion learning and standard Pavlovian conditioning also seem to reflect task, rather than process, differences. The major process factor, the evident dissimilarity of taste and nontaste stimuli, is a perceptual or cognitive property rather than something directly related to learning or memory.)

It is still conventional in psychology texts to discuss the topics in this chapter—memory, representation, discrimination, and generalization—in separate sections. But, recent work in neural modeling is beginning to show how these different phenomena may simply be different aspects of the same thing, namely an adaptive network with many connected units that learns by changing a distributed representation consisting of connection weights. This approach has certainly been highly successful at the engineering level: It produces systems that perform useful tasks. But, it is still too early to know if it is in fact an accurate model for the neural mechanisms of behavior. Although, even in a simplified form, the idea of a distributed representation enlarges our notions about how adaptive behavior might be produced, and it certainly adds a new and exciting dimension to psychological theory.

We still have much to learn about how animals learn about the world and how they translate this knowledge into action. Early research, derived as it was from a fundamentally stimulus–response view of behavior, has taught us much about the action of reward and punishment but relatively little about cognition. Research in cognition and machine intelligence—and distributed models—has shown that even the behavior of simple animals requires much more than simple S–R links. To recognize hundreds or even thousands of different situations and respond rapidly, precisely, and adaptively to them demands a sophisticated world model as well as a substantial repertoire of stimulus–response routines. We have made much progress in understanding animal behaviors, but we are still groping to understand what they know.

7

Stimulus Control and Performance

In the last chapter we concluded that animals develop internal representations of their worlds that guide their behaviors. The properties of such representations are still uncertain, and we cannot yet be sure of the effects of reward and punishment on them. It seems likely that the representation of simple objects is independent of reward and punishment—animals need no special training to recognize simple objects—whereas representations of complex objects may perhaps be acquired only through a history of explicit reinforcement. For example, the perceptual learning through which trained archeologists develop uncanny skill in picking out fossils may be possible only because of the excitement (positive reinforcement) such discoveries induce. Medieval teachers believed that Latin was learned only through the sting of a whip (i.e., negative reinforcement), and the view that complex (i.e., difficult) learning requires strong motivation was almost universal until recently. Still, for recognition of simple stimuli, no special training seems to be required. In such cases, reward and punishment seems to give value to certain objects or places as represented, it does not appear to create or modify the representations themselves.

Is discrimination performance then determined solely by the animal's external environment, as internally represented? In this chapter, we discuss two other factors that must be taken into account: response constraints and competition among activities for available time. These factors together account for many, if not all, experimental results on operant generalization and discrimination. The chapter also discusses how these factors contribute to such well-established phenomena as behavioral contrast, discrimination, and peak shift.

Animals need to know both when to act and when not to act; hence, stimuli can have both excitatory and inhibitory effects. But as we will see, if animals are not performing one activity, they are usually performing another. Thus efficient allocation of behavior sets the stage for *competition* among tendencies to action. If an activity is especially pressing, such as finding something to eat when you're hungry, it will have a suppressive effect on all other behavior, for example, you would probably stop reading this text. Thus, the excitatory or inhibitory effects of stimuli on behavior must be examined in relation to other activities. Typically, animals are highly "aroused" under the conditions of operant-conditioning experiments. For instance, hunger, combined with periodic access to small amounts of food, sets the stage for intense behavioral competition. The animals have a lot to do and limited time in which to do it. A stimulus that signals the absence of food ($S-$) not only lets the animal know that it need not act in ways related to food, it also tells it that other activities are free to occur. The effects of inhibitory stimuli are thus both excitatory and inhibitory.

THE FEATURE-NEGATIVE EFFECT

Because organisms are able to perform more than one activity, and since these tendencies to action usually coexist, it is difficult to decide whether a stimulus that suppresses activity A acts directly on A by inhibiting it, or whether it acts indirectly by facilitating some other, antagonistic activity, which in turn suppresses A. The problem of indirect and even reverse effects of external stimuli is characteristic of any complex system in which the elements exert effects on one another and are also acted on by external forces. For example, in California a few years ago, strenuous efforts were made to eradicate the Mediterranean fruit fly, (a crop pest commonly called the Medfly) by killing it with insecticide—a direct inhibitory effect on the fly. However, Medflies are also preyed on by other insects. These predators naturally found it easier to catch those Medflies already weakened by the insecticide. For this reason and because a single predator will normally consume several prey, insecticide accumulated even faster in the bodies of Medfly predators than in the Medfly population itself. Hence, the predator population dropped sharply, disinhibiting the Medfly population, which actually increased under ill-conceived attacks of the insecticide campaign.

In short, since we have no direct access to the chain of internal causation that links activities to one another and to external stimuli, it is quite difficult,

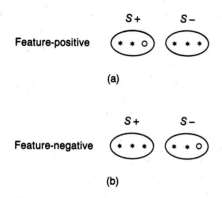

FIGURE 7.1   Examples of (**a**) feature-positive and (**b**) feature-negative stimulus displays.

even in principle, to disentangle apparently direct effects of stimuli on behavior. Apparently, inhibitory effects may actually be the result of a direct excitatory effect plus an indirect inhibitory one, or the reverse. Nevertheless, psychologists have devised tests for inhibitory and excitatory effects, and even though we cannot always be sure of what the results mean, we can make some useful generalizations.

For example, it is easier to establish inhibitory stimulus control, that is, control whereby presentation of a stimulus suppresses ongoing activity, if the inhibitory stimulus can also act to facilitate antagonistic activities. A curious phenomenon known as the *feature-negative effect* shows the converse: an inability to produce inhibitory control in the absence of antagonistic activities. In a series of studies, Jenkins and Sainsbury (1970) trained pigeons on a simple discrimination procedure of the following sort. At random intervals averaging 60 sec, a response key was illuminated with one of two stimuli. Four pecks on the positive stimulus ($S+$) produced food, whereas four pecks on the negative stimulus ($S-$) turned off the stimulus but had no other effect. In either case, if the animal failed to peck the keys four times, the stimulus went off after 7 sec.

The birds quickly learned not to peck during the dark-key intertrial interval. Did they also learn not to peck $S-$ (which amounts to inhibitory control by $S-$)? Not always, and the conditions when they did and did not suggest the importance of behavioral competition.

Figure 7.1 shows two kinds of $S+$, $S-$ stimulus pairs that Jenkins used: Figure 7.1a may be termed *feature-positive*, in the sense that the feature distinguishing $S+$ from $S-$ appears on $S+$; Figure 7.1b is *feature-negative*, since the distinctive feature appears on $S-$. Pigeons easily learn the feature-positive discrimination, pecking on $S+$ and not on $S-$, but they fail to learn the feature-negative discrimination, pecking indiscriminately on $S+$ and $S-$ (thus the term "feature-negative effect"). Why?

The Feature-Negative Effect and Perception

There seem to be three reasons for the feature-negative effect. One is perceptual: The displays in Figure 7.1 consist of separate elements; their dimensions are separable, not integral. That is, the elements of each display are not treated as a single perceptual unit. Moreover, $S+$ and $S-$ share elements in addition to those in the display. For example, they are usually on for about the same time, and they both appear on a white-lighted key (as opposed to the dark key used during the intertrial interval). Separability means that the elements are responded to separately; that is, $S+$ and $S-$ are not treated by the animal as discrete entities, rather, they are treated in terms of the elements they contain. Since $S-$ contains two of the three separable elements in $S+$, any tendency to respond to $S+$ must generalize powerfully to $S-$, because most of the features are common to both.

The Feature-Negative Effect and Sign Tracking

The second reason for the feature-negative effect is that pigeons naturally peck at features that signal food, which is called *sign tracking* (Hearst & Jenkins, 1974). Sign tracking is the basis for the phenomenon called *autoshaping,* which was briefly discussed in Chapter 6 ("Measurement of Stimulus Control"), and it may be another example of hill-climbing (behaving in a manner that best predicts a reward). Thus in the feature-positive case, the animals learn to peck at the distinctive element in the $S+$ display (the open circle in Figure 7.1), even before they show much decline in pecking $S-$. In the feature-negative case, the stimulus element that signals food is present in both the $S+$ and $S-$ displays; thus restriction of pecking this feature is therefore incompatible with refraining from pecking $S-$. However, pigeons can master a feature-negative discrimination if the display elements are close together, so that $S+$ and $S-$ are perceived as one unit (i.e., they become integral rather than separable). Pecking then is directed at the entire $S+$ complex, not to individual elements within it.

The Feature-Negative Effect and Competition

A third reason for the feature-negative effect may be the weakness of competing activities in $S+$ and $S-$. The discrimination procedure used in the pigeon experiment allows much time during the intertrial interval (ITI) for activities other than key pecking: The ITI averages 60 sec, whereas $S+$ and $S-$ are at most 7 sec in duration. The birds soon learn not to peck during the ITI, so that the time is free for other activities. Hence, the animal's tendency to engage in other activities during the relative brief $S+$ and $S-$ periods is relatively low, and any contribution to discrimination performance made by the facilitation of antagonistic activities in $S-$ is also small. In other words, the animal doesn't lose much by pecking during both $S+$ and $S-$. In support of this idea are data that show that the feature-negative effect is not obtained in more conventional successive discrimination procedures, in which $S+$ and $S-$ simply alternate at, perhaps, 60-sec

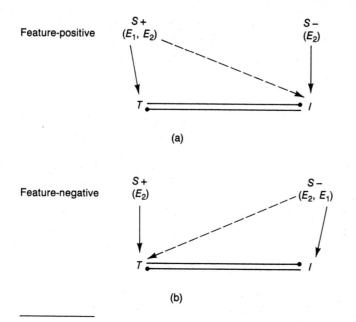

FIGURE 7.2   Excitatory control of terminal (T) and interim (I) activities by stimulus elements in (**a**) feature-positive and (**b**) feature-negative discriminations.

intervals, with no intervening ITI. In this case, the animal learns to peck for food only during $S+$, and it performs other activities during $S-$, when the likelihood of receiving food is quite low (we describe some of these data shortly).

The competition argument is diagrammed in Figure 7.2. Figure 7.2a shows the stimulus-control factors that act in the feature-positive case: $S+$ is made up of two kinds of elements (E_1, the distinctive feature [the open circle in Figure 7.1] and E_2, the element common to both $S+$ and $S-$; $S-$ is made up of just E_2, the common element. E_1 controls T, the *terminal response* of pecking; E_2 controls the *interim activity*, the collective term for activities other than the food-related terminal response (more on terminal responses and interim activities in the section called "Terminal Response and Interim Activities"). The horizontal lines symbolize the reciprocal inhibition (competition) between T and I activities. In the feature-positive case there is obviously nothing to facilitate key pecking (T) in the presence of $S-$. This situation is not true of the feature-negative case (Figure 7.2b). In that figure, pecking must be controlled by E_2, the common element, so that suppression of pecking in $S-$ must depend on reciprocal inhibition from interim activities. If these inhibitions are weak, there is every reason to suppose that pecking will occur in $S-$ as well as in $S+$, which it does.

The general point is that discrimination performance is determined by two factors:

1. The nature of the stimuli: How discriminable are they? Are they integral or separable?

2. The availability of competing (interim) activities: How strong are they? What aspects of $S-$ are likely to control them?

The level of responding to $S-$ is simply the sum of the two factors—discriminability, which if it is low may be a positive factor (favoring stimulus generalization from $S+$), and competition, which is a small negative factor if there are opportunities for interim activities other than in the presence of $S-$, but which is a large negative factor if there are no other opportunities.

Several predictions follow from the idea of behavioral competition as an essential component of discrimination performance:

1. Discrimination performance should be better when a substantial competing activity is available than when it is not.

2. The operant response rate in one component of a successive discrimination (multiple schedule) should generally increase when the reinforcement rate in the other component is reduced. This much-studied phenomenon is termed *behavioral contrast.*

3. Inhibitory generalization gradients (to be described shortly) should generally be less steep than their excitatory counterparts.

4. Discrimination gradients obtained following training in which $S+$ and $S-$ are on the same dimension should differ in predictable ways from gradients obtained after training with $S+$ and $S-$ on separate dimensions.

Let's look at the arguments behind these predictions and the experimental results that bear on them.

STIMULUS CONTROL AND BEHAVIORAL CONTRAST

About 30 years ago, when the operant-conditioning movement was enjoying its first flush of success, stimulus control was thought of in a simple fashion: A stimulus came to control an operant response when the response was reinforced in its presence. Each stimulus was assumed to be an independent entity, maintaining behavior strictly according to the conditions of reinforcement associated with it. Many data appeared to support this view. For example, if the schedule associated with one stimulus were a variable-interval schedule, and if the schedule associated with an alternating stimulus were a fixed-interval schedule, then the behavior in each stimulus soon became appropriate to the schedule in force. During the fixed-interval stimulus, the animal would show "scallops" of accelerating responding between food deliveries; during the variable-interval component, a steady response rate would prevail.

It was therefore quite a surprise when George Reynolds (1961) published a simple experiment that violated the rule of stimulus independence. His experi-

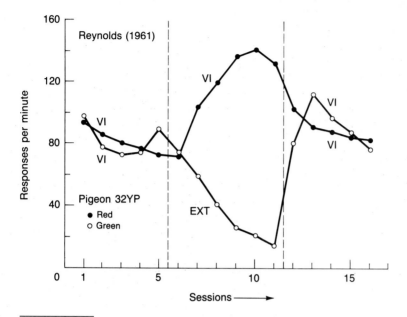

FIGURE 7.3   Positive behavioral contrast. Filled circles: response rate in the
unchanged (VI VI) component. Open circles: response rate in the changed (VI
EXT) component. Right third of the figure shows that the rate changes produced
by the shift to extinction in the changed component are reversible (from Reynolds,
1961b).

ment had two conditions. In the first (the *prediscrimination phase*), hungry
pigeons were trained to peck a key for food delivered according to a moderate
(e.g., 60-sec) VI schedule. The stimulus on the key was either a red or a green
light; the components alternated every 60 sec (a multiple VI VI schedule). When
a reinforcement schedule consists of two alternating schedules, such as this one,
it is called a *multiple schedule.* In the second condition (the *discrimination
phase*), the schedule in one stimulus (green, say) was changed from VI to extinction; conditions in the other stimulus remained unchanged (multiple VI EXT
schedule). The result was a reliable and substantial increase in response rate in
the unchanged (VI) component (*positive behavioral contrast*) (Figure 7.3).
The figure shows the response rate in the two components before and after the
shift from VI VI (VI food in both components) to VI EXT (VI food in one component, extinction in the other). Before the shift, the response rate is roughly the
same in both components, as would be expected. Afterward, however, as the response rate decreases in the extinction component, it increases in the (unchanged) VI component.

   Reynolds also demonstrated the converse effect, that of *negative contrast,*
which occurs when the rate of food delivery in one component is improved
rather than degraded. For example, when a multiple VI 60 VI 60 sec schedule is

changed to multiple VI 60 VI 20 sec, the usual result is a decrease in response rate in the (unchanged) VI 60 component.

Behavioral contrast is a widespread but not universal effect. For example, it is generally easier to demonstrate with pigeons pecking keys than with rats pressing levers or pigeons pressing a treadle. (There are some exceptions: Rats in runways and with appropriate stimuli in multiple schedules show contrast effects). In addition, if the food rate in the VI–VI condition is quite high (e.g., VI 15 sec), contrast effects are typically not obtained.

What is the reason for these changes? Why should responding increase or decrease in one component when food rate decreases or increases in the other component? What are the boundary conditions? For example, does contrast sometimes fail to occur?

There are two alternative explanations for contrast: One is based on response-rate change, the other is based on food-rate change. The response-change account rests on the implicit hypothesis that the animal has only so many responses to "spend," so that if it spends fewer in one component (because responses are no longer reinforced there), it will have more to spend in the still-reinforced component.

The food-change account rests on the general notion that response rate is guided by relative, rather than absolute, food rate. When the two components signal the same rate of food (VI 60 and VI 60), the relative rate of food is the same. When one component is shifted to extinction, the relative rate of food in the VI component increases from 50 percent to 100 percent, producing an increase in response rate during that component.

Reynolds and others have attempted to discriminate between these two hypotheses by experimentally separating the response-rate and food-rate drops in the changed component. For example, in one experiment (Reynolds, 1961), pigeons were reinforced for *not* responding for 6 sec, that is, all periods of 6 sec without a key peck ended with the delivery of food. This schedule effectively abolished pecking, but it failed to produce an increase in responding in the unchanged component; in other words, there was no behavioral contrast, even though a decrease occurred in the response rate in the changed component. Subsequent experiments by others have used other methods to reduce responding in the changed component (while maintaining food rate), but they have also failed to produce contrast. The general conclusion is that a change in relative food rate is usually sufficient to produce contrast, but a change in response rate unaccompanied by a change in food rate is usually ineffective.

STIMULUS CONTROL AND BEHAVIORAL COMPETITION

Behavioral competition seems to be a major factor in all these effects, although it is probably not the only process involved in contrast. The idea of competition can be illustrated by looking at how pigeons behave under periodic-food schedules (Skinner, 1948; Staddon & Simmelhag, 1971; Timberlake & Lucas, 1985). When hungry pigeons are exposed for an hour or so each day to a schedule in

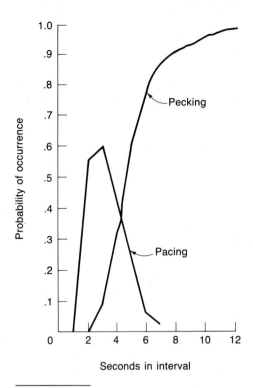

Seconds in interval

FIGURE 7.4   Average behavior of a single hungry pigeon receiving food every 12 sec. Each curve shows the probability that the activity will occur in each of the 12 sec between food deliveries (from Staddon and Simmelhag, 1971).

which they receive brief access to food every 15 sec or so (fixed time: FT 15), they spend a good portion of their time near the feeder. If food delivery is frequent and they are sufficiently hungry, they will often peck the wall in front of the feeder as the time for food approaches, even though the pecks are both unnecessary and ineffective.

Typical results of such an experiment are shown in Figure 7.4. The figure shows the behavior of a single, well-trained pigeon averaged across three, 30-min daily sessions of a FT 12-sec schedule. Each curve refers to a separate activity of the animal, which was assessed by visual observation. The curves show the probability of occurrence of each activity in each of the 12 sec between food deliveries. Thus, pecking never occurred during the first two seconds after food was received, but thereafter it occurred with increasing frequency, reaching a probability of nearly 1 by the end of the interval.

Terminal Response and Interim Activities

All the pigeons used in such experiments showed the same pattern, namely, two classes of behavior within each interfood interval: a single activity that increases in frequency up to the time that food is delivered (*terminal response*) and other activities that occur during earlier parts of the interval (*interim activities*). Thus, pecking is the terminal response; pacing and other movement patterns monitored in the experiment are interim activities. This division into terminal and interim activities has subsequently been demonstrated with rats and hamsters as well as pigeons. The specific activities that fall into the terminal and interim classes differ from species to species. Nevertheless, all activities become less vigorous at longer interfood intervals; and the terminal response need not always be identical to the response normally elicited by food, although that general pattern is well established. Terminal responses are obviously food-related, and they occur at times when food delivery is likely. Interim responses are not (with a few exceptions) food related, and they occur at times when food delivery is unlikely. For these reasons, we labeled those activities controlled by $S+$ as "terminal" and those controlled by $S-$ as "interim" in Figure 7.2.

When food delivery depends on a response (a fixed-interval schedule rather than fixed-time schedule), this response follows the same time course as the terminal response in Figure 7.4. The time taken up by food-related (i.e., terminal) activities is little affected by whether or not a response is necessary to receive food, although, of course, the type of response shown is likely to depend on the response contingency. When food delivery is aperiodic, as in a variable-time schedule, the same division into terminal and interim activities can often be seen, especially if there are definable periods when the probability of food delivery is zero. For example, if the shortest interval between food deliveries is 5 sec., say, then interim activities will typically occur during the first two or three seconds following food delivery. When food deliveries are random in time, no definable postfood period is available for interim activities; but, food probability does increase with postresponse time. Perhaps in response, interim activities, usually in some sort of vestigial form, occur in alternation with food-related activities. Thus, pigeons responding on a VI schedule often show brief turning-away movements alternating with key pecking.

Whether food delivery is periodic or aperiodic, whether a response is required or not, animals spend much time in food-related activities. The rest of their time is spent in activities that tend to occur at times or in the presence of stimuli that signal the absence of food. The competition between these two classes of activity seems especially intense in conditioning situations, in which small amounts of food are delivered frequently to hungry animals.

Motivation for Competing Activities and Behavioral Contrast

The existence of interim and terminal responses, with the properties just described, together with the general properties of any motivated behavior (see the discussion of Lorenz's hydraulic model in Box 6.1), sets the stage for contrast effects. (The argument can also be made from a functional point of view, using the economic property of *diminishing marginal returns:* The more you perform any activity, no matter how pleasurable, the less attractive each additional increment becomes.)

The motivational argument for behavioral contrast is as follows: Recall that a general property of any motivated behavior is that the tendency to engage in it increases with time, so long as it is not occurring (deprivation), but that the tendency decreases when it is occurring (satiation). Since the animals in these experiments are kept quite hungry and they only receive small amounts of food, satiation of food-motivated (i.e., terminal) behavior is slight. Their interim activities tend to be weakly motivated, and the tendency to engage in them certainly decreases substantially once they begin to occur. In the prediscrimination condition, with the same VI schedule operative in both components, interim activities must compete with the terminal response in *both* components. Thus, the tendency to engage in interim activities is relatively high, because there is no opportunity for complete satiation. The interim activities are therefore strongly competitive with the terminal response, which keeps its rate down in both components. But when one component is changed to extinction, the tendency to make the terminal response during that component is greatly weakened. Hence, interim activities are free to occur at will—and to satiate—during the extinction component, so their tendency to occur in the VI component is reduced. Since the food-motivation factors that sustain the terminal response in the unchanged component have not altered, but its competitor has become less effective, the rate of the terminal response must increase in the unchanged component. This situation represents a positive contrast, which is produced by a process of behavioral (as opposed to stimulus) *disinhibition*. (The way to make the functional argument in terms of diminishing returns is to say that the more total time allocated to interim activities, the less competitive they become. Because, in $S-$, the animal has extra time for interim activities when one of the VI components is changed to extinction, interim activities are less competitive in the unchanged component, hence terminal responding increases.)

A similar argument accounts for negative contrast. When the reinforcement rate in one component is increased, key pecking takes up more time. Hence, interim activities can claim less time and consequently become more competitive in the unchanged component, suppressing pecking. This situation represents a negative behavioral contrast, which is produced by a process of behavioral inhibition.

Figure 7.5 shows the results of an experiment by John Hinson and John Staddon (1978) that demonstrated directly the role of competition in contrast and discrimination. Rats were run in the standard two-component, two-condition contrast paradigm: first trained with VI 60 sec in both components of a multiple schedule, then shifted to EXT in one component. The experiment was performed both with and without a running wheel available to the rats. The top panels in the figure show the levels of lever-pressing and wheel-turning in the unchanged component. With a wheel (left quarter), the lever-press rate (solid line) is relatively low, because of competition from running, but the contrast effect following the shift to VI EXT is substantial. As the response rate increases in the second panel, the rate of wheel-turning (open circles) decreases. With no running wheel available (right quarter), the lever-press rate is higher, and the contrast effect (proportional increase in response rate in the unchanged component) is small.

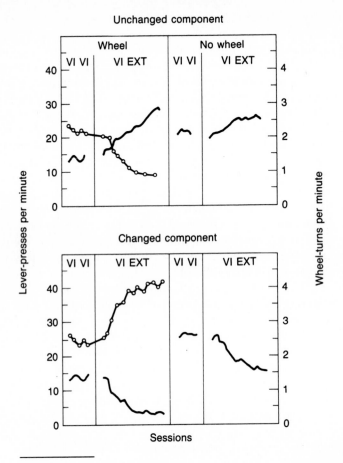

FIGURE 7.5   Reallocation of competing behavior during behavioral contrast. Mean daily rates of lever-pressing (solid line) and wheel-turning (open circles) for four rats in changed and unchanged components, with and without a running wheel available (from Hinson and Staddon, 1978).

The lower panels show the concomitant changes in the changed component. With a wheel (left quarter), wheel-turning increases and lever-pressing decreases substantially in the extinction component, thus discrimination performance is good. With no wheel (right quarter), the lever-press rate decreases little in the extinction component, thus discrimination performance is poor. Therefore, the availability of a strong interim activity can both improve discrimination performance and facilitate behavioral contrast.

The competition account of contrast is mechanistic not functional, although it makes functional sense. The competitiveness of the terminal response in each component is assumed to be directly related to the reinforcement obtained for terminal responses. The competitiveness of the interim activity is assumed to be related to its overall rate. In other words, the lower the rate of interim activities, the more competitive they become; the higher their rate, the less competitive they become. This process is economically efficient, as it allocates resources among different temporal periods in a manner that tends to maximize benefit to the individual (economists call such allocation "efficient *intertemporal resource allocation*"; you may call it common sense). For example, the efficient executive will read reports or dictate memos on his or her commuter train, when he or she cannot engage in other species-typical activities such as telephoning, chairing committees, or eating at lunch meetings. In like fashion, the rat trapped in $S-$ might as well perform interim activities, so it can put in more time pressing the lever in $S+$. Behavioral competition allows this problem to be solved in a manner that requires no foresight and puts no load on memory.

The competition process is clearly a major ingredient of behavioral contrast, but contrast may also occur for other reasons. We consider in the next section one theory, the additivity theory, because it has received considerable attention and serves to introduce a different way of looking at operant behavior. (Further discussions of these and other mechanisms of behavioral contrast can be found in Fantino and Logan [1979], Schwartz [1982], and Williams [1983].)

TWO-FACTOR THEORIES OF BEHAVIORAL CONTRAST

The basic idea of *two-factor theory* is attractively simple, as there are only two kinds of possible *contingencies* in learning experiments: *stimulus–stimulus* and *stimulus–response*. These contingencies roughly correspond to Pavlovian (classical) and operant (instrumental) conditioning procedures. But, it is often difficult to separate these contingencies unless special steps are taken. For example, a Pavlovian procedure may involve unwanted operant contingencies. In Pavlov's original experiment, salivation may improve the taste of the food powder, so that salivation may actually be partially under operant control. It is possible to eliminate response-reinforcer (operant) contingencies from Pavlovian procedures. However, Pavlovian elements found in operant-conditioning experiments are harder to eliminate, because any response-produced reward (US) must occur in the presence of some stimulus. Therefore, it may be that many of the responses officially designated as "operant" are actually a product of Pavlovian stimulus–stimulus (CS–US) contingencies and not operant ones. Indeed, some theorists (e.g., Bindra, 1972) have proposed that all operant behavior is the product of such contingencies.

Additivity Theory

Additivity theory is a less ambitious version of two-factor theory. According to additivity theory, behavioral contrast occurs when the effects of response and stimulus contingencies combine to affect the level of so-called Pavlovian key pecks. This theory is based on a two-process view of operant conditioning that has perhaps been more successful in application to aversively motivated behavior than to food-rewarded behavior. The idea here is simply that key pecking (the theory applies best here) can occur for two independent reasons. The conventional reason is the response contingency between pecking and food. The other reason is Pavlovian: Pigeons will peck a stimulus simply because it predicts (i.e., is correlated with) food delivery. Barry Schwartz proposed a few years ago that the physical pecks associated with these two sources of "strength" were different. He said that classically induced "autopecks" are shorter in duration than operantly produced pecks. This distinction has not held up well, but it is not essential to the hypothesis. The hypothesis merely asserts that when the stimulus contingency is changed in a multiple schedule, as it is when the reinforcement frequency in one component is altered, changes in pecking in the other component will be in the direction predicted by Pavlovian principles.

In George Reynolds's original experiment (see "Stimulus Control and Behavioral Contrast"), one of the VI schedules was changed to extinction, which meant that the Pavlovian correlation between food and the stimulus that signaled the unchanged component was thereby increased. During the prediscrimination phase, each component of the multiple schedule was signaled by a red or a green key light. Because the conditions of reinforcement never really changed (VI 60 to VI 60), the stimuli were not predictive of anything. On the other hand, during the discrimination phase, the stimuli signaled either VI 60 or extinction, and it was therefore predictive of reinforcement and nonreinforcement. This stimulus–reinforcer (CS–US) relation set the stage for Pavlovian conditioning, in which additional responses add to those already maintained by the operant contingency. Thus, it is the addition of responses maintained by Pavlovian conditioning to those maintained by operant conditioning that produces the increase in responding seen during the discrimination phase of Figure 7.3.

A major problem for the additivity theory of behavior contrast has been finding good tests for the interaction of operant and Pavlovian contingencies. Do the two contingencies produce responses that have different physical characteristics? Or, do they differ only with respect to the theoretical processes that control them? If the two kinds of pecks are not measurably different, then the theory does little more than restate Reynolds's empirical conclusion that relative food rate is the critical independent variable (McSweeney, Ettinger & Norman, 1981).

Opponent-Process Theory

A more sophisticated version of two-factor theory, called *opponent-process theory* (Solomon & Corbit, 1974), can answer some theoretical questions more effectively than additivity theory can. This theory has found useful application in a number of other areas such as drug addiction, love and attachment, and Pavlovian conditioning. It shares a number of elements with some of the other theories we have discussed in this book, such as the Rescorla–Wagner model and the hydraulic model. It is briefly described in Box 7.1.

STIMULUS CONTROL AND DISCRIMINATION

Performance on reinforcement schedules (as well as in many natural settings) is determined by the joint effects of external stimuli and competition for available time. The message of preceding sections is that the competitiveness of an ac-

B   O   X

7.1

Opponent-Process Theory

Richard Solomon and J. Corbit (1974) came up with the opponent-process theory to account for some commonplace facts. Most people are aware that a strong emotional experience is often followed by a cyclic reversal of affect. Everyone is also aware that almost every event, no matter how exciting, becomes habitual and unexciting with time (habituation).

(There is a rude and doubtless apocryphal story told of President Calvin Coolidge and his wife that illustrates habituation. The presidential couple were being shown around an agricultural breeding establishment. Mrs. Coolidge, observing the vigor with which the male hog went about his work, commented: "You should tell Mr. Coolidge about that!" Silent Cal, hearing of his wife's remark, responded laconically: "Tell Mrs. Coolidge that the sow is always new. . . .")

But, the habituation after excitement is not simply the restoration of a passive ground state. For example, after the initial thrill of a desirable gift, an attachment forms that shows itself as extreme unhappiness when the gift is lost or damaged. The same is true of a successful love affair: Even after two lovers have settled down to an apparently routine and undemonstrative existence, the loss of one will cause extreme grief in the other. These effects are characteristic of unpleasant as well as pleasant effects. The initial unhappiness of someone caught in an unpleasant situation, say, a hostage or a prisoner, after a while gives way to resignation. Upon his release, the hostage or prisoner will be elated, and up to a point, his or her elation is likely to be greater the longer the period of incarceration.

Solomon and Corbit proposed that these two effects—the elicitation of high affect followed by habituation and a release of affect in the opposite direction when the eliciting stimulus is removed—are connected. They proposed that the two effects are a consequence of a fundamentally regulatory, or *homeostatic,* mechanism. Let's imagine that any hedonic event elicits a reaction, which may remain constant while the stimulus is present or may decay with time. Solomon and Corbit called this process the "A" process; we call it x. The A-process in turn causes an internal "B" process (which we call y) that opposes the A-process, in the sense that the observed reaction depends on their difference $(x - y)$. Now let's imagine that these two processes correspond to integrators, with which you are thoroughly familiar. That is,

$$x_{N+1} = ax_N$$

where $0 < a < 1$, a "leaky bucket," and

$$y_{N+1} = bx_N + y_N(1 - b)$$

where $0 < b < 1$, a "regulator." We also know that the observed reaction (z) is $z = x - y$.

continued

BOX 7.1 (*continued*)

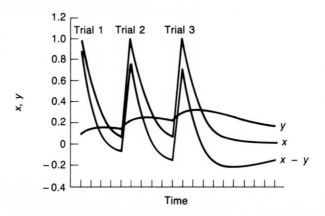

FIGURE B7.1   The opponent-process theory. The three curves show the A-process (x), the B-process (y), and the net affective reaction ($x - y$), as modeled by the x- and y-equations in the text. Parameter a (speed of the A-process) for these curves was 0.5; parameter b (speed of the B-process) was 0.1. Notice that the successive peaks of curve x (A-process) are reduced, because the level of curve y (B-process) is increasing. As a result, the after-reaction ($x - y$) also continues to increase.

The properties of this system of equations are simple. Variable x is a re-action that habituates: We let $x = 1$ when a hedonic event occurs, and then we let it decay afterward. On the other hand, variable y is a regulatory variable that attempts to "track" x: We could have written the second equation as $\Delta(y) = b(x - y)$ to indicate that y changes in such a way as to reduce the difference between x and y. Since the observed response depends on the dif-ference between x and y, the response magnitude will tend to decrease with repeated hedonic stimulus presentations (reinforcers)—a regulatory effect. The theory also assumes that parameter a is generally larger than parameter b, that is, the A-process is quick, whereas the B-process is slower.

The combined effect of these two processes will be that as hedonic events (reinforcers) occur repeatedly, the animal's initial reaction will de-crease (regulation), but the after-reaction will increase, (Figure B7.1). The fig-ure shows three equally spaced reinforcers, followed by an extinction period. Notice the strong negative after-reaction ($x - y$ curve) by the third trial.

This theory provides a neat explanation for the withdrawal effects of drug addiction: As the response to the drug diminishes, so the severity of the withdrawal increases. If we assume (as Schull, 1979, has proposed) that the B-process, which is generated by the animal in response to the stimulus-induced A-process, can itself become classically conditioned to situational cues, some quite surprising results follow. For example, an addict who is used to a highly concentrated drug dose will have a vigorous B-process (which under-lies the phenomenon of drug tolerance); if he or she unknowingly uses a much

continued

BOX 7.1 (*continued*)

weaker dose, the physiological effects of the B-process, now not balanced by a strong A-process, may be debilitating (withdrawal symptoms). Conversely, if the addict shoots up the drug in unfamiliar circumstances, so that his or her B-process (which is conditioned to a familiar situation) is not fully activated, he or she may lose tolerance—such that the usual drug dose (which may be much larger than the amount that can be tolerated by a nonaddict) can prove fatal. This effect may account for many drug-related overdose deaths, which are often not associated with larger-than-usual drug amounts (Siegel, 1983).

It seems clear that opponent-process theory does indeed capture something critical about the effects of highly affective stimuli and events. Nevertheless, much is left unstated. The process does not make obvious functional sense: For example, why must the development of habituation come at the cost of a severe opposite-sense after-reaction? The after-reaction depends on the slower speed of the B-process: Why shouldn't the B-process be as fast or even faster than the A-process? The answer may be that if the B-process is not slower, then it will not remain at a high level long enough to reduce the initial "spike" of A-reaction to later reinforcer presentations.

It is reasonable that organisms should *not* be well-adapted to nonbiological events that are evolutionarily recent, such as the injection of psychotropic drugs. It is less obvious why the organism should deal in an apparently maladaptive way with pair-bonding and like events that must have been common in the evolution of the species.

There are many unanswered questions about drug effects. For example, we do not know why the effects of opiate drugs conform to opponent-process theory, but nicotine and alcohol, in many ways just as addictive, do not. Nor can we yet identify the A- and B-processes with consistent physiological changes, although recent work on elicited and conditioned form of behavioral response shows some promising possibilities. Nevertheless, the opponent-process model is a provocative and readily modifiable theoretical framework that continues to raise interesting research questions.

---

tivity is directly related to the reinforcement for it, which is inversely related to its overall rate. Can we find a comparably simple way to describe the effects of external stimuli on behavior?

In the steady-state, multiple-schedule situation previously discussed, discrimination is perfect or near perfect: The stimuli are easy to tell apart, and changes in response rate reflect not failures of discrimination but efficient allocation of behavior. Even when a rat continues to respond in $S-$ (e.g., Figure 7.5, bottom right), the responding is not because it cannot tell the difference between $S+$ and $S-$ but rather because the cost of lever-pressing is quite low and it has nothing more appealing to do. In a generalization test, the response rate falls off gradually rather than abruptly (see Figure 6.4); yet given appropriate training with the opportunity to engage in competing activities, extremely sharp gradients can be produced. Presumably, the discriminability of the stimulus continuum (i.e., the cognitive and perceptual properties discussed in Chapter 6) has not altered, so this change in the shape of generalization gradients from gradual to steep reflects a change in behavioral competition.

The analysis of behavioral allocation developed in this chapter provides a relatively simple way to deal with these interactions among stimuli, competing activities, and differential reinforcement for those activities. Figure 7.6, which is a simplified version of Figure 7.2, provides a starting point. The figure shows the factors that affect the terminal (x) and the interim (z) activities in a successive discrimination (multiple schedule) of the sort already discussed. S_1 and S_2 represent *disjoint* (i.e., perfectly discriminable) elements that differentiate $S+$ and $S-$: For example, if $S+$ is a dark pecking key with a white star in the center and $S-$ a green key, then we can assume that there is zero perceptual overlap between these two stimulus elements (green and star). In addition, we can assume that since color/image is the only aspect that is different in the positive and negative schedule components, then this aspect must be the basis for any discrimination. Thus, x is controlled (facilitated might be a more accurate term) only by S_1, and z is facilitated only by S_2. As well, each activity is inhibited (because of competition for time) by the other. The variable C refers to all those stimulus factors that have effects on both x and z (i.e., common factors). Let's consider how the diagram in Figure 7.6 applies to an experiment with a simple, successive discrimination procedure.

In an experiment by Werner Honig and his colleagues (1963), two groups of pigeons were exposed to two alternating stimuli: one associated with VI food, the other with extinction (a multiple VI EXT schedule). For one group of animals, $S+$ was a vertical line and $S-$ a blank key; for the other group, $S-$ was a vertical line and $S+$ a blank key. Since the vertical line is the distinctive feature, the first group is feature-positive and the second feature-negative.

After sufficient training to produce good discrimination between $S+$ and $S-$ (i.e., few $S-$ responses), both groups of animals were given generalization tests in which their peck rate was measured in the presence of different line tilts (Figure 7.7). The result for the feature-positive group is the familiar excitatory gradient, with a peak at $S+$. However, the feature-negative group shows an inhibitory gradient, in which the response rate increases as the test stimulus departs from $S-$; moreover (and this is typical of many similar subsequent studies), the inhibitory gradient is somewhat shallower than the excitatory one, even though the experiment followed the same procedure for both groups of animals.

The diagram in Figure 7.7 implies that in the feature-positive group, the vertical line will facilitate x (the operant response), whereas z (the interim activities) will be facilitated by the blank key. Any variation in line tilt during a test should therefore weaken the key-peck rate much more than other activities, yielding the usual decremental gradient for x. In the feature-negative group, however, the vertical line must facilitate other activities much more than key pecking. Consequently, any variation in line tilt for the feature-negative case must weaken z much more than x, allowing x to increase (since its facilitating factors—the blank key and the vertical line—are still present) and producing the inhibitory gradient shown in the figure.

The shallower slope of the inhibitory rather than the excitatory gradient is also easily explained. The excitatory gradient directly measures the effect of

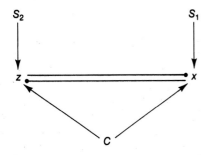

FIGURE 7.6   Causal factors in disjoint stimulus control: Each activity is facilitated by a disjoint stimulus element (S_1 or S_2) and common factors (C) and is inhibited by the other activity.

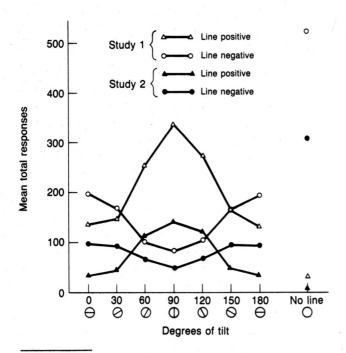

FIGURE 7.7   Inhibitory generalization gradients. Open triangles: excitatory line-tilt generalization gradient for a group of pigeons trained on multiple VI EXT, with a vertical line as $S+$, a blank key as $S-$ (feature-positive group). Open circles: inhibitory line-tilt generalization gradient for a group trained with a vertical line as $S-$, a blank key as $S+$ (feature-negative group). Closed symbols are from a repeat experiment (from Honig, Boneau, Burstein & Pennypacker, 1963).

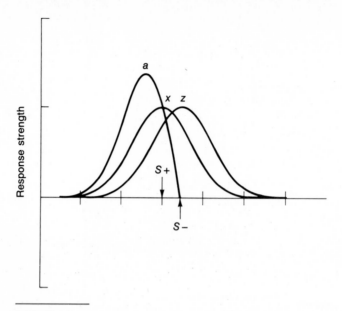

FIGURE 7.8   Peak shift (a) predicted from the interaction of generalization gradients surrounding $S+$ (activity x) and $S-$ (activity z).

stimulus variation on the activity controlled ($x:$ pecking). However, the inhibitory gradient is an indirect measure of the effect of $S-$ variation on z (an interim activity) and the activity it controls, because we are measuring only key-peck rate. If we were to measure interim activities directly (which has unfortunately not been done in these experiments), we would expect to see an excitatory gradient as the $S-$ feature is varied. But unless the interim activity controlled by $S-$ and the terminal response controlled by $S+$ are not only mutually exclusive but also exhaustive (there are no other activities), a given increase in z will produce a smaller decrease in x. This fact is true because a given increase in z will cause decreases in both terminal response x and interim activities other than z. Hence even if the excitatory effect of $S+$ on x is the same (i.e., shows an equally steep generalization gradient) as the excitatory effect of $S-$ on z, the inhibitory effect of $S-$ on x will be less steep than the excitatory effect of $S+$ on x. This effect is illustrated in Figure 7.8.

STIMULUS CONTROL AND PEAK SHIFT

Thus far we have discussed cases that illustrate behavioral contrast and generalization gradients that are based on successive discrimination training with disjoint stimuli. In these experiments, $S+$ and $S-$ are easy to tell apart, and it is unlikely that the animals ever get confused as to which is which. However, when $S+$ and $S-$ differ only slightly on only a single dimension, the resulting generalization gradient is different in important ways.

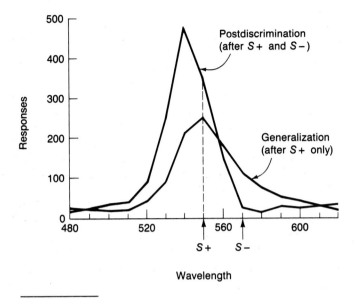

FIGURE 7.9   Wavelength generalization gradients after exposure to $S+$ only and after exposure to successive discrimination involving $S+$ and $S-$. The difference between the two gradients illustrates positive contrast and peak shift (after Hanson, 1959).

Figure 7.9 shows the result of a classic experiment on generalization after discrimination training with similar stimuli (Hanson, 1959). In the control condition, a group of pigeons was trained with $S+$ alone (simple VI) then was given a generalization test. For the control condition, $S+$ was a green light of 550 nm. The result of the generalization test is the lower gradient in the figure, which is peaked at $S+$. Other pigeons were trained on the familiar, multiple VI EXT procedure: $S+$ was the same green light of 550 nm; $S-$ was a greenish-yellow light of a slightly longer wavelength, 570 nm. The results of the generalization test following the multiple VI EXT training are a higher gradient in the figure, with its peak at about 540 nm. That is, the gradient shifted from $S+$ in a direction away from $S-$. Why the difference in gradients?

The increased responding in $S+$ in the postdiscrimination gradient is the positive behavioral contrast illustrated in Figure 7.3. As we have seen, this increased responding can usually be explained by the efficient reallocation of terminal and interim activities between the $S+$ and $S-$ periods. The *peak shift* is a related effect of competition between the activities controlled by $S+$ (terminal response) and by $S-$ (interim activities). Thus far, we have established that

1.   Both terminal responses and interim activities have controlling stimuli.
2.   Variation in these stimuli yields excitatory generalization gradients.
3.   Because of competition, an excitatory gradient in terms of one response will usually be associated with a (shallower) inhibitory gradient in terms of other responses.

B   O   X

7.2

Kenneth Spence and the Theory of Transposition

In the 1930s, arguments raged between two groups of psychologists—the stimulus–response theorists and the gestaltists—who had two very different approaches to discrimination learning. The *gestalt* psychologists (a group of German emigrés whose best-known representatives are Wolfgang Köhler and Kurt Koffka) devised several clever perceptual demonstrations to refute simple-minded ideas about the passivity of perception. (Many of the illusions you probably saw in an introductory psychology class were discovered by the gestalt psychologists.) The word *gestalt* means *whole,* and the gestaltists argued that perception—and discrimination—involve properties of the whole stimulus array that cannot be derived from properties of stimulus elements. The gestalt psychologists seized on an effect called *transposition* in support of their position. Transposition, although measured in a simultaneous rather than a successive discrimination, is quite similar to peak shift.

The setup was as follows: Rats were trained to respond to the larger, say, of two squares. After training, the animals were then confronted with two new squares, the smaller of which was equal in size to the larger of the previous pair. The question: Will the animals respond to the same-size square (absolute responding, which is congenial with stimulus–response theory) or to the still-larger square (i.e., transposition, which is relational responding congenial with gestalt theory)? Of course, the clever animals usually picked the larger square, giving aid and comfort to the gestaltists and until Kenneth Spence, spreading gloom and despondency among S–R theorists.

Spence's (1937) insight was that this kind of result can be derived from suitable assumptions about the properties of stimulus elements: If reinforcing responses to $S+$ causes the development of an excitatory gradient, then non-reinforcement of responses to $S-$ should produce an inhibitory one. If these two gradients are smooth and the slope of the inhibitory gradient is greater than the slope of the excitatory one (at least in the vicinity of $S+$), then the difference between the two gradients, which determines measured preference, will have its peak not at $S+$ but shifted from $S+$ in a direction away from $S-$. Therefore, given $S+$ and a still larger stimulus, Spence's model predicted that the response strength associated with the larger stimulus might well be greater than the response strength associated with $S+$. Moreover, (and this fact was the strong point of the model), Spence's model also predicted that if the new stimulus were too large, the animal would not transpose but would show *transposition reversal,* preferring the original $S+$. Indeed, animals act in this manner, and Spence's model received solid support.

More than 20 years later, after the invention of the technique of free-operant, generalization testing by Norm Guttman and Harry Kalish and the discovery of peak shift following intradimensional discrimination, Spence's theory was applied to peak shift. But here, Spence's model has several flaws. The least important weakness in the model is that it was devised for simultaneous situations, but peak shift does not occur in operant-concurrent experiments. A more critical flaw is its requirement that the inhibitory gradient be steeper than the excitatory one and that responding to $S+$ after the formation of a discrimination be at a lower level than before. As we have seen, measured inhibitory gradients are generally shallower than excitatory ones, and post-discrimination $S+$ responding is generally at a higher level than before (positive contrast). Nevertheless, John Staddon (1977) showed that these defects can be corrected while retaining the essentials of Spence's theory, which therefore remains the best account for peak shift and inhibitory generalization gradients.

Still, many data cannot be easily explained by the simple interaction of excitatory and inhibitory gradients. Experiments in which animals can learn to recognize complex stimulus categories, such as "people" or "trees" (Herrnstein, Loveland & Cable, 1976; Cerella, 1979; Delius, 1985), and studies in which they learn to pick the "odd" stimulus or one of intermediate value in a set of three show that animals do appear to possess the complex perceptual abilities favored by the gestaltists. Nevertheless, the recent development of multidimensional versions of interacting-gradient theory (Heinemann, 1984) suggests that such gradient models can explain much more than was at one time believed. The gestaltists' explanations remain inadequate in principle. No matter what the merits of his theory, Spence was quite correct in rejecting "relational responding" as a satisfactory explanation for anything. It's fine to show that pigeons can solve tricky perceptual problems; but to term this behavior relational responding and not explain it further leaves us with no satisfactory answers. A proper explanation must, like Spence's, get down to the physical properties of the stimulus and its transformation by the animal. We are still far from being able to fulfill this task, even for activities such as object recognition.

To see in addition how these processes may lead to peak shift, look at Figure 7.8, which shows the interaction between generalization gradients that represent both $S+$ and $S-$. The theory sketched in Figure 7.8 is a recent development based on an early theory proposed by Clark Hull's student Kenneth Spence (Box 7.2).

The two symmetrical, bell-shaped curves in the figure represent the generalization gradients for $S+$ and $S-$ (measured in terms of the responses they control) presented alone. The higher, asymmetrical curve is the postdiscrimination gradient produced when $S+$ and $S-$ alternate on a multiple schedule. It is higher than the underlying gradient for $S+$ because of the behavioral contrast discussed earlier: The animal allocates key pecking to the $S+$ component and other activities to the $S-$ component of the multiple schedule. The curve is steeper for the same reason. The peak of the postdiscrimination gradient for $S+$ is shifted away from $S-$ because of the interaction between activities controlled by $S+$ and by $S-$. Wherever the two gradients overlap, there is a subtractive effect on the activities controlled by $S+$ by the activities controlled by $S-$. It is hard to see intuitively how these two effects—behavioral competition and overlap of gradients—combine to yield the peak shift, but it can be shown mathematically in a fairly straightforward manner. Thus, the basic properties of discrimination performance, inhibitory control, and generalization gradient peak shift all seem to reflect behavioral competition and direct excitatory control of behavior by stimuli.

Several other effects also fit into this general picture. For example, some years ago Herbert Terrace performed an experiment in which pigeons were first trained to peck a distinctive $S+$ (e.g., a key illuminated with a white vertical line) for food presented on a VI schedule. Once this pecking was established, Terrace occasionally presented a brief $S-$ with a very different appearance (e.g., a dark key). Pecks on this stimulus did not lead to food, but in fact most animals never pecked it. Terrace then progressively increased the duration of $S-$ and faded the color of the key. In this way, he was able to establish discriminations without the animals making any "errors" ($S-$ responses). His procedure became known as *errorless discrimination.* The animals turned away from the key as soon as $S+$ went off, so that presumably no activity came under the explicit control of $S-$. Perhaps for this reason, these animals failed to show inhibitory generalization gradients. They also failed to show behavioral contrast. Other work has confirmed that contrast and inhibitory gradients usually occur together. The present analysis suggests they should, because they both depend on stimulus control by $S-$ of activities antagonistic to the terminal response. Contrast and peak shift also tend to go together, although there are some cases in which they can be disassociated.

SUMMARY

In this chapter we argued that many of the properties of performance on successive discrimination tasks, such as a multiple schedule, can be derived from three assumptions:

1. That inhibitory stimulus control, the suppression of an ongoing activity by presenting a stimulus, is associated with excitatory control of antagonistic activities. That is, inhibitory control of activity A is excitatory control of competing activity B. The two competing classes of behavior correspond to the terminal and interim activities observed in periodic-food experiments.

2. The competitiveness of an activity decreases as its level increases. This change in level is a consequence of the satiation-deprivation property characteristic of all motivated behavior. It can be expressed in functional terms as the concept of diminishing marginal returns: That is, the more one engages in an activity, the less attractive it becomes.

3. That the competitiveness of an activity is directly related to its rate of reinforcement. For example, the more food is available for a given activity, the more competitive it becomes.

In most operant-conditioning situations, competition between activities is especially severe. Hungry pigeons or rats have much to do, such as key pecking or pressing a lever for food (terminal activities), as well as their other activities, such as grooming, preening, or perhaps drinking (interim activities). Over the course of the conditioning experiment, animals begin to allocate terminal activities to times when food is more likely, and they allocate interim activities to other times. This reallocation during successive (multiple-schedule) discrimination experiments appears to account for some instances of behavioral contrast, the characteristics of inhibitory generalization gradients, and the interactions between excitatory and inhibitory gradients that produce peak shift.

There is still no general agreement on whether the intermediary role we have assigned to interim activities is either necessary or invariable. Our predictions could be derived in the same fashion by assuming the existence of some inhibitory process, which might or might not correspond to observable activity. Such an alternate path is taken by the opponent-process theorists, for example. Nevertheless, interim activities usually occur, and they make sense: Even hungry animals perform other activities than looking for food, and in a suitable environment we can observe them. The properties of the inhibitory process are just what we would expect of such activities, assuming that they behave like other motivated activities. All in all, it seems simpler to include them than to leave them out.

CHAPTER

8

Learning and Behavior

Thus far we have shown how behavior in a range of situations appears to be guided by the animal's internal representation of its world—from fixed-interval schedules to the radial maze, to conditioning experiments with rats and bees. Studies of Pavlovian conditioning in Chapter 5 showed how conditioning can be regarded from a functional point of view as an inference process that allows an animal to incorporate something about the causal texture of the environment into its representation. In this chapter, we examine the relation between operant and Pavlovian conditioning, and we discuss how actions can be derived from representations. The chapter presents "learning" as a circular process in which surprise and novelty cause an animal to update its representation of the situation, which in turn leads to new activity, a new situation, perhaps more surprises, and so on. These updates can be seen in a series of iterations that usually converges on an adaptive behavioral pattern. We begin with a brief description of several classic experiments that forced a reevaluation of the relation between operant and Pavlovian conditioning. These experiments provided the context for a new approach to the study of learning.

THE RELATION BETWEEN
OPERANT AND PAVLOVIAN CONDITIONING

Autoshaping

Several years ago a very simple experiment shocked workers in animal learning. Paul Brown and Herb Jenkins (1968) presented hungry, experimentally naive pigeons in a Skinner box with a 7-sec stimulus (a colored light) on a single response key at intervals averaging one minute (VI 60-sec). At the end of the 7 sec, the food hopper appeared for 4 sec. Food delivery was independent of the animal's behavior; that is, the pigeon could neither prevent nor aid operation of the feeder. The procedure is clearly Pavlovian in that a CS (the key light) is reliably paired with a US (food)—even though the bird and the Skinner box are more usually associated with operant-conditioning procedures. The surprising feature of the experiment was not the procedure but the results. After as few as 10 light–food pairings, the pigeons began to peck the lighted response key and continued to do so indefinitely, even though pecking had no effect on food delivery. Brown and Jenkins called this effect *autoshaping*, because the procedure automatically "shaped" the pigeon to peck the response key. Autoshaping is in contrast to *handshaping*, which is the traditional training procedure, in which closer and closer approximations to key-pecking are successively reinforced by the experimenter.

Autoshaping was surprising because it was believed that key-pecking was an operant response and thus conditionable only by operant procedures. Indeed, C. B. Ferster and B. F. Skinner's work on operant conditioning, *Schedules of reinforcement* (1957), is almost entirely about pigeons that peck keys for food reinforcement. Brown and Jenkins showed that this prototypical operant response could also be shaped by Pavlovian procedures. The implications of this result for our understanding of how operant conditioning actually works were to be profound.

Williams and Williams (1969) made a small change in the autoshaping procedure that changed it from a Pavlovian procedure to an operant one. In their procedure, on trials when the pigeon did peck the key, food did *not* occur, and the key light was turned off. If the pigeon did not peck on a trial, the key light remained on, and food arrived as usual after 7 sec. The Williamses procedure is termed *omission training,*[1] and it is a traditional control procedure in Pavlovian-conditioning experiments. Clearly, it pays for the pigeon *not* to peck under these conditions, since pecking prevents food delivery. If pecking is truly an operant response, that is, one whose rate is determined by its consequences, then key-pecking should cease. But, it did not. The pigeons pecked less often than before, but they continued to peck the key in spite of the omission of food (*negative*

---

[1] Note that *omission training* is not the same as the reinforcement *omission effect* discussed in Chapter 6 in connection with temporal control.

(a)   (b)

FIGURE 8.1 Typical food and water autoshaped responses as they appear at the moment of key contact. (**a**) Responses to the left key, which was paired with water. (**b**) Responses to the right key, which was paired with food (from Jenkins & Moore, 1973).

automaintenance). Thus, the purely "operant" nature of key-pecking was seriously called into question.

Autoshaping is not unique to pigeons and key-pecking. Subsequent experiments under appropriate conditions have shown autoshaping in rats, monkeys, and even people. However, the type of response that can be conditioned by the autoshaping procedure is limited and seems to resemble an anticipatory response to the US. For example, if the US is food in an autoshaping experiment, the pigeon pecks in a manner similar to pecking at grain. On the other hand, if the US is water, the pigeon pecks the key as if it were drinking. These two responses are illustrated in Figure 8.1, which shows photographs of key-pecking in anticipation of water reinforcement (Figure 8.1a: closed bill) or food (Figure 8.1b: open bill).

Voluntary and Involuntary Behavior

To understand the impact of these autoshaping experiments it helps to know something about the historical context. For many years it was thought that Pavlovian- and operant-conditioning arrangements exerted their effects on different types of behavior. The Pavlovian procedure was thought to be uniquely effective on behavior controlled by the autonomic nervous system (e.g., salivation, changes in skin resistance and heart rate, pupillary dilation). Such responses are *involuntary*, because they are not directly controllable; that is, you cannot directly increase or decrease heartrate or pupil constriction. On the other hand, operant behavior is *voluntary* in the sense that we feel we can produce it at will. Voluntary behavior usually involves the skeletal muscles. B. F. Skinner proposed a similar, although supposedly more objective, distinction between

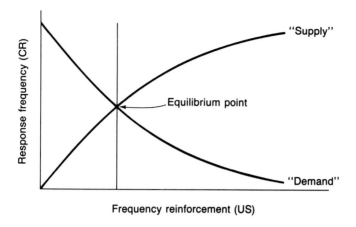

FIGURE 8.2   The equilibrium point, where the amount of salivation supplied permits a reinforcement frequency just able to sustain it.

emitted (voluntary) and *elicited* (involuntary) behaviors. We use these two sets of terms interchangeably.

Defining voluntary and involuntary in an objective manner is difficult, to say the least, since the terms are by their very nature subjective (Kimble & Perlmutter, 1970). On the other hand, when we are dealing with human behavior, we can say that voluntary behavior is behavior people can produce quickly, on demand. Therefore, we can say that involuntary behavior cannot always be produced at will—sexual impotence is the most embarrassing example—and it sometimes occurs when we would wish it did not—blushing, for example. Of course, there are people who claim to be able to produce behavior at will that in others is involuntary, but such actors' tricks usually rely on an indirect method. For example, such tricks include imagining oneself in an embarrassing situation to achieve blushing or imagining oneself in a sad situation to produce tears.

Involuntary responses such as salivation are insensitive to purely operant contingencies. For example, if food is always omitted on each trial when the animal salivates in the presence of the CS, it usually salivates anyway, the amount determined by the actual frequency with which food occurs in the presence of the CS. The equilibrium frequency of salivation (or any other purely Pavlovian response) is thus determined by the intersection of two curves: one of "supply" (how much salivation will occur at a given reinforcement frequency) and the other of "demand" (how much reinforcement will be given at a given salivation frequency). The names "supply" and "demand" are arbitrary, of course, but the curves in an omission-training experiment look quite similar to economic supply-and-demand curves, in which the supply curve is an increasing one. Therefore, the more frequent the reinforcement, the more the animal salivates. The demand curve in such a scenario (on an omission schedule) is declining: the more frequent the salivation, the less often the animal is reinforced. The equilibrium is the intersection point of the two curves, where the amount of salivation supplied permits a reinforcement frequency just able to sustain it (Figure 8.2).

The typical finding for responses such as salivation is that the amount of salivation in an omission experiment is exactly what would be obtained in a purely Pavlovian (response-independent) schedule that provided reinforcement at the equilibrium rate, that is, at the rate indicated by the vertical line in the figure. In other words, the omission contingency has no independent effect on the animal. Its only effect is to reduce the frequency of the US (food), which has an effect on CR (salivation) frequency. In practice, this comparison must be made between two procedures at different times or between two different groups of animals in what is termed a *yoked-control procedure.* This procedure involves two animals: the experimental animal is exposed to an omission schedule; but the control animal is on a *partial-reinforcement,* Pavlovian-conditioning schedule, whose reinforcement frequency is determined by the reinforcements actually obtained by the experimental animal. In other words, when the experimental animal is reinforced, so is the control animal. The question is whether the frequency of responding (CR) is the same for both animals (or *less* for the experimental animal—which would indicate some sensitivity to the omission contingency. For a response such as salivation, the control and experimental animals respond identically.

This outcome is different from what we would expect of an operant response, which should decrease under the omission contingency. Several yoked-type studies of autoshaped key-pecking have been conducted, and the consensus seems to be that there is only a small effect of the omission contingency above and beyond the large effect of reinforcement frequency. (Operant conditioners should perhaps not have been quite so surprised at this outcome, since they produced a similar result with *spaced-responding schedules,* i.e., schedules in which food is delivered for key-pecks separated by more than T-sec. When T is greater than about 20 sec, pigeons, at least, are unable to restrain their pecking, and they respond at a rate high enough to prevent almost all food deliveries [Staddon, 1965].)

Clearly, some skeletal responses are strongly affected by Pavlovian contingencies. However, there is less evidence for crossovers in the other direction, that is, for direct operant conditioning of autonomic activities. The proposition that heartrate can be modified directly by operant means is difficult to test, because changes in skeletal responses often have correlated autonomic effects. For example, changes in breathing pattern can have effects on heartrate; a person can change his or her heartrate and skin resistance by imagining (an operant, voluntary activity) a frightening scene or tensing muscles. When *biofeedback* (feeding back to the subject information about his or her autonomic processes) is successful, it is often via one of these intermediary processes, although it seems to be true that part of the problem in the voluntary control of autonomic activities is that we are normally unaware of them. In other words, biofeedback can help make people aware of their heartrate or level of galvanic skin response (GSR).

One way to test the direct reinforcibility of autonomic effects is to eliminate skeletal muscle activity by injecting a derivative of the paralytic drug curare. For example, an experiment by Miller and Banuazizi (1968) used curarized rats with electrical brain stimulation as the operant reinforcer. Heartrate changes or intestinal contraction or relaxation were the reinforced, autonomic responses for different groups of animals. Heartrate increased when the brain stimulation depended on increases, and it decreased when stimulation depended on decreases. Intestinal motility showed similar effects. Unfortunately, the drastic curare treatment is subject to side effects that make positive results difficult to interpret. Several of the dramatic early experiments of Miller and his associates have turned out to be seriously flawed. Workers in Miller's own laboratory have not been able to repeat some of these early results (see Obrist et al., 1974).

Thus, autonomic responses do not seem to be directly affected by operant contingencies, nor should we expect them to be, given their adaptive function. Autonomic activities are concerned with regulating the internal, not the external, economy of the organism. Heartrate, skin resistance, intestinal motility, pupillary dilation, or any of the other autonomic responses used in Pavlovian experiments do not typically have any direct effect on the external environment, as skeletal muscle movements do. Therefore, it seems unlikely that these processes would be modifiable in exactly the same way as muscle movements.

The internal economy is of course indirectly involved in operant behavior. "Fight or flight" reactions to external threat are more efficient if the body is suitably prepared in advance. For example, the animal will fight more efficiently if its heart and breathing rates are high (so the blood is well charged with oxygen), if its digestive and other vegetative functions are suppressed (releasing metabolic resources for the struggle), if its pupils are dilated for better vision, and if its body hair is erect, ready to intimidate its opponent and shed the heat from impending exertions. Karen Hollis (1984) has recently shown that male gouramis (an Indian anabantid fish frequently kept in home aquaria) are more successful in defending their territory if they receive notice of an imminent intrusion in the form of a Pavlovian CS. There are also several other examples in which a CS facilitates a species-specific behavior, often via the preactivation of slow-to-act hormonal systems. It makes sense, therefore, that Pavlovian-conditioned responses should be anticipatory and guided by the predictiveness of situational cues, as they almost invariably are. Similar changes take place in anticipation of food, water, and other hedonic events.

The conclusion appears to be that under the proper conditions many skeletal responses such as key-pecking are sensitive to Pavlovian contingencies. However, autonomic activities are probably not directly sensitive to operant contingencies, even though heartrate, blood pressure, and some other autonomic responses can be influenced indirectly by operant procedures (e.g., biofeedback).

If operant and Pavlovian conditioning cannot be neatly identified with skeletal and autonomic responses, we are left with the problem of understanding the relations between Pavlovian- and operant-conditioning procedures. In Chapter 4, we proposed that Pavlovian conditioning sets the stage for operant conditioning by allowing the animal to identify the kind of situation it is in, that is, to classify it. In Chapter 5, Pavlovian conditioning was presented as an inference process in which situations and objects are assigned values depending on the animal's prior knowledge and the temporal relations prescribed by the conditioning procedure. In the next section, we see that situations with different motivational significances automatically activate different behavioral repertoires. These repertoires involve both autonomic and skeletal activities. The skeletal activities and the cognitive processes that often underlie them are then candidates for strengthening or weakening by the temporal (contiguity) relations enforced by operant-conditioning procedures. Thus, the functional significance of Pavlovian conditioning (i.e., sensitivity to stimulus–stimulus relations) seems to be that it provides the behavioral raw material for operant conditioning (selection of an appropriate action).

BEHAVIORAL VARIATION: THE ORIGINS OF BEHAVIOR

A standing criticism of purely cognitive views of behavior is that they imply no action. For example, Edward Tolman's early cognitive-map idea was criticized because it left the rat sitting in the maze "lost in thought." The rat knew where everything was, but it had no reason to go anyplace. This issue is one of performance, which was discussed in Chapter 7. In this section, we see that the same inference processes that allow the animal to identify potential conditioned stimuli can also permit it to identify potential operant responses. That is, the rat not only knows what a stimulus is but also what it should do about it.

The function of Pavlovian learning seems to be the development, by the animal, of an accurate model of its world. But, action is also part of the animal's representation. As we saw at the end of Chapter 5, for a bee, to know a good flower is to seek it out. All organisms approach good things and withdraw from bad ones. Certain kinds of situations automatically entail certain kinds of action. All Pavlovian conditioning carries implications for action, which were often concealed from Ivan Pavlov and his successors by the restrictions they imposed on their animals. Pavlov's dogs were restrained in a special harness so that their salivation could be measured easily. (Pavlov worked in this manner because he believed in the reflex model for behavior: By isolating this one element, he thought, he could eventually understand all behavior). Yet, salivation is probably the least important aspect of what Pavlov's dogs learned. A visitor to Pavlov's laboratory reported the reaction when a dog previously trained to salivate at the sound of a metronome was released: The animal at once approached the metronome, wagged its tail at it, barked and behaved in every way as it might toward an individual who feeds it. Clearly, the major effect of conditioning was to assign a food value to the metronome. Given this valuation and the physical properties of the object, the animal's behavior followed from its innate repertoire of food-related behavior and the nature of the object. (In this case, the object itself probably had little modulating effect; but if the signal had been social, e.g., the appearance of another dog or a human, then the food-begging component of the animal's behavior would probably have been enhanced [see Timberlake, 1983, for discussion and examples]).

Autoshaping is thus only a special case of the built-in tendency for all animals to approach (and behave appropriately in other ways) objects of positive value and withdraw from objects of negative value. The inference mechanisms of Pavlovian conditioning allow the animal to detect which objects have value. The amount and type of value (food, water, a predator, or a potential mate) is sufficient by itself to produce approach and withdrawal as well as other, specialized patterns such as autoshaped pecking, flight or fight, "freezing," or other species-specific reactions.

What determines which action shall occur in a given situation? The rules are essentially the same as those discussed in Chapter 5. Let's now look at how to represent the inference problem in the contingency space first discussed in Chapter 4 and then extend the same principles to operant conditioning.

Inference and Pavlovian Conditioning

The occurrence of an hedonic event (US) such as food or shock poses an inference problem for the animal: Which environmental feature, of those present now and in the recent past, is the best predictor or probable cause of the US (the assignment of credit problem)? The animal has two kinds of information available to it to solve this problem: prior knowledge and any temporal relations between the valued event (US) and its potential cause or predictor, which may have been either a CS or an operant response. Let's look at how the animal might use both kinds of information to solve the problem.

PRIOR KNOWLEDGE AND CONDITIONABILITY   As we have already seen, prior knowledge refers to innate priors and previously learned priors, both of which contribute to the animal's current representation of its environment. The animal's evolutionary history provides it with predispositions to connect certain kinds of events with certain kinds of outcomes. For example, pain is more likely to be associated with another animal than with an inanimate stimulus (recall the hedgehog experiment discussed in Chapter 5). A related finding is *shock-induced fighting*. When a pair of rats is placed in a cage and briefly shocked through their feet, they will usually attack one another (Ulrich & Azrin, 1962). Pain, in the presence of a probable cause, elicits the behavior that is preprogrammed for that situation—namely attack directed at the cause. If the situation is familiar or is similar in terms of the animal's representation of a familiar one, the probable cause may be partly determinable. For example, a rat shocked in the presence of two others, one familiar and the other not, is more likely to attack the novel animal. A similar effect can be seen in taste-aversion learning: Given two potential taste CSs, an aversion develops to the novel one. Blocking has the converse effect: Given a CS element already associated with the US, little or no conditioning occurs to the novel CS element.

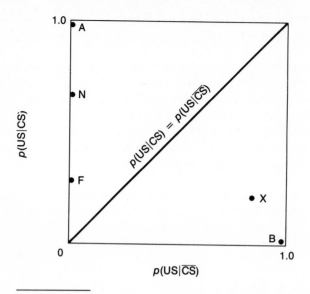

FIGURE 8.3   The contingency space representing Pavlovian conditioning.

The way in which prior knowledge guides future conditioning can be represented in the contingency space first described in Chapter 4 and shown again here as Figure 8.3. Given a US, the animal has prior estimates for each potential CS as the best predictor of that US, that is, estimates of the probability of that US in the presence, or absence, of a specific CS. Complete conditioning, which is the consequence of a history of perfect prediction of the US by the CS, is indicated by point A in the figure. For this case, $p(\text{US}|\overline{\text{CS}}) = 0$ and $p(\text{US}|\text{CS}) = 1$. Any other situation represents something less than complete excitatory conditioning. Complete conditioning of a safety signal (CS$-$) is indicated by point B in the figure.

The ease with which a stimulus (or response, as we will see in a moment) can become conditioned as a CS+ depends on its distance from point A in the space. However, the conditionability of one stimulus is not independent of the conditionability of others. As we saw in Chapter 7, cues (CSs) compete with one another for conditioning. The function of conditioning is to determine action, which means the animal must generally decide which of two things is a better or a worse predictor of the US. A conclusion that both are equally predictive is not helpful as a guide to choice. Thus, ease of conditioning should depend on the distance of a cue from point A in the contingency space of Figure 8.3. Let's look at some of the cases described in Chapter 5 from this point of view.

Blocking. In the blocking experiment, the already-conditioned stimulus lies at point A; the novel, unconditioned stimulus, lies at point X. The position of X depends on several factors: First, the vertical position is determined by the prior probability of X causing the US. This probability is the innate prior probability if X is a completely novel stimulus. Second, the horizontal position of X is determined by the animal's preexposure to the US. That is, the probability of the US in the absence of X $p(\text{US}|\overline{\text{CS}})$ must be quite high, because the US has occurred on several trials without X already. Since stimulus A in Figure 8.3 is already perfectly conditioned and X is a long way from the point of perfect conditioning, the conditionability of X is clearly low—as blocking implies.

Conditioning to Novel Tastes. If a familiar and a novel taste both precede poisoning, aversion develops to the novel taste. The familiar taste (F) can be represented by point F in Figure 8.3, in which $p(\text{US}|F)$ is low, and $p(\text{US}|\overline{F}) = 0$ if this exposure is the animal's first to sickness. The novel taste (N) can be represented by point N, since its (innate) prior association with sickness is presumed high. Clearly, point N is closer to A than point F, so that aversion develops to the novel taste (N).

Latent Inhibition. Preexposure of the CS in the absence of the US retards conditioning. If a novel CS is located at N in the contingency space, then preexposure without the US must displace its location to some lower point on the vertical axis, say F, since experience with the CS in the absence of the US should reduce the animal's estimate of $p(\text{US}|\text{CS})$. Consequently, CS preexposure should retard conditioning—as it does.

Preexposure to the US. This case is similar to the conditioning to stimulus X in the blocking experiment. Preexposure to the US in the absence of X moved X further from point A and closer to point B: That is, the probability of the US in the absence of the CS is greater than the probability of the US in the presence of the CS. Hence, we might expect US preexposure to retard conditioning—as it usually does. Thus, the contingency space provides a useful summary for the effects of novelty and preexposure on CS conditionability.

TEMPORAL RELATIONS   The temporal relations between a potential CS and the US are the second source of information available to the animal in making its inference. As we saw in previous chapters, relative proximity of the CS to the US is important for conditioning: Better conditioning occurs if the CS closely precedes the US than if it closely follows the US (Figure 8.4). The part of the gradient in the figure before the US represents forward conditioning, with better conditioning occurring with a shorter CS–US delay. The portion of the gradient after the US represents backward conditioning, which rarely occurs.

In summary, animals use prior information, either innate or from previous experience, together with information about temporal relations between CS and US, to guide conditioning. *Candidates* for conditioning, that is, predictors or potential causes, are identified either before or after US occurrence, as illustrated in Figure 8.4. Identification of CS candidates is an active process: Pavlov termed the behavior associated with noticing and processing novel stimuli the *orienting reflex*, which correctly reflects its automatic character; most animals cannot help gathering information. Magicians take advantage of this automatic information gathering by providing signals that distract their human audience while they carry out sleight of hand tricks. The orienting reflex, and indeed all new learning,

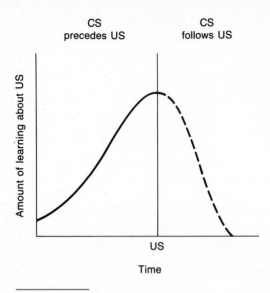

FIGURE 8.4   Schematic representation of the delay-of-reinforcement gradient.

seems to be motivated by surprise, that is, a perceived discrepancy between reality and the animal's representation of it.

The details of the process by which candidates are selected and the precise composition of the candidate set are not known. In fact, it is a simplification to talk of a candidate set as if it contained a number of independent stimulus elements, when what seems to be changing during conditioning is some form of representation in which stimulus elements are probably dependent on one another. In other words, most stimuli are represented in terms of context not as individual elements. For example, a CS in one context may be only partially effective in another context. All we know for sure is that Pavlovian conditioning does involve selection from among a set of possibilities, that the selection is biased by innate factors and previous experience, and that the temporal relations between a possible CS and the US are important, although not necessarily decisive, determinants of learning.

Inference and Operant Conditioning

This functional approach applies with little change to the learning of activities. The problem for the animal is still to decide which of several possibilities caused or predicted the US. The main difference is that when a stimulus signals another stimulus, we can only speak safely about prediction of A by B (because the animal cannot actively manipulate A); but when a response is a signal for something it becomes a potential cause, because the animal controls its own responding. Pavlovian conditioning is nothing more than observation, whereas operant conditioning involves action.

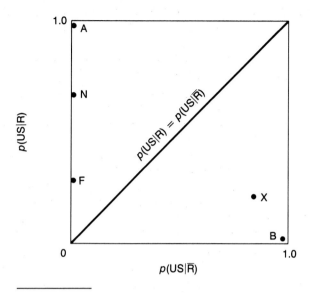

FIGURE 8.5   The contingency space representing operant conditioning.

Figure 8.5 illustrates how contingencies work in operant conditioning. It is similar to Figure 8.3, except that the axes are now $p(US|\bar{R})$ and $p(US|R)$. The delay between response and reinforcer (US) and prior information about the response both guide learning as with Pavlovian conditioning.

Therefore, the major difference between operant and Pavlovian conditioning is in the selection of candidates for conditioning. In the Pavlovian case, the candidates (potential CSs) in some sense already exist and merely have to be attended to by the animal (not really, of course, since the animal's perceptual apparatus must analyze the world in the appropriate way). In the operant case, through activity the animal may change its environment, thus changing the set of candidates as well as the place the candidate activity sits in contingency space. For example, if the animal increases the rate of activity A, and A is in fact not a cause of hedonic event B, then $p(B|A)$ will decline. Conversely, if A is a cause of B, $p(B|A)$ may change when the frequency of A changes. And if A doesn't occur at all, the animal cannot find out if it causes B or not. This logical *priority of action* is the functional basis for variable, spontaneous activity, which as we saw in Chapter 3, underlies all operant behavior.

PRIOR KNOWLEDGE AND OPERANT CONDITIONING   As in Pavlovian conditioning, prior knowledge is associated with any candidate. For example, if food is given to a pigeon just after it has pecked and preened (in either order), it is much more likely to associate the food with the pecking than with the preening, even though the preening may be closer to the food. Priors contribute to the selection of one response over another as the probable cause of the US.

Prior knowledge can also be used to originate a response, as we saw in autoshaping. The CS in an autoshaping experiment is a signal for food, and the pigeon comes equipped by its evolutionary and personal history with a repertoire of activities that have proven useful in food situations. These activities involve both the internal economy of the animal and its relations to the external world: The internal activities are the traditional province of Pavlovian conditioning. Skeletal activities such as pecking and a few others such as pacing and bill-swiping make up a repertoire that has proven useful to ancestral pigeons in food situations. Consequently, pigeons have evolved so that these activities occur in any situation in which (by the animal's estimate) food is probable. Behavior of this sort might be termed *situation-induced*. It forms the response pool out of which operants (habitual patterns), as functional units with stimulus and response components, will emerge. Every situation generates its own range of activities, and from this set a single activity or a small number of activities will eventually emerge as the learned response.

Induced Behavior. Inducing situations are of two main types: the outcome of Pavlovian training, in which the reinforcer significance of a stimulus has been established by a prior predictive history, or simply the immediate result of the presentation of a reinforcer such as food. Because food often occurs in patches, or "runs," finding one piece of food is often a signal for others. Many animals innately treat food as a signal for more food, thus food delivery (especially in a novel context) elicits the full range of food-related activities. For example, a hungry chicken when given a little grain will at once become active and start scratching at the floor and pecking at small objects. The unexpected occurrence of other hedonic stimuli, such as shock, water, or a member of the same species, similarly arouses a set of specific activities.

It is hardly conceivable that animals could be constructed so as *not* to make use of prior information in this manner. Life in a changing environment (and the animal changes its environment merely by moving through it) constantly poses fresh problems. Finding food or a mate and the avoidance of predators are ever-present challenges. All problems can be thought of as a search through a set of potential solutions. Sometimes the solution set is quite well defined, as in finding a source of food; in this case, the animal moves at a certain rate of speed in a uniform environment, can scan an area per unit of time, and there is a certain density of food sources. At other times, if the environment is not uniform, or if the type of response required to obtain food is not specified, the solution set is much harder to define. Animals have limited computational resources and time, and without some means of limiting their search, most such problems would take too long to solve. Animals can only reduce their problems to a reasonable level of difficulty by making use of prior knowledge, both learned and innate.

Instinctive Drift. Numerous experiments have demonstrated the spontaneous emergence of food-related behaviors in food situations and fear-related behaviors in frightening situations. Some of the most dramatic come from attempts to train animals such as pigs and raccoons to do tricks. Marion and Keller Breland, early collaborators with B. F. Skinner, describe a number of failures to condition (by operant means) several "arbitrary" activities: For example, a raccoon was being trained to pick up a wooden egg and drop it down a chute. At first the animal easily released the egg and went at once to the feeder for its bite of food. But the second time, the animal was reluctant to let loose the egg: "He kept it in his hand, pulled it back out, looked at it, fondled it, put it back in the chute, pulled it back out again, and so on; this went on for several seconds" (Breland & Breland, 1966, p. 67). Animals of other species, such as otters, pigs, and squirrel monkeys, are equally reluctant to let go an object that has become a reliable predictor of food.

In another experiment, a chicken had been trained to make a chain of responses, leading at last to standing on a platform for 15 sec, at which time food was delivered. After training, the chicken showed vigorous ground scratching while waiting on the platform. Ground scratching is apparently an innate food-seeking activity.

The activity observed depends on all aspects of the situation. For example, in another experiment the Brelands trained a chicken to operate a firing mechanism that projected a ball at a target. A hit produced food. All went well at first, but when the animal had learned the temporal association between ball and food, it could not refrain from pecking directly at the ball. Thus when a chicken must stand and wait for food, it ground-scratches, but when it has a foodlike object that signals food, it pecks at it. In mammals and birds, information from all sources—from both the US and the CS—contributes to the selection of a response.

The Brelands first reported these apparent failures of the reinforcement principle in a paper called "The misbehavior of organisms" (Breland & Breland, 1961), whose title was a parody of Skinner's masterwork. Most of these examples of "misbehavior" have in common the property that the application of response-contingent reinforcement at first strengthens the reinforced activity, but after a while that activity is supplanted by an innate food-related behavior, such as "washing" the token (raccoons) or pecking at it (pigeons). The Brelands termed this pattern *instinctive drift.*

Species-specific Defense Reactions. In situations associated with electric shock, animals show so-called *species-specific defense reactions,* that is, built-in reactions to potentially dangerous situations (Bolles, 1970). There are three main reactions to danger: flight, fight, or "freeze." Which one is chosen depends on the magnitude and certainty of the threat and the escape routes and cover available. For example, baby chicks are likely to freeze in any threatening situation, unless cover is available, in which case they are likely to run to it. Rats flee from a superior opponent, fight an inferior one, and freeze if the source of danger is uncertain.

The reactions are quite specific both to the type of hedonic stimulus and the other features of the situation. Even in the apparently simple pigeon-autoshaping situation, the type of US makes a difference: Pigeons attack a grain CS with an open bill, whereas they suck the water CS with a closed bill (see Figure 8.1). Other experiments have shown that types of food that require different handling also elicit matching autoshaped responses. Even lights and tones favor different types of conditioned response in rats (Holland, 1980).

Behavioral Variation: Sampling and Stereotypy

Learning is a way for animals and people to use their limited resources efficiently. Once stimuli are identified as predictors of hedonic events, specific activities are more or less likely to occur in their presence depending on the event. As we have just seen, food-related activities occur when food is likely, defense reactions when there is threat, and so on. In this manner, energy is conserved, and risk is minimized. But *sampling,* variation in behavior so as to discover the properties of a situation, and *exploitation,* making use of what has been learned, are necessarily in opposition (this point has been emphasized by the behavioral ecologists: see chapters by Krebs & McCleery and Shettleworth, in Krebs & Davies, 1984, for example). Without sampling, nothing can be learned; but without exploitation, there is no benefit to learning. An animal can make two kinds of mistakes during the learning process: It can sample too much, wasting resources, or it can sample too little, making mistakes by settling for less than the best strategy. Lacking omniscience, there is no way for animal (or a human) to be certain of avoiding these errors. The best it can do is settle for the optimal trade-off. For example, when the cost of error is severe and it has developed some way of coping, it should stick with it—that is, don't mess with a winning (or at least, not-losing) combination. Decision theorists have termed this settling for "good enough" *satisficing* (Simon, 1956). When costs of error are severe, the result may be highly stereotyped behavior. For example, in human social life, the more serious the decision, the more it is surrounded with form and ritual: From cockpit drills to marriage, when the outcome is important, a rigid pattern or ritual tends to emerge.

This proneness to a fixed behavioral pattern in critical situations reflects intelligence, not stupidity. Simple animals don't show these rigidities because their representation of the world is so primitive that they cannot afford to rely on it. In place of rigid patterns, tied to well-specified situations, these simple animals must waste resources in excessive amounts of random sampling. This activity protects them from traps, but it limits their ability to allocate their resources efficiently.

SAMPLING AND HUMAN BEHAVIOR   Recent work in human decision making has amply documented how even human beings limit their sampling in ways that can lead to poor decisions. For example, consider how competitive research grants are awarded, how students are admitted to a selective college, or how personnel are selected. In every case, the criterion on which a decision is based (*selection measure*) is usually different from the final behavior that is the goal of the selection process (*performance measure*): Research performance is the performance measure for the research grant, success in college and in later life for college admission, and on-the-job performance for personnel selection. But since performance cannot be measured at the time of selection, some indirect measure must be used, such as evaluation of a research proposal by a peer group (for a research award) or some combination of test scores and scholastic record (for college admission). Typically, a selection measure is chosen that allows appli-

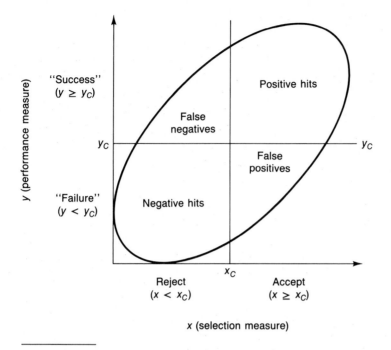

FIGURE 8.6   The relation between selection and performance measures and criteria for selection and performance, given an imperfect selection measure (after Einhorn & Hogarth, 1978).

cants to be ranked. Such a procedure assumes that the measure is directly re-lated to the criteria, that is, people with high selection-measure scores are also likely to score highly in terms of the performance measure. Thus, highly ranked students should do well in college, and highly ranked research proposals should lead to high-quality research. As you may have guessed, this is not always the case.

The decision situation is illustrated in Figure 8.6. The horizontal axis shows the selection measure (e.g., test score), and the vertical axis shows the perfor-mance measure (e.g., grade-point average). The performance- and selection-criterion values are shown by the crossed lines. Each individual can be repre-sented by a point in this space, whose coordinates are his or her scores on the test and in reality (performance score). The oval area shows the region in which most individuals lie, assuming that the test has some validity (selection measure is positively correlated with performance) but is less than perfect. If the measure were perfect, all points would lie on a diagonal line.

The decision maker has two tasks: One is to find the best rule for picking people (to make the oval region as narrow as possible); the second is to pick the best people (to get individuals in the top-right corner). These two tasks are in opposition, as they are the dichotomy between sampling and exploitation we have already discussed. To pick the best people, the decision maker sets his or her selection criterion as high (as far to the right) as possible. In this manner, his or her proportion of positive hits (people above the performance criterion) will be as high as possible. But to estimate the validity of the selection measure, the decision maker must also sample individuals to the left of the criterion; that is, he or she needs to estimate the proportion of false negatives. The variability of this calculation would require that the decision maker admit some students with poor scores or award research grants for poorly rated proposals. Therefore, the necessary sampling of people to the left of the selection criteria almost never occurs, partly because of the cost of false positives to the decision maker (bad things happen to the personnel manager who hires a loser, but a missed winner costs relatively little), and partly because many decision makers are unaware of the need to keep up to date on the validity of their decision rules (Box 8.1).

People are as dumb as animals in their unawareness of how poorly they are sampling. For example, in a well-known experiment by Wason (see Wason & Johnson-Laird, 1972, for a general review), subjects were presented with four cards lying on a table. A single letter or number (A, B, 2, or 3) was visible on each card. The subjects were told to check the truth of the statement "Only cards with a vowel on one side have an even number on the other." To check positive instances, the card with "A" should be turned over—which all subjects did. But to check negative instances, the appropriate choice is the "3" card, which could determine whether vowels occur on cards with odd numbers as well. None of the subjects turned over the "3" card. Many chose the "2" card, which of course added nothing to their knowledge about the truth of the statement.

This error can be eliminated by casting the situation as one in which it is important to spot cheaters. For example, suppose the problem is set up as follows:

> Drinking alcohol is illegal for those under age. You are in a bar that contains four people: A, B, C, and D. What information should you look for?

Almost anyone will conclude that you need IDs only for those who are drinking. In the jargon of cognitive psychology, it is fairly obvious that human intelligence, like animal intelligence, is *domain specific*, that is, people behave more rationally in some situations than in others, even if the same rule is required in all. There is still dispute about why people make these errors; perhaps the best suggestion is that they reflect what Cosmides (see Cosmides & Tooby, 1987) has called *Darwinian algorithms*, which are domain-specific rules that have evolved to deal with situations frequently encountered by our ancestors. Thus, people look for positive instances in the card situation because it looks like one in which these have the most value—even though the instructions are worded otherwise. But if the negative instances are emphasized, as in the drinking example, people treat it like a "catch-the-cheaters" problem and follow the logically correct train of experimentation.

If a situation can be identified with precision and there is a unique solution, then evolution will tend to build that solution into the organism, especially if the risks associated with rigidity are negligible and/or the costs of error are high. For example, the identification of one's own species is generally either innate or de-

Applied and Basic Research

The dichotomy between sampling and exploitation can be broadly applied to the distinction between *applied research* (including application) and basic research, a distinction that is crucial to national science and technology policy. Applied research is much more expensive and easier to justify (because of its obvious relevance to practical problems) than basic research is; but applied research in the absence of a knowledge of basic laws is usually doomed to futility (which may be one of the reasons for slow progress in the fight against cancer, despite weekly "breakthroughs"). Consequently, a proper balance between applied research and basic research is essential to effective science policy. Basic research is the equivalent of sampling, an activity carried on solely to produce knowledge. Applied research and its application is largely exploitation of what is already known. As we have seen, sampling and exploitation are necessarily at odds.

Because the techniques used and many of the subproblems encountered in applied and basic research are the same, and because most people like to appear "positive" and to be for unity rather than division, there is a strong tendency to argue that there is no real difference between basic and applied research. Basic research defines its own problems and studies things that promise to reveal general principles. But, the essence of applied research is to achieve concrete results, to solve a predefined problem, and to this end it uses whatever basic knowledge is available. It may incidentally add to that knowledge (that's one reason for the confusion), but adding to the storehouse of knowledge is not its chief purpose. For example, a physician given two possible treatments, and not knowing which is more effective, may well elect to administer both—which is terrible basic science (if the patient gets better, the clinician has no idea which treatment was responsible)—but it might be very responsible medicine. Like the personnel manager who wants the best selection rule, the basic scientist must often try solutions he or she already knows may have no effect (the control group), so that he or she may properly understand those activities that do have effect (the experimental group).

The confusion between basic science and application has caused special difficulties in the field of psychology, in which a spurious unity has been built into the educational system in the form of the so-called *scholar–professional model.* This idealistic concept grew out of a meeting in Boulder, Colorado, some years ago at which the objective was to decide how clinical psychologists should be educated. The conclusion was that they should be educated both in research and psychotherapy and that this education could best be carried out in academic (i.e., basic research) departments of psychology. Unfortunately, although an individual might be both a clinician and a basic researcher at different times, there is no way (for the reasons just discussed) that he or she can be both simultaneously. The natural tendency to attempt the impossible by living up to the scholar–professional ideal has led to decades of tension between clinical and nonclinical psychologists and much confusion in research activity.

pends in a rigid way on early experience, as in imprinting (Chapter 5). Protective reflexes, as we saw in Chapter 2, are almost impossible to modify.

CONCLUSION   Organisms define situations both in terms of their actual experience with them and in terms of weightings inherited from their evolutionary past—which means that reasoning, even human reasoning, is often domain specific. A situation in which the outcome is relatively certain and of high value (positive or negative) is not a situation that encourages variability in behavior. If the outcome is positive (as with a food schedule), then behavioral variation will result in a substantial loss in the positive outcomes. If the outcome is negative (as on a shock-avoidance schedule), variations from the effective response will result in an increase in negative outcomes encountered.

The rule is that high-valued situations tend to produce a rigid pattern of activity specific to the situation, which is called *behavioral stereotypy*. This rule accounts for the two phases in the Brelands' experiments. For example, when the raccoon first learned to drop its egg down the chute, nothing much depended on it. But after a few tries, with food following every egg, the egg became a rich predictor of food. The raccoon's genes tell it that when something looks like food, is strongly associated with food, and can be handled like food, hang onto it! So it did. But when it did so, it failed to receive more food, became less reluctant to let go of the egg, dropped a couple of eggs, received more food, and the egg became valuable again, and so on. This effect of high hedonic value also accounts for the feature-negative effect, which occurs when $S+$ is a rich predictor of food, not when it is a poorer predictor, and for omission autoshaping.

The same rule applies to reinforcement schedules. A hungry pigeon pecking a key for food on a relatively rich schedule should spend little time doing anything else, because the food given up is certain, whereas the prospect of a better alternative is tenuous. Similarly, a well-trained squirrel monkey pressing a lever to avoid shock also has little incentive to explore as time out from pressing will soon be punished, and long training has taught the animal the futility of looking for a better game in this situation. The rule that high hedonic value leads to stereotyped behavior applies to negative as well as to positive values and to schedules involving electric shock as well as to hungry animals on frequent-food schedules. In Chapter 10, we will see that this rigidity can have surprising and sometimes maladaptive consequences.

As outcomes become less certain and/or the hedonic value is not so great, the variability in behavior tends to increase. For example, as a food-reinforcement schedule is changed to extinction, in which food is no longer available for lever-pressing, animals tend to perform many activities in addition to pressing the lever—hence the decrease in the rate of lever-pressing observed during extinction. This increase in behavioral variability often leads to a new response that is effective in producing reinforcement. For example, in nature as the seasons change and the supply of flying insects decreases, flycatchers, which normally forage exclusively on flying insects, begin to forage for seeds and ground bugs. Certain types of reinforcement schedules can also favor variability, as we see in the next section.

Reinforcing Variable Behavior

That reinforcement tends to produce behavioral stereotypy has been known for a long time. Indeed, Barry Schwartz (1986) has used this fact as a criticism of Skinnerian theory and applications of reinforcement principles in the workplace, arguing that motivating workers purely by means of the reward schedule for their product is dehumanizing and inefficient, because it encourages rigidity. Some have doubted that reinforcement could ever, no matter what the schedule, produce anything but stereotyped behavior. Yet, there are contradictory data. For example, in an ingenious experiment some years ago, Pryor, Haag, and O'Reilly (1969) rewarded porpoises every day for doing something new, that is, something different from what they had done on previous days. The animals soon learned to produce a wide variety of breaching and surface-swimming patterns, many never before observed in the species (interestingly, some of these patterns are common in closely related species).

The type of reinforcement schedule is crucial. All successful attempts to use reinforcement to generate variable behavior have used some type of frequency-dependent schedule in which infrequent acts are favored. In dealing with porpoises, a highly intelligent species, Pryor, Haag, and O'Reilly were able to impose the toughest of criteria—not just infrequent behavior, but only behavior *never* seen before. But even pigeons, when trained on a least-frequent schedule, can show quite variable behavior. For example, Donald Blough (1966; Platt, 1973), performed an experiment in which pigeons received food only following pecks that terminated specific interresponse times (IRTs: times between key pecks). These IRTs were continuously sorted by a computer into bins, such as $0-1$'s, $1-2$'s, ..., $> T$'s, which could at any instant find the category that had the smallest count and then set up reward preferentially for any key peck that terminated an IRT in that category. The result was a distribution of IRTs that closely resembled purely random responding. More recently, using similar methods, Allen Neuringer (e.g., Page & Neuringer, 1985) trained pigeons to peck two different response keys in highly variable sequences.

The conditions necessary to reinforce behavioral variability underscore the many parallels between selection by reinforcement and natural selection. Population biologists are familiar with the idea of frequency-dependent selection, which is usually a stabilizing force and one that can under some conditions promote diversity. For example, the concept of *search image* arose from Luuk Tinbergen's (1960) observation of a biased relation between the representation of prey species in the environment and in the diet of predators: Woodland birds often seemed to take too few rare insects and too many common ones. Tinbergen suggested that this fact might be because the birds have to learn to see cryptic (i.e., camouflaged) prey, and they cannot do so when the prey density is quite low (because they then do not receive enough practice in seeing it). The details of Tinbergen's mechanism remain controversial, but there seems to be little doubt that under many conditions rare prey types have a selective advantage, and this fact of course favors the evolution of more rare types, that is, morphological diversity. The extreme polymorphism of many cryptic prey species is generally attributed to this selective process. In evolution as in reinforcement schedules, selecting rare types favors variation.

THE GUIDANCE OF ACTION

We are now in a position to pull together the threads of an account of learning. The account has three ingredients:

1. The *initial state* of the animal that corresponds to the set of candidates, both external stimuli and aspects of the animal's own behavior, that serve as predictors of the hedonic stimulus (the US or reinforcer).

2. The *selection rules* that determine how the set of candidates is changed.

3. For operant conditioning, *response-reinforcer* contiguity, that is, the temporal relation between a response and reinforcement.

Let's look at each of these ingredients.

The Initial Behavioral State

Situations vary in familiarity. If the situation is novel, then animals seem to have available a variety of built-in activities that serve the function of testing the situation in various manners. Small animals subject to predators are naturally cautious at first. For example, a rat, especially a feral rat, placed in a laboratory environment at first hides or at least remains immobile for some time. If nothing bad happens, the animal probably explores, not entirely randomly but according to rules that depend on the nature of the place. As we have already seen, in a maze rats tend to avoid recently visited locations. They also have a fairly stereotyped routine elicited by novelty that includes rearing, sniffing, and nosing into holes. This activity is almost entirely innate and *endogenous* (internally generated as opposed to elicited by the environment in an automatic and unavoidable way). If the environment contains another animal, then a repertoire of social "probes" is called into play that serves to identify the sex and status of the stranger.

These activities serve the function of exposing the animal to stimuli that allow it to build up an internal representation of the environment. As we have seen, the experimental evidence for a maplike spatial representation is now quite strong for rats, other mammals, and even some invertebrates such as honeybees. Of course, the behavior is also guided by this developing representation. Other things being equal, the animal is likely to seek out parts of its environment that are relatively less familiar, either because they have not been visited recently or because they have never been visited.

At some point, perhaps as a consequence of action by the animal, something of value may occur (e.g., the delivery of food, electric shock, or the appearance of another member of the species). The situation is now both more familiar (e.g., the animal has experience with other food situations) and one in which it

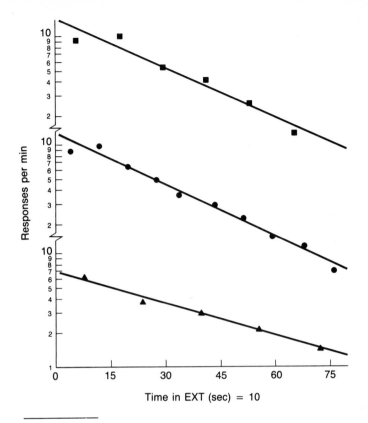

Responses per min

Time in EXT (sec) = 10

FIGURE 8.7   General activity as a function of time after a single, isolated feeding. Each curve is the average of several pigeons in similar experiments (from Killeen, Hanson, & Osborne, 1978). (Note the logarithmic vertical axis.)

pays the animal to invest additional efforts, both of thought (computation) and activity. That is: "There is something good (or bad) here, and I had better find out about it!"

This additional effort is termed *arousal,* and it can be measured both physiologically (via electrical measures of brain activity) and behaviorally. For example, in an experiment by Peter Killeen and his associates (Killeen, Hanson, & Osborne, 1978), a hungry pigeon was placed in a Skinner box equipped to measure the amount of the bird's movement: The floor was divided into six hinged plates, so that as the bird walked from plate to plate, switches were depressed and released. After about 30 min, which allowed the pigeon time to settle down, the bird was given a single feeding and was allowed to remain in the apparatus for another 30 min. This procedure was repeated for several days. The records of switch operations for these days were then averaged to show how the amount of movement declined with postfood time. The results are strikingly regular. Food delivery produces an immediate increase in activity that declines exponentially with postfood time (Figure 8.7).

The regularity of these curves depends on considerable averaging, because the effect of a single food delivery on the behavior of an individual pigeon is by no means orderly. The functional argument tells us that the animal should "try harder" after food, but this effort involves both computation and activity; hence activity is only an indirect measure of the total effect of the single feeding. There are also good reasons why both computation and activity should involve random elements. As we saw in earlier chapters, all adaptation involves selection from a variable set of possibilities. The activity or arousal produced by food suggests that the animal is generating "candidate causes" for the food at a high rate.

Hedonic stimuli are not the only things that arouse animals. The first encounter each day with the Skinner box is itself arousing. Any situation reentered after a delay is to some degree novel, and it thus generates the exploratory action appropriate to a novel situation.

The general rule is that arousal is elicited by situations of potential importance (in the evolutionary sense) to the animal. These situations include novel situations, surprising situations, and situations that involve hedonic stimuli such as food, shock, or a conspecific. As we have seen, both surprise and novelty motivate learning, that is, they change in the animal's internal representation, which reduces surprise and novelty.

Selection Rules for Behavior

If a reinforcer is delivered to an animal for the first time in a new situation, the animal becomes aroused. We see this arousal as an increase in behavior and more attention to external stimuli. But, these effects are selective; they are guided by the prior knowledge appropriate to the reinforcer. Therefore, certain kinds of stimuli command more attention than others, certain kinds of action are more likely than others, and some actions are more likely than others to be considered as potential causes of the reinforcer.

As additional reinforcers occur, the temporal relations between behavior and reinforcement (contiguity) have an effect in reducing the set of candidates: Candidates that closely precede the reinforcer are preferentially retained. The principles of memory—recency, primacy, and frequency—also begin to alter prior knowledge, favoring some activities over others. Thus, additional weight is given to the first activity that the animal performs in a given situation (primacy), as well as the most recent (recency) and the most frequent, and these assessments change dynamically, moment by moment, as different activities occur and are or are not rewarded. If reinforcers are delivered according to a simple rule, such as a fixed-interval schedule, then the set of candidates will eventually be reduced, so that activities consistent with the rule are retained and others are lost.

The concept of "candidate" here is necessarily vague, because it refers neither to responses nor stimulus–response connections but to whatever "computational elements" the animal uses to guide its behavior. The relation between candidates and responses thus parallels the relation between phenotype and genotype in biology. Overt behavior occurs and acts on the environment and determines whether or not reinforcement occurs. But what is selected is not the responses themselves but whatever memorial (i.e., transmissible across time) elements underlie the reinforced responses. Similarly, in natural selection it is phenotypes that occur and reproduce, but it is genes (that contain the instructions for phenotype assembly) that are passed on through time.

Response-Reinforcer Contiguity

Contiguity with the reinforcer is one of the factors that affects the selection of candidates, but because it is so important and has received so much attention historically, it deserves a section to itself. The temporal relation between response and reinforcer was once thought to be the only factor in conditioning, yet we now know that several other factors are also important. Animals are sensitive to immediate contiguity between their actions and stimulus changes, but this sensitivity is clearly not the only manner in which they assess cause–effect relations.

When animals have ample opportunity to sample and factors such as autoshaping don't create a strong bias in favor of a specific response, an animal's ability to detect response-dependent stimulus changes is excellent. For example, in another experiment by Killeen (1978), pigeons pecked the center key of a three-key display. One out of 20 pecks was unpredictably followed by darkening of the center key and illumination of the two outside keys. As the pigeon pecked the center key, a computer generated random pseudo-pecks at the same rate. Thus, one-half the time, the stimulus change depended on the bird's peck (according to a variable-ratio 20 schedule) and one-half the time on the computer's pecks (also a VR 20 schedule). If the stimulus change on the center key was contingent on a response (i.e., dependent on the pigeon's peck), a peck on the right-hand key provided immediate food, but a peck on the left-hand key caused a brief timeout, which delayed the next food opportunity. Conversely, if the stimulus change was independent of responding (i.e., produced by the computer's pecks), a peck on the left-hand key produced food, and a response on the right-hand key produced a timeout. The contingencies in this experiment are shown in Figure 8.8.

Killeen's pigeons had little difficulty in responding accurately in this experiment, which indicates that they could distinguish whose pecks (theirs or the computer's) caused the stimulus to change. The only cue available to the birds was the brief time between a peck and stimulus change, which was short and constant for the response-produced changes but variable and on average longer for the computer-produced changes. Small as these temporal differences were, they were sufficient for the birds to detect with high accuracy which changes were caused by them and which were caused by the machine.

CONTIGUITY, CONTINGENCY, AND THE "SUPERSTITION" EXPERIMENT   Pigeons' great sensitivity to response-reinforcer contiguity makes implausible B. F. Skinner's explanation for a well-known effect that he called pigeon "superstition" (Skinner, 1948). In Skinner's original experiment, experimentally naive, hungry pigeons were placed in a box and given brief access to food at fixed periods (15 sec for some animals, longer periods for others). This *temporal conditioning* is a Pavlovian procedure, since the animal's behavior has no effect on food delivery

Choice

Stimulus change was	Left	Right
Response dependent	Timeout	Food
Response independent	Food	Timeout

FIGURE 8.8   Contingencies for Peter Killeen's experiment.

(other than the necessity to approach the feeder and eat when food appears). Despite the absence of an operant contingency, all of Skinner's animals developed strikingly stereotyped, "superstitious" activities in between feeder operations. On its face, this experiment might seem a considerable embarrassment to standard reinforcement theory, which places great emphasis on the role of the response contingency.

It is a mark of his ingenuity that Skinner was not only unworried by this result but was also able to present it as support for his views ("Every crisis is an opportunity," said Winston Churchill, which means that the ingenious theorist will act accordingly). The demonstration of superstitious behavior was not devastating, because reinforcement theory existed in two forms: contingency theory and contiguity theory. *Contingency theory* emphasized the importance of contingency, that is, the dependence of reinforcement on the occurrence of the response. In contingency theory, reinforcement strengthens the behavior on which it is dependent. In all practical matters, this view prevails. For example, in clinical behavior modification, an undesirable behavior is abolished by omitting reinforcers that are normally contingent on it or by delivering contingent punishment; a desirable behavior is strengthened by making reward contingent on it.

Response contingency is a procedural feature, not a behavioral process—contingencies must act through some mechanism. The *contiguity theory* of reinforcement emphasized the mechanism, which was widely thought to be simply the strengthening through response-reinforcer contiguity. This view implies that response contingencies function because they ensure that when the reinforcer is delivered, the contingent response is always contiguous with it. As we saw in Chapter 4, a similar view once prevailed about the learning of CS–US relations in Pavlovian conditioning. At the time of Skinner's original superstition experiment, the operant equivalent of Robert Rescorla's (1967) "truly random control" experiment had not yet been run, so the empirical inadequacy of simple contiguity theory was not apparent.

Skinner explained the vigorous, stereotyped behavior of his pigeons in between periodic food deliveries by means of *adventitious reinforcement,* that is, accidental contiguity between food and a behavior that originally occurs for "other reasons." The argument ran as follows: The pigeon is not a passive creature, especially when hungry and in a situation in which it receives occasional food. Suppose it happens to be performing an activity toward the end of an inter-food interval and food is delivered. The behavior is contiguous with the food, and thus (according to the contiguity theory of reinforcement) it is more likely to occur again. If the next food delivery comes quite soon, this same behavior might still be occurring, and so receive another accidental pairing with food, be further strengthened, occur again in the next interval, and so on. By means of this positive feedback process, some behavior might be raised to a very high probability.

Since there is no real causal relation between behavior and reinforcer, Skinner called the behavior "superstitious," by analogy to human superstitions, which he believed to arise in a similar manner.

Killeen's demonstration that pigeons are good at telling whether food occurs contiguously with a peck or not should make us suspicious of Skinner's "accidental contiguity" explanation for superstition. Pigeons on these schedules not infrequently fail to show "superstitious" behavior within a given interfood interval, and even if they do show it, it is not always contiguous with food. Thus, the pigeons have ample opportunity to detect the lack of any true temporal relationship between what they do and the delivery of food. There are also other problems with Skinner's explanation. His account was not based on direct observation of the process he described. No one had actually recorded these accidental response-reinforcer contiguities or the progressive increase in response strength that was supposed to follow them. In addition, Skinner never defined his contiguity theory in an adequate manner.

The contiguity view was also defended in a way that rendered it almost impossible to disprove. For example, even in 1948 there was some understanding that the delivery of "free" reinforcers on a response-contingent schedule might tend to weaken the instrumental (i.e., reinforced) response (which was demonstrated experimentally several years later). The free-reinforcers effect was explained by the hypothesis that if, for some reason, a behavior other than the instrumental response should happen to occur, then by chance it would sometimes be contiguous with the occasional free reinforcers. This occurrence would tend to strengthen other behaviors and thus, by competition, weaken the reinforced response. No careful observations were made at that time to substantiate this hypothesis (Did such behaviors occur? How often were they contiguous with free food? What is the form of behavioral competition? Did the frequency of the instrumental response drop before or after such accidental pairings?). As well, no quantitative details were given (How many accidental pairings are needed to produce how great an increment in strength? How often should unreinforced "other" behaviors be expected to occur?). This lack of observations and detail made the contiguity view difficult to refute. Subsequently, a few supporting observations have appeared (cf. Henton & Iversen, 1978), but the weight of evidence remains against Skinner's idea.

The contiguity account of reinforcement in its original form poses a difficult methodological problem. It is a causal hypothesis in which the cause, the response-reinforcer contiguity, is not under experimental control: The experimenter can control the contiguity aspect, but the animal determines when it makes the response. The inability to control the occurrence of the response makes it impossible to be sure of the effect of response-reinforcer contiguity. For example, suppose the response occurs and we at once deliver a reinforcer, thus ensuring response-reinforcer contiguity. Suppose that additional responses then occur: Have we demonstrated a strengthening effect of contiguity? Not at all; perhaps this response just happens to occur in runs, so that one response is usually followed by others, quite apart from any reinforcing effect. This situation is not uncommon, for example, a pigeon will rarely peck only once. Suppose we reinforce a second response, just to be sure. After a few repeats, without doubt the pigeon is pecking away at a good rate. Have we then demonstrated an effect of contiguity? Again, not really. By repeating the pairings of response and reinforcer we hope to have established a true dependency between the two, but perhaps the increase in pecking is simply the result of some other process that allows the pigeon to detect such contingencies. In addition, we have also established a stimulus contingency between situational stimuli and food, and of course this contingency will also tend to facilitate pecking.

These difficulties would not be serious if careful observation revealed the kind of process implied by Skinner's argument. If each response-reinforcer pairing produced a predictable and measurable increase in the rate of the reinforced response, the account would be assured. There have been few careful observational studies, and those familiar to the authors have completely failed to find the systematic effects implied by the contiguity view. Instead, the reinforced response emerges in an apparently chaotic manner from an unpredictble mix of variable activities. Moreover, the pattern of its emergence shows little uniformity from individual to individual.

John Staddon and Virginia Simmelhag (1971) repeated Skinner's superstition experiment, they carefully observed the pigeons' behavior in each interfood interval from the beginning of training. They found three aspects that differed from Skinner's account:

1.   The activities that developed are of two kinds: interim activities that occur in the first two-thirds or so of the interfood interval and a single terminal response that occurs during the last third (see Chapter 7).

2.   The terminal response is either pecking or a stereotyped pacing activity obviously related to it (cf. Timberlake & Lucas, 1985). The terminal response does not differ from animal to animal in the irregular fashion implied by Skinner's account.

3.   Terminal pecking does not develop in the accidental manner implied by the adventitious reinforcement hypothesis.

This experiment was discussed in Chapter 7 and presented in Figure 7.4. The figure showed the behavior of one of their pigeons in the last 2 sec of a 12-sec interfood interval over the entire course of the experiment. For the first seven sessions, the pigeon placed its head in the food magazine to receive food. We know from other studies that this response is perfectly "reinforcible"—if pigeons are required to get food by putting their heads into the feeder opening, they have no difficulty in learning to do so. This behavior occurred reliably within 2 sec or less of food delivery. Yet on the eighth day, the pigeon ceased to place its head in the feeder and began a completely new pecking response. Obviously, contiguity with food is both ineffective in maintaining the pigeon's head in the feeder and makes essentially no contribution to the strengthening of pecking. In fact, the pecking is an instance of autoshaping with a temporal stimulus (post-food time) rather than a visual one. As well, Staddon and Simmelhag found that contiguity also makes no contribution to the genesis of interim activities, since these activities are almost never contiguous with food. Data such as these, together with the manifest incompleteness of the contiguity account of reinforcement, have led to the abandonment of "adventitious reinforcement" as an explanation. Although contiguity is a factor in both operant and Pavlovian conditioning, it is not the only factor. Animals detect contingencies with the aid of a mixture of mechanisms, one of which involves the temporal relation between response and reinforcer. The contiguity versus contingency debate is now seen as an ill-formed contest for two reasons. First, the two explanations are of different types: Contiguity is a mechanism, albeit a primitive and incomplete one, for the detection of contingent relations, which is a procedural feature. To show the dominance of contingency over contiguity is not to provide an alternative mechanism for conditioning but simply to show the inadequacy of contiguity as a mechanism. Second, the adventitious-reinforcement account is incomplete as an explanation, because the original cause of the adventitiously reinforced behavior is undefined, and because the quantitative properties of the contiguity-strengthening process are completely unspecified.

The Acquisition of Behavior

The moment-by-moment effect of reinforcer contiguity is demonstrated dramatically in the well-known animal-training technique of shaping by successive approximations. Shaping, a standard classroom demonstration as well as a traditional method of circus trainers, proceeds in two steps. First a hungry pigeon or rat is allowed to become familiar with its environment, the presence of the trainer, and so on. Then the trainer settles on some trick he or she wishes the animal to perform. The trick is often something that animals occasionally do spontaneously (most circus tricks are of this sort, e.g., seals balancing balls and dolphins leaping). If the animal is inactive, it may be given some food, which usually produces activity via the arousal mechanism already described. If the target act then occurs, it is immediately reinforced by feeding the animal as soon as it behaves in the desired fashion. Consistent reinforcement for the act soon produces an animal that behaves in the desired manner, however little "new" behavior has been created. The training has merely brought an existing behavior under the stimulus control of the trainer; that is, the hungry seal now balances the ball when the trainer feels like it, not at the whim of the seal.

These examples do not represent the limits of shaping. All too often, the desired act does not occur spontaneously in its entirety, which is where *successive approximations* enter the picture. As before, the trainer decides on a target behavior, but instead of waiting for perfection, he or she reinforces any behavior that approximates or is a component of the desired behavior. For example, if we want a pigeon to walk in a figure-eight pattern, we begin by giving the bird a bit of food every time it turns in one direction. Once that pattern is well established, we wait until the animal initiates a turn in the opposite direction after completing the first turn, and then we reinforce that behavior. And so on, until the complete pattern is established. Before autoshaping was discovered, key-pecking was shaped in this way: First the bird was fed immediately following any movement in the general direction of the key. Then once it had learned to position itself in front of the key, any head movement was reinforced, then movement directed toward the key, and finally pecking the key. The possibilities of shaping indicate that the set of stimulus and response candidates is not closed. That is, the animal does not at once show everything of which it is capable in a given situation.

Most human education is a process of shaping: The problem is not so much a "strengthening" of the behavior (the task studied in most learning experiments and described by most learning theories) as getting it to occur *for the first time*. Even the term "behavior" is misleading here, because the objective of other than skill learning is the attainment of that special change in internal state known as "understanding." Understanding something is not keyed to any specific behavior, but rather it is the creation of a whole new repertoire of behavior—the child who has learned long division has learned not just to divide the specific pairs of numbers but to divide any pair of numbers.

The main difficulty in getting children to understand something like long division is finding the necessary precursor behaviors, that is, the proper sequence of subtasks that will lead to mastery of long division. If the subject is well structured (like mathematics or shaping of key-pecking in the pigeon), there is less difficulty than if the subject has no obvious structure. In teaching mathematics, addition and subtraction are essential prerequisites to division and multiplication. Even so, you can imagine several ways to get children to understand addition—manipulation of counting sticks, logical explanation, examples, rote memorization of tables, playing with calculators, and so on. There is no unique sequence at any level to guide the teaching of some subjects such as history, writing, or psychology. Different students may have different initial expectations (prior knowledge) about such fields, so that different sequences might be appropriate for different people. Thus, the problem of the proper training sequence is at least as important to the success of shaping as the timely delivery of reinforcers. In fact, in human learning, the sequence is much more important.

Experimenting with shaping and the development of novel behavior is difficult, but there have been a few recent attempts to explore this question that was once a major concern of animal psychologists (e.g., Hull, 1935). An entertaining example of the problem and the sort of solution that can be found for it is provided by some experiments on pigeons by Robert Epstein and his collaborators. Their point of departure was a series of famous experiments with chimpanzees by the German gestalt psychologist Wolfgang Köhler (1925). Köhler did his postdoctoral research at the German biological station on the tropical island of Tenerife, off the northern coast of Africa. World War I was declared while he was there, and the dominance of the British Fleet meant that he could not leave. He was trapped on Tenerife for seven years, and during this long sojourn he studied the problem-solving abilities of chimpanzees. His "box and banana" problem has become a classic. The chimp is provided with a box in one corner of its cage and a banana, hanging just out of reach, in the other. Köhler found that the brighter chimps, after puzzling for a while, would suddenly move the box under the banana, climb on it, and get the banana. Köhler called this sort of activity *insight learning,* and he supposed that only the higher primates were capable of such "creative" learning.

Whether or not Köhler's speculation is true, his analysis is scientifically uninformative: Labeling a kind of learning "insight" aids us little in understanding it, and "creative" behavior can usually be traced to the rearrangement of old elements in new combinations. Nevertheless, Köhler's hypothesis was a good place for Epstein to begin further experimentation on the shaping of behavior. Epstein therefore tried to see if a nonprimate, the pigeon, could be supplied with the appropriate elements in such a way that it would show "insightful" behavior. He describes one of his experiments as follows:

> [We] . . . reported that pigeons with appropriate training histories can solve the classic box-and-banana problem in an insightful, humanlike fashion. [We] assessed the contributions of different experiences by varying the training histories of different birds. Three birds had learned (a) to push a box toward a small green spot placed at random positions around the base of a large cylindrical chamber, (b) to climb onto a box and peck a small facsimile of a banana suspended overhead, and (c) not to jump or fly toward the banana when it was suspended out of reach in the absence of the box; all three solved the problem in what has traditionally been called an "insightful" manner . . . (Epstein, 1987, p. 197).

In a subsequent experiment, Epstein showed that a pigeon pretrained to acquire four repertoires—to peck a picture of a banana, to climb on a box, to open a door, and to push a box toward targets—could solve a still more complex problem in which the banana was out of reach and the box was behind a door.

There is little that is mysterious about the process of "insight," once it is analyzed in this fashion. The trained bird in the second experiment does what it has been trained to do. In the first experiment, it learns to push the box about. Since there is no green spot to peck at in this new situation, the only food predictor available is the banana. One food predictor being similar to another, the bird therefore pushes the box toward the banana. Once the box gets close to the banana, the situation is again one for which the bird has been trained: When the box is under the banana, the pigeon jumps on it, pecks the banana, and gets the food.

The occurrence of the various repertoires seems to follow conventional learning principles: Recently learned acts are more probable than older ones, but older ones recur if the new ones prove ineffective. Stimuli that predict food are treated similarly. We still have no good theory about how a repertoire, as a class of related actions, evolves out of a limited set of specific training experiences.

But granted that it does so and that repertoires behave as functional units, the rest of the process seems straightforward. The chief differences between pigeons and chimpanzees seem to be that the chimp is innately provided with exploratory routines that allow it to build up a "library" of repertoires without special training, and, we suspect, the chimp's brain can hold a larger library than the pigeon's.

A DYNAMIC MODEL FOR REINFORCED LEARNING

We have discussed a number of concepts and findings in this chapter that relate to the idea of *reinforcement.* For example, arousal, autoshaping, contiguity, contingency, behavioral repertoire, instinctive drift, and the differences between autonomic (elicited) and skeletal (emitted) behaviors have been discussed from both functional and mechanistic points of view. The functional analysis is certainly useful, but it is ultimately unsatisfying: We would like to know not only what different types of reinforced learning are for but also how they work. Of course, there is no settled answer to the question of mechanism. Indeed, there is no general theory that attempts to explain all these diverse phenomena. Nevertheless, it may be useful to attempt to create a working model for at least those aspects of learning that do not involve long-term memory. In this way, we may fix in our minds a possible set of relationships among these various phenomena. Francis Bacon, the prototype philosopher of science, said more than 400 years ago: "The truth shall come sooner from error than confusion." History has borne out the wisdom of his words: Once a science is well supplied with basic data, it is better to propose and attempt to improve a wrong model than to have no model at all.

Our objective here is to show how four basic properties of operant behavior—variability, arousal, competition, and adaptation—taken together are sufficient to account for several of the learning phenomena we have already discussed. These phenomena encompass sensitivity to contingency, the difference between elicited and emitted behavior, autoshaping, "superstition" and instinctive drift, high sensitivity to temporal contiguity, and the variability-inducing effects of frequency-dependent schedules.

To see the essentials of the reinforcing process, it is necessary to simplify. We therefore consider only local effects, the visible change in behavior you might expect to see within a single experimental session. The model does not directly incorporate long-term memory—whether the response-enhancing effects are situation-specific and whether they will recur in the same situation tomorrow—nor does it specify just what it is that is enhanced—response, association, expectation, or whatever. We do assume that the enhancement is reflected in an observable activity, and we concentrate on the minimal properties necessary for something, some activity or activity substrate, to be selectively enhanced by the response-contingent presentation of an hedonic event. In conclusion, we will see that this minimal process has enough flexibility to account for most of the phenomena we have discussed in the chapter.

Positive reinforcement is usually defined by three effects:

1. When the occurrence of a reinforcer is made to depend on the occurrence of a specific response, the response rate increases.

2. When the reinforcer is no longer presented or is presented independently of responding, response rate declines—often, but not necessarily, to zero (extinction).

3. The property that reinforcement must be reversibly selective for at least one pair of activities, that is, capable of strengthening reinforced activity A at the expense of activity B that is not reinforced, and vice versa.

It turns out that a minimal process that satisfies (1) and (2) also satisfies (3). A set of assumptions sufficient to produce these effects is as follows (for simplicity we discuss two responses, although the same ideas can easily be generalized to any number):

1. *Variability.* We assume that our model organism has at least two modes of behavior (activities), A and B. We represent the strengths of these two activities by two stochastic (random-in-time) variables, $V_A(t)$ and $V_B(t)$. That is, the strengths of A and B vary irregularly with time (t). This assumption is represented by variable E in our model.

2. *Competition.* The activity with the higher strength (V) is the one that actually occurs.

3. *Arousal.* We assume that the occurrence of a positive reinforcer produces an increase in the strength of both activities and that strength is directly related to their current strengths. In other words, positive reinforcers act like amplifiers, increasing the strength of all tendencies to action. This concept is represented by parameter b.

4. *Adaptation.* The strength increment caused by an individual reinforcer presentation dissipates with time. In other words, the boost a reinforcer gives eventually dissipates, which is crucial, although not necessarily at the same rate, for every activity. This idea is represented by parameter a.

The preceding assumptions boil down to a simple system of integrators, a type of mechanism with which you should now be quite familiar. For each activity, in each instant of time (t), assume:

Following nonreinforcement: $V(t + 1) = aV(t) + E$

$$\text{where } 0 < a < 1 \qquad (8.1)$$

Following reinforcement: $V(t + 1) = aV(t) + E + bV(t)$ (8.2)

The term $aV(t)$, on the right-hand side of Equation 8.1 is our old favorite, the leaky bucket: At each instant, the strength (V behavior) "leaks out" a bit (the smaller a, the faster the leak). The term E is a factor that includes all sources of strength other than the effects of reinforcement. We consider E to be a random factor, so that the strengths of the two activities vary from moment to moment, which allows both of them to occur from time to time, as one or the other has the higher strength. E embodies the assumption of variability. Equation 8.1 also embodies the idea of adaptation, since any transient effect on V (some water poured into the bucket) always dissipates eventually. Notice that when a is high, V values change only slowly so that any reinforcer-induced change is persistent; when a is small, V values in successive ticks (t) are only weakly correlated, and the effects of a reinforcer are transient. Since we assume that different activities have different values for a, some activities are naturally labile, changing strength rapidly from moment to moment (under the influence of E), whereas others are naturally "sticky," changing only slowly from moment to moment (under the influence of $V(t)$).

Equation 8.2 is the same as Equation 8.1, except for the additional term $bV(t)$, which represents arousal. That is, it represents the increment to all strengths caused by a positive reinforcer. The increment is proportional to the current strength, so that reinforcement acts as an amplifier. Since different activities generally have different values for the constant of proportionality (b), which represents the amplification factor (the gain), some activities are strongly facilitated by a given reinforcer, others are strengthened only weakly.

Predictions from the Model

Consider first the case in which both activities are identical, for example, pecking the left key versus pecking the right key, where the animal has no preference as to side. In this case, parameters a and b are the same for both activities. Under free conditions (i.e., no reinforcement), the activities alternate at random, first one, then the other, with neither occurring more frequently than the other. Consider now what happens if we reinforce activity A. At the instant of reinforcement, by the competition assumption, the strength of A is greater than the strength of B: $V_A > V_B$. Since the effects of reinforcement are assumed to be multiplicative (amplifying), A therefore receives a larger absolute increment in strength than B does. This change in increment happens every time a reinforcer is presented. If parameter a is sufficiently large that the effects of reinforcement do not dissipate immediately, V_A slowly increases until activity A becomes the predominant activity. Thus, the model shows enhancement of an activity by response-contingent reinforcement. Obviously, we would have gotten the same result if we had chosen to reinforce activity B, in that the model shows selectivity (property (3) in the preceding list). The model demonstrates that reinforced activity increases in frequency relative to the unreinforced activity.

Notice that if the two activities are truly identical, then even slight contiguity differences are detectable. If A is reinforced with zero delay, but B is reinforced with a delay that is on average slightly longer (as in Killeen's contiguity-detection experiment), then if parameter a is large enough (so that effects can cumulate strongly), activity A eventually predominates. In other words, the model is potentially highly sensitive to temporal contiguity differences.

Consider now the case in which the two activities are different. Activity A has a low value for parameter a_A, but it has a high value for parameter b_A. The low a value makes activity A labile from moment to moment, since V_A is determined largely by the random element E (plus any increment due to reinforcement) and little determined by its previous value (activity A is like a bucket with a large leak). The high b value means that each reinforcement causes a large increase in V_A, but this increase is transient because a_A is small. In this case, we let activity B remain as before, with moderate a and b values. (We also apply a correction factor to E, so that the steady-state, unreinforced V values for both activities remain the same, but this procedure need not concern us here.) What is the effect of presenting a reinforcer? Because parameter b_A is large, each reinforcement almost always causes a large increase in V_A, so that activity A almost always occurs when a reinforcer is presented, whether or not the reinforcer is contingent on activity A. On the other hand, activity B is not much enhanced by occurrence of the reinforcer, unless the reinforcer is actually contingent on activity B, in which case it eventually predominates, because its higher a value allows the effects of each reinforcer presentation to cumulate. The difference between activity A and activity B corresponds to the difference between elicited and emitted behavior. Elicited behavior (e.g., salivation) is reliably produced by reinforcer presentation, but it is not strengthened by response-contingent reinforcement; emitted behavior (e.g., lever-pressing) is not elicited by reinforcement, but it can be strengthened by response-contingent reinforcement.

Notice that the model, right or wrong, is nevertheless an advance over the simple emitted/elicited dichotomy, because it also allows for other possibilities, for example, behavior that is both elicited by a reinforcer and capable of being selectively strengthened. Pecking is one example of the emitted/elicited dichotomy, since it is both elicited by grain (in a hungry pigeon) and is also reinforceable by grain presentation.

If you have understood the argument thus far, you will also be able to see that this model accounts for the effects of contingency and delay of reward. Consider again the first case with two identical activities. Suppose that we degrade the contingency between activity A and reinforcement either by making reinforcement intermittent (e.g., every second occurrence of A) or by delivering "free" reinforcers. It should be clear that either of these changes will tend to weaken the superiority of activity A over activity B, either because the enhancing effects on A dissipate because of less frequent reinforcement or because the enhancement is almost as likely to be of B as of A (when free reinforcers are given). Therefore, the observed difference in rates between the two activities is reduced. Similarly, if we delay reinforcement, when reinforcement actually occurs it is as likely to strengthen B more than A as the reverse, unless parameter a is quite large (so that V_A changes only very slowly). In short, as the delay between response A and subsequent reinforcement increases, the facilitating effect on A must get less and less, which is the delay-of-reward gradient.

The most interesting outcome from this model is the misbehavior that was labeled instinctive drift by the Brelands. The process operates as follows: Suppose that activity A has moderate a and b values but that activity B has high a and low b values. Suppose that reinforcement is contingent on activity A. Since b_A is much greater than b_B, and since reward is contingent on activity A, the first

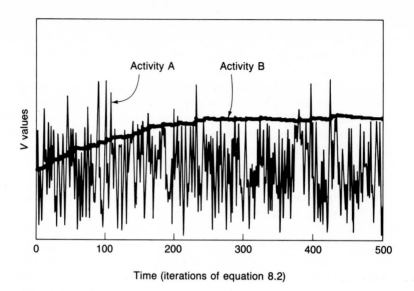

FIGURE 8.9   The strengths of activities A and B, which start from the same initial values. Initially activity A predominates; eventually activity B supersedes.

effect is an increase in the level of activity A, with a concomitant increase in reward frequency. Now, because b_B is much less than b_A, these rewards produce only small increments in V_B. But because a_B is much greater than a_A, these small increments in V_B cumulate strongly, so that V_B eventually exceeds V_A, and activity B displaces activity A, the rewarded activity, which thereafter occurs only infrequently. In other words, the explicitly reinforced response increases at first, as the reinforcement principle requires, but then it is irreversibly superseded by a competing "unreinforced" response.

The effect is illustrated in Figure 8.9, which shows the strengths of both activities starting from the same initial value. The strength of activity B shows a slow and not-very-variable rise (slow because b_B is small; not-variable because a_B is large). The strength of activity A (the reinforced activity) shows a rapid but variable rise (rapid because b_A is large; variable because a_A is small). The behavioral outcome is that "hare" activity A predominates at first, but it is eventually superseded by "tortoise" activity B. This same combination of parameter values, one activity labile (small a_A), the other slow-changing (large a_B), also yields Skinner's "superstition" result: When reinforcers are delivered periodically and if the period is short enough (for a given a_B), activity B will come to predominate. This situation occurs because the small increments in strength activity B receives cumulate more rapidly than the larger increments received by activity A.

You should also be able to see that frequency-dependent schedules tend to promote diverse behavior when using this model, as they do in reality. That is, once an activity is effectively strengthened, so that it begins to predominate, the schedule automatically switches to reinforcing something else. It should also be obvious that a behavior for which the gain (b) *or* the lability (a) is quite small will be almost impossible to reinforce. If either of these parameter values depends on both the activity and the reinforcer, we have the conditions necessary for the kinds of so-called *constraints on learning* demonstrated by Sara Shettleworth (1975) and others. For example, Shettleworth has shown that an activity such as grooming in hamsters is almost impossible to strengthen via food reinforcement, whereas other activities, such as rearing and digging, can be strengthened relatively easily. Our model implies that one or both of the two parameters should be smaller for grooming than for rearing and other food-reinforcible activities.

Finally we should note that the model can account for many of the effects of punishment, which is defined as a response-contingent presentation of an aversive event. In terms of the model, punishment is simply a case in which parameter b is negative. Response-contingent presentation of such an aversive event tends to suppress the response on which it is contingent, and because of competition, to facilitate all other responses. The model animal can learn to make an avoidance response because all other responses are eventually suppressed. The learning is rather inefficient, however, even if there are only two responses—but avoidance learning is often inefficient if the to-be-learned response is not one elicited by the reinforcer (we apply this model to punished behavior in Chapter 10).

Conclusion

Why take up time with a model that certainly falls short of being a complete explanation even for short-term learning effects? We believe there are several valid reasons:

1. To understand learning we need to think in terms of dynamic processes, that is, the way that tendencies to action change over time.

2. When we begin to perceive learning in this manner, we see immediately that activities require at least two parameters to describe their dynamics: a parameter that says how labile they are from moment to moment (a) and a parameter that says how they are affected by a given hedonic event (b). In fact, we probably need other parameters as well to describe different types of competitive and cooperative interactions between behavior systems, to describe the difference between long-term and short-term learning, to describe the effects of remote past experience, to describe periodicities, and so on.

3. Even a simplistic model shows that the reinforcibility of behavior is unlikely to be a simple, absolute property, as labels such as "preparedness" and "belongingness" have sometimes suggested. The reinforcibility of behavior A by reinforcer X depends on at least two properties of activity A (lability and gain: a_A and b_A) but also on the properties of other potential activities, both absolutely (how labile they are, etc.) and in relation to X (how affected they are by X).

4.   Even a simple model shows that reinforcement can act either directly or indirectly: An activity can change its frequency either because it is directly facilitated or suppressed or because other, competing, activities are directly facilitated or suppressed.

SUMMARY

In this chapter we looked at the specifics of operant conditioning from both functional and mechanistic points of view. Considered functionally, reinforced learning proceeds through four repeating stages: Three of these stages are in the animal; one is in the environment. These stages are, in order, surprise (or novelty), inference, action, new situation. After "new situation," we begin again with surprise, and so on. Any new situation first elicits a program of protective and then of exploratory activities that serve to build up a representation of the situation and perhaps to change the value of the situation. The value of a situation may be changed by causing the delivery of food or electric shock, for example. Causes for or predictors of this change in value in the environment and the animal's own behavior are identified by the inference principles described in this chapter and in Chapter 5. Potential candidates as causes of this change in value are evaluated according to their salience, their prior relation to valued events, and their relative temporal proximity to the US.

Pavlovian (classical) conditioning is the name we give to those processes that allow animals to attribute motivational significance to stimulus situations. The combination of situational properties and the type of motivational significance gives rise to a set of candidate activities, which may change the situation (hence lead to new Pavlovian conditioning), and also allows for response selection (via contiguity and other selection rules). The response-selection aspect of the process is termed operant conditioning. The process stabilizes when the action induced by this inference process maintains the conditions of the environment that initially gave rise to it, that is, when the animal is no longer surprised by what happens to it and the pattern of action generates feedback (reinforcement) that sustains that action.

Researchers have built up a catalog of phenomena that show the inferential properties of both Pavlovian and operant conditioning: overshadowing, blocking, US and CS preexposure, and latent inhibition (best demonstrated in Pavlovian-conditioning experiments); autoshaping, instinctive drift, and constraints on learning (best demonstrated in operant-conditioning experiments). We have shown how prior knowledge and present contingencies seem to act in combination to produce these different effects.

Operant learning involves a necessary opposition between sampling (behavior designed to reveal properties of the environment) and exploitation (behavior intended to obtain something of value). We saw how animals must settle for a feasible tradeoff between the two activities, with the result being often highly stereotyped behavior in situations in which costs and benefits are high.

Experiments with people show that we are also subject to this sampling/exploitation limitation, and humans frequently sample much less than they should, settling for a rule that works rather than the best possible rule. Decision theorists have called this activity satisficing (settling for "good enough") as opposed to optimizing (settling for the best possible).

Positive reinforcement has been criticized as a training technique because it supposedly induces stereotypy. But, we showed that there are situations—frequency-dependent schedules, for example—in which reinforcement can encourage variability, such as in the shaping of novel behavior. We saw that a promising beginning has been made toward understanding this type of learning through the concept of behavioral repertoires and their spontaneous rearrangement in novel combinations.

The chapter concluded with a simple model for reinforcement that attempted to show the kinds of mechanistic links that must exist among various reinforcement-related phenomena. These phenomena include "superstition," sensitivity to response-reinforcer contiguity, reinforcement of variability, instinctive drift, the delay-of-reward gradient, the difference between emitted and elicited behavior, and so-called constraints on learning. The model is based on a simple process, the integrator, which has turned up several times in earlier chapters. It illustrates the importance of dynamics, and it shows that "reinforcibility" is not an absolute property of a given response-reinforcer combination but depends on the whole set of potential activities.

Large unknowns remain as to the properties of the animal's internal representation of the situation and the processes of memory by which remote past events affect present action. The arguments in this and preceding chapters have suggested that both action and learning are guided by the animal's knowledge of the world. Learning occurs when this knowledge fails to match reality, and actions occur when knowledge (innate and learned) indicates something to approach, or avoid, or do. In Chapter 9, we continue to examine some experimental results that tell us a bit more about the animal's internal representation and how reinforcement contingencies affect it and behavior is guided by it.

9

Conditioned Reinforcement, Chain Schedules, and Extinction

In this chapter we expand on two topics introduced in Chapters 6 and 7: stimulus control and temporal discrimination. We show how temporal discrimination and discrimination between nontemporal stimuli interact to determine behavior on more complex procedures, in which stimulus changes are produced by the animal's own behavior (chain schedules). Experimental results have implications for theories of choice, human as well as animal, and for what has been termed *self-control:* the refraining from choosing a small, immediate reward in favor of a larger, delayed reward. The chapter also further explores the problem of extinction, which is the waning of a previously reinforced activity when reinforcement is withdrawn. We begin by looking at how external signals modulate the effects of food delivery that is delayed or periodic.

CONDITIONED REINFORCEMENT

Delayed Reinforcement

Animals will use any available cue to help them allocate their behavior efficiently. For example, you have already learned that when food is delivered at fixed time intervals, animals behave differently during early and late parts of the interfood interval: During the late part of the interval they engage in food-related activities; during the early part they engage in activities less directly related to food. This behavioral allocation is under the control of time, measured from a time marker that, on FI schedules, is the delivery of food. Time acts like a stimulus that guides the allocation of behavior.

You have already encountered this pattern on schedules in which two or more stimuli, such as lights or sounds, alternate on multiple schedules. Food-related behavior is more likely in the presence of a stimulus that signals food, whereas other activities occur in the presence of a stimulus that signals no-food.

Both of these processes, control by time and control by a food-signaling stimulus, are involved in more complex procedures that are called *chain schedules,* in which stimulus changes are under the animal's control. The complex patterns of behavior on chain schedules and related procedures illustrate four functions of stimuli:

1. As aids or impediments to memory
2. As sources of value (conditioned reinforcement)
3. As guides to behavioral allocation (behavioral contrast)
4. As time markers

These four functions and the behavioral mechanisms associated with them allow us to explain a wide variety of experimental results from complex reinforcement schedules.

We introduce chain schedules by first considering a simpler procedure called *delayed reinforcement.* Suppose we attempt to train a pigeon to peck a white key for food reward, but we delay the food for 5 sec after each peck. We call this type of schedule a delayed-reinforcement schedule. Even if the animal does eventually peck the key, the effect of each reward is likely to be small. Thus, the pigeon will peck the key only a few times and will consequently receive few food deliveries. The functional reason for the weak effect of delayed reinforcement is that it is difficult for the animal to pick out the peck, which is a brief event preceded and followed by other activities, as the best predictor of food that occurs several seconds later (the assignment-of-credit problem). The animal is likely to perceive other events or behaviors, closer to the time of reinforcer delivery, as predictors of food. But since the peck is the only effective response, the rate of reinforcement drops if pecking is displaced by other activities, so that the pigeon may eventually cease to respond at all (i.e., behavior extinguishes). We described a mechanism for delayed reinforcement at the end of Chapter 8. How can we make the delayed-reinforcement schedule easier for the pigeon?

Chain-Reinforcement Schedules: Stimuli as Memory Aids and Sources of Value

We can make the bird's task easier by altering the procedure slightly. Suppose that pecks on the white key are now immediately followed by a change in the color of the key to green. After the green stimulus has been in effect for 5 sec, food is presented as before. That is, a peck now produces a stimulus change plus

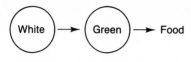

FIGURE 9.1   Two-link chain schedule.

food after 5 sec. After receiving food, the white key reappears, as shown in the two-link chain schedule illustrated in Figure 9.1. This procedure is called a chain schedule because the first contingency for food, a response, is linked to an additional contingency, in this case time, that is associated with a signal, the green light. The time relations between pecking and food are exactly the same as in the delayed-reinforcement procedure, yet the pigeon will rapidly learn to peck the white key if given the green key as a prefood signal.

The change from the white to the green stimulus is used as a reinforcer, and the stimulus seems to have some of the properties of a reinforcer. However, the green stimulus gains its power not innately (or early in development), as does food reinforcement, but by virtue of its pairing with food. Therefore, a food-signaling stimulus is termed a *conditioned,* or *secondary, reinforcer* (to be contrasted with *primary reinforcers,* such as food). Why is this conditioned-reinforcement procedure more effective than the simple delay procedure?

The green-key conditioned reinforcer appears to aid conditioning for two reasons. First, it bridges the temporal gap between the peck (the real cause of the food) and its consequence (the food). It therefore serves as an aid to memory. Rather than having to remember a brief event that occurs 5 sec before its consequence, the animal has only to remember that pecking leads to stimulus change (and that the stimulus is associated with food). Because peck → stimulus change, delay is negligible, thus presenting little difficulty for memory. Second, because the rate of food delivery in the presence of the green stimulus is much higher than in the presence of the white stimulus, the green stimulus acquires a higher hedonic value—greater significance—than the white. The value is relatively transient and depends on reliable delivery of the food. That is, if food ceases to occur, the green stimulus quickly loses its value: The pigeon pecks to produce the green stimulus, because by doing so it turns off a stimulus with a low (zero) rate of food delivery and turns on one with a higher rate. We have seen many other examples in which behavior is guided by this kind of hill-climbing process in previous chapters.

Several procedural tricks allow conditioned stimuli to retain their value for some time after the primary reinforcement has ceased. These tricks depend on memory confusions like those we discuss shortly in connection with second-order schedules. (See discussions of second-order conditioning, e.g., Rescorla, 1982).

The factors that maintain behavior are often different from those that give it birth. The pigeon learns to peck to achieve the green stimulus because it has more value than the white stimulus it replaces. But once the bird has learned to peck the key, other factors come in to play. For example, the duration of the green stimulus is fixed, thus time can begin to play a role, and the role it plays is in some respects surprising. What would you expect to be the effect of increasing the duration of the green stimulus from 5 sec to 10 sec, for example? Will this change have any effect on how long the animal waits in the presence of the white key before pecking to produce the green? It makes no sense for the animal to wait for any but the shortest time before pecking the white key, since the delay for food during the green key's illumination is fixed—every second the bird waits before pecking the white key unnecessarily delays food by the same amount of time. Nevertheless, the longer the green stimulus, the longer the bird will wait with the white key before pecking to produce the green. This behavior is an example of proportional timing, which plays a dominant role in chain-schedule performance. (We describe proportional timing in more detail in the next section.) Now let's look in more detail at the factors that maintain (as opposed to initiate) performance on chain schedules. The function of stimuli as sources of value is much less important than other functions, such as stimuli as memory aids or impediments and stimuli as time markers. Pigeons on multilink chain schedules behave in ways that are not easily reconciled with the idea that pecking in link N is reinforced by the production of link $N + 1$. Consider a chain schedule with three links: Pecking in link 3 (S_3) is reinforced by food; pecking in link 2 (S_2) is reinforced by the production of link 3; pecking in link 1 (S_1) is reinforced by the production of link 2. In principle, there is nothing wrong with extending such a chain indefinitely, for example, to six links (Figure 9.2a). Suppose that each link (S_1, S_2, etc.) is T sec long. That is, the first peck after T sec in the presence of S_1 causes it to change to S_2, and so on—which is called a *chain FI schedule*. How many such fixed-interval links can be strung together and still maintain responding in S_1, the stimulus most remote from food?

The answer, for even quite short values of T, is not more than five or six links. Figure 9.3a shows a cumulative record from a pigeon trained with six fixed-interval, 15-sec links (a blip in the record indicates each stimulus change; the recorder pen is reset after food). Long pauses occur after food is received, and the times between food deliveries are always much longer than the 90-sec minimum prescribed by the schedule. An additional link would have caused the pigeon to stop responding altogether. With longer fixed intervals, five links are the upper limit. What causes this breakdown? We get some clues by changing the procedure slightly—by eliminating the different stimuli that signal each link in the chain. This new procedure is called a *tandem FI schedule* (Figure 9.2b).

TANDEM SCHEDULES   Figure 9.3b shows a typical performance on a six-link tandem FI schedule. On a tandem FI schedule, the timer for the second link doesn't begin until the animal has responded after time T in the first link, and so on, but the stimulus on the response key is always the same. Performance on the tandem schedule is different from performance on the chain in two main ways. First, there are no pauses at the onset of each link, because there are no stimulus changes to serve as time markers. Second, the response rate at the end of the interfood interval is much lower on the tandem schedule, but the postfood pause is much shorter than on the chain schedule. You can see these differences in the figure: the last fixed interval before receiving food has a much steeper slope in

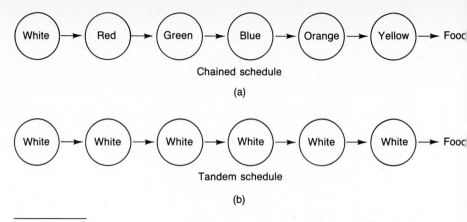

FIGURE 9.2 Six links of FI 15 sec **(a)** Multilink chain schedule. **(b)** Multilink tandem schedule.

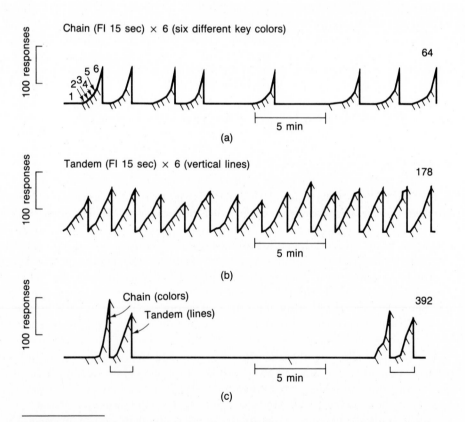

FIGURE 9.3 **(a)** Cumulative record from a well-trained pigeon on a five-link chained, fixed-interval, 15-sec schedule. The recorder pen resets to the bottom after food is received. The blips indicate a stimulus change. **(b)** Cumulative record from a well-trained pigeon on a five-link tandem schedule. A single stimulus was presented throughout the successive, fixed-interval links. **(c)** Cumulative record from a well-trained pigeon exposed to both the chained schedule and the tandem schedule in alternation (from Catania, 1979).

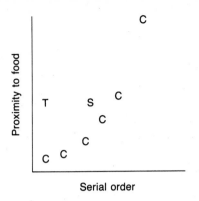

FIGURE 9.4   Stimuli arranged according to their serial order and proximity to food in three procedures: chained schedule (C), tandem schedule (T), and a scrambled schedule (S).

the chain than the tandem record, for example. These differences appear even more clearly in Figure 9.3c, which shows both types of schedule successively in the same pigeon.

Clearly, one problem with the simple, conditioned-reinforcement idea is that it cannot explain results like those that appear in Figure 9.3. Why should five or six chain links be the limit? Why should the pigeons respond *less* in the first chain link than in the first tandem link? These problems are usually handled by factors in addition to the value-added property of conditioned reinforcement. Three differences between chain and tandem schedules have been suggested as reasons for the different behavior they produce:

1. The relative proximity to reinforcement (food) of each stimulus in the series (stimuli early in the chain are far from the next delivery of food, later stimuli are successively closer)
2. The pairing, or lack of pairing, of a stimulus with food
3. The contingency between pecking and a transition to a stimulus closer to food delivery

The last two factors—paring with food and contingency—define conditioned reinforcement in the strict sense. Pairing with food is important because a reinforcer must have value, and value is derived from direct association with food. The contingent relation between response and reinforcer is important *for learning*, because reinforcers are usually assumed to act through response contingency. However, we have already seen that once the response has been learned, contingency is no longer always necessary to maintain the response. Thus, we should not be surprised to see that contingency becomes relatively unimportant for conditioned reinforcement.

Pairing of a stimulus with food is important, and it seems to exert the major effect. Figure 9.4 plots the serial order of each stimulus against its temporal proximity to food. The figure shows that in the case of the chain schedule, the serial order is perfectly correlated with proximity to food, and the response rate is perfectly correlated with both the serial order and the proximity to food: The closer to food, the more responding to the stimulus (Figure 9.3). In the case of the tandem schedule in the figure, a single stimulus has a moderate temporal proximity to food, and it sustains a moderate rate of pecking. In the case of a "scrambled" chain schedule, the proximity to food of all six chain stimuli in the figure is scrambled from interval to interval—so that each stimulus occurs in each serial position $\frac{1}{6}$ of the time. Once again, proximity to food seems to be the major factor, because all six stimuli sustain the same middling response rate under these conditions.

Charles Catania (1980) has demonstrated the relatively weak role of the response contingency on chain FI schedules. So long as the response contingency for food is maintained in the final link of a chain FI schedule, the contingency can be omitted in the earlier links with little effect on key-pecking. That is, fixed-interval schedules can be replaced with fixed-time schedules in all but the final link, and the pigeon will continue to peck in each link much as before. If the stimuli truly serve as "reinforcers," in the sense that their effect depends on the contingent relation between peck and stimulus change, the response rate should have decreased when the contingency was removed. Catania found that it changed little, suggesting that other factors, temporal proximity to food and pairing with food, are more important.

Thus, data from chain and tandem schedules all point to relative temporal proximity to reinforcement as the major factor that maintains pigeon behavior. We now show in more detail how this timing process works.

Dynamics of Chain and Tandem Schedules: Stimuli as Time Markers

All reinforcement schedules present stimuli and reinforcers to the subject in a temporal sequence. On most schedules, this sequence is quite regular. We know that mammals and birds readily detect temporal regularity—the phenomenon is termed *temporal discrimination*. For example, we know that on FI schedules animals always pause before beginning to respond and that the pause is roughly proportional to the interfood interval (see Chapter 6). We will term this temporal discrimination process *proportional timing*. The terms *scalar timing* (Gibbon, 1977) or *linear waiting* (Wynne & Staddon, in press) have also been used for more sophisticated versions of the same idea.

Let's examine how proportional timing might work on chain schedules. Consider a two-link chain FI schedule, in which the interval duration is T sec. The first response after T sec in the presence of S_1, the first stimulus after food delivery, causes a change to S_2. The first response after T sec in S_2 yields food. We also know that the pause is determined by time, since a *time marker,* on FI schedules, is simply the delivery of the reinforcer. But on our two-link chain schedule, there are two time markers. The reinforcer (usually food) determines the first pause, and then the transition from S_1 to S_2 determines the second pause. For simplicity, let's suppose that our animal pauses just one-half the ex-

TABLE 9.1   Behavior on Two- and Three-Link FI 100-Sec Chains
(pause fraction: 0.5)

Cycle	Stimulus	Expected Time to Food	Pause	Link Length
Two-Link Schedule				
1	S_1	200	100	100
	S_2	100	100	100
		Interfood interval:		**200**
2	S_1	200	100	100
	S_2	100	100	100
		Interfood interval:		**200**
Three-Link Schedule				
	S_1	300	**150**	150
1	S_2	200	100	100
	S_3	100	50	100
		Interfood interval:		**350**
	S_1	350	**175**	175
2	S_2	200	100	100
	S_3	100	50	100
		Interfood interval:		**375**
	S_1	375	**188**	188
3	S_2	200	100	100
	S_3	100	50	100
		Interfood interval:		**388**

pected time to food delivery. Because the expected time to food immediately following food delivery is *at least* $2T$ (the minimum duration of the two fixed intervals), the first pause in the chain schedule should be T sec. The second pause
should be $T/2$, because the expected time to food delivery after the stimulus
change from S_1 to S_2 is T sec.

   With these values, the timing process is both stable and optimal, in the sense
that our hypothetical pigeon behaves in such a way that food is delivered as soon
as the schedule permits—with this pattern, it receives food after $2T$ sec. But,
notice what happens if we add one more FI link, making the chain a three-link
chain. If the animal rapidly updates its expectation about the time to food delivery,
from interfood interval to interfood interval, the pattern of pausing is no longer
stable at the original values, and it is certainly not optimal. The sequence of pause
values and times to food delivery is shown in Table 9.1, which compares hypothetical performance in successive cycles on two- and three-link FI 100-sec schedules.

   The key times (interfood intervals) in the table are in **boldface.** We assume
that in the first cycle the animal expects the minimum possible times to food.
That is, on the two-link schedule, the minimum expected time to food delivery is

200 sec at the onset of S_1 and 100 sec at the onset of S_2. On the three-link schedule, the minimum expected time to food delivery is 300 sec at the onset of S_1, 200 sec at the beginning of the second link, and 100 sec at the beginning of the last link. But, notice what happens in the second cycle: On the two-link schedule, the pause remains the same; but on the three-link schedule, because the pause in the first link (150 sec—one-half the 300 sec expected time to food delivery at the onset of S_1) was longer than the 100 sec FI value, the total interfood interval is increased from 300 (the minimum prescribed by the three FI 100 links) to 350 sec. In response to this occurrence, the first pause in the second cycle increases to 175 sec, which means that that cycle is still longer than the preceding one: 375 versus 350 sec. The third cycle is longer still. It is easy to show that the process illustrated in Table 9.1 stabilizes with an initial pause of 200 sec, giving a total interfood interval of 400 sec which is suboptimal because it is 100 sec longer than the minimum permitted by the schedule. The equilibrium interfood interval deviates still more from the minimum permitted by the schedule when we add additional links, because the animal begins to show pauses longer than T (100 sec in the table) in links after the first.

We know from previous chapters that proportional timing is a reliable feature of performance on periodic-food schedules. We have just shown that it explains one characteristic of chain schedules: the excessive pausing in early links. But our explanation still lacks something, because it makes identical predictions for chain and tandem schedules. Moreover, the simple proportional timing process always stabilizes at a finite value. Thus, timing alone cannot predict the extinction that is such a dramatic feature of performance on multilink chain schedules. Animals also do not respond in the rigid way implied by a constant pause fraction; that is, pause duration varies somewhat from link to link. Real animals also do not adapt to changes in interfood interval as rapidly as our ideal pigeon, and their average pause may well be less than 50 percent of the typical time to food delivery. All these deviations from the simple model tend to mitigate its predictions and to shorten postfood pausing on multilink chains. Nevertheless, practice pigeons, at least, are unable to maintain their responding on chain schedules of more than five or six links. What is missing?

What seems to be missing is a factor that reflects whether or not food actually occurs in the presence of a stimulus: In a tandem schedule, food does in fact occur in the presence of the stimulus; but in a chain schedule, food only occurs in the presence of the final stimulus in the chain. The pairing between a stimulus and food contributes positively to performance on the tandem schedule but is lacking for stimuli other than the terminal one on chain schedules. The absence of this factor plus remoteness from food produce extinction in the earliest component of a multilink chain. The fact that food actually occurs in the presence of the stimulus accounts for the maintenance of behavior on multilink tandem schedules and on chain schedules in which the components are scrambled from cycle to cycle.

This analysis and the weak effects of the contingency between response and conditioned reinforcer deemphasize the role of conditioned reinforcement as a "strengthener." It seems that behavior on chain schedules is determined largely by pairing with food (or its absence) and by temporal proximity to food.

The higher response rate in the final link of a chain schedule, compared with the corresponding tandem schedule, also reflects the allocation of terminal and interim activities. The process is the same as the one we have already seen in behavioral contrast on multiple schedules (Chapter 7). Interim and terminal activities are segregated into early and late links on chain schedules, because the early stimuli are never paired with food; interim and terminal activities are less-well segregated on tandem schedules, in which only (postfood) time distinguishes early and late links. Hence, terminal responding suffers less reduction from competition, and it therefore occurs at a higher rate in the late links of the chain.

It is also worth noting that a reliable temporal pattern for well-trained animals on multiple schedules, high response rates in anticipation of a "rich" component and low rates in anticipation of a "lean" component, follows from the kind of timing process described in Table 9.1. The response rate is high just before the transition to a rich component, because the expected time to food delivery is short; the response rate is low before a transition to a lean component, because the expected time to food delivery is long (cf. Williams, 1979).

Second-Order Schedules:
Stimuli as Impediments to Memory

Stimuli that signal delayed reinforcement facilitate the acquisition of behavior because they aid recall. Figure 9.5 shows the results of a procedure that is superficially similar to a chain schedule, in which response-produced stimuli seem to facilitate responding by interfering with recall. Figure 9.5a shows the relatively high response rate and scalloped pattern produced in a well-trained pigeon by splitting up a fixed-interval, 60-min schedule into 15 fixed-interval schedules with 4-min components, each terminated by a brief (0.5 sec) response-contingent stimulus. Food follows (that is, is paired with) the last such brief stimulus in the 15-component cycle. This arrangement is called a *second-order schedule*, which differs from a chain schedule in that the component-change stimulus is brief and is always the same. Figure 9.5b shows behavior on a comparable tandem schedule, in which the performance indicates that without the brief stimuli, the response rate is low, and in the absence of time markers other than food there are no 4-min scallops within the longer 60-min interfood interval.

The brief stimuli in this experiment seem to act by interfering with the animal's recall for the most recent food delivery. In Chapter 6, we showed how the scalloped pattern on fixed-interval schedules depends on the animal's ability to recall the most recent time marker. In the second-order schedule shown in the figure, the most reliable time marker is food delivery. However, food is temporally remote (the interval is 60 min long), and the time is filled with periodic brief stimuli. Moreover, the last brief stimulus is also a potential time marker, because food is always preceded by a brief stimulus 4 min earlier. The brief

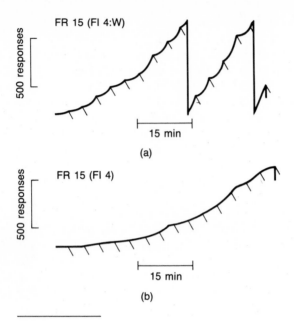

FIGURE 9.5   **(a)** Cumulative record from a well-trained pigeon on a second-order, FI 60-min (FI 4-min) schedule. Every 4 min a peck produced a brief (0.7 sec) stimulus on the response key, which are represented by the blips on the record. At the end of the 15th stimulus, food was presented. Thus, the brief stimulus was paired with food once every hour. **(b)** Performance on the same schedule, but with no brief stimulus presentations. The blips show the unsignaled FI 4-min components (from Kelleher, 1966).

stimulus is less reliable than food as a temporal predictor—food only follows one of the 15 brief stimuli—but it is a great deal closer in time, in other words, when food occurs after a brief stimulus, it does so after only 4 min, as opposed to 60 min. The greater validity of food as a time marker seems to be outweighed by the greater frequency and closer proximity to food delivery of the less-valid brief stimulus. The brief stimulus seems to interfere retroactively with recall for food delivery as the effective time marker. Because the animal does not know where it is in the interval, it must treat each brief stimulus as if it were the last— hence the animal anticipates food at each stimulus presentation. Since a brief stimulus occurs every 4 min, the response rate is naturally higher than on the tandem schedule, which is treated much like an FI 60-min schedule. The effects of the second-order stimuli on behavior can be so great that the term *quasi-reinforcement* was once suggested for them (Neuringer & Chung, 1967; Staddon, 1972).

In summary, the effects of brief stimuli were at one time attributed to the pairing of the final stimulus with food. Subsequent work has shown that pairing seems to be important only for the initial acquisition of the pattern of responding (Squires, Norborg, & Fantino, 1975; Stubbs, 1971). Conditioned reinforcers seem to aid the acquisition of behavior because they act as aids to memory, that is, aids to solving the assignment-of-credit problem, and as signals for food. They aid the maintenance of behavior under some conditions because they signal conditions of more-frequent reinforcement, but they also impair behavior on extended chain schedules because early links in the chain are both remote from and unpaired with food. Under other conditions, second-order stimuli can maintain behavior by confusing the animal, that is, interfering with the animal's ability to recall the time of food delivery.

In our discussion of delayed reinforcement and the beneficial effects of adding a chain link (i.e., a signal during the response-produced delay), we described the "reinforcing" effect of the stimulus in hill-climbing terms. We saw how the pigeon pecks the white key to produce a green key because the green key is associated with a higher frequency of food reinforcement than the white key. Will animals respond only for "good news"—a situation clearly better than the current one—or will they also respond for information, good or bad news, about the conditions of reinforcement? This issue has been pursued by several researchers beginning many years ago with experiments on what was called observing behavior (Wyckoff, 1952).

Observing Behavior: Information or Conditioned Reinforcement?

In an observing-behavior experiment, pigeons are offered the opportunity to produce a stimulus that tells them whether or not a reinforcer is likely, but this information has no effect on the actual availability of the reinforcer. Responding sustained by the production of such an *informative stimulus* is termed *observing behavior.* For example, suppose that food for hungry pigeons is scheduled on a variable-interval, 60-sec (VI 60) schedule for pecking on the left key, which is normally white. Pecks on the right key have no effect on food delivery, but they turn the left key green if the variable interval is due to make food available within the next 30 sec. Under favorable conditions, pigeons soon learn to peck the right key. Does this behavior indicate that information is reinforcing in and of itself, or can we deduce this result from familiar principles? The answer is that we do not need to postulate a desire for information on the part of the bird. The delay to food delivery in the presence of the green key is less than its delay in the situation as a whole. Hence, pigeons should peck the right key, turning the left key green, even though the observing response has no effect on the overall rate of reinforcement. According to our hill-climbing idea, responding is maintained on the observing key by an overall reduction in the delay to reinforcement. The reduction is only apparent, of course, but the pigeon is not in a position to know that.

A better way to test for pigeons' quest for "information" is to use a procedure in which the left key is normally white, as before, but a peck on the right key turns the left key (the "observing" key) green if food is *not* to become available in the next 30 sec. This "bad news" procedure gives the bird the same amount of information as the "good news" procedure just described, but pigeons will not peck the "observing" key under these conditions, because it is associated with a delay to reinforcement longer than the overall average. Pigeons prefer "good news" information, in the same way that humans do (Chapter 8). It also reflects the underlying hill-climbing process discussed in Chapter 2: Organisms act in ways that lead to an improvement in their overall situation. Pigeons, at least, have little use for information in the abstract.

Proportional Timing and Ratio Schedules

We have seen how proportional timing seems to be the major factor in performance on fixed-interval and chain FI schedules. (In the next section we describe how it can help us understand the complex patterns of data on choice procedures.) It may also underlie behavior on procedures that seem to have nothing whatever to do with timing, namely *ratio schedules*. Let's pursue the argument with the aid of our "ideal pigeon." We use the term *ideal pigeon* in the way that physicists use the term *ideal gas,* which is one that obeys the gas laws perfectly, as real gases do not. Nevertheless, the ideal is close enough to the reality to provide interesting predictions. Our ideal pigeon obeys the principle of proportional timing perfectly. It always waits a fixed fraction of the expected time to food delivery before responding; and when it responds, it does so at a steady rate until the next food delivery. We also assume (following the argument in Table 9.1) that our pigeon updates its estimate of the expected time to food delivery each time it receives food. In a moment we will see that the ideal pigeon mimics the behavior of real pigeons in many concurrent chain experiments. What will such a predictable bird do when it receives food following every peck, that is, on an FR 1 schedule?

The first food delivery doesn't tell the pigeon much, because it has no time marker (other than the beginning of the session) to tie it to. But, the second food delivery occurs time t_1 after the first, where t_1 is the time between the first peck and the second. Now, the pigeon has a time marker—food (or a peck, since they occur simultaneously)—and an estimated time to food delivery—t_1. Proportional timing says that the pigeon's next peck will be after a time t_2 that is shorter than t_1, because the pause is always a fraction of the expected time to food delivery. By the same process, the next pause, t_3, is shorter still, and so on in a positive-feedback process that will soon have the animal responding as rapidly as possible. Rapid responding is of course the main characteristic of performance on ratio schedules.

Now, suppose we slowly increase the ratio size, first to two pecks to food, then to three, and finally to 10, say. We have two time markers: food, which signals a relatively long time to the next food (because the animal must complete the 10-peck ratio in between), and the peck, which still signals a short time to the next food opportunity (assuming that the animal cannot count, thus cannot tell one peck within the ratio "run" from another). The short minimum peck → food time implies that once the animal begins to respond, it should continue to respond at a high rate. But, the longer food → food time implies that the first postfood peck will be delayed, that is, the animal should develop a postfood pause. The fixed ratio thus begins to look like a two-link chain schedule: The first link is the time between food and the first peck; the second link is the ratio "run," once pecking has begun. Moreover, the larger the ratio size (the longer the second link), the longer the pause should be. Postfood pause is indeed directly related to ratio size on fixed-ratio schedules.

How long can we continue this process? That is, how large can we make the ratio before behavior collapses and the bird stops responding? Here the simple theory is less accurate, but it is at least possible to calculate how the postfood pause should increase with ratio size. Suppose the animal always waits one-half the expected time to food delivery (i.e., $E/2$), and suppose that it cannot peck faster than one peck every t sec. If the ratio size is N, the time taken up by each ratio "run" is therefore Nt sec. Hence, the expected time to food delivery (E) is $t_p + Nt$, where t_p is the postfood pause. But by our hypothesis, the postfood pause is always one-half the expected time to food delivery (i.e., $t_p = E/2$). Thus, we must solve two equations to find the actual value of the pause:

$$E = t_p + Nt$$
$$t_p = E/2$$

We must eliminate E from these equations to solve for t_p as a function of N. The answer: $t_p = Nt$. That is, the pause is proportional to the ratio value, as the verbal argument led us to expect. In general, if the pause fraction is A, where A is between 0 and 1, the relation is $t_p = ANt/(1 - A)$. For example, consider our ideal pigeon responding on an FR 50 schedule at a maximum rate of 60 responses per minute. For this case, $t = 1$ (1 response/sec = 60/min), $N = 50$, and $A = 0.3$, say. Therefore, $t_p = 0.3 (50 \times 1)/(1 - 0.3)$, or $t_p = 21.43$ sec.

Experimental results also show that the pause fraction (A) depends on the size of the food delivery the animal receives: The larger the food delivery, the smaller the pause fraction (Powell, 1969). We will have use for this relationship between pause fraction and reward magnitude when we discuss self-control later in the chapter.

This proportional-timing process is stable—no matter how high the ratio, the ideal pigeon should continue to respond—so long as our assumption that the animal cannot discriminate one peck from another holds true. But at very large ratios, the first peck in the ratio "run" occurs a long time after food delivery, and it may perhaps become discriminable from later pecks. Nevertheless, this first peck signals a long time to food delivery, so that a pause may begin to develop after this peck—just like the pause that follows the onset of the second link in a multilink chain schedule. This pause lengthens the total time between food deliveries and thus the postfood pause. *Ratio strain* is the name given to the pausing that begins to occur during the ratio run at high ratio values. It is usually a sign that the animal is almost at its limit of ratio size and that further increases are likely to lead to extinction. It is presumably the cumulative effects of the development of pausing during the ratio run that lead to the eventual breakdown of ratio-schedule performance at high ratios. Other processes, such as the sheer effort involved in a long run of pecking, may also contribute.

What behaviors can we see with pigeons on variable-ratio schedules? Here the positive-feedback process that produces a high response rate operates just as it does on a fixed-ratio schedule, but food delivery is no longer a reliable signal for a long expected time to food, because some ratio values are quite small. Hence, proportional timing implies no postfood pause. And in fact, pausing does not occur on VR schedules, although the response rate is indeed high, just like with fixed-ratio schedules. Thus, the main properties of responding on *both* fixed- and variable-ratio schedules, the high "running" rate and the fixed-ratio postfood pause, are directly traceable to the proportional timing process.

DELAYED REINFORCEMENT AND CHOICE

Chain schedules have been used extensively in choice procedures intended to discover quantitative principles of reinforcement. Some of these procedures are complicated, but their basic design—and many of their results—can be understood quite easily by beginning with an idealized, two-choice procedure. Examine the FI schedule diagrammed in Figure 9.6a, which shows how the ideal pigeon will respond during a single interfood interval. The bird waits for a fixed fraction, say $\frac{1}{4}$, of the time to food delivery before beginning to peck, and then (we assume) pecks at a constant rate until food is delivered at the end of the interval. The steady rate of pecking is represented by the shaded area that begins $T/4$ sec into the T-sec interval.

Now look at Figure 9.6b, which shows a concurrent FI FI schedule: two response keys, left and right, each of which allows access to its own, independent FI schedule. The two schedules are not of equal length: One is T_L sec, the other T_R sec; and $T_R > T_L$. How will the pigeon respond in this situation? The answer tells us a great deal about how animals treat more complex procedures.

The simplest assumption we can make is that our ideal pigeon treats each key in the concurrent situation in exactly the same way it would treat it in isolation. That is, the pigeon waits $T_L/4$ sec after food delivery before beginning to respond on the FI T_L key. It waits $T_R/4$ sec before beginning to respond on the FI T_R key; since the pigeon cannot respond at the same time on both keys, there will inevitably be competition for available time after $T_R/4$ sec, when the bird must peck on both keys (we ignore this factor for the moment, since it affects both keys equally). But, there is an ambiguity: Clearly the animal will receive food earlier after pecking the left, FI T_L, key than after pecking the right, FI T_R, key. Thus, there are two ways that the procedure might work:

1. The FI T_R timer could continue even after food delivery for a left key response, until a peck eventually produces food on the right key
2. *Both* scheduling timers, right key as well as left key, could be reset, so that the two FI schedules are timed from a food delivery produced by either key

It is important to notice that this procedural difference makes a great deal of difference to how the animal is likely to behave.

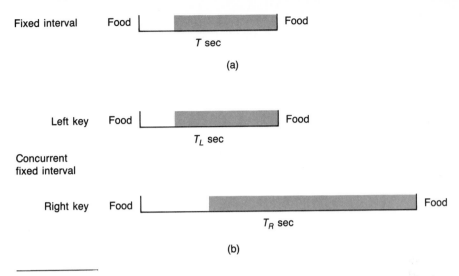

FIGURE 9.6   **(a)** A single cycle of simple and **(b)** concurrent fixed-interval schedules.

If we adopt programming method (1), resetting the left FI timer only when food is produced by a left key response and the right FI timer only when food is produced for a right key response, then we favor some responding to both keys. The reason is that even if the animal starts out by responding almost exclusively on the left (short FI) key, after only a few food deliveries a single peck on the right key will produce food—because the right key timer continues to run until food is produced by a right key response. A pigeon with some initial tendency to peck both keys soon detects this feature, hence continues to respond on both the right as well as the left keys. This mixture of left and right key responding is termed a *partial preference.*

Conversely, if we reset both timers after food delivery, according to programming method (2), with the response pattern shown in Figure 9.6 the immediate result is that the animal only receives food for a left key response—because the left key timer is always timed out first and food delivery resets both timers. Thus, a right key peck is never followed by food delivery, and the right key becomes a stimulus that is never paired with food—therefore, pecking the right key eventually drops out entirely. Hence, programming method (2) favors *exclusive choice* of the left key.

Pigeons behave as these arguments suggest—showing partial preferences on procedures programmed according to method (1) and tending toward exclusive choice on procedures programmed according to method (2). We explore several examples of both effects later in the section.

Let's now look at a chain-schedule version of the two-choice procedure. Figure 9.7a shows a single interfood interval on a two-link chain FI schedule: an initial link of t-sec duration, in the presence of stimulus S_1, followed by a response-produced transition to a second link of T-sec duration in the presence of stimulus S_2. The two response records show the hypothetical performance of our ideal

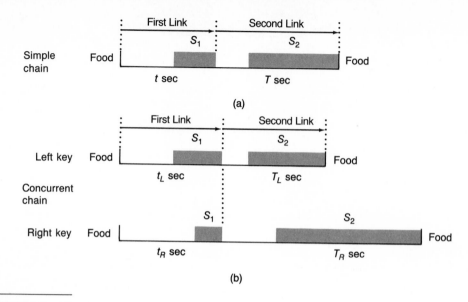

FIGURE 9.7   **(a)** A single cycle of simple and **(b)** concurrent chain FI FI schedules. Responding is indicated by the shaded areas.

pigeon, who follows the now familiar pattern described in Table 9.1. After the initial time marker (food), the pigeon pauses a fixed fraction (say $\frac{1}{4}$) of the total time to food delivery (i.e., $(t + T)/4$ sec), and it thereafter responds at a steady rate until it reaches the response-produced transition from S_1 to S_2. When S_2 begins, the pigeon pauses the same fraction of the remaining time to food (i.e., $T/4$ sec). (We ignore the additive effect of the pairing of S_2 with food because that fact has no bearing on behavior in S_1, which is what we are interested in here.)

Figure 9.7b shows a concurrent-chain schedule with two keys that is programmed in the same manner as the single key chain in Figure 9.7a, but with different values for the duration of the second link, which is T_L on the left key and T_R on the right key. The procedure has an additional feature that was not necessary on the single-link, concurrent FI FI schedule: When the pigeon successfully produces a transition to *either* second link (i.e., either S_{L2} or S_{R2}), the other key is turned off until after food delivery, when both keys return to their initial-link stimuli. Thus, once the animal has produced a second link, it is committed to it until food is delivered. The programming rule for the t-sec timer in the first link is method (1) from our previous discussion, that is, when food is delivered in either second link, both first-link FI timers are reset.

The response records for our ideal pigeon in Figure 9.7 show how it behaves using this new procedure. The major result is clear: It waits much longer before beginning to respond in the first link on the right key, which leads to the longer second link. Because the proportion of time taken up by responding (the shaded area) is larger on the left key than on the right key, the ideal pigeon seems to respond at a higher rate in the first link on the left key (which has a short second link) than on the right key (which has a longer second link). Notice that because of the "commitment" feature of the procedure (once a second link is begun, the other key becomes ineffective), the animal continues to receive about 50 percent of its food for pecking on the right key. Nevertheless, because of the pigeon's late start at pecking on the right key, its proportion of responses is obviously much smaller on the key that leads to the longer second link.

This result—some responding on both keys, but more on the key that leads to the shorter second link—is not surprising, although responding on both keys is not always optimal behavior under these conditions. Nevertheless, this behavior is in fact true to life, although the schedules used are little more complex than the ones shown in Figure 9.7. In the usual concurrent-chain experiment, the delays in the second links are often fixed, as in our example, but the first-link schedules are usually on variable- rather than on fixed-interval schedules. The reasons are largely historical—the first experiments were performed in this fashion (e.g., Herrnstein, 1964)—but this difference does not affect our conclusion, which depends only on the animal setting its waiting time in the two initial links to a fixed fraction of the expected time to food delivery.

Optimal Policy on Concurrent-Chain Schedules

How should pigeons respond on concurrent-chain schedules with equal first links? What should they do so as to minimize the average time between food deliveries? The pigeon really has only two options in this situation: either ignore the key leading to the longer second link or sample both in such a way as to enter each second link as soon as it is available. Let's call the first strategy *fixate* (on the short-link key) and the second *sample*. It is relatively clear from Figure 9.7 that with fixed-duration, equal-length first links that are reset with each food delivery, there is absolutely no reason ever to respond to the key that has the longer second link. But, what if the first links are variable- rather than fixed-interval links? In this case, responding depends on the relative durations of the first and second links. The argument is straightforward: For the fixate strategy, the average interfood interval is simply $t + T_L$, where t is now the value of both first-link VI schedules. For the sample strategy, the average interfood interval is the average of two numbers: a number that represents the average time the animal spends in the first link, plus a second number that is the average of the two second-link delays. The first number, when the first links are equal VI t seconds, is one-half the VI value, since the two VI schedules are independent and each begins once every t sec. Thus, the average interfood interval under the sample strategy is $(t + T_L + T_R)/2$. The fixate strategy is better than the sample strategy if the corresponding interfood interval $(t + T_L)$ is less than $(t + T_L + T_R)/2$, which reduces to the condition:

$$t + T_L < T_R$$

In short, the animal should be more likely to fixate as the duration of the first-link VI schedule (t) decreases, which makes intuitive sense. By waiting long enough, the animal can ensure that a single peck on the right key activates the second link. But, such pecking is only worthwhile if the delay the pigeon must then suffer (T_R) is shorter than the expected time to food delivery for simply continuing to respond in the first link on the left key ($t + T_L$).

What is interesting about this prediction is that this shift, away from fixation toward indifference as t (the first-link VI schedule) is increased, is precisely the pattern that pigeons show on these procedures (Fantino, 1969). We show in a moment that this pattern, and a number of other results from experiments with concurrent chain schedules, is also what we would expect from our ideal pigeon—who behaves nearly optimally under these far-from-natural conditions. Of course, the ideal pigeon is not optimizing at all; rather, it is simply following blindly the proportional-timing rule, which happens to work well in the situations we have discussed so far. Naturally there are situations in which proportional timing does not work as well; and in these situations, the ideal pigeon behaves suboptimally. It is interesting that in such situations real pigeons also fail to maximize their rate of food delivery. (We return to these topics in a moment.)

CHAIN SCHEDULES AND NATURAL FORAGING   The choice between two chain VI FI schedules is formally the same as the problem of choosing between two different prey types that have different profitabilities. The problem is a classic one in behavioral ecology, the problem of diet selection (see Stephens & Krebs, 1986, for an excellent survey of theoretical and experimental work). For example, imagine a predator, a squirrel, say, that has two types of nuts available to it. Let's for the moment assume that both nuts have the same nutritive value (food amount) but that nut A has a thicker shell than nut B, thus nut B takes longer to crack (i.e., has a longer handling time). To simplify the situation further, let's assume that the two types of nuts are equally abundant. When should our squirrel eat either type of nut whenever it encounters it, and when should it specialize on only the more profitable type? (*Profitability* is the ratio of energetic value, E, to *handling time*, h: profitability $= E/h$.) If each type of nut is encountered on the average every t sec, the squirrel's rate of energy intake if it specializes on B is $R_B = E/(t + h_B)$, where h_B is the handing time for B. That is, R_B is equal to the energy expended cracking each nut (E), divided by the average time between cracking nuts (encounter interval t, plus handling time h_B) (Figure 9.8). On the other hand, if the squirrel generalizes, accepting both A and B, its rate of energy intake is E, divided by the average encounter time, which is now $t/2$ (since we count encounters with either equally abundant type), plus the average handling time, which is ($h_A + h_B$)/2—therefore, $R_A = 2E/(t + h_A + h_B)$. The animal should specialize if $R_B > R_A$, which reduces to $t + h_B < h_A$, which is the same as the condition for the fixate policy in our preceding chain-schedule analysis. The main ecological implication of this analysis is that as food density decreases (i.e., encounter time, $t/2$, increases), the animal should be less likely to specialize and more likely to accept any food it encounters, even the least profitable. Numerous experiments have confirmed this qualitative prediction in several species (see Stephens & Krebs, 1986).

A more general diet-selection problem—the so-called optimal-diet problem—provides the initial impetus for the field of *optimal foraging theory* (MacArthur & Pianka, 1966). Consider two prey types, one of which is highly profit-

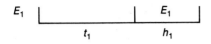

FIGURE 9.8   A typical cycle of foraging for a food type with profitability E_1/h_1, encountered on the average every t_1 sec.

able (low handling time and/or high energy content) and the other less profitable: $E_1/h_1 > E_2/h_2$. These two types have different abundances: Type 1 is encountered on the average of every t_1 sec, type 2 every t_2 sec. Under what conditions should the animal select both types: whenever it encounters them (generalize) or should it select only the more profitable one (specialize)? The analysis is similar to our preceding example, but it also allows us to introduce a new technique, the *method of marginal value*. We first derive an expression for the expected food rate under the specialize strategy. The situation is like the simple chain schedule shown in Figure 9.8. It is clear from the diagram that the expected rate of energy acquisition under the specialize strategy is $R_1 = E_1/(t_1 + h_1)$: that is, the energy in one prey item (E_1), divided by the time between items (t_1), plus the time it takes to eat an item (h_1).

The *generalize* strategy is a bit more difficult to explain, because we must somehow average the payoff from both types of items. At first blush, it might seem that our predator should always select both items, but that is because we forget what economists call the *opportunity cost* of eating a low profitability prey item. The opportunity cost is incurred by the item's handling time (h_2): If h_2 is long, then it might be better for our optimal predator to spend the time looking for the more profitable prey, rather than waste time struggling to eat the less profitable one. The easiest way to see the optimal strategy is to use the marginal value argument, which says that under most conditions an animal can maximize its rate of return by always picking, moment by moment, the option with the highest expected reward rate. The base comparison is, of course, with the specialize strategy: If the animal ignores the less profitable item, it can always find food at a rate $R_1 = E_1/(t_1 + h_1)$. Thus when an animal encounters a less profitable item, it should compare R_1 with the expected food rate once it has already encountered the less profitable item (namely E_2/h_2, which is the profitability of the lesser food type). This argument yields the counterintuitive result that in a situation like this one, the abundance of the less profitable item (determined by t_2) should have no effect on the animal's willingness to take it—only the abundance of the more profitable item (determined by t_1) should have any effect.

Under many conditions this prediction seems to hold true. For example, John Krebs and his colleagues (1977) performed a laboratory prey-selection experiment with great tits (*Parus major*), small insectivorous European birds. The birds were presented with artificial prey (mealworms) that passed in front of them on a small conveyor belt. There were two types of prey: "bigs" and "smalls." The experimenters varied the frequency of the "bigs" to see if there was indeed a critical frequency above which the birds would suddenly cease to take any "smalls." They did find a transition, but it was smooth, rather than sudden. (You can probably think of many reasons for the gradualness of the change: e.g., how well could the birds estimate frequency?) In another experiment, Werner and Hall (1974) looked at bluegill sunfish feeding on *Daphnia* (water fleas) of three different sizes in a tank. There were equal numbers of each size flea. The more fleas there were in the tank, the less likely the fish were to take the smaller sizes.

Thus, optimal-foraging analysis can be extended to make predictions about what animals should do when the two food types have different abundances or are of different nutritive values. The case in which encounter rates are the same, but nutritive values and handling times are different, resembles the self-control experiments we discuss later in the chapter. Of course, these optimality arguments don't say anything about the mechanisms or rules that underlie the animal's behavior. In the next section we see that proportional timing, which is the main mechanism that seems to drive choice in these procedures, does not always produce optimal behavior. We can therefore expect optimal-foraging predictions to fail under some experimental conditions.

Parametric Effects on Concurrent-Chain Schedules

Pigeons will peck a key to produce a stimulus if the stimulus signals a higher rate of food delivery than the prevailing rate. This finding led researchers to assume that the value of a conditioned reinforcer is directly related to the rate of primary reinforcement in its presence. They believed that

1. Pecking to produce conditioned reinforcers is maintained by the value of the conditioned reinforcers
2. The value of a conditioned reinforcer is related to the rate of primary reinforcement that it signals

As you have seen, it now seems unlikely that the reinforcing property of conditioned reinforcers is as important to the maintenance of pecking as their proximity to food. Nevertheless, you need to know the theoretical presumptions that have led to a long series of experiments aimed at measuring the value of conditioned reinforcers. The reasoning was along the following lines: Perhaps stimulus A, in whose presence food occurs after T sec, is about one-half as valuable as stimulus B, in whose presence the same food occurs after a delay of only $T/2$ sec. If true, perhaps pigeons will work twice as hard for B as for A. How can we verify this prediction, researchers wondered? We might ask pigeons, on a trial-by-trial basis, to choose between two keys: one displaying stimulus A, the other stimulus B. But even the dimmest pigeon is likely to choose stimulus B exclusively, which tells us something about the relative values of A and B— namely that B is greater than A—but it does not tell us *how much* greater. Something more subtle was needed.

Richard Herrnstein (1964) proposed an ingenious solution to the problem of measuring the value of a conditioned reinforcer, based on an earlier result with primary (food) reinforcement. He and his colleagues had already shown that if pigeons are allowed to respond concurrently on two independent variable-interval schedules, they will approximately match their ratio of key pecks, right/left, to the ratio of obtained food reinforcements (if the VI schedules are different) or to the ratio of food magnitudes (if the VI schedules are the same) (see Herrnstein (1970) for a review). If we denote rates of responding on right and left keys by x and y and rates of reinforcement obtained by $R(x)$ and $R(y)$, the *matching law* says that

$$x/y = R(x)/R(y)$$

We say more about the matching law in Chapter 11.

The matching-law result with schedules of primary reinforcement suggested to Herrnstein a procedure to measure the value of *conditioned* reinforcers: Why not ask pigeons to choose between two conditioned reinforcers, each delivered according to the same VI schedule? Such a chain is simply the concurrent-chain procedure we have been discussing thus far but with VI, rather than FI, schedules in the first link. The matching result implies, Herrnstein argued, that the ratio of key pecks in the first links should provide an accurate measure of the ratio of conditioned reinforcing values of the second links.

In his first experiment Herrnstein (1964) found, as he had expected, that the ratio of pecks on the right and left keys in the equal-VI first links matched the inverse ratio of second-link delays. Thus, if the second link delays were $T_L = T$ and $T_R = T/2$, the ratio of right key pecks to left key pecks in the first links were 1:2. Evidently, the value of a conditioned reinforcer is indeed inversely related to the food delay in its presence.

However, subsequent experiments soon showed that this conclusion is valid only under certain specialized conditions. From a present-day perspective, we can see that Herrnstein's result was unlikely to be universal because it rested on a functional argument that explained behavior in terms of its outcome. Like any functional principle—such as the principle of reinforcement itself—Herrnstein's simple rule took no account of the mechanisms that underlie performance. Just as reinforcers sometimes fail to reinforce (cf. the discussion of instinctive drift and superstition at the end of Chapter 8), so too conditioned reinforcers will sometimes fail to act in the expected manner. Just as the failures of the reinforcement principle have told us something about the mechanisms that underlie reinforcement, so too the failures of conditioned reinforcement tell us something about how *it* works.

The first experiment to cause problems showed that the quantitative preference for the shorter-second-link key diminishes as the length of the first-link VI schedule is increased: the longer the first links of a concurrent-chain schedule, the more the animal tends to be indifferent between the two first-link keys (Fantino, 1969). As we have seen, this outcome makes intuitive sense, because if the first links are quite long relative to both second links, then the animal's optimal policy is to exit the first-link (in this case, either first-link) as soon as possible. This policy follows directly from the optimality condition for fixation on the short-link key we derived earlier, in which $t + T_L < T_R$: the longer the value of t, the first-link delay, the less likely the animal is to respond on only one

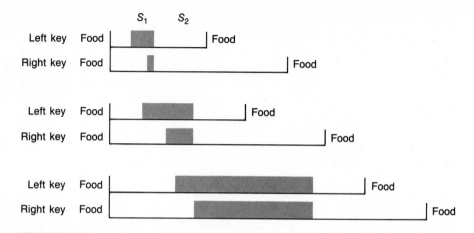

FIGURE 9.9   The effect of first-link duration on concurrent-chain schedule performance. First-link responding begins after $\frac{1}{4}$ time to food delivery.

key. This kind of result poses severe difficulties for the simple, conditioned-reinforcement idea. The difficulties come from the fact that the value of a conditioned reinforcer depends on more than the rate of primary reinforcement that it signals. The conditioned-reinforcing value is evidently a relative rather than an absolute property. However, the difficulties are not insuperable because we can simply revise our functional principle to accommodate this relativity, and numerous attempts have been made to do so. But, the cost is greatly increased theoretical complexity and loss of predictive power.

Over the years several other limitations on Herrnstein's original conclusion have appeared. First-link preference is affected by the absolute (as well as relative) durations of the second links, by the variability of second-link delays, as well as by the absolute value of first-link delays. First-link preference is surprisingly little affected by the number, as opposed to the delay, of second-link reinforcers.

We now show how all these effects can be derived from our proportional-timing mechanism. The arguments are discussed in the following subsections.

EFFECT OF FIRST-LINK DELAY   Figure 9.9 shows how our ideal pigeon should respond on three concurrent-chain schedules with the same pair of unequal second-link delays and increasing but equal first-link delays. As before, we assume that first-link responding begins when $\frac{1}{4}$ of the expected time to food delivery has elapsed. The period of responding during each first link is indicated by the shaded region. It is easy to see that the ratio of first-link pecks approaches indifference (1:1) as the first-link delays increase.

EFFECT OF SECOND-LINK DELAY   Figure 9.10 shows how our ideal pigeon adapts to increasing the absolute duration of the two second links, while keeping the equal first links constant. It is easy to see that as the absolute durations of the two

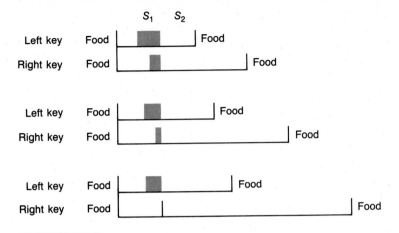

FIGURE 9.10   The effect of second-link duration on concurrent-chain schedule performance. The ratio of second-link delays is constant. First-link responding begins after $\frac{1}{4}$ time to food delivery.

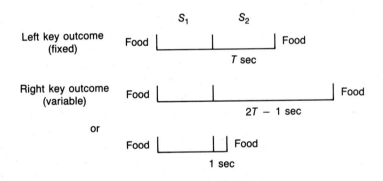

FIGURE 9.11   Concurrent-chain procedure with variable versus fixed second links. The two variable, right-key second links occur with equal probability and have the same average duration as the fixed, left-key second link.

second links increase, preference should shift toward exclusive choice. This result is basically the same as that seen in Figure 9.9: In the first case, the second links were held constant and the first links increased; in this case, the first links are held constant and the second links increased. Real pigeons show both of these effects (Fantino, 1972; MacEwen, 1972).

EFFECT OF VARIABLE VERSUS FIXED SECOND-LINK DELAY   Figure 9.11 shows the time relations in a concurrent-chain experiment with equal first links. The second link on the left key is a constant delay (T). On the right key, two different delays, $2T - 1$ or 1, averaging T, occur with equal probability. Numerous exper-

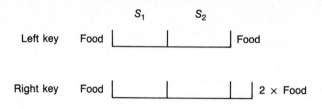

FIGURE 9.12   Concurrent-chain procedure in which the second link for the right key provides two food deliveries for every link of the left key.

iments have shown that pigeons have a strong preference for the variable alternative, that is, the one that leads to either a short or long second link with equal probability. Our ideal pigeon also shows this effect, because it begins responding in the initial link in anticipation of the first food opportunity (providing that opportunity is not too infrequent). Since the variable response key provides the first food opportunity, responding should begin much earlier on that key. The ideal pigeon becomes indifferent between the two alternatives only when the fixed alternative is almost equal in value to the shorter of the two variable alternatives (rather than equal to their mean, as the optimal policy requires).

James Mazur (1984) developed a negative-feedback, or *titration*, procedure that allowed him to estimate the point of indifference in procedures like the one just described. Mazur's schedule is complicated, but its essential feature is that if the animal shows a preference for the variable key, then the duration of the fixed second-link delay is reduced; conversely, if the animal prefers the fixed key, then its duration is increased. In this way, the animal is driven toward indifference. Mazur found that given a choice between a variable alternative with 0 and 20-sec delays, pigeons become indifferent only when the fixed delay is set to a little over 1 sec, a strikingly large departure from the optimal policy, which implies indifference when the fixed delay is 10 sec. In another confirmation of the proportional-timing hypothesis, Gibbon, Church, Fairhurst, and Kacelnik (1987), who have also developed an elegant quantitative theory of scalar timing, have shown that pigeons greatly prefer a distribution of variable-length delays where short delays predominate to a distribution with equal mean and variability where long delays predominate. This result shows quite clearly that the pigeons' behavior in Mazur's experiment does not in any way imply a preference for variability as such. The birds prefer the short-delay distribution because the expected time to the first food opportunity is shorter than in the long-delay distribution.

EFFECT OF NUMBER OF SECOND-LINK REINFORCERS   Figure 9.12 shows a procedure that one might expect to produce a strong right-key preference (but also see Box 9.1). In this figure, first- and second-link delays are the same, but for the right key two reinforcers are delivered in close succession before the first link reappears. Optimal responding here implies a strong right-key preference, although our ideal pigeon shows an outcome close to indifference, because the first food opportunity occurs after the same delay for both keys. The second second-

B   O   X

9.1

What Do We Mean by *Preference?*

Note that what we have referred to as *preference* in this chapter really isn't anything like the conventional term. Cognitive psychologists Kahneman and Tversky (1984) have pointed out the importance of what they term *framing,* the way that people confronted with a choice conceptualize the problem: For example is the problem one of loss (the glass half empty) or gain (the glass half full)? But there is a more fundamental frame, common to all real choices— namely the comparison between alternatives. Our proportional-timing analysis of these supposed choice experiments involves *no* comparison at all: We have been able to derive our results on the assumption that the pigeon treats each alternative as though it were present in isolation. Moreover, although these procedures are explicitly designed in terms of a choice phase (the first link) and an outcome phase (the second link), our analysis shows that from the pigeon's point of view, both phases merge into one. The pigeon does not seem to be first *choosing* and then *receiving* the food; rather at every instant, the pigeon pecks in anticipation of where (according to the timing mechanism plus additive stimulus factors) it anticipates food will be.

The general point is that the experimenter's view of a procedure may not coincide with the animal's view. Our analysis suggests that from the pigeon's viewpoint, these complex procedures are not choice procedures at all. They are merely situations in which food occurs at different times for pecking different keys. The animal acts as if its task is not so much to choose as simply to be there when food becomes available.

link food delivery does have a slight effect, which becomes weaker as the delay between it and the first food delivery becomes larger (Mazur, 1986; Moore, 1982).

Conclusion

In accordance with our policy throughout this book, we have explained the major behavioral mechanisms that underlie a class of experimental phenomena (Box 9.2). The mechanisms that underlie conditioned reinforcement, as measured in concurrent-chain schedule experiments, turn out to be two in number, and both are quite simple:

1. An effect due to the pairing of a primary reinforcer (food) with a stimulus

B   O   X

9.2

What Is an Explanation?

The discussion of conditioned reinforcement in this chapter is our most ambitious attempt so far to show you how a simple principle can explain a wide
range of experimental results. Less elaborate examples are the dynamic model
for short-term learning described at the end of Chapter 8 and the integrator
model for *Stentor* escape behavior in Chapter 3. These models do not refer
directly to physiology, to neurons and synapses. Nor do they predict precise
trajectories, like the equations of Newtonian physics. In what sense, then, are
they explanations? They explain in the sense that they reduce a set of diverse
and apparently unrelated facts to the operation of a simple rule or a small set
of rules. Of course, the grandest theory of this type is Charles Darwin's explanation of the vast diversity of organic life by the twin processes of variation
and natural selection. Like Darwin's theory, our theories explain patterns of
results (e.g., see Figures 9.14–9.16) and suggest relations between procedures
that might otherwise seem unrelated (e.g., between ratio schedules and chain
schedules). These theories make qualitative, rather than quantitative, predictions. Whereas most highly quantitative theories are rather limited in application—they explain a few things precisely—these theories are more comprehensive—they explain a number of things, but in a qualitative fashion.

Both types of theory have their uses. In biology, the Hodgkin–Huxley
equations for nerve action comprise a theory of the first type: They explain
one thing, the nerve action potential. This theory has led to enormous advances in our understanding of the molecular mechanisms that allow neurons
to transmit signals. The theories we have described in this text are of the second type. They are too large scale to tell us much about the details of nervous-
system function, but they do tell us something about what exactly the nervous

2.   An effect due to the delay between a time marker and the primary
     reinforcer

Pairing adds value and reinforces to the extent that the rate of food delivery in
the presence of a to-be-produced stimulus is greater than the food rate in the
current stimulus (the hill-climbing strategy). Reinforcer delay acts through a
timing process that causes the animal to wait an approximately fixed proportion
of the expected time to food delivery before responding (proportional timing).
The effects on well-trained pigeons of many experimental manipulations—of
first- and second-link length, of second-link variability, and of number of second-
link reinforcers—are all explicable by the influences of delay alone.

system is doing when the hungry animals adapts to periodic food schedules. They also give some clues to the large-scale organization of the brain. For example, they tell us that time is critically involved in the way that pigeons and rats adapt to all reinforcement schedules. For instance, neuroscientists need to look for internal clocks. They tell us that these internal clocks must be affected by time markers, so we must look for internal connections between stimulus inputs to the brain and whatever the animal uses to measure time. They tell us that damage to this system—caused by an experimental lesion, for example—is likely to have a multiplicity of effects, since proportional timing is involved in so many situations. They also tell us that the ability of a given event to act as a time marker is limited by proactive and retroactive interference from earlier and later events, so that our timing and stimulus-input mechanisms must also be connected in some way to brain regions that subserve long-term memory.

As yet, few theories of whole-organism behavior have contributed directly to our understanding of how the nervous system produces adaptive behavior, but work in this area is moving at a rapid pace. As we saw in the earlier discussion of distributed representations and connectionist modeling (Chapter 6), researchers have learned a lot recently about how sets of neuronlike elements can show adaptive behavior. And as you have seen in this book, behavioral models have also grown in power and comprehensiveness. Researchers are gaining confidence both in their behavioral models and in their understanding of how populations of neurons work. It will not be long before these two understandings begin to collaborate actively. The result is likely to be an explosive increase in our knowledge about brain–behavior relations.

Nevertheless, we have had to omit much. This area of research is quite active, and the issues and experimental procedures can become complex. There is some evidence for effects that cannot be reduced to our two processes; but, it is fair to say that these effects are less powerful and reliable than the ones we have described. Pairing and proportional timing seem to be by far the most important processes involved in the performance of pigeons on chain schedules.

It is noteworthy that these behavioral mechanisms, simple though they are in outline, are sufficient to produce behavior that is close to optimal under many conditions. It is also noteworthy that the situations in which behavior is optimal have close parallels in nature (e.g., simple concurrent chains resemble the optimal-diet problem), whereas those in which behavior is suboptimal have no obvious natural parallel (e.g., concurrent chains with fixed versus variable second links or links with different numbers of reinforcers).

The Self-Control Problem

People's inattention to delayed consequences poses a chronic problem for psychologists and public policy makers. People smoke, drink, and take drugs for the present pleasure they give, and they ignore their future detriments, which are not only delayed but often are only probabilistic. For example, cigarette smoking gives *some* people cancer; it may not give *me* cancer. Individual economic decisions also are often made unwisely because of a failure to evaluate future events realistically: We may impulse-buy now and fail to pay our rent or tuition loan later. These obvious practical applications have maintained research interest in self-control as a separate problem area, even though, in the present context, it is but one of many possible variations on the concurrent-chain procedure.

A typical self-control experiment is depicted in Figure 9.13 (Green & Snyderman, 1980). It is a minor variation on the second-link-duration problem depicted in Figure 9.10. The only difference is that in this figure the procedure compares second links that differ not only in the delay to food but also in the amount of food. A successful peck on the left key, say, produces a small reward (E_L) delivered after a short delay (T). A successful peck on the right key produces a larger reward (E_R) delivered after a longer delay (KT). That is, $K > 1$; $E_R/E_L = A > 1$). The presumption is that under most conditions it pays to show self-control and to choose the longer delay to receive the larger reward rather than be impulsive and choose the short-delay alternative. In a moment we will see that the optimal policy depends on a number of criteria and that sometimes impulsiveness does pay.

Proportional timing seems at first to aid us little in predicting the results of self-control experiments, because the small reward always comes sooner than the larger. Strict application of the rule would have the ideal pigeon always showing impulsiveness, that is, picking the short-delay alternative. So long as the two reinforcers are of equal size and the initial link is not too long, this behavior of course holds true. To account for any alternative result, we must include a factor that biases the animal in favor of the other choice. The simplest possibility is that the amount of food affects the proportion of time the animal waits before beginning to respond. If it waits 2 sec before beginning to respond in anticipation of a small amount of food delivered after 10 sec, it might wait only 1 sec for a large amount delivered with the same delay. That is, increasing the amount of food delivered reduces the pause fraction. This assumption seems to account for most of the results from the extensive manipulations of second-link delay in the Green and Snyderman (1980) experiment.

Green and Snyderman studied three ratios of long to short second-link delay (denote the short link by T, the long by KT). The three values for K were 1.5, 3, and 6. For each value of relative delay (K) the researchers studied several values of T, which is absolute delay. They already knew the earlier results on varying second-link delay (T) with equal rewards from pecking both keys; what

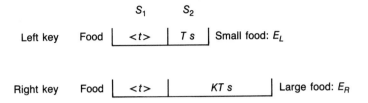

FIGURE 9.13   The self-control problem. S_1 is present during the initial equal delay (usually equal VI t-sec schedules). A successful response produces one of the two delays and associated food amounts in a single second link.

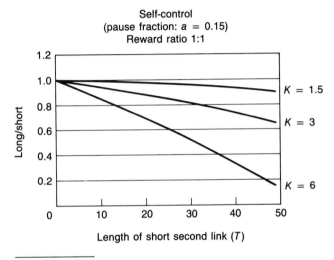

FIGURE 9.14   Predictions of proportional timing for the concurrent-chain procedure with constant-ratio second links. Graph shows three long/short ratios (K) of first-link responses (long/short) as the absolute value of the second links (T) is varied.

they were interested in here was how these results are changed by delivering unequal reward amounts for the short and long delays. We have already seen that when the rewards are equal, increasing T always produces a shift of prefer-ence toward the shorter link. Our ideal pigeon shows exactly this pattern of re-sults in Figure 9.14, using a pause fraction of 0.15. The downward slope of the curves indicates that as absolute second-link duration (T) increases, preference shifts away from the longer-link alternative at all three K (relative delay) values. (The formulas used are described in Box 9.3, which can be skipped by those without mathematical interests.)

Green and Snyderman found that when the shorter link led to 2-sec access to food and the longer link to 6-sec access, the results were slightly different from those shown in Figure 9.14: At the smallest K value (1.5), preference for the

B   O   X

9.3

Proportional Timing and Optimal Policy in Self-Control Experiments

We assume that the animal treats each key independently and that the initial-key VI schedule can be treated as an FI schedule, but with a smaller proportional-waiting constant (a). Thus, for the procedure in Figure 9.13:

$$\text{Pause on the left key:}\quad a_L(t + T) \tag{B9.1a}$$

$$\text{Pause on the right key:}\quad a_R(t + KT) \tag{B9.1b}$$

where K is the ratio of long/short second links. We also assume that the pause constants a_L and a_R are inversely related to the reward magnitudes on the left and right keys. If the ratio $a_L/a_R = A$, and we rewrite a_R as a for simplicity, equation 9.1 reduces to

$$\text{Pause on the left key:}\quad Aa(t + T) \tag{B9.2a}$$

$$\text{Pause on the right key:}\quad a(t + KT) \tag{B9.2b}$$

From our assumption (and ignoring competition) in the first link, the response rate is proportional to the time spent responding to each key, which is $t -$ pause time. The ratio of responding is simply the ratio of these quantities:

$$\text{Left key/right key} = \frac{t - Aa(t + T)}{t - a(t + KT)} = \frac{t(1 - Aa) - aAT}{t(1 - a) - aTK} \tag{B9.3}$$

(Competition tends to make preferences more extreme, because it favors response to the key with the shorter pause; but competition affects both keys equally when pauses are equal.) Equation B9.3, with the indicated parameter values, generates the curves in Figures 9.13–9.15. Note that if $T = 0$, this equation reduces to $L/R = (1 - Aa)/(1 - a)$, which is unity if the two rewards are equal and shows a bias toward the larger-reward key if $A > 1$.

longer link increased as T was increased; however, at the other two K values, preference shifted toward the shorter link, as it does when both rewards are equal. The ideal pigeon also shows this pattern, assuming that the pause fraction in anticipation of the larger reward is one-half the pause for the smaller reward (Figure 9.15). The prediction on the assumption that the larger-reward pause is

Optimal Policy in the Self-Control Procedure

Three strategies are possible here: impulsive (always pick the short-delay key), self-control (always pick the long-delay key), and sample (pick both). The sample strategy is only possible with VI initial links. For the simple FI case, the comparison between impulsive and self-control options is straightforward:

Impulsive: $\dfrac{1}{t + T}$

Self-control: $\dfrac{A}{t + KT}$

where $A, K \geqslant 1$ and A is the ratio of large/small reward magnitude and K is the ratio of long/short second-link length. These two ratios suggest when to switch: Select the impulsive option if

$$\frac{t < T(K - A)}{A - 1} \quad \text{or} \quad \frac{t}{T} < \frac{K - A}{A - 1} \tag{B9.4}$$

Note that the choice here does not depend on the absolute values of T and t but only on their ratio, which is different both from the data and the proportional-timing prediction. Moreover, if $K \leqslant A$, the animal should never select the impulsive option, and if $A \leqslant 1$, it should always select it.

The equations for predicting the sample option using VI schedule first links is too complicated to discuss here. Suffice it to say that the food rate for the sample option is given by a generalized version of the argument we gave earlier for chain VI FI with identical rewards for both keys. In the present case, it yields $A/(t + 2KT) + 1/(t + 2T)$ for the sample option food rate, which in turn gives rise to quadratic expressions when compared with the food rates for the other two strategies.

one-third the smaller-reward pause is shown in Figure 9.16, in which preference shifts toward the longer key at two of the three K values. There is some reason to believe that the effectiveness of food rewards is less than proportional to their physical magnitudes (see Chapter 11), as we had to assume to obtain correct predictions of Green and Snyderman's results.

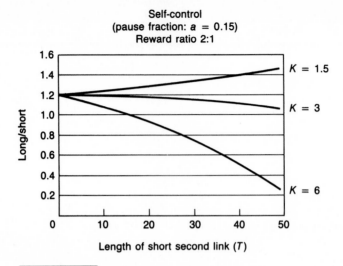

FIGURE 9.15   Predictions of proportional timing for the self-control, concurrent-chain procedure with constant-ratio second links and 2:1 long/short reward ratio. Graph shows three long/short ratios (K) of first-link responses as the absolute value of the second links (T) is varied.

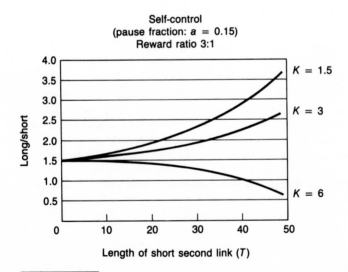

FIGURE 9.16   Predictions of proportional timing for the self-control, concurrent-chain procedure with constant-ratio second links and 3:1 long/short reward ratio. Graph shows three short/long ratios (K) of first-link responses as the absolute value of the second links (T) is varied.

CONCLUSION   Proportional timing, in the form of our ideal pigeon, seems to handle the rather complex pattern of experimental results on self-control procedures, as it does for other concurrent-chain schedule data. Of course, there are many differences between real and ideal pigeons: Real pigeons show considerable variability in timing, although their average pause is related to the minimum time to food delivery in the same way as for our ideal bird; real pigeons don't adjust their waiting time simply interval by interval but also day by day (they show long-term as well as short-term effects); and limitations on memory mean that some time markers are better than others. These differences mean that some of the most direct predictions from our ideal pigeon—that pausing, not just average response rate, for example, should vary in the first link of concurrent-chain schedules—are not as well supported as the more indirect predictions about patterns of results (although, to be fair, no one seems to have looked carefully at anything *but* average rate).

There are also other, more elaborate descriptive theories of performance on chain schedules. The *scalar-timing theory* of John Gibbon and his associates is equivalent to proportional timing, but it makes additional assumptions about the stochastic properties of the timing process (1987). Edmond Fantino's *delay-reduction* theory under many conditions reduces to the optimal policy (Fantino & Abarca, e.g., 1984). Peter Killeen's *incentive theory* is also a delay-based theory that makes many of the same predictions as our simplified ideal pigeon (e.g., 1985). Many details remain to be resolved; but the overwhelming importance of reward delay in self-control and other chain-schedule procedures is now well established.

Although interest in the self-control problem is fueled by its obvious similarity to human situations in which delayed consequences sometimes fail to affect people's behavior as we feel they should, we cannot generalize directly from the animal results to the human situation. The reason goes beyond these experiments: Simply speaking, what we can generalize about, if anything, is not the specific result of any animal experiment but the principles and mechanisms that underlie the result. It is not sufficient to show that pigeons or rats show self-control or impulsiveness under this or that condition. To generalize, we must know *why* they show these effects, before we can confidently apply what we have learned to the human case.

Although the theoretical problems in this area are far from settled, our ability to predict many results from the idea of proportional timing supports the hypothesis that this mechanism underlies these effects. But, proportional timing cannot operate until the animal has had the opportunity to learn about the time intervals involved, which means repeated cycles of exposure to each alternative and its outcome. This scenario is almost never possible in those cases of most urgent interest to public policy, such as the smoking habit or prudent personal spending. We cannot run people through several lifetimes so that they can compare at first hand the consequences of smoking versus abstinence or profligacy versus prudence. Therefore, we may have to look elsewhere than laboratory self-control experiments—with people or pigeons—for public policy recommendations on how to eliminate bad habits with long-delayed consequences. The major problem may not be people's assessment of delayed consequences as much as their assessment of things about which they have been told, but which they have never actually experienced.

What we *can* take away from this discussion is the overwhelming importance to organisms of strongly valued events, such as food for a hungry animal. These choice situations may not, from the pigeon's point of view, involve any real choice at all. The pigeon is not much distracted by our colored lights and response contingencies remote from food. It keeps its eye on the ball and for the most part allocates its behavior in relation to the ultimate goal, food, rather than the intermediate ones we have set up for it. People, on the other hand, all too often mistake the pointing finger for the moon and toil at subgoals while losing sight of the ultimate objective (see Box 9.1). It is unclear whether this fact is a reflection of the greater cognitive complexity of human beings, which allows them better to compartmentalize their tasks, or whether it is simply because their goals (at least in psychology experiments) are not as important to them as food is for an underweight pigeon. Because we cannot ethically manipulate human motivation to the extent that we can alter the hunger of a pigeon, we cannot really answer this question directly, with human subjects. We therefore have little choice but to continue to pursue through animal experiments the problem of how organisms choose between highly attractive alternatives.

EXTINCTION

The term *extinction* is used to refer both to an experimental procedure and to its effect on behavior. The procedure is simply the elimination of an existing reinforcement schedule. For example, changing from fixed-interval reinforcement to no reinforcement. The behavioral definition of extinction is the decrease in the previously reinforced response that usually follows the elimination of reinforcement.

The rat that learns to press the lever for food reward is the same rat that learns not to press the lever when food is no longer forthcoming. Extinction involves the same learning mechanisms as the original acquisition of the response. The major differences are in the behavioral repertoire with which the animal confronts the changed situation and the animal's history at the time the change occurs. During the acquisition of a response, the initial repertoire is variable and exploratory, appropriate to a novel situation. At the beginning of extinction, a single response class, the learned response, typically dominates. During acquisition, the animal's task is to detect a positive contingency between behavior and reinforcer. During extinction, the task is to detect a change in such a contingency. The task during extinction is more difficult in the sense that during acquisition there is a "right answer," whereas during extinction there is none. Some say that extinction is slower than operant conditioning, but there is no real evidence for this statement, because the tasks are so different—and different in a way that usually favors conditioning. The animal's history at the beginning of extinction also exerts effects in ways we return to shortly.

Let's describe some of the basic phenomena associated with extinction and then discuss possible theoretical interpretations of them.

"Superstitious" Maintenance of Behavior

A response such as lever-pressing or key-pecking is typically acquired through the enforcement of a response contingency between the lever-press and immediate food reward. A striking feature of extinction, especially with key-pecking in pigeons, is the greatly decreased importance of the response contingency once the response has been acquired. If the contingency, but not the actual delivery of food, is abolished, pigeons that have learned to peck for food on an FI schedule, for example, hardly change their responding at all. In other words, the change from a fixed-interval schedule, for instance, in which pecking is essential for food delivery, to a fixed-time schedule, in which pecking is irrelevant but food delivery remains periodic, produces little change in behavior. A greater change is produced if the situation involves rats that must press levers to receive food, but the decline in lever-pressing is still much less than if food delivery ceases entirely. This persistence is often termed "superstitious" (Herrnstein, 1966), because it resembles B. F. Skinner's "superstitious" behavior, which we discussed in Chapter 8.

These experimental results are usually interpreted as showing the importance of food as a stimulus: Just as changing the color of the response key causes an immediate decline in pecking (see earlier discussions of generalization decrement in Chapter 6), so too does elimination of food as a stimulus produce a decline in responding. But, superstitious maintenance is also an expected consequence of the dynamics of reinforcement (Chapter 8). We return to this topic shortly.

Spontaneous Recovery

Extinction, like conditioning, is rarely immediate. For example, given a pigeon that is well trained to peck on a variable-interval schedule, the cumulative record of responding on the first day of extinction typically follows a pattern of slow decline, with a complete cessation of responding only after several hours. However, when the animal is returned to the apparatus the next day, responding resumes at almost its old, preextinction, pace. This recovery of response rate after a delay to near preextinction levels is termed *spontaneous recovery,* which makes great sense from a functional viewpoint. After all, something may have changed today, say, and perhaps the mass of previous successful experience before the single extinction day is worth more than one negative experience. The resemblance of extinction to habituation and the recovery from habituation after a lapse of time is also striking.

The Partial-Reinforcement Effect

Food reinforcement has many effects on behavior, but the most obvious one is its strengthening effect. Strengthening implies that the more, or more frequently, a behavior has been reinforced, the stronger it should be and the longer, therefore,

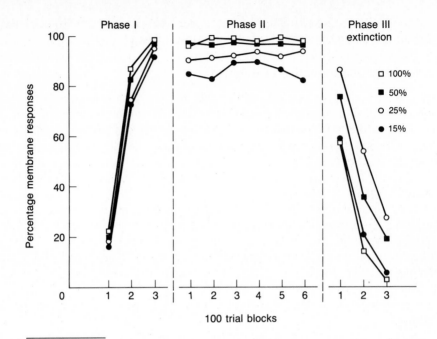

FIGURE 9.17   Three phases of a Pavlovian-conditioning experiment with the rabbit–nictitating membrane response. Phase I: acquisition with 100 percent reinforcement. Phase II: maintenance with either 100 percent, 50 percent, 25 percent, or 15 percent reinforcement. Phase III: extinction (from Gibbs, Latham, & Gormezano, 1978).

it should take to extinguish when reinforcement is withdrawn. Under some conditions, this expectation is confirmed. For example, a group of rats that has just learned to press a lever for food-pellet reward and has each received a total of 20 pellets on the average presses more times in extinction than a similar group that has received only one pellet each.

But under other conditions, the opposite result is obtained. For example, rats trained to respond for food on a VI 60-sec schedule take very much longer to extinguish than rats given the same number of pellets on a continuous-reinforcement (CRF: one pellet per response) schedule. Thus, the type of schedule makes a great deal of difference to resistance to extinction. In general, intermittent schedules produce greater resistance to extinction, which is known as the *partial-reinforcement effect* (*PRE*).

Sometimes results are mixed. Figure 9.17 shows the results of a Pavlovian-conditioning experiment that illustrates both the PRE and its opposite: Animals that received reinforcement on either 25 percent or 50 percent of the trials were more resistant to the effects of the extinction procedure than the animals that received reinforcement on either 15 percent or 100 percent of the trials. The superiority of the 25–50 percent groups to the 100 percent group shows the PRE; the superiority of the 50 percent group to the 15 percent group shows its opposite. Obviously, the PRE is not invariable but depends on how intermittent the food delivery is. Other schedule properties also make a difference: For instance, variable-interval schedules yield better resistance to extinction than fixed-interval schedules, and variable-ratio schedules yield better resistance than fixed-ratio schedules.

Previous Experience and the Rate of Extinction

The obvious functional explanation for the PRE is that it is simply more difficult to tell when extinction has begun after a partial-reinforcement schedule than after continuous reinforcement. A good way to make this account more precise is in terms of decision theory—the kind of argument we developed earlier to analyze the limits on temporal control. The animal's task (from this point of view) is thus to decide whether or not the period without food it is currently experiencing represents a change. After CRF, even a single, unreinforced response is something completely outside the animal's previous experience, so it should suffice to tell it that something has changed. But after VI reinforcement, even a few minutes without food may be within the range of previous experience, and so an unreinforced response is an unreliable signal that the conditions of reinforcement have changed.

The key term here is "previous experience." It was once thought that the important determiner of resistance to extinction is simply the similarity between the most recent schedule and extinction. An animal that is switched from partial reinforcement to extinction should always extinguish more slowly than an animal that is switched from continuous reinforcement to extinction. Since partial reinforcement is more similar to extinction than CRF is, so partial reinforcement should produce greater persistence. But, what matters to the animal is *all* its experience, not just the most recent segment. For example, suppose we have three groups of rats: Group P–C receives some experience with partial reinforcement, followed by some experience with continuous reinforcement; Group C–P receives twice the same reinforcements as P–C but in reverse order; and Group C–C receives twice the amount of CRF. Which group will show the greatest persistence? In fact, Groups C–P and P–C are quite similar, and both more persistent than Group C–C (whether P–C or C–P is more persistent depends on the relative durations of the two conditions). It is not only the most recent experience that determines how the animal will behave but all its experience in this and other similar situations.

Prior history not only affects resistance to extinction, it also affects the kinds of behavior that an animal will show once reinforcement is withdrawn. For example, suppose an animal is successively trained to make reponse A (lever-pressing), then response B (chain-pulling, lever-pressing is now ineffective), and then C (nosing). Each of these behaviors receives numerous reinforcements in succession, say, three sessions of A, followed by three of B, and three of C. What will now happen if reinforcement is completely withdrawn? Response C diminishes, of course, but what succeeds it is not random: Responses A and B are likely to be the first to reappear. This sort of observation led early learning theorist

Clark Hull to the concept of *habit-family hierarchy*. As we saw in Chapter 8 in the discussion of acquisition, past history contributes to the behavioral repertoire with which an animal confronts a new situation.

Theories of Extinction

We have described a number of features of extinction that demand explanation: the PRE, both when it occurs and when it fails to occur; superstitious maintenance; spontaneous recovery; and the various effects of reinforcement history on resistance to extinction and the repertoire of behavior. How can the processes we have already identified, in this and earlier chapters, help us to understand these phenomena?

SUPERSTITIOUS MAINTENANCE   Let's begin with superstitious maintenance. We have already given a functional account in terms of the stimulus effects of reinforcement, which are retained if only the contingency, but not the delivery of food, is abolished in "extinction." But, there is also a mechanistic explanation, in terms of the dynamic model we described at the end of Chapter 8. Recall the importance in the model of parameter a, which determined the "viscosity" of an activity. Parameter a determined how rapidly its strength (V value) changes from moment to moment: the higher the a value, the more slowly the strength of the behavior changes from one instant to the next. Now imagine what is likely to happen with a reinforced activity that has a reasonably high a value. Such an activity is slow to decrease in strength. Once it has gained predominance (through the selective action of reinforcement), it therefore is slow to extinguish. If reinforcement continues to be delivered (albeit independently of behavior), the previously strengthened activity is in fact the one that usually occurs and that therefore continues to be differentially strengthened. In short, under many conditions the dynamics of reinforcement have a "ratchet" property, which means that it takes much less to maintain an already predominant activity than to raise an activity to predominance in the first place. The technical term for ratchet effects like this one is *hysteresis*, which means "lagging behind." Almost any dynamic model of the reinforcement process is likely to show this kind of hysteresis.

SPONTANEOUS RECOVERY   Spontaneous recovery may also remind you of a familiar principle: Jost's memory law. When reinforcement is first withdrawn, the previously reinforced behavior sooner or later declines in frequency. Perhaps by the end of the first extinction session it has ceased to occur at all. We might explain this decline dynamically: In the absence of any strengthening effect, the natural decay in the strength of each behavior eventually reduces all behavior to original values. But the decline in strength once reinforcement is withdrawn can also be looked at as a long-term memory effect, because it involves influences that go beyond the short-term memory of the simple integrator. In Chapter 6 we saw that recent events have a dominant effect in memory: Hence in extinction, the most recent event (absence of reinforcement) has an effect, and the reinforced behavior ceases. But, Jost's law tells us that with the passage of time, a later event loses influence relative to earlier events. After 24 hours, we should not be surprised to see that the effect of extinction during the previous day has decreased, relative to the many earlier days when the response was reinforced, and therefore behavior recovers. But once again, absence of the reinforcer exerts its effect, and behavior again extinguishes. On the third day, the animal has a recent past that comprises two successive days with no food, not just one, as on the previous day. Hence, the earlier experience with food should now have a smaller effect, spontaneous recovery should be less, and the elimination of the previously reinforced response should come about more quickly. After a few days with no food, spontaneous recovery is completely abolished, and the animal seems to have returned to its initial state.

But the earlier experience with reinforcement is never completely abolished. Its effect can be seen if we simply deliver one or two "free" (i.e., not response-contingent) reinforcers: At once, the previously reinforced response recurs, and the animal can easily be retrained—much more easily than in the first instance. Evidently, the effects of the early experience with reinforcement and the later extinction are nearly in balance: Extinction is sufficient to drive the previously reinforced response only "just below zero," so that very little is required to bring it into play once again. Notice that this account, in terms of Jost's law, also explains the recovery of previously reinforced responses once the most recently reinforced response is extinguished.

What is the relation between short-term processes, represented by our dynamic model, and the long-term processes represented by Jost's law? What are the dynamics that underlie long-term memory? Several suggestions have been postulated in the cognitive psychology literature (e.g., Alan Wagner's SOP model [Wagner & Larew, 1985]; John Anderson's [1983] ACT model; and several others). The most enduring suggestion is that extinction is not simply a reduction in strength but rather the creation of an active, opponent process—which itself slowly dissipates with time, thus producing spontaneous recovery. As yet, there is no consensus on the best way to integrate long- and short-term processes.

THE PRE   Figure 9.17 gives us one clue to the basis of the partial-reinforcement effect. Look at the center panel of the graph (Phase II). Notice that although the reinforcement probability varies over quite a wide range, from 15–100 percent, the steady-state level of responding varies over a much smaller range, from about 85 percent (for the 15 percent group) to 95 percent (for the 100 percent group). This pattern of responding is typical not only of many Pavlovian-conditioned responses, as in the figure, but also of operant conditioning. For example, Figure 9.18 shows some well-known data from an experiment by Charles Catania and George Reynolds (1968), in which the key-pecking of pigeons was successively maintained on variable-interval schedules ranging from about 10 food reinforcements per hour to 300 per hour. Over the range from about 80–300 per hour, this bird's pecking rate varied hardly at all, and the result is typical. Over most of the range, response rate varies much less than reinforcement rate.

Now, let's think about the stimulus factors that might control this rate of responding (as we did in Chapter 5 in connection with the Rescorla–Wagner

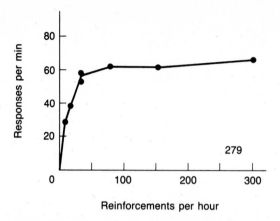

FIGURE 9.18   The relation between response rate and reinforcement rate on a partial-reinforcement schedule. The graph shows the average rate of pecking on a single response key of a single pigeon given many days of training at each of several values of a variable-interval schedule of food reinforcement. The x-axis shows the rate of reinforcements the pigeon obtained; the y-axis shows how many pecks per hour it made (from Catania & Reynolds, 1968).

model of Pavlovian conditioning). Two kinds of stimuli are involved in the control of the responding illustrated in Figure 9.18: the response key with features of the experimental apparatus and the actual presentation of food. We can think of these types of stimuli as like the two elements of a stimulus compound. The level of responding is like the upper limit of associative strength (V_{max}) in the Rescorla–Wagner model. This total strength must be partitioned in some way between the two elements: reinforcement (R) and nonreinforcement cues (N). We don't know the proportions exactly, but we do know that $N + R$ effects is approximately constant, because response rate is almost constant. Hence, if R takes up x percent of the total response rate when the animal is reinforced 10 times per hour, then it must take up $2x$ percent when it is reinforced 20 times per hour. Other things being equal, the contribution of R to the total number of responses should be proportional to the rate of reinforcement, which means that the absolute amount attributable to reinforcement must be less when the reinforcement rate is low than when it is high. In other words, the decrement in response strength to be expected when reinforcement no longer occurs must be less when the reinforcement rate is low than when it is high. This difference is the partial-reinforcement effect.

The argument can be illustrated by example. Suppose that the total response rate is 100 per minute, over the range from 5–100 reinforcements per minute. Suppose that R, as a stimulus, contributes 1 response per minute for every reinforcement per minute. Thus at the highest reinforcement rate, all 100 responses per minute are under the control of R, so that elimination of R causes

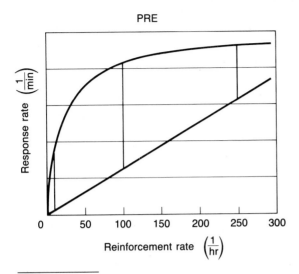

FIGURE 9.19   How the relative constancy of the response rate at different reinforcement rates interacts with the stimulus effects of reinforcement to produce the PRE. Curved line: response rate as a function of reinforcement rate on simple VI schedules (idealized data). Straight line: proportional contribution of reinforcement. Notice that when reinforcement is omitted, much more response strength is left at the 100 responses per minute schedule than on the 250 responses per minute schedule (PRE), but less is left at the 10 responses per minute schedule than the 100 responses per minute (no PRE) schedule, because the response rate is so much lower at 10 responses per minute.

a generalization decrement all the way to zero. But at 5 reinforcements per minute, only 5 of the 100 responses per minute are controlled by R, so that elimination of R only causes a drop in response rate from 100 to 95 responses per minute.

Of course, we still have not explained *why* response rate varies so much less than reinforcement rate. But, this kind of relation is so general in biology that we at least should not be surprised at it. After all, the rate of responding is limited by physical factors, whereas the rate of reinforcement can be almost anything we please. It is not surprising, therefore, to find some kind of negatively accelerated function that relates the response rate to reinforcement rate, such that as the reinforcement rate increases from zero, the response rate at first increases rapidly but then flattens out at an upper limit. (An example of such a function and a description of how it can help us account for the PRE as well as its opposite is shown in Figure 9.19.) Nor have we explained exactly how reinforcement can act as a stimulus. Our best guess is that it has something to do with its role as a time marker in the proportional-timing process we have discussed. The details remain obscure, and we defer further discussion of this point until Chapter 11, when we take up the issue of behavioral allocation.

SUMMARY

In this chapter, we have taken up in more detail three phenomena introduced earlier: temporal control, stimulus control, and extinction. In the first section, we showed how temporal control (in the form of proportional, or scalar, timing) and stimulus control combine in well-trained animals to produce the effect known as conditioned reinforcement on chain schedules. We showed how conditioned reinforcers act as aids to memory when animals learn to respond on delayed-reinforcement schedules and how memory limitations may underlie the effects of second-order schedules. We showed how proportional timing seems to determine performance even on ratio schedules. We discussed in some detail a variety of experimental results on simple and concurrent-chain procedures.

We showed that most, perhaps all, of the concurrent effects do not represent choice in the usual sense. The animals do not seem to be comparing alternatives; rather, they seem to treat each alternative as if it occurred in isolation. We were able to derive quite complex patterns of apparent preference and preference shift from an "ideal pigeon" that behaves according to proportional timing. We also showed how our analysis relates to the optimal policy on chain schedules, that is, the pattern of responding that maximizes food rate: It turns out that proportional timing almost always produces a close-to-optimal pattern of choice. We showed the similarities between the optimal policy for animals on chain-reinforcement schedules and the optimal-foraging theory predictions about diet selection. The last part of the section discussed the self-control problem—preference for small-immediate versus larger-delayed rewards—and showed how the same proportional-timing rule applies here.

In the last section we returned to the phenomenon of extinction, which is the decrease in a previously reinforced response once reinforcement is withdrawn. We discussed several well-known phenomena related to extinction: "superstitious" maintenance of behavior by the presentation of response-independent food, spontaneous recovery, the partial-reinforcement extinction effect (PRE), and some effects of different histories of reinforcement. Both short-term and long-term processes seem to be involved in extinction: The short-term processes can be modeled dynamically, as we showed in Chapter 8; the long-term processes involve memory processes described by Jost's law. Short-term processes may account for superstitious maintenance; Jost's law implies spontaneous recovery. Additive stimulus–control factors combined with relative constancy of response rate over a wide range of reinforcement rates provide one account for the PRE. Nevertheless, the relation between short-term and long-term processes is still unclear, and we lack anything approaching an adequate dynamic account for the memory mechanisms that are involved in extinction.

10

Aversive Stimuli

In the preceding chapters we have not been greatly concerned with whether the valued events to which behavior adapts (reinforcers or USs) are "good" or "bad." But, it makes a difference to our research and to the animal subjects, who must either suffer a diet—if we hope to use food as a reinforcer—or occasional electric shocks—if we intend to study the effects of aversive stimuli. Many humans not only go on diets but also pay money to do so, and their health is usually improved thereby. Therefore, we need not be too concerned about imposing moderate starvation on rat and pigeon subjects in the interests of science. On the other hand, in recent years researchers and the general public have become increasingly aware of the ethical problems involved in imposing painful treatments on animals. People are especially concerned for animal species that are kept as pets, such as cats and dogs, or that seem to resemble human beings, such as the higher primates. Of course, there is little scientific basis for such a distinction: A pig is as intelligent as a poodle, but it cannot call up as vocal a political constituency on its behalf as can the poodle. Nevertheless, partly in reaction to ethical concerns, and partly because few wholly new principles seem to be involved, research interest in aversive procedures has diminished in recent years. Pavlovian-conditioning experiments, once dominated in the U.S. by the conditioned-suppression procedure with electric shock as the unconditioned stimulus, are now largely carried out using autoshaping, with food as the US, for example.

The procedures used to study the effects of aversive stimuli are quite different from the positive-reinforcement procedures that have been our focus thus far. The effects of aversive stimuli are obviously quite different from the effects of positive-reinforcement. There is obvious practical justification for studying such aversive effects, since much human suffering is caused by painful events such as bereavement or the horrors of war—and the only ethical way to study these effects is with animals.

Unpleasant events and the steps we take to avoid or mitigate them are an inevitable part of everyday life. Many (perhaps most!) of the arrangements under which people live are much closer to escape or avoidance schedules than to schedules of positive reinforcement. For example, consider all the procedures that involve taking precautions: boating drills; fire drills; cockpit routines; insurance; vaccination and inoculation; taking medicines for chronic, symptomless ailments such as high blood pressure; brushing your teeth; and watching your cholesterol. All these activities are motivated by the desire to avoid future harm—not to secure present gain. Such activities are sustained by avoidance schedules of one sort or another. The modern bureaucratic state imposes its own set of aversive schedules to which activities like attending class, preparing for exams, getting to work on time, submitting tax returns, meeting deadlines, and keeping to the speed limit are responses. The criminal justice system is an intricate, institutionalized set of aversive contingencies, to which honest and law-abiding behavior is the usual response. The religious concepts of sin and retribution serve a similar social function. The hippie generation of the 1960s might almost be defined by its rejection of all avoidance schedules!

Animals also have an extensive repertoire of behavior adapted to the avoidance of harm. The next time you are watching wild birds at a feeding station, notice how wary they are, how cautiously they look around before taking a crumb; and how they fly off with it to a safer place if it's big enough to be worth the effort. People who have tried to domesticate wild animals like wolves, for example, remark on their extreme sensitivity to anything novel. Reportedly, a domesticated wolf will not enter a familiar room for days if even one piece of furniture has been moved. We have already discussed taste-aversion learning and the well-adapted pattern of sampling that feral rats show when confronted with a novel food. These activities are not motivated by hunger or strengthened by food reinforcement; they have evolved to protect the animal from poison or predators. Obviously, no account of learning and adaptive behavior would be complete without some discussion of how organisms adapt to schedules of aversive events.

In this chapter, we discuss the main phenomena and experimental arrangements that have emerged from the study of the effects of aversive stimuli. The aversive stimulus is almost always a brief electric shock, delivered either through a floor grid or through electrodes (on the animal's tail for rats, implanted in a

wing muscle for pigeons). A few comparisons have been made with other aversive stimuli, such as immersion in water, change in g-force (when the animal's
cage is allowed to free-fall for a short distance), and "slapping," but few consistent differences have been found. Consequently, most experiments have used
electric shock, largely for its convenience. We first examine procedures used to
measure so-called conditioned emotional responses. We then examine escape
and avoidance procedures. We also look at the effects of punishment procedures
on behavior. In the final section, we will see that the effects of aversive stimuli fit
resaonably well within the dynamic framework for reinforcement effects that we
introduced in Chapter 8.

CONDITIONED SUPPRESSION

Some experiments on Pavlovian conditioning use a procedure in which the effects of a CS are assessed indirectly. Rather than measuring its direct effect on
an autonomic response such as salivation or pupillary dilation, it is often more
convenient to study the CS's effects on some ongoing behavior. For example, rats
are first trained to press a lever for food, which is delivered on a VI schedule. As
we have seen (Chapter 4), after a little training this schedule maintains a moderate, steady rate of response. Therefore, the VI schedule makes an ideal baseline
for the study of other variables. In a conditioned-suppression test, stimuli of, say,
60-sec duration are occasionally superimposed on this VI baseline. Rats soon habituate to the added stimulus, and their response rate is the same in the presence of the superimposed stimulus as in its absence. In the final phase, a brief
electric shock is delivered in the presence of the superimposed stimulus (CS).
Within a few stimulus–shock pairings, the onset of the CS causes a reduction in
the rate of lever-pressing. This effect has been termed *conditioned suppression* or a *conditioned emotional response* (*CER*), because it was originally believed that the CS elicited an emotional response such as fear, which was responsible for the suppression in bar-press rate. In fact, the first study of conditioned
suppression by William Estes and B. F. Skinner (1941) was titled "Some quantitative properties of anxiety." As the title suggests, the conditioned-suppression
procedure was believed to produce fear or anxiety that interferes with ongoing
operant behavior.

Suppression Ratio

The decrease, or suppression, in the rate of lever-pressing during the CS, relative
to the preceding baseline period, supposedly provides a measure of the amount
or strength of the conditioned emotional response. The greater the CER, the
greater the suppression of bar-pressing during the CS. The results of conditioned-
suppression experiments are typically presented in terms of a *suppression
ratio*, which represents the ratio of responding in the presence of the CS to responding during both the presence and the absence of the CS: Suppression ratio,

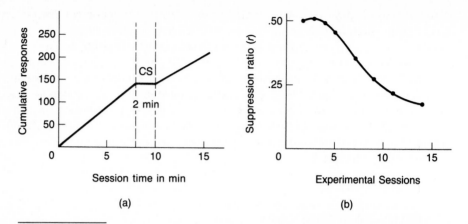

FIGURE 10.1   (a) Typical cumulative record of a rat showing suppression in the presence of a 2-min CS that signals the occurrence of a brief electric foot shock. (b) Change in suppression ratio across experimental sessions.

$r = x_{CS}/(x_{CS} + x_0)$, where x_{CS} is the response rate in the presence of the CS and x_0 is the response rate in its absence. For example, suppose that during a 2-min period preceding the CS, the bar-press rate was 30 responses per minute, and suppose that during a 2-min period with the CS, the bar-press rate decreased to 10 responses per minute. The suppression ratio for this example is $10/(10 + 30)$ = 0.25. A suppression ratio of 0.5 represents no conditioning to the CS (because the response rate is the same in the presence of the CS as in its absence), and a suppression ratio of zero represents complete suppression of bar-pressing by the CS. Figure 10.1 shows the results of a typical conditioned-suppression experiment. You may recall that the conditioned-suppression procedure and the suppression-ratio measure were used by Leon Kamin and Robert Rescorla in their pioneering studies of blocking and contingency (Chapter 5).

On the face of it, conditioned suppression makes little adaptive sense: The rat has ample opportunity to learn that it cannot avoid or escape from the shock during the CS. By reducing its lever-press rate, the animal loses needed food reinforcers. What is the reason for this apparently maladaptive suppression? Does it add anything to our understanding of conditioned suppression to attribute it to an emotional response such as fear?

By now, the functional answer, at least, may be clear. The superimposed stimulus is a CS for shock. Once the animal has learned this relation, therefore, we may expect to see candidate defense reactions induced by the CS, according to the Pavlovian inference mechanisms discussed in Chapters 4 and 5. Robert Bolles (1970) has termed the responses made to aversive stimuli or the signals for such responses *species-specific defense reactions* (*SSDRs*). These reactions generally interfere with lever-pressing, and they therefore appear as a depression in lever-press rate. Even though they have no effect on shock, these defense reactions persist for the same reason that key-pecking persists under an autoshaping-omission contingency. The prior knowledge associated with a stimulus that predicts imminent shock simply outweighs the opposing effects of the food contingency for lever-pressing.

This argument, the phenomenon of autoshaping, and data of the Brelands discussed in Chapter 8 suggest that similar suppression effects may be produced by a food stimulus on a food-reinforced baseline. For example, if a feeder light comes on 5 sec before the feeder operates, a hungry rat will soon learn to approach the feeder as soon as the light comes on. If such stimulus–food pairings are superimposed on a VI 60-sec baseline, no one would be startled to observe a reduction in lever-pressing during the stimulus—which is indeed what occurs. Conversely, if the light were placed on the response lever rather than on the feeder, lever-pressing might well *increase* during the CS, because the rat now approaches the lever (and presses it), rather than approaching something incompatible with lever-pressing.

Both suppressive and facilitatory effects of a food CS have been widely observed. As these examples suggest, the magnitude and direction of the effect depends on the durations of the CS and the between-CS period, the type of CS (e.g., tone, light, localizable versus unlocalizable), the location of the CS relative to the feeder and the lever, and the magnitude and frequency of food in the presence of the CS. The general rule is that if the food rate in the presence of the stimulus is significantly higher than the rate in its absence (e.g., on the baseline VI schedule), the stimulus tends to induce food-related behavior. The effect of the stimulus on lever-pressing depends on the nature of the induced behavior: If the induced behavior is physically compatible with lever-pressing, the effect of the CS is to facilitate lever-pressing; if it is not, its effect is to suppress lever-pressing.

Of course, it may be that a specific emotional state is associated with each pattern of induced activities. But, it is the activities themselves that provide useful explanatory work, not the hard-to-measure emotions that go with them.

ESCAPE AND AVOIDANCE

Schedules of aversive events are of two kinds: escape and avoidance. *Escape schedules* ensure that the subject always receives shock, but the shock can be turned off by making a specific response. *Avoidance schedules* ensure that the subject receives shocks if it does nothing; but if it makes the appropriate response, shocks can be avoided entirely or at least greatly reduced in frequency (in which case the schedule may be termed either escape or avoidance). We first look at the functional properties of avoidance and escape and then discuss their properties in detail.

The Functional Aspects of Escape and Avoidance

Animals find it difficult to learn the correct response on most avoidance schedules. Two factors contribute to this difficulty: one is a characteristic of the procedure, the second has to do with the adaptive function of avoidance. The first factor is the poor feedback that comes with success; successful avoidance simply means that something bad does *not* happen. But, suppose that nothing bad was going to happen anyway? The truly successful avoider might never find out. You may remember the following joke: A man in a railway carriage (this is really old!) is throwing banana peels out the window. A puzzled fellow passenger asks him why. He responds, "to keep the elephants away." His companion responds, "but there are no elephants." The man replies, "works great, doesn't it!" This is the problem with being too good an avoidance learner.

The adaptive problem with avoidance learning is that often in nature the animal doesn't get a second chance. The bird that systematically compares the results of two policies (fleeing the cat and not fleeing the cat) is unlikely to contribute any genes to posterity. The well-adapted bird flees without reflecting on the alternatives. In short, under many conditions, the appropriate response must be ready-made if it is to be effective. Therefore, we should not be surprised to find that much avoidance behavior is either not learned at all—and occurs in more or less final form as a direct effect of the aversive event—or else occurs as a Pavlovian-conditioned response to a stimulus situation that signals an aversive event. The role of consequences, of the response contingency, is often less on aversive schedules than it is on positive-reinforcement schedules.

It is no surprise to find that the most frequently used aversive stimulus, electric shock, has a number of paradoxical effects that all derive from its strong behavior-inducing effects. Shock and stimuli that signal shock produce stereotyped reactions (SSDRSs) from most animals: flight, fight, or freeze. (We discuss flight—leaving the area—shortly.) If a plausible cause for the aversive event, such as another animal, is in the vicinity, a shocked rat may attack it, which is termed *shock-induced attack*. But under usual experimental conditions, immobility—freezing—is the dominant response, especially if the shock is frequent or severe. Thus, if a rat is presented with a series of brief electric shocks that can be turned off by some operant response, it may only learn the necessary escape response if it is part of the defense reactions normally induced by shock. If the required response is to press a lever, the rat will learn the behavior much more easily if simply holding the lever is sufficient rather than a depression followed by a release—because holding the lever is compatible with the induced reaction of freezing. In contrast, actual lever-pressing requires that the animal periodically release the lever so that it can be depressed again. The inducing effects of shock are often incompatible with the response requirement on shock-motivated operant schedules, so that conditioning with aversive stimuli is often difficult for most animals. The ease of conditioning depends heavily on whether or not the response to be learned is compatible with the induced response.

THE ROLE OF THE INSTRUMENTAL RESPONSE   Let's look first at an avoidance experiment by Bolles (1970) in which two groups of rats were trained to avoid shock in a running wheel. For one group, the avoidance response was running in the wheel; for the other, it was standing up. Both of these responses occur naturally in this situation, yet only the running group learned the behavior. The animals that were required to stand up to avoid shock not only failed to learn, but the frequency of standing up actually decreased with training, resulting in more shocks. The explanation for this apparently maladaptive strategy seems to be that the standing response is part of the animal's natural exploratory repertoire, not part of the repertoire induced by aversive events. That is, the rats were looking for an escape route. Once this task (looking) was completed, even though an escape was not found, the natural exploratory response, which includes standing, decreased in frequency. Although the rats' failure to learn the standing response appears unintelligent, it may well be that under natural conditions freezing is the best response if an escape cannot be found.

THE ROLE OF RESPONSE CONTINGENCY   Under other conditions, however, the consequences of an escape response do have an effect. For example, in a classic experiment conducted by Brogden, Lipman, and Culler (1938; see also Sheffield, 1948), the researchers studied the escape behavior of guinea pigs in a revolving cage. For all animals, the basic procedure involved repeated trials in which a 2-sec buzzer signal (the CS) was followed by electric shock (the US). One group of animals was trained in a strictly Pavlovian fashion: The shock occurred whether or not they ran. The other group was trained on an avoidance schedule: If they ran when the buzzer sounded, they escaped the shock entirely. The avoidance group learned more quickly and ran faster than the Pavlovian group. This result is usually taken to indicate that avoidance conditioning is not to be explained entirely by the elicitation of avoidance activities by the CS.

But, the preceding discussion does not explain the whole story. For example, we know that the pattern of activities elicited by a stimulus depends on quantitative issues. Not only do we need to know that the CS signals shock, we also must know how strong and how frequent the shock is. If the shock is both strong and frequent, then the stimulus may elicit passive activities; whereas if it is weak and infrequent, the CS may elicit something more active, like running. Notice that the animals in the Brogden groups received shocks at quite different rates: Because of the avoidance contingency, the avoidance group received many fewer shocks than the Pavlovian group. Perhaps this difference alone accounts for the greater running of the avoidance group? It might have been better to compare the avoidance group with a Pavlovian, yoked-control group (see Chapter 11) that received the same shocks independently of their responding. A number of experiments of this sort have been performed in situations that are more or less similar to those of the Brogden experiment, and they usually find small, or no, differences between the Pavlovian and avoidance conditions. There are also problems with the yoked-control method that tend to favor the leader (i.e., avoidance) animal over the follower (Pavlovian) animal. Therefore, the evidence for a substantial effect of the operant contingency is quite weak. But as we shall see, the real solution to this problem is to think a bit more deeply about the possible dynamics of the process. Later on in the chapter, we suggest some possibilities.

THE ROLE OF THE SCHEDULE   Animals should find it easier to learn to escape a series of brief electric shocks than to avoid or postpone them because the feedback is much better: A change from two shocks per second (say) to zero shocks should be easy to perceive. Under some conditions, animals easily learn to escape—when the induced behavior is consistent with success—but under other conditions they do not. Parametric considerations (How often are the animals shocked? How intense is the shock?) are also more important under these schedules than under comparable positive-reinforcement schedules.

FLIGHT   In all shock experiments, the animal's highest priority is to escape from the training apparatus entirely—which is precisely what one might expect not only from natural selection but from the principles of reinforcement. In nature, "bad" things are usually correlated with specific places, hence a change of place is almost always the best way to escape from something aversive. In a food situation, animals detect the stimulus most predictive of food and approach it. In an aversive situation, they detect the stimulus or situation most predictive of shock and escape from it. This rule prescribes flight from the experimental apparatus, which is the only place the animal normally experiences shock. Because escape from the apparatus is always prevented, anything the animal does in the experimental situation is in a sense second best, and thus is not an ideal measure of the effect of the shock schedule.

Studies of positive reinforcement don't suffer from this problem. A hungry animal is typically happy to be in a box in which it receives food. There is a wonderful sign in France that warns at railroad crossings: *Un train peut cache un autre,* which means "one train can hide another." The saying has become a national proverb, and it of course means that if your attention is focused on one thing you are much more likely to miss something else. Everyone can think of many examples of such situations from their own experiences. What this saying means for avoidance and escape behavior is that if you (i.e., Monsieur Rat) are obsessed with escaping from the apparatus, you will naturally find it difficult to learn the silly tricks the experimenter wants you to perform while restrained in it.

Avoidance Procedures

The difference between an escape response and an avoidance response is that an escape response always follows exposure to the reinforcer (e.g., shock); whereas an avoidance response prevents exposure to the reinforcer. For example, animals shocked at one end of a long shuttlebox soon learn to run to the other (safe) end as soon as they are placed in the box. Rats often learn this one-way avoidance response after a few trials (Figure 10.2). In contrast, a two-way avoidance response is one in which the animal must run back and forth from one end of the shuttlebox to the other whenever a signal sounds (Figure 10.3). This more complicated response is much harder for animals to learn because there is no safe place (within the shuttlebox) and the animal's dominant response (flight) is blocked.

What factors maintain avoidance responding? Is avoidance behavior maintained by the termination of signals that predict shock (i.e., the termination of an aversive CS)? Or, is it maintained by a reduction in shock frequency alone?

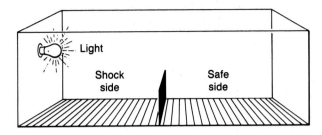

FIGURE 10.2   One-way shuttle box. Animal is placed in the left compartment at the beginning of each trial. Shock can be avoided by crossing to the right compartment after the light (CS) comes on. No shocks are administered on the right side.

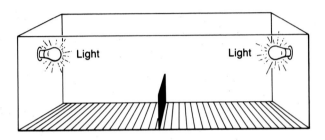

FIGURE 10.3   Two-way shuttle box. Shock can be administered on either side of the box following CS (light) onset. Crossing to the opposite compartment only temporarily avoids shock.

The first view, that offset of a shock-signaling CS is always the effective event, is attractive as long as the model for all learning is strengthening by positive reinforcement. Avoidance, especially unsignaled avoidance (which we discuss shortly), poses problems because there seems to be no tangible event (e.g., delivery of food) that can serve the strengthening function. Nevertheless, as long as a CS is found, then its offset provides the necessary strengthening event. Even if no external event is available, perhaps fear and its reduction by the performance of an avoidance response can serve the strengthening function? This view is known as *two-factor theory* (which we briefly discussed in connection with autoshaping in Chapter 8). According to two-factor theory, two processes are involved in maintaining avoidance responses. The first process is the conditioning of fear to an aversive CS, which may be an external stimulus but may also be temporal cues or simply the absence of an avoidance response (i.e., any situation that is correlated with the occurrence of shock). The second process is the strengthening of the operant response by CS termination.

    An account of avoidance behavior sometimes called *one-factor theory* asserts that avoidance responding is maintained by the reduction in shock rate alone. We now examine several experiments that test each of these theories. At

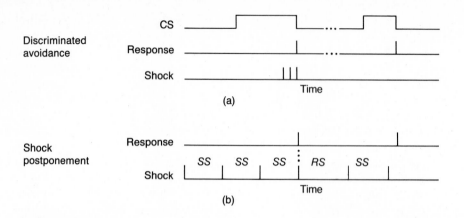

FIGURE 10.4   Shock-avoidance procedures. (a) discriminated avoidance. A response during the CS turns off the shock (avoidance). Shock occurs at the end of the CS until a response occurs (escape). (b) Shock postponement. Shock occurs at fixed intervals (the shock-shock—SS—interval) unless a response occurs. Each response postpones the next shock for a fixed interval (the response-shock—RS—interval) (from Staddon, 1983).

the end of the chapter, we conclude that neither theory is adequate. Yet you must study this theoretical context to understand the reasons behind the procedures we describe.

DISCRIMINATED AVOIDANCE   There are two classes of operant avoidance procedures: discriminated avoidance and shock postponement. In *discriminated avoidance,* a stimulus such as a tone or a light is occasionally presented and then followed, after several seconds, by shock. After a few seconds of the stimulus with shock, both the stimulus and the shock terminate (Figure 10.4). If an operant response occurs during the brief stimulus period before shock onset, shock is avoided on that trial. The two-factor explanation for responding with discriminated-avoidance procedures is the same as the standard explanation for conditioned reinforcement. The animal is presented with two situations: first, a low-value CS period in which shock is likely, and second, a higher-value period in which shock is unlikely. A response during the low-value period produces the higher-valued one. The response-contingent transition from CS to no CS ensures that the animal can remember the effective response, and the higher value of (lower shock rate in) no CS ensures that once the response occurs, it is maintained.

There is little doubt that animals value a shock-free period. For example, consider an experiment by Pietro Badia and his associates (Badia, Coker, & Harsh, 1973). For initial training, Badia and his colleagues exposed rats to a variable-time, 4-min (VT 4) schedule of brief shocks (i.e., the animals received a brief shock on the average of once every 4 min). Each shock was preceded by a 5-sec tone stimulus. After three sessions of this *signaled-shock procedure,* the animals were shifted to a procedure in which the same VT schedule delivered shocks, but now without the 5-sec warning stimulus (*unsignaled-shock procedure*). During this second phase, a lever-press response turned on a cue light for 3 min. The cue light shocks were delivered as before, but they were now preceded by the tone signal. The rats consistently pressed the lever to turn on the signal. Badia interpreted this result as due to a preference for the signaled, shock-free periods (light but no tone) that were produced by the response that turned on the light. This preference turned out to be quite strong. In subsequent conditions, Badia varied the VT schedule in the presence of the light: Even when signaled shocks came every 2 min, the rats preferred to turn on the light rather than receive unsignaled shocks at the much lower rate of once every 4 min.

In our discussion of conditioned reinforcement in Chapter 9, we saw that the two-factor explanation is not fully adequate, especially for maintained behavior. Other factors such as memory and temporal delay seem to be much more important to the maintenance of behavior than the added value of the stimulus change produced by a response. Despite the rats' clear preference for stimuli that signaled a shock-free period, similar caveats apply to two-factor theory as a general explanation for avoidance. For example, some experiments seem to show that reduction in the rate of shock alone is sufficient to maintain responding, which leaves little role for a two-factor explanation. We examine some of these experiments next.

Shock Postponement and Reduction Procedures

SIDMAN AVOIDANCE   There are two major shock-postponement procedures. One is illustrated in Figure 10.4b. In this procedure, brief shocks occur at fixed-time intervals of, say, 20 sec—the *shock-shock (SS) interval.* If the rat responds, usually by pressing a lever, the shock timer is reset, and the next shock is rescheduled for, say, 30 sec later—the *response-shock (RS),* or *postponement, interval.* The postponement interval need not be longer than the shock-shock interval, although it usually is. This procedure is usually termed *Sidman avoidance,* after its inventor. However, a more descriptive label might be *fixed-interval shock postponement.* Sidman avoidance is an avoidance procedure because shocks can be avoided entirely by pressing the lever. Notice that no matter how short the *RS* interval, if the animal always responds before the interval elapses, that is, has no interresponse time longer than the *RS* interval, it is never shocked.

How well do animals perform on Sidman-avoidance schedules? What can performance on such schedules tell us about how avoidance behavior is maintained? Figure 10.5 illustrates the performance of two animals in an experiment reported by Sidman (1966). Each of the animals displays quite different patterns of responding. The figure shows two animals: one that learned to avoid most of the shocks and another that failed to learn altogether. The steeper slope of the cumulative record for animal H-28 indicates a faster response rate; the smaller number of "blips" in the record indicates that it also received fewer shocks. Animals that fail to learn the shock-postponement response are often observed in a crouched or "frozen" position typical of behavior induced by unavoidable shock.

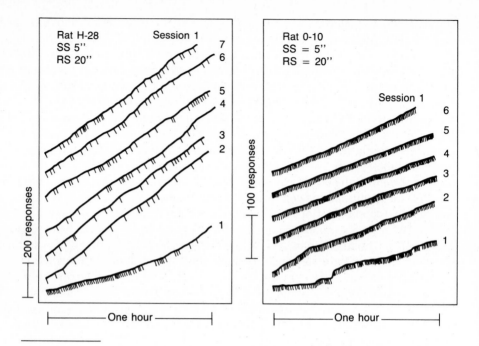

FIGURE 10.5   Cumulative records of lever-pressing for two rats the first time they were exposed to a nondiscriminated-avoidance procedure. Numerals at the right indicate successive hours of exposure to the procedure. Oblique slashes indicate delivery of shock (from Sidman, 1966).

These results are difficult for two-factor theory to handle because there is no explicit CS correlated with shock or a reduction in shock rate as there is for discriminated-avoidance schedules. However, it can be argued that time serves as a CS in Sidman's procedure, because the response-shock interval is always 20 sec: By always responding before 20 sec, the animals escape from the aversive, post-20-sec temporal "stimulus." Such results present an example of temporal conditioning (Chapter 4). Because of the fixed interval between responding and the next scheduled shock, it is not inconceivable that the animals are responding to reduce fear that is produced by temporal conditioning on Sidman-avoidance schedules. We next look at a procedure that attempts to preclude temporal conditioning.

RANDOM-INTERVAL SHOCK REDUCTION   The *random-interval shock-reduction procedure* is similar to the Sidman-avoidance procedure, but the time intervals involved are random rather than fixed. The easiest way to understand this procedure is by analogy to coin-tossing. The scheduling computer has two "biased coins" that it can toss: Coin A has probability 0.9 of a tail (no shock) and probability 0.1 of a head (shock); coin B has probability 0.8 of a tail (no shock) and 0.2 of a head (shock). The schedule works as follows. If the animal (rat or pigeon) does nothing, the computer tosses coin B once per second (say), so that the animal receives a brief shock on the average of once every 5 sec—$p(\text{shock}) = 0.2$—which is quite a high rate. However, if the animal responds to the stimulus, the computer begins to toss coin A, which means that the next shock occurs on average after 10 sec—$p(\text{shock}) = 0.1$. If the animal responds before the shock, the computer keeps tossing coin A; but if the shock occurs before it responds, then after the shock the computer begins to toss coin B again.

The point of this procedure is to show that responding has no effect on any specific shock. A response simply selects a rate of shock delivery. In fact, responding always selects a lower rate than failure to respond, as in our example.

In an experiment conducted by Richard Herrnstein and Philip Hineline (1966), the computer tossed the imaginary coin every 2 sec. The no-responding coin had a shock probability of 0.3 (shock on the average of every 6.7 sec); the responding coin had a shock probability of only 0.1 (shock on the average of every 20 sec). Figure 10.6 shows how three rats in Herrnstein and Hineline's experiment adjusted to this procedure. As we have seen before with avoidance procedures, the individual animals were quite different, some doing quite well, others quite poorly. However, all the animals developed a fairly stable pattern of avoidance responding by the 10th session.

What maintains the responding shown in Figure 10.6? Can the reduction in shock rate alone serve to maintain responding? Or, is responding maintained by the termination of an aversive CS? Unlike the Sidman-avoidance procedure, there is no obvious role here for temporal conditioning. Responding in this procedure appears to be maintained by a reduction in shock rate alone.

However, to say that rats can learn to respond to reduce shock rate—or that reduction in shock rate is an explanation for avoidance—is not adequate for at least two reasons. First, we know little about how shock rate is assessed by the animal; therefore, as it stands, such an explanation is merely a redescription of the results of shock-rate-reduction experiments. These data seem to rule out other accounts, such as simple versions of two-factor theory, but they provide no obvious alternative. Second, as we have already seen in the Badia experiment discussed earlier in the chapter, when responding produces a signaled, shock-free period, rats can be trained to respond even if the overall shock rate is thereby *increased.* Hineline (1977) has reviewed similar results in terms of signaled delays: Rats respond to delayed shock, even if the overall shock rate is thereby increased. In one experiment, Hineline's rats received a single shock after a short delay if they did nothing; but if they pressed a retractable lever, they received several closely spaced shocks that were delivered after a delay. The rats continued to press the lever, despite the fact that by doing so they increased the overall shock rate. Hineline's results are reminiscent of the results with positive reinforcement on concurrent schedules discussed in Chapter 9. You may recall from that chapter the puzzling finding that pigeons are almost indifferent between two choices for which the time to the first food delivery is the same but the number of food deliveries per schedule cycle is different. These data emphasize the importance of the expected time to food delivery. Clearly, the expected time of the aversive event is equally important to avoidance responding.

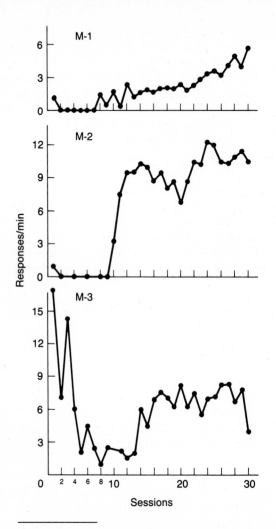

FIGURE 10.6   Responses per minute for three rats (M-1, M-2, and M-3) during the
first 30 sessions of conditioning with shock probabilities equal to 0.3–0.1. Each
point represents a 100-min session (from Herrnstein and Hineline, 1966).

AVOIDANCE PERFORMANCE   Effective avoidance performance on a shock-postponement schedule means that the animal receives few shocks; however, the few
shocks that are received are important. Even well-trained rats show a reliable
"warm-up" effect in each session, responding slowly or not at all at first. The few
shocks received at this time induce avoidance responding so that later in the session almost all shocks are avoided. Suppose we take such an animal and turn off
the shock generator, except for a few response-independent shocks at the beginning of each session. The animal now has almost no information to tell it that the
world has changed so that it need not respond to avoid shock. Because respond-

ing never fails to occur during the experiment, the animal cannot learn that responding is no longer necessary. There is nothing to produce surprise in this
situation, the first requirement for learning. The animal's only protection against
this bind is to sample the environment by *not* responding occasionally later in
the session. But, sampling is the result of having a large candidate set, and we
have already established that schedules of severe shock and long-term training
greatly reduce the candidate set. Therefore, the animal does not sample, and the
lack of contingency between responding and no shock go unnoticed. Avoidance
responding persists almost indefinitely under these conditions. People are especially prone to this insensitivity to changes in avoidance contingencies and may
persist in avoidance behavior long after the contingencies have changed. This
fact has led many researchers to conclude that aspects of human psychopathol-
ogy may be related to avoidance conditioning.

ROLE OF CONTIGUITY   Both the shock-postponement and the shock-reduction
procedures provide an opportunity for response selection by contiguity. For example, the effective response is always the one most remote in time from the
shock. If proximity to shock tends to exclude (by punishment) an activity from
the candidate set, then the animal should eventually arrive at the correct response (avoidance) as the one least contiguous with shock. This response is generally effective in reducing overall shock rate. Similarly, contiguity is the process
by which punishment (response-contingent presentation of an aversive stimulus) selectively eliminates the punished activity. For example, activity that causes
or is correlated with punishment is soon eliminated, leaving other behaviors that
have no contingent relation to punishment free to increase in rate. At the end of
the chapter, we show how the dynamic reinforcement model introduced in Chapter 8 can account for avoidance, escape, and punishment schedules solely through
the effects of contiguity and competition.

Avoidance and Escape: Conclusion

Rats learn to respond on both Sidman-avoidance and shock-rate-reduction procedures, although with some difficulty. Judging by the proportion of animals that
completely fail to learn, these procedures are more difficult even than the two-
way shuttlebox, and they are much more difficult than one-way shuttle avoidance or avoidance in which the response is running in a wheel. The source of the
difficulty seems to be that lever-pressing is not one of the candidate responses
made by animals in shock situations. Weaker shocks often aid learning, presumably by diminishing the tendency for shock to induce rigidly stereotyped behavior (freezing). Strong shocks seem to induce behavior that is incompatible with
the operant response required for avoidance.

In a general sense, escape and avoidance behavior seem to follow the same
rules as behavior on positive-reinforcement schedules. Shock is an hedonic stimulus and both arouses the animal (although the effects seem depressive rather
than excitatory) and elicits specific activities. However, the elicited activities are
often passive ("freezing"), and they may dominate unless special steps are taken

to prevent them, such as reducing the intensity of the shock or making the operant response compatible with shock-induced activity. The most common active
behaviors induced by shock are attempts to withdraw from the source or escape from the experimental situation. Because these tendencies are invariably
blocked, the set of remaining candidates may be small. From this set, effective
members are selected in ways not fully understood. However, we shall soon see
how competition and selective suppression of activities contiguous with shock
are sufficient to produce most of the observed effects. The usual result of this
candidate-selection process is a behavior that leads to a reduction in shock rate.

We can conclude that the temporal relations between response and shock
clearly play some role in escape and avoidance learning, but the role of temporal
contiguity is rather weak under many conditions. In discriminated avoidance,
animals learn to respond to produce a shock-free stimulus.

RESPONSE-PRODUCED SHOCK

Behavior maintained by the production of electric shock provides the most striking example of the effects of shock schedules in minimizing behavioral variation.
In an experiment by McKearney (1969), squirrel monkeys restrained in a chair
were first trained to lever-press on a schedule of shock postponement. In this
experiment, the shock-shock interval was 10 sec and the postponement interval
was 30 sec. When the typical, steady response rate had developed, a 10-min,
fixed-interval schedule of shock production was superimposed. That is, a response at the end of each 10-min interval now produced shock. Eventually, the
shock-postponement schedule was phased out, leaving only the FI 10-min, shock-
production schedule. The monkeys nevertheless continued to respond on the
fixed-interval, shock-production schedule, and their behavior soon became organized with respect to it (Figure 10.7). That is, lever-pressing followed the typical

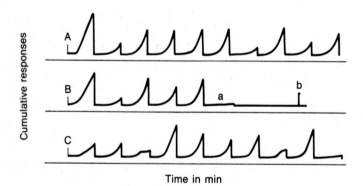

FIGURE 10.7   Samples of performance from three different sessions of responding
under a FI 10-min schedule of shock presentation (from McKearney, 1969).

scalloped pattern, increasing up until the moment of the reinforcer delivery, as on food-reinforcement schedules. As with food reinforcement, the shorter the fixed-interval duration, the higher the response rate. When shock was omitted entirely, the behavior soon ceased.

Rats in the typical Skinner box are less prone to the kind of rigidity shown by monkeys and cats in these experiments. However, rats can be trained to produce electric shocks in a shuttlebox apparatus. Similar behavior has been established in humans. This so-called self-punitive behavior is not an isolated phenomenon.

In McKearney's experiment, long training, physical restraint, and the highly aversive electric shock all act to reduce behavioral variation. In addition, the transition from simple shock postponement to shock postponement plus FI shock is barely perceptible. Because the monkeys occasionally failed to avoid shocks on the postponement schedule, an additional shock every 10 min made little difference. Moreover, even if the shocks produced by the FI schedule were detected, the animal could not cease responding without receiving many more shocks through the shock-postponement contingency. Thus, responding in the face of occasional response-contingent shocks is maintained. If there was a sufficient reservoir of behavioral variation, the monkey might have detected that almost any new behavior would lead to less shock than lever-pressing. The monkeys' failure to sample suggests that training on the shock-postponement schedule had so reduced the candidate set that the necessary variation in behavior was lacking.

Behavior maintained by response-produced shock is not masochistic: That is, the shock does not become pleasurable or positively reinforcing. Squirrel monkeys are transported to the experimental apparatus in restraining chairs partly because they would not otherwise choose to stay. The behavior is a misfiring of mechanisms that normally lead to adaptive escape and avoidance responses.

A major puzzle is that the pattern of behavior displayed in Figure 10.7 looks just like the FI "scallop" on schedules of positive reinforcement: It looks as if the monkey is "working for" the shock, even though we know it to be aversive. The reason: We know from studies with shock postponement that the shorter the response-shock interval, the faster the animal responds. As postshock time increases using McKearney's procedure, the expected time to shock decreases. The animal's previous training has established performance appropriate to shock postponement (the animal "thinks" it is on an avoidance schedule). Hence, the decreasing time to shock produces the higher response rate appropriate to a shorter RS interval.

Shock in these studies seems to play two roles. First, it provides a discriminative stimulus. The major discriminative property of shock is to define the situation. Its most important characteristic for this purpose is its aversiveness, but when shock is periodic (as in McKearney's experiment), it also acts as a time marker. Second, shock motivates behavior. Even highly effective avoidance behavior eventually extinguishes when shock is omitted, but behavior maintained by response-produced shock persists indefinitely—many months in most of these experiments.

LEARNED HELPLESSNESS

We have been arguing that learning involves selection from among a set of stimulus and response candidates, and we have seen that surprising results can come from procedures that seem to reduce severely the size of the candidate set. What if the set of response candidates is reduced to zero? The requirements for such a reduction should now be clear: very severe, response-independent shock. Severe shock ensures that the candidate set will be small, and response independence ensures that it will be empty, or at least contain only the "behavior of last resort" (in rats, usually freezing). These two characteristics define the phenomenon known as *learned helplessness*, which was discovered first as an effect and then advocated as a hypothesis by Martin Seligman (1968). In Seligman's original experiment, dogs were first restrained in a harness and given a series of severe, inescapable shocks. The next day, the dogs were placed in a simple, discriminated-avoidance situation. On each trial, when a CS came on, shock followed after 10 sec unless the dogs jumped over a low barrier. If they failed to jump, the CS remained on, and shocks continued for 50 sec. Thus, the animals had an opportunity either to avoid or escape from the shock by jumping the barrier.

Normal dogs, that is, dogs without day-before exposure to inescapable shock, have no difficulty learning first to escape from shock and then to avoid it by jumping as soon as they hear the CS. But, the dogs pretrained with inescapable shock almost invariably failed to jump at all. Similar effects have been shown with a variety of species and aversive stimuli in experimental situations. The effects often generalize from one highly aversive stimulus such as water immersion (unpleasant for rats) to another stimulus such as shock. This pattern suggests that the aversive property of the situation is the defining one for most animals.

Learned helplessness is a dramatic example of the impairment of learning by *US preexposure*, which was discussed earlier in Chapter 5 as *latent inhibition*. The dogs that received shock in the absence of the CS subsequently found it more difficult to detect the predictive properties of the CS. The magnitude of the impairment in learning is surprising, but the severity of the shock can perhaps account for it.

Learned helplessness follows from the candidate-selection idea because pretraining with inescapable shock reduces the candidate set. Subsequent training in a situation that permits avoidance or escape from shock is perceived as essentially the same, because the presence of electric shock defines the situation, therefore inaction persists. Because sampling does not occur, surprise (no shock) cannot occur. Shock continues to occur because the animal fails to avoid the shock, so the process is stable—a self-fulfilling prophecy.

Some species are less prone to learned helplessness than others are. For example, rats in the usual lever-pressing situation are less likely to show learned helplessness than monkeys and even people (unless the escape response is made especially difficult). People are much more susceptible to effects like learned helplessness even than dogs, and they show the effects even with very weak positive or negative reinforcers. The reason is that people learn more rap-

TABLE 10.1   Luchins's Set Experiment with Water Jars

Problem	GIVEN: Empty jars	TO OBTAIN:	Method
1	29, 3	9	Repeated subtraction from largest
2	127, 21, 3	100	" "
3	163, 25, 14	99	" "
4	43, 18, 10	5	" "
5	42, 9, 6	21	" "
6	59, 20, 4	31	" "
7	49, 23, 3	20	One subtraction from middle jar
·	· · ·	·	
·	· · ·	·	
·	· · ·	·	

idly, and they rely more on their ability to learn than "lower" animals do. The experiments that have purported to show learned helplessness in people do not, and do not need to, use severely unpleasant stimuli. The effects are examples of a long-known phenomenon, which used to be called *set* (or *Einstellung,* from the German): rigidity produced by earlier experience.

The phenomenon of set works as follows. Imagine a group of subjects that is asked to solve a series of similar problems. Luchins (1942) used simple quantitative "word problems" of the following sort: Imagine that you have a series of measuring jars of various capacities. The task is to produce a given amount of water by pouring water from one jar to another. For example, suppose you have two jars, one of 29 pints and the other of 3 pints, and the task is to obtain 20 pints. Obviously, the easiest procedure to follow is to fill the 29-pint jar, then pour out three 3-pint jars worth, leaving 20 pints in the large jar. Luchins selected his "jar" problems so as to teach his subjects a simple repetitive strategy. He then slipped in new problems that could be solved in the old, repetitive, fashion—but could also be solved much more simply. For example, one of Luchins's problem series began as shown in Table 10.1. Notice that all the problems can be solved by filling the largest jar, then subtracting repeatedly using the smaller ones. For example, Problem 2, 100 pints can be obtained by filling 127 pints, then subtracting first 21 pints, then 2 × 3 pints. Problem 7 is the critical one: It can be solved by filling the largest jar, then subtracting 23 pints and 2 × 3 pints; but, it can also be solved much more easily by filling the 23 pints and subtracting 3 pints. Without exception, Luchins's subjects failed to see this simpler method of solving the problem. After performing the first six problems, all the subjects blindly applied the same, and now inefficient, rule to the seventh. Training on the first six problems had reduced behavioral variation to the point that Luchins's subjects—faculty members and graduate students—all failed to "see" the simple solution, which they would have found at once if Problem 7 had been the first instead of the seventh.

Systematic training is one way to reduce behavioral variation. Strong motivation, especially of an aversive sort, is another. Highly intelligent, trainable species such as humans can be fooled by a clever training regimen. Less intelligent species may require the constricting effects of a strongly aversive stimulus to reduce behavioral variation. The effect of strong motivation, especially aversive motivation, on the ability to solve problems has been known for a long time as the *Yerkes–Dodson law*. In 1908, Yerkes and Dodson found that animals learned to escape from shock most rapidly if the shock was of intermediate intensity. Learned helplessness is an example of what happens when the shock intensity is quite high.

Learned helplessness and response-produced shock can both be abolished by increasing behavioral variation. For example, helplessness can be overcome by physically helping the dog over the barrier—forcing it to sample. In addition, prior training with escapable shock leads to a reservoir of behavior that prevents helplessness (in Chapter 9, we saw a similar effect of prior training with partial reinforcement on resistance to extinction following continuous reinforcement). Other experiments have shown that changes in shock intensity and other features of the situation may minimize helplessness. In short, these maladaptive behaviors are metastable; that is, if behavior is disrupted in some way, it may not return to its previous form. For example, if responding that produces electric shock is somehow prevented from occurring for several trials, the behavior is likely to disappear.

For a number of years controversy raged over whether learned helplessness is simply an effect of the suppression by punishment of effective responses or whether in some cognitive sense the animals "really learn" that they have no control over what happens to them. The latter idea is known as the *learned-helplessness (LH) hypothesis,* which must be distinguished from the experimental *learned-helplessness effect.* There is no doubt about the effect, but the status of the hypothesis is more problematic. In most cases, the LH effect is indeed associated with a severe reduction in the level or variety of motor output of the animal, but there are a few experiments in which controls seem to rule out this possibility. However, these conflicting results have little bearing on the hypothesis's central problem, which is that it is weak as an explanation: If we knew what it really meant to "know" something (as in "know that you cannot control shock occurrence"), then the LH hypothesis would have some validity. As it is, it merely substitutes the appearance of familiarity (most people *think* they know what it means "to know something") for a bald admission that we don't really know why the recent experience of traumatic shocks renders dogs unable to learn a simple escape response.

A Behavioral Model of Depression?

Much of the interest in learned helplessness derives from Seligman's persuasive arguments (e.g., Seligman & Weiss, 1980) that learned helplessness constitutes a model for an intractable and life-threatening human problem: clinical depression. Everybody gets "the blues" once in a while, especially when bad things happen (e.g., fail an exam, boyfriend or girlfriend leaves for someone else, lose a loved one). But, most people recover from such traumas quite rapidly, and few people feel sad for no discernible reason. Clinical depression is much more severe and often occurs without any plausible external cause. Depressives cannot sleep, they are always tired, they get sudden attacks of unreasoning panic, they cannot remember things, they feel life is not worth living, they often cannot attend even to routine tasks—and they may even kill themselves. Depression afflicts hundreds of thousands of people every year and the only effective treatments are drugs, which often have side effects and may encompass traumatic procedures reminiscent of the medieval driving out of devils. One such traumatic procedure is electroconvulsive shock (ECT), which destroys recent memories but often relieves the worst symptoms of the depression, at least for a few days or weeks. If you are interested in studying clinical depression, take a look at Stewart Sutherland's fascinating book *Breakdown* (1976). Sutherland, a British experimental psychologist, describes his personal struggle with manic depression, a cyclic form in which the sufferer cycles between "high" spirits and "low" depression over a period of weeks. In the book, Sutherland describes the pharmacological and psychological treatments he received and also gives an acute, critical view of the scientific status of clinical psychology that is well worth reading.

Depression is clearly a major medical problem, so that anything that promises to shed light on it is sure to command wide attention. Seligman has argued that the behavior of "helpless" dogs, which often seem severely depressed, can provide useful guides to comparable treatments for depressed people. Perhaps much of human depression has similar causes, or at least may be alleviated by similar means. This idea gained considerable support because drugs and other forms of behavioral intervention that were known to alleviate human depression also alleviate helplessness in animals. However, the parallel should make you suspicious for reasons we have already discussed—it is based on an analogy between similar phenomena, and such analogies can be dangerous. To be confident that something done with animals can also be applied to people, we must ensure that similar principles or processes operate in both domains. Since we do not fully understand even the animal phenomenon of helplessness, we must be cautious about applying what we learn from the animal experiments to this pressing human problem.

The Concept of a Behavioral Model

The idea of a behavioral model is worth some discussion in its own right. First a few words about models, then a comment on the validity of the learned-helplessness model of human depression.

What does it take to generalize from one situation (e.g., a dog receiving electric shocks) to another (e.g., a human consulting a physician about symptoms of depression)? There are two ways to generalize about this topic: one only partly satisfactory, the other completely satisfactory.

First, the generalization is probably valid if both situations have been extensively studied and comparison has revealed exact parallels from one to the other. For example, the development of food aversions in people has many properties in common with taste-aversion learning in rats. The aversion often follows the experience of sickness; the taste (rather than the sight or the locale) of the food becomes unpleasant; novel tastes are more likely to become aversive than familiar ones; and so on. Such models of similar properties but no guarantee of identical processes are called *analogical models.*

Second, the generalization is certainly valid if the underlying processes are known to be the same. For example, the process of energy metabolism in humans can be studied in vitro using material from many other species, because the basic biochemistry is known to be the same throughout the animal kingdom. Molecular genetics can be studied in *Drosophila* or *E. coli* for the same reason: DNA and RNA are universal, and no leap of faith is involved in generalizing from the basic biochemistry. The behavior of a bridge can be studied by a miniature replica because the laws of physics are the same for both. These types of models are called *substantive models.*

The model of learned helplessness is an analogical model, at best. Although there are many similarities between shocked dogs and depressed people (e.g., lack of behavior, "depressed" appearance, inability to learn new tasks), there are also many differences. The effects are found in animals only in response to massively aversive treatment. Human depression often occurs under more mild circumstances. Learned helplessness is usually situation-specific; human depression appears to be much less so. Learned helplessness wears off after 24 hours; human depression can last for years. Thus, there is no evidence of identity at a fundamental level. Indeed, rather little research has been devoted to understanding the processes (behavioral and physiological) that underlie learned helplessness. This lack of research is unfortunate because it is these processes, rather than superficial analogies between procedures and results, that may provide the real link between animal research and human problems.

The message: Anything short of a substantive model can be dangerous. Partial knowledge based on an analogy can be helpful, but it is often misleading and may distract attention away from research on fundamental processes.

PUNISHMENT

Punishment has received much less attention from researchers than reinforcement, and our current understanding reflects this fact. What are the effects of punishment on behavior? Are they opposite to the effects of positive reinforcement? In the remainder of this chapter, we examine the relation between punishment and reinforcement. We will see that although some controversy over the interpretation of experiments on punishment still exists, the effects of punishment fit well within the framework we have developed.

Punishment has been defined both as a procedure—that is, the presentation of an aversive stimulus—and as an effect—the suppression of behavior on which the aversive stimulus is contingent. We usually use the term *punish-*

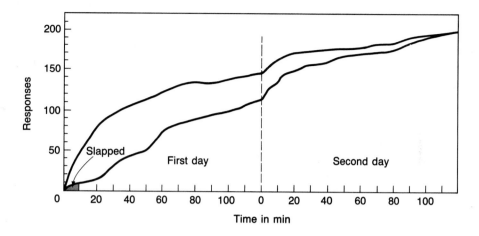

FIGURE 10.8   Effect of punishment on extinction. The two curves are from groups of four rats each, with the same experimental history. All responses made by one group during the first 10 min of extinction were "slapped." The rate is depressed for some time but eventually complete recovery is made (from Skinner, 1938).

ment to mean the suppression of behavior by the presentation of a response-contingent, aversive stimulus. In this sense, the response-produced shock procedure used by McKearney (1969) was not a punishment procedure because the rate of the operant response did not decrease. For the same reason, avoidance procedures are not considered examples of punishment because the rate of the avoidance response increases in the presence of aversive stimulation.

The Negative Law of Effect

The study of punishment can be traced to Edward Thorndike's original *law of effect* (see Chapter 4). According to Thorndike, the effects of punishment are opposite to those of reinforcement: That is, reinforcement serves to strengthen associations, punishment serves to weaken them. However, Thorndike's later work seems to suggest that the effects of punishment are not symmetrical to those of reinforcement. Thorndike (1932) and Skinner (1938) argued that punishment, unlike positive reinforcement, is not an effective procedure for controlling behavior. Thus, the negative aspect of the law of effect was abandoned.

An early experiment by Skinner (1938) suggests why the effects of punishment were considered to be weak. Figure 10.8 shows cumulative records for two groups of rats from Skinner's experiment. Both groups received several sessions of lever-press training on a VI schedule of food reinforcement. Following VI training, both groups received two sessions of extinction (i.e., food reinforcement was eliminated for bar-pressing). In addition, animals in one of the groups received a mild punishment (a "slap" administered by the response lever) for lever-pressing during the first 10 min of extinction. The figure shows that this mild punishment was effective in decreasing bar-press rate during the 10-min period when it occurred. However, the effects of the punishment were only temporary: That is, both groups produced the same number of responses by the end of the second session of extinction, as shown by the merging of the cumulative records in the figure. The punishment did not appear to decrease the "strength" of the bar-press response at all.

Skinner's experiment obviously presents only a small piece of evidence. The punishment was brief and mild, and Skinner's interpretation has been rightly criticized on these grounds. Subsequent work has shown that had punishment continued, responding would have ceased. In any case, even the effects of positive reinforcement wear off when reinforcement is discontinued. Severe punishment clearly suppresses behavior on which it is contingent, although the suppression may not continue indefinitely when punishment ceases.

For example, Nathan Azrin (1960), using pigeon subjects, compared the effects of several intensities of shock on key-pecking maintained by VI schedules of food reinforcement. Figure 10.9 shows that the rate of responding is inversely related to the intensity of the punishment. High shock intensities virtually eliminated responding, whereas low-intensity shock had little effect. Can Skinner's failure to produce permanent suppression be attributed to the weak punishment he used? Perhaps not. Look at Figure 10.10, from Azrin's experiment. The procedure consisted of alternating periods of punishment superimposed on a VI schedule of food reinforcement. That is, hungry pigeons could still obtain food according to a VI schedule. During punishment periods, responding was suppressed. However, when punishment was discontinued briefly, responding resumed at a high rate. These results suggest that the effects of punishment on a well-trained animal, like the effects of positive reinforcement, are determined by the response contingency: Shock must occur and must be contingent on responding to have a persistent effect. When shock ceases, responding resumes. The results of Skinner's (1938) experiment can also be interpreted in this fashion. When the punishment ceased after 10 min, responding resumed. Too much should probably not be made of the apparent compensation for the depressive effects of punishment because of the brevity and mildness of the punishment.

The effects of four important factors—contingency, delay, partial punishment, and type of response—are symmetrical for punishment and positive reinforcement. We consider each in turn and then show how a dynamic reinforcement model can handle these effects.

CONTINGENCY   Free food does not normally produce lever-pressing. We have already seen that the addition of free positive reinforcers tends to suppress lever-pressing that is maintained by response-contingent reinforcement. Punishment shows similar effects: Response-independent punishment has a smaller suppressive effect on lever-pressing than response-contingent punishment that occurs at the same rate. For example, Russell Church (1969) compared three groups of rats that all responded to food reinforcement on a VI 1-min schedule. Group A received no punishment; Group B received a random shock every 2 min, on the average; Group C received the shock on a VI 2-min schedule, that is, every 2 min, as for Group B, but on a response-contingent rather than response-independent ba-

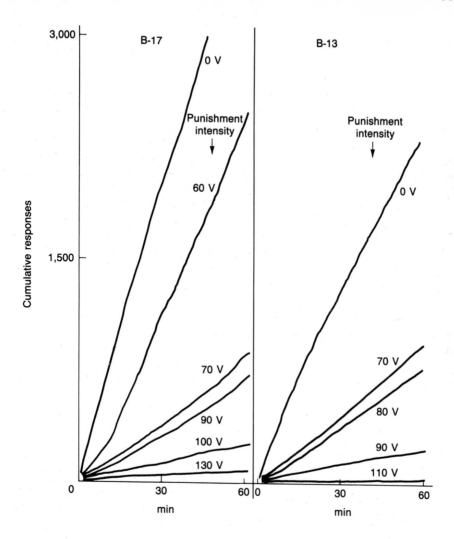

FIGURE 10.9 Response rate as a function of punishment intensity (in volts) for two subjects. Each curve is the cumulative-response record for a 1-hour period of concurrent food reinforcement and punishment (from Azrin, 1960).

sis. The order of lever-press rates was A > B > C: Response-contingent shock suppressed lever-pressing more effectively than response-independent shock did.

DELAY   The effects of delay on punishment are also similar to the effects of delay of positive reinforcement. Delayed punishment is less effective than punishment that occurs immediately following the punished response (cf. Church, 1969).

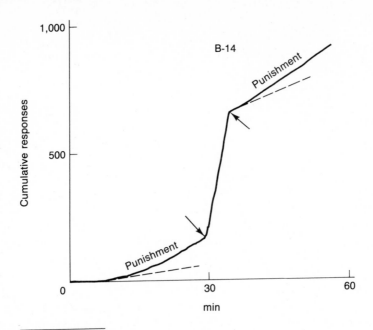

FIGURE 10.10   Effect of a brief period without punishment. The responses are reinforced throughout by a 1-min, variable-interval schedule of food reinforcement. The actual delivery of these reinforcements is not indicated. The lower arrow marks the moment at which the punishment is discontinued. The upper arrow marks the moment at which the punishment was reinstated. The dotted lines are a projection of the response rates at the start of the session and at the start of the reinstated punishment period. During the period of punishment, the brief punishing stimulus is delivered following every response (from Azrin, 1960).

PARTIAL PUNISHMENT   Azrin and his associates (Azrin, Holz, & Hake, 1963) have shown that when punishment is administered on various fixed-ratio schedules (from 1 to 1,000) to pigeons pecking a key for food, the response rate is directly related to the ratio value: The less frequent the punishment, the higher the rate. Interestingly, the pigeons do not seem to be sensitive to the fixed-ratio aspect of punishment under these conditions; for example, they do not show a higher key-peck rate immediately following each shock, which would be the punishment counterpart to the fixed-ratio pause on a positive-reinforcement schedule. The effect of the punishment seems to depend on its frequency rather than on the manner in which it is scheduled.

RESPONSE TYPE   As we might expect from the SSDR idea, some responses are more resistant to the effects of punishment than others are—just as some responses are easier to strengthen through positive reinforcement. For example, Sara Shettleworth (1978), who has conducted several experiments on the differential susceptibility to reinforcement of different types of behavior, studied the effects of electric shock on the response repertoire of hamsters. She found that a pattern called open rearing (rearing up on the hind legs without touching a wall) was less susceptible to punishment than scrabbling (a sort of digging pattern)—presumably because open rearing is an SSDR for hamsters.

THE DYNAMICS OF PUNISHMENT AND AVOIDANCE [1]

Probably no topic in the study of learning has been so conceptually confused as the effects of aversive stimuli. We are not completely sure of the reason, but a symptom of the confusion is the long and fruitless search for something analogous to a positive reinforcer for avoidance behavior. How can the *absence* of something strengthen behavior? Theorists have pondered this topic, accepting without question that *strengthening* is an appropriate explanation for the effects of positive reinforcement. Perhaps the primary error arises because giving food to a hungry animal in return for a simple response such as lever-pressing seems to have such a direct effect on the reinforced response. So direct, in fact, that theorists have taken this situation as a model for all reinforcement procedures, negative as well as positive. What the model neglects is that repeated presentation of any hedonic event, positive or negative, acts on the animal's entire repertoire of behavior. The eventual emergence of one dominant activity is likely to be an outcome not simply of effects on that activity but of effects on the ensemble. The processes that permit this emergence of a dominant activity are of two kinds: processes that govern the effects of hedonic stimuli on specific activities and processes that govern how different activities interact with one another. These processes, taken together, account not only for reinforcement but also for failures to reinforce. It is these underlying processes (not the "strengthening" metaphor) that should generalize from the positive to the negative case.

A Dynamic Model for Punishment

At the end of Chapter 8 we discussed a simple, dynamic model based on the idea that hedonic events have effects on the entire behavioral repertoire. The model easily explains not just positive reinforcement—the strengthening of an activity on which an hedonic stimulus is made contingent—but also several types of reinforcement failure. These reinforcement failures include elicited behavior (which is stimulated to occur by a hedonic event but is not permanently strengthened when the event is response contingent), autoshaping and superstition (the strengthening of a behavior by response-independent stimulus presentation), and instinctive drift (apparently successful strengthening of a response by response-contingent reinforcement, followed by its subsequent displacement by another activity). We now show that the same model can account for all the basic

---

1. A sketch of this model, applied to positive-reinforcement effects, appears in Staddon (1988).

effects of aversive stimuli, including unsignaled avoidance behavior—the situation that has remained most puzzling for traditional reinforcement theory. As before, the model does not attempt to account for stimulus effects or effects that involve long-term memory. For example, it does not explain responding to produce a shock-free stimulus, but effects of this type are not particularly puzzling to theorists.

Our model is based on the assumption that the effects of positive and negative hedonic stimuli—reinforcers and punishers—are essentially symmetrical. Whatever we previously assumed for reinforcers, we now assume for punishers, but with opposite effect: Where reinforcers had positive, additive effects, punishers have negative, subtractive ones. To make the parallels clear, let's repeat our argument from Chapter 8, substituting punishment for reinforcement.

Punishment can be defined by three effects:

1. When the occurrence of punishment is made contingent on a specific response, the rate of that response decreases.

2. When the punisher is no longer presented or is no longer response contingent, the rate of the response returns to its previous value (which is the procedural definition of extinction of punishment).

3. Punishment must be reversibly selective for at least one pair of activities: suppressing punished activity A relative to unpunished activity B, and vice versa.

A process that satisfies both (1) and (2) also satisfies (3).

From assumptions about variability, adaptation, arousal, and competition in Chapter 8, we derived a system of simple integrators that determined the "strengths" (V value) of each activity. The activity with the highest V value is the one that actually occurs (competition). Each integrator expresses the V value of each activity at each instant of time ($t + 1$) as a function of what happened in the previous instant (t). Thus, for each activity,

Following nonpunishment: $V(t + 1) = aV(t) + E$
where $0 < a < 1$ (10.1)

Following punishment: $V(t + 1) = aV(t) + E + bV(t)$
where $b < 0$ (10.2)

The first term in Equation 10.1 (aV) is again our "leaky bucket." At each instant in time (t), the "strength" (V) of our behavior decreases (leaks out) a bit (adaptation). The smaller variable a, the faster the leak. When the values of a are high, the V values change only slowly. The second term in the equation (E) is our assumption of variability. Variable E represents the effects of all other sources of reinforcement and punishment that affect the "strengths" of activities. These effects are assumed to vary at random and affect the strength of each activity differently at any instant, so that each activity is occasionally the one with the highest V and thus occurs from time to time. The terms t and $t + 1$, as before, refer to instants of time ("ticks").

Equation 10.2 is similar to Equation 8.2 with the exception that now the term $bV(t)$ is *subtracted* from V, not added to it (because $b < 0$). The term $bV(t)$ now represents the multiplicative *decrement* in strength caused by punishment, whereas before it represented the increment due to reinforcement. If positive reinforcement causes arousal ($b > 0$), punishment is assumed to cause the opposite effect ($b < 0$). Because different activities may have different values for b, which represents how much of an effect reinforcement or punishment can have on a given activity, some activities may be greatly decreased (large b value) by punishment and some only little affected (smaller b value).

PUNISHMENT   Let's now consider a simple example with two activities, as we did in Chapter 8. We assume that activities A and B are occurring at a relatively high rate (perhaps because they are both being maintained by similar VI schedules of food reinforcement). Activity A might be pecking a right key and activity B pecking a left key. Consider what happens when we superimpose punishment on activity A (pecking the right key). At the time of punishment, activity A has a greater "strength"—$V_A > V_B$—as implied by the competition assumption. Activity A therefore receives a greater decrement than activity B because $bV_A < bV_B < 0$. If parameters a and b are the same for both activities, activity A therefore decreases at a faster rate than activity B. If there are only two activities, then activity B must increase as A decreases.

Thus, we have reproduced two well-known effects of punishment: its suppressive effect on the punished activity and its facilitating effect on an alternative activity. Notice that if there are more than two activities, not all the unpunished ones will increase. If all a values are equal, activities with large (negative) b values tend to decrease, whether or not punishment is contingent on them, and the other activities tend to increase. If the a values are not the same for all the activities, then complex interactions, resembling instinctive drift, are possible.

PARTIAL PUNISHMENT AND DELAY   It should be clear that this process is sensitive to the probability of punishment in the way we have already described: The less probable the punishment, the smaller the suppression of the punished response. Because the mechanism is sensitive to contiguity, it is also sensitive to punishment delay: The longer the delay, the smaller the suppressive effect.

EFFECTS OF CONTINGENCY   It should also be clear that "free" (response-independent) punishment is much less effective in suppressing behavior than response-contingent punishment is. Indeed, if all activities are identical, it is completely ineffective, because it then has the same suppressive effects on all activities. Since the activity that occurs is simply the one with the highest momentary V value, equal suppression of all V values leaves the distribution of activities unchanged. In terms of our model, conditioned suppression implies the existence of an activity other than lever-pressing that has a lower (negative) b value, hence less susceptible to suppression by punishment. Clearly, SSDRs are by definition less susceptible to punishment than something like lever-pressing, so they

B   O   X

10.1

Contingency and Contiguity

Because of the leaky-bucket assumption, our dynamic model is in effect a contiguity model for reinforcement. In the recent history of learning theory, there was much discussion and confusion about the relationship between contiguity and contingency as explanations for reinforcement: Do reinforcers "strengthen" just by being contiguous in time with the reinforced activity, or must there be a real dependence of the reinforcer on the reinforced activity (contingency)? We touched on this debate in Chapter 8. It is worth noting, therefore, that adding a competition assumption to a contiguity theory changes it to a contingency theory. Now, the activity strengthened by the reinforcer is not necessarily the activity contiguous with the reinforcer but the activity *most contiguous* with the reinforcer. In other words, contingency, as it is usually defined, is nothing but *relative contiguity*.

should increase, and thus suppress lever-pressing, when punishment is response independent.

We have already seen that the effects of punishment, like those of positive reinforcement, are reduced by degrading the contingency between the response and the outcome: Occasional "free" food deliveries depress the rate of food-reinforced lever-pressing; occasional free shocks increase the rate of a response punished by response-contingent shock. Our model accounts for this effect: If punishment is contingent on response A, it is depressed relative to response B. But because free shocks are just as likely to suppress activity B as activity A, the addition of free shocks must reduce the *difference* between the strengths of A and B (see Box 10.1). Table 10.2 lists typical data from a simulation. For the simulation, we studied 1,000 iterations of Equations 10.1 and 10.2 for a set of three identical (same a and b) activities, A, B, and C. Every instance of activity A was punished, but we varied the frequency of "free" punishment, which was either absent (0) or occurred with probability 0.2 or 0.5 per iteration. The table shows the average proportion of time taken up by activity A. With no punishment (NP), A occurs about one-third (33 percent) of the time. With response-contingent punishment only, A occurs 20.4 percent of the time. But when free punishment is added to the response-contingent punishment, the frequency of the punished activity increases, first to 24 percent and then to almost 35 percent.

EFFECTS OF RESPONSE   Conditioned suppression implies that some activities have more negative b values than others do, hence should be more susceptible to

TABLE 10.2   Proportion of Time Taken Up by One of Three Identical Activities*

	Probability of "Free" Punishment			
	NP	0	0.2	0.5
% Activity A	33	20.4	24.0	34.7

*With no punishment (NP) or punishment with three levels of "free" punishment. Each number is the average of 100 iterations for 10 "stat" animals. Parameter $a = 0.9$ and $b = -0.1$ for all activities.

the effects of punishment. As we described earlier, Shettleworth (1978) and others have shown this condition explicitly for several species. Differential susceptibility to reinforcement and punishment is an expected consequence of the type of model we have been describing.

UNSIGNALED AVOIDANCE   Our model explains unsignaled avoidance by two properties: punishment and competition. In the Sidman procedure, for example, the avoidance response is always separated from shock by the $R*S$ interval. Hence, other activities are generally punished more effectively than the avoidance response. And since the behavior that actually occurs is determined by competition, suppression of all activities other than the avoidance response must entail an increase in its level. Figure 10.11 shows a cumulative record for three identical activities from a typical simulation, under the conditions described for our model. The record shows cumulative instances of activity A, the avoidance response. When all activities occur equally often, the expected curve is the shallow straight line, with a slope of $\frac{1}{3}$. However, as you can see, by about half way through the simulation, activity A has become the dominant activity.

The same process explains shock-rate-reduction procedures: The avoidance response is punished selectively less than other activities because it is always followed by shock after a longer time than the shock that follows other activities. Note that this model also explains another distinctive feature of responding on shock-rate-reduction schedules: The response rate is directly related to the difference between postshock and postresponse shock rates. Obviously, when these two rates are identical, we have a simple response-independent punishment situation, which produces no increase in any response. Conversely, when the response-shock distribution is at a low rate, the difference between the punishment of avoidance and nonavoidance responses is maximal.

Conclusion: Dynamics of Punishment and Avoidance

Our model for the effects of hedonic stimuli on behavior is intended to make two main points. First, to understand reinforcement, punishment, and all the other effects of hedonic stimuli we have described, it is essential to frame the problem

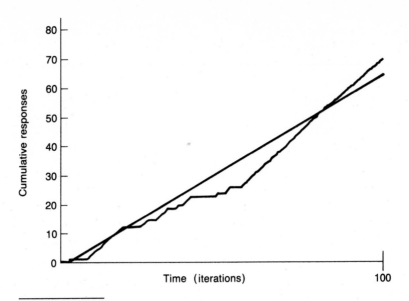

FIGURE 10.11   Cumulative record of an avoidance response from a simulation of the dynamic model discussed in the text. The graph shows 100 iterations. Parameter values are $a = 0.95$ and $b = -1$. The RS interval and SS interval are two iterations.

as one of understanding the effects of certain stimuli (not in a manner that confuses an explanation—strengthening via reinforcement—with the effect to be explained). The problem is not to find the "reinforcer" for avoidance responding but rather to see why aversive stimuli, scheduled in this peculiar fashion, usually facilitate the avoidance response. The second point of our model is to emphasize the importance of two factors: competition among tendencies to action and arousal (or its opposite) caused by hedonic events. Competition is essential; without it, suppression of one activity could have no facilitating effects on others. Arousal is necessary to account for the generalized effects of hedonic stimuli on behavior.

The other factors in our model—adaptation (the leaky-bucket process) and additive variability—are necessary to make the model work, but there are probably other assumptions that could work as well. (Indeed, in Chapter 11, we discuss how our current assumption of time-independent variability is incorrect in many respects. Fortunately, that assumption doesn't compromise the integrity of this chapter). The term E in Equations 10.1 and 10.2 is like a place marker in an incomplete piece of software: It indicates one place at which the model must be extended. Another place is the competition assumption. We have assumed that activities interact in the simplest possible way: The highest V value wins. But, there are many other possibilities for interaction, including cooperative interactions between some activities. The leaky-bucket assumption is probably necessary in some form, because we need something to capture the different "viscosities" of different activities and to account for the effects of contiguity, although there are undoubtedly better (if not simpler) ways to capture these properties. It seems likely that a more adequate model may need more than one process to accommodate the effects of contiguity and the viscosity of response strength.

DYNAMIC MODELS AND NEURAL MODELS   At the end of Chapter 6, we briefly described some of the work on neural models for behavior. Here and in Chapter 8, we have described a dynamic model. These two approaches are much more similar than they may appear. You will remember that the "neurons" used by the neural modelers have only a rather distant relation to real neurons: For example, they are usually much simpler; they are often assumed to fire in synchrony; they may be connected bidirectionally (real neurons are unidirectional); and they may have fewer modes of action (on/off) rather than have the possibility of a range of firing rates. In reality, even the neural models are simply systems of equations that share certain general properties with neural networks, most notably parallelism—many computations occur simultaneously—and nonlinearity—the effects are generally not simply additive.

Our model also is parallel, because we assume that Equations 10.1 and 10.2 are computed simultaneously for every available tendency to action. In addition, our model is nonlinear (even though the equations are linear) because of the "highest value wins" competition rule. In fact, the neural models and our dynamic model are completely interchangeable. We could have represented our model by a set of formal neurons, one for each action tendency, each connected by inhibitory connections, and all activated by reinforcement or punishment inputs. We did not represent our model in the fashion of neural models simply because such a description adds little to the equations that encompass it.

Therefore, it is no accident that the features of our model—competition, parallelism, leaky-bucket decay, and global activation—have also been studied extensively by neural modelers (see the books by Stephen Grossberg (1988) and by David Rumelhart and James McClelland (1986) that were referred to in Chapter 6). Competition, especially, has been found to be an essential component of many learning networks. Decay of connection weights with time has also turned out to be a useful assumption.

Our model has two main deficiencies: It does not attempt to explain the effects of stimuli that involve long-term memory, and it does not explain extinction effects. For example, Herrnstein & Hineline (1966) showed with their shock-rate-reduction procedure that the smaller the difference between the postshock and postresponse shock rates, the lower the rate of the avoidance response, but also the longer the period of extinction when the difference is reduced to zero. The first effect follows easily from our model, but the second does not. As well, there are other implications of our model that need to be explored. But to show that a model does not explain everything is not to say that it explains nothing. We believe that the essential features of this model—competition, arousal, some notion of behavioral viscosity—are likely to form part of any successful theory of reinforcement and punishment.

SUMMARY

Much, perhaps too much, of human life is dominated by arrangements that resemble avoidance schedules. Much human suffering is caused by traumatic aversive events. Much animal behavior is adapted to the avoidance of harm. The
study of aversive stimuli is therefore an important part of the study of adaptive
behavior and learning. This chapter has been organized around the various procedures used to study aversive effects. To understand many of the procedures, it
was also necessary to describe the theoretical concerns that gave rise to them.
Historically, the dominant theoretical issue derived from the parallel between
aversively motivated and appetitively motivated procedures. Until the growing
awareness of learning constraints in the mid-1970s, the latter seemed satisfactorily explained by the idea of strengthening via contiguity: The rat learns to
press the bar because bar-pressing is immediately followed by food, a positive
reinforcer, which somehow strengthens the tendency to bar-press. Two-factor
theory applied this account to discriminated avoidance: The buzzer that signals
shock was assumed to acquire aversive properties through Pavlovian conditioning. Turning off the now-aversive buzzer strengthened lever-pressing. The wish
to test this idea led to the invention of a variety of unsignaled-avoidance procedures. These provide no external safety signal, thus they do not lend themselves
to a two-factor account. Nevertheless, rats learn to avoid shock delivered on
unsignaled-avoidance schedules. Temporary reprieve for two-factor theory was
provided by the suggestion that time might serve as a signal in Sidman-avoidance
schedules, but this escape route was effectively closed by the shock-rate-
reduction procedure of Herrnstein and Hineline in which shocks occurred at unpredictable times.

   Although two-factor theory can be rescued even from the attack of the
shock-rate reducers, we argue that the entire controversy is based on a miscon-
ception. Even the effects of food reinforcement are not well explained by the
simple strengthening idea, as the vast literature on learning constraints such as
autoshaping, superstition, and instinctive drift now attests. In Chapter 8, we proposed a simple, dynamic model for all these effects. In this chapter, we showed
that the same model provides an acceptable account for the various effects of
aversive stimuli, including unsignaled-avoidance responding, which poses the
major difficulty for two-factor theory.

   The chapter discusses a number of other topics related to aversive stimuli,
notably the effects of response-produced shock and learned helplessness as theory and phenomena. Both these effects reflect the Yerkes–Dodson law that says
that strong motivation reduces behavioral variation, hence impairs problem solving. If variation is reduced in the context of an avoidance schedule, squirrel
monkeys can be trained to produce electric shocks indefinitely. If variation is reduced under conditions in which neither escape nor avoidance are possible, dogs
become passive and "helpless." We also point out the resemblance between the
variation-reducing effects of strong shock and of prolonged training, which is
termed set. We discuss learned helplessness as a model for the problem of clinical

depression in humans, and we note the many differences between learned helplessness in animals and human depression. We also discuss the concept of an animal model to study human depression. We note the important differences between models that are merely analogies and substantive models, such as a miniature bridge used to model the behavior of a real bridge, in which the underlying principles are known to be the same. We conclude that the animal phenomenon of learned helplessness is at best an analogical model for human depression. Seligman and his associates seem recently to have come to a similar conclusion (cf. Peterson & Seligman, 1984).

11

Behavioral Allocation and Choice

Perhaps no topic in the field of operant learning has received more attention during the last 10 years than *choice*. The study of choice is the study of the factors that make animals and people do one thing rather than another. In this sense, all of psychology is the study of choice—but as we will see, special experimental arrangements allow us to compare the factors that make alternative actions more or less attractive.

In common speech, choice implies conscious deliberation. Humans often ponder decisions: Shall we go out for dinner or eat at home? Or, shall I stay home tonight and study or go out to the game and have a good time? But animals also choose, and here the role of conscious comparison between alternatives becomes less clear. Indeed, in Chapter 9 we concluded that in many choice experiments animals seem to treat each alternative independently; these experiments may not involve any direct comparisons. In any case, whether the subjects are animals or people, the central scientific questions are

1. What measurable, external factors determine choice?

2. What mechanisms underlie choice behavior?

We attempt to answer these questions in this chapter.

For our discussion, we study the notion of choice in two kinds of situations: implicit choice and explicit choice. *Implicit choice* refers to the allocation of behavior under relatively free conditions, that is when many activities are free to occur. This kind of choice is implied by examples such as the following: How should the organism spend its time? How much time should it spend sleeping, eating, drinking, mating, and so on? Are there preferred patterns of time allocation? For example, does the animal like to sleep at regular intervals and for fixed periods of time, or is it sufficient that it spend a certain percentage of time in each activity? What factors determine the preferred pattern? How might it be altered?

Explicit choice refers to special experimental arrangements (such as the concurrent-chain schedules discussed in Chapter 9) that allow us to measure the effects on preference of factors such as reward amount, probability, delay and type.

The chapter is divided into three parts. The first part discusses implicit choice and the molar allocation of behavior. It concludes with a discussion of optimality models for the allocation of behavior under free conditions and on reinforcement schedules. The second part takes up the optimality theme and shows how it is related to the economic approach to behavior. In this section, the much-studied matching law and some potential explanations for it and related findings are discussed. It turns out that optimality and economic models can provide a comprehensive account for behavioral allocation, although like all functional accounts, they fail under some conditions. Optimality accounts provide a good description of what animals manage to achieve on reinforcement schedules, but they say nothing about the mechanisms they use to achieve it. Therefore, the last part of the chapter explores the question of mechanism, the moment-by-moment rules that animals use to adapt to reinforcement schedules. Recent advances are beginning to reveal what seem to be quite simple rules underlying the apparently complex behavior on reinforcement schedules. The chapter concludes by pointing out some promising directions for future research.

The study of behavioral allocation and choice is one of the most highly developed areas in the biopsychology of learning. It is not possible to discuss it in any depth without going into technical matters and some mathematics. Nevertheless, we believe the basic ideas can be conveyed through text, graphs, and diagrams and can be understood even by students unfamiliar with mathematical methods. But be warned: there are several equations in the pages ahead! None requires more than the simplest high school algebra. Understanding some of the issues involved will require effort from those who have had little exposure to quantitative science.

IMPLICIT CHOICE: THE ALLOCATION OF BEHAVIOR

People and animals choose things that have value, and they prefer things of higher value to things of lower value. Thus, the study of choice is also the study of reinforcement, which we have defined as the effect on behavior of valued events. Yet organisms perform activities all the time, and many of these activities do not seem to be directed at any specific goal; much behavior seems to exist "for its own sake" and not for its consequences. Some years ago David Premack (1965) posed the following question: Perhaps there are conditions under which *all* activities (not just consummatory activities like eating or copulation) are reinforcing? He argued that essentially all activities have some value and that the necessary and sufficient condition for positive reinforcement is simply the opportunity to exchange a less valuable activity for a more valuable one. His work has led to major advances in our understanding of the functional basis for reinforcement. Extensions of it, in the form of economic and optimality accounts, have revealed unsuspected relationships between implicit and explicit choice, that is, between how animals allocate their time and how their choice behavior is guided by reinforcement.

The Premack Principle

Imagine an animal such as a rat in a seminatural environment in which it can perform several activities each of which we can record and make available or unavailable. We can conduct two kinds of experiments with such a situation:

1. Add or remove the opportunity to perform various activities and study the effect on the amount and temporal pattern of the remaining activities.

2. Impose contingencies between pairs of activities and see if the operant response increases in rate. For example, make the animal run to get access to water and see if it runs more.

Premack was the first to see a connection between the pattern of activities under free conditions—measured in experiments of the first type—and the effect of making one activity contingent on another—the second type of experiment. In studies with rats and monkeys, Premack showed that the effect of making access to one activity contingent on performance of another depends on the levels of the activities under unconstrained conditions. Let's examine one of Premack's experiments and then describe the ways in which the imposition of a reinforcement contingency can be expected to change the levels of the activities involved.

In this experiment, Premack (1965) studied the reinforcing relations among the activities of Cebus monkeys. The monkeys were in individual cages, and there were four items they could play with: a lever (L), a plunger (P), a hinged flap (F), and a horizontally operated lever (H). Access to each item was controlled by the experimenter. Premack's idea was that "reinforcement" is not an absolute property of a consummatory activity (e.g., eating food) but is simply the relation between a more probable activity and a less probable one. In other words, for a hungry animal, eating is more probable than, say, lever-pressing—thus hunger makes eating reinforcing, not something special about eating itself. Premack's experimental situation with the monkeys was more convenient for testing this idea than the usual Skinner box, both because more activities were available, and because different animals showed different preferences for the different activities.

Premack compared the proportions of total time spent in each activity under free conditions with the proportions after he had imposed a 1:1 contingency between the several possible pairs of activities. (The free situation, with which the contingent situation is to be compared, is known as the *paired-baseline condition.*) The contingency was similar to an FR 1 schedule, although the units were time rather than responses. For example, the animal might be required to accumulate 10 sec of performing activity A before it would be allowed 10 sec of activity B. Activity A here is termed the *operant,* or *instrumental, response;* B is the *contingent response.* Premack wrote:

> The clearest predictions possible were those for Chicko, who in the first procedure [free access to all activities—paired baseline] showed three reliably different response probabilities [proportions of time spent]. Indeed, Chicko's protocol made possible three kinds of contingencies: contingent response [the reinforcer] higher than, less than, and, in one case, about equal to the free [operant] response. . . . The outcomes for the three types of contingencies were as follows: (1) contingent response higher than free response produced . . . an increment in the free response; (2) contingent less probable than free response produced . . . a decrement . . . ; (3) the one case in which the responses were about equal produced little or no change, increment or decrement (1965).

Thus, a monkey that spent 10 percent of its time playing with L and 20 percent playing with P under free conditions, increased its level of L when L, the operant response, had to occur for several seconds in order for P, the contingent response, to be available for several seconds. Evidently, access to a high-probability activity served to reinforce a low-probability activity. For example, if you watch TV for, say, 3 hours each day and study for only 1 hour, we can increase the amount of time you allocate to studying by making access to your baseline (3 hours) TV allocation contingent upon 3 hours of study. You may wind up watching TV less, and you will also study more. The reinforcing effect of a high-probability activity on a low-probability one exemplifies the *Premack principle,* which Premack proposed as a general principle of reinforcement.

Do Premack's results really represent "reinforcement" in the familiar sense? Are there any limits to the principle: Is behavior probability really what determines reinforcing effectiveness, for example?

The Premack Principle and Reinforcement

Let's discuss this question of reinforcement and look first at the simplest possible theoretical case. (We return to the question of limits to the Premack principle in the section entitled "Dynamics of Behavioral Allocation.") In this experiment, the animal can perform only two activities, and it always performs one or the other. That is, the activities are mutually exclusive and exhaustive. The situation under free conditions is illustrated in Figure 11.1, which shows the amounts of time devoted to each activity along the horizontal and vertical axes. A given activity distribution is thus a single point whose coordinates are the times taken up by the two activities. The time constraint is shown by the line of negative slope. The term *time constraint* refers to the fact that if the animal increases the amount of one activity, the other must decrease by the same amount

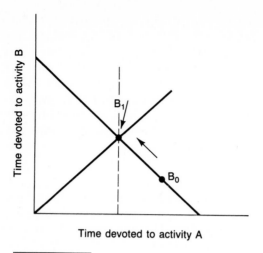

FIGURE 11.1   Schedule and time allocation constraints with only two available activities.

(can you figure out the equation for the constraint line?) The *free-behavior point* (B₀) represents the times taken up by each activity under free conditions. As we've drawn it, the animal spends more of its time in activity A than in activity B. The line of unit slope through the origin represents the *schedule constraint* imposed by the 1:1 contingent relation between the activities. Remember, we stipulated that x units of operant activity are required for x units of contingent activity, which implies a feedback function of unit slope—the feedback function for an FR 1 schedule (cf. Chapter 4).

The animal's behavior must satisfy both the schedule constraint and the time constraint. The only point that satisfies both is the intersection of the two constraints (B₁). The arrow indicates the forced change in the proportions of the two activities implied by the shift from B₀ to B₁: Activity A (the contingent and more frequent activity) decreases, and activity B (the operant and less frequent activity) increases.

Notice two things about Figure 11.1. First, by making the more frequent activity contingent on the less frequent one, we cause the less frequent one to increase. Second, notice that this increase is *not* a "reinforcing" effect of the more probable activity on the less probable one. It is not an adaptive response but merely a forced change that is caused by the two constraints. Because the schedule makes operant and contingent activities occur equally often, and because the contingent activity occurs more often than the operant activity does under free conditions, the first effect of the 1:1 schedule constraint is artificially to restrict the time devoted to the contingent activity. Because the animal must engage in one activity or the other, restriction of the contingent activity forces an increase in the operant response. This forced change in activity levels is called a *restriction effect.*

It should be clear that the two constraints, time allocation plus the FR 1 schedule, exhaust the degrees of freedom available to the animal in this simple situation. In a moment, we will see that to get something more than restriction effects we must have more activities than constraints (at least three activities, if we have a schedule constraint in addition to the ever present time constraint).

There is a simple experimental test for whether a given increase is a restriction effect or something more. The test asks whether the increase in the operant response associated with the imposition of a contingency is greater than or merely equal to the increase produced by restricting the proportion of time the animal can devote to the contingent activity. The restriction effect is illustrated in Figure 11.1 by the dashed vertical line through B_1. Under these conditions (two mutually exclusive and exhaustive activities), restriction of the contingent response to the level attained under the contingency condition yields the same increase in the operant response, despite the lack of any contingent relation between the two activities.

THE YOKED-CONTROL PROCEDURE.   This test is easy to state in principle, but it is not so obvious how we would go about it in practice. We want to compare the level of the operant response, activity B (e.g., lever-pressing) obtained under the contingency with its level when the contingent response, activity A (e.g., wheel-running), is artificially kept at the same level as it is under the contingency. One way to conduct such an experiment would be by comparing the two conditions successively. First, in phase 1, we impose the contingency and measure the level of activity A, which may require several daily experimental sessions to get reliable data. During this phase, we record the time of every occurrence of activity A. In a second phase, we use a timer to restrict access to A (i.e., lock and unlock the running wheel) to the same level it attained in the first phase. For a fair comparison, we also want to control the temporal pattern of A, to keep it the same as it was in the first phase (the reason for our recording of every occurrence of A). This method works quite well as long as we are sure that the animal's experience in phase 1 has not changed it in some way so that its behavior in phase 2 is different from what it would have been if we had run phase 2 first. For Premack, such a situation was not usually a problem. But when it is, an alternative method is available that requires us to use two animals: One animal is called the *leader,* the other the *follower.* The leader and the follower are housed in two separate boxes, both controlled by the same computer. The leader works under the contingency: To get access to A, it must engage in B. The follower cannot control access to A; but it gets access to A whenever the leader gets access to A. Thus, the follower gets exactly the same temporal distribution of A as the leader, but it gets it independently of any behavior.

We can now compare the level of behavior B for the leader and the follower. If both are equal, we conclude that any elevation in B relative to paired-baseline levels is simply a restriction effect. But if the leader shows a higher level of B than the follower does, we conclude that we have a real reinforcing effect, termed a *contingent effect*—which is the main topic of this chapter.

Both procedures described are known as *yoked-control procedures:* The first is *within-animal,* the second *between-animals.* Both have their limitations. The within-animal method fails if our effects are not completely reversible, that is, if the effect of either treatment depends on prior experience. The between-animals method fails if (as Premack in fact found) our two animals are not identical (e.g., if one animal has a higher free level of A than the other). We can mitigate this between-animals problem somewhat by looking at average data from several leader–follower pairs, although such a solution is not always a good idea. We must rely on our knowledge of the animals and the activities we are studying to judge which is more appropriate in any specific instance.

Premack's early experiments lacked the necessary controls to rule out restriction effects. Nevertheless, later work has borne out his principle that a more probable activity generally reinforces a less probable one on which it is contingent and that this increase is greater than that expected merely from restriction.

Premack thought of reinforcement as being particularly associated with activities not with events: for example, with eating rather than the availability of food or with running rather than the availability of a running wheel. But, the important aspect is the preferred levels of events, which may be activities but can also be the presentation of stimuli. For example, let's consider the case of *punishment:* Receiving electric shock is not an activity. Nevertheless, animals clearly have a preferred rate for such an event, which is zero. With this sole quantitative difference, electric shock can be treated as the reverse of reinforcement. It requires an animal to engage in a low-probability act or to experience an event that is generally avoided to gain access to a higher-probability act that has a reinforcing effect on the low-probability act but has a punishing effect on the high-probability act. Reinforcement and punishment are thus two sides of the same contingent coin; the only difference is a practical one. Commonly used punishments like shock are usually events that can be delivered to the animal without its cooperation. However, this difference is not an essential one between reinforcement and punishment. Animals can be punished by forcing them to engage in more of a low-probability activity than they would like (just like the schoolchild required to write a sentence 100 times), and they can be positively reinforced by hypothalamic brain stimulation that requires as little cooperation as electric shock does.

Notice that the imposition of a contingency allows the animal a range of possible options. In Figure 11.2, the free levels of two mutually exclusive, but not exhaustive, activities are indicated by the free-behavior point (B_0). A ratio contingency—access to Y depends on performance of X—is indicated by the line through the origin. If it is much more important to the animal to regulate the rate of Y than the rate of X, then we may expect X to increase to the level indicated by B_2, which allows Y to continue to occur at its baseline rate. But if regulation of X is much more important than regulation of Y, X will remain at its baseline rate, forcing a large drop in the rate of Y. In practice, either extreme result is rare, and animals usually settle for a compromise solution, such as B_3, at which point activity X occurs above its preferred level and activity Y below its preferred level. We discuss some explanations for this kind of compromise shortly.

In addition to the explicit assumptions we have already discussed, Premack's hypothesis contains an important implicit assumption: that reinforcing

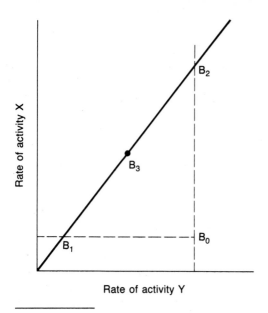

FIGURE 11.2   Potential adaptations to a ratio-schedule constraint.

effects depend only on *molar measures* such as the total proportion of time devoted to an activity. He was not at all concerned with molecular properties such
as the pattern in time of specific activities or contiguity relations between the
operant and contingent responses. We have already seen in earlier chapters that
contiguity relations are often quite important. A few experiments have also
shown that the temporal pattern of an activity, not just its average frequency, can
be important. Thus, we may suspect that Premack's theory is at least incomplete.
Nevertheless, his emphasis on molar analysis has proven to be a useful approach
that has led to several advances in our understanding of behavioral regulation
and the functional properties of reinforcement schedules. We take up these topics and the molecular analysis of behavioral allocation and choice in later sections of this chapter. But first, we need to say something about the dynamic processes that underlie behavioral allocation.

Dynamics of Behavioral Allocation

Over a 30-min period, animals like rats or pigeons typically show a varied pattern
of activity. A rat, at the appropriate time in its daily cycle, may groom itself, run
in a running wheel, drink, and eat. What causes the transition from one behavior
to the next? What determines the distribution of activities over this time, that is,
the proportions of time spent in running, eating, and so on? We can get an idea of
these possibilities by artificially preventing the animal from performing one activity, such as eating. We can expect two kinds of effects:

1.   Some change in the distribution of the remaining activities
2.   A compensating change when the blocked activity is restored

If access to one activity is blocked, then the time devoted to at least one other activity must increase. The process by which a mix of activities was generated in the reinforcement model discussed at the end of Chapter 8 illustrates the simplest rule for behavior reallocation. In that model, two or more activities compete for expression. The "strength" of each activity depends on a variable (V) that varies in random fashion; the activity with the highest V value is the one to occur. When there are three activities whose strengths vary according to the same random process, then each will obviously occur for about one-third the time. Suppose we block one activity. The situation is then reduced to one with two activities, whose strengths vary randomly. Clearly these activities will now split the time equally, which suggests a general rule for behavioral reallocation: The relative proportions of time taken up by the activities remaining after one or more has been blocked will remain constant. This rule is variously termed *Luce's principle* (Luce, 1959, 1977), the *independence of irrelevant alternatives*, or the *axiom of choice*. For example, suppose we have three activities A, B, and C that take up the following percentages of the total time—A: 50 percent, B: 25 percent, C: 25 percent. If we block C, Luce's rule implies that A will increase to 67 percent and B to 33 percent.

Experimental results are sometimes in agreement with Luce's principle, but there are some striking exceptions. For example, suppose that the blocked activity is eating and one of the remaining activities is drinking. If our subjects are rats, eating and drinking are loosely linked under free conditions—rats typically drink before and after meals—so that omission of eating usually reduces rather than increases the level of drinking, a clear violation of the principle. Luce's principle also assumes a closed set of activities; for example, it cannot account for the appearance of a novel activity. Yet without the possibility of novel activities occurring, little operant learning could ever take place.

What happens when the blocked activity is restored? Our simple model says that the previous distribution of activities will be immediately reestablished; there will be no aftereffect of the period of deprivation. Once again, experimental results vary. For example, if the blocked activity is eating, then after a period of deprivation, the animal will eat a lot more than normal: The first meal after deprivation will be quite long (Le Magnen, 1985). This result is typical: A period of deprivation is almost always followed by a compensatory increase when the blocked acitivity is restored (see Mook, 1987, for an excellent review of recent research on such motivational systems).

This result may remind you of something we have already discussed: Konrad Lorenz's hydraulic model (Box 6.1). We concluded from that discussion that the tendency to engage in any motivated activity is not constant but increases so long as it is *not* occurring (and decreases when the activity occurs). If we are to stick with our general approach in terms of competing V values, then a compensatory increase implies that the V value for an activity must increase during a period of deprivation. It seems clear that although our dynamic model may be adequate as a reinforcement model, it will not do as a model for behavior allocation.

But now, we can begin to see the outlines of a dynamic basis for behavioral allocation and regulation: If activities that are *not* occurring increase in strength (a deprivation effect), and if activities that *are* occurring decrease in strength (a satiation effect), we have a potentially self-regulating or homeostatic system. The system is regulatory because it changes in such a way as to oppose the effects of any imposed change. If an activity cannot occur, its strength (i.e., the tendency for it to occur) increases; if it is forced to occur, its strength decreases. The result in either case is to diminish the effect of the imposed change. Although the details remain obscure, it is clear that a dynamic satiation–deprivation process underlies behavioral regulation.

But what of reinforcement? What does such a process say about the effects of making one activity contingent on the performance of another? The simple answer is that without additional assumptions, it says nothing. A blocked activity generally takes priority once the block is removed, and it then occurs for an extended period of time. But the satiation–deprivation idea has no other implications for the effect of a contingent relation. In particular, it provides no mechanism for strengthening the operant response. It is easy to suggest additional processes that have the desired effect. For example, deprivation causes the V value of the blocked activity to rise to an unusually high level. Suppose that gaining access to an activity with a large V value elevates all V values. If the elevation takes the form of amplification, we are back to the strengthening process discussed in Chapter 8. Although this assumption seems to work, we don't know enough to rule out a number of other possibilities. The dynamical basis for the Premack principle is an area that needs more theoretical and experimental work.

Behavioral Regulation: The Molar Analysis of Behavioral Allocation

Premack only studied schedules in which an amount of time devoted to the operant response gave the animal access to an equal amount of the contingent response (i.e., an FR 1 schedule). But, our graphical method of analysis allows us to make predictions about what should happen with other schedules. Look again at Figure 11.2. Suppose responses X and Y were to be related by a ratio schedule chosen so that its feedback function goes through point B_0. For example, suppose that under paired-baseline conditions the animal spends 40 percent of its time engaging in Y and 10 percent in X. This ratio implies that access to Y should be reinforcing for X, because Y is the higher-probability activity. But if we require 1 sec of X for access not to 1 sec of Y but to 4 sec of Y, will there be a contingent increase in X? Probably not, because by continuing to engage in X at the paired-baseline level (i.e., 10 percent), the animal continues to receive as much access to Y as it needs to maintain the paired-baseline level (i.e., 40 percent).

What about the converse possibility? Suppose we require the animal to engage in response Y (high probability) for access to response X (low probability) but make the terms of the exchange so unfavorable that the animal can only maintain X by increasing the level of Y? For example, we require 5 units of Y for access to 1 of X. Even though X is of a lower probability than Y (thus should not be able to reinforce Y, according to Premack), our analysis suggests that Y should in fact be reinforced under these conditions, because the paired-baseline ratio of the two is $4:1$, which is less than the $5:1$ ratio imposed by our schedule. Experiments have shown that under these conditions the level of Y usually increases. These results led William Timberlake and James Allison (1974) to propose a generalized version of the Premack principle that they called *response deprivation*. Their version of the theory proposed that a contingency between one activity and another should change the level of the operant response if the animal cannot attain its paired-baseline levels without changing the level of the operant response. In terms of Figure 11.2, response deprivation amounts to the assertion that the operant response will increase if the schedule constraint (feedback function) lies above the free-behavior point and will decrease if the schedule constraint lies below the free-behavior point.

Response deprivation is a regulatory hypothesis, since the core idea is that animals act so as to maintain a certain distribution of activities: If the imposition of a contingency means that any activity is pushed below the animal's preferred (paired-baseline) level, other activities will be reallocated to as to reduce the discrepancy. For example, if we measure an animal's amount of drinking and bar-pressing during a baseline session, we are likely to find that it drinks at a specific rate and bar-presses very little. If we make drinking at the baseline rate contingent on bar-pressing above the baseline rate, bar-pressing is likely to increase. But how much will it increase? What will be the effect on other activities such as wheel-running and sleeping? Response deprivation is only qualitative: It predicts when there will be a change and what its direction will be, but it does not say *how much* change there will be. We turn now to regulatory theories that attempt to answer these questions.

BEHAVIORAL CONSERVATION   Behavioral conservation is a model of behavioral regulation proposed by Allison (1980). *Conservation theory* assumes that animals attempt to conserve some property of the set of activities. Allison has tentatively proposed energy expenditure as the conserved dimension (although we also discuss an alternative suggestion). If energy is conserved, then the energy expended on all activities in the paired-baseline session should be the same as the energy expended when access to water is contingent on bar-pressing. The conservation model is formalized by the following equation:

$$kND + NP = kO_d + O_p \tag{11.1}$$

where O_d and O_p represent the amounts of drinking and lever-pressing that occur during the paired-baseline session, and D and P are the amounts "traded" during each cycle of the contingency session (e.g., 5 sec of drinking for 10 sec of lever-pressing), and N is the number of cycles. Notice that the quantity ND is simply the total amount of D in the contingency session, and NP is the total amount of P. Notice also that the right-hand side of the equation is constant, since k is constant and so are the baseline levels of the two activities. Thus, Equation 11.1 says that the total amounts of D and P during the contingency session are equal to the total amounts during the paired baseline, with D given a weight of k relative to P in both cases. Constant k represents how energetic D is relative to P. For example, suppose each instance of D (lick) takes one-half the energy required for each instance of P (lever-press); then conservation says that $2 \times$ number of licks + number of lever-presses will be constant over any fixed time period.

This notation is cumbersome. It is easier to see what is going on if we deal in total amounts of activity and ignore the number of cycles (N), which is irrelevant to the theory. With this simplification, Equation 11.1 reduces to $ky + x =$ constant, where y is the total amount of P (i.e., NP in the contingency session, O_p in the baseline session) and x is the total amount of D (i.e., ND in the contingency session and O_d in the baseline session). We can therefore rewrite the conservation model as a linear relation between the total amount of drinking (x) and lever-pressing (y):

$$y = K - \frac{x}{k} \tag{11.2}$$

where K is a constant proportional to session length and k is a constant that represents the relative importance of x and y. Equation 11.2 says that the amount of the operant response (Y) is related to the amount of the contingent response (X) by straight line with negative slope $-1/k$.

Numerous experimental results appear to support this linear relation. An example is shown in Figure 11.3. In this experiment, rats were exposed to either VI 7 sec or VI 14 sec schedules in which one lever-press produced access to either 25 or 50 licks of water. As you can see, no matter how much water the animals received for each effective lever-press, the total number of lever-presses was related to the total number of licks by the same straight line of negative slope. The fit of the data looks excellent, yet conservation theory is not generally accepted as a valid model for reinforcement. What might be wrong?

An obvious problem is that conservation theory says nothing about the schedule that relates the two behaviors, X and Y. It says that the relation between x (the rate of X) and y is linear, no matter what the schedule relating the two. Yet, as we will see in a moment, numerous experimental results show that the schedule makes a great deal of difference to the relation between the behaviors. For example, animals always respond faster on ratio schedules than on interval schedules, even if both schedules yield the same rate of reinforcement. If in a more elaborate experiment, we measure the rate of lever-pressing under a range of ratio schedules and plot it against the rate of food delivery obtained on each schedule, we usually get a different function than if we plot lever-pressing against food delivery over a range of variable-interval schedules. Conservation theory must predict the same relation for both; yet many data, such as those in Figure 11.3, seem to support conservation and show the same function for interval and ratio schedules. How can this contradiction be resolved?

The conditions under which the data in Figure 11.3 were gathered provide a clue to the answer. The variable-interval schedules Allison used to collect these data were quite short—7 sec–15 sec—compared to typical VI values, which are usually in the range of minutes; in addition reinforcement—25 licks or 50 licks—was rather long. Rats were undoubtedly pressing their levers at a high

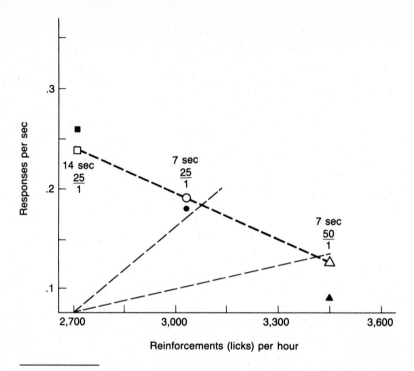

FIGURE 11.3   A test of the conservation model. The closed symbols represent the observed rates of each activity and the open symbols represent the predicted rates. The triangle represents the performance observed under a 7-second variable-interval schedule that allowed 50 licks per lever press (from J. Allison, 1980).

rate on such rich schedules, and they perhaps had little time for anything except drinking and lever-pressing. But if animals were in effect engaging in two mutually exclusive and exhaustive activities, then the situation is a familiar one. The case is simply the one described in Figure 11.1, in which the relation between the two behaviors is completely determined by the time constraint. When the time constraint is dominant, then the schedule indeed makes no difference—and X and Y are related by a straight line with negative slope, just as conservation theory implies.

We can conclude that conservation theory probably amounts to a time constraint: Something is conserved, but it may be nothing more than the total time available. The constant k then represents the relative durations of the two activities. For example, if a lick (X) takes only one-half the time of a lever-press (Y), the conservation relation must be $2x + y =$ constant, where x and y are the rates (number per minute) of the two activities. Therefore, the conservation principle tells us nothing about the nature of reinforcement but only something about the limitations on our methods for studying it.

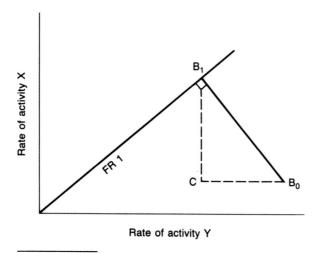

Rate of activity Y

FIGURE 11.4   Relations between the schedule constraint (line through the origin) and the distribution of activities under paired-baseline conditions (B_0). In most of the discussion, we assume that the schedule is *reciprocal* (e.g., on FR 1, one unit of Y is required for access to one unit of X, which must be taken up before access to Y is possible again). On standard reinforcement schedules, the constraint is usually only one-way: There is a requirement to engage in activity X (e.g., lever-pressing) for access to activity Y (eating), but X is always available. Since Y is always highly preferred, the reciprocal contingency is assumed to be unnecessary.

Optimal Policy on Ratio and Interval Schedules

We turn now to more sophisticated regulatory models that can deal with the different molar patterns generated by different reinforcement schedules. Let's look again at Figure 11.2. Recall that if a ratio contingency is imposed that forces behavior away from the free-behavior point (B_0), animals typically settle for the sort of compromise represented by B_3. The contingent response (Y) decreases somewhat (but not as much as if X had remained at its paired-baseline level, i.e., not to B_1), and the operant response (X) increases (but not as much as necessary to maintain the level of Y at its paired-baseline level, i.e., not to B_2). John Staddon (1976) was one of the first to diagram reinforcement schedules in this fashion, and the diagram immediately suggested a simple hypothesis. The hypothesis: Suppose that the animals just get *as close as possible* to the free-behavior point, which all theories acknowledge as the animal's preferred state (economists call points like this *bliss points*). This prediction is illustrated in Figure 11.4: It amounts to dropping a perpendicular from B_0 to B_1 on the straight-line, ratio-schedule feedback function. B_1 corresponds to the compromise position B_3 in Figure 11.2. The *minimum-distance* (*MD*) *prediction* (Staddon, 1979) always falls somewhere in between the two extreme possibilities.

Let's test the prediction by seeing if an FR 1 produces the predicted increase in response X.

The first predictions are discouraging. If response X is key-pecking and response Y is eating, by a pigeon at 80 percent of its normal weight, the predicted increase in the level of key-pecking is much too small. But, the reasons are not far to seek. The first problem is one of units. In conventional operant-conditioning experiments, key-pecking is measured as pecks per unit of time and reinforcement rate is measured as food deliveries per unit of time, but there is nothing that makes these two equivalent. A peck does not take up as much time as a food reinforcement (which is typically 3 or 4 sec access to a grain hopper). At the very least, the predicted number of pecks must be increased to reflect the shorter duration. But even with this correction in the vertical scale, the predicted increase in pecking falls far short of what is observed. For example, on an FR 2 schedule, a hungry pigeon may peck almost twice as fast as on an FR 1 schedule, yet the uncorrected MD model shows the pigeon responding at about the same rate. Evidently, something is still missing.

The Premack principle equates the reinforcing value of an activity with its probability—how much time the animal spends in the activity. Yet a little reflection suggests that this equation cannot be the whole story. The cartoon cat Garfield spends most of his time resting, but we know that food is what he finds reinforcing. Under many conditions, probability is correlated with reinforcing strength, but anyone can think of counter examples (e.g., sexual activity, which is relatively infrequent yet highly reinforcing). The important difference between rest and eating has to do not with the free levels of each but with the degree to which those levels are regulated. Garfield can tolerate interruptions of his rest a great deal better than curtailment of his food supply—and humans are probably the same. How can we incorporate this property into the MD model?

Look at the triangle B_1B_0C in Figure 11.4. It makes visible the separate deviations of behaviors X and Y from their free levels forced by the FR schedule: Distance CB_0 is the deviation in the level of Y (eating), distance CB_1 is the deviation in the level of X (key-pecking). With an FR 1 schedule, these deviations are equal. Which deviation is more upsetting to our hungry pigeon? Clearly CB_0, the shortfall in eating rate, is likely to be a great deal more important than CB_1, the surplus of key-pecking. It is relatively easy to modify the MD model to take care of the different *costs of deviation* (*CoD*) in the levels of the two behaviors. To see how this modification is made, we must explain two new concepts: the concept of cost and the concept of an objective function.

COST AND OBJECTIVE FUNCTIONS   The conservation model assumes that there is some property of the set of activities that is conserved (maintained constant) in any closed situation. It turns out that the quantity conserved is probably the total time taken up, but it might just as well be the total energy expended or something even more complicated. The MD model takes an important step beyond this assumption and assumes that some quantity associated with the set of activities is *minimized*. This minimization assumption represents a great advance, because now the properties of the reinforcement schedule enter in as constraints on the minimization—so that minimization (optimality) models do indeed make different predictions about performance on different reinforcement schedules.

We have already encountered the idea of minimization in Chapter 9, in our discussion of reward-rate maximization (which is equivalent to interfood time minimization). In that chapter, we calculated the optimal policy for the animal to minimize the time between food deliveries on several concurrent-chain schedules. But the quantity to be minimized, which is known as the *cost function* or *currency*, doesn't need to be interfood interval. There are other, better possibilities.

Let's look at the general method for conducting such an *optimality analysis*. The method involves four steps:

1. First, decide on what property (or properties) of behavior is free to vary—which is termed the *dependent variable*. In the present case, the dependent variable is rate of key-pecking.

2. Then decide what is to be minimized (or maximized). This quantity is termed the *cost function* (or *value function*). The choice of cost function is critical and also difficult, because there are always many possibilities. We begin with the simplest possibility, namely interfood interval, and then look at the effect of modifying it.

3. Then identify the constraints in the situation. For the present case, there are two: time (the time taken by all mutually exclusive and exhaustive activities must add up to the session length) and the fixed-ratio schedule (which constrains the relation between peck rate and food rate). We ignore the time constraint in this elementary discussion because its effects are usually minimal, and we focus on the reinforcement schedule.

4. Then derive a quantitative expression for the total cost as a function of the level of the dependent variable, subject to the constraints. This procedure sounds complicated, but in the present case, it simply means deriving an expression for the average interfood interval (cost) as a function of peck rate (dependent variable) when food rate depends on peck rate according to a fixed-ratio schedule (constraint). This expression, which relates the behavior to the total costs, subject to the operative constraints, is termed the *objective function*, because it defines the quantity that must be minimized.

On an FR schedule, the time interval between food deliveries, which we call $I(x)$ (to indicate that it is a function of x), depends on response rate (x) according to the following relation:

$$I(x) = \frac{M}{x} \tag{11.3}$$

where M is the number of responses in the ratio. That is, if the animal responds 10 times a minute and receives food on an FR 5 schedule, it will receive food at

30-sec intervals. Equation 11.3 is the objective function for interfood-interval minimization on FR schedules.

It doesn't take any knowledge of calculus to see that to minimize the objective function, x should be as large as possible: The animal should respond as fast as it can. This conclusion also makes common sense: If receiving food as fast as possible is what is important, then on a ratio schedule, you must respond as fast as possible. This conclusion is not very helpful, because it gives the same answer for any ratio value: No matter what the value of M, the optimal policy is to perform the activities as fast as possible. But, we know that animals perform at different rates on different ratio schedules. So what's wrong with our analysis?

One answer may be that we have ignored the time constraint, but since that affects every activity, it doesn't actually alter anything. What about the cost function? A possibility is that we have neglected the cost of key-pecking: Food delay may be costly, but surely key-pecking, especially at the high rate characteristic of ratio schedules (at least we know this prediction is correct) is also costly. So, let's add the assumption that pecking incurs a cost proportional to its rate, which means we must add a term Qx to the objective function, where Q represents the cost of each peck per unit time and x is peck rate. Our cost function now has two components: time (interfood interval) and response, scaled in time–cost units (Q). Thus, the new delay-plus-response-cost objective function, $C(x)$, is as follows:

$$C(x) = \frac{M}{x} + Qx \qquad\qquad (11.4)$$

We call this model the *response–cost (RC) model.* Now we can easily find the value of x for which $C(x)$ is a minimum. Calculus tells you to take the first derivative of $C(x)$ with respect to x, set it equal to zero, and solve for x. But, everyone can see the same result graphically in Figure 11.5, which shows Equation 11.4 plotted for three values of the ratio value ($M = 2, 4, 8$). Notice two things about these curves:

1. The minimum cost occurs at a finite response rate. When each response is costly it doesn't pay to perform as fast as possible all the time.

2. The response rate that minimizes cost increases with ratio value. (The reason: $C(x)$ is made up of two components—M/x, which declines as x increases, and Qx, which increases with x. The point at which the influence of the Qx component becomes dominant shifts to the right as M increases.)

Both these features are encouraging. The response rate on ratio schedules is high, but usually less than "as fast as possible." As well, empirical results from rats, pigeons, and several other species all show that over most of the typical range of ratio values, the response rate does indeed increase with ratio value. (If you have some mathematical background you might want to try to derive the actual equation that relates M and x; it's not too difficult, and the answer is provided in the legend to Figure 11.6.)

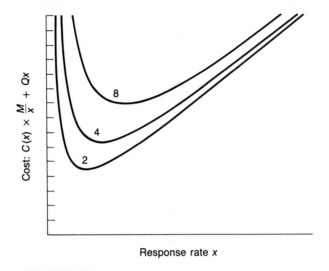

FIGURE 11.5   The effect of response rate on cost, where cost = interfood interval + response rate, weighted by a factor Q: $C(x) = M/x + Qx$, where M is the ratio value. The three curves are for ratio values of 2, 4, and 8. $Q = 0.5$.

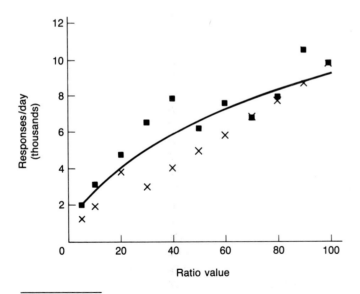

FIGURE 11.6   Daily number of lever-presses on an ascending series of ratio schedules of water reinforcement for a group of guinea pigs. Filled squares: Group that received 10-sec access to water as reinforcement; x's: Group that received 20-sec access (replotted from Hirsch & Collier, 1974, Figure 1). The heavy curved line is the optimal policy predicted from a response–cost model: $x = \sqrt{M/Q}$, where M is the ratio value and Q is the cost of each response.

Some typical experimental results with ratio schedules are shown in Figure 11.6. The data are from a group of guinea pigs each pressing a lever for water reinforcement. The animals had access to the lever all day and obtained all their water ration via the schedule. The figure shows the number of responses per day plotted against the ratio value. As you can see, the response rate increases with the ratio value. The heavy curved line is the prediction of the response–cost (RC) optimality model. It fits the general form of the data quite well, even though it is not, in fact, a very good model. As we saw with conservation theory, the fact that a model can generate a simple curve that fits data well is a rather weak kind of support for the model. It is much more important that a model provide an accurate picture of a pattern of experimental results. The response–cost model does much better than conservation theory in this respect, but it does not do quite as well as the minimum-distance model or more elaborate economic models.

Now that you have a good understanding of the idea of an objective function, we can return to the problems of the minimum-distance model. Look again at Figure 11.4, and recall the basic assumption that the animal minimizes the deviation B_0B_1 (i.e., the distance between B_0 and B_1). Remember from geometry that the shortest distance between two points is a straight line, which is determined by the minimum-distance equation. Thus, B_0B_1 is simply the square root of the sum of the squares of the two other sides of the triangle, CB_0 and CB_1, that is, $(x_1 - x_0)^2 + (y_1 - y_0)^2$, where x_1 and y_1 are the coordinates of B_1 and x_0 and y_0 are the coordinates of B_0. If we minimize the square root of something, we also minimize the thing itself; thus the objective function for the simple, minimum-distance model is the following:

$$C(x) = (x_0 - x_1)^2 + (y_0 - y_1)^2$$

If we add a parameter to reflect the greater importance of regulating activity Y (say, if Y is eating and X is key-pecking), then we arrive at a formula:

$$C(x) = (x_0 - x_1)^2 + c(y_0 - y_1)^2 \tag{11.5}$$

which is the objective function for the MD model. Parameter c is the CoD for activity Y. Notice that there are three features about the MD objective function that are different from the simple RC model. First, it is a two-parameter model, since each activity is characterized by two parameters: its paired-baseline level (e.g., y_0) and its CoD (e.g., c). The RC model has only one parameter (Q), which represents the relative importance of the response cost and the reward delay. Second, it is based on the rates of activities rather than on their delays. And third, it is nonlinear in the sense that it assumes that the cost of a given deviation increases as the square of the deviation, so that doubling the deviation increases the cost by a factor of four. The latter makes good intuitive sense. A drop in feeding rate of 10 gm/hour is clearly more costly to the inhabitant of a prison camp, starving on a subsistence diet, than to a well-fed suburbanite. The further the feeding rate from the bliss point, the more costly additional deviations become. This idea of positively accelerated cost (which is equivalent to negatively accelerated value) has interesting implications for choice behavior, as we will see in the next section.

The objective function with the CoD parameter solves the problems with the MD model we identified earlier. If the CoD parameter (c) is much larger than unity, an MD animal will freely increase the rate at which it makes low-CoD response X so as to maintain approximately constant the level of high-CoD response Y. If c is great enough, an MD animal will almost double its response rate when we increase the FR value from 1 to 2, for example, thus maintaining an almost constant reinforcement rate. With these amendments, the MD model makes tolerable predictions of the empirical relations between response and reinforcement rates on variable-interval, variable-ratio, and many other reinforcement schedules. In most cases, the predicted relation is an inverted-U: Response rate is low at very low and very high reinforcement rates and is quite high at intermediate rates.

The MD model is not simple algebraically, nor does it make better predictions than some other optimality and economic models. But, it is important historically as one of the first attempts to show how well-known patterns of behavior on reinforcement schedules may be explained by an optimality analysis. It also brings out an important difference between strong reinforcers (e.g., food for a hungry pigeon) and weak reinforcers (e.g., the opportunity to play with a plunger for a Cebus monkey: feeding is a highly regulated activity; play is not). In Premack's original view, everything of importance about an activity is contained in its free, paired-baseline level: point B_0 in Figure 11.4 and coordinates x_0 and y_0 in Equation 11.5 (the bliss point). The MD model shows that activities differ in more than one way: in their free levels, as Premack pointed out, but also in the degree to which they are regulated, which is indicated by a parameter that represents the different costs of deviation from the bliss point. The higher the CoD parameter, the better an activity will be regulated—the harder the animal will work to maintain it at its free level. Strong reinforcers like food may or may not have high operant levels; they certainly have high costs of deviation. Weak reinforcers, like the opportunity to run in a wheel, may or may not have low operant levels; they will certainly have low CoD parameters.

The details of the MD model may now be largely of historical interest. Two things survive:

1. the basic notion that an adequate molar theory of behavioral regulation requires at least two parameters for each activity
2. the notion that a comprehensive optimality model must assume a nonlinear cost function

We are now in a position to see in detail how an optimality analysis can be used to make predictions about how animals should behave on different reinforcement schedules. But because the MD model is algebraically difficult, we use our simple response–cost model—which is a bit less accurate than the MD model, but not as different as it might appear—to make our points. You have already seen how to derive the prediction that on ratio schedules the response rate should be directly related to the ratio value (Figure 11.6).

FIGURE 11.7   Components of the average interfood interval on variable-interval schedules.

MOLAR OPTIMAL POLICY ON VARIABLE-INTERVAL SCHEDULES.   Let's tackle a more difficult case: variable-interval schedules. To do so, we follow the four steps described for conducting an optimality analysis. Luckily, everything is the same as for ratio schedules, except the schedule constraint. How does interfood interval depend on response rate on VI schedules? We have already done the work when we derived the molar feedback function of VI schedules (Equation 4.4). We repeat it here with the aid of Figure 11.7, which shows that on a VI schedule the average interfood interval is the sum of two delays: the average delay set by the VI timer (I), plus the average delay between setup and the reinforced response (which is determined by the animal's average response rate, x). If the response rate is random in time, this average delay is equal to one half of the reciprocal of the average response rate. Summing these two delays, we arrive at the following expression for the average interfood interval:

$$I(x) = I + \frac{1}{x} \tag{11.6}$$

To find the optimal policy, we can now plug this expression into Equation 11.4 in place of M/x, the expression for interfood interval on ratio schedules. The result:

$$C(x) = I + \frac{1}{x} + Qx \tag{11.7}$$

We can then go through the same graphical analysis as we did before and arrive at a simple conclusion. To minimize the cost function, our animal should respond at a constant rate for all VI schedules: $x = \sqrt{(1/Q)}$ (as opposed to $\sqrt{(M/Q)}$ for the ratio schedule). How do the data from VI and FR schedules compare with these predictions?

We have already seen the relevant data for pigeons, key-pecking for food reinforcement on VI schedules, (Figure 9.18): The rate of key-pecking is a negatively accelerated function of obtained reinforcement rate. But the function is indeed approximately constant over quite a wide range as the RC model implies it should be. The function in Figure 9.18 is a reliable finding for both rats and pigeons on VI schedules. (However, it does depend on exactly how the response rate is measured. This function holds at very high reinforcement rates only if the time spent eating is excluded from the time denominator.) The data from ratio schedules are somewhat more variable, depending on exactly how they are obtained, whether in a so-called *closed economy*—in which the animal is able to respond throughout the day and must get all its food via the schedules—or in an *open economy*—with short, daily experimental sessions and supplemental feed-

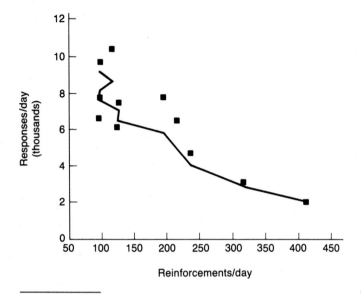

FIGURE 11.8   Data from Figure 11.6 replotted as response rate versus rate of reinforcement obtained for the 10-sec access condition. The solid line is the optimal policy according to the response–cost model, as before.

ing after the session to make up any nutritional shortfall (Hursh, 1984). Figure 11.6 is typical of closed-economy data, which invariably show that response rate is directly related to ratio value and, usually, inversely related to the rate of reinforcement actually obtained. The data from Figure 11.6 are regraphed as Figure 11.8 with response rate plotted versus obtained food rate. Data from open-economy experiments are often of this form, but sometimes they also turn down at low reinforcement rates (corresponding to high ratio values: cf. Timberlake & Peden, 1987). As you can see in Figures 11.6 and 11.8, the RC prediction is quite good.

Let's compare directly the predictions of the RC model for VI and FR (or VR) schedules. On FR schedules, the response rate is determined according to the relation $x = \sqrt{(M/Q)}$, where M is ratio value and Q is response cost. The relation for VI is similar: $x = \sqrt{(1/Q)}$. In other words, the RC model says that the animal should treat a VI schedule just like an FR 1 schedule. Notice what these two equations predict about the relative response rates on VI and VR schedules: For any ratio value greater than 1, the response rate should always be higher on the ratio. This fact is one of the oldest and most reliable findings about ratio and interval schedules. Several careful comparisons have been made (e.g., Catania, Matthews, Silverman, & Yohalem, 1977; Lea & Tarpy, 1982). For example, in the yoked-control study conducted by Catania and his associates, the key-peck rates of a leader and a follower pigeon were compared. The leader produced food reinforcement according to a variable-ratio schedule. Reinforcement for the leader constituted schedule "setup" for the follower, who collected the reinforcement with the next peck. Thus, the leader received food on a VR schedule, the follower on a VI schedule that was approximately matched to the VR both for temporal pattern of food deliveries and the average rate. Catania found that the VR leader pigeons always developed faster key-peck rates than their VI followers. Almost any optimality model that includes the time between reinforcements in its cost function will predict this result.

Thus, both the MD and RC optimality models predict the most obvious difference between interval and ratio schedules: the fact that animals always respond faster on ratio schedules. They do so because the different feedback functions enter into the objective functions as different constraints. We will be more explicit about how these different constraints give rise to different predictions when we discuss marginal utility in the next section of the chapter. Both optimality models also do a reasonable job of predicting other molar properties, such as the way response rate increases with ratio value and the approximate constancy of response rate on variable-interval schedules. However, you may have noticed that there are some inconsistencies in the data: Animals in so-called open economies behave rather differently than animals in closed economies, for example. We return to these issues later when we discuss optimality in the context of behavioral economics.

Behavioral Allocation: Conclusion

What have we learned from this account of behavioral allocation? The first step was taken by Premack, who took to heart Edward Thorndike's conclusion that reinforcement must be defined in terms of the organism's own behavior (Chapter 4). Premack saw that at the instant an organism initiates an act, that act is by definition the most preferred. If reinforcement is defined by preference (as Thorndike believed), then this act at that moment must be the most reinforcing activity in the organism's repertoire. How might this insight be used to redefine the concept of reinforcement? We can reconstruct Premack's reasoning as follows: At the instant of choice, the act that occurs is the most probable act. Probability cannot be measured instant by instant, but we can get an idea of what is most probable by looking at the proportion of time taken up by different activities. Perhaps the most frequent act is also the most preferred, hence the most reinforcing? And so it proved, in the situations Premack and his successors chose to study.

But now that the links in this chain of argument are exposed, you can probably see its weaknesses. The argument blurs the distinction between molecular (the instant of choice) and molar (the frequency of an activity). It also blurs the distinction between behavioral dynamics and what we might call behavioral *statics*. The momentary-probability definition of reinforcement is about dynamics and the molecular structure of behavior. The activity-frequency definition is about static, molar properties of behavior. Once we agree to look at averages, that is, at molar behavior, we at once encounter the problem of the averaging *window,* the time period over which we are to count activities. The window size makes a great deal of difference. Premack's intuition about the reinforcing effect of the highest-probability act implicitly assumed a time window short enough to encompass only the instant of choice. But to test his theory, Premack had to average his results over much longer time intervals. The fact that his predictions were generally confirmed is fortunate and implies that preferences may change relatively slowly. But as we have seen, to extend his theory to "strong" reinforcers like food and water requires additional assumptions.

The real meaning of the molar-molecular distinction cannot be properly clarified until we have a full, dynamic understanding of behavioral allocation. But historically, the weak points in Premack's original position were shored up by adding assumptions to the molar theory. The response-deprivation hypothesis allowed for schedules other than FR 1, and the minimum-distance model added a parameter (CoD) that took into account differences between overall frequency and momentary priority. MD models allow for activities that are frequent, but not urgent, and the converse; whereas for the Premack principle and response deprivation, frequency and urgency are one and the same. Premack set the study of behavioral allocation on a molar path. The MD analysis and the work of Howard Rachlin and his associates (Rachlin, 1978; Rachlin, Battalio, Kagel, & Green, 1981) on economic models showed the possibilities of molar optimality analysis as a way of understanding the varied effects of different reinforcement schedules on behavior.

We have taken you through a simple optimality analysis of interval and ratio schedules, and although the fit to data is not exact in any case, the analysis shows the variety of predictions derivable from a simple model and their approximate correctness. Simple optimality analyses like this one are the pigeon *equivalent* of the economists' *rational man:* no real man, woman, or pigeon behaves in this fashion, but the model provides a rough sketch of reality that is close enough to be useful. When a mechanistic model is developed, you may be sure that it will approximate the predictions of the optimality model under many conditions—just as our ideal pigeon in Chapter 9 frequently approximated the optimal policy.

There are still a number of situations for which we have no adequate mechanistic account (e.g., choice between rewards of different types or occurring in variable amounts). These are the province of behavioral economics, to which we now turn.

BEHAVIORAL ECONOMICS

One question at the core of economics is: What is the source of value? For example, why is it that diamond jewelry, which is of little practical use, is highly valued, whereas bread, without which humans cannot live, is priced inexpensively? One theory has to do with what we call the *inputs* necessary to produce a commodity, labor and time: Bread is cheap because it is easy to produce; diamonds are dear because they are hard to find. But then, four-leaf clovers are hard to find, and they have no market price at all. Scottish scholar Adam Smith, the first modern economist, in his great work *An inquiry into the nature and causes of the wealth of nations* (1776), solved this problem. We cannot know anything about value, he argued, we can only know about price. (Oscar Wilde once remarked that a cynic is a man who knows the price of everything and the value of nothing; perhaps his cynic was a Smithian economist.) About price, Smith came to the same conclusion that we have come to about reinforcement: In the end, it is defined by people's behavior. (We will soon come to the same conclusion about value.) He reasoned as follows:

> The market price of every particular commodity is regulated by the proportion between the quantity which is actually brought to market, and the demand of those who are willing to pay the . . . price. . . . When the quantity of any commodity . . . falls short of the effectual demand . . . the market price will rise . . . (1776/1976, p. 73).

In modern terms, the price of a commodity is explained as an equilibrium between two curves: a rising curve, which says how much will be produced at a given price and is called the *supply curve;* and a falling curve, which says how much will be bought at a given price and is called the *demand curve.* The higher the price consumers are willing to pay, the more items will be produced; conversely, the higher the price rises, the fewer the customers willing to pay it. The price at the point the two curves cross is the *market clearing price,* which is the price at which all who wish to sell are able to sell and all who wish to buy are able to buy. The demand curve is at the heart of *microeconomics,* the study of how the behavior of individual economic units determines the state of the economy as a whole.

About 10 years ago, several researchers pointed out that behavioral data from animals working on ratio-reinforcement schedules conform to the law of demand: As the "price" (work requirement) increases, the amount "bought" falls (cf. Lea, 1978). Figure 11.9 shows an example that is replotted from a data set we have already seen. It shows the number of reinforcements per day obtained ("bought") under different ratio schedules ("prices") in the Hirsch and Collier (1974) experiment. The curve is typical: As the ratio value increases, the amount of food obtained falls. The "demand law," that as price increases effective demand falls, is almost as general in the world of reinforcement schedules as in the economic world. (However, even in economics, there are a few exceptions. So-called *Giffen goods*[1] are bought for more, not less, as their price increases. Narcotics and prestige items are often Giffen goods.)

Demand curves illustrate the essentially regulatory character of responding on ratio schedules, although not perhaps as directly as the response rate versus reinforcement rate plotted in Figure 11.2. A horizontal demand curve indicates a perfectly regulated activity: No matter what the cost, the amount bought holds constant. If we had to pay for the oxygen we breathe, it would show highly *inelastic* demand (amount holds constant) (Figure 11.10a). A downward-slop-

---

[1] After Robert Giffen (1837–1910), British statistician and economist.

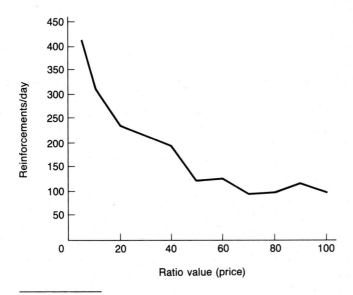

FIGURE 11.9   Molar ratio-schedule performance plotted as a demand curve. The data from Figure 11.6, for the 10-sec condition, are plotted as reinforcements obtained per day versus "price," that is, ratio value.

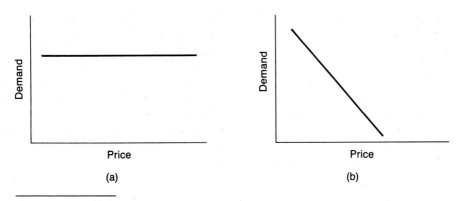

FIGURE 11.10   **(a)** An inelastic demand curve—as price increases, demand remains constant. **(b)** An elastic demand curve—as price increases, demand decreases.

ing demand curve indicates imperfect regulation, which is elastic demand (Figure 11.10b).

There is another economic analogy that has been applied to data such as these. A plot of response rate against ratio value (e.g., Figure 11.6) can be compared to what is termed the *labor-supply curve,* which shows how the amount of labor supplied (response rate) depends on the wage rate (ratio value). The

B   O   X

─11.1─────────────────

The Laffer Curve

The *Laffer curve* was reportedly sketched by California economist Arthur Laffer on a paper napkin as he vigorously argued the case for lower tax rates to a colleague over lunch. He justified his proposal using the following argument. Suppose that people's willingness to work productively depends on the effective wage rate in the backward-bending fashion of the standard labor supply curve. The effective wage rate depends on the tax rate, since we can only spend what is left after income tax has been extracted. Tax rates are (nominally) highly progressive, so that the higher the wage rate the higher the proportion that is lost (to the earner) in taxes. Hence, there must be a point at which higher taxes begin to depress the total amount of productive work. If the total amount of work decreases enough, then the total tax "take" will begin to decrease, even though the tax rate is high.

The key question: When is the tax rate too high? That is, when is it so high that the depressive effect on total amount of labor supplied exceeds the added revenue brought in by virtue of the high rate? Laffer argued that that time is *now*, so that taxes ought to be reduced.

Laffer's argument appears to be an economic one, but it clearly has a large, and crucial, psychological component, because it hinges on the size of the reduction in work associated with the loss of income to taxes. If people remain willing to work hard, even though a large chunk of their income goes to taxes, then Laffer's argument fails. The current consensus seems to be that people are more willing to work than Laffer expected. Yet, major legislation has been enacted based on little more than a collective conjecture about how people might react to a small increase in take-home pay.

idea is that when the wage rate is low, people are not willing to work much—thus the labor supply (by an individual or a group) is low. As the wage rate rises, the amount of labor supplied rises to a maximum; but when the wage rate is very high, labor is withdrawn, because now people have enough money to want to take time off to spend what they have earned. (The labor-supply curve is closely related to another curve—the Laffer curve [Box 11.1]—that has become notorious as part of the "voodoo economics" of which the Reagan administration was accused during its early years.)

A reinforcement schedule that fits the labor-supply analogy is shown in Figure 11.11. It shows data from a single pigeon pecking a response key for food reinforcement on a wide range of random-ratio schedules, ranging from 12.5 to 400. The data are typical of results from open-economy experiments in which

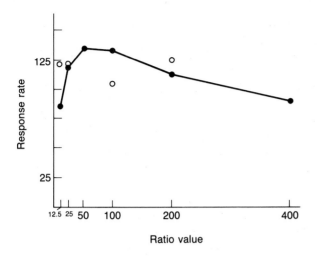

FIGURE 11.11 Molar ratio-schedule performance plotted as a labor supply curve. Response rate versus random-ratio value for a single pigeon exposed for many experimental sessions to each of a series of random-ratio schedules is plotted (from Green, Kagel, & Battalio, 1982, Figure 18.3).

the animals are given many sessions of exposure to each ratio value. The functions are an inverted-U shape: The animals respond at a low rate when the ratio value is very high or very low; they respond at a high rate at intermediate ratio values. Notice that these data are different from the monotonically increasing response rate versus ratio value function depicted in Figure 11.6. These two sets of data raise two questions:

1. Why are the data in Figure 11.10 different in form from the data in Figure 11.6?

2. Which economic analogy is valid, demand curve or labor-supply?

As always when attempting to understand behavioral data, the first step to study is the procedure: How, exactly, were these data obtained? The data for the demand curve (Figures 11.6 and 11.9) were obtained from a group of guinea pigs in a closed economy (24–hour access to the reinforcer) with water reinforcement. The labor-supply data (Figure 11.11) were obtained from a pigeon working for food in an open economy (short, daily sessions, supplemented by extra food after the experimental session if necessary). We obviously have a lot to choose from in deciding which of these many procedural differences—species, type of reinforcer, length of session, type of economy, individual versus group— was responsible for the different results obtained. In fact, other data pinpoint the type of economy as the indirect cause for the different results—*indirect* because in a closed economy there is a limit to the ratio value that can be tried. If the ratio is so high that the animal cannot obtain its minimum daily requirement of water (or whatever the reinforcer is) in the experiment, then it, and the experiment, will soon end. This problem does not occur in the open-economy experiment, because any shortfall during the experimental session can always be made up by supplemental feeding or watering afterward. Because supplemental feeding is not possible with a closed economy, the ratio values used in closed-economy experiments are always moderate and to the left of the peak in the labor-supply curve, on the rising part of the function. Over this range, the pattern in open and closed economies is the same (compare Figure 11.6 with Figure 11.11 at ratios of 50 and below). In addition to the range problem, it is also possible that the post-session supplemental feedings given in the open-economy situation may have a suppressive effect on behavior at high ratios, especially if the feedings are given soon after the end of the experimental session (which may be another effect of the proportional-timing process discussed in Chapter 9).

Notice that we cannot directly compare the absolute values of the ratios between open- and closed-economy experiments, because we cannot equate either the values of water and food reinforcement for the two species or the relative effort of pecking and lever-pressing. The forms of the two curves, not the absolute values, are the features of interest.

If the "true" function that relates response rate and ratio value is an inverted-U, does it mean that the labor-supply analogy is true and the law of demand analogy is false? The answer: Both are simply *analogies,* and what we are interested in is *principles.* What common principles underlie both these functions, and do they apply to behavior on these schedules? In fact, the common principles are the same as those behind the optimality analyses we have already discussed, although here they are refined in the context of human economic analysis.

Preference Structure and Indifference-Curve Analysis

We turn now to the concept of preference structure that economists have used to explain the downward-sloping demand curve. Economics is about value or, as economists term it, *utility.* Psychologists and philosophers differ on whether it makes sense to give numbers to utilities. Some psychologists say you can, most philosophers say you can't, and economists agree with the philosophers. Economists have devised a method that allows them to make predictions based only on value relations of "equal" and "greater than." The method: Consider two goods such as bread and milk. Even if we can't give numbers to the utility of a given quantity of milk or bread, everyone seems to agree that we can always equate the value of bundles of goods. For example, 2 quarts of milk and 3 loaves of bread may be judged equal to another bundle with 4 quarts of milk and 2 loaves, in the sense that we are indifferent as to which *commodity bundle* we receive. There exists an entire set of bundles of this sort, differing in the proportions of bread and milk, but they are the same in that we are indifferent among them. This set defines an individual *indifference curve.*

An indifference curve represents a set of commodity bundles that are equal in value. Figure 11.12 shows several indifference curves. Any point on one curve

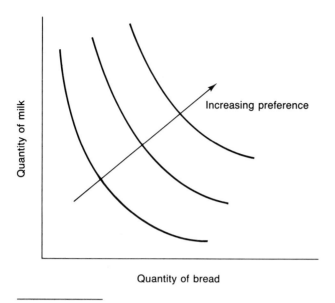

FIGURE 11.12   Conventional indifference curves.

is of equal value to all other points on the same curve. Everyone agrees that
bundles of goods, or of activities, can be rank ordered—A being preferred to B,
B to C, and so on—even if we cannot be sure by how much A is preferred. When
bundles of goods are ranked in order of value, they occupy different indifference
curves. For example, if we now compared 5 quarts of milk and 4 loaves of bread
with 4 quarts and 2 loaves we would prefer the first, as the 5,4 bundle must occupy a point on a *higher* indifference curve. Thus, a set of indifference curves is
defined by the relation of value equality—among bundles on the same curve—
and greater than (or less than)—for bundles on different curves.

The point of maximum value is represented by the point in the upper right
corner of Figure 11.12. The *preference structure* for bread and milk, or any
other pair of goods, can therefore be represented by a sort of contour map of
indifference curves, such as those illustrated in the figure. The arrow indicates
the direction of increasing preference, which for most real commodities (but not
for activities) is generally in the direction of more of both goods. The analogy to
contours is exact: Like contours, indifference curves cannot cross one another.
Like contours, they represent equal values on a third dimension: height or value.
A set of indifference curves is a contour map lacking a vertical scale: We know
where the mountains are and which contour line is above which, but we don't
know how much higher one is than another.

Knowledge of an individual's preference structure is not by itself sufficient
to predict behavior. We also must know what constraints the individual is under. However, once a constraint is specified, the optimal solution is clearly to
settle on the highest indifference curve consistent with the constraint. For

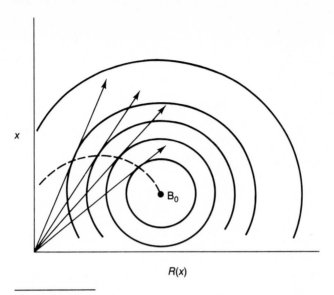

FIGURE 11.13   Indifference curves derived from the minimum-distance model.
Rays through the origin are ratio constraints. The dashed curve is the expected
response location.

reinforcement-schedule constraints, the optimal solution implies an equilibrium
at the point at which the feedback function is tangent to the highest indifference
curve. Figure 11.13 illustrates this tangent, equilibrium point for operant responding on the vertical axis and reinforcement on the horizontal axis. The indifference curves are circles centered on B_0. Notice that B_0 is such that the reinforcement rate is high and operant responding is low. The constraint lines are
simply the feedback functions for different ratio schedules. The dashed line is
the locus (path) of points traced by a series of different ratio schedules in this
space; this locus is termed the ratio-schedule *response function.*

If you think about it, you will realize that circular indifference curves correspond to the minimum-distance model shown earlier in Figure 11.4, because
circular curves correspond to the assumption that points equidistant from the
free-behavior (bliss) point are all of equal cost. Since equal cost obviously corresponds to equal utility, it makes no difference whether we perform our analysis
in terms of cost or utility; the indifference curves, and therefore the predictions,
remain the same.

Notice that the response function traced in Figure 11.13 is an inverted-U
shape. So also is the comparable function that relates response rate to ratio
value—which is not shown, but you can see that response rate declines at high
ratio values (steep feedback lines), rather than continuing to increase. In other
words, the minimum-distance model predicts a labor-supply–type relation between response rate (labor supply) and ratio value (wage rate).

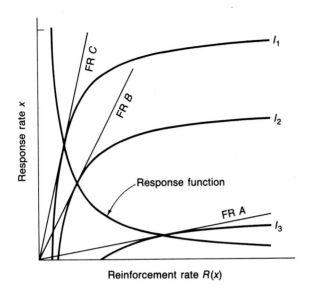

FIGURE 11.14   Indifference curves (I_1, I_2, I_3) for the response–cost model (Equation 11.9 with C = 3, 10, and 15; Q = 0.5). Feedback functions for three fixed-ratio values (FR A, FR B, FR C) are shown. The downward-sloping line is the response function.

How does the response–cost model compare? We can easily derive indifference curves from the cost function (Equation 11.4):

$$C(x) = I + Qx$$

where I is the interfood interval, Q is a cost parameter, and x is the rate of the operant response. The interfood interval is 1/reinforcement rate, that is, $1/R(x)$, so that the equation becomes

$$C(x) = \frac{1}{R(x)} + Qx \qquad\qquad (11.8)$$

To plot an indifference curve, we simply pick a value for the cost, say C, set the right-hand side of Equation 11.8 equal to C, and rearrange to get x as a function of $R(x)$. The result:

$$x = \frac{C - \dfrac{1}{R(x)}}{Q} \qquad\qquad (11.9)$$

which we can then plot. Each time we change the value of C, we get another indifference curve. Indifference curves for three values of C are plotted in Figure 11.14. The response function goes through the points at which the three fixed-ratio schedule feedback functions are tangent to the three indifference curves.

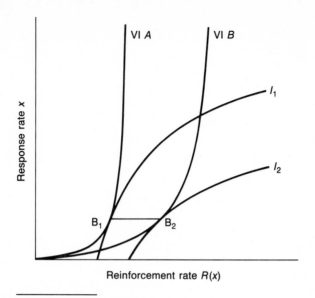

FIGURE 11.15   Indifference curves (I_1, I_2) for the response–cost model and two VI molar feedback functions (VI A, VI B) that are tangent to them. B_1 and B_2 are two points on the response function.

As we showed earlier, the RC response function slopes downward to the right, like a demand curve.

Indifference curve analysis makes it easy to separate the cost function, which is the essence of the model, from the constraints. The set of indifference curves represents the cost function; the constraint lines then define on which indifference curve and where on the curve behavior will lie. So far, we have only discussed fixed-ratio schedule constraints, but it is almost as easy to derive predictions for other schedules, such as variable-interval schedules. Figure 11.15 shows two indifference curves for the RC model that are tangent to two VI feedback functions. Both points of tangency are at the same response rate, which is in agreement with the optimal VI policy we derived earlier in the chapter for the RC model. This prediction, however, is only in approximate agreement with actual performance.

Notice that the VI feedback functions in Figure 11.15 have a shape that makes sense, based on what you know of VI schedules: When the response rate is very low, the reinforcement rate is almost proportional to the response rate. For example, on a VI 1-min schedule, if an animal increases its response rate from once per hour to twice per hour, its reinforcement rate approximately doubles. But as its response rate approaches the maximum reinforcement rate specified by the schedule, the reinforcement rate rises more slowly, approaching as an *asymptote* the maximum rate permitted by the VI schedule.

We are now in a position to see the real difference between the labor-supply curve and the demand curve analogies—which is the form of preference

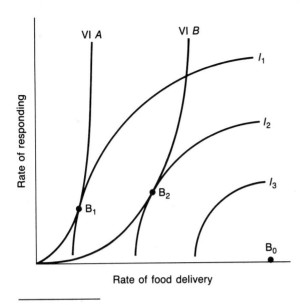

FIGURE 11.16   Indifference curves for the minimum-distance model and VI molar feedback functions that are tangent to two of them. B_1 and B_2 are two points on the response function. B_0 is the preferred point.

structure each implies. The inverted-U, labor-supply function implies indifference curves that resemble those of the MD model; the downward-sloping, demand curve function implies indifference curves like those of the RC model. As you can see in Figure 11.16, the indifference curves for the MD model differ slightly from those of the RC model in such a way as to produce a VI schedule response function that rises over most of the range (response rate at point $B_2 >$ B_1), rather than being constant (as in Figure 11.15). On balance, the MD analysis and related economic models fit experimental results a bit better than the response–cost model.

All the optimality analyses we have discussed thus far—interfood interval minimization, response cost, and minimum distance—imply a certain preference structure. As you have just seen, given the form of the cost function, we can easily derive the form of indifference curves. So why do we need yet another method for doing the same thing? What can we do with an indifference-curve analysis that we can't do using a cost function?

1. *The indifference-curve method is potentially experimental.* It tells us (at least in principle) how to measure an organism's preference structure by equating commodity bundles. This method is known as *revealed preference,* which is the closest that economists come to being pure behaviorists. Like reinforcement theorists, economists are now unanimous in agreeing that the only way to assess value is through the

individual's expressed preferences, represented by indifference curves. In fact, neither economists nor psychologists use the direct method of asking people or animals to equate commodity bundles.

2.   *A set of indifference curves need not follow any specific mathematical form.* The form can be anything of our choosing, subject to the logical limitation that indifference curves, like contour lines, cannot cross. Although some behavior theorists have favored preference structures formally derived from assumptions such as minimum distance or response cost, others have favored the greater flexibility of a graphical approach in which indifference curves are simply drawn in a plausible fashion.

3.   *Because indifference curves directly represent the cost function, they show the real similarities between models.* You can see the similarity easily by comparing Figures 11.15 and 11.16. The indifference curves derived from MD and RC analysis are clearly quite similar, even though the equations that describe the two models do not appear similar at all.

Marginal Value and Substitutability

It is no accident that the indifference curves we have been discussing are all convex, that is, they curve outward from the region of maximum value. *Convexity* represents an important property of cost, usually expressed as the *law of diminishing marginal utility* (or *increasing marginal cost*). What this law means is that the more you have of something, the less each additional increment is worth. Conversely, the more you lose of something, the greater the cost of each additional bit of loss.

Figure 11.17 illustrates diminishing marginal utility, and it shows a negatively accelerated utility function. The vertical lines indicate increments of a "good" (e.g., food-rate increments). The two small vertical lines indicate two increments in utility associated with successive equal increments in that good. As you can see, the first utility increment (α), is greater than the next (β), and this pattern continues across the entire curve. Thus, going up and to the right from A (increasing utility), the curve shows diminishing marginal utility; going down and to the left from A, the same curve shows increasing marginal cost. Diminishing marginal utility is sometimes termed *satiation,* and there is a close relationship between this property and the dynamic property of satiation that we discussed earlier in the chapter in the section on dynamics of behavioral allocation: Both imply behavioral diversity, as we discuss further in a moment.

The concept of marginal utility is important because it tells us how to allocate resources for maximum satisfaction. For example, given $100 to spend on any mixture of three commodities (e.g., bread, milk, and beer), maximum satisfaction is assured if we are indifferent on whether to spend our last dime on more milk, bread, or beer. Indifference means that we have equated the marginal values of the three commodities. Those familiar with differential calculus will

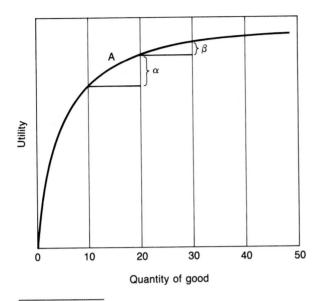

FIGURE 11.17   A negatively accelerated utility function. Successive increments in utility (α and β) are produced by equal increments in the quantity of a good.

recognize that equating marginal value is simply the mathematical operation of equating the partial derivatives of the value (or cost) function with respect to each commodity.

Marginal value can be understood without getting into higher mathematics. For example, consider how you should allocate a fixed total amount of time between two activities whose utilities are each proportional to time spent. If value functions were linear, then the best strategy is to devote all the time to one activity or the other, depending on which line has the steeper slope. However, it is more typical for value functions to be *negatively accelerated,* as shown in Figure 11.17, in which case, the more one does of something, the smaller the marginal benefit. For example, the more you eat of something, the less tasty each additional morsel becomes. It is obvious that most goods show diminishing marginal utility: The first ice cream is wonderful, the next is nice, and the 10th may make you sick. Moreover, if two goods show diminishing marginal utility, then when you must allocate limited resources among them, your optimal policy is to spend some money on both, that is, to show a *partial preference* rather than an *exclusive choice* of one or the other. If the goods are activities, each of which shows diminishing marginal utility, then clearly the optimal policy is to spend some time in each activity, to show behavioral diversity rather than behavioral stereotypy.

The relation between partial preference, diminishing marginal utility, and convex indifference curves is illustrated in Figure 11.18. The figure shows an indifference curve for two goods, A and B, each of which shows diminishing mar-

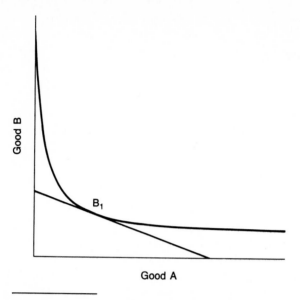

FIGURE 11.18   An indifference curve for two partially substitutable goods.

ginal utility of the form shown in Figure 11.17. As you can see, the curve is convex. The diagonal line represents what economists call the *budget constraint,* which is a fixed sum of money that must be spent on A and B. The slope of the line represents the relative prices of A and B: If both prices are equal, the line will intersect both axes at the same value. If A and B are activities that are measured as proportions of time spent, the budget constraint corresponds to the time-allocation constraint discussed earlier in the chapter. The optimal allocation of resources is at B_1, at which point the constraint line is tangent to the indifference curve. B_1 obviously represents a partial preference.

What is the form of the indifference curve when utilities do *not* show diminishing returns? In Figure 11.17, the utility of each activity was simply proportional to the amount of activity: $U_1 = aT_1$ and $U_2 = bT_2$, where U_1 and U_2 are the utilities of investments, T_1 and T_2 are the times invested, and a and b are the ratios of the utility to time spent. Now recall how we derive indifference curves from utility (or cost) functions. First, we select a total utility (or cost) (C), and then we set the combined utilities equal to C:

$$C = U_1 + U_2 = aT_1 + bT_2$$

rearranging terms gives the following:

$$T_1 = \frac{C - bT_2}{a}$$

which is a straight line. There is obviously no way that a straight-line budget constraint can be tangent to a straight-line indifference curve. Hence, the optimal policy in this case is to choose activity 1 or activity 2 exclusively. (As an exercise, satisfy yourself that you can derive this prediction from the indifference-curve analysis.)

Note that a straight-line indifference curve need not imply that the goods it relates are not subject to diminishing marginal utility. It may also mean that the goods are not independent, so that consumption of one causes satiation for both. For example, consumption of coffee may cause satiation for tea.

Economists have names for the different kinds of indifference curves. Two goods related by a straight-line indifference curve, in which the optimal policy is exclusive choice, are termed *perfect substitutes*. Examples are two equivalent brands of gasoline: You simply pick the one with the lowest price. Two goods related by a convex indifference curve are termed *partial substitutes*, because a change in price (slope of the budget line) causes a change in preference that falls short of a complete switch from one to the other. Coffee and tea are partial substitutes: If tea becomes more expensive, you may drink more coffee. Two goods related by an extreme convex indifference curve (i.e., a corner made up of a vertical and a horizontal line) are termed *complements*. The idea here is that there is a preferred ratio of the two goods (e.g., equal number of left and right shoes), so that we are indifferent to additional quantities of either good: A bundle of 105 left shoes and 100 right shoes has the same value as a 100:100 bundle.

Note: These terms are not very useful for analyzing the kinds of animal behaviors we've been discussing in the text, because the terms say more than they mean. For example, *substitution* implies *functional equivalence* (i.e., that consumption of one good satiates for both), but all it really means is a specific form of indifference curve. As we have seen, a given indifference curve may be generated in several ways, only some of which correspond to functional equivalence. On the other hand, since these terms are used commonly, you should be familiar with them.

Implications for Behavioral Allocation and Choice

We have already pointed out the most obvious implication of imperfect substitutability for implicit choice: Partial substitutability implies behavioral diversity. These ideas can also help us understand the results of explicit choice experiments in which the reinforcers are of different types or are delivered in different amounts. Let's consider first one of the simplest choice situations, the two-armed bandit, and the effect of different types of reward.

A *two-armed bandit* is a two-choice version of the familiar Las Vegas one-armed bandit, that is, a situation in which the animal has two choices (e.g., two levers or two response keys), each of which delivers reward on a probabilistic (i.e., random-ratio) schedule. For example, our subject may be a rat that must respond on one lever to receive cherry cola and on another lever to receive either cherry cola or Tom Collins mix. Suppose the two random-ratio schedules are the same (e.g., 25), so that the rat receives access to either reinforcer with probability 0.04 for pressing the appropriate lever. What should the rat do if both levers produce only cherry cola? Well, it really doesn't matter, and chances are that after much experience our rat will develop a *position preference* and respond exclusively on one or other lever. Such position preference in cases for which two rewards are perfect substitutes is practically guaranteed if the two ratio schedules are unequal (e.g., 15 and 25): Most rats eventually fixate on the higher-probability lever.

If the animal has only a fixed number of responses to expend, then the constraint line is like the budget line in Figure 11.18: x responses on the left lever means $N - x$ on the right lever, where N is the total number of responses permitted and the prices (ratio values) are equal. In this case, if the two rewards are perfect substitutes, then the indifference curve is also a straight line, so that the prediction will almost always be exclusive choice of one option or the other.

What happens if the rewards for the two responses are different (cherry cola and Tom Collins mix)? Now, the indifference curve may be convex—complete satiation on cherry cola may leave our rat still with some appetite for Tom Collins mix, and vice versa. The prediction for equal-ratio schedules is now partial preference rather than exclusive choice. Moreover, if the partial preference favors cherry cola, say, then we can increase the ratio for that lever without abolishing responding. Indeed, the change in preference for a given change in "cost" allows us to estimate the indifference curve directly. It turns out that the behavior of rats is consistent with this simple economic analysis (Rachlin, Battalio, Kagel, & Green, 1981).

Now let's look at different food reinforcer amounts for each choice, with equal ratio values for each. No matter what the form of the utility curve for food amount, so long as more is preferable to less, our ideal "rational rat" should always pick the larger food-amount option exclusively—and rats (after sufficient experience) usually do. But, we can see the effect of the utility function if we change the procedure slightly: For pressing the left lever, the animal continues to receive a small amount of food, say, a 20-mg food pellet; for pressing the right lever, the animal receives either a small (10 mg), or a large (30 mg) pellet, with equal probability. So now, 25 responses on the left lever on average buys our rat 20 mg of food; 25 responses on the right lever buys it either 10 or 30 mg of food, which averages out to the same amount. The question: Which lever should the rat prefer? The answer depends on how the utility of food depends on its amount.

Look again at the negatively accelerated utility curve in Figure 11.16. Let's see how much utility (as opposed to how much food) our rat receives with the two options described. For the left lever, the rat receives amount A of food (Figure 11.16), which is about 0.8 on the utility axis. For the right lever, it receives either $0.8 - \alpha$ or $0.8 + \beta$. But since α is plainly always greater than β (given a negatively accelerated utility function), then the average of $0.8 - \alpha$ and $0.8 + \beta$ must be *less* than 0.8. Thus, the rat should prefer the lever with the fixed food amount to the lever with variable amounts albeit the same average—and rats do. This aversion to variability is known to decision theorists as *risk aversion,* and it is a common result whether the decision agents are people or animals. This explanation for risk aversion is quite old, as psychological explanations go, being first offered by the Swiss mathematician Daniel Bernoulli in 1738.

RISK AVERSION   Risk aversion can easily be demonstrated with human subjects. For example, the two psychologists Daniel Kahneman and Amos Tversky (1979) have become famous for a series of experiments in which they asked college students deceptively simple questions about decisions involving gambles—and received some surprising answers. In one experiment, students were asked to decide between the following two outcomes:

> Which would you prefer: $3,000 for sure, or a 0.8 chance for $4,000?

Since $0.8 \times 4,000 = 3,200$, the gamble has the higher expected value. Nevertheless, the great majority of subjects opted for the sure bet.

Risk aversion is evidently a widespread characteristic. It makes good adaptive sense for at least two reasons. First, the future is uncertain: "A bird in the hand is worth two in the bush." Second, the value of reinforcements such as food depends not just on their amount but also on their distribution in time. An individual may consume 100 kg of food per year, say, but he is unlikely to trade a regimen of 0.3kg per day (total: 109.5 kg) for 200 kg delivered at year's end. A large food reward should be less valuable than two half-size rewards delivered twice as often, although the difference may well be small if the amounts and delays are also small. Since any repeated gamble involves a change in temporal distribution as well as distribution of amounts, risk aversion is often adaptive.

The Matching Law

Convex indifference curves and linear constraints yield partial preference. Let's look again at variable-interval schedules and see how this rule may apply when an animal must choose between two independent VI schedules. Figure 11.15 shows how the reinforcement rate obtained on a VI schedule depends on the response rate. If you can imagine the axes reversed, with response rate on the x-axis and reinforcement rate on the y-axis, you can see that the VI feedback function has the same form as the negatively accelerated utility function in Figure 11.17. As responding increases from zero, reinforcment rate at first rises rapidly but then more slowly as it approaches the maximum prescribed by the VI schedule, Let's see if we can figure out what an animal should do when confronted with two concurrent VI VI schedules. We assume the simplest possible utility function: average reinforcement rate. The animal is to allocate its responding to receive as many reinforcements as possible within a fixed time. Given a fixed total number of responses to "spend," the animal should spend them so that the marginal reinforcement rate gain on each of the two VI schedules is equal. This result is illustrated in Figure 11.19. Since the two feedback functions are both negatively accelerated, the outcome must yield a partial preference: Some responding on both VI schedules, more on the richer one. In fact, with the molar VI feedback function described in Figure 11.14, maximization of the reinforcement rate predicts that the animal should match the ratio of the responses made to the reinforcements obtained: $x/y = R(x)/R(y)$, where x and y are the total number of responses to left and right keys and $R(x)$ and $R(y)$ are the total number of reinforcements obtained (Staddon & Motheral, 1978). In other words, if we find

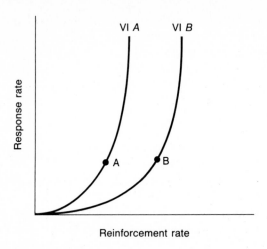

FIGURE 11.19   Marginal gains on two VI schedules. Points A and B have equal marginal rate gains, that is, the slopes at A and B are equal.

that our rational pigeon receives 40 reinforcements for pecking on right keys and 20 for pecking on left keys, we expect that it has made twice as many pecks on the right key as on the left key. Rewritten in terms of proportions, the following is the well-known *matching law* for responding on concurrent VI VI schedules:

$$\frac{x}{x + y} = \frac{R(x)}{R(x) + R(y)} \qquad (11.10)$$

The matching law was discovered by Richard Herrnstein (1961), and his original data, taken from pigeons pecking two keys for food reinforcement delivered on VI schedules, are shown in Figure 11.20. Each data point plots the proportion of left and right key pecks against the proportion of reinforcements obtained after several weeks of daily exposure to a given pair of VI values. To minimize changes in the overall response rate, the total rate of food delivery for left and right key pecks combined was held approximately constant. The diagonal line indicates perfect matching, and as you can see, the data from the three pigeons conform closely to it.

The matching law has been the focus for an extraordinary amount of experimental and theoretical work in the more than 25 years since it was first discovered. The law itself, originally just an empirical finding, has even been used as the basis of a molar theory for reinforcement-schedule performance in general.

Generalized Matching: The Relative Law of Effect

Let's turn now to a different kind of molar approach, which we term *molar descriptive theories* of behavioral allocation and choice. (We then will be ready to delve into the final section of the chapter on molecular and dynamic analyses.)

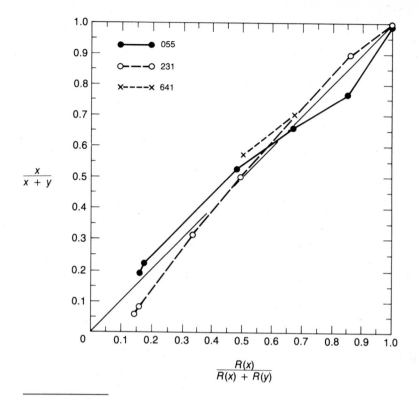

FIGURE 11.20   Results from three pigeons on concurrent VI VI schedules. Each point represents a different condition. The diagonal line represents perfect matching (from Herrnstein, 1961).

The simplicity and reliability of the matching law suggested to Herrnstein and his students that it might well form the basis for a general theory of behavior on reinforcement schedules. Recall Equation 11.10: $x/(x + y) = R(x)/[R(x) + R(y)]$. Suppose we replace the denominator on the left-hand side of the equation with a term that represents *all* behavior in a given situation and the denominator on the right-hand side with a term that represents *all* sources of reinforcement:

$$\frac{x_1}{\Sigma x_i} = \frac{R(x_1)}{\Sigma R(x_i)}$$

where x_1 is one response, Σx_i is the sum of all responses, and $\Sigma R(x_i)$ is the sum of all reinforcements. If we add the single assumption that the sum of all responses is constant and then move the constant to the other side of the equation, the equation reduces to the following:

$$x_1 = \frac{kR(x_1)}{\Sigma R(x_i)}$$

(11.11)

where k is now a constant of proportionality. In other words, the equation says that the rate of a given response (x_1), is proportional to its rate of reinforcement *relative* to the reinforcement for all other responses. Herrnstein (1970) called this relationship the *relative law of effect.*

Herrnstein had to make two assumptions to get from the simple matching result to the relative law. The first is to assume the constancy of the term Σx_i, which is the sum of all responses. The second is to assume that all sources of competition are also sources of reinforcement. Activities such as grooming or sleeping, which take away time from the operant response, must therefore be treated as sources of reinforcement. The latter assumption is hard to verify, and it is probably unnecessary to the theory as a formal description of results. The first assumption is *incorrect*, unless each activity is scaled in terms of the time it takes up. Therefore, the constant (k) in Equation 11.11 does double duty: It represents the total period of observation, divided by the duration of one instance of activity X_1.

The simplicity of the relative law of effect has proven quite attractive, and strenuous attempts have been made to extend it to a wide variety of schedules. Here, we consider only its extension to responding on single-response (i.e., not concurrent) VI schedules. In this case, the term $\Sigma R(x_i)$ simplifies to $R(x) + R_0$, where R_0 is the sum of reinforcers for activities other than response X. Equation 11.11 is thus reworked to represent a single response:

$$x = \frac{kR(x)}{R(x) + R_0} \tag{11.12}$$

where x is the response rate and $R(x)$ is the reinforcement rate, as usual.

Equation 11.12 is sometimes known as *Herrnstein's hyperbola*. When $R(x)$ is low relative to R_0 (i.e., a low reinforcement rate for X), the equation reduces to $x = kR(x)/R_0$—that is, response rate is proportional to reinforcement rate. Conversely, when $R(x)$ is large relative to R_0, the equation reduces to $x = k$. These two properties should be familiar by now: They correspond to the negatively accelerated pattern of response rate versus reinforcement rate we have already seen for pigeons and rats on VI schedules (see Figures 9.18 and 9.19). It seems that the quantitative law of effect provides an accurate account of response rate versus reinforcement rate functions not only for concurrent VI VI schedules but also for simple VI schedules. How far can this idea be extended?

Herrnstein has proposed extensions to explain behavioral contrast on multiple schedules (Chapter 7), but these extensions have not been well supported by experimental work. The principle also fails on simple ratio schedules and interlocking schedules. As we saw earlier, response rate on ratio schedules is either a declining function of reinforcement rate or an inverted-U; response functions on interlocking schedules follow the linear declining form shown in Figure 11.21 on page 401. The problem is that Equation 11.12 has no provision for the reinforcement schedule: Like conservation theory discussed earlier in this chapter, it predicts the same result for any reinforcement schedule. Thus, the relative law of effect has failed to provide us with a general principle of reinforcement. Nevertheless, the function it predicts for simple VI schedules (Equation 11.12) is accurate. Later in the next section we suggest a reason why this equation works for simple VI schedules.

Conclusions About the Matching Law

The derivation of matching from simple, reinforcement-rate maximization gives a great boost to the optimality approach. It turns out that many maximization models predict matching, because of the negatively accelerated form of the VI molar feedback function. However, closer study soon reveals difficulties. As we have seen, optimality models fail under some conditions because they are functional—not mechanistic—models. Molar reinforcement-rate maximization fails to predict matching in a situation that is closely related to concurrent VI VI: concurrent VI VR. When one alternative is a variable-interval schedule but the other is a variable-ratio schedule, pigeons spend too much time on the ratio alternative: Maximization predicts more responding on the ratio schedule (in which responses count more) than on the VI schedule (in which they count less). Nevertheless, pigeons, blindly obedient (apparently) to the matching principle, continue to match response ratios to ratios of obtained reinforcements, with a slight bias in favor of the ratio: $x/y = kR(x)/R(y)$, where k is greater than 1, and x is the ratio-reinforced response (Herrnstein & Heyman, 1979).

Stephen Lea (1976) has investigated the matching idea in a more subtle fashion. His pigeons could respond on either of two keys. On the left key, say, they received food according to a random-ratio schedule with constant probability (p). On the right key, they received food according to an adjusting ratio: With each food delivery on the right key, the ratio increased; with each food delivery on the left key, the ratio on the right key decreased. This procedure is termed a *titration procedure* (we encountered a titration schedule in an experiment by Mazur, 1984, discussed in Chapter 9). The point is that the optimal strategy here is for the animal to work for some time on the left key, until the ratio on the right key has reached a low value, then to switch and collect a few "cheap" reinforcements before switching back to the right key and repeating the process. Instead of maximizing in this way, Lea's pigeons alternated back and forth in such a way that the net payoff probability on the right key (adjusting) matched the probability on the left key (constant). If we denote payoff probability on the right key by q and on the left key by p, then $p = q$ represents the birds' steady-state behavior. But, p is equal to the ratio of reinforcements to reponses on the left key, $R(x)/x$, and similarly for q, so that Lea's result is simply another example of the matching law:

$$x/R(x) = y/R(y) \quad \text{or}$$
$$x/y = R(x)/R(y)$$

Although Lea's data disprove molar maximizing as an account of choice, they are perfectly consistent with what has been termed *local*, or *molecular*, *maximizing*. If the pigeon allocates its pecking on a moment-by-moment basis to the alternative that offers the highest probability of reinforcement, then the titration schedule ensures that the average payoff probability will be the same on both keys, which implies matching. This same molecular-maximizing process was suggested many years ago as the basis for matching on concurrent VI VI schedules (Shimp, 1966). We will return to molecular processes shortly, but first, let's see if there is any good evidence that marginal changes in molar variables such as reinforcement rate have direct effects on behavior.

Is Behavior Directly Sensitive to Marginal Molar Changes?

The fundamental assumption of molar optimality is that behavior is sensitive to marginal quantities, measured at the molar level. How valid is this assumption? Ettinger, Reid, and Staddon (1987) recently carried out a direct test. They chose a schedule that has linear molar feedback functions, because many optimality models predict an especially simple adaptation to such schedules: a straight-line response function. These models all predict that a change in the slope of the molar feedback function (i.e., a change in its marginal rate of return) should always cause some change in the slope of the response function.

Ettinger and his colleagues used what are called *interlocking schedules,* which is a combination interval-ratio schedule: If the animal does nothing, the schedule is effectively a fixed-interval one, but, the interfood time is reduced by every response, as it is on a ratio schedule. For example, if the animal does nothing, food becomes available for the first response after 60 sec, say. But if the animal makes one response before the 60 sec mark, then food becomes available after 55 sec; if it makes two responses, food is available after 50 sec, and so on. Thus, the interfood interval is determined according to the formula $I = T - am$, where m is the number of responses that are actually made (excluding the response that actually procures the reinforcer), T is the minimum interfood interval if no responses are made, and a is a parameter that says how much each response reduces the time to food.

The results of one of the Ettinger experiments are shown graphically in Figure 11.21. The figure shows feedback functions for two sets of interlocking schedules that differ in the slope parameter, T (two sets of positive-slope lines). Within each group, the slopes are the same, but the intercepts (parameter a) differ. Response functions predicted from the MD model are sketched in as dashed lines. Other optimality models predict different changes in the slope of the response function. The point is that all molar optimality models predict *some* change in slope between the two conditions. Yet the results are clear: (1) the obtained response functions are indeed approximately linear, but (2) there seems in fact to be only one linear function, which is the *same* for both sets of schedules. All the data points seem to lie on the same straight line with negative slope. The difference in molar marginal rate of reinforcement between the two series evidently has no effect on response-function slope. These data strongly suggest that here, as with the chain schedules discussed in Chapter 9 and Lea's titration schedule, we must look at the local, molecular level to understand how reinforcement schedules actually affect behavior.

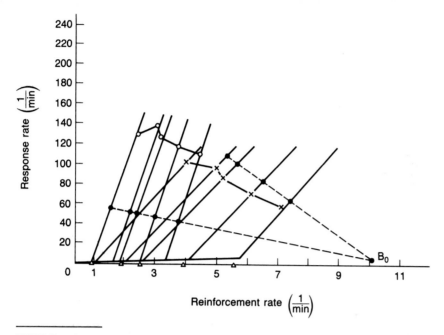

FIGURE 11.21 Results from one animal on two sets of interlocking schedules. The interlocking schedules are represented by the two sets of five lines with positive slopes. The minimum-distance predictions are represented by dashed lines. The obtained response functions are represented by the solid lines that connect the symbols (from Ettinger, Reid, & Staddon, 1987).

Molar Optimality: Conclusion

What can we conclude about the status of molar optimality as a valid model for implicit and explicit choice? We must first acknowledge the general conclusion that no optimality model works in every situation. Animals are rarely, if ever, "literal optimizers:" They don't remember the average payoff associated with a given pattern of responding and compare it with the payoffs for other patterns (from a well-defined set of possibilities) and then pick the best pattern, as some views of optimal responding often seem to imply. Under most conditions, people don't behave in this way either. Moreover, the data from the Ettinger experiment discussed previously strongly suggest that the real causal relations are not at the molar level at all. Nevertheless, as we saw in Chapter 9, the simple local rules animals often use perform remarkably well in a wide range of situations. Hence, molar-optimality analyses also perform rather well. Optimality analyses have also revealed unsuspected relationships between implicit and explicit choice, and they still provide the simplest account for choice between partially substitutable reinforcers and for the analysis of choice behavior under risk. Optimality models show unequivocally that reward value is a negatively accelerated function of reward amount, so that doubling the amount increases the value by a factor less than 2. Recall that we needed to assume a less-than-proportional relation between reward size and reward effect in Chapter 9 to get correct predictions of self-control results from the proportional-timing model. In short, optimality models provide a tolerably good picture of what animals manage to achieve—but a poor picture of how they actually achieve it. Animals often behave optimally, but they almost never optimize in any literal sense (Staddon & Hinson, 1983).

Behavioral economics is simply optimality theory by another name and with a slightly different bag of theoretical tricks: indifference curves instead of objective and cost functions. But the rationale, the results, and the limitations of behavioral economics are exactly the same as those of optimality—only the names and connotations are different. "Labor-supply" and "demand curve" suggest different things than "response cost" and "minimum distance," but the principles behind them are the same.

In our discussion of behavioral economics we have tried to show you the intimate relation between the psychology of behavioral allocation and economic analyses of choice. It should be clear that the economic analysis that underpins legislative acts touches all our lives (e.g., The Tax Reform Act of 1986), and it often rests on unacknowledged psychological assumptions about the mechanisms of behavioral allocation. It should also be clear that we need to understand a great deal more about choice before the underpinnings can be based on something more sound than a curve sketched on a paper napkin.

MOLECULAR MECHANISMS OF BEHAVIORAL ALLOCATION

Matching of response ratios to reinforcement ratios is a robust finding on concurrent VI VI and concurrent VI VR schedules, which is why the matching law was proposed as a general reinforcement principle. Yet, the attempt failed. Can there be other reasons why matching is such a reliable result? We have two places to look: in the procedure and in the animal. Perhaps the procedure is such that many patterns of behavior inevitably result in matching? Perhaps the animal is following some simple local rule that results in matching? Let's examine the procedure.

You will remember from earlier chapters that one of the basic properties of behavior is *variation*, which serves many adaptive functions but one of the most important is that it helps animals to detect regularities. Pigeons in choice experiments show some moment-by-moment variation in both their overall rate of responding and their allocation of responses to each key. What effects might this variation have, given the known properties of VI schedules? To answer this question, we must reexamine the feedback function for VI schedules. The VI feedback function has two general properties: When response rate is low, the schedule is in effect an FR ratio 1 schedule (i.e., every response is reinforced); when response rate is high, reinforcement rate is almost constant. Consequently, if our pigeon reponds at a low rate on each key, it will receive food for almost every response. If it receives food for every response on each key, then it *must* match reponse ratios to (obtained) reinforcement ratios. Therefore, we can safely conclude that when the response rate is low, matching is an artifact of the properties of the VI schedule. This possibility has been well known for many years. Proponents of matching as a general principle have therefore focused on the second possibility offered by VI schedules, namely that when the reponse rate is high, the reinforcement rate is almost constant and therefore independent of the response rate. But, the reality of behavioral variation means that we cannot assume a constant, high response rate—we must assume a range of rates, as well as some bias in favor of the higher-reinforcement-rate alternative. The issue is quantitative, and it involves at least two properties of behavior: its amount (how fast does the pigeon peck?) and its bias (how much does it prefer the higher-reinforcement-rate key?). The issue is not one easily settled by verbal arguments, but we can get some insights into it with the aid of simulation: writing a computer program to "respond" at various rates with different biases and deliver "reinforcers" at random times. Simulations (e.g., Hinson & Staddon, 1983b) have shown that on concurrent VI VI schedules, at least, almost any pattern of responding that satisfies two conditions will result in matching. The two conditions:

1. That the response rate on a given key is some positive function of the rate of reinforcement obtained,
2. That if no reinforcement is obtained, the response rate is zero

Both these properties of operant behavior were well established long before the matching result was obtained. Hence, the matching law has been valuable more for the research it has stimulated than for what it is has revealed about the actual mechanisms of reinforcement. It is a law about the behavior of a system—animal plus schedule—rather than about the animal itself.

  If animals are not molar matchers, then what are they? In this final section, we discuss the molecular mechanisms of choice that may underlie all the molar patterns we have been discussing. The first two, momentary maximizing and melioration, are examples of hill-climbing processes, that is, processes that move behavior in the direction of the better alternative. The last, linear waiting, is a slight extension of the proportional-timing process discussed in Chapter 9.

Momentary Maximizing

We have already seen that animals will usually settle for the high-probability alternative in the two-armed-bandit situation. Given one key that pays off with probability $\frac{1}{10}$ and another that pays off with probability $\frac{1}{20}$, pigeons eventually learn to peck only the high-probability key. In 1966, Charles Shimp proposed that pigeons follow this rule consistently, even on VI schedules in which it does not seem to apply in any obvious manner. He called his hypothesis *momentary maximizing*. How does momentary maximizing work? The simplest way to understand this theory is to begin with a procedure that is quite similar to the concurrent VI VI schedule: concurrent FI FI. We discussed concurrent FI FI at the beginning of Chapter 9 (see Figure 9.6).

Recall that the concurrent FI FI schedule could be programmed in two ways: Either the two programming timers could both be reset with reinforcement for either response, or the timers could be independent, the timer on the left only resetting following reinforcement for a left-key response and similarly for the right key. Recall also that the method using independent timers favors responding to both keys—partial preference—whereas the other method favors exclusive choice. Let's consider why by taking a simple example of a concurrent FI 3–min, FI 1–min schedule. Assume that our pigeon is initially naive and knows nothing about either alternative, other than being willing to peck both keys without preference. For this behavior, the bird receives food after 1 min of pecking on the right key, which may cause it to shift its preference slightly to the right key. After 2 min, the bird receives a second reinforcement on the right key. But presumably, two food deliveries are insufficient to produce an exclusive preference, so it still pecks the left key once in a while. After 3 min, the bird receives a third reinforcement on the right key, but this time, its next peck on the left key also procures food, because the FI 3–min timer has been running right along and the time is now out. If we were to continue to watch the pigeon, we might begin to see more complex patterns develop. If the bird can keep both keys and the timers "in synch," then it can learn that a peck on the left key is only reinforced some time after two reinforcements on the right key—thus we might see the development of a sequential pattern. But even without such a pattern, it should be obvious that our bird will continue to peck on both keys.

Let's complicate the situation a bit. Instead of a concurrent FI FI schedule, let's now look at a concurrent VI VI schedule. The general argument still applies. The pigeon should clearly sample both alternatives, but now there is absolutely no possibility of learning any kind of response sequence like "peck on the right key until you receive two reinforcements, then try the left key," because the reinforcers now occur at unpredictable times on both keys. Thus, two left-key reinforcers may sometimes occur in close succession. What information can the pigeon use to help it?

Shimp's (1966) insight was to see that although reinforcement is always uncertain on a VI schedule, the probability of reinforcement changes in a predictable fashion. As Staddon, Hinson, and Kram (1981) showed 15 years later, the critical aspect on VI schedules with truly random distributions of reinforcers is the *time since the last response* on each key. The longer the time since the animal last responded on a given key, the higher the probability that a response will be reinforced. You can see the truth of this statement when you look at the concurrent FI FI case: On both keys, the longer the postreinforcement time, the more likely a response will be reinforced. Postreinforcement time is critical here, because the FI timers run from one food delivery to the next. On the other hand, post*response* time is critical on random-interval (RI) schedules because of a curious property of randomness.

People get confused on this point because of something called the gambler's fallacy. Suppose someone is tossing a coin and you have been assured that it is a truly unbiased coin. Nevertheless, you have just witnessed five heads in a row: What is the probability that the next toss will be tails? Clearly, the answer depends in part on how much you trust the person who assured you the coin is unbiased. But trust us: It *is* unbiased. So what is the probability of a tails on the next toss? Many people may guess that the probability of tails is now greater than one-half, because of the prior preponderance of heads. Such theorizing is known as the *gambler's fallacy,* because (of course) the probability of tails really is always one-half.

The counterpart to the gambler's fallacy with random-interval schedules is to believe that reinforcement is more likely the longer the time that has elapsed without reinforcement. However, this statement is not true so long as the animal continues to respond. It *is* true as long as the animal *does not* respond. Let's see why. On a random-interval schedule, reinforcement availability is determined by a process quite like a sequence of coin tosses. One difference is that the tosses are much more likely to turn up tails (no food) than heads (food), and they are made extremely rapidly by a computer. Most important, on interval schedules of all kinds, once the timer has run its course, it does not start again until a response occurs. Therefore, once a head turns up, reinforcement is available for the next response, whenever it occurs.

Let's suppose the scheduling computer tosses its imaginary coin once per second and the probability of heads is $\frac{1}{10}$. Then, as long as the animal responds at least once per second, it will receive food on the average of once every 10 sec, that is, the pigeon is on a random-interval (RI), 10–sec schedule. Moreover, if the bird responds exactly once every second, the probability that each peck will result in food is a constant $\frac{1}{10}$. But suppose the bird is interrupted and doesn't respond, how will the probability of payoff change? Well, even if you're not a student of probability theory, you can see that for the first second, the payoff probability is $\frac{1}{10}$, but if the bird doesn't respond, then after 2 sec, the payoff probability has increased (because food could have been made available in the first second—the pigeon doesn't know because it didn't respond—or the second second). The situation is like tossing a coin twice and asking: What is the probability of getting heads at least once?

The algebra is in fact quite simple: The probability of at least one head in two tosses is one minus the probability of two tails. For our RI schedule, the probability of a tail is $\frac{9}{10}$; and the probability of a tail on the second toss is also $\frac{9}{10}$. Hence, the probability of tossing two tails is $(\frac{9}{10})^2 = 0.81$. Thus, the probability of at least one head is $1 - 0.81 = 0.19$, which is a considerable increase over 0.1. The increment in p(head) as a function of postresponse time is shown graphically in Figure 11.22. As you can see, after 20 sec of no response, the probability of payoff is quite high, almost 0.9.

On a concurrent random-interval schedule, there are two schedules like the one shown in Figure 11.22. Therefore, for pressing each key, the probability of reinforcement is rising, so long as the animal does not respond. As soon as it responds, then the probability returns to zero and starts the same function again. The difference between a rich RI schedule and a poor one is in the probability setting of the "coin tosser": The higher the probability of a head, the faster the

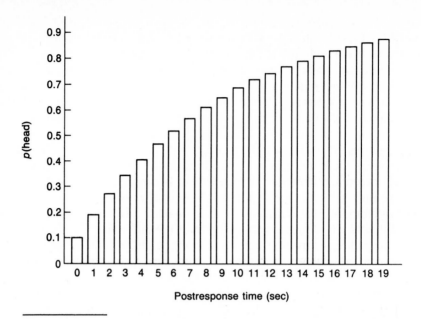

FIGURE 11.22   Probability of at least one head after 1–20 tosses of a biased coin in which p(heads) = 0.1 and p(tails) = 0.9.

curve rises to its maximum value of 1. For example, if p(head) = $\frac{1}{2}$, then p(head) after 1, 2, 3 (etc.) sec of nonresponding is 0.5, 0.75, 0.875, and so on.

The hypothesis of momentary maximizing says that whenever the animal decides to respond, it will always pick the alternative with the highest momentary probability of payoff and that probability of payoff is determined by a rising function like the one shown in Figure 11.22. Notice that the hypothesis is incomplete in an important way: It says which key will be chosen, once the animal decides to respond; it does not say at what time or how fast the animal will respond. Nevertheless, it turns out that there is a simple way to see whether an animal is responding according to this rule. For example, suppose that the two VI (really RI) schedules are 1–min for the right key and 3–min for the left key. Thus when the animal responds on the left key (the longer-time-to-food-delivery key), the time since its previous response on the left key should be at least three times as long as the time since its previous response on the right key. Conversely, when the animal responds on the right key, the time since its last right-key response should be at least one-third the time since its last left-key response. Under most conditions, following this rule implies that the animal will make three times as many responses on the right key as on the left key. This relationship should sound familiar: It is the ubiquitous matching result once again. In other words, momentary maximizing, like essentially every other reinforcement rule, predicts matching in the concurrent RI RI situation.

What do the data say? We know that pigeons and rats match, but do they match because they are also momentary maximizing? The answer seems to be "sometimes, but perhaps not every time." Hinson and Staddon (1983a, 1983b) conducted a series of experiments in which they measured the times of every key peck in a concurrent RI RI situation. They found that pigeons followed the momentary-maximizing rule—although not very well. In their study, as in many others, the animals tended to *undermatch*, that is, the proportion of left key pecks and right key pecks is closer to 50:50 (indifference) than to the proper proportion of the reinforcers.

Melioration

Rachlin (1973) and Herrnstein (Herrnstein & Vaughan, 1980) have suggested an alternative mechanism for matching that is somewhere in between the purely molecular mechanism of momentary maximizing and the purely molar relative law of effect (see Staddon, 1988, for a formal statement of this theory). Herrnstein calls this idea *melioration*, meaning "to make better." The closest analogy, for those of you familiar with elementary chemistry, is to the idea of diffusion. You may remember that if you have a concentrated solution on one side of a semipermeable membrane and a dilute solution on the other, water will diffuse from the more dilute into the more concentrated because of osmotic pressure. The concentrated solution is for Herrnstein and Rachlin like the richer of two reinforcement schedules, and the flow of solute is like the shift of responding. Thus, melioration is a shift in preference toward the alternative in which the "cost" of reinforcement—that is, responses made divided by reinforcements obtained—is less.

Note that this theory is similar to momentary maximizing in that the driving factor, the "cost" of reinforcement, is simply the reciprocal of the reinforcement probability. But, this theory is different in that it does not specify over what time period the shift in preference should take place. In short, it is really a molar theory, because it contains unspecified assumptions about an averaging window over which reinforcement probability and response proportions are assessed. (To be fair, momentary maximizing is also silent about the averaging window within which a payoff probability is measured.)

What is the evidence for melioration? The strongest evidence is that it so obviously gives the right answer: If preference shifts so that the cost of reinforcement is equal on both keys, that is, $R(x)/x = R(y)/x$, then we automatically have matching. Melioration cannot explain systematic deviations like the ubiquitous undermatching that is found in most experiments unless explicit steps are taken to prevent it (we discuss these steps in a moment). Melioration is supported by the results of Lea's (1976) titration experiment, which we described earlier; but it has failed in one direct test.

The test used what is called a *frequency-dependent (FD) schedule* (Staddon, 1988), which is like the two-armed bandit we have discussed. The pigeon has the choice of two keys to peck, and payoffs for each choice are delivered probabilistically. The difference between the keys is that the payoff probabilities depend on the animal's current preference. Current preference is measured by the controlling computer, which keeps a record of the last 32, say, choices. The

FD schedule used by Horner and Staddon (1987) worked in the following way. The payoff probability on the left key varied from close to zero to 0.2, say: It was zero if the animal's current preference were 100 percent for the left key; it was 0.2 if its current preference were 100 percent for the right key; it was proportionately less for intermediate values. The payoff probability on the right key followed a similar, linear function: Zero if preference were 100 percent for the left key, and 0.1 if its preference were 100 percent for the right key. Thus no matter what the animal's current preference, the payoff probability was always twice as high on the left key as it was on the right key.

Notice that this FD schedule poses an especially acute problem for a hill-climbing animal. If such an animal always picks the alternative with the higher payoff probability, then it must always pick the left key. But by selecting the left key, it drives down the payoff probability ever lower. Indeed, when preference is exclusively for the left key, the payoff probability is zero for both responses. A meliorating animal should therefore extinguish completely. A momentary-maximizing animal is also doomed to the same fate.

The fact is that Horner and Staddon's pigeons did *not* extinguish. They showed some preference for the left key, but that preference fell far short of the exclusive choice predicted by the two hill-climbing theories. Evidently, the birds were not blindly following either melioration or momentary maximizing. Horner and Staddon proposed an alternative, probabilistic learning rule they call *ratio invariance* that is consistent with their results but is too technical to pursue here. For now, it is sufficient to say that neither melioration nor momentary maximizing are adequate to account for probabilistic choice.

Linear Waiting

In Chapter 9 we showed how proportional timing seems to underlie a wide variety of effects on chain-reinforcement schedules. Since this process is so ubiquitous, we must see what it predicts for the situations we have been discussing in this chapter. For example, what does proportional timing imply for molar measures of performance on RI and FR schedules? What does it imply for the allocation of behavior on concurrent RI RI schedules? Is it consistent with the matching law? We take each of these cases in turn.

SIMPLE RI SCHEDULES   Behavior on RI schedules is the easiest to understand in terms of proportional timing. First, we must decide on the time marker. In our discussion of momentary maximizing, we showed that postresponse time is the critical variable on RI schedules. Proportional timing, then, just says that pigeons (and rats) will set their average interresponse time to be a fixed proportion of the expected time between a response and reinforcement. If the reinforcement is delivered on a random basis, then the expected time to reinforcement is 1/reinforcement rate. Thus, proportional timing implies that the response rate should be proportional to the reinforcement rate on RI schedules. This statement is close to the truth when the reinforcement rate is low; it is not true when the reinforcement rate is high. What have we forgotten?

We have forgotten that there is an upper limit on response rate, which is a lower limit on the time between responses. When typical waiting times are long, on FI schedules, for example, we can ignore this constraint. But when they are short, on RI schedules, for example, we must include it. If we add in a term for the minimum time between responses, we have a modified version of proportional timing that Wynne and Staddon (1988) have called *linear waiting*. If we denote the expected time to reinforcement by I and the time between responses by t, linear waiting is as follows:

$$t = AI + B \tag{11.13}$$

where A is the proportion of the expected time to food that the animal waits, as before, and B is the shortest possible interresponse time. Thus even if I is zero, the animal will wait at least time B between successive responses.

Let's look at what Equation 11.13 predicts for simple VI schedules: t is 1/response rate, x; I is 1/reinforcement rate, $R(x)$. Making these substitutions yields $1/x = A/R(x) + B$, or

$$x = \frac{R(x)}{A + BR(x)} = \frac{\dfrac{1}{B}R(x)}{\dfrac{A}{B} + R(x)} \tag{11.14}$$

Equation 11.14 should look quite familiar: It is Herrnstein's hyperbola (the matching law prediction for simple VI schedules: Equation 11.12), with $1/B = k$ and $A/B = R_0$. As we have seen, this equation gives a good description of molar responding on most VI schedules (cf. Figure 9.18). Moreover, the parameters $1/B$ and A/B have the same significance as Herrnstein's parameters k and R_0. Recall that R_0 was supposed to represent the effect of "other" reinforcers; hence, increasing the magnitude of the reinforcer for response X should in effect reduce R_0. Increasing reinforcement magnitude reduces the waiting proportion *(A)*, as we saw earlier, hence reduces A/B. Parameter k is assumed to represent the maximum possible response rate; the linear-waiting parameter B represents the shortest possible interresponse time, so that $1/B$ has the same significance as k.

FIXED-RATIO SCHEDULES   One of the main problems with the single-response matching equation (Equation 11.12) is that it does not provide an accurate prediction of how response rate varies with reinforcement rate on fixed-ratio schedules (Timberlake, 1977). And since it has no term for the schedule itself, it obviously cannot describe the relation between response rate and ratio value. However, it is not difficult to derive these predictions from linear waiting.

In Chapter 9 we argued that fixed-ratio schedules are treated by animals in a fashion quite similar to two-link chain schedules. We can use this analysis to work out how overall response rate should depend on ratio value and how it should be related to obtained reinforcement rate as the ratio value is varied (i.e., the response function). The algebra involved is too lengthy to go into here (for those who wish, the relevant equations are summarized in Box 11.2), but the conclusions are quite simple:

B   O   X

—11.2—

Linear Waiting
and Fixed-Ratio Schedules

Responding on FR schedules is made up of two components: the postreinforcement pause of length t and the ratio "run." The run is N responses long, where N is the ratio value. The time between successive "run" responses is d. The value of d is determined by the positive feedback process described in Chapter 9. To illustrate, consider the case of FR 1, where $d = t$. Linear waiting says that $t = d = AE + B$, where A is the pause fraction, B is the shortest possible wait, and E is the expected time to food. But on FR 1, $E = d$. Solving for d therefore yields $d = B/(1 + A)$ as our estimate of the time between run responses. On higher ratios, the pause time (t) is determined in a similar way, $t = AE + B$, where E is now made up of two components: the pause time (t) plus the time taken up by a "run," (Nd, where N is the ratio value). Thus on an FR N schedule, the five equations we have to work with are as follows.

linear waiting for pause: $t = AE + B$

components of interreinforcement time: $E = t + Nd$

"run" interresponse time: $d = \dfrac{B}{1 - A}$

overall response rate: $x = \dfrac{N}{E}$

overall reinforcement rate: $R(x) = \dfrac{1}{E}$

Solving for response rate (x) as a function of ratio value we get the following:

$$x = \frac{N(1 - A)^2}{B[(1 - A) + N]} \tag{B11.1}$$

which is a positive, negatively accelerated function. Solving for x as a function of obtained reinforcement rate we get the following:

$$x = \frac{(1 - A)^2}{B} - (1 - A)\,R(x) \tag{B11.2}$$

which is a linear function with negative slope (see Figure 11.23).

1. Linear waiting predicts a positive relation between ratio value and re-
    sponse rate (Equation B11.1).

2. Linear waiting predicts a linear relation, with negative slope, between
    response rate and obtained reinforcement rate (Equation B11.2).

The validity of these predictions depends on conditions being such that parameters A and B are constant. They will not be constant if the animal's motivational
state is allowed to vary—for example, if the experimental session is so long or
the reinforcement rate so high that the animal is more or less hungry at the end
of the session than it was at the beginning.

    You have already seen data consistent with the first prediction in the Hirsch
and Collier experiment (Figure 11.6). As well, numerous others reviewed by
Hogan and Roper (1978), show that the response rate increases with the ratio
value over most of the range in most experiments with food or water reinforcement. The second prediction, a linear-response function of negative slope, has
also been repeatedly confirmed in ratio-schedule experiments by Allison that are
not open to the artifactual objection we discussed earlier (see Allison, 1983) and
by Ettinger and Staddon (1983). Ettinger and Staddon used a novel procedure in
which rats working for food reinforcement were repeatedly exposed to an ascending and descending cycle of six ratio values, (2, 4, 8, 16, 32, and 64). By comparing cycles early and late in the session, we can ensure that performance is the
same at the beginning as at the end, permitting the six cycles/session to be
averaged.

    The results are illustrated in Figure 11.23, which shows three straight-line
response functions. The rightmost line was obtained with very hungry rats (80
percent of free-feeding weight), the parallel one to the left was obtained with the
same rats eating food adulterated with bad-tasting quinine. The third function,
the one of lower slope, was obtained when the rats were less hungry (95 percent
of free-feeding weight). What is the effect of hunger in terms of the linear-
waiting model? Recall that in Chapter 9 we used the fact that the waiting fraction
(A) is smaller for large reinforcements to explain some properties of self-control
on chain schedules. We use similar reasoning here, because the reinforcer must
change in effective value as the animal becomes satiated. Hence, parameter A
should be larger for a satiated animal than for a hungry one. What is the effect of
an increase in body weight? Parameter A must increase, because the reinforcer
is now less effective. But an increase in A means a lower value for the term $1 - A$,
which means a shallower line—which is just what we see in Figure 11.23. What
about the y-intercept (b): $(1 - A)^2/B$? It also changes when A changes, and
Ettinger and Staddon found that as well. But notice that anything that affects
only parameter B affects *only* the y-intercept—and not the slope. Apparently a
noxious taste, such as quinine, does just that, as shown by the leftmost parallel
response function in Figure 11.23. All is not perfect, however, because the negative FR response-function slope predicted by linear waiting is too shallow.

CONCURRENT RI RI SCHEDULES   We have already seen that any reinforcement rule
that satisfies two not-very-restrictive conditions—that response rate be positively related to reinforcement rate and that the intercept zero—is sufficient to

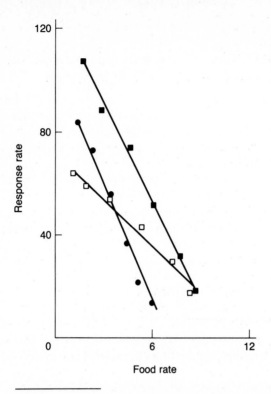

FIGURE 11.23   Each point is the average lever-press rate for a group of four rats trained on a cyclic-ratio schedule. Each point represents a different ratio value: for example, the points at the bottom of the graph are for FR 2, the points at the top for FR 64. The straight lines are fitted to the data. The rightmost line is for rats at 80 percent of their free-feeding weights; the inner line parallel to it is for the same rats that are receiving food adulterated with quinine. The line of most shallow slope is for the rats at 95 percent of their free-feeding weights (from Ettinger & Staddon, 1983).

produce matching on concurrent RI RI schedules. Linear waiting satisfies these conditions: The interresponse time is positively related to the reinforcement delay, and any infinite delay (zero reinforcement rate) should produce infinite waiting (no responses). Hence, linear-waiting, like numerous other reinforcement rules, predicts matching of response ratios to ratios of obtained reinforcement on concurrent RI RI schedules.

We have also seen that behavior on concurrent RI RI schedules often conforms quite well to momentary maximizing. Does this result conflict with the linear-waiting hypothesis? Not at all, because an animal that follows the linear-waiting rule will also show momentary maximizing. For example, suppose the RI schedule on the left key is 3 min and on the right key is 1 min. Linear waiting implies that the time between interresponse times on the left key will be on average about three times longer than interresponse times on the right key. Such a pattern is not *required* by momentary maximizing—recall that the actual times when a "decision" to respond is made are not prescribed by momentary maximizing—but it is perfectly consistent with momentary maximizing. The response that actually occurs satisfies the momentary-maximizing condition because it is made to the alternative with highest payoff probability.

Molecular Mechanisms: Conclusion

We have discussed three molecular mechanisms for behavioral allocation: momentary maximizing, melioration, and linear waiting. The first two are hill-climbing processes; they act to shift preferences in the direction of the locally better alternative. Therefore, both predict fixation on the richer alternative in the two-armed bandit situation. In the form of the relative law of effect, melioration can account for molar behavior on simple RI schedules, but it fails to account for behavior on simple FR schedules because it treats all schedules alike. Momentary maximizing is also unable to account for performance on simple schedules. Neither melioration nor matching can explain performance on a frequency-dependent schedule in which the probability of payoff on the left key is always higher than on the right key and increasing left-key preference reduces the absolute values of both payoff probabilities.

The timing process called linear waiting accounts for some differences between molar patterns on simple schedules. It explains why Herrnstein's hyperbola works so well on RI schedules, and also suggests one reason for why the FR and RI response functions are different. On concurrent RI RI schedules, linear waiting is quite similar to momentary maximizing and makes similar predictions. It can also account for the effects of the changeover delay, which tends to produce good matching, and the effects of low absolute-reinforcement rates, which tend to produce undermatching. However, we do not know (it is not easy to solve the problem analytically) whether linear waiting can account for the complex patterns of behavior produced by some frequency-dependent schedules, nor is it clear whether it can account for biased matching on concurrent VI VR schedules. Whether these failures reflect a fundamental error or the need for auxiliary assumptions is not clear as yet.

SUMMARY

This chapter has been about implicit and explicit choice. Implicit choice refers to the processes that determine the proportions of time that animals spend on different activities, the factors that maintain that distribution, and the effects of disturbing it by blocking activities or making access to one activity contingent on the performance of another. We saw that under many conditions the activity distribution is stable, and the organism resists in various ways perturbations that threaten to change the distribution from its paired-baseline level. The first attempt to understand these effects was made by David Premack, who concluded that higher-probability activities always reinforce lower-probability activities. This molar principle was extended first by the qualitative principle of response deprivation and then by a variety of quantitative optimality and economic analyses. The first of these, the minimum-distance model, gave a special status to the paired-baseline levels, or bliss point.

Optimality analysis is a general tool that can be applied to any adaptive system. It has allowed us to see common principles that underlie implicit choice and explicit choice, that is, special experimental arrangements to compare the effects on preference of things such as the type and amount of a reinforcer. Robust experimental findings such as the matching law turn out to be generally consistent with optimality models. Similar adaptive principles—diminishing marginal utility of reward frequency and amount—seem to underlie both the situations studied by Premack and more conventional schedules of operant reinforcement.

Despite their many successes, all optimality models fail under some conditions, because they are functional models, not models of mechanism. Animals and people are rarely, if ever, literal optimizers, systematically comparing the long-term payoffs associated with different policies. Thus, although matching on concurrent VI VI schedules fits in with a number of optimal policies, matching on concurrent VI VR does not. We described a number of other experiments in which animals clearly behave nonoptimally.

The last part of the chapter looked at the mechanisms of choice and behavioral allocation. Our first conclusion was that marginal changes in molar variables probably do not have any direct effect on behavior, underscoring the conclusion that even good optimality models, especially molar optimality models, only describe what animals achieve, not how they achieve it. The last part of the chapter therefore focused on molecular mechanisms of behavioral allocation: momentary maximizing, melioration, and linear waiting. Momentary maximizing and linear waiting make similar predictions in choice situations, but linear waiting promises to be more general. We have already seen the importance of this process to conditioned reinforcement in Chapter 9. Quite apart from the quantitative details, it is clear that the expected time to the reinforcer, assessed through a memory-constrained timing mechanism, plays a dominant role in all the complex patterns of behavior generated by a variety of reinforcement schedules.

"Further research is needed" is the cliché with which every tired undergraduate has at one time or another thankfully ended an overdue term paper. The theoretical and experimental analysis of learning and adaptive behavior in mammals and birds is now a mature field. At times it has seemed as if little more needed to be, or could be, done to understand behavior at the purely behavioral level. Further progress, many assumed, had to come through deeper understanding of the brain mechanisms behind behavior. We hope that our account of the lively theoretical discussions of the mechanisms underlying adaptive behavior have persuaded you otherwise. There is still more to be learned from the relatively impoverished patterns of pigeons in Skinner boxes than was believed even 10 years ago. More research, especially theoretical research, is indeed needed to learn about these behavioral mechanisms. Even the relatively little that we do know is beginning to bring into clearer focus the real task for the neural machinery, which is not "to produce behavior" or "to respond to stimuli" but to implement the rules that behavior follows. If these rules are as simple and powerful as those we have discussed in this text, perhaps it will not be long before we know how the brains of rats, pigeons—and people—actually go about the computations that underlie adaptive behavior.

References

Allison, J. (1980). Conservation, matching, and the variable-interval schedule. *Animal Learning and Behavior, 8,* 185–192.

Allison, J. (1983). *Behavioral economics.* New York: Praeger.

Anderson, J. R. (1983). *The architecture of cognition.* Cambridge, MA: Harvard University Press.

Azrin, N. H. (1960). Effect of punishment intensity during variable-interval reinforcement. *Journal of the Experimental Analysis of Behavior, 3,* 123–142.

Azrin, N. H., Holz, W. C., & Hake, D. (1963). Fixed-ratio punishment. *Journal of the Experimental Analysis of Behavior, 6,* 141–148.

Badia, P., Coker, C., & Harsh, J. (1973). Choice of higher density signalled shock over lower density unsignalled shock. *Journal of the Experimental Analysis of Behavior, 20,* 47–55.

Bernoulli, D. (1954). Exposition of a new theory on the measurement of risk. *Econometrica, 22,* 23–36. (Original work published 1738).

Blough, D. S. (1966). The reinforcement of least-frequent interresponse times. *Journal of the Experimental Analysis of Behavior, 9,* 581–591.

Boag, P. T., & Grant, P. R. (1981). Intense natural selection in a population of Darwin's finches (Geospizinae) in the Galapagos. *Science, 214,* 82–84.

Boakes, R. (1984). *From Darwin to behaviorism: Psychology and the minds of animals.* Cambridge: Cambridge University Press.

Bolles, R. C. (1970). Species-specific defense reactions and avoidance learning. *Psychological Review, 77,* 32–48.

Braitenberg, V. (1984). *Vehicles: Experiments in synthetic psychology.* Cambridge, MA: The MIT Press.

Brandt, H. (1934). Die lichtorientierung der mehlmotte. *Ephestia kuehniella. Zeitschrift für Vergleichende Physiologie, 20,* 646–673.

Breland, K., & Breland, M. (1961). The misbehavior of organisms. *American Psychologist, 16,* 661–664.

Brogden, W. J., Lipman, E. A., & Culler, E. (1983). The role of incentive in conditioning and extinction. *American Journal of Psychology, 51,* 109–117.

Brown, P. L., & Jenkins, H. M. (1968). Auto-shaping of the pigeon's key-peck. *Journal of the Experimental Analysis of Behavior, 11,* 1–8.

Campbell, D. T. (1975). On the conflicts between biological and social evolution and between psychology and moral tradition. *American Psychologist, 30,* 1103–1126.

Caplan, A. I., & Ordahl, C. P. (1978). Irreversible gene repression model for the control of development. *Science, 201,* 120–130.

Catania, A. C. (1979). *Learning.* Englewood Cliffs, NJ: Prentice-Hall.

Catania, A. C., Mathews, T. J., Silverman, P. J., & Yohalem, R. (1977). Yoked variable-ratio and variable-interval responding in pigeons. *Journal of the Experimental Analysis of Behavior, 28,* 155–161.

Catania, A. C., & Reynolds, G. S. (1968). A quantitative analysis of the behavior maintained by interval schedules of reinforcement. *Journal of the Experimental Analysis of Behavior, 11,* 327–383.

Catania, A. C., Yohalem, R., & Silverman, P. J. (1980). Contingency and stimulus change in chained schedules of reinforcement. *Journal of the Experimental Analysis of Behavior, 33,* 213–219.

Church, R. M. (1969). Response suppression. In B. A. Campbell & R. M. Church (Eds.), *Punishment and aversive behavior.* New York: Appleton-Century-Crofts.

Church, R. M. (1978). The internal clock. In S. H. Hulse, H. Fowler, & W. K. Honig (Eds.), *Cognitive processes in animal behavior.* Hillsdale, NJ: Erlbaum.

Cosmides, L., & Tooby, J. (1987). From evolution to behavior: Evolutionary psychology as the missing link. In J. Dupré (Ed.), *The latest on the best: Essays on evolution and optimality.* Cambridge, MA: Bradford.

Crutchfield, J. P., Farmer, J. D., Packard, N. H., & Shaw, R. S. (1986). Chaos. *Scientific American, 255*(6), 46–57.

D'Amato, M. R. (1973). Delayed matching and short-term memory in monkeys. In G. H. Bower (Ed.), *The psychology of learning and motivation: Advances in research and theory.* New York: Academic Press.

Darwin, C. (1951). *The origin of the species.* Reprinted from the 6th ed., 1872. Oxford: Oxford University Press.

Darwin, C. (1875). *The movements and habits of climbing plants.* London: John Murray.

Dews, P. B. (1962). The effect of multiple S^Δ periods on responding on a fixed-interval schedule. *Journal of the Experimental Analysis of Behavior, 5,* 369–374.

Dickinson, A. (1980). *Contemporary animal learning theory.* Cambridge, Eng.: Cambridge University Press.

Einhorn, H. J., & Hogarth, R. M. (1978). Confidence in judgment: Persistence of the illusion of validity. *Psychological Review, 85,* 395–416.

Epstein, R. (1987). The spontaneous interconnection of four repertoires of behavior in a pigeon (*Columba livia*). *Journal of Comparative Psychology, 101,* 197–201.

Estes, W. K., & Skinner, B. F. (1941). Some quantitative properties of anxiety. *Journal of Experimental Psychology, 29,* 290–400.

Ettinger, R. H., Reid, A. K., & Staddon, J. E. R. (1987). Sensitivity to molar feedback functions: A test of molar optimality theory. *Journal of Experimental Psychology: Animal Behavior Processes, 13,* 366–375.

Ettinger, R. H., & Staddon, J. E. R. (1983). Operant regulation of feeding: A static analysis. *Behavioral Neuroscience, 97,* 639–653.

Fantino, E. (1969). Choice and rate of reinforcement. *Journal of the Experimental Analysis of Behavior, 12,* 723–730.

Fantino, E., & Abarca, N. (1985). Choice, optimal foraging, and the delay-reduction hypothesis. *The Behavioral and Brain Sciences, 8,* 315–330.

Fantino, E., & Logan, C. A. (1979). *The experimental analysis of behavior: A biological perspective.* San Francisco: W. H. Freeman.

Fantino, E., Squires, N., Delbrück, N., & Peterson, C. (1972). Choice behavior and the accessibility of the reinforcer. *Journal of the Experimental Analysis of Behavior, 18,* 35–43.

Ferster, C. B., & Skinner, B. F. (1957). *Schedules of reinforcement.* New York: Appleton-Century-Crofts.

Fraenkel, G. S, & Gunn, D. L. (1940). *The orientation of animals.* Fair Lawn, NJ: Oxford University Press, Dover edition: 1961.

Frank, J., & Staddon, J. E. R. (1974). The effects of restraint on temporal discrimination behavior. *Psychological Record, 23,* 123–130.

Galef, B. G. (1988). Evolution and learning before Thorndike: A forgotten epoch in the history of behavioral research. In R. C. Bolles & M. D. Beecher, *Evolution and learning.* Hillsdale, NJ: Erlbaum.

Garcia, J., Kimmeldorf, D. J., & Hunt, E. L. (1961). The use of ionizing radiation as a motivatory stimulus. *Psychological Review, 68,* 383–385.

Garner, W. R. (1962). *Uncertainty and structure as psychological concepts.* New York: Wiley.

Gibbon, J. (1977). Scalar expectancy theory and Weber's law in animal timing. *Psychological Review, 84,* 279–325.

Gibbon, J., Berryman, R., & Thompson, R. L. (1974). Contingency spaces and measures in classical conditioning. *Journal of the Experimental Analysis of Behavior, 21,* 585–605.

Gibbon, J., Church, R. M., Fairhurst, S., & Kacelnik, A. (1988). Scalar expectancy theory and choice between delayed rewards. *Psychological Review, 95,* 102–114.

Gibbs, C. M., Latham, S. B., & Gormezano, J. (1978). Classical conditioning of the rabbit nicitating membrane response: Effects of reinforcement schedule on response maintenance and resistance to extinction. *Animal Learning and Behavior, 6,* 209–215.

Gleick, J. (1987). *Chaos: Making a new science.* New York: Viking.

Gottlieb, G. (1966). Species identification by avian neonates: Contributory effect of perinatal auditory stimulation. *Animal Behavior, 14,* 282–290.

Gould, J. L., & Gould, C. G. (1982). The insect mind: Physics or metaphysics? In D. R. Griffin (Ed.), *Animal mind–human mind.* Berlin/Heidelberg/New York: Springer-Verlag.

Green, L., Kagel, J. H., & Battalio, R. C. (1982). Ratio schedules of reinforcement and their relation to economic theories of labor supply. In M. L. Commons, R. J. Herrnstein, & H. Rachlin (Eds.), *Quantitative analyses of behavior: Vol. II. Matching and maximizing accounts.* Cambridge, MA: Ballinger.

Green, L., & Snyderman, M. (1980). Choice between rewards differing in demand and delay: Toward a choice model of self-control. *Journal of the Experimental Analysis of Behavior, 34,* 135–147.

Grossberg, S. (Ed.). (1987). *The adaptive brain* (Vols. I–II). Amsterdam: North-Holland.

Guttman, N., & Kalish, H. I. (1956). Discriminability and stimulus generalization. *Journal of Experimental Psychology, 51,* 79–88.

Hanson, H. M. (1959). The effects of discrimination training on stimulus generalization. *Journal of Experimental Psychology, 58,* 321–334.

Harlow, H. F., & Harlow, M. K. (1959). Love in infant monkeys. *Scientific American, 200,* 68–74.

Harrison, R., & Nissen, H. W. (1941). Spatial separation in the delayed response performance of chimpanzees. *Journal of Comparative Psychology, 31,* 427–435.

Hearst, E., Koresko, M. B., & Poppen, R. (1964). Stimulus generalization and the response-reinforcement contingency. *Journal of the Experimental Analysis of Behavior, 7,* 369–380.

Hearst, E., & Jenkins, H. M. (1974). Sign-tracking: The stimulus-reinforcer relation and directed action. *Psychonomic Society Monograph.*

Hebb, D. O. (1949). *The organization of behavior.* New York: Wiley-Interscience.

Henton, W. W., & Iversen, I. H. (1978). *Classical conditioning and operant conditioning.* New York: Springer-Verlag.

Herrnstein, R. J. (1961). Relative and absolute strength of response as a function of frequency of reinforcement. *Journal of the Experimental Analysis of Behavior, 4,* 267–272.

Herrnstein, R. J. (1964). Secondary reinforcement and rate of primary reinforcement. *Journal of the Experimental Analysis of Behavior, 7,* 27–36.

Herrnstein, R. J. (1966). Superstition: A corollary of the principles of operant conditioning. In W. K. Honig (Ed.), *Operant behavior.* New York: Appleton-Century-Crofts.

Herrnstein, R. J., & Heyman, G. M. (1979). Is matching compatible with reinforcement maximization on concurrent variable interval, variable ratio? *Journal of the Experimental Analysis of Behavior, 31,* 209–223.

Herrnstein, R. J., & Hineline, P. N. (1966). Negative reinforcement as shock-frequency reduction. *Journal of the Experimental Analysis of Behavior, 9,* 421–430.

Herrnstein, R. J., & Vaughan, W. (1980). Melioration and behavioral allocation. In J. E. R. Staddon (Ed.), *Limits to action: The allocation of individual behavior.* New York: Academic Press.

Hilgard, E. R., & Marquis, D. G. (1940). *Conditioning and learning.* New York: Appleton-Century-Crofts.

Hineline, P. (1977). Negative reinforcement and avoidance. In W. K. Honig & J. E. R. Staddon (Eds.), *Handbook of operant behavior.* New York: Appleton-Century-Crofts.

Hinson, J. M., & Staddon, J. E. R. (1978). Behavioral competition: A mechanism for schedule interactions. *Science, 202,* 432–434.

Hinson, J. M., & Staddon, J. E. R. (1983a). Hill-climbing by pigeons. *Journal of the Experimental Analysis of Behavior, 39,* 25–47.

Hinson, J. M., & Staddon, J. E. R. (1983b). Matching, maximizing and hill-climbing. *Journal of the Experimental Analysis of Behavior, 40,* 321–31.

Hirsch, E., & Collier, G. (1974). Effort as determinant of intake and patterns of drinking in the Guinea pig. *Physiology and Behavior, 12,* 647–655.

Hogan, J. A., & Roper, T. J. (1978). A comparison of the properties of different reinforcers. In J. S. Rosenblatt, R. A. Hinde, E. Shaw, & C. Beer (Eds.), *Advances in the study of behavior: Vol. 8.* New York: Academic Press.

Holland, P. C. (1980). Influence of visual conditioned-stimulus characteristics on the form of the appetitive Pavlovian conditioning in rats. *Journal of Experimental Psychology: Animal Behavior Processes, 6,* 81–97.

Hollis, K. L. (1984). Representation-mediated overshadowing and potentiation of conditioned aversions. *Journal of Experimental Psychology: Animal Behavior Processes, 9,* 1–13.

Honig, W. K., Boneau, C. A., Burstein, K. R., & Pennypacker, H. S. (1963). Positive and negative generalization gradients obtained after equivalent training conditions. *Journal of Comparative and Physiological Psychology, 56,* 111–116.

Honig, W. K., & Thompson, R. K. R. (1982). Retrospective and prospective processes in animal working memory. In G. H. Bower (Ed.), *The psychology of learning and motivation: Vol. 16,* pp. 167–197. New York: Academic Press.

Horner, J. M., & Staddon, J. E. R. (1987). Probabilistic choice: A simple invariance. *Behavioral Processes, 15,* 59–92.

Hovland, C. I. (1951). Human learning and retention. In S. S. Stevens (Ed.), *Handbook of experimental psychology.* New York: Wiley.

Hull, C. L. (1935). The mechanism of assembly of behavior segments in novel combinations. *Psychological Review, 42,* 219–245.

Hursh, S. R. (1984). Behavioral economics. *Journal of the Experimental Analysis of Behavior, 42,* 435–452.

Jenkins, H. M., & Moore, B. R. (1973). The form of the autoshaped response with food or water reinforcers. *Journal of the Experimental Analysis of Behavior, 20,* 163–181.

Jenkins, H. M., & Sainsbury, R. S. (1970). Discrimination learning with the distinctive feature on positive or negative trials. In D. I. Mostofsky (Ed.), *Attention: Contemporary theory and analysis.* New York: Appleton-Century-Crofts.

Jennings, H. S. (1976). *Behavior of the lower organisms.* Reprint of the 1906 edition. Bloomington: Indiana University Press.

Kahneman, D., & Tversky, A. (1979). Prospect theory: An analysis of decision under risk. *Econometrica, 47,* 263–291.

Kahneman, D., & Tversky, A. (1984). Choices, values and frames. *American Psychologist, 39,* 341–350.

Kamin, L. J. (1969). Predictability, surprise, attention and conditioning. In B. A. Campbell & R. M. Church (Eds.), *Punishment and aversive behavior.* New York: Appleton-Century-Crofts.

Keith-Lucas, T., & Guttman, N. (1975). Robust-single-trial delayed backward conditioning. *Journal of Comparative and Physiological Psychology, 88,* 468–476.

Kelleher, R. T. (1966). Chaining and conditioned reinforcement. In W. K. Honig, (Ed.), *Operant behavior: Areas of research and application.* New York: Appleton-Century-Crofts.

Kello, J. (1973). Observation of the behavior of rats running to reward and nonreward in an alleyway. Doctoral dissertation, Duke University.

Killeen, P. R. (1978). Superstition: A matter of bias, not detectability. *Science, 199,* 88–90.

Killeen, P. R. (1985). Incentive theory: IV. Magnitude of reward. *Journal of the Experimental Analysis of Behavior, 43,* 407–417.

Killeen, P. R., Hanson, S. J., & Osborne, S. R. (1978). Arousal: Its genesis and manifestation as response rate. *Psychological Review, 85,* 571–581.

Kimble, G. A. (1961). *Hilgard and Marquis' conditioning and learning.* (2nd. ed.). New York: Appleton-Century-Crofts.

Kimble, G. A., & Perlmutter, L. C. (1970). The problem of volition. *Psychological Review, 77,* 361–384.

Kohler, W. (1925). *The mentality of apes.* Trans. by E. Winter. New York: Harcourt, Brace, & World.

Konishi, M. & Nottebohm, F. (1969). Experimental studies in the ontogeny of avian vocalization. In R. A. Hinde (Ed.), *Bird vocalization.* Cambridge: Cambridge University Press.

Koshland, D. E. (1977). A response regulator model in a simple sensory system. *Science, 196,* 1055–1063.

Krebs, J. R., & Davies, N. B. (1984). *Behavioural ecology: An evolutionary approach* (2nd ed.). Sunderland, MA: Sinauer Associates.

Krebs, J. R., Erichsen, J. T., Webber, M. I., & Charnov, E. L. (1977). Optimal prey selection by the great tit (*Parus major*). *Animal Behaviour, 25,* 30–38.

Kuo, Z. Y. (1932). Ontogeny of embryonic behavior in Aves: IV. The influence of embryonic movements upon the behavior after hatching. *Journal of Comparative Psychology, 14,* 109–122.

Le Magnen, J. (1985). *Hunger.* Cambridge, Eng.: Cambridge University Press.

Lea, S. E. G. (1978). The psychology and economics of demand. *Psychological Bulletin, 85,* 441–446.

Lea, S. E. G., & Tarpy, R. M. (1982). Different demand curves from rats working under ratio and interval schedules. *Behaviour Analysis Letters, 2,* 113–121.

Lett, B. T. (1975). Long-delay learning in the T-maze. *Learning and Motivation, 6,* 80–90.

Levine, M. W., & Shefner, J. M. (1981). *Fundamentals of sensation and perception.* Philippines: Addison-Wesley.

Lockhead, G. R. (1970). Identification and form of multidimensional discrimination space. *Journal of Experimental Psychology, 85,* 1–10.

Lorenz, K. (1950). The comparative method in studying innate behavior patterns. *Symposium for the Society for Experimental Biology, 4,* 221–268.

Lowe, C. F., Davey, G. C., & Harzem, P. (1974). Effects of reinforcement magnitude on interval and ratio schedules. *Journal of the Experimental Analysis of Behavior, 22,* 553–560.

Luce, R. D. (1959). *Individual choice behavior: A theoretical analysis.* New York: Wiley.

Luce, R. D. (1977). The choice axiom after twenty years. *Journal of Mathematical Psychology, 15,* 215–233.

Luchins, A. S. (1942). Mechanization in problem solving: The effect of Einstellung. *Psychological Monographs, 54* (No. 248).

MacArthur, R. H., & Pianka, E. R. (1966). Optimal use of a patchy environment. *American Naturalist, 100,* 603–609.

MacEwen, D. (1972). The effects of terminal-link fixed-interval and variable-interval schedules on responding under concurrent chained schedules. *Journal of the Experimental Analysis of Behavior, 18,* 253–261.

Mackintosh, N. J. (1974). *The psychology of animal learning.* New York: Academic Press.

MacNab, R. M., & Koshland, D. E. (1972). The gradient-sensing mechanism in bacterial chemotaxis. *Proceedings of the National Academy of Sciences, USA, 69,* 2509–2512.

Maki, W. S., Jr., & Leith, C. R. (1973). Shared attention in pigeons. *Journal of the Experimental Analysis of Behavior, 19,* 345–349.

Marler, P., & Tamura, M. (1964) Culturally transmitted patterns of vocal behavior in sparrows. *Science, 146,* 1483–1486.

Marr, D. (1982). *Vision: A computational investigation into the human representation and processing of visual information.* San Francisco: W. H. Freeman.

Mast, S. O. (1911). *Light and the behavior of organisms.* New York: Wiley.

Mazur, J. E. (1984). Tests of an equivalence rule for fixed and variable reinforcer delays. *Journal of Experimental Psychology: Animal Behavior Processes, 10,* 426–436.

Mazur, J. E. (1986). Choice between single and multiple delayed reinforcers. *Journal of the Experimental Analysis of Behavior, 46,* 67–78.

McClelland, J. L., Rumelhart, D. E., & the PDP Research Group. (1986). *Parallel distributed processing: Explorations in the microstructure of cognition.* (Vols. 1 & 2). Cambridge, MA: MIT/Bradford.

McCulloch, W. S., & Pitts, W. (1943). A logical calculus of ideas immanent in nervous activity. *Bulletin of Mathematical Biophysics, 5,* 115–133.

McKearney, J. W. (1969). Fixed-interval schedules of electric shock presentation: Extinction and recovery of performance under different shock intensities and fixed-interval duration. *Journal of the Experimental Analysis of Behavior, 12,* 301–313.

McSweeney, F. K., Ettinger, R. H., & Norman, W. D. (1981). Three versions of the additive theories of behavioral contrast. *Journal of the Experimental Analysis of Behavior, 36,* 285, 297.

Miller, N. E., & Banuazizi, A. (1968). Instrumental learning by curarized rats of a specific visceral response. *Journal of Comparative and Physiological Psychology, 65,* 1–7.

Mook, D. G. (1987). *Motivation: The organization of action.* New York: Norton.

Moore, E. F. (1956). Gedanken-experiments on sequential machines. In C. E. Shannon & J. McCarthy (Eds.), *Automata studies.* Princeton, NJ: Princeton Annals of Mathematics Studies.

Moore, G. E. (1903). *Principia ethica.* Cambridge: Cambridge University Press.

Moore, J. (1982). Choice and number of reinforcers. *Journal of the Experimental Analysis of Behavior, 37,* 115–122.

Morris, R. G. M. (1981). Spatial localization does not require the presence of local cues. *Learning and Motivation, 12,* 239–260.

Müller, A. (1925). Uber lichtreaktionen von landasseln. *Zeitschrift für Vergleichende Physiologie, 3,* 113–144.

Neuringer, A. J., & Chung, S. H. (1967). Quasi-reinforcement: Control of responding by a percentage-reinforcement schedule. *Journal of the Experimental Analysis of Behavior, 10,* 45–54.

Obrist, P. A., Howard, J. L., Lowler, J. E., & Galozy, R. A. (1975). Operant conditioning of heart rate: Somatic correlates. *Psychophysiology, 12,* 445–455.

Olton, D. S., & Samuelson, R. J. (1976). Remembrance of places past. Spatial memory in rats. *Journal of Experimental Psychology: Animal Behavior Processes, 2,* 97–116.

Osgood, C. E. (1953). *Method and theory in experimental psychology.* New York: Oxford University Press.

Page, S., & Neuringer, A. (1985). Variability is an operant. *Journal of Experimental Psychology: Animal Behavior Processes, 11,* 429–452.

Peterson, C., & Seligman, M. E. P. (1984). Causal explanations as risk factors for depression. *Psychological Review, 91,* 347–374.

Platt, J. R. (1973). Percentile reinforcement: Paradigms for experimental analysis of response shaping. In G. H. Bower (Ed.), *Psychology of learning and motivation: Advances in research and theory: Vol. 7.* New York: Academic Press.

Popper, K. R. (1968). *The logic of scientific discovery.* New York: Harper & Row.

Powell, R. W. (1969). The effect of reinforcement magnitude upon responding under fixed-ratio schedules. *Journal of the Experimental Analysis of Behavior, 12,* 605–608.

Premack, D. (1965). Reinforcement theory. In D. Levine (Ed.), *Nebraska symposium on motivation: Vol. 13.* Lincoln: University of Nebraska Press.

Pritchard, R. M. (1961). Stabilized images in the retina. *Scientific American, 203,* 72–78.

Pryor, K. W., Haag, R., & O'Reilly, J. (1969). The creative purpose: Training for novel behavior. *Journal of the Experimental Analysis of Behavior, 12,* 653–661.

Rachlin, H. (1973). Contrast and matching. *Psychological Review, 80,* 217–234.

Rachlin, H., Battalio, R. C., Kagel, J. H., & Green, L. (1981). Maximization theory in behavioral psychology. *The Behavioral and Brain Sciences, 4,* 371–388.

Rachlin, H., & Burkhard, B. (1978). The temporal triangle: Response substitution in instrumental conditioning. *Psychological Review, 85,* 22–48.

Ralston, A. (1986). Discrete mathematics: The new mathematics of science. *American Scientist, 74,* 611–618.

Rescorla, R. A. (1967). Pavlovian conditioning and its proper control procedures. *Psychological Review, 74,* 71–80.

Rescorla, R. A. (1968). Probability of shock in the presence and absence of CS in fear conditioning. *Journal of Comparative and Physiological Psychology, 66,* 1–5.

Rescorla, R. A. (1982). Simultaneous second-order conditioning produces S–S learning in conditioning suppression. *Journal of Experimental Psychology: Animal Behavior Processes, 8,* 23–32.

Rescorla, R. A., & Wagner, A. R. (1972). A theory of Pavlovian conditioning: Variations in the effectiveness of reinforcement and nonreinforcement. In A. Black & W. R. Prokasy (Eds.), *Classical conditioning II.* New York: Appleton-Century-Crofts.

Revusky, S. H. (1971). The role of interference in association over delay. In W. K. Honig & P. H. R. James (Eds.), *Animal memory.* New York: Academic Press.

Reynolds, G. S. (1961). Behavioral contrast. *Journal of the Experimental Analysis of Behavior, 4,* 57–71.

Richelle, M., & Lejeune, H. (1980). *Time in animal behavior.* Oxford: Pergamon.

Riley, D. A., & Roitblat, H. I. (1978). Selective attention and related processes in pigeons. In S. H. Hulse, H. Fowler, & W. K. Honig (Eds.), *Cognitive processes in animal behavior.* Hillsdale, NJ: Erlbaum.

Roitblat, H. L. (1982). The meaning of representation in animal memory. *Behavioral and Brain Sciences, 5,* 353–506.

Rosenblatt, F. (1959). Two theorems of statistical separability in the perceptron. In *Mechanization of thought processes: Proceedings of a symposium held at the National Physical Laboratory, November 1958: Vol. 1,* pp. 421–456. London: H. M. Stationery Office.

Rosenblueth, A., Wiener, N., & Bigelow, J. (1943). Behavior, purpose, and teleology. *Philosophy of Science, 10,* 18–24.

Schwartz, B. (1982). Failure to produce response variability with reinforcement. *Journal of the Experimental Analysis of Behavior, 37,* 171–181.

Schwartz, B. (1986). *The battle for human nature.* New York: Norton.

Seligman, M. E. P., & Meier, S. F. (1967). Failure to escape traumatic shock. *Journal of Experimental Psychology, 74,* 1–9.

Seligman, M. E. P., & Weiss, J. (1980). Coping behavior: Learned helplessness, physiological activity, and learned inactivity. *Behavioral Research and Theory, 18,* 459–512.

Shaw, G. B. (1946). *The black girl in search of God and some lesser tales.* Reprinted from *The adventures of the black girl in her search for God,* first published in 1932. Harmondsworth, Eng.: Penguin.

Sheffield, F. D. (1948). Avoidance training and the contiguity principle. *Journal of Comparative and Physiological Psychology, 41,* 165–177.

Shepard, R. N. (1987). Evolution of a mesh between principles of the mind and regularities of the world. In J. Dupre (Ed.), *The latest on the best: Essays on evolution and optimality.* Cambridge, MA: Bradford.

Shepard, R. N., & Metzler, B. (1971). Mental rotation of three-dimensional objects. *Science, 171,* 390–398.

Sherrington, C. S. (1906). *The integrative action of the nervous system.* Reprinted from the 1947 edition. New Haven, CT: Yale University Press.

Shettleworth, S. J. (1978). Reinforcement and the organization of behavior in golden hamsters: Punishment of three action patterns. *Learning and Motivation, 9,* 99–123.

Shettleworth, S. J. (1983). Memory in food-hoarding birds. *Scientific American, 248,* 102–110.

Shimp, C. P. (1966). Probabilistically reinforced choice behavior in pigeons. *Journal of the Experimental Analysis of Behavior, 9,* 443–455.

Sidman, M. (1966). Avoidance behavior. In W. K. Honig (Ed.), *Operant behavior: Areas of research and application.* New York: Appleton-Century-Crofts.

Siegel, S. (1983). Classical conditioning, drug tolerance, and drug dependence. In Y. Israel, F. B. Glaser, H. Kalant, R. E. Popham, W. Schmidt, & R. G. Smart (Eds.), *Research advances in alcohol and drug problems: Vol. 7.* New York: Plenum.

Simon, H. A. (1956). Rational choice and the structure of the environment. *Psychological Review, 63,* 129–138.

Skinner, B. F. (1938). *The behavior of organisms.* New York: Appleton-Century-Crofts.

Skinner, B. F. (1948). "Superstition" in the pigeon. *Journal of Experimental Psychology, 38,* 168–172.

Smith, A. (1976). *An inquiry into the nature and causes of the wealth of nations.* Reprint of 1776 edition. Oxford: Oxford University Press.

Solomon, R. L. & Corbit, J. D. (1974). An opponent process theory of motivation: Temporal dynamics of affect. *Psychological Review, 81,* 119–145.

Sperry, R. W. (1969). A modified concept of consciousness. *Psychological Review, 76,* 532–536.

Squires, N., Norbert, J., & Fantino, E. (1975). Second-order schedules: Discrimination of components. *Journal of the Experimental Analysis of Behavior, 24,* 157–171.

Staddon, J. E. R. (1965). Some properties of spaced responding in pigeons. *Journal of the Experimental Analysis of Behavior, 8,* 19–27.

Staddon, J. E. R. (1970a). Temporal effects of reinforcement: A negative "frustration" effect. *Learning and Motivation, 1,* 227–247.

Staddon, J. E. R. (1970b). Effect of reinforcement duration on fixed-interval responding. *Journal of the Experimental Analysis of Behavior, 13,* 9–11.

Staddon, J. E. R. (1972a). Reinforcement omission in temporal go–no-go schedules. *Journal of the Experimental Analysis of Behavior, 18,* 223–229.

Staddon, J. E. R. (1972b). Temporal control and the theory of reinforcement schedules. In R. M. Gilbert & J. R. Millenson (Eds.), *Reinforcement: Behavioral Analysis.* New York: Academic Press.

Staddon, J. E. R. (1974). Temporal control, attention and memory. *Psychological Review, 81,* 375–391.

Staddon, J. E. R. (1975). A note on the evolutionary significance of supernormal stimuli. *American Naturalist, 109,* 541–545.

Staddon, J. E. R. (1983). *Adaptive behavior and learning.* Cambridge: Cambridge University Press.

Staddon, J. E. R. (1987). Brain models and behaviorism: A review of vehicles, by Valentino Braitenberg. *Behaviorism, 15,* 63–66.

Staddon, J. E. R. (in press). On the process of reinforcement. *Behavioral and Brain Sciences.*

Staddon, J. E. R. (1988). Quasi-dynamic choice models: Melioration and ratio-invariance. *Journal of the Experimental Analysis of Behavior, 49,* 303–320.

Staddon, J. E. R., & Ayres, S. (1975). Sequential and temporal properties of behavior induced by a schedule of periodic food delivery. *Behavior, 54,* 26–49.

Staddon, J. E. R., & Frank, J. (1974). Mechanisms of discrimination reversal. *Animal Behavior, 22,* 802–828.

Staddon, J. E. R., & Innis, N. K. (1969). Reinforcement omission on fixed-interval schedules. *Journal of the Experimental Analysis of Behavior, 12,* 689–700.

Staddon, J. E. R., & Hinson, J. M. (1983). Optimization: A result or a mechanism? *Science, 221,* 976–977.

Staddon, J. E. R., Hinson, J. M., & Kram, R. (1981). Optimal choice. *Journal of the Experimental Analysis of Behavior, 35,* 397–412.

Staddon, J. E. R., & Motheral, S. (1978). On matching and maximizing in operant choice experiments. *Psychological Review, 85,* 436–444.

Staddon, J. E. R., & Simmelhag, V. L. (1971). The "superstition" experiment: A reexamination of its implications for the principles of adaptive behavior. *Psychological Review, 78,* 3–43.

Stephens, D. W., & Krebs, J. R. (1986). *Foraging theory.* Princeton, NJ: Princeton University Press.

Stubbs, D. A. (1971). Second-order schedules and the problem of conditioned reinforcement. *Journal of the Experimental Analysis of Behavior, 16,* 289–313.

Stubbs, D. A. (1976). Response bias and the discrimination of stimulus duration. *Journal of the Experimental Analysis of Behavior, 25,* 243–250.

Sutherland, S. (1976). *Breakdown: A personal crisis and a medical dilemma.* London: Weidenfeld & Nicolson.

Suzuki, S., Augerinos, G., & Black, A. H. (1980). Stimulus control of spatial behavior on the radial-arm maze in rats. *Learning and Motivation, 6,* 77–81.

Thorndike, E. L. (1898). Animal intelligence: An experimental study of the associative processes in animals. *Psychological Monographs, 2,* 109.

Thorndike, E. L. (1932). *The fundamentals of learning.* New York: Teachers College, Columbia University.

Timberlake, W. (1983a). Rat's response to a moving object related to food or water: A behavior-systems analysis. *Animal Learning & Behavior, 11,* 309–320.

Timberlake, W. (1983b). The functional organization of appetitive behavior: Behavior systems and learning. In M. D. Zeiler & P. Harzem (Eds.), *Advances in analyses of behaviour: Vol. 3.* Chichester, Eng.: Wiley.

Timberlake, W., & Allison, J. (1974). Response deprivation: An empirical approach to instrumental performance. *Psychological Review, 8,* 146–164.

Timberlake, W., & Lucas, G. A. (1985). The basis of superstitious behavior: Chance contingency, stimulus substitution, or appetitive behavior? *Journal of the Experimental Analysis of Behavior, 44,* 279–299.

Timberlake, W., & Peden, B. F. (1987). On the distinction between open and closed economies. *Journal of the Experimental Analysis of Behavior, 48,* 35–60.

Tinbergen, L. (1960). The natural control of insects in pinewoods: I. factors affecting the intensity of predation by songbirds. *Archives Neerlandaisis de Zoologie, 13,* 265–343.

Tolman, E. C. (1959). Principles of purposive behaviorism. In S. Koch (Ed.), *Psychology: A study of a science* (Vol. 2). New York: McGraw-Hill.

Toulmin, S. (1967). Neuroscience and human understanding. In G. Quarton, F. Schmitt, & E. Melnechuk (Eds.), *Neuroscience: A study program.* New York: Rockefeller University Press.

Ulrich, R. E., & Azrin, N. H. (1962). Reflexive fighting in response to aversive stimulation. *Journal of the Experimental Analysis of Behavior, 5,* 511–520.

Vaughan, W., & Greene, S. L. (1984). Pigeon visual memory capacity. *Journal of Experimental Psychology: Animal Behavior Processes, 10,* 256–272.

Verplanck, W. S. (1955). Since learned behavior is innate, and vice versa, what now? *Psychological Review, 52,* 139–144.

Waddington, C. H. (1960). Evolutionary adaption. In S. Tax (Ed.), *Evolution after Darwin: Vol. 1. The evolution of life.* Chicago: University of Chicago Press.

Wagner, A. R., & Larew, M. B. (1985). Opponent processes and Pavlovian inhibition. In R. R. Miller & N. E. Spear (Eds.), *Information processing in animals: Memory mechanisms.* Hillsdale, NJ: Erlbaum.

Wason, P. C., & Johnson-Laird, P. N. (1972). *Psychology of reasoning: Structure and content.* London: Batsford.

Watson, J. B. (1919). *Psychology from the standpoint of a behaviorist.* Philadelphia: Lippincott.

Weinberger, N. M., McGaugh, J. L., & Lynch, G. (Eds.) (1985) *Memory systems of the brain: Animal and human cognitive processes.* New York: Guilford Publications.

Werner, E. E., & Hall, D. J. (1974). Optimal foraging and the size selection of prey by the bluegill sunfish (*Lepomis machrochirus*). *Ecology, 55,* 1042–1052.

West, M. J., King, A. P., Eastzer, D. H., & Staddon, J. E. R. (1979). A bioassay of isolate cowbird song. *Journal of Comparative and Physiological Psychology, 93,* 124–133.

Wickens, D. D., & Wickens, C. D. (1942). Some factors related to pseudoconditioning. *Journal of Experimental Psychology, 31,* 518–526.

Williams, B. A. (1979). Contrast, component duration, and the following schedule of re-inforcement. *Journal of Experimental Psychology: Animal Behavior Processes, 5,* 379–396.

Williams, B. A. (1983). Another look at contrast in multiple schedules. *Journal of the Experimental Analysis of Behavior, 39,* 345–384.

Williams, D. R., & Williams, H. (1969). Auto-maintenance in the pigeon: Sustained pecking despite contingent nonreinforcement. *Journal of the Experimental Analysis of Behavior, 12,* 511–520.

Wyckoff, L. B., Jr. (1952). The role of observing responses in discrimination learning. Part 1. *Psychological Review, 59,* 431–442.

Wynne, C. D. L., & Staddon, J. E. R. (1988). Typical delay determines waiting time on periodic-food schedules: Static and dynamic tests. *Journal of the Experimental Analysis of Behavior,* 197–210.

Yerkes, R. M., & Dodson, J. D. (1908). The relation of strength of stimulus to rapidity of habit formation. *Journal of Comparative and Neurological Psychology, 64,* 458–82.

Copyrights and Acknowledgments

Chapter 1

Figure 1-2 C. H. Waddington in S. Tax (ed.) *Evolution After Darwin Vol. 1: The Evolution of Life.* University of Chicago Press. 1960 "Four typical Drosophila wing types induced by heat stress.

Chapter 2

Figure 2-1 J. E. R. Staddon (1983) *Adaptive Behavior and Learning.* Cambridge: Cambridge University Press.

Figure 2-3 D. E. Koshland (1977) A response regulator model in a simple sensory system. *Science, 196,* 1055–1063.

Figure 2-4 H. S. Jennings (1976) *Behavior of the Lower Organisms.* Indiana University Press (reprint of 1906 ed.).

Figure 2-5 S. O. Mast (1911) *Light and the Behavior of Organisms.* John Wiley & Sons, Inc.

Figure 2-6 M. W. Levine & J. M. Shefner (1981) *Fundamentals of Sensation & Perception.* Philippines: Addison-Wesley.

Figure 2-7 A. Müller (1925) Uber lichtreaktionen von landasseln. *Zeitschrift für Vergleichende Physiologie, 3,* 113–144. Adapted by permission of Springer-Verlag, N.Y., Inc.

Figure 2-8 H. Brandt Die lichtorientierung der mehlmotte *Ephestia kuehniella. Zeitschrift fur Vergleichende Physiologie, 20,* 646–673. Adapted by permission of Springer-Verlag, N.Y., Inc.

Figure 2-9 C. Darwin (1951) *The Origin of Species.* Oxford University Press, Oxford. (reprinted from the 6th ed., 1872).

Chapter 3

Figure 3-1 H. S. Jennings (1976) *Behavior of the Lower Organisms.* Indiana University Press (reprint of the 1906 ed.).

Figures 3-2, 3-3, 3-4, 3-5, 3-6, 3-7 J. E. R. Staddon (1983) *Adaptive Behavior and Learning.* Cambridge: Cambridge University Press.

Chapter 4

Figures 4-2, 4-3, 4-5, 4-6, 4-7 J. E. R. Staddon (1983) *Adaptive Behavior and Learning.* Cambridge: Cambridge University Press.

Figure 4-8 J. Gibbon, R. Berryman & R. L. Thompson (1974) Contingency spaces and measures in classical conditioning. *Journal of the Experimental Analysis of Behavior, 21,* 585–605.

Figures 4-9, 4-10, 4-11 J. E. R. Staddon (1983) *Adaptive Behavior and Learning.* Cambridge: Cambridge University Press.

Figure 4-13 E. L. Thorndike (1898) Animal intelligence: an experimental study of the associative processes in animals. *Psychological Monographs, 2,* 109.

Figure 4-16 J. E. R. Staddon (1983) *Adaptive Behavior and Learning.* Cambridge: Cambridge University Press.

Figure 4-17 B. F. Skinner (1938) *The Behavior of Organism.* New York: Appleton-Century-Crofts.

Figure 4-18 J. E. R. Staddon (1983) *Adaptive Behavior and Learning.* Cambridge: Cambridge University Press.

Figure 4-19 C. B. Ferster & B. F. Skinner (1957) *Schedules of Reinforcement.* New York: Appleton-Century-Crofts.

Figures 4-22, 4-23, 4-24 J. E. R. Staddon (1983) *Adaptive Behavior and Learning.* Cambridge: Cambridge University Press.

Chapter 5

Figure 5-1 M. Konishi & F. Nottebohm (1969) Experimental studies in the autogeny of avian vocalization. In R. A. Hinde (ed.), *Bird Vocalization.* Cambridge: Cambridge University Press.

Figure 5-2 P. Marler, M. Kreith, and M. Tamura (1964) Culturally transmitted patterns of vocal behavior in sparrows. *Science, 146,* 1483–1486.

Figure 5-3 J. E. R. Staddon (1983) *Adaptive Behavior and Learning.* Cambridge: Cambridge University Press.

Figure 5-4 S. H. Revusky (1971) The role of interference in association over delay. In W. K. Honig & P. H. R. James (eds.), *Animal Memory.* New York: Academic Press.

Chapter 6

Figure 6-1 M. J. West, A. P. King, D. H. Eastzer & J. E. R. Staddon (1979) A bioassay of isolate cowbird song. *Journal of Comparative and Physiological Psychology, 93,* 124–133. Copyright 1979 by the American Psychological Association. Printed with permission.

Figure 6-2 J. E. R. Staddon (1983) *Adaptive Behavior and Learning.* Cambridge: Cambridge University Press.

Figures 6-4 & 6-5 E. Hearst, M. B. Koresko & R. Poppen (1964) Stimulus generalization and the response-reinforcement contingency. *Journal of the Experimental Analysis of Behavior, 7,* 369–380.

Figures 6-6 & 6-7 W. S. Maki Jr. & C. R. Leith (1973) Shared attention in pigeons. *Journal of the Experimental Analysis of Behavior, 19,* 345–349.

Figure 6-9 J. E. R. Staddon & N. K. Innis (1969) Reinforcement omission on fixed-interval schedules. *Journal of the Experimental Analysis of Behavior, 12,* 689–700.

Figure 6-10 J. E. R. Staddon (1972a) Reinforcement omission in temporal go-no-go schedules. *Journal of the Experimental Analysis of Behavior, 18,* 223–229.

Figure 6-11 A. C. Catania & G. S. Reynolds (1968) A quantitative analysis of the behavior maintained by interval schedules of reinforcement. *Journal of the Experimental Analysis of Behavior, 11,* 327–383. Figure 19.

Figure 6-12 J. E. R. Staddon (1972b) Temporal control and the theory of reinforcement schedules. In R. M. Gilbert & J. R. Millenson (eds.) *Reinforcement: Behaviorial Analysis.* New York: Academic Press.

Figure 6-13 J. E. R. Staddon (1975) A note on the evolutionary significance of supernormal stimuli. *American Naturalist, 109,* 541–545. Figure 3.

Figure 6-14 D. A. Stubbs (1976) Response bias and the discrimination of stimulus duration. *Journal of the Experimental Analysis of Behavior, 25,* 243–250.

Figure 6-15 J. E. R. Staddon (1983) *Adaptive Behavior and Learning.* Cambridge: Cambridge University Press.

Figures 6-16 & 6-17 J. E. R. Staddon & J. Frank (1974) Mechanisms of discrimination reversal. *Animal Behavior, 22,* 802–828.

Chapter 7

Figures 7-1 & 7-2 J. E. R. Staddon (1983) *Adaptive Behavior and Learning.* Cambridge: Cambridge University Press.

Figure 7-13 G. S. Reynolds (1961) Behavioral contrast. *Journal of the Experimental Analysis of Behavior, 4,* 57–71.

Figure 7-4 J. E. R. Staddon & V. L. Simmelhag (1971) The "superstition" experiment: a re-examination of its implications for the principles of adaptive behavior. *Psychological Review, 78,* 3–43. Copyright 1971 by the American

Psychological Association. Reprinted with permission.

Figure 7-5 J. M. Hinson & J. E. R. Staddon (1978) Behavioral competition: A mechanism for schedule interactions. *Science, 202*, 432–434.

Figure 7-6 J. E. R. Staddon (1983) *Adaptive Behavior and Learning.* Cambridge: Cambridge University Press.

Figure 7-7 W. K. Honig, C. A. Boneau, K. R. Burstein & H. S. Pennypacker (1963) Positive and negative generalization gradients obtained after equivalent training conditions. *Journal of Comparative and Physiological Psychology, 56,* 111–116.

Figure 7-8 J. E. R. Staddon (1983) *Adaptive Behavior and Learning.* Cambridge: Cambridge University Press.

Chapter 9

Figure 9-3 A. Charles Catania (1984) *Learning,* (2nd ed.) 180. Adapted by permission of Prentice-Hall, Inc., Englewood Cliffs, N.J.

Figure 9-4 J. E. R. Staddon (1983) *Adaptive Behavior and Learning.* Cambridge: Cambridge University Press.

Figure 9-5 R. T. Kelleher (1966) Chaining and conditioned reinforcement. In W. K. Honig (ed.) *Operant Behavior: Areas of Research and Application.* New York: Appleton-Century-Crofts.

Figure 9-17 C. M. Gibbs, S. B. Latham & I. Gormenzano (1978) Classical conditioning of the rabbit nicitating membrane response. *Animal Learning and Behavior, 6,* 209–215.

Chapter 10

Figure 10-4 J. E. R. Staddon (1983) *Adaptive Behavior and Learning.* Cambridge: Cambridge University Press.

Figure 10-5 M. Sidman (1966) Avoidance behavior. In W. K. Honig (ed.) *Operant Behavior: Areas of Research and Application.* New York: Appleton-Century-Crofts.

Figure 10-6 R. J. Herrnstein & P. N. Hineline (1966) Negative reinforcement as shock-frequency reduction. *Journal of the Experimental Analysis of Behavior, 9,* 421–430.

Figure 10-7 J. W. McKearney (1969) Fixed-interval schedules of electric shock presentation: extinction and recovery of performance under different shock intensities and fixed-interval duration. *Journal of the Experimental Analysis of Behavior, 12,* 301–313.

Figure 10-8 B. F. Skinner (1938) *The Behavior of Organism.* New York: Appleton-Century-Crofts.

Figures 10-9 & 10-10 N. H. Azrin (1960) Effect of punishment intensity during variable-interval reinforcement. *Journal of the Experimental Analysis of Behavior, 3,* 123–142.

Chapter 11

Figures 11-1 & 11-2 J. E. R. Staddon (1983) *Adaptive Behavior and Learning.* Cambridge: Cambridge University Press.

Figure 11-3 J. Allison (1980) Conservation matching and the variable-interval schedule. *Animal Learning and Behavior, 8,* 185–92. Reprinted by permission of Psychonomic Society, Inc.

Figures 11-11 & 11-12 J. E. R. Staddon (1983) *Adaptive Behavior and Learning.* Cambridge: Cambridge University Press.

Figure 11-18 R. J. Herrnstein (1961) Relative and absolute strength of response as a function of frequency of reinforcement. *Journal of the Experimental Analysis of Behavior, 4,* 267–272.

Figure 11-19 R. H. Ettinger, A. K. Reid & J. E. R. Staddon (1987) Sensitivity to molar feedback functions: a test of molar optimality theory. *Journal of Experimental Psychology: Animal Behavior Processes, 13,* 366–375. Copyright 1987 by the American Psychological Association. Reprinted with permission.

Author Index

Subject Index